1001 Great Family Days Out

Produced by AA Publishing

Advertisement Sales: advertisingsales@theAA.com
Editorial: lifestyleguides@theAA.com

The Automobile Association would like to thank the following photographers,
companies and picture libraries for their assistance in the preparation of this book.
1 AA/N Hicks; 2 AA/C Jones; 3 Paignton Zoo; 5 At-Bristol; 6 AA/J Tims;
202 AA/A Burton; 203 AA/A Baker; 233 AA/C Warren; 253 AA/C Coe;
Front Cover Photo: AA/John Wood
Every effort has been made to trace the copyright holders, and we apologise in
advance for any accidental errors. We would be happy to apply any corrections in
the following edition of this publication.

Printed and bound in China by Everbest Printing Company Limited
Directory compiled by the AA Lifestyle Guides Department, managed in the Librios
Information Management System and generated from the
AA establishment database system.

theAA.com/shop

Published by AA Publishing, a trading name of AA Media Limited
whose registered office is Fanum House, Basing View, Basingstoke, Hampshire,
RG21 4EA

Registered number 06112600.

A CIP catalogue record for this book is available from the British Library

ISBN 978-0-7495-6454-4
A04298

Contents

How to Use the Guide

The AA 1001 Great Family Days Out Guide provides useful information for museums, art galleries, theme parks, national parks, visitor centres, stately homes and other attractions across Britain and Ireland. Entries include contact details, along with a short description and details of opening times, prices and special facilities. We hope this guide will help you and your family get the most out of your visit.

The Directory

The directory is arranged in countries, counties, and in alphabetical location order within each county.

1 Telephone Numbers have the STD code shown before the telephone number. (If dialling Northern Ireland from England use the STD code, but for the Republic you need to prefix the number with 00353, and drop the first zero from the Irish area code).

2 Directions may be given after the address of each attraction and where shown have been provided by the attractions themselves.

3 Opening Times quoted in the guide are inclusive - for instance, where you see Apr-Oct, that place will be open from the beginning of April to the end of October.

4 Fees quoted for the majority of entries are current. If no price is quoted, you should check with the attraction concerned before you visit. Places which are open 'at all reasonable times' are usually free, and many places which do not charge admission at all may ask for a voluntary donation. Remember that prices can go up, and those provided to us by the attractions are provisional.

Admission prices followed by a star relate to 2009. It should be noted that in some entries the opening dates and times may also have been supplied as 2009. Please check with the establishment before making your journey.

Free Entry FREE

These attractions do not charge a fee for entry, although they may charge for use of audio equipment, for example. We have not included attractions that expect a donation in this category.

5 Facilities This section includes parking, dogs allowed, refreshments etc. See page 5 for a key to Symbols and Abbreviations used in this guide.

SOUTH MOLTON

Quince Honey Farm

EX36 3AZ

1 ☎ 01769 572401 📠 01769 574704
e-mail: info@quincehoney.co.uk
web: www.quincehoney.com
2 **dir:** 3.5m W of A361, on N edge of South Molton

Follow the story of honey and beeswax from flower to table. The exhibition allows you to see the world of bees close up in complete safety; hives open at the press of a button revealing the honeybees' secret life. After viewing the bees at work, sample the fruits of their labour in the café or shop.

3 **Times** Open daily, Apr-Sep 9-6; Oct 9-5; Shop only Nov-Etr
4 9-5, closed Sun. Closed 25 Dec-4 Jan.* **Fees** £4 (ch 5-16
5 £3, pen £3.50)* **Facilities** 🅿 ⛽ 🍴 (outdoor) ♿ (partly **6** accessible) (no lift to exhibition on first floor) toilets for disabled shop ⊗

---

6 Visitors with Mobility Disabilities should look for the wheelchair symbol showing where all or most of the establishment is accessible to the wheelchair-bound visitor. We strongly recommend that you telephone in advance of your visit to check the exact details, particularly regarding access to toilets and refreshment facilities. Assistance dogs are usually accepted where the attractions show the 'No Dogs' symbol ⊗ unless stated otherwise. For the hard of hearing induction loops are indicated by a symbol at the attraction itself.

7 Credit & Charge cards are taken by a large number of attractions for admission charges. To indicate which do not accept credit cards we have used this symbol at the end of the entry 💳

Photography is restricted in some places and there are many where it is only allowed in specific areas. Visitors are advised to check with places of interest on the rules for taking photographs and the use of video cameras.

Special events are held at many of these attractions, and although we have listed a few in individual entries, we cannot hope to give details of them all, so please ring the attractions for details of exhibitions, themed days, talks, guided walks and more.

Attractions with *italic* headings. These are entries that were unable to provide the relevant information in time for publication.

...and finally Opening times and admission prices can be subject to change. Please check with the attraction before making your journey.

Key to Symbols

☎	Telephone number	♛	The National Trust for Scotland
♿	Suitable for visitors in wheelchairs	🏛	Historic Scotland
🅟	Parking at Establishment		
Ⓟ	Parking nearby		**Abbreviations**
☕	Refreshment		**BH** Bank Hoildays
🛋	Picnic Area		**PH** Public Holidays
🍽	Restaurant		**Etr** Easter
⊗	No Dogs		**ex** except
🚌	No Coaches		**ch** Children
✳	Admission prices relate to 2009		**Pen** Senior Citizens
⊜	No Credit cards		**Concessions** (Students, unemployed etc)
⊕	Cadw (Welsh Monuments)		
#	English Heritage		
🎗	National Trust		

To see the effect - look down the tube and watch the magnet as it falls.

Cheddar Gorge, Somerset

England

BEDFORDSHIRE

LEIGHTON BUZZARD

Leighton Buzzard Railway

Pages Park Station, Billington Rd LU7 4TN
☎ 01525 373888 🖹 01525 377814
e-mail: station@lbngrs.org.uk
web: www.buzzrail.co.uk
dir: 0.75m SE on A4146 signed in and around Leighton Buzzard, near rdbt junct with A505

The Leighton Buzzard Railway offers a 70-minute journey into the vanished world of the English light railway, with its sharp curves, steep gradients, level crossings and unique roadside running. Built in 1919 to serve the local sand industry, the railway has carried a steam passenger service, operated by volunteers, since 1968. Special events throughout the year.

Times Open mid Mar-Oct, Sun; Etr wknd, early & late May & Aug BH, also Sat & Mon; 3-24 Aug, Tue; 7 & 14 Apr, 2 Jun-25 Aug, 27 Oct, Wed; 3 Jun, 5-26 Aug, Thu. Xmas trains in Dec. **Fees** Return ticket £8 (ch 2-15 £4, ch under 2 free, pen £6). Family & day Rover tickets available. Different prices at Xmas. **Facilities** ❷ ⏛ 🛤 (outdoor) ♿ (partly accessible) (some museum exhibits not suitable, platform & train access for wheelchairs) toilets for disabled shop

LUTON

Stockwood Discovery Centre   FREE

Stockwood Park, London Rd LU1 4LX
☎ 01582 548600 🖹 01582 546763
e-mail: museum.gallery@luton.gov.uk
web: www.luton.gov.uk/museums
dir: signed from M1 junct 10 & from Hitchin, Dunstable, Bedford, Luton town centre

Stockwood Discovery Centre is a museum and visitor attraction that includes new gardens featuring world, medicinal and sensory gardens, a visitor centre with a shop and café selling locally produced free range products and an outdoor discovery play area. It also features fascinating interactive displays about the history of Luton and the surrounding areas as well as exciting events and special exhibitions.

Times Open all year; Apr-Oct, Mon-Fri 10-5, Sat-Sun 11-5, until 8 on 1st Thu of mth; Nov-Mar, Mon-Fri 10-4, Sat-Sun 11-4.* **Facilities** ❷ ⓟ ⏛ 🛤 (outdoor) ♿ toilets for disabled shop ⊗

OLD WARDEN

The Shuttleworth Collection

Old Warden Park SG18 9EP
☎ 01767 627927 🖹 01767 627949
web: www.shuttleworth.org
dir: 2m W from rdbt on A1, Biggleswade by-pass

Housed in eight hangars on a classic grass aerodrome, 40 working historic aeroplanes span the progress of aviation with exhibits ranging from a 1909 Bleriot to a 1941 Spitfire. A garage of roadworthy motor vehicles explores the eras of the 1898 Panhard Levassor to the Railton sports car of 1937. The 19th-century coach house displays horse-drawn vehicles from 1880 to 1914. Flying displays of historic aeroplanes are held on the first Sunday of the month between May and October.

Times Open Apr-Oct 10-5 (last admission 4), Nov-Feb 10-4 (last admission 3). Closed Xmas-New Year. **Fees** £10 (concessions £9). Flying displays £20.* **Facilities** ❷ ⏛ 🍴 licensed 🛤 (outdoor) ♿ toilets for disabled shop ⊗

SANDY

RSPB The Lodge Nature Reserve

The Lodge SG19 2DL
☎ 01767 680541 🖹 01767 683508
e-mail: thelodgereserve@rspb.org.uk **web:** www.rspb.org.uk
dir: 1m E of Sandy, on B1042 Potton road

The headquarters of the Royal Society for the Protection of Birds. Explore peaceful woodlands, colourful gardens and the Iron Age hill fort on Galley Hill. The house and buildings are not open to the public, but there are waymarked paths and formal gardens. Two species of woodpecker, nuthatches and woodland birds may be seen, as may rare breed sheep. Various events include Shakespeare plays and Feed the Birds.

Times Open all year, Nature Reserve: dawn-dusk. Shop: Mon-Fri 9-5, Sat, Sun & BHs 10-5. Closed 25-26 Dec. **Fees** Reserve, Gardens & parking: £4 per motor vehicle (RSPB members free). **Facilities** ❷ 🛤 (outdoor) ♿ (partly accessible) (gardens some steps, nature trails some steep sections) toilets for disabled shop ⊗

Bedfordshire

WHIPSNADE

Whipsnade Wild Animal Park

LU6 2LF
☎ **01582 872171** 📄 **01582 872649**
e-mail: marketing@zsl.org
web: www.whipsnade.co.uk
dir: signed from M1 junct 9 & 12

Located in beautiful Bedfordshire countryside, Whipsnade is home to more than 2,500 rare and exotic animals and is one of the largest conservation centres in Europe. Hop aboard the Jumbo Express, a fantastic steam train experience, and see elephants, rhino, yaks, camels and deer, along with wild horses, and learn about their lives in the wilds of Asia and Africa. Other highlights include the Lions of the Serengeti, the sealion pool, and Birds of the World. The Discover Centre is home to tamarins, turtles, big snakes and sea horses among others. Visitors can also enjoy the picnic areas, keeper talks and animal shows.

Times Open all year, daily. (Closed 25 Dec). Closing times vary.*
Facilities 🅿 ☐ 🛱 (outdoor) toilets for disabled shop ⊗

WILDEN

Wild Britain

65A Renhold Rd MK44 2PX
☎ **01234 772770** 📄 **01234 772773**
e-mail: enquiries@wild-britain.co.uk
web: www.wild-britain.co.uk
dir: From A421 take Gt Barford slip road. Follow brown signs

Join the Adventures of Urchin the hedgehog as he explores the countryside. Meet British animals in the presentation shows. Visit the steamy tropical butterfly house to experience what the future could hold for Britain. Children's arts and craft activities every day.

Times Open Etr-Oct, 10-5. **Fees** £6 (ch16 £4.95, under 2s free, concessions £5.50).* **Facilities** 🅿 ☐ 🚻 toilets for disabled shop ⊗

WOBURN

Woburn Abbey

MK17 9WA
☎ **01525 290333** 📄 **01525 290271**
e-mail: admissions@woburnabbey.co.uk
web: www.woburn.co.uk
dir: Just off M1 junct 12/13

Set in a beautiful 3,000 acre deer park, Woburn Abbey has been home to the Dukes of Bedford for over 300 years and is currently occupied by the 15th Duke and his family. The Abbey houses one of the most important private art collections in the world including paintings by Canaletto, Gainsborough, Reynolds, Van Dyck and Cuyp and collections of silver, gold and porcelain. Woburn was the setting for the origin of "Afternoon Tea", introduced by Anna Maria, wife of the 7th Duke. An audio tour is available (charged) and guided tours on request. There are extensive informal gardens, pottery and a fine antiques centre representing over 70 dealers. Various events throughout the year include Plays in the Park season between June and August.

Times Open 15 Mar-3 Apr & 5-25 Oct, wknds only. 4 Apr-4 Oct, daily, 11-5.30 (last entry 4).* **Fees** £13 (ch 3-15 £6, pen £11). Passport ticket for Woburn Abbey and Woburn Safari Park allows one visit to each attraction on same or different days £22.50 (ch £15.50, pen £19). Please phone or check website for further details.* **Facilities** 🅿 ☐ 🍽 licensed 🛱 (outdoor) ♿ (partly accessible) (limited access to house, only 3 rooms on ground floor. Other areas can only be accessed by means of stairs) toilets for disabled shop ⊗

Woburn Safari Park

MK17 9QN
☎ **01525 290407** 📄 **01525 290489**
e-mail: info@woburnsafari.co.uk
web: www.woburn.co.uk
dir: Signed from M1 junct 13

Enjoy a Safari Adventure at Woburn Safari Park and enjoy the beauty of wild animals in real close-up. Tour the reserves from the safety of your car and experience the thrill of being alongside white rhino, buffalo, giraffe or Siberian tiger. The Leisure Park has indoor and outdoor adventure playgrounds, walkthrough areas with wallabies, squirrel monkeys and lemurs, and a full programme of keeper talks and demonstrations. The sea lions and the penguins are very popular. All attractions are included in the entry price including the new Mammoth Play Ark, Great Woburn Railway and the Swanboats.

Times Open 7 Mar-1 Nov 10-5 (last entry), Winter wknds 11-3 (Nov-early Mar).* **Fees** £10.50-£18.50 (ch 3-15 £8.50-£13.50, pen £8.50-£15). Passport ticket for Woburn Safari Park and Woburn Abbey allows one visit to each attraction on same or different days £22.50 (ch £15.50, pen £16-£19). Please phone or check website for further details.* **Facilities** 🅿 ☐ 🍽 licensed 🛱 (indoor & outdoor) ♿ (partly accessible) (some steeper hills in leisure area) toilets for disabled shop ⊗

BERKSHIRE

BRACKNELL

The Look Out Discovery Centre

Nine Mile Ride RG12 7QW
☎ 01344 354400   📄 01344 354422
e-mail: thelookout@bracknell-forest.gov.uk
web: www.bracknell-forest.gov.uk/be
dir: 3m S of town centre. From M3 junct 3, take A322 to Bracknell and from M4 junct 10, take A329M to Bracknell. Follow brown tourist signs

A hands-on, interactive science and nature exhibition where budding scientists can spend many hours exploring and discovering over 80 fun filled exhibits within five themed zones, linked to the National Curriculum. Zones include Light and Colour, Forces and Movement and the Body and Perception. A new exciting zone, Woodland and Water; has a vortex, stream, ant colony and many more interactive exhibits. Climb the 88 steps to the Look Out tower and look towards Bracknell and beyond or enjoy a nature walk in the surrounding 1,000 hectares of Crown Estate woodland. Interactive shows for the public and schools running throughout the year. Please note the tower is closed when wet.

Times Open all year 10-5 (Closed 24-26 Dec, 11-15 Jan).
Fees £5.95 (ch & concessions £3.95). Family (2ad+2ch or 1ad+3ch) £15.85. **Facilities** 🅿 ⬚ 🎪 (outdoor) toilets for disabled shop ⊗

HAMPSTEAD NORREYS

The Living Rainforest

RG18 0TN
☎ 01635 202444   📄 01635 202440
e-mail: enquiries@livingrainforest.org
web: www.livingrainforest.org
dir: follow brown tourist signs from M4/A34

By providing education and supporting research into the relationship between humanity and the rainforests, this wonderful attraction hopes to promote a more sustainable future. Visitors to the Living Rainforest will see plants and wildlife that are under threat in their natural habitat, and be encouraged to take part in a large variety of activities, workshops and exhibitions.

Times Open all year daily 10-5. (Closed 24-26 Dec) **Fees** £8.75 (ch 3-4 £5.75, ch 5-14 £6.75, concessions £7.75). Family ticket £27.50* **Facilities** 🅿 ⬚ 🎪 (outdoor) ♿ toilets for disabled shop ⊗

LOWER BASILDON

Basildon Park

RG8 9NR
☎ 0118 984 3040   📄 0118 976 7370
e-mail: basildonpark@nationaltrust.org.uk
web: www.nationaltrust.org.uk/basildonpark
dir: 7m NW of Reading on W side of A329 between Pangbourne & Streatley

This 18th-century house, built of Bath stone, fell into decay in the 20th century, but has been beautifully restored by Lord and Lady Iliffe. The classical front has a splendid central portico and pavilions, and inside there are delicate plasterwork decorations on the walls and ceilings. The Octagon drawing room has fine pictures and furniture, and there is a small formal garden. The house more recently featured in the 2005 film adaptation of Jane Austen's Pride and Prejudice. Please contact for details of special events.

Times House open mid Mar-Oct, Wed-Sun & BH Mon 12-5. Park & garden, shop & tea room mid Feb-mid Dec, Wed-Sun & BH Mon 11-3. **Fees** House & grounds £8.80 (ch £4.40). **Facilities** 🅿 🍴 licensed 🎪 (outdoor) ♿ (partly accessible) (grd floor ramped access to exhibition rooms, tea rooms & shop) toilets for disabled shop 🐾

Beale Park

Lower Basildon RG8 9NH
☎ 0870 777 7160   📄 0870 777 7120
web: www.bealepark.co.uk
dir: M4 junct 12, follow brown tourist signs to Pangbourne, A329 towards Oxford

Beale Park is home to an extraordinary collection of birds and animals including peacocks, swans, owls and parrots. It also offers a steam railway, rare breeds of farm animals, a great pet corner, meerkats, wallabies, ring-tailed lemurs, a deer park, three splash pools, a huge adventure playground, acres of gardens, and sculptures in a traditional, family park beside the Thames. There are summer riverboat trips and excellent lake and river fishing.

Times Open Mar-Oct.* **Facilities** 🅿 ⬚ 🍴 licensed 🎪 (outdoor) toilets for disabled shop ⊗

Berkshire

READING

Museum of English Rural Life   FREE

University of Reading, Redlands Rd RG1 5EX
☎ 0118 378 8660   🖹 0118 378 5632
e-mail: merl@reading.ac.uk
web: www.merl.org.uk
dir: close to Royal Berkshire Hospital, museum 100mtrs on right

Recently moved to larger premises, this museum houses a national collection of agricultural, domestic and crafts exhibits, including wagons, tools and a wide range of other equipment used in the English countryside over the last 150 years. Special facilities are available for school parties. The museum also contains extensive documentary and photographic archives, which can be studied by appointment. There is a regular programme of events and activities, please see website for details.

Times Open all year, Tue-Fri, 9-5, Sat & Sun 2-4.30 (Closed BHs & Xmas-New Year).* **Facilities** ❷ 🎪 (outdoor) ♿ toilets for disabled shop ⊗

RISELEY

Wellington Country Park

RG7 1SP
☎ 0118 932 6444   🖹 0118 932 6445
e-mail: info@wellington-country-park.co.uk
web: www.wellington-country-park.co.uk
dir: signed off A33, between Reading & Basingstoke

350 acres of woodland walks and parkland ideal for a family outing. Attractions appealing to younger and older children include; a miniature railway, a variety of play areas, crazy golf and nature trails. There is also an 80-acre family campsite, a nature trail maze and animal corner.

Times Open Feb-Nov, daily 9.30-5 in low season, 9.30-5.30 in high season. **Fees** £6.50 (ch 2 and under free, 3-15 £5.50, pen £6) Family ticket (2ad+2ch) £21.50* **Facilities** ❷ 🖵 🎪 (outdoor) ♿ (partly accessible) (most walks are forest floor but park area stone surface) toilets for disabled shop ⊗

WINDSOR

LEGOLAND Windsor

Winkfield Rd SL4 4AY
🖹 01753 626119
e-mail: customer.services@legoland.co.uk
web: www.legoland.co.uk
dir: on B3022 (Windsor to Ascot road) signed from M3 junct 3 & M4 junct 6

With over 50 interactive rides, live shows, building workshops, driving schools and attractions. Set in 150 acres of beautiful parkland, LEGOLAND Windsor is a different sort of family theme park. An atmospheric and unique experience for the whole family, a visit to LEGOLAND Windsor is more than a day out, it's a lifetime of memories.

Times Open daily 12 Mar-5 Nov* **Facilities** ❷ ❷ 🖵 🍴 licensed 🎪 (outdoor) toilets for disabled shop ⊗

The Royal Landscape

**The Savill Garden, Wick Ln,
Englefield Green TW20 0UU**
☎ 01784 435544 & 439746
e-mail: enquiries@theroyallandscape.co.uk
web: www.theroyallandscape.co.uk
dir: M25 junct 13, signed off A30 between Egham & Virginia Water

The work of master landscape gardener, Sir Eric Savill, this is one of the greatest woodland gardens in England. It was created in the 1930s and offers year-round interest with colourful displays of interesting and rare plants. The Savill Building is a visitor centre built to a unique and innovative gridshell design, made with timber harvested from Windsor Great Park. The Royal Landscape is an area of a thousand acres of gardens and parkland accessible to the public, at the southern end of Windsor Great Park. It includes the Savill Garden, the Valley Gardens and Virginia Water, and was shaped and planted over a period of 400 years.

Times Open all year, daily 10-6 (10-4.30 Nov-Feb). Closed 25-26 Dec* **Fees** For information on prices, please call, email or visit website. **Facilities** ❷ 🖵 🍴 licensed 🎪 (outdoor) ♿ toilets for disabled shop ⊗

Windsor Castle

SL4 1NJ
☎ **020 7766 7304** 📄 **020 7930 9625**
e-mail: bookinginfo@royalcollection.org.uk
web: www.royalcollection.org.uk
dir: M4 junct 6 & M3 junct 3

Covering 13 acres, Windsor Castle is the official residence of HM The Queen, and the largest occupied castle in the world. Begun as a wooden fort by William the Conqueror, it has been added to by almost every monarch since. A visit takes in the magnificent State Apartments, St George's Chapel, Queen Mary's doll's house, the Drawings Gallery, and from October to March, the semi-state rooms created by George IV.

Times Open daily except Good Fri & 25-26 Dec. Nov-Feb, 9.45-4.15 (last admission 3); Mar-Oct, 9.45-5.15 (last admission 4). May be subject to change at short notice (24hr info line: 01753 831118) **Fees** £16 (ch under 17 £9.50, under 5s free, concessions £14.50) Family (2ad+3ch) £42 **Facilities** ℗ ♿ toilets for disabled shop ⊗

BRISTOL

BRISTOL

Arnolfini

16 Narrow Quay BS1 4QA
☎ **0117 917 2300 & 0117 917 2301** 📄 **0117 917 2303**
e-mail: boxoffice@arnolfini.org.uk
web: www.arnolfini.org.uk
dir: From M32 follow brown signs

In a fantastic location at the heart of Bristol's harbourside, Arnolfini is one of Europe's leading centres for the contemporary arts. Arnolfini stages art exhibitions, cinema, live art and dance performances, talks and events and has one of the country's best art bookshops. Entrance to the galleries is free, making Arnolfini a great place to spend a few minutes or a few hours.

Times Open all year, Tue-Sun, 10-6 & BHs. **Fees** Galleries free, Cinema £6 (concessions £4.50).* **Facilities** ℗ 🚻 🍽 licensed ⊓ ♿ toilets for disabled shop ⊗

Bristol's City Museum & Art Gallery   FREE

Queen's Rd, Clifton BS8 1RL
☎ **0117 922 3571** 📄 **0117 922 2047**
e-mail: general.museum@bristol.gov.uk
web: www.bristol.gov.uk/museums
dir: follow signs to city centre, then follow tourist board signs to City Museum & Art Gallery

Regional and international collections representing ancient history, natural sciences, and fine and applied arts. Displays include dinosaurs, Bristol ceramics, silver, and Chinese and Japanese ceramics. A full programme of special exhibitions take place throughout the year. Ring for details.

Times Open all year, daily 10-5. (Closed 25-26 Dec). **Facilities** ℗ 🚻 ♿ (partly accessible) (level access entrance, lift to some floors) toilets for disabled shop ⊗

Bristol Zoo Gardens

Clifton BS8 3HA
☎ **0117 974 7399** 📄 **0117 973 6814**
e-mail: information@bristolzoo.org.uk
web: www.bristolzoo.org.uk
dir: M5 junct 17, take A4018 then follow brown elephant signs. Also signed from city centre

There are over 450 exotic and endangered species in the 12-acre grounds of Bristol Zoo. Visit the primates in Monkey Jungle, stroll through the lemur garden, and visit the Seal and Penguin coast. Other favourites include Gorilla Island, the Asiatic lions, Bug World, Butterfly Forest, Twilight World, the Reptile House and the children's play area. Follow the footsteps of jungle adventurers at the new Explorers' Creek exhibit, home to three exciting areas; Splash, a water-play area, Forest of Birds, and feed the Lorikeets, a truly unique experience.

Times Open all year, daily (ex 25 Dec). 9-5.30 (British Summer Time), 9-5 (standard hrs)* **Fees** £12.50 (ch 3-14yrs £7.75, under 3 free, concessions £11). Family ticket (2ad+2ch) £36.50.* **Facilities** ℗ 🚻 🍽 licensed ⊓ (outdoor) ♿ toilets for disabled shop ⊗

Bristol continued

Brunel's ss Great Britain

Great Western Dock, Gas Ferry Rd BS1 6TY
☎ 0117 926 0680 📠 0117 925 5788
e-mail: admin@ssgreatbritain.org
web: www.ssgreatbritain.org
dir: off Cumberland Rd

Built and launched in Bristol in 1843, Isambard Kingdom Brunel's maritime masterpiece was the first ocean-going, propeller-driven, iron ship. Launched in 1843 to provide luxury travel to New York, the world's first great ocean liner set new standards in engineering, reliability and speed. Find out about passengers and crew - from the rich and famous to those leaving 1850s England to begin a new life. Steer the ship on a westerly course, prepare her for sail and climb to the crow's nest. Descend beneath the glass 'sea' for a close up view of the ship's giant hull and propeller and the state-of-the-art equipment which will save her for the next hundred years. Another feature is the Dockyard Museum charting the history of Brunel's Masterpiece. A replica of the square rigger 'Matthew' is moored at the same site when in Bristol. Special events are held all year - please see the website for details.

Times Open all year daily 10-6, 4.30 in winter. (Closed 17, 24-25 Dec).* **Facilities** ❷ ⓟ ☑ ⑁ toilets for disabled shop ⊗

At-Bristol

Anchor Rd, Harbourside BS1 5DB
☎ 0845 345 1235 📠 0117 915 7200
e-mail: information@at-bristol.org.uk
web: www.at-bristol.org.uk
dir: from city centre, A4 to Anchor Rd. Located on left opposite Cathedral

At-Bristol is one of the UK's most exciting hands-on science centres, and is located on Bristol's historic Harbourside. Discover interactive exhibits and special exhibitions, take in a Planetarium show or join the Live Science team for fun experiments and activities. Explore involves people of all ages in an incredible journey through the workings of the world around us. The centre celebrates its 10th Anniversary in 2010.

Times Open all year, term-time wkdays 10-5, wknds & school hols 10-6. (Closed 24-26 Dec).* **Fees** With Gift Aid £11.90 (ch £7.70, concessions £9.90). Family ticket £34.* **Facilities** ❷ ⓟ ☑ ⋒ (outdoor) ⑁ (partly accessible) toilets for disabled shop ⊗

HorseWorld

Staunton Manor Farm, Staunton Ln, Whitchurch BS14 0QJ
☎ 01275 540173 📠 01275 540119
e-mail: visitor.centre@horseworld.org.uk
web: www.horseworld.org.uk
dir: A37 Bristol to Wells road, follow brown signs from Maes Knoll traffic lights

Set in beautiful stone farm buildings on the southern edge of Bristol, HorseWorld's Visitor Centre is an award winning attraction that offers a great day for everyone. Meet the friendly horses, ponies and donkeys.

Times Open all year Apr-Oct daily 10-5; Nov-Mar daily (ex Mon & Tue) 10-4. **Fees** £6.95 (ch 3-15yrs £4.95, concessions £5.95). Family (2ad+2ch) £20.95.* **Facilities** ❷ ☑ ⑽ licensed ⋒ (indoor & outdoor) ⑁ toilets for disabled shop

BUCKINGHAMSHIRE

AYLESBURY

Tiggywinkles Visitor Centre & Hedgehog World Museum

Aston Rd HP17 8AF
☎ **01844 292511**
e-mail: mail@sttiggywinkles.org.uk **web:** www.tiggywinkles.com
dir: Turn off A418 towards Haddenham then follow signs to 'Wildlife Hospital'

Look through the glass into bird and mammal nursery wards in the hospital. Find out all about the hospital, the patients and their treatment on education boards dotted around the gardens. See some of the other hospital wards on CCTV monitor. Wander round the world's first Hedgehog Memorabilia Museum, or watch the foxes in their permanent enclosure. Try to catch a glimpse of one of the resident badgers or see the deer in the recovery paddocks. The animals live as natural a life as possible, so don't be surprised if they do not come out to visit.

Times Open Etr-Sep, daily 10-4* **Facilities** ❷ 🛏 shop ⊗

BEACONSFIELD

Bekonscot Model Village and Railway

Warwick Rd HP9 2PL
☎ **01494 672919** 📄 **01494 675284**
e-mail: info@bekonscot.co.uk **web:** www.bekonscot.com
dir: M40 junct 2, 4m M25 junct 16, take A355 and follow signs to Model Village

A miniature world, depicting rural England in the 1930s. A Gauge 1 model railway meanders through six little villages, each with their own tiny population. Rides on the sit-on miniature railway take place at weekends and local school holidays. Remote control boats are available.

Times Open 13 Feb-Oct, 10-5. **Fees** £8 (ch £4.50, concessions £5)* **Facilities** ❷ ❿ ⊑ 🛏 (indoor & outdoor) ⴙ toilets for disabled shop ⊗

BLETCHLEY

Bletchley Park

The Mansion, Bletchley Park MK3 6EB
☎ **01908 640404** 📄 **01908 274381**
e-mail: info@bletchleypark.org.uk
web: www.bletchleypark.org.uk
dir: Approach Bletchley from V7 Saxon St. At rdbt, southern end of Saxon St under railway bridge towards Buckingham & follow signs to Bletchley Park

Known as 'Station X' during World War II, this was the home of the secret scientific team that worked to decipher German military messages sent using the Enigma code machine. Visitors can find out more about the Enigma machine; the 'bombes', computers used to crack the code; Alan Turing, one of the leading mathematicians of his day, who worked on the project; as well as see a number of other displays including the use of pigeons during the war, wartime vehicles, and a Churchill collection.

Times Open daily 9.30-5.30 (Tours at 11 & 2). Wknds open 10.30-5. Closed 25 & 26 Dec.* **Facilities** ❷ ❿ ⊑ 🍴 licensed 🛏 toilets for disabled shop

CHALFONT ST GILES

Chiltern Open Air Museum

Newland Park, Gorelands Ln HP8 4AB
☎ **01494 871117** 📄 **01494 872774**
e-mail: coamuseum@netscape.net
web: www.coam.org.uk
dir: M25 junct 17, M40 junct 2. Follow brown signs

Chiltern Open Air Museum is an independent charity, established over 30 years ago, with the aim of preserving some of the historic buildings that are unique examples of the heritage of the Chilterns. The museum is now home to more than 30 historic buildings all rescued from demolition and re-erected on this 45-acre woodland and parkland site. Events take place weekends and school holidays throughout the season, please check website for details.

Times Open 27 Mar-29 Oct, daily 10-5 (last admission 3.30). **Fees** £7.50 (ch 5-16, under 5's free) £5 , concessions £6.50) Family ticket (2ad+2 ch) £22.* **Facilities** ❷ ⊑ 🛏 (indoor & outdoor) ⴙ (partly accessible) (Some paths/areas and buildings not accessible for all on this 45 acre site - full details on website or phone) toilets for disabled shop ⊗

The Roald Dahl Museum & Story Centre

81-83 High St HP16 0AL
☎ **01494 892192** 🖹 **01494 892191**
e-mail: admin@roalddahlmuseum.org
web: www.roalddahlmuseum.org
dir: From London/Amersham turn left off A413 into Great Missenden link road

This award-winning museum is aimed at 6 to 12 year olds and their families. Two interactive and biographical galleries tell the fascinating story of Roald Dahl's life, while the Story Centre puts imagination centre-stage, and encourages everyone (young and old) to dress up, make up stories, words and poems, or get arty in the craft room. Situated in Great Missenden where Dahl lived for over 36 years, it was created as a home for the author's archive (which visitors can see on regular tours) and as a place to inspire creativity and a love of reading in children, about which Dahl was passionate. 13th September every year - Roald Dahl Day national celebrations.

Times Open all year, Tue-Sun & BH Mon 10-5.* **Facilities** Ⓟ ⊑ ⚠ (indoor & outdoor) toilets for disabled shop ⊗ 🛒

HIGH WYCOMBE

Hughenden Manor

HP14 4LA
☎ **01494 755573** 🖹 **01494 474284**
e-mail: hughenden@nationaltrust.org.uk
web: www.nationaltrust.org.uk
dir: 1.5m N of High Wycombe, on W side of A4128

This fascinating Victorian manor was home to Prime Minister Benjamin Disraeli from 1848 to 1881. Many of his possessions are still on display, along with beautiful gardens designed by his wife Mary-Anne. Other facilities include circular woodland walks, family tracker packs, I-spy sheets in the Manor and an exhibition revealing Hughenden's role in WWII. See website for special event details.

Times House open 17 Feb-Oct, Wed-Sun & BH Mon 12-5 (last admission 4.30); 3 Nov-19 Dec 11-4. Gardens 17 Feb-Oct, 11-5. Park open all year. **Fees** £8 (ch £4.10). Family ticket £20. Garden only £3.20 (ch £2.20). Park free. **Facilities** Ⓟ ⦿ licensed ⚠ (outdoor) ♿ (partly accessible) (Ground floor only fully accessible) toilets for disabled shop ⊗ 🛒

MIDDLE CLAYDON

Claydon House

MK18 2EY
☎ **01296 730349** 🖹 **01296 738511**
e-mail: claydon@nationaltrust.org.uk
web: www.nationaltrust.org.uk
dir: M40 junct 9 off A413 in Padbury, follow National Trust signs. Entrance by north drive only

The rather sober exterior of this 18th-century house gives no clue to the extravagances that lie inside, in the form of fantastic rococo carvings. Ceilings, cornices, walls and overmantels are adorned with delicately carved fruits, birds, beasts and flowers by Luke Lightfoot. The Chinese room is particularly splendid. There is also a spectacular parquetry staircase. 2010 is the centenary of Florence Nightingale's death. She was a regular visitor to the house from 1859-1890. 2010 sees the introduction of Costume Collection Displays where many costumes will be on display for the first time.

Times House open 7 Mar-1 Nov, Sat-Wed 1-5. (Last admission 4.30).* **Fees** £6 (ch £2.90). Family ticket £14.75. Private Gardens £3.50. Half price for wheelchair guests.* **Facilities** Ⓟ ⊑ ⦿ licensed ⚠ (outdoor) ♿ (partly accessible) (ground floor accessible) toilets for disabled 🛒

QUAINTON

Buckinghamshire Railway Centre

Quainton Road Station HP22 4BY
☎ 01296 655720 & 655450 📄 01296 658569
e-mail: office@bucksrailcentre.org
web: www.bucksrailcentre.org
dir: Signed off A41 (Aylesbury-Bicester road) at Waddesdon, 7m NW of Aylesbury

Housed in a former Grade II listed building, the Centre features an interesting and varied collection of about 20 locomotives with 40 carriages and wagons from places as far afield as South Africa, Egypt and America. Items date from the 1800s up to the 1960s. Visitors can take a ride on full-size and miniature steam trains, and stroll around the 20-acre site to see locomotives and rolling stock. The Centre runs locomotive driving courses for visitors. Regular 'Days out with Thomas' events take place throughout the year.

Times Open with engines in steam Apr-Oct, Sun & BH; also Wed in school hols 10.30-4.30. (Open most days for restricted viewing). **Fees** Steaming Days: £7 (ch £4.50, under 5s free, concessions £6). Family ticket (2ad+up to 4 ch) £18. Special events £9 (ch £6, under 5's free, concessions £8). Family ticket £24.* **Facilities** ℗ ⌖ †◎¹ licensed ⊼ (outdoor) ♿ (partly accessible) (some trains not accessible) toilets for disabled shop

WADDESDON

Waddesdon Manor

HP18 0JH
☎ 01296 653211, 653226 & 653203 📄 01296 653212
e-mail: waddesdonmanor@nationaltrust.org.uk
web: www.waddesdon.org.uk
dir: entrance off A41, 6m NW of Aylesbury

Built in the 19th century by Baron Ferdinand de Rothschild, this French-style chateau was created as a showcase for his fine collection of French decorative arts. The Victorian gardens are known for seasonal displays, a parterre, walks, views, fountains and statues. The aviary is stocked with species that were once part of Baron Ferdinand's collection and the wine cellar contains Rothschild wines dating back to 1868. Special events throughout the year.

Times Gardens: 3 Jan-29 Mar, wknds only; Apr-23 Dec, Wed-Sun & BHs; 27-31 Dec, Wed-Sun & 28-29 Dec, 10-5. House: Apr-1 Nov, Wed-Sun & BHs. Bachelors Wing Apr-1 Nov, Wed-Fri; 11 Nov-23 Dec, Wed-Fri 12-4; Sat-Sun, 21-22 Dec; 27-31 Dec Wed-Sun & 28-29 Dec, Sat-Sun 11-4 & Wed-Fri 12-4.* **Fees** Gardens, 6 Jan-18 Mar (wknds only) 21 Mar-23 Dec, 27-31 Dec (Wed-Fri) £5.50, (ch £2.75). Family £13.75. 19 Mar-23 Dec, 27-31 Dec (wknds & BHs) £7, (ch £3.50). Family £17.50. House & gardens, 21 Mar-28 Oct (Wed-Fri) £13.20, (ch £9.35), wknds & BHs £15, (ch £11).* **Facilities** ℗ †◎¹ licensed ♿ toilets for disabled shop ⊗ ✿

CAMBRIDGE

Fitzwilliam Museum   FREE

Trumpington St CB2 1RB
☎ 01223 332900 📄 01223 332923
e-mail: fitzmuseum-enquiries@lists.cam.ac.uk
web: www.fitzmuseum.cam.ac.uk
dir: M11 junct 11, 12 or 13. Near city centre

The Fitzwilliam is the art museum of the University of Cambridge and one of the oldest public museums in Britain. It contains magnificent collections spanning centuries and civilisations, including antiquities from Ancient Egypt, Greece and Rome; sculpture, furniture, armour, ceramics, manuscripts, coins and medals, paintings, drawings and prints.

Times Open all year Tue-Sat 10-5, Sun 12-5. (Closed Mon ex BH, & 24-26, 31 Dec & 1 Jan).* **Facilities** ℗ ⌖ ⊼ (outdoor) ♿ toilets for disabled shop ⊗

Scott Polar Research Institute Museum

Lensfield Rd CB2 1ER
☎ 01223 336540 📄 01223 336549
e-mail: enquiries@spri.cam.ac.uk
web: www.spri.cam.ac.uk
dir: 1km S of city centre

An international centre for polar studies, including a museum featuring displays of Arctic and Antarctic expeditions, with special emphasis on those of Captain Scott and the exploration of the Northwest Passage. Other exhibits include Inuit work and other arts of the polar regions, as well as displays on current scientific exploration. Public lectures run from October to December and February to April. Departure of Captain Scott's Terra Nova from London on 1 June 1910 will be celebrated by the opening of a new Polar Museum on the centenary.

Times Open: Tue-Fri 11-1 & 2-4. Sat 12-4. Closed BH wknds, public hols & University hols. Please call 01223 336540 or check the website for further details. **Fees** Free admission, donations welcome. **Facilities** ℗ ♿ toilets for disabled shop ⊗

Cambridgeshire

DUXFORD

Imperial War Museum Duxford

CB22 4QR
☎ **01223 835000** 📄 **01223 837267**
e-mail: duxford@iwm.org.uk
web: www.iwm.org.uk/duxford
dir: off M11 junct 10, on A505

Duxford is Europe's premier aviation museum with many original buildings such as the control tower and hangars which are still in use, alongside state-of-the-art, award-winning exhibition buildings including AirSpace and the American Air Museum. A collection of nearly 200 aircraft includes over 50 historic aircraft that regularly take to the sky. Duxford also has one of the finest collections of tanks, military vehicles and artillery in the UK. The Museum holds four air shows throughout the summer plus other special events such as American Air Day, Military Vehicle Show and car shows and more.

Times Open all year, 15 Mar-26 Oct, daily 10-6 (last admission 5); 28 Oct-14 Mar, daily 10-4 (last admission 3). Closed 24-26 Dec.* **Fees** £16 (ch under 16 free, concessions £12.80). Events & airshow prices vary.* **Facilities** Ⓟ ♤ ⦿◎ licensed ⌂ (indoor & outdoor) & toilets for disabled shop ⊗

ELY

Oliver Cromwell's House

29 St Mary's St CB7 4HF
☎ **01353 662062** 📄 **01353 668518**
e-mail: tic@eastcambs.gov.uk
web: www.visitely.org.uk
dir: follow brown tourist signs from main roads. Adjacent to Saint Mary's Church

Cromwell inherited the house and local estates from a maternal uncle and moved here in 1636, along with his mother, sisters, wife and eight children. There are displays and period rooms dealing with Cromwell's life, the Civil War and domestic life in the 17th century, as well as the history of The Fens and the house itself, from its medieval origins to its role as an inn in the

19th century. Various special events are held during the year including Living History days.

Times Open all year: Apr-Oct, daily 10-5; Nov-Mar, Mon-Fri 11-4, Sat 10-5. Sun, 11.15-4.* **Fees** £4.30 (ch £3, concessions £3.85). Family ticket £12.50* **Facilities** Ⓟ & (partly accessible) (wheelchair access to two rooms) shop ⊗

LINTON

Linton Zoological Gardens

Hadstock Rd CB21 4NT
☎ **01223 891308** 📄 **01223 891308**
web: www.lintonzoo.co.uk
dir: M11 junct 9/10, on B1052 off A1307 between Cambridge & Haverhill, signed

Linton Zoo places emphasis on conservation and education where visitors can see a combination of beautiful gardens and a wealth of wildlife from all over the world. There are many rare and exotic creatures to see including tapirs, snow leopards, tigers, lions, zebra, tamarin monkeys, lemurs, owls, parrots, giant tortoises, snakes, tarantulas and many others. The zoo is set in 16 acres of gardens with plenty of picnic areas, children's play area and bouncy castle.

Times Open all year, daily 10.30-4, (last admission 3). Hours extended during summer. Closed 25-26 Dec.* **Facilities** Ⓟ ♤ ⌂ (outdoor) & toilets for disabled shop ⊗

PETERBOROUGH

Flag Fen Archaeology Park

The Droveway, Northey Rd PE6 7QJ
☎ **01733 313414** 📄 **01733 349957**
e-mail: info@flagfen.org
web: www.flagfen.org
dir: From A1139 exit at Boongate junct. At rdbt 3rd exit, through lights, turn right. At T-junct turn right, Flag Fen signed

Although visitors enter this site through a 21st-century roundhouse, the rest of their day will be spent in the Bronze Age, some 3,000 years ago. Flag Fen's Museum contains artefacts found over the last 20 years of excavating on site, and includes among them the oldest wheel in Britain. In the Park there is a reconstructed Bronze Age settlement and Iron Age roundhouse, while in the Preservation Hall visitors can see the excavated Bronze Age processional way that spanned over one mile. The Hall also contains a 60-ft mural depicting the fens in ancient times.

Times Open daily Mar-Oct 10-5 (last admission 4). **Fees** £5.50 (ch £4.15, concessions £4.95). Family £15.15. Prices include gift aid.* **Facilities** Ⓟ ♤ ⌂ (outdoor) & toilets for disabled shop ⊗

Railworld

Oundle Rd PE2 9NR
☎ 01733 344240 & 319362   📄 01733 319362
e-mail: railworld@aol.com
web: www.railworld.net
dir: from A1(M) Peterborough onto A1139 then exit at junct 5
to city centre. At 1st rdbt, follow "Little Puffer" tourist signs.
Entrance for Railworld off Oundle Rd at city end through car park

Railworld is a sustainable transport centre and 21st-century
rail showcase. Its main focus is on the future of rail transport
and how it can meet the challenges of climate change and
other environmental issues. It features a large model railway,
displays on rail history, showcases of rail technology and
innovation, an environmental maze, hovertrains, and much
more.

Times Open Mar-Oct ,daily 11-4; Nov-Feb, Mon-Fri 11-4. Closed
Good Fri & 25-31 Dec unless by appointment.* **Fees** £5 (ch
£2.50, concessions £4). Family £13 (up to 4 ch).* **Facilities** 🅿 Ⓟ
🗠 🖰 (outdoor) ♿ toilets for disabled shop ⊗

RAMSEY

Ramsey Abbey Gatehouse

Abbey School PE17 1DH
☎ 01480 301494   📄 01263 734924
e-mail: ramseyabbey@nationaltrust.org.uk
web: www.nationaltrust.org.uk
dir: SE edge of Ramsey, at Chatteris Road & B1096 junct

The ruins of this 15th-century gatehouse, together with the
13th-century Lady Chapel, are all that remain of the abbey.
Half of the gatehouse was taken away after the Dissolution.
Built in ornate late-Gothic style, it has panelled buttresses and
friezes.

Times Open Apr-Sep, first Sun of the month 1-5 (Group visits by
appt only other wknds)* **Fees** Free but donations appreciated.
Facilities ⊗ ♨

THORNHAUGH

Sacrewell Farm & Country Centre

PE8 6HJ
☎ 01780 782254   📄 01780 781370
e-mail: info@sacrewell.org.uk
web: www.sacrewell.org.uk
dir: E of A1/A47 junct. Follow brown tourist signs from both
directions

Treasures of farming and the country await discovery at this
farm and 18th-century watermill. All aspects of agriculture and
country life through the ages are here, listed buildings, working
watermill, mill house and farm bygones. Farm animals,
tractor rides, mini maze and pedal tractors are just a few of
the activities to be experienced. Events throughout the year
include lambing at Easter, Halloween rides and a Christmas
spectacular.

Times Open all year daily Mar-Sep, 9.30-5; Oct-Feb 10-4. Closed
24 Dec-2 Jan.* **Fees** £6.50 (ch £4.85, ch under 3 free pen
£5.50).* **Facilities** 🅿 🗠 🍽 licensed 🖰 (indoor & outdoor) ♿
(partly accessible) (upstairs in watermill not accessible) toilets for
disabled shop

WATERBEACH

The Farmland Museum and Denny Abbey

Ely Rd CB25 9PQ
☎ 01223 860988   📄 01223 860988
e-mail: info@farmlandmuseum.org.uk
web: www.dennyfarmlandmuseum.org.uk
dir: on A10 between Cambridge & Ely

Explore two areas of rural life at this fascinating museum. The
Abbey tells the story of those who have lived there, including
Benedictine monks, Franciscan nuns, and the mysterious
Knights Templar. The farm museum features the craft
workshops of a wheelwright, a basketmaker, and a blacksmith.
There is also a 1940s farmworker's cottage and a village shop.
Special events on Easter, May and August Bank Holidays.

Times Open daily, Apr-Oct, 12-5.* **Facilities** 🅿 🗠 🖰 (outdoor)
♿ (partly accessible) toilets for disabled shop

Cambridgeshire

WICKEN

Wicken Fen National Nature Reserve

Lode Ln CB7 5XP
☎ **01353 720274**
e-mail: wickenfen@nationaltrust.org.uk
web: www.nationaltrust.org.uk
dir: S of Wicken A1123

An ancient fenland landscape and internationally renowned wetland site, Wicken Fen is home to the Wicken Vision Project, the Trust's most ambitious landscape-scale habitat restoration project.

Times Reserve and Visitor Centre open all year daily 10-5.
Fees £5.75 (ch 5-17yrs £2.95). Family £14.70. NT members free.
Facilities ❶ ♿ 🍴 (outdoor) ♿ (partly accessible) (boardwalk 0.75m circular walk suitable for wheelchairs) shop ✿

WIMPOLE

Wimpole Hall

SG8 0BW
☎ **01223 206000** 📠 **01223 207838**
e-mail: wimpolehall@nationaltrust.org.uk
web: www.nationaltrust.org.uk/wimpole
dir: M11 junct 12, 8m SW of Cambridge off A603

Wimpole Hall is one of the grandest mansions in East Anglia, and has 360 acres of parkland devised and planted by no less than four celebrated landscape designers, Charles Bridgeman, Lancelot 'Capability' Brown, Sanderson Miller and Humphry Repton. The house dates back to 1640, but was altered into a large 18th-century mansion with a Georgian façade. The chapel has a trompe l'oeil ceiling.

Times Hall 28 Feb-15 Jul, 29 Aug-1 Nov, Mon-Wed, Sat & Sun 10.30-5; 18 Jul-27 Aug, Mon-Thu, Sat & Sun 10.30-5. Garden 1-25 Feb, 2 Nov-23 Dec, 2-31 Jan, Mon-Wed, Sat & Sun 11-4; 28 Feb-15 Jul, Mon-Wed, Sat & Sun; 18 Jul-27 Aug, 10.30-5. BH Mon & Good Fri 10.30-5 (Hall 11-5 & Good Fri 1-5). Park: all year dawn-dusk daily.* **Fees** Hall & Garden: £8.80 (ch £4.95) Family £25.50. Hall, garden & farm £13.30 (ch £7.20). Family £35. Garden & farm £7.30 (ch £4.95) Family £22.50. Garden only £3.70 (ch £1.95)* **Facilities** ❶ ♿ 🍴 licensed 🍴 (outdoor) ♿ (partly accessible) toilets for disabled shop ⊗ ✿

Wimpole Home Farm

SG8 0BW
☎ **01223 206000** 📠 **01223 207838**
e-mail: wimpolefarm@nationaltrust.org.uk
web: www.nationaltrust.org.uk/wimpole
dir: M11 junct 12, 8m SW of Cambridge off A603

When built in 1794, the Home Farm was one of the most advanced agricultural enterprises in the country. The Great Barn, now restored, holds a display of farm machinery and implements of the kind used at Wimpole over the past two centuries. On the farm there are rare breeds of domestic animals, and visitors can see the new lambs in spring, and sheep shearing in June. Please ring for details of special events.

Times Open 1-25 Feb, Sat & Sun 11-4; 28 Feb-15 Jul, Mon-Wed, Sat & Sun 10.30-5; Jul-27 Aug, Mon-Thu, Sat & Sun 10.30-5; 29 Aug-1 Nov, Mon-Wed, Sat & Sun 10.30-5; 7 Nov-20 Dec, Sat-Sun 11-4; 27-31 Dec, Tue-Thu, Sat & Sun 11-4; 2-31 Jan, Sat-Sun 11-4. BH Mon & Good Fri 10.30-5.* **Fees** £7.30 (ch £4.95) Family £22.50. Hall & Farm: £13.30 (ch £7.20) Family £35* **Facilities** ❶ ♿ 🍴 licensed 🍴 (outdoor) toilets for disabled shop ⊗ ✿

WOODHURST

The Raptor Foundation

The Heath, St Ives Rd PE28 3BT
☎ **01487 741140** 📠 **01487 841140**
e-mail: heleowl@aol.com
web: www.raptorfoundation.org.uk
dir: B1040 to Somersham, follow brown signs

Permanent home to over 250 birds of which there are 40 different varieties. This is a unique opportunity to meet and learn about birds of prey. Depending on weather and time of year flying demonstrations are held, usually three times a day and audiences have the chance to participate in displays. There are nearly 60 birds in the flying team, so each display has a different set of birds. Educational trail linking to new education room. New indoor flying area. Ask about activity days, membership and adoption.

Times Open all year, daily 10-5. Closed 25-26 Dec & 1 Jan.* **Fees** £4.50 (ch £2.75 ages 2-4 £1, concessions £3.50). Family ticket £12.50.* **Facilities** ❶ ♿ 🍴 licensed 🍴 (outdoor) ♿ toilets for disabled shop ⊗

BEESTON

Beeston Castle

Chapel Ln CW6 9TX
☎ **01829 260464**
web: www.english-heritage.org.uk
dir: on minor road off A49 or A41

Known as the 'Castle of the Rock', Beeston Castle is at the top of an impressive crag which enjoys breathtaking views over eight counties, from the Pennines to the Welsh mountains. An exhibition details 4,000 years of Beeston Castle's history, from Bronze Age settlement to Iron Age hill fort. Legend tells of a vast treasure hidden here by King Richard II, but a treasure more easily found is the 40 acres of unspoiled woodland full of wildlife and trails to explore.

Times Open all year, Apr-Sep, daily 10-6; Oct-Mar, Thu-Mon 10-4. Closed 24-26 Dec & 1 Jan. **Fees** £5 (concessions £4.30, ch £2.50). Please call 0870 333 1181 for the most up to date prices and opening times when planning your visit. **Facilities** Ⓟ ⧫ shop ⊗ ▓

CHESTER

Chester Zoo

Upton-by-Chester CH2 1LH
☎ **01244 380280** ▤ **01244 371273**
e-mail: marketing@chesterzoo.org
web: www.chesterzoo.org
dir: 2m N of city centre off A41& M53 junct 10 southbound, junct 12 all other directions

Chester Zoo is the UK's number one charity zoo, with over 7,000 animals and 400 different species, some of them amongst the most endangered species on the planet. There's plenty to see and do, like the Realm of the Red Ape enclosure, home to the Bornean and Sumatran orang-utans. Experience the sights and sounds of Assam, with the herd of Asian Elephants, Hornbills, Tree Shrews and rare fish inside Elephants of the Asian Forest. View the world's fastest land mammal, the cheetah, from the new Bat's Bridge. See a wide variety of beautifully coloured African birds housed in African Aviaries and Philippine crocodiles in their new enclosure in the Tropical Realm.

Times Open all year, daily from 10. Last admission varies with season. (Closed 25-26 Dec). **Fees** £14.95 (ch £11.30). Family £50* **Facilities** Ⓟ Ⓟ ⧫⧫ licensed ⧫ (indoor & outdoor) ♿ toilets for disabled shop ⊗

Dewa Roman Experience

Pierpoint Ln, (off Bridge St) CH1 1NL
☎ **01244 343407** ▤ **01244 347737**
e-mail: info@dewaromanexperience.co.uk
web: www.dewaromanexperience.co.uk
dir: city centre

Stroll along reconstructed streets experiencing the sights, sounds and smells of Roman Chester. From the streets of Dewa (the Roman name for Chester) you return to the present day on an extensive archaeological 'dig', where you can discover the substantial Roman, Saxon and medieval remains beneath modern Chester. Try on Roman armour, solve puzzles and make brass rubbings and make mosaics in the hands-on/ activity room. Roman soldier patrols available.

Times Open all year, daily Feb-Nov 9-5, Dec-Jan 10-4 . (Closed 25-26 & 31 Dec & 1 Jan).* **Facilities** Ⓟ shop ⊗

CHOLMONDELEY

Cholmondeley Castle Gardens

SY14 8AH
☎ **01829 720383** ▤ **01829 720877**
e-mail: office@cholmondeleycastle.co.uk
web: www.cholmondeleycastle.com
dir: off A49 Tarporley to Whitchurch road

Dominated by a romantic Gothic Castle built in 1801 of local sandstone, the gardens are laid out with fine trees and water gardens, and have been replanted with rhododendrons, azaleas, cornus, and acer. There is also a rose and lavender garden, lakeside and woodland walks, and unusual breeds of farm animals. The Duckery, a derelict 19th-century lakeside pleasure ground has recently been developed and restored. The castle is not open to the public. Plenty of events throughout the year, including classic car rallies, open-air theatre and fireworks. Please contact for details.

Times Open 2 Apr-26 Sep, Wed-Thu, Sun & BHs 11-5. **Fees** £5 (ch £2).* **Facilities** Ⓟ ⧫ ⧫ (outdoor) ♿ (partly accessible) (designated wheelchair route) toilets for disabled shop

DISLEY

Lyme Park

SK12 2NX
☎ **01663 762023 & 766492** 📄 **01663 765035**
e-mail: lymepark@nationaltrust.org.uk
web: www.nationaltrust.org.uk
dir: off A6, 6.5m SE of Stockport. 12m NW of Buxton. House & car park 1m from entrance

Originally Tudor, Lyme Park now resembles a huge, Italianate palace following its transformation in the 18th century. Inside, a colourful family history is brought to life in beautifully furnished rooms. Outside, enjoy the opulent Victorian and Edwardian gardens with their sunken parterre, lake, and Wyatt-designed orangery. The surrounding deer park stretches up to the moors and is stocked with native species of deer.

Times Open 27 Feb-Oct, house Fri-Tue, garden daily, 11-5. Park: open all year daily 8-8. **Fees** House & Garden £8 (ch £4). Family ticket £20. House £5.80 (ch £2.90). Garden £5.50 (ch £2.75). **Facilities** 🅿 ▯🍴 licensed ⩎ (outdoor) ♿ (partly accessible) (access restricted, no lift to other floors, grounds have some slopes and uneven gravel paths) toilets for disabled shop ⊗ ⚏

ELLESMERE PORT

Blue Planet Aquarium

Cheshire Oaks CH65 9LF
☎ **0151 357 8800** 📄 **0151 356 7288**
e-mail: info@blueplanetaquarium.co.uk
web: www.blueplanetaquarium.com
dir: M53 junct 10 at Cheshire Oaks, M56 junct 15 follow Aquarium signs

A voyage of discovery on one of the longest moving walkways in the world. Beneath the waters of the Caribbean Reef, see giant rays and awesome sharks pass inches from your face, stroke some favourite fish in the special rock pools, or pay a visit to the incredible world of poisonous frogs. Divers hand feed the fish throughout the day and can answer questions via state of the art communication systems. Home to Europe's largest collection of sharks, including the large sand tiger sharks. We offer at least two special events in each season please check website for details.

Times Open all year, daily from 10. (Closed 25 Dec). Seasonal variations in closing times, please call to confirm. **Fees** £14.50 (ch £10.50, concessions £12.50). Family ticket £48 (2ad+2ch). Groovy grandparent ticket (2+2) £44. Please check website for further details.* **Facilities** 🅿🅿 ▯🍴 licensed ⩎ (outdoor) ♿ toilets for disabled shop ⊗

The National Waterways Museum

South Pier Rd CH65 4FW
☎ **0151 355 5017** 📄 **0151 355 4079**
e-mail: bookings@thewaterwaystrust.org
web: www.nwm.org.uk
dir: M53 junct 9

The National Waterways Museum aims to bring Britain's canal history to life. The fascinating museum is set within a 200-year-old seven acre dock complex and includes the world's largest floating collection of canal craft. With the dock workers cottages, blacksmiths forge, boat trips and events throughout the year there is something for everyone to enjoy. Check website or telephone for details of future events.

Times Open Summer daily 10-5. Winter Thu-Sun 10-4. Closed 1 Jan.* **Facilities** 🅿 ▯⩎ (indoor & outdoor) ♿ (partly accessible) (85% of the site is accessible to wheelchairs) toilets for disabled shop

JODRELL BANK

Jodrell Bank Visitor Centre & Arboretum

SK11 9DL
☎ **01477 571339** 📄 **01477 571695**
web: www.manchester.ac.uk/jodrellbank
dir: M6 junct 18, A535 Holmes Chapel to Chelford road

At Jodrell Bank, a scientific and engineering wonder awaits you - the magnificent Lovell telescope, one of the largest radio telescopes in the world. A pathway leads you 180 degrees around the telescope as it towers above you surveying and exploring the universe. Then, the visitor can wander along pathways amongst the trees of the extensive arboretum. The Centre is currently under a redevelopment, which will take 2-3 years to complete.

Times Open daily Nov-mid Mar 10.30-3, wknds 11-4; mid Mar-end Oct 10.30-5.30* **Facilities** 🅿 ▯⩎ (outdoor) ♿ toilets for disabled shop ⊗

KNUTSFORD

Tatton Park

WA16 6QN
☎ 01625 374400 & 374435   📄 01625 374403
e-mail: tatton@cheshireeast.gov.uk
web: www.tattonpark.org.uk
dir: Signed on A556, 4m S of Altrincham. Entrance to Tatton Park on Ashley Rd, 1.5m NE of junct A5034 with A50

Tatton Park is one of England's most complete historic estates, with gardens and a 1,000-acre country park. The centrepiece is the Georgian mansion, with gardens laid out by Humphry Repton and Sir Joseph Paxton. More recently, a Japanese garden with a Shinto temple was created. The Tudor Old Hall is the original manor house, where a guided tour is available. There is also a working 1930s farm and a children's adventure playground. Special events most weekends include the RHS flower show and open air concerts. The Second Tatton Park Bienniale takes place in summer 2010 bringing contemporary art back to the Estate.

Times 28 Mar-4 Oct, 10-7; 5 Oct-26 Mar 11-5* **Fees** Car entry £4.50. Each attraction £4.50 (ch £2.50). Family ticket £11.50. Totally Tatton Ticket (up to 3 attractions) £7 (ch £3.50). Family £17.* **Facilities** 🅿 🍽 licensed 🎪 (outdoor) ♿ (partly accessible) (old hall & areas of farm not accessible) toilets for disabled shop ♨

NANTWICH

Hack Green Secret Nuclear Bunker

French Ln, Hack Green CW5 8AP
☎ 01270 629219   📄 01270 629218
e-mail: coldwar@hackgreen.co.uk
web: www.hackgreen.co.uk
dir: from Nantwich take A530 towards Whitchurch, follow brown signs

One of the nation's most secret defence sites. Declassified in 1993, this underground bunker would have been the centre of regional government had nuclear war broken out. Observe the preparations the government made for nuclear war and step into the lives of people who worked here. View the Minister of State's office, life support, communication centre, decontamination facilities, telephone exchange and much more.

Times Open 20 Apr-30 Oct, daily 10.30-5.30; Nov, Jan, Feb wknds, 11-4. Closed Dec.* **Fees** £6.30 (ch £4.50, concessions £5.90). Family £19* **Facilities** 🅿 🅿 🍽 licensed 🎪 (outdoor) ♿ (partly accessible) (1st floor & bistro partly accessible) toilets for disabled shop ⊗

Stapeley Water Gardens

London Rd, Stapeley CW5 7LH
☎ 01270 623868 & 628628   📄 01270 624919
e-mail: info@stapeleywg.com
web: www.stapeleywg.com
dir: off M6 junct 16, 1m S of Nantwich on A51

There is plenty to do at Stapeley Water Gardens. The Palms Tropical Oasis is home to piranhas, parrots, skunks and exotic flowers, as well as tamarin monkeys, poisonous frogs and a crocodile. The two-acre Water Garden Centre houses a fantastic collection of water-lilies, as well as Koi carp and other water features. There is also a large garden centre, and various children's activities, including 'Meet the Keeper', which take place during school holidays.

Times Open Summer: Mon-Sat 9-6, BHs 10-6, Sun 10-4, Wed 9-8; Winter: Mon-Sat 9-5, BHs 10-5, Sun 10-4. The Palms Tropical Oasis open from 10.* **Fees** The Palms Tropical Oasis £4.95 (ch £2.95, concessions £4.45). Family ticket (2ad+2ch) £12.60 (2ad+3ch) £15. Discounts for groups 15+* **Facilities** 🅿 ⊡ 🍽 licensed 🎪 (outdoor) ♿ toilets for disabled shop ⊗

NORTHWICH

Salt Museum

162 London Rd CW9 8AB
☎ 01606 271640   📄 01606 350420
e-mail: cheshiremuseums@cheshire.gov.uk
web: www.saltmuseum.org.uk
dir: on A533, 0.5m S of town centre & 0.5m N of A556. Well signed from A556

Britain's only Salt Museum tells the fascinating story of Cheshire's oldest industry. Models, reconstructions, original artefacts and audio-visual programmes throw new light on something we all take for granted. Various temporary exhibitions are held here, please contact for details.

Times Open Tue-Fri 10-5, wknds 2-5 (Sat & Sun, 12-5 in Aug). Open BH & Mons in Aug 10-5.* **Facilities** 🅿 ⊡ 🎪 (outdoor) ♿ toilets for disabled shop ⊗

RUNCORN

Norton Priory Museum & Gardens

Tudor Rd, Manor Park WA7 1SX
☎ 01928 569895 📠 01928 589266
e-mail: info@nortonpriory.org
web: www.nortonpriory.org
dir: from M56 junct 11 towards Warrington, follow brown signs

Thirty-eight acres of peaceful woodland gardens are the setting for the medieval priory remains, museum and Walled Garden. Displays tell the story of the transformation of the priory into a Tudor manor house and then into an elegant Georgian mansion.

Times Open all year, Apr-Oct, Mon-Fri 12-5; Sat, Sun & BHs 12-6; Nov-Mar daily 12-4. Closed 24-26 Dec & 1 Jan. Walled Garden open Apr-Oct, daily 1.30-4.30.* **Fees** £5.50 (ch 5-16, concessions £3.95). Family ticket (2ad & 3) £13.50.* **Facilities** 🅿 Ⓟ ♿ 🎏 (outdoor) ♿ toilets for disabled shop ⊗

STYAL

Quarry Bank Mill & Styal Estate

SK9 4LA
☎ 01625 527468 & 445896 📠 01625 539267
e-mail: quarrybankmill@nationaltrust.org.uk
web: www.quarrybankmill.org.uk
dir: 1.5m N of Wilmslow off B5166, 2.5m from M56 junct 5. Follow heritage signs from A34 & M56

Founded in 1784, Quarry Bank Mill is one of the finest surviving cotton mills of the period. Inside the water and steam-powered mill there are hands-on exhibits and demonstrations that show how traditional spinning and weaving was transformed through the ingenuity of early textile engineers. Using the most powerful working waterwheel in Europe, two mill engines bring the past to life. At the Apprentice House you can discover what home life was like for the pauper children who worked in the mill in the 1830s. Visit the Mill Owner's secret garden, a picturesque valley retreat. After all this history take a walk through surrounding woods and farmland along the River Bollin.

Times Open Mar-Oct, daily 11-5; Nov-Feb, Wed-Sun 11-4 (last admission 1hr before closing). Apprentice House timed tours. Garden open Mar-Oct.* **Fees** Mill & Apprentice House or Garden £10 (ch £5). Family ticket £24. Mill only £7 (ch £3.70). Family ticket £17.70. **Facilities** 🅿 ♿ 🍴 licensed 🎏 ♿ (partly accessible) (Apprentice House level access to ground floor only) toilets for disabled shop ⊗ 🐾

FALMOUTH

National Maritime Museum Cornwall

Discovery Quay TR11 3QY
☎ 01326 313388 📠 01326 317878
e-mail: enquiries@nmmc.co.uk web: www.nmmc.co.uk
dir: follow signs from A39 for park/float ride and museum

Recently voted the south west's Visitor Attraction of the Year, this museum offers something for everyone from ever changing exhibitions, hands-on family activities, talks, lectures, displays, events, crabbing and the opportunity to sail and see marine and bird life. Admire the views from the 29 metre tower, descend the depths in one of only three natural underwater viewing galleries in the world and discover Cornwall, journey through time, explore the seas and go mad about boats. The purchase of a full price individual ticket gives you free entry to the Museum for a year.

Times Open daily 10-5. Closed 25-26 Dec.* **Fees** £8.75 (ch under 5 free, ch 6-15 & students £6, pen £7). Family ticket £24.* **Facilities** 🅿 Ⓟ ♿ 🍴 licensed ♿ toilets for disabled shop ⊗

Pendennis Castle

Pendennis Headland TR11 4LP
☎ 01326 316594 📠 01326 212044
web: www.english-heritage.org.uk
dir: 1m SE

Together with St Mawes Castle, Pendennis forms the end of a chain of castles built by Henry VIII along the south coast as protection from attack from France. Journey through 450 years of history and discover the castle's wartime secrets.

Times Open all year, Apr-Jun & Sep, daily 10-5 (Sat 10-4); Jul-Aug, daily 10-6 (Sat 10-4); Oct-Mar, daily 10-4. Closed 24-26 Dec & 1 Jan. **Fees** £5.70 (ch £2.90, concessions £4.80). Family £14.30. Please call 0870 333 1181 for the most up to date prices and opening times when planning your visit. **Facilities** 🅿 ♿ 🎏 ♿ (partly accessible) (two steep steps ticket point, spiral staircase, difficult steps to upper floor) toilets for disabled shop ⊗ ♿

GWEEK

National Seal Sanctuary

TR12 6UG
☎ **01326 221361 & 221874** 📄 **01326 221210**
e-mail: slcgweek@merlin-entertainments.com
web: www.sealsanctuary.co.uk
dir: pass RNAS Culdrose, take A3293, then B3291 to Gweek. Sanctuary signed from village

Britain's first rescue centre dedicated to the rehabilitation and release of grey seals. The Sanctuary offers a unique, educational experience and is a fun opportunity to learn more about the UK's largest mammal. Visit the UK's only Arctic hooded seal and the most diverse collection of pinnipeds (members of the seal family) in the UK, as well as Asian short-clawed otters, goats, ponies and sheep.

Times Open all year, daily from 10. Closed 25 Dec. **Fees** £12.90 (ch under 3 free, 3-14 £10.75, concessions £11.85). Family ticket (2ad+2ch) £38.70.* **Facilities** ❷ ⊡ ㅈ (outdoor) ♿ toilets for disabled shop

---

HELSTON

The Flambards Experience

Culdrose Manor TR13 0QA
☎ **01326 573404** 📄 **01326 573344**
e-mail: info@flambards.co.uk
web: www.flambards.co.uk
dir: 0.5m SE of Helston on A3083, Lizard road

Three award-winning, all-weather attractions can be visited on one site here. Flambards Victorian Village is a recreation of streets, shops and houses from 1830-1910. Britain in the Blitz is a life-size wartime street featuring shops, a pub and a living room complete with Morrison shelter. The Science Centre is a science playground that brings physics alive for the whole family. Along with the Thunderbolt and Extreme Force, Flambards also offers the Hornet Rollercoaster, the Family Log Flume, Go-Kart circuit, and rides and play areas for the very young. The Wildlife Experience show features lizards, snakes, large spiders and birds of prey. See the website for special events.

Times Open Etr-Nov, summer opening. Nov-Mar, winter opening.* **Fees** £16 (ch 3-15 £11.50). Family from £36.*
Facilities ❷ ⊡ ㅈ (indoor & outdoor) ♿ (partly accessible) (some rivers not accessible) toilets for disabled shop ⊗

Goonhilly Satellite Earth Station Experience

Goonhilly Downs TR12 6LQ
☎ **0800 679593** 📄 **01326 221438**
e-mail: goonhilly.visitorscentre@bt.com
web: www.goonhilly.bt.com
dir: From Helston follow the brown direction signs

Future World is on the site of what was the largest satellite earth station in the world, with over 60 dishes, which makes a dramatic impression on the Lizard Peninsula landscape. Enter a world of historic predictions, past inventions and ideas and see artefacts from jet packs and space helmets to the Sinclair C5 and the first mobile phones, complete with 'brick' size batteries. Journey into a zone of interactive displays where you can record your own visions of the future. Discover the history and heritage of Goonhilly itself in the main visitors' centre, and learn how international communications have developed over the past 200 years. You an also book a tour into the heart of 'Arthur', the Grade II listed iconic satellite dish.

Times Open 15 Mar-27 Jun & 6 Sep-31 Oct 10-5; 28 Jun-5 Sep 10-6; Nov-27 Mar 11-4.* **Facilities** ❷ ⊡ ⁜꘡ licensed ㅈ (outdoor) ♿ toilets for disabled shop ⊗

Trevarno Estate Garden & Museum of Gardening

Trevarno Manor, Crowntown TR13 0RU
☎ **01326 574274** 📄 **01326 574282**
e-mail: enquiry@trevarno.co.uk
web: www.trevarno.co.uk
dir: E of Crowntown. Leave Helston on Penzance road signed B3302

Victorian gardens with the splendid fountain garden conservatory, unique range of crafts and the National Museum of Gardening. In the tranquil gardens and grounds, follow the progress of restoration projects, visit craft areas including handmade soap workshop, explore Britain's largest and most comprehensive collection of antique tools, implements, memorabilia and ephemera, creatively displayed to illustrate how gardens and gardening influences most people's lives. Adventure play area for the youngsters, extended estate walk and viewing platform. Home of the national daffodil collection showgarden (flowering Jan-mid May).

Times Open daily 10.30-5. Closed 25-26 Dec **Fees** £6.50 (ch 5-14 £2.25, concessions £5.75, disabled £3.25). Group 12+*
Facilities ❷ ⊡ ㅈ (outdoor) ♿ toilets for disabled shop

Cornwall

LANHYDROCK

Lanhydrock

PL30 5AD
☎ **01208 265950** 🖃 **01208 265959**
e-mail: lanhydrock@nationaltrust.org.uk
web: www.nationaltrust.org.uk
dir: 2.5m SE of Bodmin, signed from A30, A38 & B3268

Part-Jacobean, part-Victorian building that gives a vivid picture of life in Victorian times. The 'below stairs' sections have a huge kitchen, larders, dairy, bakehouse, cellars, and servants' quarters. The long gallery has a moulded ceiling showing Old Testament scenes, and overlooks the formal gardens with their clipped yews and bronze urns. The higher garden, famed for its magnolias and rhododendrons, climbs the hillside behind the house.

Times House open 13 Mar-Oct daily (ex Mon) 11-5 (Apr-Sep 5.30), open BH Mon & Mon during school hols. Gardens open all year, daily 10-6. **Fees** House & Grounds £10.90 (ch £5.40). Family tickets available. Garden & Grounds £6.40 (ch £5.80). Reduced rate when arriving by cycle or public transport. **Facilities** ❷ ⓟ ⬚ 🍴 licensed 🆎 (outdoor) ♿ toilets for disabled shop ⊗ 😾

LAUNCESTON

Tamar Otter & Wildlife Centre

North Petherwin PL15 8GW
☎ **01566 785646**
e-mail: info@tamarotters.co.uk
web: www.tamarotters.co.uk
dir: 5m NW off B3254 Bude road

Visitors to this wildlife centre will see British and Asian short-clawed otters in large natural enclosures. They will also be able to see fallow and Muntjac deer, and wallabies roaming around the grounds. There are also owls, peacocks, and a large selection of waterfowl on two lakes. Otters are fed at noon and 3pm and this is accompanied by an informative talk.

Times Open Apr-Oct, daily 10.30-6 (dates extended in accordance with school hols). Opens Good Fri if earlier than 1 Apr.* **Fees** £7 (ch 3-15yrs £3.50, concessions £6) Family (2 ad+3 ch) £18* **Facilities** ❷ ⬚ 🆎 (outdoor) ♿ (partly accessible) (steep slope to otter pens/woodland walk) toilets for disabled shop ⊗

LOOE

The Monkey Sanctuary Trust

St Martins PL13 1NZ
☎ **01503 262532** 🖃 **01503 262532**
e-mail: info@monkeysanctuary.org
web: www.monkeysanctuary.org
dir: signed on B3253 at No Man's Land between East Looe & Hessenford

Visitors can see a colony of Amazonian woolly monkeys in extensive indoor and outdoor territory. There are also conservation gardens, children's play area, activity room, a display room and vegetarian cafe. The Monkey Sanctuary Trust is also a rescue centre for ex-pet capuchin monkeys rescued from the UK pet trade. In addition a bat cave is on site where visitors can watch a colony of rare horseshoe bats.

Times Open Sun-Thu from the Sun before Etr-Sep. Also open Autumn Half Term.* **Facilities** ❷ ⬚ 🆎 (outdoor) ♿ (partly accessible) toilets for disabled shop ⊗

MARAZION

St Michael's Mount

TR17 0HT
☎ **01736 710507 & 710265** 🖃 **01736 719930**
e-mail: mail@stmichaelsmount.co.uk
web: www.stmichaelsmount.co.uk
dir: access is by Causeway on foot at low tide. 0.5m S of A394 at Marazion or by motorboat in summer

After the Norman Conquest, the abbey on St Michael's Mount was granted to the Benedictine order and the church on the island's summit was built by the French abbot in charge of the abbey. Miracles, said to have occurred here in the 1260s, increased the island's religious attraction to pilgrims. The Mount was besieged in 1473 during the War of the Roses, in 1588 it was the place where the first beacon was lit to warn of the arrival of the Spanish Armada, and in the Civil War it was a Royalist stronghold attacked by Cromwell's forces. Today it is the home of the St Aubyn family who have lived here since the 17th century. The island is separated from the mainland by a causeway which is covered by the sea at high tide.

Times Open: Castle 29 Mar-1 Nov 10.30-5. (last entry 45mins before closing). Winter Tue & Fri by guided tour only. Garden May-June, Mon-Fri, Jul-Oct Thu & Fri 10.30-5.* **Fees** £6.60 (ch £3.30) Family ticket £16.50 (1ad family £9.90). Groups 15+ £5.60. Garden £3 (ch £1). Castle & gardens free to NT members.* **Facilities** ⓟ ⬚ 🍴 licensed 🆎 (outdoor) shop ⊗ 😾

MAWNAN SMITH

Trebah Garden

TR11 5JZ

☎ 01326 252200   📄 01326 250781

e-mail: mail@trebah-garden.co.uk

web: www.trebah-garden.co.uk

dir: signed at Treliever Cross rdbt at junct of A39/A394 & follow brown tourist signs

A 26-acre wooded valley garden, descending 200 feet from the 18th-century house down to a private cove on the Helford River. The cascading Water Garden has pools of giant koi and exotic water plants, winding through two acres of blue and white hydrangeas to the beach. There are glades of sub-tropical tree ferns and palms, as well as rhododendrons and many other trees and shrubs from all over the world. The beach is open to visitors and there are children's trails and activities all year.

Times Open daily 10-5 (last admission). In winter 10 til dusk. **Fees** Mar-Oct £7.50 (ch £2.50, ch under 5 free, disabled £3.50, concessions £6.50; Nov-Feb £3 (ch & disabled £1, ch under 5 free, concessions £2.50). **Facilities** 🅿 Ⓟ 🚻 †◎† licensed ⅋ (outdoor) ♿ (partly accessible) (disabled easy access route) toilets for disabled shop

NEWQUAY

Blue Reef Aquarium

Towan Promenade TR7 1DU

☎ 01637 878134   📄 01637 872578

e-mail: newquay@bluereefaquarium.co.uk

web: www.bluereefaquarium.co.uk

dir: from A30 follow signs to Newquay, follow Blue Reef Aquarium signs to car park in town centre. Satellite Navigation TR7 1JQ. Disabled access please ring.

Take the ultimate undersea safari at the Blue Reef Aquarium. Discover Cornish marine life from native sharks and rays to the incredibly intelligent and playful octopus. From here journey through warmer waters to watch the magical seahorses, unusual shape shifting, jet-propelled cuttlefish and the vibrant, swaying tentacles of living sponges and anemones. Continue your safari through the underwater tunnel below a tropical sea. Here you will encounter the activities of a coral reef alive with shoals of brightly coloured fish and the graceful, black tip reef sharks which glide silently overhead. Daily talks and regular feeding demonstrations bring the experience to life. Events all year, please see website for details.

Times Open all year, daily 10-5. (Closed 25 Dec). Open until 6 during summer holidays. **Fees** £8.95 (ch £6.95, concessions £7.95).* **Facilities** Ⓟ 🚻 ⅋ (outdoor) ♿ (partly accessible) (small area, only accessible via steps) toilets for disabled shop ⊗

Dairy Land Farm World

Summercourt TR8 5AA

☎ 01872 510246   📄 01872 510349

e-mail: info@dairylandfarmworld.co.uk

web: www.dairylandfarmworld.com

dir: Signed from A30 at exit for Mitchell/Summercourt

Visitors can watch while the cows are milked to music on a spectacular merry-go-round milking machine. The life of a Victorian farmer and his neighbours is explored in the Heritage Centre, and a Farm Nature Trail features informative displays along pleasant walks. Children will have fun getting to know the farm animals in the Farm Park. They will also enjoy the playground, assault course and indoor play areas.

Times Open daily, late Mar-Oct 10-5. (Bull pen additional winter openings Thu-Sun & school hols, please telephone for more information)* **Facilities** 🅿 🚻 ⅋ (indoor & outdoor) toilets for disabled shop ⊗

Newquay Zoo

Trenance Gardens TR7 2LZ

☎ 01637 873342   📄 01637 851318

e-mail: info@newquayzoo.org.uk

web: www.newquayzoo.org.uk

dir: off A3075 and follow signs to Zoo

Newquay Zoo is set among exotic lakeside gardens with animals from all around the world. Enjoy fascinating talks, animal encounters and feeding times throughout the day. See the otter family playing in the stream in the Oriental Garden, look out for meerkats on sentry duty, try to spot the secretive red panda, and glimpse the endangered lemurs and fossa. Kids will enjoy the Tarzan Trail, the village farm and the dragon maze. Other highlights include penguin, zebra, Sulawesi-crested macaques, tapirs, marmosets, tamarim and a new African Savanna and Philippines exhibits.

Times Open all year Apr-Sep, daily 9.30-6, (last entry 5); Oct-Mar, 10-5. **Fees** Under review please contact for details. **Facilities** Ⓟ 🅿 🚻 †◎† licensed ⅋ (outdoor) ♿ (partly accessible) (stairs in Tropical House & upto the Owls & Tarzan Trail) toilets for disabled shop ⊗

PENDEEN

Geevor Tin Mine

TR19 7EW
☎ 01736 788662   📠 01736 786059
e-mail: bookings@geevor.com
web: www.geevor.com
dir: From Penzance take A3071 towards St Just, then B3318 towards Pendeen. From St Ives follow B3306 to Pendeen

A preserved tin mine and museum provide an insight into the methods and equipment used in the industry that was once so important in the area. The Geevor Tin Mine only actually stopped operation in 1990. Guided tours let visitors see the tin treatment plant, and a video illustrates the techniques employed. A museum of hard rock mining has recently opened, and the underground tour is well worth the trip.

Times Open daily (ex Sat) 9-5 (9-4 Nov-Mar). Closed 21-26 Dec & 1 Jan **Fees** £8.50 (ch & students £4.50, concessions £7.50) Family ticket £25. **Facilities** ❷ ℗ 🖵 🍽 licensed 🗛 (outdoor) ♿ (partly accessible) (access to new museum, shop & cafe) toilets for disabled shop ⊗

PENTEWAN

The Lost Gardens of Heligan

PL26 6EN
☎ 01726 845100   📠 01726 845101
e-mail: info@heligan.com
web: www.heligan.com
dir: signed from A390 & B3273

Heligan, seat of the Tremayne family for more than 400 years, is one of the most mysterious estates in England. At the end of the 19th-century its thousand acres were at their zenith, but only a few years after the Great War, bramble and ivy were already drawing a green veil over this sleeping beauty. Today the garden offers 200 acres for exploration, which include productive gardens, pleasure grounds, a sub-tropical jungle, sustainably-managed farmland, wetlands, ancient woodlands and a pioneering wildlife project. Please telephone for details of spring-time and harvest-time events and for summer evening theatre.

Times Open Apr-Sep, daily 10-6 (last tickets 4.30); Oct-Mar, daily 10-5 (last tickets 3.30)* **Fees** £8.50 (ch £5, pen £7.50). Family £23.50 (2ad+3ch)* **Facilities** ❷ ℗ 🖵 🗛 (indoor & outdoor) ♿ (partly accessible) (northern gardens, wildlife project, shop, plant sales & tearooms all accessible) toilets for disabled shop ⊗

ST AUSTELL

Charlestown Shipwreck & Heritage Centre

Quay Rd, Charlestown PL25 3NJ
☎ 01726 69897   📠 01726 69897
e-mail: admin@shipwreckcharlestown.com
web: www.shipwreckcharlestown.com
dir: signed off A390 from St. Austell close to Eden Project

Charlestown is a small and unspoilt village with a unique sea-lock, china-clay port, purpose built in the 18th century. The Shipwreck and Heritage Centre was originally a dry house for china clay built on underground tunnels. Now it houses the largest display of shipwreck artefacts in the UK, along with local heritage, diving exhibits, and an RMS Titanic display. A recent addition is a Nelson display which commemorates the 200th anniversary of the Battle of Trafalgar.

Times Open Mar-Oct, daily 10-5. (Last admission 1 hour before closing) **Fees** £5.95 (ch under 10 free if accompanied by paying adult, ch under 16 £2.50, concessions £3.95) group prices on request. **Facilities** ❷ ℗ 🖵 🍽 licensed ♿ toilets for disabled shop

The China Clay Country Park

Carthew PL26 8XG
☎ 01726 850362   📠 01726 850362
e-mail: info@chinaclaycountry.co.uk
web: www.chinaclaycountry.co.uk
dir: 2m N on B3274, follow brown signs 'China Clay Museum'

This museum tells the story of Cornwall's most important present-day industry: china clay production. The open-air site includes a complete 19th-century clayworks, with huge granite-walled settling tanks, working water-wheels and a wooden slurry pump. There is a fully interactive gallery, nature trails and a children's adventure trail. Exhibition halls and interactive displays depict the life of claypit workers from 1800 to the present.

Times Open all year 10-6, last admission summer 4, winter 3* **Facilities** ❷ ℗ 🖵 🍽 licensed 🗛 (outdoor) ♿ toilets for disabled shop

Eden Project

Bodelva PL24 2SG
☎ **01726 811911** 🖹 **01726 811912**
e-mail: information@edenproject.com
web: www.edenproject.com
dir: overlooking St Austell Bay signposted from A390/A30/A391

An unforgettable experience in a breathtaking location, the Eden Project is a gateway into the fascinating world of plants and human society. Space age technology meets the lost world in the biggest greenhouse ever built. Located in a 50 metre deep crater the size of 30 football pitches are two gigantic geodesic conservatories: the Humid Tropics Biome and the Warm Temperate Biome. This is a startling and unique day out. There's an ice-rink in the winter (Nov-Feb) and concerts in the summer - see the website for details.

Times Open Mar-Oct, daily 9-6 (last admission 4.30). Nov-Mar 10-4.30 (last admission 3). 20 Jul-4 Sep open until 8 on Tue, Wed & Thu. Closed 24-25 Dec & 25-26 Jan. **Fees** £16 (ch £5, under 5's free, student £8 concessions £11). Family ticket (2ad+ up to 3ch) £38. Annual membership available.* **Facilities** ℗ ⏍ ⑩ licensed 🍴 (indoor & outdoor) ♿ (partly accessible) toilets for disabled shop ⊗

ST IVES

Park your car at Lelant Station and take advantage of the park and ride service. The fee includes parking and journeys on the train between Lelant and St Ives during the day.

Tate St Ives

Porthmeor Beach TR26 1TG
☎ **01736 796226** 🖹 **01736 794480**
e-mail: tatestivesinfo@tate.org.uk
web: www.tate.org.uk/stives
dir: M5 to Exeter, then A30 onto Penzance & St Ives. Located on Porthmeor Beach

Home of post-war British Modernism, St Ives provides the artistic foundations for Tate St Ives. Built in 1993, the gallery celebrates the surroundings and atmosphere that inspired the Modernists, and its unique architecture recalls the 'White

Relief' work of Ben Nicholson as well as the unexpected twists and turns of the town itself. The gallery presents a varied programme of both Cornish and international artists, from the past and present, including displays on loan from Tate Modern.

Times Open Mar-Oct, daily 10-5.30; Nov-Feb, Tue-Sun 10-4.30. Closed 24-26 Dec* **Facilities** ℗ ⏍ ⑩ licensed toilets for disabled shop ⊗

TINTAGEL

Tintagel Castle

PL34 0HE
☎ **01840 770328** 🖹 **01841 772105**
web: www.english-heritage.org.uk
dir: on Tintagel Head, 0.5m along uneven track from Tintagel, no vehicles

Overlooking the wild Cornish coast, Tintagel is one of the most spectacular spots in the country and associated with King Arthur and Merlin. Recent excavations revealed Dark Age connections between Spain and Cornwall, alongside the discovery of the 'Arthnou' stone suggesting that this was a royal place for the Dark Age rulers of Cornwall.

Times Open all year, Apr-Sep, daily 10-6; Oct-1 Nov, daily 10-5; 2 Nov-Mar, daily 10-4. Closed 24-26 Dec & 1 Jan. Beach cafe open daily, Apr-Oct (closes 1/2hr before castle) Nov-Mar 11-3.30. **Fees** £4.90 (concessions £4.20, ch £2.50). Family ticket £12.30. Please call 0870 333 1181 for the most up to date prices and opening times when planning your visit. **Facilities** ℗ shop ⊗ ⚎

Tintagel Old Post Office

PL34 0DB
☎ **01840 770024**
e-mail: tintageloldpo@nationaltrust.org.uk
web: www.nationaltrust.org.uk
dir: In centre of Tintagel village

A rare survival of Cornish domestic medieval architecture, this 14th-century yeoman's farmhouse is well furnished with local oak pieces. One room was used during the Victorian era as the letter receiving office for the district.

Times Open daily, 13-21 Feb & 13 Mar-2 Apr 11-4; 3 Apr-28 May 10.30-5; 29 May-1 Oct 10.30-5.30; 2-31 Oct 11-4. **Fees** £3.20 (ch £1.60, under 5's & NT members free). Family tickets available. Group 10+ £2.60. **Facilities** ℗ ♿ (partly accessible) (partly accessible with ramp) shop ⊗ ⚘

TORPOINT

Mount Edgcumbe House & Country Park

Cremyll PL10 1HZ
☎ 01752 822236 📄 01752 822199
e-mail: mt.edgcumbe@plymouth.gov.uk
web: www.mountedgcumbe.gov.uk
dir: from Plymouth via Cremyll Foot Ferry, Torpoint ferry or Saltash Bridge. Via Liskeard to A374, B3247 follow brown heritage signs

Covering some 800 acres, the country park surrounding Mount Edgcumbe contains a deer park, an amphitheatre, formal gardens, sculpture, the 18th-century Earl's Garden, and woodlands containing California redwoods. The coastal footpath runs along the shores of the Park from Cremyll to Whitsand Bay. Sir Richard Edgcumbe of Cotehele built Mount Edgcumbe between 1547 and 1553. It survived a direct hit by bombs in 1941, and was restored in the 1950s. It now contains antique paintings and furniture, 16th-century tapestries, and 18th-century porcelain. Events and exhibitions held each year.

Times Open: House & Earl's Garden Apr-Sep, Sun-Thu & BH Mon, 11-4.30. (Closed Fri & Sat). Country Park open all year.*
Facilities 🅿 🅟 ⬛ 🍽 licensed ⛱ (outdoor) toilets for disabled shop ⊗

TRERICE

Trerice

TR8 4PG
☎ 01637 875404 📄 01637 879300
e-mail: trerice@nationaltrust.org.uk
web: www.nationaltrust.org.uk
dir: 3m SE of Newquay off A3058 at Kestle Mill

Trerice was built in 1571 by Sir John Arundell IV and, having suffered no major changes since then due to a succession of absentee landlords, it appears very much the same as when it was built. The plaster ceilings in the Great Hall and Great Chamber are of particular merit and the façade of the building is thought to be the oldest of its kind in the country. The house contains many fine pieces of furniture and a large collection of clocks, and the garden is planted to provide colour and interest throughout the year, and features an orchard with many varieties of Cornish apple trees.

Times Open Mar-Oct, daily (ex Fri) 11-4.30 **Fees** House £7.40 (ch £3.70) Family & group tickets available. Reduced rate when arriving by cycle or public transport. **Facilities** 🅟 ⬛ 🍽 licensed ⛱ (outdoor) ♿ toilets for disabled shop ⊗ 🌿

WENDRON

Poldark Mine and Heritage Complex

TR13 0ER
☎ 01326 573173 📄 01326 563166
e-mail: info@poldark-mine.com
web: www.poldark-mine.com
dir: 3m from Helston on B3297 Redruth road, follow brown signs

The centre of this attraction is the 18th-century tin mine where visitors can join a guided tour of workings which retain much of their original character. The site's Museum explains the history of tin production in Cornwall from 1800BC through to the 19th century and the fascinating story of the Cornish overseas. In addition to the Museum, the audio-visual presentation gives more insight into Cornwall's mining heritage. Ghost tours through July and August, please phone for details.

Times Open Etr-end Oct, 10-5.30 (last tour 4).* **Facilities** 🅟 ⬛ 🍽 licensed ⛱ (indoor & outdoor) ♿ (partly accessible) (surface area only) toilets for disabled shop

ZENNOR

Wayside Folk Museum

TR26 3DA
☎ 01736 796945
dir: 4m W of St Ives, on B3306

Founded in 1937, this museum covers every aspect of life in Zennor and the surrounding area from 3000BC to the 1930s. Over 5000 items are displayed in 12 workshops and rooms covering wheelwrights, blacksmiths, agriculture, fishing, wrecks, mining, schools, dairy, domestic and archaeological artefacts. A photographic exhibition entitled 'People of the Past' tells the story of the village. The museum also contains a watermill to which visitors have access.

Times Open Etr-end Oct, daily 10.30-5.30.* **Fees** £3.75 (ch £2.25). Family ticket (2ad+2ch) £11. Party rates 10+* **Facilities** 🅟 ⛱ (outdoor) shop

CUMBRIA

ALSTON

Nenthead Mines

Nenthead CA9 3PD
☎ **01434 382726** 📠 **01434 382043**
e-mail: mines@npht.com
web: www.npht.com/nentheadmines
dir: 5m E of Alston, on A689

Set in 200 acres in the North Pennines, this hands-on heritage centre contains exhibitions and displays on geology, local wildlife, and social history. Visitors can operate three enormous water wheels, gaze down a 328ft deep brewery shaft, and take an underground trip through the Nenthead mines, last worked for lead in 1915. Special events take place throughout the year.

Times Open Etr-Oct, daily 11-5 (last entry to mine 3.30).*
Facilities 🅿️ Ⓟ 🚻 🎠 (indoor & outdoor) ♿ (partly accessible) (ltd disabled access underground) toilets for disabled shop

South Tynedale Railway

The Railway Station, Hexham Rd CA9 3JB
☎ **01434 381696**
web: www.strps.org.uk
dir: 0.25m N, on A686

Running along the beautiful South Tyne valley, this narrow-gauge railway follows the route of the former Alston to Haltwhistle branch. At present the line runs between Alston and Kirkhaugh.

Times Open Etr-Oct, wknds & BHs; mid Jul-Aug daily. Please enquire for exact details **Fees** Return £5.50 (ch 3-15 £2.50). Single £3.30 (ch 3-15 £1.50). All day £9 (ch 3-15 £4). Family ticket £15.* **Facilities** 🅿️ Ⓟ 🚻 🎠 (outdoor) ♿ toilets for disabled shop

BARROW-IN-FURNESS

The Dock Museum   FREE

North Rd LA14 2PW
☎ **01229 876400** 📠 **01229 811361**
e-mail: dockmuseum@barrowbc.gov.uk
web: www.dockmuseum.org.uk
dir: A590 to Barrow-in-Furness. Follow brown tourist signs

Explore this museum and relive the fascinating history of Barrow-in-Furness. Discover how the industrial revolution prompted the growth of the town from a small hamlet into a major industrial power through models, graphics and computer kiosks.

Times Open mid Apr-Nov, Tue-Fri 10-5, Sat-Sun 11-5; Nov-Mar, Wed-Fri 10.30-4, Sat-Sun 11-4.30.* **Facilities** 🅿️ Ⓟ 🚻 🎠 (outdoor) ♿ toilets for disabled shop ⊗

BASSENTHWAITE

Trotters World of Animals

Coalbeck Farm CA12 4RD
☎ **017687 76239** 📠 **017687 76598**
e-mail: info@trottersworld.com
web: www.trottersworld.com
dir: follow brown signs on A591/A66 from Bassenthwaite Lake

Home to hundreds of friendly creatures including lemurs, wallabies, zebras, otters and other exotic animals along with reptiles and birds of prey and a family of gibbons which will keep families amused for hours. Informative, amusing demonstrations bring visitors closer to the animals. "Clown About" is an indoor play centre with soft play area and ballpools for toddlers upwards.

Times Open all year, except 25 Dec & 1 Jan, 10-5.30 or dusk if earlier.* **Facilities** 🅿️ 🚻 🍽️ licensed 🎠 (outdoor) ♿ toilets for disabled shop ⊗

BORROWDALE

Honister Slate Mine

Honister Pass CA12 5XN
☎ **01768 777230** 📠 **01768 777958**
e-mail: info@honister.com
web: www.honister.com
dir: from Keswick take B5289 through Borrowdale & Rosthwaite, follow road to top of pass. From Cockermouth take B5292 towards Keswick for 4m, turn right onto B5289 to Low Larton & Buttermere. Follow road to top of pass

The last working slate mine in England. Fully guided tours allow you to explore the caverns hacked out by Victorian miners. Learn the history of the famous Honister green slate, how to rive slates, and see local skills in action.

Times Open Mon-Fri 9-5, wknds 10-5. Closed 19 Dec-12 Jan.* **Facilities** 🅿️ Ⓟ 🚻 🍽️ licensed 🎠 ♿ (partly accessible) toilets for disabled shop

CARLISLE

Tullie House Museum & Art Gallery

Castle St CA3 8TP
☎ 01228 618718 📠 01228 810249
e-mail: enquiries@tulliehouse.co.uk **web:** www.tulliehouse.co.uk
dir: M6 junct 42, 43 or 44 follow signs to city centre. Car park in Devonshire Walk

Set in newly re-designed Roman and Jacobean gardens, Old Tullie House is home to an impressive collection of Pre-Raphaelite art, with many of the classical features of the 17th century building still remaining, including a stunning staircase. Along with painting and sculpture, there are interactive exhibits that explore Roman life as well as 'Freshwater Life'. Lots of events through the year, contact for details.

Times Open Nov-Mar, Mon-Sat 10-4, Sun 12-4; Apr-Jun & Sep-Oct, Mon-Sat 10-5, Sun 12-5; Jul-Aug, Mon-Sat 10-5, Sun 11-5. Closed 25-26 Dec & 1 Jan.* **Fees** Ground floor (including Art Gallery & Old Tullie House) Free. Upper floors & New Millennium Gallery £5.20 (ch under 18 free, concessions £3.60).* **Facilities** ℗ ⚏ ⏐❍ licensed ♿ (partly accessible) (Old Tullie House restricted access) toilets for disabled shop ⊗

COCKERMOUTH

Wordsworth House

Main St CA13 9RX
☎ 01900 820882 📠 01900 820883
e-mail: wordsworthhouse@nationaltrust.org.uk
web: www.wordsworthhouse.org.uk
dir: W end of Main Street

William Wordsworth was born here on 7th April 1770, and happy memories of the house had a great effect on his work. The house is imaginatively presented for the first time as the home of the Wordsworth family in the 1770s. It offers a lively and interactive visit with hands-on activities and costumed living history.

Times Open 27 Mar-28 Oct, 11-4.30. Jul, Aug & BHs Mon-Sat, other times Tue-Sat.* **Fees** £6.20 (ch £3.10). Family ticket £15.50. **Facilities** ℗ toilets for disabled shop ⊗ 🌷

DALTON-IN-FURNESS

South Lakes Wild Animal Park

Crossgates LA15 8JR
☎ 01229 466086 📠 01229 461310
e-mail: office@wildanimalpark.co.uk
web: www.wildanimalpark.co.uk
dir: M6 junct 36, A590 to Dalton-in-Furness, follow tourist signs

A day you'll never forget at one of Cumbria's top attractions. Hand feed giraffes, penguins and kangaroos every day. Get up close to rhinos, tigers, bears, hippos, monkeys, vultures, and lemurs. There are new aerial walkways and viewpoints, the Wild Things gift shop and Maki restaurant, all overlooking a recreated African Savannah where rhinos, giraffes and baboons wander.

Times Open all year, daily 10-5 (last admission 4.15); Nov-Feb 10-4.30 (last admission 3.45). Closed 25 Dec. **Fees** £11.50 (ch & concessions £8). **Facilities** ℗ ℗ ⚏ ⏽ (indoor & outdoor) ♿ toilets for disabled shop ⊗

GRASMERE

Dove Cottage, The Wordsworth Museum and Art Gallery

LA22 9SH
☎ 015394 35544 📠 015394 35748
e-mail: enquiries@wordsworth.org.uk
web: www.wordsworth.org.uk
dir: A591 S of rdbt for Grasmere village

Dove Cottage was the inspirational home of William Wordsworth between 1799-1808, and it was here that he wrote some of his best-known poetry. The cottage has been open to the public since 1891, and is kept in its original condition. The museum displays manuscripts, works of art and items that belonged to the poet. There is a changing programme of special events, both historical and modern. Please visit website for details.

Times Open daily 9.30-5.30 (last admission 5). Closed 24 Dec & Jan. **Fees** £7.50 (ch £4.50). Family ticket £17.20. Discounts for pre-bkd groups. **Facilities** ℗ ℗ ⚏ ⏐❍ licensed ♿ (partly accessible) (Museum, galleries & ground floor of cottage accessible) toilets for disabled shop ⊗

HAWKSHEAD

Beatrix Potter Gallery

Main St LA22 0NS
☎ 015394 36269   ▤ 015394 36811
e-mail: beatrixpottergallery@nationaltrust.org.uk
web: www.nationaltrust.org.uk
dir: on main street in village centre

An annually changing exhibition of Beatrix Potter's original illustrations from her children's storybooks, housed in the former office of her husband, solicitor William Heelis.

Times Open 13 Feb-25 Mar, Sat-Thu 11-3.30; 27 Mar-Oct, Sat-Thu 10.30-4.30. Admission by timed ticket including NT members. **Fees** £4.20 (ch £2.10). Family ticket (2ad+3ch) £10.50.
Facilities ℗ ♿ (partly accessible) shop ⊗ ✿

HOLKER

Holker Hall & Gardens

Cark in Cartmel, Grange over Sands LA11 7PL
☎ 015395 58328   ▤ 015395 58378
e-mail: publicopening@holker.co.uk
web: www.holker-hall.co.uk
dir: from M6 junct 36, follow A590, signed

Dating from the 16th century, the new wing of the Hall was rebuilt in 1871, after a fire. It has a notable woodcarving and many fine pieces of furniture which mix happily with family photographs from the present day. There are magnificent gardens, both formal and woodland, and the Lakeland Motor Museum, exhibitions, deer park and adventure playground are further attractions.

Times Open Apr-28 Oct, Garden open 10.30-5.30. Hall open 12-4.* **Fees** Gardens & Grounds £5.95 (ch 6-15 £3) Family ticket £15.50. All 3 attractions £11.50 (ch £6.50) Family ticket £32.*
Facilities ℗ ☖ ⊙ licensed ⊟ (outdoor) toilets for disabled shop ⊗

KENDAL

Museum of Lakeland Life

Abbot Hall LA9 5AL
☎ 01539 722464   ▤ 01539 722494
e-mail: info@lakelandmuseum.org.uk
web: www.lakelandmuseum.org.uk
dir: M6 junct 36, follow signs to Kendal. Located at south end of Kendal beside Abbot Hall Art Gallery

The life and history of the Lake District is captured by the displays in this museum, housed in Abbot Hall's stable block. The working and social life of the area are well illustrated by a variety of exhibits including period rooms, a Victorian Cumbrian street scene, a farming display, Arts and Crafts movement textiles and furniture and a recreation of Arthur Ransome's study, furnished with many of his personal possessions.

Times Open 13 Jan-12 Dec, Mon-Sat 10.30-5. (Closing at 4 Jan-Mar & Nov-Dec)* **Fees** £4.75 (ch £3.40). Family ticket £13.60.*
Facilities ⊙ ℗ ☖ ♿ (partly accessible) toilets for disabled shop ⊗

KESWICK

Cars of the Stars Motor Museum

Standish St CA12 5LS
☎ 017687 73757   ▤ 017687 72090
e-mail: cotsmm@aol.com
web: www.carsofthestars.com
dir: M6 junct 40, A66 to Keswick, continue to town centre, close to Bell Close car park

This unusual museum features celebrity TV and film vehicles. Some notable exhibits to look out for are Chitty Chitty Bang Bang, James Bond's DB5 Aston Martin, Harry Potter's Ford Anglia, Del Boy's Robin Reliant, A-Team van and Batmobiles. Each vehicle is displayed in its individual film set. Newly open "The Bond Museum".

Times Open Feb half term, daily Etr-Nov (wknds Dec) 10-5
Fees £6 (ch £4)* **Facilities** ℗ ♿ shop

Keswick continued

Cumberland Pencil Museum

Southey Works, Greta Bridge CA12 5NG
☎ **017687 73626** 📠 **01900 602489**
e-mail: kes_museum@acco.com
web: www.pencilmuseum.co.uk
dir: M6 N onto A66 at Penrith. Left at 2nd Keswick exit, left at
T-junct, left over Greta Bridge

Investigating the history and technology of an object most of
us take utterly for granted, this interesting museum includes
a replica of the Borrowdale mine where graphite was first
discovered, the world's longest pencil, children's activity
area, and various artistic techniques that use pencils. Artist
demonstrations and workshops will take place throughout the
year.

Times Open daily 9.30-4 (hours may be extended during peak
season). (Closed 25-26 Dec & 1 Jan). **Fees** £3.50 (concessions
£2.25). Family ticket (2ad+3ch) £9.25. Annual membership
£14.75. **Facilities** 🅿 Ⓟ ▯ 🍴 (outdoor) ♿ toilets for disabled
shop

Mirehouse

CA12 4QE
☎ **017687 72287**
e-mail: info@mirehouse.com
web: www.mirehouse.com
dir: 3m N of Keswick on A591

Visitors return to Mirehouse for many reasons: close links to
Tennyson and Wordsworth, the spectacular setting of mountain
and lake, the varied gardens, changing displays on the Poetry
Walk, free family trail, four woodland playgrounds, live
piano music in the house, generous Cumbrian cooking in the
tearoom, and a relaxed, friendly welcome. Please contact for
details of special events.

Times Open Apr-Oct. Grounds: daily 10.30-5.30 House: Wed,
Sun, (also Fri in Aug) 2-last entry 4.30.* **Fees** House & grounds
£6 (ch £3). Grounds only £3 (ch £1.50). Family ticket £17 (2ad &
up to 4ch)* **Facilities** 🅿 ▯ 🍴 (outdoor) ♿ toilets for disabled Ⓧ

LAKESIDE

Lakes Aquarium

LA12 8AS
☎ **015395 30153** 📠 **015395 30152**
e-mail: info@lakesaquarium.co.uk
web: www.lakesaquarium.co.uk
dir: M6, junct 36, take A590 to Newby Bridge. Turn right over
bridge, follow Hawkshead Rd to Lakeside

Re-launched in 2008, the Lakes Aquarium is now home to
creatures that live in and around freshwater lakes across the
globe! See things that swim, fly and bite in beautifully-themed
displays. Discover mischievous otters in the Asia area, piranhas
in the Americas and cheeky marmosets in the rainforest
displays, not forgetting all your favourite creatures that live a
bit closer to home. This includes diving ducks in the spectacular
underwater tunnel and fresh water rays and seahorses in the
Seashore Discover Zone. Don't miss the worlds first virtual
dive bell! Experience a spectacular interactive adventure and
come face to face with awesome virtual creatures including a
terrifying shark, charging hippo and fierce crocodile - without
getting wet. Special themed events take place throughout the
year, please see website for details.

Times Open all year, daily from 9-5 (winter) 9-6 (summer) last
admission 1hr prior to closing. Closed 25 Dec.* **Fees** £8.75 (ch
3-15 £5.75, concessions £7.25). Family ticket (2ad+2ch £24.95)*
Facilities 🅿 ▯ 🍴 licensed 🎃 (outdoor) ♿ toilets for disabled
shop Ⓧ

NEAR SAWREY

Hill Top

LA22 0LF
☎ **015394 36269** 📠 **015394 36811**
e-mail: hilltop@nationaltrust.org.uk
web: www.nationaltrust.org.uk
dir: 2m S of Hawkshead. or 2m from Bowness Car Ferry.

This small 17th-century house is where Beatrix Potter wrote
many of her famous children's stories. It remains as she left it,
and in each room can be found something that appears in one
of her books.

Times House open 13 Feb-25 Mar, Sat-Thu 11-3.30; 27 Mar-Oct,
Sat-Thu 10.30-4.30. Garden open 13 Feb-25 Mar, daily 11-4;
26 Mar-Oct, daily 10-5; Nov-24 Dec, daily 10-4 **Fees** £6.20 (ch
£3.10). Family ticket £15.50 (2ad+3ch). Entry to garden free
on Fri when house is closed. **Facilities** 🅿 ♿ (partly accessible)
(access by arrangement) shop Ⓧ 🌿

The Rheged Centre

Redhills CA11 0DQ
☎ **01768 868000** ▤ **01768 868002**
e-mail: enquiries@rheged.com
web: www.rheged.com
dir: M6 junct 40, on A66 near Penrith

Rheged's ten shops reflect the unique nature of the region, while the indoor and outdoor activities provide challenges for children of all ages. The centre has introduced large format 3D films, three films show twice a day. From a relaxed family lunch to a quick coffee and cake, Rheged's three cafes offer fresh food, made on the premises using the finest local ingredients. 2010 celebrates the 10th birthday of Rheged.

Times Open daily 10-5.30. Closed 25-26 Dec & 1 Jan **Fees** £4.95 (ch £3, pen £3.95). Family ticket £17 3D large format films*
Facilities ❷ ⊑ ❑ licensed 🅰 (outdoor) ⅋ toilets for disabled shop ⊗

Wetheriggs Animal Rescue & Conservation Centre   FREE

Clifton Dykes CA10 2DH
☎ **01768 866657** ▤ **01768 866657**
web: www.wetheriggsanimalrescue.co.uk
dir: approx 2m off A6, S from Penrith, signed

Wetheriggs is an animal rescue centre with a mixture of farm and exotic animals. All proceeds go towards rescuing and looking after the animals. You can also learn about the heritage of the steam-powered pottery and engine room, and paint your own pot. There is a newt pond, play area and a petting farm and reptile house, café and gift shop, all set in 7.5 acres of the beautiful Eden Valley.

Times Open daily, Apr-Oct 10-4; Nov-Mar 10-3. Closed 25-26 Dec & 1 Jan.* **Facilities** ❷ ⊑ 🅰 (outdoor) toilets for disabled shop

Ravenglass & Eskdale Railway

CA18 1SW
☎ **01229 717171** ▤ **01229 717011**
e-mail: steam@ravenglass-railway.co.uk
web: www.ravenglass-railway.co.uk
dir: close to A595, Barrow to Carlisle road

The Lake District's oldest, longest and most scenic steam railway, stretching from the coast at Ravenglass, through two of Lakeland's loveliest valleys for seven miles to Dalegarth Visitor Centre and the foot of England's highest mountains. At least seven trains daily from March to November, plus winter weekends and holiday periods. Packages for walkers and cyclists, children's activities with the Water-vole Stationmaster and special event days.

Times Open: trains operate daily mid Mar-early Nov, most winter wknds, daily between Xmas & New Year & Feb half term. **Fees** Return fare £10.20 (ch £5.10, under 5's free). Family discounts available* **Facilities** ❷ ℗ ⊑ ❑ licensed 🅰 (outdoor) ⅋ toilets for disabled shop

Sizergh Castle & Garden

LA8 8AE
☎ **015395 60951**
e-mail: sizergh@nationaltrust.org.uk
web: www.nationaltrust.org.uk
dir: 3.5m S of Kendal, signed from A590

The castle has a 60-foot high tower, built in the 14th century, but most of the castle dates from the 15th to the 18th centuries. There are panelled rooms with fine carved overmantles and adze-hewn floors, and the gardens, laid out in the 18th century, contain the National Trust's largest limestone rock garden.

Times Open Apr-Oct, Sun-Thu 1.30-5.30; Garden open Apr-Oct, from 12.30. (Last admission 5).* **Fees** House & Garden £7.50 (ch £3.80). Family ticket £18.80. Garden only £4.90 (ch £2.50). **Facilities** ❷ ⊑ 🅰 toilets for disabled shop ⊗ ❦

Cumbria

WHITEHAVEN

The Beacon

West Strand CA28 7LY
☎ **01946 592302** 📄 **01946 598150**
e-mail: thebeacon@copelandbc.gov.uk
web: www.thebeacon-whitehaven.co.uk
dir: A595, after Parton right onto New Rd. Follow one way system & town museum tourist signs

Home to Copeland's museum collection, The Beacon traces the area's history from prehistoric times up to modern day using interactive displays and activities. Enjoy panoramic views of the town and coast from the fourth floor gallery. Regular art exhibitions are held in the Harbour Gallery.

Times Open all year, Tue-Sun 10-4.30. Closed Mon except school & BHs. Closed 25-26 Dec.* **Fees** Art gallery free. Museum £5 (under 16's free, concessions £4)* **Facilities** ℗ ℗ ❙○❙ licensed & toilets for disabled shop ⊗

The Rum Story

27 Lowther St CA28 7DN
☎ **01946 592933** 📄 **01946 590595**
e-mail: dutymanagers@rumstory.co.uk
web: www.rumstory.co.uk
dir: A595, follow town centre signs

Set in the original shop, courtyards, cellars and bonded warehouses of the Jefferson family - the oldest rum trading family in the UK - this fascinating story takes the visitor back in time to the early days of the rum trade, its links with the slave trade, sugar plantations, the Royal Navy, barrel-making and more. Set pieces include a tropical rainforest, an African village, a slave ship, and a cooper's workshop.

Times Open daily, 10-4.30. Closed 25-26 Dec & 1 Jan. Also closed 3rd wk in Jan for maintenance. **Fees** £5.45 (ch £3.45, concessions £4.45) Family £16.45. (2ad+2ch). Group rate 15+ £3.50, Child group 15+ £2.50 **Facilities** ℗ ❙□❙○❙ licensed & toilets for disabled shop ⊗

WINDERMERE

Lake District Visitor Centre at Brockhole

LA23 1LJ
☎ **015394 46601** 📄 **015394 43523**
e-mail: infodesk@lake-district.gov.uk
web: www.lake-district.gov.uk
dir: on A591, between Windermere and Ambleside, follow brown tourist signs

Set in 32 acres of landscaped gardens and grounds, on the shore of Lake Windermere, this house became England's first National Park Visitor Centre in 1969. It offers permanent and temporary exhibitions, lake cruises, an adventure playground and an extensive events programme. Contact the Centre for a copy of their free events guide. Boats available for hire in summer, weekends and school holidays.

Times Open 14 Feb-1 Nov, daily 10-5. Grounds & gardens open all year.* **Facilities** ℗ □❙○❙ licensed 🛏 (indoor & outdoor) & toilets for disabled shop

DERBYSHIRE

BOLSOVER

Bolsover Castle

Castle St S44 6PR
☎ 01246 822844 📠 01246 241569
web: www.english-heritage.org.uk
dir: on A632

This award winning property has the air of a romantic storybook castle, with its turrets and battlements rising from a wooded hilltop. See the stunning Venus garden with its beautiful statuary and fountain. State of the art audio tours are available.

Times Open all year, Apr-Jun & Sep-1 Nov, dailly 10-5, (Fri-Sat 10-4); Jul-Aug, daily 10-6, (Fri-Sat 10-4), 2 Nov-Mar, Thu-Mon 10-4. (Part of the Castle may close for 1hr if event is booked, please phone to check.) Fees £7 (concessions £6, ch £3.50). Family £17.50. Please call 0870 333 1181 for the most up to date prices and opening times when planning your visit. Facilities ♿ ⬚ ㆒ ♿ (partly accessible) (little castle not accessible to wheelchair users, some steps) shop ⊗ ⌗

BUXTON

Poole's Cavern (Buxton Country Park)

Green Ln SK17 9DH
☎ 01298 26978 📠 01298 73563
e-mail: info@poolescavern.co.uk
web: www.poolescavern.co.uk
dir: 1m from Buxton town centre, off A6 and A515

Limestone rock, water, and millions of years created this natural cavern containing thousands of crystal formations. A 45-minute guided tour leads the visitor through chambers used as a shelter by Bronze Age cave dwellers, Roman metal workers and as a hideout by the infamous robber Poole. Attractions include the underground source of the River Wye, the 'Poached Egg Chamber', Mary, Queen of Scots' Pillar, the Grand Cascade and underground sculpture formations. Set in 100 acres of woodland, Buxton Country Park has leafy trails to Grinlow viewpoint and panoramic peakland scenery.

Times Open Mar-Oct, daily 9.30-5; Nov-Feb wknds 10-4.* Fees £7.50 (ch £4.50, concessions £6). Family ticket £22. Please check website or telephone for current details* Facilities ♿ ⬚ ⍾ licensed ㆒ (outdoor) ♿ (partly accessible) (access to visitor centre & 1st 100mtrs of cave tour to main chamber, no access to woods) toilets for disabled shop ⊗

CALKE

Calke Abbey

DE73 7LE
☎ 01332 863822 📠 01332 865272
e-mail: calkeabbey@nationaltrust.org.uk
web: www.nationaltrust.org.uk
dir: on A514 between Swadlincote and Melbourne

A country house and estate preserved in 20th century decline. A place poised somewhere between gentle neglect and downright dereliction, telling the tale of an eccentric family who amassed a huge collection of hidden treasures. The house has had little restoration portraying a period when great country houses struggled to survive. In the walled gardens explore the Orangery, the flower and kitchen gardens or walk around the fragile habitats of Calke Park National Nature Reserve. All visitors (including NT members) require a ticket for the house and garden or garden only from the Visitor Reception.

Times Open 1-9 Mar, Sat-Sun; 15 Mar-2 Nov, Mon-Wed & Sat-Sun & Good Fri. House 12.30-5; Gardens & Church 11-5; Restaurant & Shop 10.30-5. Note: Timed house tickets apply and delays on entry will occur at busy times and BHs.* Fees With Gift Aid donation: £8.50 (ch £4.20). Family ticket £21.50. Garden only £5.30 (ch £2.70). Family ticket £13.30.* Facilities ♿ ⍾ licensed ㆒ (outdoor) ♿ (partly accessible) (Access to 3 rooms on ground floor only. Stairs to other floors. Grounds toilets for disabled shop ⊗ ✿

CASTLETON

Blue-John Cavern & Mine

Buxton Rd S33 8WP
☎ 01433 620638 & 620642 📠 01433 621586
e-mail: lesley@bluejohn.gemsoft.co.uk
web: www.bluejohn.gemsoft.co.uk
dir: follow brown 'Blue-John Cavern' signs from Castleton

A remarkable example of a water-worn cave, over a third of a mile long, with chambers 200ft high. It contains 8 of the world's 14 veins of Blue John stone, and has been the major source of this unique form of fluorspar for nearly 300 years.

Times Open all year, daily, 9.30-5 (or dusk). Guided tours of approx 1hr every 10 mins tour. Closed 25-26 Dec & 1 Jan. Fees £8 (ch £4, pen & students £6) Family ticket £22. Party rates on request.* Facilities ♿ ⬚ ⬚ shop

Castleton continued

Peak Cavern

S33 8WS
☎ **01433 620285**
e-mail: info@peakcavern.co.uk
web: www.devilsarse.com
dir: on A6187, in centre of Castleton

One of the most spectacular natural limestone caves in the Peak District, with an electrically-lit underground walk of about half a mile. Ropes have been made for over 500 years in the 'Grand Entrance Hall', and traces of a row of cottages can be seen. Rope-making demonstrations are included on every tour.

Times Open all year, daily 10-5. Nov-Mar limited tours, please call in advance for times. Closed 25 Dec.* **Fees** £7.25 (ch £5.25, other concessions £6.25). Family ticket (2ad+2ch) £22.* **Facilities** 🅿 🅟 🍴 (indoor & outdoor) ♿ (partly accessible) (number of stairs throughout the cave) shop

Speedwell Cavern

Winnats Pass S33 8WA
☎ **01433 620512** 📠 **01433 621888**
e-mail: info@speedwellcavern.co.uk
web: www.speedwellcavern.co.uk
dir: A625 becomes A6187 at Hathersage. 0.5m W of Castleton

Descend 105 steps to a boat that takes you on a one-mile underground exploration of floodlit caverns part of which was once a lead mine. The hand-carved tunnels open out into a network of natural caverns and underground rivers. See the Bottomless Pit, a huge subterranean lake in a huge, cathedral-like cavern.

Times Open all year, daily 10-5 (Closed 25 Dec). Phone to check winter opening times due to weather. Last boat 4pm **Fees** £7.75 (ch £5.75).* **Facilities** 🅿 🅟 ♿ (partly accessible) (105 steps in one flight down to boat & back up again to surface) shop ⊗

Treak Cliff Cavern

S33 8WP
☎ **01433 620571** 📠 **01433 620519**
e-mail: treakcliff@bluejohnstone.com
web: www.bluejohnstone.com
dir: 0.75m W of Castleton on A6187

An underground world of stalactites, stalagmites, flowstone, rock and cave formations, minerals and fossils. There are rich deposits of the rare and beautiful Blue John stone, including 'The Pillar', the largest piece ever found. Show caves include the Witch's Cave, Aladdin's Cave, Dream Cave and Fairyland Grotto. These caves contain some of the most impressive stalactites in the Peak District. Visitors can also polish their own Blue John stone in school holidays, and purchase Blue John stone jewellery and ornaments in the Castleton Gift Shop.

Times Open all year, Mar-Oct, daily 10-last tour 4.20; Nov-Feb daily - call for special tour times. All tours are guided & last about 40 mins. Enquire for last tour of day & possible closures. Closed 24-26 & 31 Dec & 1 Jan. All dates & times are subject to change without notice.* **Fees** £7.95 (ch 5-15 £4). Family ticket (2ad+2ch) £22.* **Facilities** 🅿 🅟 ⊒ 🍴 (indoor & outdoor) ♿ (partly accessible) (no wheelchair access, walking disabled only) shop

Chatsworth

DE45 1PP
☎ 01246 565300   📄 01246 583536
e-mail: visit@chatsworth.org
web: www.chatsworth.org
dir: 8m N of Matlock off B6012. 16m from M1 junct 29, signposted via Chesterfield, follow brown signs

Home of the Duke and Duchess of Devonshire, Chatsworth contains a massive private collection of fine and decorative arts. There is a splendid painted hall, and a great staircase leads to the chapel, decorated with statues and paintings. There are pictures, furniture and porcelain, and a trompe l'oeil painting of a violin on the music room door. The park was laid out by 'Capability' Brown, but is most famous as the work of Joseph Paxton, head gardener in the 19th century. The park is also home to the Duke and Duchess' personal collection of contemporary sculpture.

Times Open mid Mar-23 Dec, House & Garden 11-5.30, Farmyard 10.30-5.30.* **Facilities** 🅿 🅟 🖵 🍴 licensed ♿ (partly accessible) toilets for disabled shop ⊗

Creswell Crags Museum and Education Centre

Crags Rd, Welbeck S80 3LH
☎ 01909 720378   📄 01909 724726
e-mail: info@creswell-crags.org.uk
web: www.creswell-crags.org.uk
dir: off B6042, Crags Road, between A616 & A60, 1m E of Creswell village

Creswell Crags, a picturesque limestone gorge with lakes and caves, is one of Britain's most important archaeological sites. The many caves on the site have yielded Ice Age remains, including bones of woolly mammoth, reindeer, hyena and bison, stone tools of Ice Age hunters from over 10,000 years ago and new research has revealed the only Ice Age rock art in Britain (about 13,000 years old). Visit the Museum and Education Centre to learn more about your Ice Age ancestors through an exhibition, touch-screen computers and video. Join a 'Virtually the Ice Age' cave tour, picnic in Crags Meadow, or try the new activity trail. Plenty of special events year round, contact for details.

Times Open all year, Feb-Oct, daily, 10.30-4.30; Nov-Jan, Sun only 10.30-4.30.* **Facilities** 🅿 🚠 ♿ (partly accessible) (accessible round Gorge. Tour may be unsuitable for mobility scooters, due to steps) toilets for disabled shop ⊗

Crich Tramway Village

DE4 5DP
☎ 01773 854321   📄 01773 854320
e-mail: enquiry@tramway.co.uk
web: www.tramway.co.uk
dir: off B5035, 8m from M1 junct 28

A mile-long scenic journey through a period street to open countryside with panoramic views. You can enjoy unlimited vintage tram rides, and the exhibition hall houses the largest collection of vintage electric trams in Britain. The village street contains a bar and restaurant, tearooms, a sweet shop, ice cream shop, and police sentry box, among others. There is also a Workshop Viewing Gallery where you can see the trams being restored. Ring for details of special events.

Times Open Apr-Oct, daily 10-5.30 (6.30 wknds Jun-Aug & BH wknds). 10.30-4 until Nov.* **Fees** £10.50 (ch 4-15 £5.50, pen £9.50). Family ticket (2ad+3ch)* **Facilities** 🅿 🅟 🖵 🍴 licensed 🚠 (outdoor) ♿ toilets for disabled shop

DENBY

Denby Pottery Visitor Centre

Derby Rd DE5 8NX
☎ 01773 740799   🖹 01773 740749
e-mail: tours.reception@denby.co.uk
web: www.denbyvisitorcentre.co.uk
dir: 8m N of Derby off A38, on B6179, 2m S of Ripley

Situated around a cobbled courtyard with shops and a restaurant. Pottery tours are available daily February to October including hands-on activities such as paint-a-plate and make-a-clay-souvenir. Extensive cookshop with free half hour demonstrations daily. There are lots of bargains on Denby seconds in the factory shop; Dartington Crystal Shop, gift shop, garden shop and hand painted Denby.

Times Centre open all year. Factory tours, Mon-Thu 10.30 & 1. Craftroom tour, daily 11-3. Visitor Centre Mon-Sat 9.30-5, Sun 10-5. No tours Nov-Jan. Closed 25-26 Dec.* **Fees** Free. Factory tour £5.95 (ch £4.95). Craftroom tour £4.95 (ch £3.95).* **Facilities** ❷ 🖵 †◎¹ licensed 🌂 (outdoor) ♿ toilets for disabled shop ⊗

HARDWICK HALL

Hardwick Hall

Doe Lea S44 5QJ
☎ 01246 850430   🖹 01246 858424
e-mail: hardwickhall@nationaltrust.org.uk
web: www.nationaltrust.org.uk
dir: 2m S M1 junct 29 via A6175. Access by Stainsby Mill entrance only

One of the most splendid houses in England. Built by Bess of Hardwick in the 1590s and unaltered since, its huge windows and high ceilings make it feel strikingly modern. Its six towers make a dramatic skyline. Climbing up through the house, from one floor to the next, is a thrilling architectural experience. Rich tapestries, plaster friezes and alabaster fireplaces colour the rooms, culminating in the hauntingly atmospheric Long Gallery. Note: The Old Hall is owned by the NT and administered by English Heritage.

Times Please telephone or see website for details. **Fees** Please telephone or see website for details. **Facilities** ❷ †◎¹ licensed 🌂 (outdoor) ♿ (partly accessible) (Ramped entrance. Ground floor accessible, stairs with handrail to other floors, Grounds partly accessible with slopes, grass paths & some cobbles.) toilets for disabled shop ⊗ 🐾

KEDLESTON HALL

Kedleston Hall

DE22 5JH
☎ 01332 842191   🖹 01332 841972
e-mail: kedlestonhall@nationaltrust.org.uk
web: www.nationaltrust.org.uk
dir: 5m NW of Derby, entrance off Kedleston Rd, signed from rdbt where A38 crosses A52, close to Markeaton Park

Take a trip back in time to the 1760s at this spectacular neo-classical mansion framed by historic parkland. Designed for lavish entertaining and displaying an extensive collection of paintings, sculpture and original furnishings, Kedleston is a stunning example of the work of architect Robert Adam. The Curzon family have lived here since the 12th century and continue to live at the Hall. Lord Curzon's Eastern Museum is a treasure trove of fascinating objects acquired on his travels in Asia and while Viceroy of India (1899-1905). Used as a key location for 2008 film, The Duchess. Note: Medieval All Saints Church, containing many family monuments is run by the Churches Conservation Trust.

Times Open all year: House; Mar-2 Nov, Sat-Wed 12-5 (last admission 4.15). Garden; same as house but open daily 10-6. Park open daily, Mar-2 Nov 10-6 & 3 Nov-27 Feb10-4. (Closed 25-26 Dec & some restrictions may apply in Dec & Jan).* **Fees** With Gift Aid donation: House & Garden £8.50 (ch £4.20). Family ticket £21.50. Park and Garden only: £3.80 (ch £1.90). Family ticket £9.60. Park (winter) £4.* **Facilities** ❷ †◎¹ licensed toilets for disabled shop ⊗ 🐾

MATLOCK BATH

The Heights of Abraham Cable Cars, Caverns & Hilltop Park

DE4 3PD

☎ 01629 582365 01629 581128

e-mail: office@heightsofabraham.com

web: www.heightsofabraham.com

dir: on A6, signed from M1 junct 28 & A6. Base station next to Matlock Bath railway station

The Heights of Abraham, a unique Hilltop Park, reached using the country's most up-to-date cable cars. Once you are at the summit you can join exciting underground tours of two spectacular show caverns. Above ground there are play areas, picnic spots, exhibitions, shops, café and summit bar all with stunning views across the surrounding Peak District. New attractions are the Heath and Heaven and Fossil Factory exhibitions, plus brand new, state-of-the-art lighting in the Great Masson Cavern which reveals its magnitude as it has never seen before.

Times Open 14-22 Feb, daily 10-4.30; 28 Feb-14 Mar, wknds 10-4.30; 21 Mar-Sep,daily 10-4.30 (later at wknds & in high season). Oct -1 Nov, daily 10-4.30. Please telephone or check website for details.* **Fees** £10.80 (ch £7.80 (5-16 yrs), under 5s free (one per full paying adult). Senior ticket £7.80. Family (2ad+2ch) £33.00, (2ad+3 ch) £39. Please telephone or check website for details.* **Facilities** licensed (outdoor) (partly accessible) toilets for disabled shop

Peak District Mining Museum

The Pavilion DE4 3NR

☎ 01629 583834

e-mail: mail@peakmines.co.uk

web: www.peakmines.co.uk

dir: On A6 alongside River Derwent

A large display explains the history of the Derbyshire lead industry from Roman times to the present day. The geology of the area, mining and smelting processes, the quarrying and the people who worked in the industry, are illustrated by a series of static and moving exhibits. The museum also features an early 19th-century water pressure pumping engine. There is a recycling display in the Pump Room.

Times Open all year, daily Apr-end Sep 10-5, Oct-end Mar 11-3. Closed 25 Dec.* **Facilities** shop

Temple Mine

Temple Rd DE4 3NR

☎ 01629 583834

e-mail: mail@peakmines.co.uk

web: www.peakmines.co.uk

dir: off A6. Please telephone for directions

A typical Derbyshire mine which was worked from the early 1920s until the mid 1950s for fluorspar and associated minerals. See examples of mining methods which give an insight into working conditions underground.

Times Open Apr-end Sep timed visits noon & 2pm daily, Oct-end Mar timed visits noon & 2pm wknds only* **Facilities**

RIPLEY

Midland Railway Butterley

Butterley Station DE5 3QZ

☎ 01773 747674 & 749788 01773 570721

e-mail: mr_b2004@btconnect.com

web: www.midlandrailwaycentre.co.uk

dir: M1 junct 28, A38 towards Derby, then signed

A regular steam-train passenger service runs here, to the centre where the aim is to depict every aspect of the golden days of the Midland Railway and its successors. Exhibits range from the steam locomotives of 1866 to an electric locomotive, with a large section of rolling stock spanning the last 100 years. Also a farm and country park, along with narrow gauge, miniature and model railways. Regular rail-related special events throughout the year. Contact for details.

Times Open all year, trains run wknds Feb-Dec & most school holidays* **Fees** £10.90 (ch 5-16 £5.50, pen £9.95) children under 2 free. Party 15+.* **Facilities** (outdoor) toilets for disabled shop

SUDBURY

Sudbury Hall and Museum of Childhood

DE6 5HT
☎ 01283 585305 ▤ 01283 585139
e-mail: sudburyhall@nationaltrust.org.uk
web: www.nationaltrust.org.uk
dir: 6m E of Uttoxeter at junct of A50 & A515

Two totally different experiences sitting side by side. The country home of the Lords Vernon features exquisite plasterwork, wood carvings, murals based classical stories and fine 17th century craftsmanship. The Great Staircase and Long Gallery are extremely impressive. The Museum of Childhood is a delight for all ages with something for everyone. Explore the childhoods of times gone by, make stories, play with toys and share your childhood with others. You can be a chimney weep, a scullion or a Victorian pupil, and be captivated by the archive film, interactives and displays.

Times Please telephone or see website for details. **Fees** Please telephone or see website for details. **Facilities** ❷ ℗ ☞ ⫪❶ licensed ᨖ (partly accessible) (Access via steps & 4 flights of steps to first floor. Lift to all Museum floors. Grounds partly accessible, grass & loose gravel paths, some steps) toilets for disabled shop ⊗ ⛿

DEVON

ARLINGTON

Arlington Court

EX31 4LP
☎ 01271 850296 ▤ 01271 851108
e-mail: arlingtoncourt@nationaltrust.org.uk
web: www.nationaltrust.org.uk
dir: 7m NE of Barnstaple, on A39

Arlington Court was built in 1823 and is situated in the thickly wooded Yeo Valley. The centrepiece is the Victorian mansion, surrounded by formal and informal gardens. Also open to visitors is the working stable yard, housing a collection of carriages and horse-drawn vehicles. The extensive parkland around the house is grazed by Jacob sheep and Red Devon cattle. Please telephone for details of events running throughout the year.

Times Open 13 Mar-Oct, daily 10.30-5. (Last admission 4.30). Grounds open Nov-Mar during daylight hours. **Fees** House, carriage museum & grounds £8.60 (ch £4.30). Family £21.50. Carriage museum & grounds £6.20 (ch £3.10). Parties 15+ pre-booked 15% discount. **Facilities** ❷ ☞ ᨖ (outdoor) ᨖ (partly accessible) (ground floor only of house) toilets for disabled shop ⊗ ⛿

BEER

Pecorama Pleasure Gardens

Underleys EX12 3NA
☎ 01297 21542 ▤ 01297 20229
e-mail: pecorama@btconnect.com
web: www.peco-uk.com
dir: from A3052 take B3174, Beer road, signed

The gardens are high on a hillside, overlooking Beer. A miniature steam and diesel passenger line offers visitors a stunning view of Lyme Bay as it runs through the Pleasure Gardens. Attractions include an aviary, crazy golf, children's activity area and the Peco Millennium Garden. The main building houses an exhibition of railway modelling in various small gauges. There are souvenir and railway model shops, plus full catering facilities. Please telephone for details of events running throughout the year.

Times Open Etr-end Oct , Mon-Fri 10-5.30, Sat 10-1. Open Sun at Etr & 30 May-5 Sep. **Fees** £6.60 (ch 4-14 £4.50, concessions £6.10, over 80 & under 4 free)* **Facilities** ❷ ℗ ☞ ⫪❶ licensed ᨖ (outdoor) ᨖ (partly accessible) (no wheelchairs on miniature railway) toilets for disabled shop ⊗

BICTON

Bicton Park Botanical Gardens

East Budleigh EX9 7BJ
☎ 01395 568465 ▤ 01395 568374
e-mail: info@bictongardens.co.uk
web: www.bictongardens.co.uk
dir: 2m N of Budleigh Salterton on B3178, leave M5 at junct 30 & follow brown tourist signs

Unique Grade I-listed, 18th-century historic gardens with palm house, orangery, plant collections, extensive countryside museum, indoor and outdoor activity play areas, pinetum, arboretum, nature trail, woodland railway garden centre and restaurant. All this set in 63 acres of beautiful parkland that has been cherished for 300 years. Open air concerts take place in July and August.

Times Open Winter 10-5, Summer 10-6. Closed 25 & 26 Dec.* **Facilities** ❷ ☞ ⫪❶ licensed ᨖ (outdoor) toilets for disabled shop

Exmoor Zoological Park

South Stowford, Bratton Fleming EX31 4SG
☎ 01598 763352   📄 01598 763352
e-mail: exmoorzoo@btconnect.com
web: www.exmoorzoo.co.uk
dir: off A361 link road onto A399, follow tourist signs

Exmoor Zoo is both personal and friendly. Open since 1982 it is an ideal family venue, catering particularly for the younger generation. The zoo specialises in smaller animals, many endangered, such as the golden-headed lion tamarins. There are new exhibits for animals such as cheetahs, maned wolves, tapirs, sitatungas and of course the "Exmoor Beast".

Times Open daily, Mar-4 May & 16 Sep-2 Nov 10-5; 3 Nov-30 Mar 10-4; 5 May-15 Sep 10-6* **Fees** £8.25 (ch £6, concessions £7.25). Family ticket (2ad+2ch) £26.50.* **Facilities** 🅿 ⛺ 🎠 (outdoor) ♿ (partly accessible) (tarmac paths on hill) toilets for disabled shop ⊗

Buckfast Butterfly Farm & Dartmoor Otter Sanctuary

TQ11 0DZ
☎ 01364 642916
e-mail: contact@ottersandbutterflies.co.uk
web: www.ottersandbutterflies.co.uk
dir: off A38, at Dart Bridge junct, follow tourist signs, adjacent to steam railway

Visitors can wander around a specially designed, undercover tropical garden, where free-flying butterflies and moths from around the world can be seen. The otter sanctuary has large enclosures with underwater viewing areas. Three types of otters can be seen - the native British otter along with Asian and North American otters.

Times Open Apr-Oct, daily 10-5 or dusk (if earlier). For rest of year please see website **Fees** £6.95 (ch £4.95, concessions £5.95). Family ticket £19.95* **Facilities** 🅿 🅿 ⛺ 🎠 (outdoor) ♿ (partly accessible) (fence height around some otter enclosures can make it difficult for w/chair users to see) shop ⊗

Buckland Abbey

PL20 6EY
☎ 01822 853607   📄 01822 855448
e-mail: bucklandabbey@nationaltrust.org.uk
web: www.nationaltrust.org.uk
dir: off A386 0.25m S of Yelverton, signed

Originally a prosperous 13th-century Cistercian Abbey, and then home of the Grenville family, Buckland Abbey was sold to Sir Francis Drake in 1581, who lived there until his death in 1596. Several restored buildings house a fascinating exhibition about the abbey's history. Among the exhibits is Drake's drum, which is said to give warning of danger to England. There is an Elizabethan garden, estate walks and a letterbox trail.

Times Open 12-21 Feb & 17-23 Dec, daily 11-4.30; 22 Feb & Nov-12 Dec, Fri-Sun 11-4.30; 14 Mar-Oct, daily 10.30-5.30. **Fees** Abbey & grounds £8.60. Grounds only £4.40 (ch 1/2 price) Party rate £7.30 each. **Facilities** 🅿 ⛺ 🍴 licensed 🎠 (outdoor) ♿ (partly accessible) (upper floors in house not accessible. Some steep slopes in grounds) toilets for disabled shop ⊗ ♒

Canonteign Falls

EX6 7NT
☎ 01647 252434   📄 01647 52617
e-mail: info@canonteignfalls.co.uk
web: www.canonteignfalls.co.uk
dir: off A38 at Chudleigh/Teign Valley junct onto B3193 and follow tourist signs for 3m

A magical combination of waterfalls, woodlands and lakes. 3 graded walks marked with colour ferns.

Times Open summer 10-5. Last admission 1 hour before closing.* **Fees** £5.75 (ch £4.50, concessions £4.75). Family £19.50.* **Facilities** 🅿 ⛺ 🍴 licensed 🎠 (indoor & outdoor) ♿ (partly accessible) (grounds partly accessible but not up to falls) toilets for disabled shop

CHURSTON FERRERS

Greenway

TQ5 0ES
☎ 01803 842382 📄 01803 661900
e-mail: greenway@nationaltrust.org.uk
web: www.nationaltrust.org.uk/devoncornwall
dir: off A3022 into Galmpton. Follow Manor Vale Rd into village then follow brown signs for gardens

Greenway House re-opened in 2009 after a major restoration project. Pre-booking for car parking is essential; those arriving by 'green' means will have slots made available to see this unique and magical property with its many collections, including archaeology, Tunbridgeware, silver, botanical china and books, the atmospheric house set in the 1950s, and the glorious woodland garden with its wild edges and rare plantings, all allow a glimpse into the private holiday home of the famous and well-loved author, Agatha Christie, and her family. Enjoy the adventure of arriving here by ferry alighting at Greenway Quay, with the dramatic views of the house from the river. Greenway is not easily accessible having some steep and slippery paths. All visitors are asked to wear walking shoes and to follow routes and directions according to their suitability on the day.

Times Open 28 Feb-19 Jul & 2 Sep-25 Oct, Wed-Sun; 21 Jul-30 Aug, Tue-Sun 10.30-5* **Facilities** 🅿 ⛱ 🎪 (outdoor) 🦽 (partly accessible) (Ground floor of house and part of garden only accessible) toilets for disabled shop ⊗ 🦮

CLOVELLY

The Milky Way Adventure Park

EX39 5RY
☎ 01237 431255 📄 01237 431735
e-mail: info@themilkyway.co.uk
web: www.themilkyway.co.uk
dir: on A39, 2m from Clovelly

Adventure park in the country with 5 major rides and live shows. Something fun and educational for everyone. Get close and personal with a bird of prey, lose yourself in a maze or take a trip out of this world whatever the weather. The Cosmic Typhoon is Devon's tallest, fastest and longest rollercoaster. Height restriction but don't worry, there's one for smaller adventurers, The Big Apple. Plenty to do even on rainy days, with indoor attractions from alien adventures on the Clone Zone Ride and Droid Destroyer Dodgems, not to mention the death defying slides and ball pools of the Time Warp and the North Coast's largest indoor play area. Under fives can enjoy ball pools, sand pits, play tractors and more on Fantasy Farm.

Times Open Etr-end Oct, daily 10.30-6. Also open wknds & school hols in winter. **Fees** £10 per person (under 3's free, concessions £8). **Facilities** 🅿 ⛱ 🎪 (indoor & outdoor) 🦽 toilets for disabled shop

COMBE MARTIN

Combe Martin Wildlife Park & Dinosaur Park

EX34 0NG
☎ 01271 882486 📄 01271 883869
e-mail: info@dinosaur-park.com
web: www.dinosaur-park.com
dir: M5 junct 27 then A361 towards Barnstaple, turn right onto A399

Come and see the UK's only full-size animatronic Tyrannosaurus Rex, along with a pair of vicious, interacting Meglosaurs, a Velociraptor and Dilophosaurus, the 'Spitting Dinosaur'. Explore 26 acres of stunning gardens with cascading waterfalls and hundreds of exotic birds and animals. There are daily sea lion shows, falconry displays, lemur encounters and handling sessions. Other attractions include the Earthquake Canyon Train Ride, Tomb of the Pharoahs, Tropical House, T Rex photographic studio, and much more.

Times Open Feb half term-7 Nov, daily 10-5 (last admission 3). **Fees** £12 (ch 3-15 £7.50, ch under 3 free, pen £8.50). Family (2ad+2ch) £34.* **Facilities** 🅿 🅿 ⛱ 🎪 (outdoor) 🦽 (partly accessible) (bottom part of park has sharp decline, not suitable for wheelchairs or severe disabilities) toilets for disabled shop ⊗

CULLOMPTON

Diggerland

Verbeer Manor EX15 2PE
☎ 0871 227 7007 📄 0901 2010 300
e-mail: mail@diggerland.com
web: www.diggerland.com
dir: M5 junct 27. E on A38 & at rdbt turn right onto A3181.
Diggerland is 3m on left

An adventure park with a difference, where kids of all ages can experience the thrills of driving real earth-moving equipment. Choose from various types of diggers and dumpers ranging from 1 ton to 8 and a half tons. Supervised by an instructor, complete the Dumper Truck Challenge or dig for buried treasure. New rides include JCB Robots, Diggerland Dodgems, Go-karts, Landrover Safari and Spin Dizzy. Even under 5's can join in, with mum or dad's help. Please telephone for details of events during school and Bank Holidays.

Times Open 12 Feb-Oct, 10-5, wknds, BHs & school hols (including half terms). **Fees** £15 - all rides & drives included in price. **Facilities** ℗ ⊡ ⼍ (outdoor) ♿ toilets for disabled shop ⊗

DARTMOUTH

Woodlands Leisure Park

Blackawton TQ9 7DQ
☎ 01803 712598 📄 01803 712680
e-mail: fun@woodlandspark.com
web: www.woodlandspark.com
dir: 5m from Dartmouth on A3122. From A38 follow brown tourist signs

An all-weather attraction packed with variety for all ages at one inclusive cost. The new Ninja Towers has three top aerial runways, sky high rope bridges and incredible slides. The baffling illusion of the Seascape Mirror Maze has bewildering pathways and weird sea monsters that disappear. There are 16 family rides, including exhilarating water coasters, Swing Ship, 500m Toboggan Run and Avalanche, and ten massive play zones to entertain the kids for hours. Great for rainy days with 100,000sq ft of undercover action. Explore the Empire, 5 floors

of challenging climbs, rides and slides, hang on to the Trauma Tower and zap your buddies in the Master Blaster. Incredible Zoo-in-a-Farm, amazing night and day creatures, insects and birds. Get close to the animals and ride big U-Drive tractors. There is also a falconry centre with fascinating flying displays; and live entertainers in the summer holidays.

Times Open daily 27 Mar-7 Nov. Winter wknds & Devon school holidays only. **Fees** £11.45-£12.25 (under 92cms free). Family ticket £43.80 (2ad+2ch).* **Facilities** ℗ ⊡ ⼍ (indoor & outdoor) ♿ (partly accessible) (some rides not suitable) toilets for disabled shop ⊗

DREWSTEIGNTON

Castle Drogo

EX6 6PB
☎ 01647 433306 📄 01647 433186
e-mail: castledrogo@nationaltrust.org.uk
web: www.nationaltrust.org.uk
dir: 5m S of A30 Exeter-Okehampton. Coaches turn off A382 at Sandy Park

India tea baron Julius Drewe's dream house, this granite castle, built between 1910 and 1930, is one of the most remarkable works of Sir Edward Lutyens, and combines the grandeur of a medieval castle with the comfort of the 20th century. A great country house with terraced formal garden, woodland spring garden, huge circular croquet lawn and colourful herbaceous borders. Standing at more than 900 feet overlooking the wooded gorge of the River Teign with stunning views of Dartmoor, and delightful walks. Lots of events in school holidays, ring for details.

Times Castle open 14 Mar-1 Nov, daily 11-5; Garden, tearooms & shop open 14 Mar-1 Nov 10.30-5.30* **Facilities** ℗ ⊡ ⼍ (outdoor) ♿ (partly accessible) (Gardens, Hall & Library fully accessible, other areas only accessible via stairs) toilets for disabled shop ⊗ ⍾

Devon

EXETER

Exeter's Underground Passages

2 Paris St EX1 1GA
☎ 01392 665887 📄 01392 265625
e-mail: underground.passages@exeter.gov.uk
web: www.exeter.gov.uk/passages
dir: Follow signs for city centre

Dating from the 14th century, these medieval passages under Exeter High Street are a unique ancient monument. No similar system of passages can be explored by the public anywhere else in Britain. The passages were built to house the pipes that brought fresh water to the city. Visitors to the Underground Interpretation Centre pass through an exhibition and video presentation before their guided tour. The centre is packed with interactive exhibits but the passages remain the same: narrow, dark and exciting.

Times Open Jun-Sep (incl school hols outside this period), Mon-Sat 9.30-5.30 (last tour 4.30). Sun 10.30-4 (last tour 3). Oct-May (closed Mon), Tue-Fri 11.30-5.30, Sat 9.30-5.30 (last tour 4.30), Sun 11.30-4 (last tour 3).* **Fees** £4.90 (ch 5-18 £3.40, under 5 free access to exhibition only, concessions £3.90). Family ticket (2ad+3ch) £14.65.* **Facilities** ℗ toilets for disabled shop ⊗

RAMM in the Library   FREE

Royal Albert Memorial Museum, Castle St EX4 3PQ
☎ 01392 665858 📄 01392 421252
e-mail: RAMM@exeter.gov.uk
web: www.exeter.gov.uk/RAMM
dir: off High Street, next to Central Library

With a range of objects on display and hands on gallery activities, RAMM in the Library is an ideal place for family visits and to catch up on news of the Royal Albert Memorial Museum's redevelopment. Many of the Museum's favourite activities can be enjoyed here during the closure.

Times Open all year Mon-Sat 10-5. Closed BHs. **Facilities** ℗ ♿ toilets for disabled ⊗

EXMOUTH

The World of Country Life

Sandy Bay EX8 5BU
☎ 01395 274533 📄 01392 227131
e-mail: info@worldofcountrylife.co.uk
web: www.worldofcountrylife.co.uk
dir: M5 junct 30, take A376 to Exmouth. Follow signs to Sandy Bay

All-weather family attraction including falconry displays, and a safari train that travels through a forty acre deer park. Kids will enjoy the friendly farm animals, pets centre and animal nursery. There is also a Victorian street, working models and thousands of exhibits from a bygone age, including steam and vintage vehicles.

Times Open Apr-1 Nov, daily 10-5.* **Fees** £9.85 (ch 3-17 & pen £7.85). Family ticket (2ad+2ch) £32.50, (2ad+3ch) £37.50.* **Facilities** 🅿 ℗ 🖥🍴 licensed 🍴 (indoor & outdoor) ♿ toilets for disabled shop ⊗

GREAT TORRINGTON

Dartington Crystal

EX38 7AN
☎ 01805 626242 📄 01805 626263
e-mail: sfrench@dartington.co.uk
web: www.dartington.co.uk
dir: Turn off A386 in centre of Great Torrington, down School Lane (opposite church). Dartington Crystal 200mtrs on left

Dartington Crystal has won many international design awards in recognition of its excellence. The all new factory experience allows visitors to watch skilled craftsmen at work from ground level or from an elevated viewing gallery. There is something for all age groups in the Visitor Centre.

Times Open all year. Visitor centre, Factory experience, Cafe and Shops Mon-Fri 9-5 (last tour 3.15), Sat 10-5, Sun 10-4 (tours closed wknds). For Xmas, New Year and BH opening please telephone for details.* **Fees** £6 (ch under 16 free, pen £5). Max 5 ch with every full paying adult.* **Facilities** 🅿 ℗ 🖥🍴 licensed 🍴 (outdoor) ♿ toilets for disabled shop ⊗

RHS Garden Rosemoor

EX38 8PH
☎ 01805 624067   🗎 01805 624717
e-mail: rosemooradmin@rhs.org.uk
web: www.rhs.org.uk/rosemoor
dir: 1m SE of Great Torrington on A3124

RHS Garden Rosemoor is 65 acres of enchanting garden and woodland set in Torridge Valley. Rich in variety with year-round interest, Rosemoor includes inspiring displays of formal and informal planting. The garden has two beautiful rose gardens, a winter garden, cottage garden, fruit and vegetable garden, lake, arboretum and much more. Over 80 events are held each year, phone 01805 626800 for details.

Times Open: Gardens all year; Apr-Sep 10-6; Oct-Mar 10-5. Closed 25 Dec. Visitor Centre as for gardens but closed 24-26 Dec.* **Fees** £6.50 (ch 6-16 £2, under 6 free). Party 10+ £5.50. **Facilities** 🅿 Ⓟ ⊑ 🍴 licensed 🛏 (outdoor) ♿ toilets for disabled shop ⊗

ILFRACOMBE

Watermouth Castle & Family Theme Park

EX34 9SL
☎ 01271 863879   🗎 01271 865864
web: www.watermouthcastle.com
dir: 3m NE off A399, midway between Ilfracombe & Combe Martin

A popular family attraction including mechanical music demonstrations, musical water show, dungeon labyrinths, Victorian displays, bygone pier machines, animated fairy tale scenes, tube slide, mini golf, children's carousel, swingboats, aeroplane ride, water fountains, river ride, gardens and a maze.

Times Open Apr-end Oct, closed Sat. (Also closed some Mon & Fri off season). Ring for further details.* **Fees** £12 (ch £10, under 92cm free & pen £8)* **Facilities** 🅿 ⊑ 🛏 (outdoor) ♿ (partly accessible) toilets for disabled shop ⊗

Killerton House & Garden

EX5 3LE
☎ 01392 881345   🗎 01392 883112
e-mail: killerton@nationaltrust.org.uk
web: www.nationaltrust.org.uk
dir: off B3181 Exeter to Cullompton road

Elegant 18th-century house set in an 18-acre garden with sloping lawns and herbaceous borders. A majestic avenue of beech trees runs up the hillside, past an arboretum of rhododendrons and conifers. The garden has an ice house and rustic summer house where the family's pet bear was once kept, as well as a Victorian chapel. Inside the house are displays from the Killerton Dress Collection, and a Victorian laundry. Please telephone for details of annual events.

Times Open: House, 10 Mar-Oct, daily (ex Tue); 27 Jul-Aug, daily 11-5 (last entry 4.30). Gardens open all year, daily, 10.30-dusk or 7. **Fees** Gift aid admission House & garden: £8.40 (ch £4.20) Family £20.70. Garden & park only: £6.20 (ch £3.10). Standard admission £7.60 (ch £3.80). Family ticket £18.80. Garden & Park only £5.60 (ch £2.80). Reduced rate if using public transport or cycle & during Nov to Feb. **Facilities** 🅿 ⊑ 🛏 (outdoor) toilets for disabled shop ⊗ 🌿

Cookworthy Museum of Rural Life

The Old Grammar School, 108 Fore St TQ7 1AW
☎ 01548 853235
e-mail: wcookworthy@talk21.com
web: www.kingsbridgemuseum.net
dir: A38 onto A384, then A381 to Kingsbridge, museum at top of town

The 17th-century schoolrooms of this former grammar school are now the setting for another kind of education. Reconstructed room-sets of a Victorian kitchen, a costume room and extensive collection of local historical items are gathered to illustrate South Devon life. A walled garden and farm gallery are also features of this museum, founded to commemorate William Cookworthy, 'father' of the English china clay industry. The Local Heritage Resource Centre with public access databases, microfilm of local newspapers since 1855 and Devon record service point are available to visitors. Please ring for details of special events.

Times Open 31 Mar-Sep, Mon-Sat 10.30-5; Oct 10.30-4. Nov-Mar groups by arrangement. Local Heritage Resource Centre open all year, Mon-Thu 10-12 & Wed also 2-4, other times by appointment. **Fees** £2.50 (ch £1, concessions £2). Family £6 (2ad+ up to 4ch).* **Facilities** ⓟ ⌐ (outdoor) & (partly accessible) toilets for disabled shop ⊗

Knightshayes Court

EX16 7RQ
☎ 01884 254665 & 257381
e-mail: knightshayes@nationaltrust.org.uk
web: www.nationaltrust.org.uk
dir: M5 junct 27, 2m N of Tiverton off A396

This fine Victorian mansion, a rare example of William Burges' work, offers much of interest to all ages. The garden is one of the most beautiful in Devon, with formal terraces, amusing topiary, a pool garden and woodland walks.

Times Open 13-21 Feb, 11-4, 13 Mar-Oct, 11-5. **Fees** House, gardens & parkland £8.60 (ch £4.30). Family (2ad+3ch) £21.50, (1ad+3ch) £12.90. Groups 15+ £7.25 (ch £3.60). Gardens & parkland only £6.85 (ch £3.45) Groups 15+ £5.75 (ch £2.70). **Facilities** ⓟ ⌐ ⦿ licensed ⌐ (outdoor) & (partly accessible) (woodland paths not accessible. Ground floor only in mansion accessible) toilets for disabled shop ⊗ ⊻

Lydford Gorge

EX20 4BH
☎ 01822 820320 & 820441 ▤ 01822 822000
e-mail: lydfordgorge@nationaltrust.org.uk
web: www.nationaltrust.org.uk
dir: off A386, between Okehampton & Tavistock

This lush oak-wooded steep-sided river gorge, with its fascinating history and many legends, can be explored through a variety of short and long walks. See the spectacular White Lady Waterfall, pass over the tumbling water at Tunnel Falls and watch the river bubble in the Devil's Cauldron. There's an abundance of wildlife to spot.

Times Open 14 Mar-Nov, daily 10-5 (Oct & Nov 10-4). Winter opening - please ring for details.* **Facilities** ⓟ ⓟ ⌐ ⌐ (outdoor) & (partly accessible) toilets for disabled shop ⊻

Morwellham Quay

PL19 8JL
☎ 01822 832766 & 833808 ▤ 01822 833808
e-mail: enquiries@morwellham-quay.co.uk
web: www.morwellham-quay.co.uk
dir: 4m W of Tavistock, off A390. Midway between Gunnislake & Tavistock. Signed

A unique, open-air museum based around the ancient port and copper mine workings in the heart of the Tamar Valley. Journey back into another time as costumed interpreters help you re-live the daily life of a 19th-century mining village and shipping quay. A tramway takes you deep into the workings of the George and Charlotte mine. Special events include music festivals, classic car shows, and a Victorian food festival.

Times Open all year (ex Xmas wk) 10-6 (4.30 Nov-Etr). Last admission 3.30 (2.30 Nov-Etr).* **Facilities** ⓟ ⌐ ⦿ licensed ⌐ (indoor & outdoor) toilets for disabled shop

NEWTON ABBOT

Prickly Ball Farm and Hedgehog Hospital

Denbury Rd, East Ogwell TQ12 6BZ
☎ 01626 362319 & 330685
e-mail: enquiries@pricklyballfarm.co.uk
web: www.pricklyballfarm.com
dir: 1.5m from Newton Abbot on A381 towards Totnes, follow brown heritage signs

See, touch and learn about this wild animal. In mid-season see baby hogs bottle feeding. Find out how to encourage hedgehogs into your garden and how they are put back into the wild. Talks on hedgehogs throughout the day, with a big-screen presentation. There is goat walking, pony grooming, lamb feeding (in season), a petting zoo and pig and sheep feeding. 2010 is the 20th anniversary.

Times Open Apr-Nov, 10-5. (Recommended last admission 3.30)*
Fees £5.95 (ch 3-14 £5.25, ch under 3 free, concessions £5.50, special needs £4.25). Family ticket £21 (2ad+2ch)* **Facilities** ℗ ⬚ 🍴 (indoor & outdoor) ♿ toilets for disabled shop ⊗

OKEHAMPTON

Museum of Dartmoor Life

3 West St EX20 1HQ
☎ 01837 52295
e-mail: dartmoormuseum@eclipse.co.uk
web: www.museumofdartmoorlife.eclipse.co.uk
dir: follow brown signs off all major roads into Okehampton. Museum on main road next to White Hart Hotel

Housed on three floors in an early 19th-century mill, the museum tells the story of how people have lived, worked and played on and around Dartmoor through the centuries. It shows how the moorland has shaped their lives just as their work has shaped the moorland. In the Cranmere Gallery, temporary exhibitions feature local history, art and crafts.

Times Open Etr-Oct, Mon-Sat 10.15-4. Phone for Winter opening times. **Fees** £3.50 (students £1). Family £7.50 (2ad+2ch)
Facilities ❶ ℗ ⬚ ♿ toilets for disabled shop

PAIGNTON

Paignton & Dartmouth Steam Railway

Queens Park Station, Torbay Rd TQ4 6AF
☎ 01803 555872   📄 01803 664313
e-mail: mail@pdsr.eclipse.co.uk
web: www.paignton-steamrailway.co.uk
dir: from Paignton follow brown tourist signs

Steam trains run for 7 miles from Paignton to Kingswear on the former Great Western line, stopping at Goodrington Sands, Churston, and Kingswear, connecting with the ferry Dartmouth. Combined river excursions available. Ring for details of events.

Times Open Jun-Sep, daily 9-5.30 & selected days Oct & Apr-May. Santa specials in Dec.* **Fees** Paignton to Kingswear £9 (ch £5.50, pen £8). Family £25. Paignton to Dartmouth (including ferry) £11 (ch £6.50, pen £10). Family £30.* **Facilities** ℗ ⬚ ♿ toilets for disabled shop

Paignton Zoo Environmental Park

Totnes Rd TQ4 7EU
☎ 01803 697500   📄 01803 523457
e-mail: info@paigntonzoo.org.uk **web:** www.paigntonzoo.org.uk
dir: 1m from Paignton town centre on A3022 Totnes road. Follow brown signs

Paignton is one of Britain's biggest zoos, set in a secluded woodland valley, where new enclosures are spacious and naturalistic. Your visit will take you through some of the world's threatened habitats - Forest, Savannah, Wetland and Desert, with hundreds of species, many of them endangered and part of conservation breeding programmes. There is a new crocodile swamp. There are regular keeper talks, a children's play area, and special events throughout the year. Visitors can obtain special joint tickets which allow them to visit nearby Living Coasts.

Times Open all year, daily 10-6 (5 in winter). Last admission 5 (4 in winter). Closed 25 Dec.* **Fees** £11.35 (ch 3-15 £7.60, concessions £9.35). Family ticket (2ad & 2ch) £34.10. Joint family saver ticket with Living Coasts £49.15.* **Facilities** ❶ ℗ ⬚ 🍴 licensed 🍴 (indoor & outdoor) ♿ (partly accessible) (footpaths have slight gradient, some steep hills) toilets for disabled shop ⊗

National Marine Aquarium

Rope Walk, Coxside PL4 0LF
☎ 01752 600301   📄 01752 600593
e-mail: enquiries@national-aquarium.co.uk
web: www.national-aquarium.co.uk
dir: A38 to Marsh Mills (Sainsbury's) then towards city centre &
follow brown signs for Barbican & Coxside car park

Europe's biggest tank has now got Europe's biggest collection
of sharks and rays - Atlantic Ocean is a must see exhibit. Next
to this is Ocean Drifters the UK's largest collection of jellyfish.

Times Open all year daily, mid Mar-Oct 10-6; Nov-mid Mar 10-5*
Fees £11 (ch £6.50, under 5's free, concessions £9). Family £30
(2ad+2ch). **Facilities** ℗ ⊑ 🞍 (outdoor) ♿ toilets for disabled
shop ⊗

Powderham Castle

EX6 8JQ
☎ 01626 890243   📄 01626 890729
e-mail: castle@powderham.co.uk
web: www.powderham.co.uk
dir: signed off A379 Exeter/Dawlish road

Set in a tranquil deer park along the Exe estuary. Built in 1391
by Sir Philip Courtenay, it has long been the family home of
the Earl of Devon. There is a beautiful rose garden and spring
walks through the woodland garden. Guided tours showcase
the castle's intriguing history, majestic interiors and fine
collection of treasures. Special events throughout the year.

Times Open Etr-Oct, 10-5.30 (last admission 4.30). Closed Sat.*
Facilities ❶ ℗ ⊑ ⦿⦿ licensed 🞍 (outdoor) toilets for disabled
shop ⊗

Quince Honey Farm

EX36 3AZ
☎ 01769 572401   📄 01769 574704
e-mail: info@quincehoney.co.uk
web: www.quincehoney.com
dir: 3.5m W of A361, on N edge of South Molton

Follow the story of honey and beeswax from flower to table.
The exhibition allows you to see the world of bees close up in
complete safety; hives open at the press of a button revealing
the honeybees' secret life. After viewing the bees at work,
sample the fruits of their labour in the café or shop.

Times Open daily, Apr-Sep 9-6; Oct 9-5; Shop only Nov-Etr 9-5,
closed Sun. Closed 25 Dec-4 Jan.* **Fees** £4 (ch 5-16 £3, pen
£3.50)* **Facilities** ❶ ⊑ 🞍 (outdoor) ♿ (partly accessible) (no lift
to exhibition on first floor) toilets for disabled shop ⊗

Tiverton Museum of Mid Devon Life

Beck's Square EX16 6PJ
☎ 01884 256295
e-mail: curator04@tivertonmuseum.org.uk
web: www.tivertonmuseum.org.uk
dir: in centre of town next to Beck's Square car park

This large and comprehensive museum now with 15 galleries,
re-opened after extensive rebuilding throughout. It is housed
in a 19th-century school and the exhibits include a Heathcoat
Lace Gallery featuring items from the local lace-making
industry. There is also an agricultural section with a collection
of farm wagons and implements. Other large exhibits include
two waterwheels and a railway locomotive with many GWR
items.

Times Open Feb-mid Dec, Mon-Fri 10.30-4.30, Sat 10-1. Open
BHs. **Fees** £4.25 (ch £1, pen £3.25). Family (2+4) £9.* **Facilities**
℗ ♿ toilets for disabled shop ⊗

TORQUAY

Babbacombe Model Village

Hampton Av, Babbacombe TQ1 3LA
☎ 01803 315315   📄 01803 315173
e-mail: sw@model-village.co.uk **web:** www.model-village.co.uk
dir: follow brown tourist signs from outskirts of town

See the world recreated in miniature. Thousands of miniature buildings, people and vehicles capture the essence of England's past, present and future, set in four acres of award-winning gardens. Various events are planned, please contact for details.

Times Open all year, times vary.* **Fees** Price varies - please contact for current prices.* **Facilities** 🅿 🅟 ⛟ 🍴 licensed ⛱ 🚻 (partly accessible) (very steep slopes but access is possible) toilets for disabled shop

'Bygones'

Fore St, St Marychurch TQ1 4PR
☎ 01803 326108   📄 01803 326108
web: www.bygones.co.uk
dir: follow tourist signs into Torquay and St Marychurch

Step back in time in this life-size Victorian exhibition street of over 20 shops including a forge, pub and period display rooms, housed in a former cinema. Exhibits include a large model railway layout, illuminated fantasyland, railwayana and military exhibits including a walk-through World War I trench. At Christmas the street is turned into a winter wonderland. A new set piece features Babbacombe's John Lee ('the man they couldn't hang') in his cell. There is something here for all the family including a 1940s/50s shopping arcade.

Times Open all year, Summer 10-6; Spring & Autumn 10-6; Winter 10-4, wknds & school hols 10-5. (Last entry 1hr before closing).* **Facilities** 🅟 ⛟ 🚻 (partly accessible) (ground floor only accessible) shop ⊗

Kents Cavern

Cavern House, 91 Ilsham Rd, Wellswood TQ1 2JF
☎ 01803 215136
e-mail: caves@kents-cavern.co.uk
web: www.kents-cavern.co.uk
dir: 1.25m NE off B3199, follow brown tourist signs. 1m from Torquay harbour

Probably the most important Palaeolithic site in Britain and recognised as one of the country's most significant archaeological areas. This is not only a world of spectacular natural beauty, but also a priceless record of past times, where a multitude of secrets of mankind, animals and nature have become trapped and preserved over the last 500,000 years. 170 years after the first excavations and with over 80,000 remains already unearthed, modern research is still discovering new clues to our past. Please visit website for details of special events.

Times Open all year daily from 10, last tour 3.30 Nov-Feb, 4 Mar-Jun & Sep-Oct, 4.30 Jul-Aug.* **Facilities** 🅿 🅟 ⛟ 🍴 licensed ⛱ (outdoor) 🚻 (partly accessible) toilets for disabled shop ⊗

Living Coasts

Beacon Quay TQ1 2BG
☎ 01803 202470   📄 01803 202471
e-mail: info@livingcoasts.org.uk
web: www.livingcoasts.org.uk
dir: once in Torquay follow A379 and brown tourist signs to harbour

Living Coasts is a coastal zoo that allows visitors to take a trip around the coastlines of the world without leaving Torquay. Specially designed environments are home to fur seals, puffins, penguins, ducks, rats, and waders among others. All the animals can be seen above and below the water, while the huge meshed aviary allows the birds to fly free over your head. Visitors can obtain special joint tickets which will allow them to visit nearby Paignton Zoo. Contact or see website for details of special events.

Times Open daily from 10. Closed 25 Dec. **Fees** £9.20 (ch over 3 £6.90, concessions £7.15). Family ticket (2ad+2ch) £28.90. **Facilities** 🅿 🅟 ⛟ 🍴 licensed 🚻 toilets for disabled shop ⊗

Torre Abbey

The Kings Dr TQ2 5JE
☎ 01803 293593   📄 01803 215948
e-mail: torre.abbey@torbay.gov.uk
web: www.torre-abbey.org.uk
dir: A389 turn right at Torre Abbey railway station, follow brown signs for 1.5m. On seafront, next to Riviera Centre

Torre Abbey is the oldest building in Torquay, founded in 1196 as a monastery and later adapted as a country house. It has a story spanning 800 years and was once the most important Abbey of its kind in England, the brothers who lived here then were known as the White Canons. Following a massive three-year restoration project visitors, can now explore the most ancient and hallowed parts of the building and gardens where some stunning finds have been unearthed.

Times Open Feb-Mar, 10-5 (last admission 4); Apr-Oct, 10-6 (last admission 5). **Fees** £5.75 (ch £2.45, concessions £4.80). Group rates available. **Facilities** 🅿 🅟 ⛟ 🍴 licensed ⛱ (outdoor) 🚻 toilets for disabled shop ⊗

Coldharbour Mill Working Wool Museum

Coldharbour Mill EX15 3EE
☎ **01884 840960**
e-mail: info@coldharbourmill.org.uk
web: www.coldharbourmill.org.uk
dir: 2m from M5 junct 27, off B3181. Follow signs to Willand, then brown signs to museum

The picturesque Coldharbour Mill is set in idyllic Devon countryside. It has been producing textiles since 1799 and is now a working museum, still making knitting wools and fabrics on period machinery. With machine demonstrations, a water wheel and steam engines, Coldharbour Mill is a wonderful and very different family day out. The Power Trail Tour is available Tue, Wed and Thu at 11.30 and 2.30. There are engines in steam regularly throughout the year plus special events, please see the website for details. The new self-guided tour of the Woollen Mill is available every day.

Times Open all year, daily 11-4.* **Fees** General visit £4 (ch £2 concessions £3.50: Power Trail Tour £5.50 (ch £2.75 concessions £5): Steam Up Event £7 (ch £4, concessions £6.50)* **Facilities** ℗ ☐ 🍴 licensed ⅌ (outdoor) ♿ (partly accessible) (indoor restaurant not accessible but assistance given) toilets for disabled shop ⊗

DORSET

ABBOTSBURY

Abbotsbury Swannery

New Barn Rd DT3 4JG
☎ **01305 871858** 🖷 **01305 871092**
e-mail: info@abbotsbury-tourism.co.uk
web: www.abbotsbury-tourism.co.uk
dir: turn off A35 at Winterborne Abbas near Dorchester. Abbotsbury on B3157 (coastal road), between Weymouth & Bridport

Abbotsbury is the breeding ground of the only managed colony of mute swans. The swans can be seen safely at close quarters, and the site is also home or stopping point for many wild birds. The highlight of the year is the cygnet season, end of May to the end of June, when there may be over 100 nests on site. Visitors can often take pictures of cygnets emerging from eggs at close quarters. There is an audio-visual show, as well as mass feeding at noon and 4pm daily, and an ugly duckling trail. Children's play area available and a new giant maze planted with willow in the shape of a swan. Find your way to the giant egg at the centre!

Times Open 20 Mar-Oct, daily 10-6 (last admission 5). **Fees** £9.50 (ch £6.50 & concessions £9). **Facilities** ℗ ☐ 🍴 licensed ⅌ (outdoor) ♿ toilets for disabled shop ⊗

BLANDFORD FORUM

Royal Signals Museum

Blandford Camp DT11 8RH
☎ **01258 482248** 🖷 **01258 482084**
e-mail: info@royalsignalsmuseum.com
web: www.royalsignalsmuseum.com
dir: signed off B3082 (Blandford/Wimborne road) & A354 (Salisbury road). Follow brown signs for Royal Signals Museum

The Royal Signals Museum depicts the history of military communications, science and technology from the Crimea to current day. As well as displays on all major conflicts involving British forces, there are the stories of the ATS, the Long Range Desert Group, Air Support, Airborne, Para and SAS Signals. D-Day and Dorset explores the Royal Signals involvement in Operation Overlord. For children there are trails and interactive exhibits.

Times Open Mar-Oct, Mon-Fri 10-5, Sat-Sun 10-4. Closed 10 days over Xmas & New Year* **Facilities** ℗ ℗ ☐ ⅌ ♿ toilets for disabled shop ⊗

BOURNEMOUTH

Oceanarium

Pier Approach, West Beach BH2 5AA
☎ **01202 311993** 🖷 **01202 311990**
e-mail: info@oceanarium.co.uk
web: www.oceanarium.co.uk
dir: from A338 Wessex Way, follow Oceanarium tourist signs

Take an underwater adventure around the waters of the world and come face to face with hundreds of awesome creatures. Home to all your favourites from flamboyant clownfish and tiny terrapins, to stunning sharks and the infamous piranha, immerse yourself in a sea of colour, with 10 spectacular recreated environments including the Great Barrier Reef underwater tunnel. Experience the world's first Interactive Dive Cage - take a virtual adventure to discover more about magnificent sea creatures, without getting wet. And don't miss the Global Meltdown experience and find out what would happen if the ice caps melted and your world was flooded with water. Spectacular theming, state of the art technology and amazing interactive displays, make Global Meltdown an experience not to be missed.

Times Open all year, daily from 10. Late night opening during school summer hols. Closed 25 Dec. **Fees** Please telephone for admission charges or visit website. **Facilities** ℗ 🍴 licensed ♿ toilets for disabled shop ⊗

BOVINGTON CAMP

The Tank Museum

BH20 6JG
☎ **01929 405096** 📄 **01929 405360**
e-mail: info@tankmuseum.org **web:** www.tankmuseum.org
dir: off A352 or A35, follow brown tank signs from Bere Regis & Wool

The Tank Museum houses the world's best collection of tanks. From the first tank ever built to the modern Challenger II, the Museum houses examples from all over the world. This definitive collection comprises of over 250 vehicles dating back to 1909. The Tank Museum is the only place where many of these rare and historic vehicles can be seen. You will come face to face with tanks that have seen action in all the major wars of the 20th century. There are plenty of live action displays all year, please see website for details.

Times Open all year, daily 10-5 (limited opening over Xmas).*
Facilities 🅿 Ⓟ 🍵 🍽 licensed 🏔 (outdoor) ♿ toilets for disabled shop ⊗

BROWNSEA ISLAND

Brownsea Island

BH13 7EE
☎ **01202 707744** 📄 **01202 701635**
e-mail: brownseaisland@nationaltrust.org.uk
web: www.nationaltrust.org.uk
dir: located in Poole Harbour

Peaceful island of woodland, wetland and heath with a rich diversity of wildlife. The island is famous for its rare red squirrels and as the site of the first Scout camp held by Lord Baden-Powell in 1907. 2010 is the Guiding centenary.

Times Open 13 Mar-Oct, daily, 10-5 (13-26 Mar boats from Sandbanks only, 27-31 Mar full boat service from Poole Quay & Sandbanks). **Fees** £4.90 (ch £2.40). Family ticket £12.20. Group £4.20 (ch £2.10)* **Facilities** 🍵 🍽 licensed 🏔 (outdoor) ♿ (partly accessible) (countryside property with rough terrain in places. Contact ferry operators to discuss carrying of wheelchairs on boats) toilets for disabled shop ⊗ 🐾

CANFORD CLIFFS

Compton Acres Gardens

164 Canford Cliffs Rd BH13 7ES
☎ **01202 700778** 📄 **01202 707537**
e-mail: events@comptonacres.co.uk
web: www.comptonacres.co.uk
dir: on B3065, follow brown tourist signs

The ten acres of Compton Acres incorporate Japanese and Italian gardens, rock and water gardens, and heather gardens. There are fine views over Poole Harbour and the Purbeck Hills. The beautiful wooded valley is an amazing place to explore the wide range of plants. The Italian garden was used as a location in Stanley Kubrick's 1975 movie, Barry Lyndon. There is also a model railway, restaurants, a tea room, and a craft shop.

Times Open Apr-Oct 9-dusk, Nov-Mar 10-4 (last entry 1hr before close). Closed 25-26 Dec. **Fees** £6.95 (ch £3.95, concessions £6.45). Party 15+ £5.95 (concessions £5.45) **Facilities** 🅿 Ⓟ 🍵 🍽 licensed ♿ toilets for disabled shop ⊗

CHRISTCHURCH

Red House Museum & Gardens   FREE

Quay Rd BH23 1BU
☎ **01202 482860** 📄 **01202 481924**
e-mail: paul.willis@hants.gov.uk
web: www.hants.gov.uk/museum/redhouse
dir: follow brown tourist signs from Christchurch, Red House is on corner of Quay Rd

A museum with plenty of variety, featuring local history and archaeology, displayed in a beautiful Georgian house. There's an excellent costume collection, some Arthur Romney-Green furniture and gardens with a woodland walk and herb garden. Regularly changing temporary exhibitions include contemporary art and crafts, plus historical displays.

Times Open Tue-Sat 10-5, Sun 2-5 (last admission 4.30). Open BHs (spring & summer) Closed 25 Dec-1 Jan & Good Fri.*
Facilities Ⓟ 🍵 ♿ (partly accessible) (ground floor and gardens accessible) toilets for disabled shop ⊗

CORFE CASTLE

Corfe Castle

BH20 5EZ
☎ **01929 481294** ▤ **01929 477067**
e-mail: corfecastle@nationaltrust.org.uk
web: www.nationaltrust.org.uk
dir: follow A351 from Wareham to Swanage. Corfe Castle approx 5m

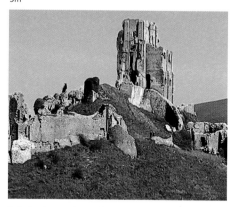

Built in Norman times, the castle was added to by King John. It was defended during the Civil War by Lady Bankes, who surrendered after a stout resistance. Parliament ordered the demolition of the castle, and today it is one of the most impressive ruins in England. Please ring for details of special events.

Times Open all year, daily Mar 10-5; Apr-Sep 10-6; Oct 10-5; Nov-Feb 10-4. (Last admission 30 mins before closing). Closed 25-26 Dec. **Fees** £6.20 (ch £3.10). Family ticket (2ad+3ch) £15.50 or (1ad+3ch) £9.30. Groups £5 (ch £2.50). **Facilities** Ⓟ Ⓟ ⌷⍩ licensed ♿ (partly accessible) (steep, uneven cobbled paths & steps, wheelchair access restricted to Outer Bailey only) toilets for disabled shop ✿

DORCHESTER

Dinosaur Museum

Icen Way DT1 1EW
☎ **01305 269880** ▤ **01305 268885**
e-mail: info@thedinosaurmuseum.com
web: www.thedinosaurmuseum.com
dir: off A35 into Dorchester, museum in town centre just off High East St

Britain's award-winning museum devoted to dinosaurs has a fascinating mixture of fossils, skeletons, life-size reconstructions and interactive displays such as the 'feelies', colour box and parasaurlophus sound. There are multi-media presentations providing an all-round family attraction with something new each year. There is a Great Dinosaur Easter Egg Hunt every Easter weekend.

Times Open all year, daily 9.30-5.30 (10-4.30 Nov-Mar). Closed 24-26 Dec. **Fees** £6.95 (ch £5.50, concessions £5.95, under 4's free). Family ticket £22.50* **Facilities** Ⓟ ♿ (partly accessible) (ground floor only accessible) shop

Dorset County Museum

High West St DT1 1XA
☎ **01305 262735** ▤ **01305 257180**
e-mail: enquiries@dorsetcountymuseum.org
web: www.dorsetcountymuseum.org
dir: off A354 signed Dorchester, attraction on right half way up main street

Displays cover prehistoric and Roman times, including sites such as Maiden Castle, and there's a gallery on Dorset writers with sections on the poet William Barnes, Thomas Hardy (with a reconstruction of his study), and 20th-century writers. Also geology, local wildlife and social history are explored in the museum. The Jurassic Coast geology gallery was opened by Sir David Attenborough in summer 2006.

Times Open all year, Mon-Sat, 10-5. Also open Sun, Jul-Sep. Closed 24-26 Dec **Fees** £6.50 (up to 2 accompanied ch free, additional ch £1, concessions £4.50)* **Facilities** Ⓟ ♿ (partly accessible) (access via lift to Geology Gallery on 1st floor) toilets for disabled shop ⊗

The Keep Military Museum

The Keep, Bridport Rd DT1 1RN
☎ **01305 264066** ▤ **01305 250373**
e-mail: keep.museum@talk21.com
web: www.keepmilitarymuseum.org
dir: near top of High West St leading out of town towards Bridport

300 years of military history with displays on the Devon Regiment, Dorset Regiment, Dorset Militia and Volunteers, the Queen's Own Dorset Yeomanry, and Devonshire and Dorset Regiment (from 1958). The Museum uses interactive and creative displays to tell the stories of the Infantry, Cavalry and Artillerymen.

Times Open Apr-Sep, Mon-Sat 10-5; Oct-Mar, Tue-Sat 10-4.30 (last admission 4 Apr-Sep & 3.30 Oct-Mar). Closed Xmas & New Year. **Fees** £6 (ch £2, under 8 free, pen £4). Family £13.* **Facilities** Ⓟ Ⓟ ♿ (partly accessible) (wheelchairs cannot access roof) toilets for disabled shop ⊗

Teddy Bear Museum

High East St & Salisbury St DT1 1JU
☎ 01305 266040   📄 01305 268885
e-mail: info@teddybearmuseum.co.uk
web: www.teddybearmuseum.co.uk
dir: off A35, museum in town centre near Dinosaur Museum

Meet Edward Bear and his extended family of people-sized bears. See them relaxing and busying themselves in their Edwardian-style house. From the earliest teddies of 100 years ago to today's TV favourites, they are all on display in this family museum.

Times Open daily, 10-5 (4.30 in winter). Closed 24-26 Dec.
Fees £5.75 (ch £4, under 4's free, concessions £5). Family £18.*
Facilities ℗ shop ⊗

Tutankhamun Exhibition

High West St DT1 1UW
☎ 01305 269571   📄 01305 268885
e-mail: info@tutankhamun-exhibition.co.uk
web: www.tutankhamun-exhibition.co.uk
dir: off A35 into Dorchester town centre

The exhibition recreates the excitement of one of the world's greatest discoveries of ancient treasure. A reconstruction of the tomb and recreations of its treasures are displayed. The superbly preserved mummified body of the boy king can be seen, wonderfully recreated in every detail. Facsimiles of some of the most famous treasures, including the golden funerary mask and the harpooner can be seen in the final gallery.

Times Open all year daily, Apr-Oct, 9.30-5.30; Nov-Mar, wkdays 9.30-5, wknds 10-4.30. Closed 24-26 Dec.* **Fees** £6.95 (ch £5.50, under 5 free, concessions £5.95). Family ticket £22.50.*
Facilities ℗ ♿ shop ⊗

ORGANFORD

Farmer Palmer's Farm Park

BH16 6EU
☎ 01202 622022   📄 01202 622182
e-mail: info@farmerpalmers.co.uk
web: www.farmerpalmers.co.uk
dir: From Poole, just off A35 straight over rdbt past Bakers Arms, signed on left, take 2nd turn, 0.5m after rdbt

Family owned and run Farmer Palmers has been specially designed for families with children 8 years and under. Many activities include meeting and learning about the animals, climbing the straw mountain, going for a tractor trailer ride and exercising in the soft play area. A fun and busy day for the family.

Times Open 6 Feb-19 Dec, daily 10-5.30 (10-4 outside main season). Closed mid Dec-early Feb. **Fees** £6.75 (ch £6.75, under 2 free, pen £5.95, disabled & carers £5.75). Family ticket (2ad+2ch) £25.* **Facilities** ❷ ℗ 🖵 ⧉ licensed 🪑 (indoor & outdoor) ♿ (partly accessible) (woodland walk & outside animal pen not level) toilets for disabled shop ⊗

Portland Castle

Castleton DT5 1AZ
☎ 01305 820539   📄 01305 860853
web: www.english-heritage.org.uk
dir: overlooking Portland harbour

Visit one of Henry VIII's finest coastal forts, in use right up to World War II. Home to the Wrens and scene of the US troops' embarkation for the D-Day invasion in 1944. Explore the Captain's House and Gardens.

Times Open Apr-Jun & Sep, daily 10-5; Jul-Aug, daily 10-6; Oct-1 Nov, daily 10-4. Closed 2 Nov- Mar. **Fees** £4 (concessions £3.40, ch £2). Family ticket £10.00. Please call 0870 333 1181 for the most up to date prices and opening times when planning your visit. **Facilities** ❷ 🖵 toilets for disabled shop ⊗ ⧉

SWANAGE

Swanage Railway

Station House BH19 1HB
☎ 01929 425800   📄 01929 426680
e-mail: info@swanage-railway.co.uk
web: www.swanagerailway.co.uk
dir: signed from A351

The railway from Swanage to Wareham was closed in 1972, and in 1976 the Swanage Railway took possession and have gradually restored the line, which now runs for 6 miles, passing the ruins of Corfe Castle. Steam trains run daily April to October, as well as week-ends most of the year. Special events throughout the year including Santa Specials.

Times Open every wknd ex Jan, daily Apr-Oct. **Fees** Swanage-Corfe/Norden £9 return (ch £7 return). Family ticket £26. Day Rover £13.50 (ch & concessions £10.50)* **Facilities** ❷ ℗ 🖵 ⧉ licensed 🪑 (outdoor) ♿ shop

Dorset

WEST LULWORTH

Lulworth Castle & Park

BH20 5QS
☎ 0845 450 1054   ◫ 01929 400563
e-mail: estate.office@lulworth.com
web: www.lulworth.com
dir: from Wareham, W on A352 for 1m, left onto B3070 to E Lulworth, follow tourist signs

Glimpse life below stairs in the restored kitchen, and enjoy glorious views from the top of the tower of this historic castle set in beautiful parkland. The 18th-century chapel is the first Catholic chapel built in England after the Reformation. Children will enjoy the animal farm, play area, indoor activity room and pitch and putt. Visit website for details of future events.

Times Open Jan-22 Mar, Sun-Fri 10.30-4; 23 Mar-26 Sep, Sun-Fri, 10.30-6; 28 Sep-Dec, Sun-Fri, 10.30-4. Closed Sat (ex Etr Sat), 24-25 Dec & 6-19 Jan.* **Fees** £8 (ch £4, concessions £5) Family ticket (1ad+3ch) £16 non-jousting season. £9.50 (ch £4.50, concessions £8) Family ticket (1ad+3ch) £18.50 jousting season (24 Jul-25 Aug)* **Facilities** ❷ ⬚ ⌷ (outdoor) ♿ (partly accessible) (access limited in castle due to grade one listing) toilets for disabled shop ⊗

WEYMOUTH

RSPB Nature Reserve Radipole Lake

The Swannery Car Park DT4 7TZ
☎ 01305 778313   ◫ 01305 778313
web: www.rspb.org.uk
dir: close to seafront & railway station

Covering 222 acres, the Reserve offers firm paths, hide and a visitor centre. Several types of warblers, mute swans, gadwalls, teals and great crested grebes may be seen, and the visitor centre has viewing windows overlooking the lake. Phone for details of special events.

Times Open daily 9-5* **Facilities** ❷ ℗ ⌷ toilets for disabled shop

Weymouth Sea Life Adventure Park & Marine Sanctuary

Lodmoor Country Park DT4 7SX
☎ 0871 423 2110 & 01305 761070   ◫ 01305 760165
e-mail: slcweymouth@merlinentertainments.biz
web: www.sealifeeurope.com
dir: on A353

A unique mix of indoor and outdoor attractions set in 7 acres. The park offers a day of fun, bringing you face to face with penguins, otters, seals and much more.

Times Open all year, daily from 10. (Closed 25 Dec).* **Facilities** ❷ ℗ ⬚ ⌷◎ licensed ⌷ (indoor & outdoor) ♿ toilets for disabled shop ⊗

WIMBORNE

Kingston Lacy

BH21 4EA
☎ 01202 883402 (Mon-Fri) & 880413 (infoline)
◫ 01202 882402
e-mail: kingstonlacy@nationaltrust.org.uk
web: www.nationaltrust.org.uk
dir: 1.5m W of Wimborne, B3082

Kingston Lacy House was the home of the Bankes family for over 300 years. The original house is 17th century, but in the 1830s was given a stone façade. The Italian marble staircase, Venetian ceiling, treasures from Spain and an Egyptian obelisk were also added. There are outstanding pictures by Titian, Rubens, Velasquez, Reynolds and Van Dyck. No photography is allowed in the house.

Times Open: House 13 Mar-Oct, Wed-Sun, 11-4. Garden & Park 13 Mar-Oct, daily, 10.30-6; 5 Feb-7 Mar, Fri-Sun 10.30-4 **Fees** House, Garden & Park £12 (ch £6) Family £30. Park & Gardens £6 (ch £3) Family £15. **Facilities** ❷ ◎ licensed ⌷ (outdoor) ♿ (partly accessible) (ground floor accessible) toilets for disabled shop ⊗ ⚘

WOOL

Monkey World Ape Rescue Centre

Longthorns BH20 6HH
☎ 01929 462537 & 0800 456600 📠 01929 405414
e-mail: apes@monkeyworld.org
web: www.monkeyworld.org
dir: 1m N of Wool on Bere Regis road

Set up in order to rescue monkeys and apes from abuse and illegal smuggling, Monkey World houses over 230 primates in 65 acres of Dorset woodland. There is the largest group of chimps outside Africa, as well as orang-utans, gibbons, woolly monkeys, lemurs, macaques and marmosets. Those wishing to help the centre continue in its quest to rescue primates from lives of misery may like to take part in the adoption scheme which includes free admission to the park for one year. There are keeper talks every half hour, and the south's largest Great Ape Play Area for kids.

Times Open daily 10-5; Jul-Aug, 10-6. (Last admission 1hr before closing). Closed 25 Dec. **Fees** £10.50 (ch 3-15 & pen £7.25, students £8.25). Family ticket (1ad+2ch) £21.50, (2ad+2ch) £31. Group rates available.* **Facilities** 🅿 ⛌ 🍴 licensed 🌲 (indoor & outdoor) ♿ (partly accessible) (woodland walk uneaven surface) toilets for disabled shop ⊗

CO DURHAM

BARNARD CASTLE

The Bowes Museum

DL12 8NP
☎ 01833 690606 📠 01833 637163
e-mail: info@thebowesmuseum.org.uk
web: www.thebowesmuseum.org.uk
dir: in Barnard Castle, just off A66

John and Josephine Bowes founded The Bowes Museum over 100 years ago. The magnificent building houses a collection of treasures from fine and decorative art to major temporary exhibitions of international quality and interest. The icon of the collection is the Silver Swan, a unique life-size, musical automaton which plays every day. There are also works by El Greco, Goya and Canaletto. The Café Bowes and beautiful grounds add to a wonderful day out for all. The Silver and Metals Gallery and Textiles and Dress Gallery can now be seen.

Times Open daily 10-5. Closed 25-26 Dec & 1 Jan. **Fees** £7 (ch under 16 free, concessions £6)* **Facilities** 🅿 Ⓟ ⛌ 🌲 (outdoor) ♿ (partly accessible) (vaults on lower ground not accessible) toilets for disabled shop ⊗

BEAMISH

Beamish Museum

DH9 0RG
☎ 0191 370 4000 📠 0191 370 4001
e-mail: museum@beamish.org.uk
web: www.beamish.org.uk
dir: off A693 & A6076. Signed from A1M junct 63.

Set in 300 acres of countryside, award-winning Beamish recreates life in the early 1800s and 1900s. Costumed staff welcome visitors to a 1913 town street, colliery village, farm and railway station; a re-creation of how people lived and worked. Ride on early electric tramcars, take a ride on a replica of an 1825 steam railway and visit Pockerley Manor where a yeoman farmer and his family would have lived.

Times Open Apr-Oct, daily 10-5; Oct-Mar 10-4 (last admission 3). Closed Mon, Fri & part of Dec.* **Fees** Summer £16 (ch £10, pen £12.50). Winter £6 (ch & pen £6). Winter visit is centred on town, colliery village & tramway only, other areas are closed.* **Facilities** 🅿 ⛌ 🌲 (outdoor) ♿ (partly accessible) (some 1st floor areas inaccessible, some ground floor areas have steeped access & narrow doorways) toilets for disabled shop ⊗

COWSHILL

Killhope The North of England Lead Mining Museum

DL13 1AR
☎ 01388 537505 📄 01388 537617
e-mail: info@killhope.org.uk
web: www.killhope.org.uk
dir: beside A689 midway between Stanhope & Alston

Equipped with hard hats and lamps, you can explore the working conditions of Victorian lead miners. The lead mine and 19th-century crushing mill have been restored to look as they would have done in the 1870s, and the 34ft water wheel has been restored to working order. There is also a visitor centre and mineral exhibition, a woodland walk, children's play area and red squirrel and bird hides. Please ring for information on workshops and events. 2010 is the 25th anniversary of Killhopes's opening.

Times Open Apr-Oct, daily10.30-5. **Fees** Mine & Site: £6.50 (ch £3.50, concessions £6). Family £17. Site: £4.50 (ch £1.50, concessions £4). Family £11.50* **Facilities** 🅿 🚻 🍴 (indoor & outdoor) 🔈 (partly accessible) (accessible hide for wildlife viewing) toilets for disabled shop

---

DURHAM

Old Fulling Mill Museum of Archaeology

The Banks DH1 3EB
☎ 0191 334 1823 📄 0191 334 5694
e-mail: archaeology.museum@durham.ac.uk
web: www.dur.ac.uk/fulling.mill
dir: On river bank directly below Cathedral

Once a key part of Durham's cloth making industry, the Old Fulling Mill is now home to Durham University's Museum of Archaeology. The collections on display provide a fascinating insight into the rich heritage of the north east of England, as well as showcasing items from across Europe. Highlights include outstanding Roman collections together with Anglo-Saxon, Medieval and Tudor finds from Durham City and the local area. Up to date details of exhibitions and the lively programme of family activities at weekends and during school holidays can be found on the museum's website.

Times Open Apr-Oct, daily 10-4; Nov-Mar, Fri-Mon 11.30-3.30* **Fees** £1 (ch & concessions 50p, students free). Family ticket £2.50.* **Facilities** 🅿 🔈 (partly accessible) (ground floor only accessible) shop ⊗

HARTLEPOOL

Hartlepool's Maritime Experience

Maritime Av TS24 0XZ
☎ 01429 860077 📄 01429 867332
e-mail: info@hartlepoolsmaritimeexperience.com
web: www.hartlepoolsmaritimeexperience.com
dir: from N A19 take A179 and follow signs for marina then historic quay. From S A19 take A689 and follow signs for marina then historic quay

Britain's maritime heritage is brought to life, with the sights, sounds and smells of an 1800s quayside. Learn about the birth of the Royal Navy, and visit the Quayside shops, the admiral's house, Europe's oldest warship afloat HMS Trincomalee and the children's Maritime Adventure Centre. Other features include regular demonstrations of sword fighting, and cannon firing. The new HMS Trincomalee exhibition is now open.

Times Open all year daily summer 10-5, winter 11-3. Closed 25-26 Dec & 1 Jan.* **Fees** £7.75 (ch £4.75, concessions £4.75-£5.75). Family ticket (2ad+3ch) £20. Museum is free.* **Facilities** 🅿 🚻 🍴 licensed 🔈 (outdoor) 🔈 (partly accessible) toilets for disabled shop ⊗

LANGLEY PARK

Diggerland

DH7 9TT
☎ 0871 227 7007   📄 09012 010300
e-mail: mail@diggerland.com
web: www.diggerland.com
dir: A1(M) junct 62. W & follow Consett signs. After 6m left at rdbt, signed Langley Park, then right into Riverside Industrial Estate

An adventure park with a difference, where kids of all ages can experience the thrills of driving real earth-moving equipment. Choose from various types of diggers and dumpers ranging from 1 ton to 8.5 tons. Supervised by an instructor, complete the Dumper Truck Challenge or dig for buried treasure. New rides include JCB Robots, Diggerland Dodgems, Go-karts, Landrover Safari and Spin Dizzy. Even under fives can join in, with mum or dad's help.

Times Open 12 Feb-end Oct, 10-5, wknds BHs & school hols only (including half terms). **Fees** £15 - All rides and drives included in price. **Facilities** ℗ ⊡ 🍴 ♿ toilets for disabled shop ⊗

SHILDON

Locomotion: The National Railway Museum at Shildon

DL4 1PQ
☎ 01388 777999   📄 01388 777999
e-mail: info@locomotion.uk.com
web: www.locomotion.uk.com
dir: A1(M) junct 68, take A68 & A6072 to Shildon, attraction is 0.25m SE of town centre

Timothy Hackwood (1786-1850) was an important figure in the development of steam travel. He constructed Puffing Billy for William Hedley, ran Stephenson's Newcastle Works, and also became the first superintendent of the Stockton & Darlington Railway. The museum and house detail Hackwood's life and the steam transport revolution, as well as displaying working models and locomotives from various periods. Steam train rides are available throughout the year, on event days. The Collections building contains 60 vehicles from the National Collection.

Times Open Apr-5 Oct, daily 10-5; 6 Oct-1 Apr, daily, 10-4. Buildings at western end of site are closed Mon & Tue in winter. **Fees** Free, small charge for train rides.* **Facilities** ℗ ℗ ⊡ 🍴 (indoor & outdoor) ♿ toilets for disabled shop ⊗

TANFIELD

Tanfield Railway

Old Marley Hill NE16 5ET
☎ 0191 388 7545   📄 0191 387 4784
e-mail: tanfield@ingsoc.demon.co.uk
web: www.tanfield_railway.co.uk
dir: on A6076 1m S of Sunniside

A 3-mile working steam railway which is the oldest existing railway in the world. The Causey Arch, the first large railway bridge of its era, is the centrepiece of a deep wooded valley, with picturesque walks. You can ride in carriages that first saw use in Victorian times, and visit Marley Hill, the home of 35 engines; inside the shed you can see the stationary steam engine at work driving some of the vintage machine tools. The blacksmith is also often at work forging new parts for the restoration work. Special events are held throughout the year, please telephone for details.

Times Open all year, Summer daily 10-5; Winter daily 10-4. Trains: Sun & Summer BHs wknds; also Thu & Sat mid Jul-Aug. Santa's Specials Sat & Sun in Dec (booking essential). Mince pie specials Boxing Day.* **Facilities** ℗ ℗ ⊡ 🍴 toilets for disabled shop

ESSEX

AUDLEY END

Audley End House & Gardens

CB11 4JF
☎ 01799 522842   📄 01799 521276
web: www.english-heritage.org.uk
dir: 1m W of Saffron Walden on B1383

One of the most significant Jacobean houses in England with 31 opulent rooms on view. Set in a 'Capability' Brown landscaped park, with walled Victorian kitchen garden.

Times Open Apr-Sep, Wed-Sun & BH 11-5 (Sat last admission 2.30); Oct-1 Nov, Wed-Sun 11-4. (Sat last admission 2.30). Closed Nov-Mar except for Festive Fun wknds (21-22, 28-29 Nov & 5-6, 12-13, 19-20 Dec). **Fees** House & Gardens: £10.70 (concessions £9.10, ch £5.40). Family £26.80. Service Wing & Gardens: £7.70 (concessions £6.50, ch £3.90). Family £19.30. Please call 0870 333 1181 for the most up to date prices and opening times. **Facilities** ℗ ⊡ 🍴 ♿ (partly accessible) (bridges either have a step or steep slope) toilets for disabled shop ⊞

CASTLE HEDINGHAM

Colne Valley Railway & Museum

Castle Hedingham Station CO9 3DZ
☎ 01787 461174
e-mail: info@colnevalleyrailway.co.uk
web: www.colnevalleyrailway.co.uk
dir: 4m NW of Halstead on A1017

Many former Colne Valley and Halstead railway buildings have been rebuilt here. Stock includes seven steam locomotives plus 80 other engines, carriages and wagons. Visitors can dine in style in restored Pullman carriages while travelling along the line. Please telephone for a free timetable and details of the many special events.

Times Open all year, daily 10-dusk. Steam days, rides from 12-4. Closed 23 Dec-1 Feb. Steam days every Sun and BH from Mothering Sun to end Oct, Wed of school summer hols & special events. Railway Farm Park open May-Sep. Phone 01787 461174 for timetable information or visit website for details. **Fees** Steam days: £7 (ch £4, pen £6) Family ticket £22. Diesel days £6 (ch £3, pen £5); Family ticket £18. **Facilities** ℗ 🖵 🍽 licensed 🎠 (outdoor) ♿ (partly accessible) (some steps) toilets for disabled shop ⊗

CHELMSFORD

RHS Garden Hyde Hall

Westerns Approach, Rettendon CM3 8AT
☎ 01245 402006   📠 01245 402100
e-mail: suecarter@rhs.org.uk
web: www.rhs.org.uk
dir: from M25 junct 29 (signed A127 Southend) or A12 junct 17 (signed A130 signed Southend/Basildon). From A130 Rettendon Turnpike rdbt, follow tourist signs towards South Woodham Ferrers on A132. At Shaw Farm rdbt turn into Willow Grove/ Creephedge Lane

RHS Garden Hyde Hall is an oasis of calm and serenity and a visit to the 360-acre estate is unforgettable in any season. The developed area of the garden, in excess of 24 acres, demonstrates an eclectic range of inspirational horticultural styles, from the formality of clipped hedges to large swathes of naturalistic planting. Highlights include the Rose Garden, colour themed herbaceous borders, ponds, dry garden and developing woodland. A range of workshops and family fun events are run throughout the year, please see the website for details.

Times Open all year (ex 25 Dec) from 10, closing times vary with season - contact garden for details.* **Fees** £5.50 (ch 6-16 £2, ch under 6 free). RHS member & guest free.* **Facilities** ℗ 🖵 🍽 licensed 🎠 (outdoor) ♿ (partly accessible) (ramps and easy access to visitor centre) toilets for disabled shop ⊗

COLCHESTER

Colchester Castle Museum

Castle Park, High St CO1 1TJ
☎ 01206 282939   📠 01206 282925
e-mail: museums@colchester.gov.uk
web: www.colchestermuseums.org.uk
dir: at E end of High St

The largest Norman castle keep in Europe - built over the remains of the magnificent Roman Temple of Claudius which was destroyed by Boudicca in AD60. Colchester was the first capital of Roman Britain, and the archaeological collections are among the finest in the country. Please telephone or visit website for details of a range of events held throughout the year.

Times Open all year, Mon-Sat 10-5, Sun 11-5. Closed Xmas/ New Year* **Fees** £5.50 (ch & concessions £3.50).* **Facilities** ℗ 🎠 (indoor & outdoor) ♿ (partly accessible) (Roman vaults not accessible) toilets for disabled shop ⊗

Colchester Zoo

Stanway, Maldon Rd CO3 0SL
☎ 01206 331292   📠 01206 331392
e-mail: enquiries@colchester-zoo.co.uk
web: www.colchester-zoo.co.uk
dir: turn off A12 onto A1124, follow elephant signs

One of England's finest zoos, Colchester Zoo has over 250 species of animal. Visitors can feed the elephants and giraffes, handle a snake, and see parrots, seals, penguins and birds of prey all appearing in informative daily displays. Enclosures include Spirit of Africa with the breeding group of African elephants, Playa Patagonia where sea lions swim above your head in a 24 metre underwater tunnel, Penguin Shores, Chimp World, and the Kingdom of the Wild, with giraffes, zebras and rhinos. There is also an undercover soft play complex, two road trains, four adventure play areas, eating places and gift shops, all set in 60 acres of gardens. Orangutan Forest is Colchester Zoo's latest new enclosure.

Times Open all year, daily from 9.30. Last admission 5.30 (1hr before dusk out of season). Closed 25 Dec. **Fees** £14.99 (ch 3-14 £7.99)* **Facilities** ℗ 🖵 🍽 licensed 🎠 toilets for disabled shop ⊗

STANSTED

Mountfitchet Castle Experience

CM24 8SP
☎ 01279 813237 🖷 01279 816391
e-mail: office@mountfitchetcastle.com
web: www.mountfitchetcastle.com
dir: off B1383, in village. 2m from M11 junct 8

Come and see a Norman motte and bailey castle and village reconstructed as it was in Norman England of 1066, on its original historic site. A vivid illustration of village life in Domesday England, complete with houses, church, seige tower, seige weapons, and many types of animals roaming freely. Animated wax figures in all the buildings give historical information to visitors. Adjacent to the castle is the House on the Hill Toy Museum, a nostalgic trip through memories of childhood days. The whole experience is a unique all-weather, all-in-one heritage entertainment complex.

Times Open daily, mid Mar-mid Nov, 10-5. **Fees** £8.50 (ch £6.50, concessions £8).* **Facilities** ❷ ⓟ ⏛ �🗚 (outdoor) ♿ (partly accessible) (partly accessible due to grassy slopes, cobbled areas & steps) toilets for disabled shop ⊗

TILBURY

Tilbury Fort

No 2 Office Block, The Fort RM18 7NR
☎ 01375 858489
web: www.english-heritage.org.uk
dir: 0.5m E off A126

View the finest example of 17th-century military engineering, a spectacular sight on the River Thames. View the World War I and II gun emplacements and even fire a real anti-aircraft gun.

Times Open all year, Apr-1 Nov, daily 10-5; 2 Nov-Mar, Thu-Mon 10-4. Closed 24-26 Dec & 1 Jan. **Fees** £3.90 (concessions £3.30, ch £2). Family £9.80. Please call 0870 333 1181 for the most up to date prices and opening times when planning your visit. **Facilities** shop ⊗ ⌗

WALTHAM ABBEY

Lee Valley Park Farms

Stubbins Hall Ln, Crooked Mile EN9 2EG
☎ 01992 892781 & 702200 🖷 01992 899561
e-mail: hayeshill@leevalleypark.org.uk
web: www.leevalleypark.org.uk
dir: M25 junct 26, follow to Waltham Abbey. 2m from Waltham Abbey on B914

Lee Valley Park offers a unique visitor experience, two farms for the price of one. Hayes Hill Farm, a traditional style farm with a variety of different animals including pigs, goats and rare breeds, as well as the Pet Centre which houses small mammals and reptiles. You can take a stroll or a tractor and trailer ride to Holyfield Hall Farm, a modern dairy and arable farm. Visit Rabbit World with the giant bunnies, explore the paddock pathways then play in the adventure play area and the new Bundle Barn soft play area.

Times Open Feb half term-Oct, daily 10-5. **Fees** £6.80 (ch 2+ £5.40, concessions £5.40). Family tickets from £11. Group & season tickets available. Contact for most recent prices **Facilities** ❷ ⓟ ⏛ 🗚 (indoor & outdoor) ♿ toilets for disabled shop

Royal Gunpowder Mills

Beaulieu Dr EN9 1JY
☎ 01992 707370 🖷 01992 707372
e-mail: info@royalgunpowdermills.com
web: www.royalgunpowdermills.com
dir: M25 junct 26. Follow signs for A121 to Waltham Abbey at rdbt, entrance in Beaulieu Drive

Set in 170 acres of natural parkland with 20 buildings of major historic importance, the site mixes fascinating history, exciting science and beautiful surroundings to produce a magical day out for all ages. Over 20 special weekend events with may living history and re-enactments, VE Day celebrations, Steam & Country Show, Rocket & Space event and a Classic Vehicle Show. Easy access, children's activities, exhibitions, guided land train tours, a woodland walk and so much more!

Times Open end Apr-end Sep, 11-5, last entry 3.30. (Wknds, BHs & Wed in summer school hols) **Fees** £7.20 (ch 5-15 £4.40, concessions £6.20, under 5's free) Family ticket (2ad & 3ch) £23.20* **Facilities** ❷ ⓟ ⏛ 🗚 (outdoor) ♿ (partly accessible) (stairs provide access to top of Wildlife Tower. Some paths on nature walk are uneven. Lift available in main exhibition, number of ramps on site) toilets for disabled shop ⊗

GLOUCESTERSHIRE

BERKELEY

Berkeley Castle

GL13 9BQ
☎ 01453 810332 🖹 01453 512995
e-mail: info@berkeley-castle.com
web: www.berkeley-castle.com
dir: M5 junct 13 or 14, just off A38 midway between Bristol & Gloucester

Berkeley Castle is the amazing fortress home of the Berkeley family, who have lived in the building since the Keep was completed in 1153. The castle is still intact, from dungeon to elegant drawing rooms, and reflects nearly a thousand years of English history: a king's murder, the American Colonies, London's Berkeley Square. Rose-clad terraces surround this most romantic castle.

Times Open 27 Mar-18 Apr, Sun-Thu 11-5.30; 18 Apr-30 May, Thu-Sun 11-5.30; 30 May-2 Sep, Sun-Thu 11-5.30; 2 Sep-24 Oct, Thu-Sun 11-5.30; 24-31 Oct, Sun-Thu 11-5.30. **Fees** Castle & Gardens & Butterfly House: £7.50 (ch 5-15 £4.50, pen £6). Family ticket (2ad+2ch) £21. **Facilities** ℗ 🅿 🖵 🎠 (outdoor) shop ⊗

BOURTON-ON-THE-WATER

Birdland

Rissington Rd GL54 2BN
☎ 01451 820480 🖹 01451 822398
e-mail: simonb@birdland.co.uk
web: www.birdland.co.uk
dir: on A429

Birdland is a natural setting of woodland, river and gardens, which is inhabited by over 500 birds; flamingos, pelicans, penguins, cranes, storks, cassowary and waterfowl can be seen on various aspects of the water habitat. Over 50 aviaries of parrots, falcons, pheasants, hornbills, touracos, pigeons, ibis and many more. Tropical, Toucan and Desert Houses are home to the more delicate species. Only group of king penguins in England.

Times Open all year, Apr-Oct, daily 10-6; Nov-Mar, daily 10-4. (Last admission 1hr before closing). Closed 25 Dec.* **Fees** £6 (concessions £5). Family ticket (2ad+2ch) £18.* **Facilities** ℗ 🖵 🎠 (indoor & outdoor) ♿ toilets for disabled shop

CHEDWORTH

Chedworth Roman Villa

Yanworth GL54 3LJ
☎ 01242 890256 🖹 01242 890909
e-mail: chedworth@nationaltrust.org.uk
web: www.nationaltrust.org.uk
dir: 3m NW of Fossebridge on A429

The remains of a Romano-British villa, excavated 1864-65 and known as 'Britains oldest county house'. Set in a beautiful wooded combe, there are fine 4th-century mosaics, two bath houses, and a temple with spring. The museum houses the smaller finds and there is an 18-minute AV programme. Telephone for further details of special events. Major redevelopment of the site will take place between 2010-2011 with a chance to see work in progress.

Times Open 13-27 Mar & 2-14 Nov, Tue-Sun 10-4; 28 Mar-Oct, Tue-Sun 10-5. (Open BH Mon). **Fees** £7 (ch £4). Family ticket £18. NT members free. **Facilities** ℗ 🖵 🎠 (outdoor) ♿ (partly accessible) (steps to mosaics and museum) toilets for disabled shop ⊗ ♣

CIRENCESTER

Corinium Museum

Park St GL7 2BX
☎ 01285 655611
e-mail: museums@cotswold.gov.uk
web: www.cotswold.gov.uk/go/museum
dir: in town centre

Discover the treasures of the Cotswolds at the new Corinium Museum. Two years and over £5 million in the making, it has been transformed into a must-see attraction. Featuring archaeological and historical material from Cirencester and the Cotswolds, from prehistoric times to the 19th century. The museum is known for its Roman mosaic sculpture and other material from one of Britain's largest Roman towns. New on display are Anglo-Saxon treasures from Lechlade bringing to life this little-known period. The museum also houses Medieval, Tudor, Civil War and 18th-19th century displays.

Times Open Mon-Sat 10-5, Sun 2-5 (closes 4pm Nov-Mar). Closed Xmas & New Year. **Fees** £4.25 (ch £2.25, students £2.75, con £3.50). Family ticket £11.50 **Facilities** ℗ 🖵 🍴 licensed ♿ toilets for disabled shop ⊗

CLEARWELL

Clearwell Caves Ancient Iron Mines

GL16 8JR
☎ 01594 832535   📠 01594 833362
e-mail: jw@clearwellcaves.com **web:** www.clearwellcaves.com
dir: 1.5m S of Coleford town centre, off B4228 follow brown
tourist signs

These impressive natural caves have also been mined since the
earliest times for paint pigment and iron ore. Today visitors
explore nine large caverns with displays of local mining and
geology. There is a colour room where ochre pigments are
still produced and a blacksmith shop. Deep level excursions
available for more adventurous visitors, must be pre-booked.
Christmas fantasy event when the caverns are transformed into
a world of light and sound.

Times Open Mar-Oct, daily 10-5; Jan-Feb, Sat-Sun 10-5; Xmas
Fantasy 1-24 Dec, daily 10-5. **Fees** £5.80 (ch £3.80, concessions
£5.30) Family ticket £17.30. **Facilities** ❷ ℗ 🛒 🎡 (outdoor)
♿ (partly accessible) (w/chair need 2 helpers on steep pathway)
toilets for disabled shop ⊗

CRANHAM

Prinknash Bird & Deer Park

GL4 8EX
☎ 01452 812727   📠 01452 812727
web: www.thebirdpark.com
dir: M5 junct 11a, A417 towards Cirencester, take 1st exit signed
A46 Stroud. Follow brown tourist signs

Nine acres of parkland and lakes make a beautiful home for
black swans, geese and other water birds. There are also
exotic birds such as white and Indian blue peacocks and crown
cranes, as well as tame fallow deer and pygmy goats. The
Golden Wood is stocked with ornamental pheasants, and leads
to the reputedly haunted monks' fishpond, which contains
trout. An 80-year old, free-standing, 16 foot tall Wendy House
in the style of a Tudor house is located near the picnic area. A
pair of reindeer, the only ones to be found in the Cotswolds,
can also be seen.

Times Open all year, summer 10-5, winter 10-4. Closed 25 Dec &
Good Fri* **Fees** £5.50 (ch £3.50, pen £4.50)* **Facilities** ❷ ℗ 🛒
🎡 (outdoor) ♿ toilets for disabled shop ⊗

DYRHAM

Dyrham Park

SN14 8ER
☎ 0117 937 2501   📠 0117 937 1353
e-mail: dyrhampark@nationaltrust.org.uk
web: www.nationaltrust.org.uk
dir: 8m N of Bath, 2m S from M4 junct 18 on A46

Dyrham Park is a splendid Baroque country house, with
interiors that have hardly altered since the late 17th century.
It has contemporary Dutch-style furnishings, Dutch pictures
and blue-and-white Delft ware. Around the house is an ancient
park with fallow deer, from where Dyrham derives its name. In
the beautiful gardens, famous for the tulip festival in April, is a
medieval church.

Times Open: House 14 Mar-2 Nov, Fri-Tue, 12-5. Garden, shop &
tearoom, 14 Mar-29 Jun, Fri-Tue, 11-5; 30 Jun- Aug, daily, 11-5;
Sep-2 Nov, Fri-Tue, 11-5; 8 Nov-14 Dec, Sat & Sun, 11-4. Park all
year, 11-5, all week.* **Facilities** ❷ 🛒 🍴 licensed 🎡 toilets for
disabled shop ⊗ 🐾

GLOUCESTER

Gloucester Folk Museum   FREE

99-103 Westgate St GL1 2PG
☎ 01452 396868 & 396869   📠 01452 330495
e-mail: folk.museum@gloucester.gov.uk
web: www.gloucester.gov.uk/folkmuseum
dir: from W - A40 & A48; from N - A38 & M5, from E - A40 &
B4073; from S - A4173 & A38

Three floors of splendid Tudor and Jacobean timber-framed
buildings dating from the 16th and 17th centuries along with
new buildings housing the dairy, ironmonger's shop and
wheelwright and carpenter workshops. Local history, domestic
life, crafts, trades and industries from 1500 to the present,
including Toys and Childhood gallery with hands-on toys and
a puppet theatre, the Siege of Gloucester, a Victorian class
room, Victorian kitchen and laundry equipment. A wide range
of exhibitions, hands-on activities, events, demonstrations and
role play sessions are held throughout the year. There is an
attractive cottage garden and courtyard for events, often with
live animals, and outside games.

Times Open all year, Tue-Sat, 10-5* **Facilities** ℗ 🎡 (outdoor) ♿
(partly accessible) shop ⊗

Gloucestershire

Gloucester continued

The National Waterways Museum

Llanthony Warehouse, The Docks GL1 2EH
☎ 01452 318200 📠 01452 318202
e-mail: gloucester@thewaterwaystrust.org.uk
web: www.nwm.org.uk
dir: From M5, A40. In city follow brown signs for historic docks

This museum takes up 3 floors of a 7-storey Victorian warehouse, and documents the 200-year history of Britain's water-based transport. The emphasis is on hands-on experience, including working models and engines, interactive displays, actual craft, computer interactions and the national collection of inland waterways. Boat trips are available (Etr-Oct).

Times Open all year, daily 10-5. (Last admission 4). Closed 25 Dec.* **Facilities** 🅿 🅿 🖵 🍴 licensed 🍴 (outdoor) ♿ toilets for disabled shop ⊗

Nature in Art

Wallsworth Hall, Tewkesbury Rd, Twigworth GL2 9PA
☎ 01452 731422 & 0845 450 0233 📠 01452 730937
e-mail: enquiries@nature-in-art.org.uk
web: www.nature-in-art.org.uk
dir: 0.5m off main A38 between Gloucester and Tewkesbury, 2m N of Gloucester. Follow brown tourist signs

Nature in Art is unique - it is the world's only museum dedicated to art inspired by nature. Within the fine Georgian mansion can be found a truly diverse range of world-class art: displays embrace two and three-dimensional work in all mediums and styles ranging from Picasso to Shepherd. Spanning 1500 years, the collection contains work by 600 artists from over 50 countries. So typically, as well as a temporary exhibition, you'll find watercolour landscapes, contemporary glass, the Flemish masters, modern abstract interpretations, bronze sculpture and even some exotic oriental treasures. With all this variety there'll be things that catch your eye and you'll certainly make some discoveries. You can also meet an artist as they work on their next creation, which can range from painting to woodcarving (Feb-Nov).

Times Open all year, Tue-Sun & BHs 10-5. Closed 24-26 Dec. **Fees** £4.50 (ch, concessions £4, ch under 8 free). Family ticket £13. Party 15+ 50p discount per person. **Facilities** 🅿 🖵 🍴 licensed 🍴 (outdoor) ♿ toilets for disabled shop ⊗

GUITING POWER

Cotswold Farm Park

GL54 5UG
☎ 01451 850307 📠 01451 850423
e-mail: info@cotswoldfarmpark.co.uk
web: www.cotswoldfarmpark.co.uk
dir: signed off B4077 from M5 junct 9

Meet over 50 breeding flocks and herds of rare farm animals. There are lots of activities for the youngsters, with rabbits and guinea pigs to cuddle, lambs and goat kids to bottle feed, tractor and trailer-rides, battery powered tractors, Touch Barn, Maze Quest, a Jumping Pillow and safe rustic-themed play areas both indoors and outside. Lambing occurs in early May, followed by shearing and then milking demonstrations later in the season. The Cotswold Farm Park also has its own 40-pitch camping and caravanning site.

Times Open mid Mar-mid Sep, daily (then open wknds only until end Oct & Autumn half term 10.30-5).* **Fees** £6.75 (ch £5.50, concessions £6.25). Family ticket £22.* **Facilities** 🅿 🖵 🍴 (outdoor) ♿ (partly accessible) toilets for disabled shop ⊗

LYDNEY

Dean Forest Railway

Forest Rd GL15 4ET
☎ **01594 843423 (info) & 845840 (enquiries)**
e-mail: info@deanforestrailway.co.uk
web: www.deanforestrailway.co.uk
dir: At Lydney, turn off A48. Follow brown tourist signs to Norchard Station, on B4234

Travel on a heritage railway operated by steam trains (and the occasional diesel) through the beautiful and historic Forest of Dean. A relaxing round trip of over 8 miles to the recently opened Parkend Station. There's free car parking at Norchard Station (near Lydney) with a well-stocked gift shop, interesting museum and cafe. Regular family events include days out with Thomas and Santa Specials.

Times Open Apr-Oct, Sun; Jun-Sep, Wed, Sat, Sun; also Thu in Aug & BHs; Dec wknds (Santa Specials) & New Year.* **Fees** £10 (under 5s free, ch £5, pen £9). Family ticket (2ad+2ch) £28. Different charges may apply to events.* **Facilities** ℗ ⊑ ⊓◎ licensed ⋒ (outdoor) ᵴ toilets for disabled shop

MORETON-IN-MARSH

Cotswold Falconry Centre

Batsford Park GL56 9AB
☎ **01386 701043**
e-mail: mail@cotswold-falconry.co.uk
web: www.cotswold-falconry.co.uk
dir: 1m W of Moreton-in-Marsh on A44

Conveniently located by the Batsford Park Arboretum, the Cotswold Falconry gives daily demonstrations in the art of falconry. The emphasis here is on breeding and conservation, and over 100 eagles, hawks, owls and falcons can be seen.

Times Open mid Feb-mid Nov, 10.30-5.30. (Last admission 5).* **Facilities** ℗ ⊑ ⋒ (outdoor) toilets for disabled shop ⊗

NEWENT

The National Birds of Prey Centre

GL18 1JJ
☎ **0870 9901992** 📄 **01531 821389**
e-mail: kb@nbpc.co.uk
web: www.nbpc.co.uk
dir: follow A40, right onto B4219 towards Newent. Follow brown tourist signs from Newent town

Trained birds can be seen at close quarters in the Hawk Walk and the Owl Courtyard and there are also breeding aviaries, a gift shop, bookshop, picnic areas, coffee shop and children's play area. Birds are flown three times daily in summer and winter, giving an exciting and educational display. There are over 80 aviaries on view with 40 species.

Times Open all year daily 10.30-5.30 (closed 25-26 Dec).* **Facilities** ℗ ⊑ ⋒ toilets for disabled shop ⊗

PAINSWICK

Painswick Rococo Garden

GL6 6TH
☎ **01452 813204** 📄 **01452 814888**
e-mail: info@rococogarden.org.uk
web: www.rococogarden.org.uk
dir: on B4073 0.5m NW of Painswick

This beautiful Rococo garden (a compromise between formality and informality) is the only one of its period to survive complete. There are ponds, woodland walks, a maze, kitchen garden and herbacious borders, all set in a Cotswold valley famous for snowdrops in the early spring. Please ring for details of special events.

Times Open 10 Jan-Oct, daily 11-5.* **Fees** £6 (ch £3, pen £5) **Facilities** ℗ ℗ ⊑ ⊓◎ licensed ⋒ (outdoor) ᵴ (partly accessible) (steep slopes) toilets for disabled shop

SLIMBRIDGE

WWT Slimbridge

GL2 7BT
☎ 01453 891900   📠 01453 890827
e-mail: info.slimbridge@wwt.org.uk   **web:** www.wwt.org.uk
dir: off A38, signed from M5 junct 13 & 14

Slimbridge is home to the world's largest collection of swans, geese, ducks and flamingos. An internationally renowned reserve with an astounding array of wildlife from water voles to waders, hares to dragonflies. Facilities include a tropical house, discovery centre, children's outdoor play area, shop and restaurant.

Times Open all year, daily from 9.30-5.30 (winter 5). Closed 25 Dec.* **Fees** £7.95 (ch £4.35, under 4's free, concessions £6.15). Family £20.50.* **Facilities** 🅿 🚼 ⛸ licensed 🎋 (outdoor) ♿ toilets for disabled shop ⊗

SNOWSHILL

Snowshill Manor

WR12 7JU
☎ 01386 852410   📠 01386 842822
e-mail: snowshillmanor@nationaltrust.org.uk
web: www.nationaltrust.org.uk
dir: 3m SW of Broadway, off A44

Arts and crafts garden designed by its owner Charles Paget Wade in collaboration with M.H. Baillie Scott, as a series of outdoor rooms to compliment his traditional Cotswold manor house filled with his unique collection of craftsmanship including musical instruments, clocks, toys, bicycles and Japanese armour. This was the first National Trust garden to be managed following organic principles. It is a lively mix of cottage flowers, bright colours and delightful scents with stunning views across Cotswold countryside.

Times Open 19 Mar-2 Nov, Wed-Sun; house 12-5, garden: 1-5.30.* **Facilities** 🅿 ⛸ licensed toilets for disabled shop ⊗ ♨

SOUDLEY

Dean Heritage Centre

Camp Mill GL14 2UB
☎ 01594 822170   📠 01594 823711
e-mail: info@deanheritagemuseum.com
web: www.deanheritagemuseum.com
dir: A40, A48 in Forest of Dean

The Dean Heritage Centre is the ideal starting point for a visit to the Forest. With five modern museum galleries, and a range of features designed to create a living history experience, there is plenty for all ages to enjoy, including Forester's Cottage, Freemine Entrance, Charcoal Burner's Camp and an adventure playground. There is a regular events programme and there are plenty of activities involving history, crafts and the Forest's wildlife. The lovely mill pond and surrounding five acres of woodland are home to lots of wildlife.

Times Open summer 10-5, winter 10-4, open BHs (ex 24-26 Dec), 1 Jan 11-4.* **Fees** £5.40 (ch £2.75, under 5's free, concessions £4.65). Family £15.40, Party 10+* **Facilities** 🅿 🅿 🚼 🎋 (outdoor) ♿ (partly accessible) (access to woodland area restricted due to uneven ground) toilets for disabled shop ⊗

TODDINGTON

Gloucestershire Warwickshire Steam Railway

The Railway Station GL54 5DT
☎ 01242 621405
e-mail: enquiries@gwsr.com
web: www.gwsr.com
dir: 10m E of M5 junct 9 near junct of B4077 & B4632 between Winchcombe & Broadway

The railway runs along a part of the former Great Western Railway's mainline from Birmingham to Cheltenham, via Stratford-upon-Avon. The line commands wonderful views of the sleepy hamlets and villages, as it runs though the beautiful Cotswold countryside. The line was primarily built (1900-1906) to improve through services from Birmingham to Bristol and the West Country.

Times Open Mar-Dec, selected days & times. Call 01242 621405 for details. **Fees** £11 (ch 5-15 £6.50, under 5 free, concessions £9.50). Family (2 ad+3 ch) £30. **Facilities** 🅿 🚼 🎋 (outdoor) ♿ (partly accessible) (steep slope to platform at Cheltenham, some uneven surfaces at Winchcombe) toilets for disabled shop

WESTONBIRT

Westonbirt, The National Arboretum

GL8 8QS
☎ **01666 880220**   🖹 **01666 880559**
web: www.westonbirtarboretum.com
dir: 3m S Tetbury on A433

Begun in 1829, this arboretum contains one of the finest and most important collections of trees and shrubs in the world. There are 18,000 specimens, planted from 1829 to the present day, covering 600 acres of landscaped Cotswold countryside. Magnificent displays of Rhododendrons, Azaleas, Magnolias and wild flowers, and a blaze of colour in the autumn from the national collection of Japanese Maples. Special events include the Festival of the Tree (Aug BH) and the Enchanted Christmas Trail (every Fri, Sat, Sun in December until Xmas).

Times Open all year, daily 10-8 or sunset. Visitor centre & shop all year. Closed Xmas & New Year.* **Facilities** 🅿 ♿ �🍴 licensed ♨ (outdoor) ♿ toilets for disabled shop

GREATER MANCHESTER

ALTRINCHAM

Dunham Massey

WA14 4SJ
☎ **0161 941 1025**   🖹 **0161 929 7508**
e-mail: dunhammassey@nationaltrust.org.uk
web: www.nationaltrust.org.uk
dir: 3m SW of Altrincham (off A56), M6 junct 19 or M56 junct 7, then follow brown signs

A fine 18th-century house, garden and park, home of the Earls of Stamford until 1976. The house contains fine furniture and silverware, and some thirty rooms, including the library, billiard room, fully-equipped kitchen, butler's pantry and laundry. The garden is on an ancient site with waterside plantings, mixed borders and fine lawns. The ancient deer park has beautiful avenues and several ponds as well as a working sawmill where the waterwheel is demonstrated on afternoons in high season.

Times Open House: 27 Feb-Oct, Sat-Wed 11-5; Garden: Nov-26 Feb, daily 11-4, 27 Feb-Oct, daily 11-5.30; Park: all year daily, 9-5; Mill: 27 Feb-Oct Sat-Wed 12-4. **Fees** House & Garden £9.40 (ch £4.70). Family £23.40. Garden only £6.60 (ch £3.30). Family £16.50. **Facilities** 🅿 🍴 licensed ♨ (outdoor) ♿ (partly accessible) (access restricted, steps with handrail to Great Hall & other floors) toilets for disabled shop ⊗ 🌱

ASHTON-UNDER-LYNE

Central Art Gallery   FREE

Central Library Building, Old St OL6 7SG
☎ **0161 342 2650**   🖹 **0161 342 2650**
e-mail: central.artgallery@tameside.gov.uk
web: www.tameside.gov.uk
dir: Near centre of town, off A635 (large Victorian building)

Set in a fine Victorian Gothic building, Central Art Gallery has three gallery spaces, each of which offers a varied programme of contemporary exhibitions. A range of tastes and styles are covered, with group and solo shows of work by artists from the region including paintings, sculpture, installation and textiles. Extensive education programmes for schools, children, families, adults and teenagers.

Times Open all year, Tue, Wed & Fri 10-5, Thu 1-7.30 & Sat 9-4.* **Facilities** 🅿 ♿ toilets for disabled shop ⊗

Museum of The Manchester Regiment   FREE

The Town Hall, Market Place OL6 6DL
☎ **0161 342 2812   & 3710**   🖹 **0161 343 2869**
e-mail: portland.basin@tameside.gov.uk
web: www.tameside.gov.uk
dir: in town centre, on market square, follow signs for museum

The social and regimental history of the Manchesters is explored at this museum, tracing the story back to its origins in the 18th century. Children can try on military headwear, experience a First World War trench, and try out the interactive 'A Soldier's Life'.

Times Open all year, Mon-Sat, 10-4. (Closed Sun).* **Facilities** 🅿 ♿ toilets for disabled ⊗

Portland Basin Museum   FREE

Portland Place OL7 0QA
☎ **0161 343 2878**   🖹 **0161 343 2869**
e-mail: portland.basin@tameside.gov.uk
web: www.tameside.gov.uk
dir: M60 junct 23 into town centre. Museum near Cross Hill Street & car park. Follow brown signs with canal boat image

Exploring the social and industrial history of Tameside, this museum is part of the recently rebuilt Ashton Canal Warehouse, constructed in 1834. Visitors can walk around a 1920s street, dress up in old hats and gloves, steer a virtual canal boat, and see the original canal powered waterwheel that once drove the warehouse machinery. Portland Basin Museum also features changing exhibitions and event programme- so there's always something new to see!

Times Open all year, Tue-Sun 10-5. (Closed Mon, ex BHs)* **Facilities** 🅿 🅿 🍴 licensed ♨ (outdoor) ♿ toilets for disabled shop ⊗

MANCHESTER

Gallery of Costume   FREE

Platt Hall, Rusholme M14 5LL
☎ **0161 224 5217**
e-mail: m.lambert@manchester.gov.uk
web: www.manchestergalleries.org.uk
dir: in Platt Fields Park, Rusholme, access from Wilmslow Rd. 2m
S of city centre

With one of the most comprehensive costume collections in
Great Britain, this gallery makes captivating viewing. Housed
in a fine Georgian mansion, the displays focus on the changing
styles of everyday fashion and accessories over the last 400
years. Contemporary fashion is also illustrated. Because of
the vast amount of material in the collection, no one period is
permanently illustrated. New temporary exhibitions programme
alongside permanent displays will start in March 2010. Platt
Fields Park celebrates its centenary in 2010.

Times Open from Apr, Wed-Sat 1.30-4.30. **Facilities** ℗ ⴹ
(outdoor) ♿ (partly accessible) (stairs with handrails to first floor)
toilets for disabled shop ⊗

Imperial War Museum North   FREE

The Quays, Trafford Wharf Rd, Trafford Park M17 1TZ
☎ **0161 836 4000** ▤ **0161 836 4012**
e-mail: iwmnorth@iwm.org.uk
web: www.iwm.org.uk
dir: M60 junct 9, join Parkway (A5081) towards Trafford Park. At
1st island take 3rd exit onto Village Way. At next island take 2nd
exit onto Warren Bruce Rd. Right at T-junct onto Trafford Wharf
Rd. Alternatively, leave M602 junct 3 and follow signs

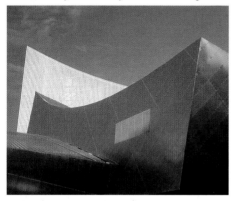

Imperial War Museum North features a wide range of
permanent and temporary exhibitions exploring all the ways
people's lives have been and still are affected by war and
conflict. The award-winning building (designed by architect
Daniel Libeskind) symbolises the world torn apart by conflict.

Times Open all year, Mar-Oct, daily 10-6; Nov-Feb 10-5. Closed
24-26 Dec. **Facilities** ℗ ℗ ⴹ ⴹ (indoor) ♿ toilets for disabled
shop ⊗

Manchester Art Gallery

Mosley St M2 3JL
☎ **0161 235 8888** ▤ **0161 235 8805**
e-mail: mag@manchester.gov.uk
web: www.manchestergalleries.org
dir: from M60 follow signs to city centre. Gallery close to Town
Hall & Central Library

Manchester Art Gallery houses the city's magnificent
art collection in stunning Victorian and contemporary
surroundings. Highlights of the collection include outstanding
Pre-Raphaelite works, crafts and design, and early 20th-century
British art. The Clore Interactive Gallery has lively exhibits and
multimedia facilities. There are also a wide range of events,
from talks and tours to hands-on activities for children and
adults. Contact for details of events and changing exhibitions.

Times Open all year, Tue-Sun, 10-5 (closed Mon ex BH). Closed
Good Fri, 24-26 & 31 Dec & 1 Jan.* **Fees** £6 (concessions £4,
under 18 & Manchester Art Gallery Friends free) **Facilities** ℗ ⴹ
◎ licensed ♿ toilets for disabled shop ⊗

Manchester Museum   FREE

The University of Manchester, Oxford Rd M13 9PL
☎ **0161 275 2634 & 2643** ▤ **0161 275 2676**
e-mail: museum@manchester.ac.uk
web: www.manchester.ac.uk/museum
dir: S of city centre on B5117

Discover the natural wonders of the world and the many
cultures it is home to. The objects in the Museum's 15 galleries
tell the story of the past, present and future of our planet.
Come face to face with live poison dart frogs, fossils of
prehistoric creatures and much more besides. Handle objects
from the collection, take part in hands-on activities or enjoy
a glass of wine or cup of coffee whilst exploring the latest
ideas in science, culture and the arts. See website for details of
family and adult events.

Times Open all year, Tue-Sat 10-5, Sun-Mon & BHs 11-4. Closed
Good Fri.* **Facilities** ℗ ℗ ⴹ ◎ licensed ⴹ (indoor) toilets for
disabled shop ⊗

Manchester United Museum & Tour Centre

Sir Matt Busby Way, Old Trafford M16 0RA
☎ **0161 868 8000** ▤ **0161 868 8861**
e-mail: tours@manutd.co.uk
web: www.manutd.com
dir: 2m from city centre, off A56

This museum was opened in 1986 and was the first purpose-built British football museum. It covers the history of Manchester United in words, pictures, sound and vision, from its inception in 1878 to the present day. Legends Tours are now available with ex players, see website for full details. 2010 is the 100th anniversary of the stadium being built.

Times Open daily 9.30-5 (open until 30mins before kick off on match days). Closed some days over Xmas & New Year. Most match days the museum is closed due to matchday hospitality. **Fees** Stadium tour & Museum: £12.50 (ch & concessions £8.50) Family ticket (4) £38, (5) £45. Museum only £9 (ch & concessions £7) Family ticket (4) £28, (5) £35. **Facilities** ⓟ ⦿ licensed ⋔ (indoor) & toilets for disabled shop ⊗

Museum of Science and Industry

Liverpool Rd, Castlefield M3 4FP
☎ **0161 832 2244** ▤ **0161 833 1471**
e-mail: marketing@mosi.org.uk
web: www.mosi.org.uk
dir: follow brown tourist signs from city centre

Uncover Manchester's industrial past and learn the fascinating stories of the people who contributed to the history and science of a city which helped shape the modern world. Located on the site of the world's oldest passenger railway station, MoSI's action-packed galleries, working exhibits and costumed characters tell the amazing story of revolutionary discoveries and remarkable inventions both past and present. There is a programme of changing exhibitions, please see the website for details.

Times Open all year, daily 10-5. Last admission 4.30. Closed 24-26 Dec & 1 Jan.* **Facilities** ⓟ ⓟ ⌷ ⦿ licensed ⋔ (indoor & outdoor) & toilets for disabled shop ⊗

Museum of Transport

Boyle St, Cheetham M8 8UW
☎ **0161 205 2122** ▤ **0161 205 1110**
e-mail: e-mail@gmts.co.uk
web: www.gmts.co.uk
dir: museum adjacent to Queens Rd bus depot. 1.25m N of city centre on Boyle St

This museum is a must-see for fans of public transport. Among the many interesting exhibits are more than 80 beautifully restored buses and coaches from the region - the biggest collection in the UK. Displays of old photographs, tickets and other memorabilia complement the vehicles, some of which date back to 1890. Please telephone for details of special events, most of which, unsurprisingly, relate to transport in some way.

Times Open all year Mar-Oct, 10-5; Nov-Feb, 10-4; Wed, Sat, Sun & BH ex Xmas* **Facilities** ⓟ ⓟ ⌷ & toilets for disabled shop ⊗

Greater Manchester

Manchester continued

People's History Museum   FREE

Left Bank, Spinningfields M3 3ER
☎ **0161 228 7212**
e-mail: info@phm.org.uk
web: www.phm.org.uk
dir: City centre, corner of Left Bank and Bridge St

The People's History Museum re-opens in late 2009 after a two-year closure and multi-million pound redevelopment. The Pump House, a former hydraulic power pumping station is being renovated to its former glory, and a new four-storey extension is being built next to it. The old and new buildings will be joined by a spectacular walkway. The Museum details the history of the British labour movement, trades unions, and other workers' organisations.

Times Open all year, Tue-Sun 10-5. **Facilities** ℗ ⊑ ㅈ (indoor) ♿ toilets for disabled shop ⊗

Urbis   FREE

Cathedral Gardens M4 3BG
☎ **0161 605 8200**   📄 **0161 605 8201**
e-mail: info@urbis.org.uk
web: www.urbis.org.uk
dir: opposite Victoria railway station

Urbis is an exhibition centre about city life. On your visit explore five floors of changing exhibitions, offering a unique insight into the culture of the modern city. Family workshops take place every weekend, see the website for details.

Times Open all year, daily 10-6.* **Facilities** ℗ ⊑ ㅣ licensed ㅈ (outdoor) ♿ toilets for disabled shop ⊗

The Whitworth Art Gallery   FREE

The University of Manchester, Oxford Rd M15 6ER
☎ **0161 275 7450**   📄 **0161 275 7451**
e-mail: whitworth@manchester.ac.uk
web: www.manchester.ac.uk/whitworth
dir: follow brown tourist signs, on Oxford Rd (B5117) to S of city centre. Gallery in Whitworth Park, opp Manchester Royal Infirmary

The gallery houses an impressive range of modern and historic drawings, prints, paintings and sculpture, as well as the largest collection of textiles and wallpapers outside London, and an internationally famous collection of British watercolours. The gallery hosts an innovative programme of touring exhibitions. A selection of tour lectures, workshops and concerts complement the exhibition programme.

Times Open all year, Mon-Sat 10-5, Sun 12-4. Closed Good Fri & Xmas-New Year.* **Facilities** ℗ ℗ ⊑ ㅈ (outdoor) ♿ toilets for disabled shop ⊗

Heaton Park   FREE

Heaton Park M25 2SW
☎ **0161 773 1085**   📄 **0161 798 0107**
e-mail: heatonpark@manchester.gov.uk
web: www.heatonpark.org.uk
dir: 4m N of Manchester city centre. M60 junct 19, S on A576, then onto A6044 & A665, into St Margaret's Road. Park 100yds on right

600 acres of rolling parkland on the edge of Manchester; a traditional park for the whole family. Facilities include a Tram Museum, sports pitches, stables, farm and animals centres, and a horticultural centre. The hall was designed by James Wyatt for Sir Thomas Egerton in 1772, the house has magnificent period interiors decorated with fine plasterwork, paintings and furniture. Other attractions include a unique circular room with Pompeian-style paintings, and the original Samuel Green organ still in working order.

Times Park: Open all year, daily 8-dusk; Hall: Open Etr-early Sep, Thu-Sun & BH 11-5.30* **Facilities** ℗ ℗ ⊑ ㅈ (outdoor) ♿ (partly accessible) (top floor not accessible) toilets for disabled shop ⊗

The Lowry   FREE

Pier Eight, Salford Quays M50 3AZ
☎ **0870 787 5774**   📄 **0161 876 2001**
e-mail: info@thelowry.com
web: www.thelowry.com
dir: M60 junct 12 for M602. Salford Quays is 0.25m from junct 3 of M602, follow brown Lowry signs

The Lowry is an award-winning building housing galleries, shops, cafés and a restaurant, plus three theatres showing everything from West End plays and musicals, comedians, ballet and live bands. With regular family activity too, you can make a whole day of your visit.

Times Open all year, daily from 10. Galleries, Sun-Fri from 11, Sat from 10. Closed 25 Dec.* **Facilities** ℗ ℗ ⊑ ㅣ licensed ♿ toilets for disabled shop ⊗

Salford Museum & Art Gallery

Peel Park, Crescent M5 4WU
☎ **0161 778 0800** 📄 **0161 745 9490**
e-mail: salford.museum@salford.gov.uk
web: www.salford.gov.uk/leisure/museums.htm
dir: from N leave M60 junct 13, A666. From S follow signs from end of M602. Museum on A6

The museum features a reconstruction of a 19th-20th century northern street with original shop fronts. Upstairs in the galleries there are temporary exhibitions and a gallery displaying paintings, sculptures and ceramics. Additions include the lifetimes gallery, featuring audio, IT zones, temporary exhibitions, a spectacular Pilkington's display and lots of hands-on activities and dressing up areas.

Times Open all year, Mon-Fri 10-4.45, Sat & Sun 1-5. Closed Good Fri, Etr Sat, 25 & 26 Dec, 1 Jan. **Fees** Free admission, some family fun days are chargeable.* **Facilities** ℗ ℗ ⬚ ♿ toilets for disabled shop ⊗

STOCKPORT

Hat Works Museum

Wellington Mill, Wellington Road South SK3 0EU
☎ **0161 355 7770** 📄 **0161 480 8735**
e-mail: bookings.hatworks@stockport.gov.uk
web: www.hatworks.org.uk
dir: M60 junct 1, on A6, Stockport town centre, follow signs for town centre. Museum opp bus station

Hat Works is the UK's only museum of the hatting industry, hats and headwear, offering an insight into a once flourishing industry. See how hats are made with a unique working collection of Victorian millinery machinery and take a tour with expert guides who will give visitors an insight into the Hatter's World. Browse an extensive collection of hats before relaxing in the Level 2 café. Exhibitions and events throughout the year, contact for details. April 2010 is the 10th anniversary of the museum.

Times Open all year, Tue-Fri 10-5, Sat, Sun & BHs 11-5. (Telephone for Xmas opening times)* **Fees** Free. (Guided tours £2.60 per person)* **Facilities** ℗ ⬚ ♿ toilets for disabled shop ⊗

HAMPSHIRE

ALDERSHOT

Aldershot Military Museum

Evelyn Woods Rd, Queens Av GU11 2LG
☎ **0845 6035635** 📄 **01252 342942**
e-mail: sally.1.day@hants.gov.uk
web: www.hants.gov.uk/museum/aldershot-museum
dir: A331 exit for 'Aldershot Military Town (North)', attraction near to North Camp

Follow the development of the 'Home of the British army' and the 'Birthplace of British aviation' through brand new displays. Also discover the fascinating local history of Aldershot and Farnborough including the first British powered flight, which took place in October 1908.

Times Open all year, daily 10-5 (last admission 4.30)* **Fees** £2 (ch under 5 free, ch & concessions £1, pen £1.50)* **Facilities** ℗ ℗ ⌷ (outdoor) ♿ toilets for disabled shop ⊗

AMPFIELD

The Sir Harold Hillier Gardens

Jermyns Ln SO51 0QA
☎ **01794 369318** 📄 **01794 368027**
e-mail: info@hilliergardens.org.uk
web: www.hilliergardens.org.uk
dir: 2m NE of Romsey, signed off A3090 & A3057

Sir Harold Hillier Gardens offers 180 acres of beauty, inspiration and discovery. Over 42,000 plants from temperate regions around the world grow in a variety of landscapes. Visit the Children's Education Garden and Europe's largest Winter Garden. Events, exhibitions and workshops all year round. During May to October visit the spectacular Art in the Garden annual outdoor exhibition, which features 150 sculptures set around the gardens. New play features include the stunning tree house.

Times Open all year, daily, 10-6 (or dusk if earlier). Closed 25-26 Dec.* **Fees** £8.25 (ch under 16 free, concessions £7.15). Group bookings £6.60* **Facilities** ℗ ⬚ ⦿ licensed ⌷ (outdoor) ♿ (partly accessible) (most pathways are fully accessible) toilets for disabled shop ⊗

ANDOVER

Finkley Down Farm Park

SP11 6NF
☎ 01264 352195   📄 01264 363172
e-mail: admin@finkleydownfarm.co.uk
web: www.finkleydownfarm.co.uk
dir: signed from A303 & A343, 1.5m N of A303 & 2m E of Andover

This fun family farm park is jam packed with things to do. You can join in with feeding time, groom a pony, or cuddle a rabbit. Lots of activities are scheduled throughout the day, or kids can just let off steam in the playground or on the trampolines. From chipmunks to chinchillas, pygmy goats to peacocks, and lambs to llamas, Finkley Down Farm has something for everyone.

Times Open mid Mar-Oct, daily 10-6 (last admission 5).*
Fees £6.75 (ch £5.75, pen £6.25). Family ticket (2ad+2ch) £24*
Facilities ❷ ⛄ 🍴 (outdoor) ♿ toilets for disabled shop ⊗

ASHURST

Longdown Activity Farm

Longdown SO40 7EH
☎ 023 8029 2837   📄 023 8029 3376
e-mail: enquiries@longdownfarm.co.uk
web: www.longdownfarm.co.uk
dir: off A35 between Lyndhurst & Southampton

Fun for all the family with a variety of hands-on activities every day, including small animal handling and bottle feeding calves and goat kids. Indoor and outdoor play areas, with trampolines and ball pools and bumpy tractor rides. Tearoom, picnic area and excellent gift shop. Farm shop selling locally sourced produce.

Times Open Feb-Oct & 12-24 Dec, daily; wknds Nov-mid Dec 10-5.* **Fees** £7 (ch 3-14 & concessions £6). Saver ticket £24 (2ad+2ch).* **Facilities** ❷ ⛄ 🍴 (indoor & outdoor) ♿ (partly accessible) (concrete path for wheelchairs) toilets for disabled shop ⊗

BASINGSTOKE

Milestones - Hampshire's Living History Museum

Basingstoke Leisure Park, Churchill Way West RG22 6PG
☎ 01256 477766   📄 01256 477784
e-mail: louise.mackay@hants.gov.uk
web: www.milestones-museum.com
dir: M3 junct 6, take ringway road (West). Follow brown Leisure Park signs

Milestones brings Hampshire's recent past to life through stunning period street scenes and exciting interactive areas, all under one roof. Nationally important collections of transport, technology and everyday life are presented in an entertaining way. Staff in period costumes, mannequins and sounds all bring the streets to life. Various events through the year. 2010 is the 10th anniversary of the museum.

Times Open all year, Tue-Fri & BHs 10-5, Sat-Sun 11-5. Closed Mon, 25-26 Dec & 1 Jan.* **Fees** £7.50 (ch 5-15 £4.50, concessions £6.75). Family ticket (2ad+2ch) £22. **Facilities** ❷ ℗ ⛄ 🍴 (indoor & outdoor) ♿ (partly accessible) toilets for disabled shop ⊗

BEAULIEU

Beaulieu : National Motor Museum

SO42 7ZN

☎ **01590 612345** 📠 **01590 612624**

e-mail: info@beaulieu.co.uk
web: www.beaulieu.co.uk
dir: M27 junct 2, A326, B3054, then follow tourist signs

Set in the heart of William the Conqueror's New Forest, on the banks of the Beaulieu River, stands this 16th-century house. It has become most famous as the home of the National Motor Museum. The site also contains the picturesque abbey building ruins, which have an exhibition on life in the middle ages, and various family treasures and memorabilia. The Secret Army Exhibition tells the story of the secret agents trained at the Beaulieu 'Finishing School' during WWII.

Times Open all year - Palace House & Gardens, National Motor Museum, Beaulieu Abbey & Exhibition of Monastic Life, May-Sep 10-6; Oct-Apr 10-5. Closed 25 Dec.* **Fees** Please contact for current prices.* **Facilities** 🅿 🅟 🖵 🍴 licensed 🏕 (outdoor) toilets for disabled shop

BUCKLERS HARD

Buckler's Hard Village & Maritime Museum

SO42 7XB

☎ **01590 616203** 📠 **01590 612624**

e-mail: info@bucklershard.co.uk **web:** www.bucklershard.co.uk
dir: M27 junct 2, A326, B3054 then follow tourist signs to Beaulieu & Buckler's Hard

An enticing port of call, the historic and picturesque shipbuilding village of Buckler's Hard is where ships from Nelson's fleet were built. Enjoy the Buckler's Hard Story, SS Persia Exhibition and the authentically reconstructed 18th-century historic cottages. Savour the sights and sounds of the countryside on a ramble along the Riverside Walk or enjoy a cruise on the Beaulieu River during the summer months.

Times Open all year daily from 10. Closed 25 Dec.* **Fees** Please contact for current prices.* **Facilities** 🅿 🖵 🍴 licensed 🏕 (outdoor) toilets for disabled shop

EXBURY

Exbury Gardens & Railway

Exbury Estate Office SO45 1AZ

☎ **023 8089 1203** 📠 **023 8089 9940**

e-mail: nigel.philpott@exbury.co.uk
web: www.exbury.co.uk
dir: from M27 W junct 2, 3m from Beaulieu, off B3054

A 200-acre landscaped woodland garden on the east bank of the Beaulieu River, with one of the finest collections of rhododendrons, azaleas, camellias and magnolias in the world - as well as many rare and beautiful shrubs and trees.

A labyrinth of tracks and paths enable you to explore the beautiful gardens and walks. Year round interest is ensured in various parts of the gardens and a steam railway has several features. Exbury is National Collection holder for Nyssa and Oxydendrum, spectacular trees for autumn colour.

Times Open Mar-mid Nov, daily 10-5; Santa Steam Specials in Dec.* **Fees** £8 (ch under 3 free, ch 3-15 £1.50, concessions £7.50). Family ticket (2ad+3ch) £18.50. Railway £3.50. The railway has 4 carriages accessible to wheelchairs.* **Facilities** 🅿 🅟 🍴 licensed 🏕 (outdoor) ♿ (partly accessible) (most pathways accessible) toilets for disabled shop

FAREHAM

Royal Armouries Fort Nelson

Portsdown Hill Rd PO17 6AN

☎ **01329 233734** 📠 **01329 822092**

e-mail: fnenquiries@armouries.org.uk
web: www.royalarmouries.org
dir: from M27 junct 11, follow brown tourist signs for Royal Armouries

Home to the Royal Armouries' collection of over 350 big guns and cannon, this superbly restored Victorian fort overlooks Portsmouth Harbour. Built in the 1860s to deter a threatened French invasion, there are secret tunnels, underground chambers and grass ramparts to explore with daily guided tours and explosive gun firings. There are free children's activity days on Tuesday and Thursday during school holidays.

Times Open all year, Apr-Oct, daily 10-5 (Wed 11-5); Nov-Mar, daily 10.30-4 (Wed 11.30-4). Closed 24-26 Dec. **Fees** Free. There may be a charge for special events/workshops. **Facilities** 🅿 🖵 🏕 (outdoor) ♿ toilets for disabled shop ⊗

GOSPORT

Explosion! Museum of Naval Firepower

Priddy's Hard PO12 4LE

☎ **023 9250 5600** 📠 **023 9250 5605**

e-mail: info@explosion.org.uk
web: www.explosion.org.uk
dir: M27 junct 11, A32 and follow signs

Explosion! The Museum of Naval Firepower is set in the green Heritage Area of Priddy's Hard in Gosport on the shores of Portsmouth Harbour, telling the story of naval firepower from the days of gunpowder to modern missiles. Come face to face with the atom bomb, the Exocet missile and the Gatling Gun and take a trip into the fascinating story of the men and women who supplied the Royal Navy. Walk around the buildings that were a state secret for 200 years and discover the Grand Magazine, an amazing vault once packed full with gunpowder, now a stunning multimedia film show.

Times Open all year, Sat-Sun only, 10-4.* **Fees** £4 (ch £2, concessions £3). Family ticket £10* **Facilities** 🅿 🖵 🍴 licensed 🏕 (outdoor) toilets for disabled shop ⊗

Gosport continued

Royal Navy Submarine Museum

Haslar Rd PO12 2AS
☎ 023 9251 0354   📄 023 9251 1349
e-mail: rnsubs@rnsubmus.co.uk
web: www.rnsubmus.co.uk
dir: M27 junct 11, follow brown tourist signs

Step inside at the Royal Navy Submarine Museum, which overlooks Portsmouth Harbour. Former submariners guide you through where they would work, eat and sleep on board HMS Alliance. Peer into the only surviving X-craft to have seen action during WWII and walk onto the Royal Navy's first submarine Holland 1.

Times Open all year, Apr-Oct 10-5.30; Nov-Mar 10-4.30. (Last tour 1 hour before closing). Closed 24 Dec & 25 Jan.* **Fees** £9 (ch & concessions £6). Family (2ad+4ch) £20.* **Facilities** 🅿️ Ⓟ 🚻 🍴 (outdoor) ♿ (partly accessible) (no wheelchair access to the Alliance WWII submarine - film version of tour available) toilets for disabled shop ⊗

HAVANT

Staunton Country Park

Middle Park Way PO9 5HB
☎ 023 9245 3405   📄 023 9249 8156
e-mail: sam.brown@hants.gov.uk
web: www.hants.gov.uk/staunton
dir: off B2149, between Havant & Horndean

Set in the Regency pleasure grounds of Sir George Staunton, 19th-century traveller, Orientalist and patron of horticulture, Staunton boasts an ornamental farm, the largest ornamental glasshouses on the South Coast, 1,000 acres of parkland, with ancient woodland and intriguing follies and much, much more. Children can feed farm animals, or visit the play area while the grown-ups stroll through the walled gardens or get lost in the Golden Jubilee Maze.

Times Open all year, daily 10-5 (4 winter). **Fees** £6.20 (ch £4.50, pen £4.60). Contact for most recent prices. **Facilities** 🅿️ Ⓟ 🚻 🍴 licensed 🪑 (outdoor) ♿ (partly accessible) (most areas accessible) toilets for disabled shop ⊗

HURST CASTLE

Hurst Castle

SO4 0FF
☎ 01590 642344
web: www.english-heritage.org.uk
dir: on Pebble Spit S of Keyhaven

Built by Henry VIII, Hurst Castle was the pride of Tudor England's coastal defences. Crouched menacingly on a shingle spit, the castle has a fascinating history, including involvement in the smuggling trade in the 17th and 18th centuries.

Times Open 21 Mar-Oct, daily 10.30-5.30.* **Facilities** 🚻 ⊗ 🚻

LIPHOOK

Hollycombe Steam In The Country

Iron Hill, Midhurst Rd GU30 7LP
☎ 01428 724900   📄 01428 723682
e-mail: info@hollycombe.co.uk
web: www.hollycombe.co.uk
dir: 1m SE Liphook on Midhurst road, follow brown tourist signs

A comprehensive collection of working steam-power, including a large Edwardian fairground, railways, one with spectacular views of the South Downs, traction engine hauled rides, steam agricultural machinery, sawmill and even a paddle steamer engine.

Times Open Apr-Oct, Sun & BHs, 4 wks to Aug BH, daily ex Mons & Sats (apart from BH w/end), 11-5. **Fees** £12 (ch 3-15 £10 & pen £10). **Facilities** 🅿️ 🚻 🪑 (outdoor) ♿ (partly accessible) (some rough paths, some rides inacessible) toilets for disabled shop ⊗

MARWELL

Marwell Zoological Park

Colden Common SO21 1JH
☎ **01962 777407** 📄 **01962 777511**
e-mail: marwell@marwell.org.uk
web: www.marwell.org.uk
dir: M3 junct 11 or M27 junct 5. On B2177, follow brown tourist signs

Marwell has over 200 species of rare and wonderful animals including tigers, snow leopards, rhino, meerkats, hippo and zebra. Highlights include The World of Lemurs, Encounter Village, Tropical World with its rainforest environment, Into Africa for giraffes and monkeys, Penguin World and Desert Carnivores. Recent additions include an exciting new snow leopard enclosure and a walkway that enables visitors to come face to face with the giraffes. Marwell is dedicated to saving endangered species and every visit helps conservation work. With road and rail trains, holiday activities, gift shop and adventure playgrounds Marwell provides fun and interest for all ages.

Times Open all year, daily 10-6 (summer), 10-4 (winter). (Last admission 90 mins before closing). Closed 25 Dec.* **Facilities** 🅿 ☕ 🍽 licensed ⛽ (outdoor) ♿ (partly accessible) toilets for disabled shop ⊗

MIDDLE WALLOP

Museum of Army Flying

SO20 8DY
☎ **01264 784421** 📄 **01264 781694**
e-mail: administration@flying-museum.org.uk
web: www.flying-museum.org.uk
dir: on A343, between Andover & Salisbury

One of the country's finest historical collections of military kites, gliders, aeroplanes and helicopters. Imaginative dioramas and displays trace the development of Army flying from before the First World War to more recent conflicts in Ireland, the Falklands and the Gulf. Sit at the controls of a real Scout or Apache attack helicopters and test your skills on the flight simulator, plus children's education centre and 1940s house.

Times Open all year, daily 10-4.30. Closed week prior to Xmas. Evening visits by special arrangement. Private functions welcome.* **Fees** £7 (ch £4.50, concessions £5) Family £21.* **Facilities** 🅿 ☕ 🍽 licensed ⛽ (outdoor) ♿ toilets for disabled shop ⊗

NEW ALRESFORD

Watercress Line

The Railway Station SO24 9JG
☎ **01962 733810** 📄 **01962 735448**
e-mail: info@watercressline.co.uk
web: www.watercressline.co.uk
dir: stations at Alton & Alresford signed off A31, follow brown tourist signs

The Watercress Line runs through ten miles of rolling scenic countryside between Alton and Alresford. All four stations are 'dressed' in period style, and there's a locomotive yard and picnic area at Ropley. Special events throughout the year including Thomas the Tank Engine, War on the Line and Santa Specials.

Times Open Jan-Oct wknds, May-Sep midwk, Aug daily.* **Fees** Unlimited travel for the day, £12 (ch £6). Family ticket £30 (2ad+2ch). Charge for dogs. Pre-booked groups 15+ discount available. **Facilities** 🅿 Ⓟ ☕ 🍽 licensed ⛽ (outdoor) ♿ (partly accessible) (ramp access to trains) toilets for disabled shop

OWER

Paultons Park

SO51 6AL
☎ 023 8081 4442   📠 023 8081 3025
e-mail: guestservices@paultons.co.uk
web: www.paultonspark.co.uk
dir: exit M27 junct 2, near junct A31 & A36

Paultons Park offers a great day out for all the family with over 50 different attractions. Many fun activities include the Edge Cobra ride, drop rides, roller coaster, 6-lane astroglide, teacup ride, log flume, pirate ship swingboat, dragon roundabout, and wave-runner coaster. Attractions for younger children include Water Kingdom, Tiny Tots Town, Rabbit Ride, the Magic Forest where nursery rhymes come to life, Wonderful World of Wind in the Willows and the Ladybird ride. In beautiful parkland setting with extensive 'Capability' Brown gardens landscaped with ponds and aviaries for exotic birds; lake and hedge maze. There is also the Village Life Museum. Something for everyone.

Times Open mid Mar-Oct, daily 10-6; Nov & Dec, wknds only until Xmas.* **Fees** £17.50 (adults & ch over 1mtr tall) (Free entry only for children under 1mtr tall). Range of Family Supersavers.* **Facilities** 🅿 ⊑ ⓘ licensed ⋒ (outdoor) ♿ (partly accessible) (some rides accessible for disabled guests) toilets for disabled shop ⊗

PORTCHESTER

Portchester Castle

Castle St PO16 9QW
☎ 023 9237 8291
web: www.english-heritage.org.uk
dir: off A27

Discover 2,000 years of history from its Roman beginnings to the years of medieval splendour. Stand where Henry V rallied his troops before setting out to the battle of Agincourt in 1415.

Times Open all year, Apr-Sep, daily 10-6; Oct-Mar, daily 10-4. Closed 24-26 Dec & 1 Jan. **Fees** £4.30 (concessions £3.70, ch £2.20). Family £10.80. Please call 0870 333 1181 for the most up to date prices and opening times when planning your visit. **Facilities** ❷ shop ⊗ ♯

PORTSMOUTH

Blue Reef Aquarium

Clarence Esplanade PO5 3PB
☎ 023 9287 5222   📠 023 9229 4443
e-mail: portsmouth@bluereefaquarium.co.uk
web: www.bluereefaquarium.co.uk
dir: on approach to city follow brown tourist signs to seafront or Aquarium. Located on Southsea seafront between D-Day Museum and The Hoverport

Spectacular underwater walkthrough tunnels offer amazing sights of exotic coral reefs - home to sharks and shimmering shoals of brightly-coloured fish. Mediterranean and tropical waters are recreated in giant ocean tanks, home to a stunning array of undersea life including seahorses, puffer fish, coral, piranhas, and incredible crustaceans. Visit the website for current special events.

Times Open all year, daily from 10. Closing times vary with season, please telephone for details.* **Fees** £8.75 (ch £6.75, pen & students £7.95)* **Facilities** ⓟ ⊑ ⋒ (outdoor) ♿ toilets for disabled shop ⊗

Charles Dickens' Birthplace Museum

393 Old Commercial Rd PO1 4QL
☎ 023 9282 7261   📠 023 9287 5276
e-mail: mvs@portsmouthcc.gov.uk
web: www.charlesdickensbirthplace.co.uk
dir: M27/M275 into Portsmouth, from M275 turn left at 'The News' rdbt. Signed

A small terraced house built in 1805 which became the birthplace and early home of the famous novelist, born in 1812. On display are items pertaining to Dickens' work, portraits of the Dickens' family, and the couch on which he died. Dickens readings are given in the exhibition room on the first Sunday of each month at 3pm.

Times Open Apr-Sep, daily 10-5.30 (Last admission 5).* **Facilities** ⓟ shop ⊗

D-Day Museum & Overlord Embroidery

Clarence Esplanade PO5 3NT
☎ 023 9282 7261 ▤ 023 9287 5276
e-mail: mvs@portsmouthcc.gov.uk
web: www.ddaymuseum.co.uk
dir: M27/M275 or M27/A2030 into Portsmouth, follow signs for seafront then D-Day museum name signs

Portsmouth's D-Day Museum tells the dramatic story of the Allied landings in Normandy in 1944. The centrepiece is the magnificent 'Overlord Embroidery', 34 individual panels and 83 metres in length. Experience the world's largest ever seaborne invasion, and step back in time to scenes of wartime Britain. Military equipment, vehicles, landing craft and personal memories complete this special story.

Times Open all year, Apr-Sep, daily 10-5.30; Oct-Mar, 10-5. Closed 24-26 Dec* **Facilities** ❷ ℗ ⛟ 🛱 (outdoor) ♿ toilets for disabled shop ⊗

Portsmouth Historic Dockyard

HM Naval Base PO1 3LJ
☎ 023 9283 9766 ▤ 023 9283 8228
e-mail: enquiries@historicdockyard.co.uk
web: www.historicdockyard.co.uk
dir: M27/M275 & follow brown historic waterfront and dockyard signs

Portsmouth Historic Dockyard is home to the world's greatest historic ships: Mary Rose - King Henry VIII's favourite ship, HMS Victory - Lord Nelson's flagship at the Battle of Trafalgar and HMS Warrior - the first iron-hulled warship. In addition, the Royal Naval Museum has the most significant, permanent collections relating to Nelson and the Battle of Trafalgar, and Action Stations gives an interactive insight into the modern day Royal Navy.

Times Open Apr-Oct, daily 10-6 (last entry 4.30); Nov-Mar, daily 10-5.30 (last entry 4).* **Fees** All inclusive ticket: £18 (ch & students £13.50 under 5 free, concessions £16) Family £50.50.* **Facilities** ❷ ℗ ⛟ 🍴 licensed 🛱 (outdoor) ♿ (partly accessible) toilets for disabled shop ⊗

The Royal Marines Museum

Southsea PO4 9PX
☎ 023 9281 9385 ▤ 023 9283 8420
e-mail: info@royalmarinesmuseum.co.uk
web: www.royalmarinesmuseum.co.uk
dir: signed from seafront

The Royal Marines Museum celebrates the famous fighting spirit and long history of the Royal Marines. Based in the lavishly decorated former Officers' Mess of Eastney Barracks, built in the 1860s for the Royal Marine Artillery, the Museum is situated in the very heart of the Corps history. With displays and exhibits highlighting the history of the Royal Marines from their beginnings in 1664 through to the present day, and the new 'The Making of the Royal Marines Commando' exhibition, the Museum brings to life the history, character and humour of the Royal Marines.

Times Open all year, daily 10-5. Closed 24-26 Dec.* **Fees** £5.95 (ch 5-16 £3.75, concessions £3.75-£4.75). Family ticket (2ad+4ch) £14.50. Registered disabled £3 (free admission for one assistant).* **Facilities** ❷ ℗ ⛟ 🛱 (outdoor) ♿ toilets for disabled shop ⊗

Spinnaker Tower

Gunwharf Quays PO1 3TT
☎ 023 9285 7520 ▤ 023 9229 8726
e-mail: info@spinnakertower.co.uk
web: www.spinnakertower.co.uk
dir: From M275 follow tourist signs for Tower

Elegant, sculptural and inspired by Portsmouth's maritime heritage, the Spinnaker Tower is a new national icon - a 'must-see' landmark for visitors worldwide. Soaring 170 metres above Portsmouth Harbour, with three viewing decks, the Spinnaker Tower is now open to view. Take the high speed internal lift and step right out into the best view in the country. Dare you 'walk on air' on the glass floor, the largest in Europe? Watch history unfold through our unique 'Time Telescopes'. Back down to earth and shop for souvenirs or talk about your travels over a snack in the waterfront Tower Café bar.

Times Open daily Feb-Jul & Sep-Jan 10-6, Aug 10-8. **Fees** £7 (ch 3-15 £5.50, ch under 3 free, concessions £6.20). **Facilities** ❷ ⛟ ♿ (partly accessible) (view deck 3 has no wheelchair access) toilets for disabled shop ⊗

RINGWOOD

Moors Valley Country Park

Horton Rd, Ashley Heath BH24 2ET
☎ 01425 470721   📠 01425 471656
e-mail: moorsvalley@eastdorset.gov.uk
web: www.moors-valley.co.uk
dir: 1.5m from Ashley Heath rdbt on A31 near Three Legged Cross

One thousand acres of forest, woodland, heathland, lakes, river and meadows provide a home for a wide variety of plants and animals, and there's a Visitor Centre, Adventure Playgrounds, picnic area, Moors Valley Railway, Tree Top Trail and 'Go Ape'-high ropes course (book on 0845 643 9215). Cycle hire is also available.

Times Open all year, 8-dusk (8pm at latest). Visitor centre open 9-4.30 (later in summer). Closed 25 Dec. **Fees** No admission charge but parking up to £8 per day. **Facilities** 🅿 ☕ 🍽 licensed 🍴 (outdoor) ♿ (partly accessible) (some footpaths in forest unaccessible) toilets for disabled shop

ROCKBOURNE

Rockbourne Roman Villa

SP6 3PG
☎ 01725 518541
web: www.hants.gov.uk/museum/rockbourne-roman-villa
dir: from Salisbury exit A338 at Fordingbridge, take B3078 west through Sandleheath & follow signs. Or turn off A354 (Salisbury to Blandford road), W of Coombe Bissett

Discovered in 1942, the site features the remains of a 40-room Roman villa and is the largest in the area. Displays include mosaics and a very rare hypocaust system. The museum displays the many artefacts found on the site during excavations. Summer Sunday activities - please ring for details.

Times Open Apr-Sep, daily 10.30-6. (Last admission 5.30) **Fees** £2.50 (concessions £1.50). Family (2ad+2ch) £7.* **Facilities** 🅿 🍴 (outdoor) ♿ toilets for disabled shop ⊗

ROWLAND'S CASTLE

Stansted Park

PO9 6DX
☎ 023 9241 2265   📠 023 9241 3773
e-mail: enquiry@stanstedpark.co.uk
web: www.stanstedpark.co.uk
dir: follow brown heritage 'Stansted House' signs from A3 Horndean exit, or A27 Havant exit

Stansted Park is set in 1750 acres of park and woodland. The mansion rooms house the Bessborough family collection of furniture and paintings, and below stairs the restored servants quarters can be found, with an extensive collection of household artefacts giving an insight into the running of the house. The ancient Chapel of St Paul was an inspiration to the poet John Keats and is open in conjunction with the house. Various events through the summer and Christmas.

Times Open Etr-Sep, Sun & BH 1-4; Jun-Aug, Sun-Wed 1-4 & by appt for schools & groups on other days. **Fees** £7 (ch £3.50, concessions £6). Family ticket (2ad+2ch) £18. **Facilities** 🅿 🍽 licensed 🍴 (outdoor) ♿ toilets for disabled ⊗

WEYHILL

The Hawk Conservancy and Country Park

SP11 8DY
☎ 01264 773850   📠 01264 773772
e-mail: info@hawkconservancy.org
web: www.hawkconservancy.org
dir: 3m W of Andover, signed from A303

The Hawk Conservancy Trust is a registered charity and award winning visitor attraction that has for many years been working in the fields of conservation, education, rehabilitation and the research of birds of prey. The Trust is set in 22 acres of woodland and wild flower meadow, where there are over 150 birds of prey on view from the tiny Pygmy Owl to the impressive European Black Vulture. A day at the Trust has a packed itinerary including three flying demonstrations that see owls, kites, hawks, falcons and eagles showing off their skills. The birds come really close and there is even an opportunity for visitors to hold a British bird of prey!

Times Open all year, mid Feb-Oct daily 10-5.30. Nov-mid Feb wknds only 10-4.30. **Fees** £10 (ch £6, pen £9.25, students £9). Family ticket (2ad+2ch) £32.* **Facilities** 🅿 ☕ 🍽 licensed 🍴 (indoor & outdoor) ♿ toilets for disabled shop ⊗

WINCHESTER

Horse Power, The King's Royal Hussars Regimental Museum   FREE

Peninsula Barracks, Romsey Rd SO23 8TS
☎ 01962 828539 & 828541 📄 01962 828538
e-mail: curator@horsepowermuseum.co.uk
web: www.krh.org.uk
dir: M3 junct 9/10 follow city centre signs, then hospital A&E red signs to Romsey Rd. Vehicle access from Romsey Rd

Horse Power, the museum of the King's Royal Hussars, tells the exciting story of an English cavalry regiment, mounted on horses and in tanks or armoured cars.

Times Open 6 Jan-18 Dec, Tue-Fri 10-4, wknds & BHs, 12-4. (Closed daily between 12.45-1.15)* **Facilities** 🅿️ ℗ 🖵 ♿ toilets for disabled shop ⊗

INTECH - Family Science Centre

Telegraph Way, Morn Hill SO21 1HZ
☎ 01962 863791 📄 01962 868524
e-mail: htct@intech-uk.com
web: www.intech-uk.com
dir: M3 junct 10 (S) or junct 9 (N) onto A31 then B3404 (Alresford road)

This purpose-built, all weather family attraction houses 100 interactive exhibits, which demonstrate the science and technology of the world around us in an engaging and exciting way. The philosophy is most definitely 'hands-on', and the motto of the centre is 'Doing is Believing'. Activities and science shows take place during school holidays. INTECH also has the UK's largest capacity planetarium. This digital cinema has a 17 metre dome making the audience feel it is floating through the universe. Dramatic, awesome and entertaining.

Times Open all year, daily 10-4. Closed 3 days at Xmas.
Fees £6.95 (ch £4.65, pen £5.50) Family ticket (2ad+2ch) £20.86* **Facilities** 🅿️ 🖵 🎋 (outdoor) ♿ toilets for disabled shop ⊗

ASHTON

Berrington Hall

Berrington HR6 0DW
☎ 01568 615721 📄 01568 613263
e-mail: berrington@nationaltrust.org.uk
web: www.nationaltrust.org.uk
dir: 3m N of Leominster, on A49

An elegant neo-classical house of the late 18th century, designed by Henry Holland and set in a park landscape by `Capability' Brown. Visitors can explore life as a servant at Berrington. The butler's pantry and bedroom tell the story of William Kemp, the butler. Join one of the "maids" on a daily below stairs tour. The corner bedroom and back stairs are brought to life with sounds and smells. Events throughout the year please contact for details.

Times Open 1-16 Mar, Sat-Sun; 17 Mar-2 Nov, Mon-Wed, wknds & Good Fri 11-5. (Last admission 30mins before closing). Garden open 11-5 (4.30 6-21 Dec). Park walk open 16 Jun-2 Nov; wknds 12-4.30 1-16 Dec. Open Good Fri.* **Fees** £6.50 (ch £2.40) Family ticket £16.25. Garden only £4.80 (ch £2.40). Joint ticket with Croft Castle £9.50* **Facilities** 🅿️ 🍽 licensed 🎋 (outdoor) toilets for disabled shop ⊗ 🐾

CROFT

Croft Castle & Parkland

Yarpole HR6 9PW
☎ 01568 780246 📄 01568 780462
e-mail: croftcastle@nationaltrust.org.uk
web: www.nationaltrust.org.uk
dir: off B4362 N of Leominster

Home to the Croft family since Domesday, the walls and towers date from the 14th and 15th centuries, while the interior is mainly 18th century. Set in 1500 acres of Herefordshire countryside, there is a splendid avenue of 350-year-old Spanish chestnuts, and an Iron Age Fort (Croft Ambrey), which may be reached by footpath. Explore the walled garden, church and parkland or enjoy a family walk. There are also many annual events, including outdoor theatre; please telephone for details.

Times Park open all year, daily dawn-dusk. Castle (on open days 11-1 by tour), Garden, shop, tea room & play area open 6 Mar-Oct, Wed-Sun 11-5; 29 Mar-11 Apr & 22 May-31 May & Jul-Aug & 23 Oct-31 Oct, daily 11-5; 6 Nov-19 Dec, Sat-Sun 11-4. Open BH Mons. Tea room & play area also open daily 2-31 Jan & 13-21 Feb; 27-28 Feb 11-4; 27-31 Dec 11-3. **Fees** Gift Aid admission House & gardens £7.80 (ch £3.60) Family ticket £17.90; groups £ 6.05). Garden & grounds: £4.20 (ch £3.15). Family ticket £10.50. Ground & garden Jan-Feb £2.10 (ch £1.05). Joint ticket with Berrington Hall £10.50. Standard prices also available, see website or display at property. **Facilities** 🅿️ 🖵 🍽 licensed 🎋 (outdoor) ♿ toilets for disabled shop ⊗ 🐾

Goodrich Castle

HR9 6HY
☎ **01600 890538**
web: www.english-heritage.org.uk
dir: 5m S of Ross-on-Wye, off A40

A magnificent red sandstone fortress rising out of a rocky outcrop above the Wye Valley. Climb the huge towers for exhilarating views and explore a maze of small rooms and passageways. Hear about the doomed Civil War lovers on our audio tour.

Times Open all year, Mar, Wed-Sun 10-5; Apr-Jun & Sep-1 Nov, daily 10-5; Jul-Aug, daily 10-6; 2 Nov-Feb, Wed-Sun 10-4. Closed 24-26 Dec & 1 Jan. **Fees** £5.20 (concessions £4.40, ch £2.60). Family £13. Please call 0870 333 1181 for the most up to date prices and opening times when planning your visit. **Facilities** ◐ shop ⊗ ✤

LEDBURY

Eastnor Castle

Eastnor HR8 1RL
☎ **01531 633160** 📄 **01531 631776**
e-mail: enquiries@eastnorcastle.com
web: www.eastnorcastle.com
dir: 2.5m E of Ledbury on A438 (Tewkesbury road)

A magnificent Georgian castle in a lovely setting, with a deer park, arboretum and lake. Inside are tapestries, fine art and armour, and the Italianate and Gothic interiors have been beautifully restored. There are an adventure playground, nature trails and lakeside walks. Events take place throughout the year.

Times Open 2-5 Apr; 2 May-26 Sep, Sun & BH; 19 Jul-Aug, Sun-Thu 11-4.30 (last admission 4). **Fees** Castle & grounds £8.50 (ch £5.50, pen £7.50) Family £22.50. Grounds only £5.50 (ch £3.50, pen £4.50). Family £13.50. **Facilities** ◐ ⊡ ⊼ (outdoor) ♿ (partly accessible) shop

HERTFORDSHIRE

HATFIELD

Hatfield House, Park and Gardens

AL9 5NQ
☎ **01707 287010** 📄 **01707 287033**
e-mail: visitors@hatfield-house.co.uk
web: www.hatfield-house.co.uk
dir: 2m from junct 4 A1(M) on A1000, 7m from M25 junct 23. House opposite Hatfield railway station

The house, built by Robert Cecil in 1611, is the home of the 7th Marquess of Salisbury and is full of exquisite tapestries, furniture and famous paintings. The 42 acres of gardens include formal, knot, scented and wilderness areas, and reflect their Jacobean history. Includes the national collection of model soldiers and children's play area. The Tudor Palace of Hatfield, close by the house, was the childhood home of Elizabeth I and where she held her first Council of State when she became Queen in 1558. Events take place throughout the year - see website for details.

Times Open Etr Sat-Sep, Wed-Sun & BH Mon, House 12-4; Park & West Garden 11-5.30.* **Fees** House, Park & Garden: £10.50 (ch £5, concessions £9.50). Park only £3 (ch £2), Park & West Garden £6 (ch £4.50).* **Facilities** ◐ ⊡ ⦿ licensed ⊼ (outdoor) ♿ (partly accessible) (lift to 1st floor) toilets for disabled shop ⊗

KNEBWORTH

Knebworth House, Gardens & Country Park

SG3 6PY

☎ 01438 812661 📄 01438 811908
e-mail: info@knebworthhouse.com
web: www.knebworthhouse.com
dir: direct access from A1(M) junct 7 Stevenage South

Home of the Lytton family since 1490, the original Tudor Manor was transformed in 1843 by the spectacular high Gothic decoration of Victorian novelist Sir Edward Bulwer-Lytton. The formal gardens, laid out by Edwin Lutyens in 1908, include a Gertrude Jekyll herb garden, a maze, an organically-run, walled kitchen garden and a dinosaur trail, comprising 72 life-size models set grazing and hunting amongst the rhododendrons and the redwoods. The 250-acres of rolling parkland include a giant adventure playground and miniature railway.

Times Open 2-18 Apr, 29 May-6 Jun, 3 Jul-Aug, daily, 20-28 Mar, 24 Apr-23 May, 12-27 Jun, 4-26 Sep, wknds & BHs; Park, gardens & playground 11-5 (last admission 4.15); House 12-5 (last admission 4). Fees House, gardens & park £10.50 (ch & pen £10) Family ticket £37. Gardens & park £8. Family ticket £28. Facilities ♿ ⏚ 🅿 (outdoor) ♿ (partly accessible) (house has no lift, history of building can be conveyed to visitors on ground floor) toilets for disabled shop ⊗

LONDON COLNEY

de Havilland Aircraft Heritage Centre

Salisbury Hall AL2 1BU

☎ 01727 826400 & 822051(info) 📄 01727 826400
e-mail: w4050.dhamt@fsmail.net
web: www.dehavillandmuseum.co.uk
dir: M25 junct 22. Follow signs for 'Mosquito Aircraft Museum' onto B556

The site of the hall and museum is a very old one. The aircraft museum opened in 1959 to preserve and display the de Havilland Mosquito prototype on the site of its conception. A working museum with displays of 20 de Havilland aircraft and sections together with a comprehensive collection of de Havilland engines and memorabilia. Selective cockpits are open to enter. Education storyboard 'maze style' gives an outline history of de Havilland Enterprise.

Times Open first Sun Mar-last Sun Oct, Sun & BHs 10.30-5.30, Tue, Thu & Sat 2-5.30.* Fees £5 (ch under 5 free, ch 5-16 £3, pen £4) Family ticket £13 (2ad+2ch)* Facilities ♿ 🅿 ⏚ 🅿 (indoor & outdoor) ♿ toilets for disabled shop ⊗

ST ALBANS

Verulamium Museum

St Michaels AL3 4SW
☎ 01727 751810   📠 01727 859919
e-mail: museum@stalbans.gov.uk
web: www.stalbansmuseums.org.uk
dir: follow signs for St Albans, museum signed

Verulamium was one of the largest and most important Roman towns in Britain - by the lst century AD it was declared a `municipium', giving its inhabitants the rights of Roman citizenship, the only British city granted this honour. A mosaic and underfloor heating system can be seen in a separate building, and the museum has wall paintings, jewellery, pottery and other domestic items. On the second weekend of every month legionaries occupy the galleries and describe the tactics and equipment of the Roman Imperial Army and the life of a legionary.

Times Open all year Mon-Fri 10-5.30, Sun 2-5.30. Closed 25-26 Dec.* **Facilities** 🅿 🛦 (outdoor) ♿ toilets for disabled shop ⊗

TRING

The Natural History Museum at Tring   FREE

The Walter Rothschild Building, Akeman St HP23 6AP
☎ 020 7942 6171   📠 020 7942 6150
e-mail: tring-enquiries@nhm.ac.uk
web: www.nhm.ac.uk/tring
dir: signed from A41

An unusual museum exhibiting a range of animals, collected by its founder Lionel Walter, 2nd Baron Rothschild, scientist, eccentric and natural history enthusiast. Home to the world-class research and collections of the Natural History Museum's Bird Group. A programme of temporary exhibitions, activities and events make any visit a unique day out.

Times Open all year, Mon-Sat 10-5, Sun 2-5. Closed 24-26 Dec. **Facilities** 🅿 🅿 🖵 🛦 (outdoor) toilets for disabled shop ⊗

KENT

BEKESBOURNE

Howletts Wild Animal Park

Beekesbourne Rd CT4 5EL
☎ 0844 8424 647   📠 01303 264944
e-mail: info@howletts.net
web: www.totallywild.net
dir: Signposted off A2, 3m S of Canterbury, follow brown tourist signs

Set in 90 acres, Howletts includes the largest group of western lowland gorillas in captivity in the world, and the largest herd of African elephants in the UK. A number of glass-fronted tiger enclosures allow for amazing views of the Sumatran and Indian tigers. In addition, Howletts is home to assorted primates, clouded leopards, tapirs, Javan langurs, black rhinos and Iberian wolves. There are plenty of other rare and endangered species from around the world. Visitors can walk in an open air enclosure where a family of amazingly agile and lively lemurs roam freely. Picnic areas are spread around the park and a variety of hot and cold dishes are available in the Pavilion Restaurant.

Times Open all year, daily 10-6 summer (last admission 4.30), 10-5 winter (last admission 3.30). Closed 25 Dec.* **Fees** £16.95 (ch £12.95 4-16yrs (must be accompanied by an adult), under 4's free, NUS card student £13.95 over 16yrs, pen £14.95). Family Ticket £54.00 (2ad+2ch)* **Facilities** 🅿 🖵 🍽 licensed 🛦 (outdoor) ♿ toilets for disabled shop ⊗

BELTRING

The Hop Farm

TN12 6PY
☎ 01622 872068   📠 01622 872630
e-mail: info@thehopfarm.co.uk
web: www.thehopfarm.co.uk
dir: on A228 at Paddock Wood

The Hop Farm is set among the largest collection of Victorian oast houses, and its attractions include museums and exhibitions, indoor and outdoor play areas, animal farm and shire horses, and restaurant and gift shop. The recently opened Driving School and Jumping Pillows offer non-stop fun for children, and for the adults there is Legends in Wax and the story of the Hop Farm. The new Great Goblin Hunt transports children into a fantasy world with 3D attractions. Events and shows all year such as the renowned War and Peace Show, Kent County Fair, The Hop Festival and Paws in the Park. For further details see website.

Times Open Apr-Nov, daily 10am. **Fees** £13. Supersaver for 4 £45, for 5 £55.* **Facilities** 🅿 🖵 🍽 licensed 🛦 (outdoor) ♿ toilets for disabled shop ⊗

Kent

BIRCHINGTON

Powell - Cotton Museum, Quex House & Gardens

Quex Park CT7 0BH
☎ 01843 842168 🖹 01843 846661
e-mail: enquiries@quexmuseum.org
web: www.quexmuseum.org
dir: A28 to Birchington right into Park Lane before rdbt in town centre. Entrance 600yds on left

Major Powell-Cotton (1866-1940) devoted his life to the study of the animals and many different cultures of Africa. This museum, founded in 1895, is his legacy, consisting of animal dioramas, ethnography, weaponry, archaeology, ceramics and artefacts from around the world. Also on display in Quex House, the family home, are collections of paintings, Eastern and Asian furniture, and English period furniture. All set within 15 acres of mature gardens, including a Victorian walled garden, fountains, children's maze and resident doves, ducks and peacocks. A full programme of family events throughout the summer can be found on the website.

Times Open Apr-Oct, Sun-Thu 11-5, Quex House 2-5. Nov-Mar museum & gardens, Sun 1-3.30 house closed.* **Fees** £7 (ch & pen £5, under 5s free). Family ticket (2ad+3ch) £18. Garden only £2.* **Facilities** 🅿 🅿 ☕🍽 licensed 🛱 (outdoor) ♿ (partly accessible) toilets for disabled shop ⊗

CANTERBURY

Canterbury Roman Museum

Butchery Ln, Longmarket CT1 2JR
☎ 01227 785575 🖹 01227 455047
e-mail: museums@canterbury.gov.uk
web: www.canterbury-museums.co.uk
dir: in centre close to cathedral & city centre car parks

Step below today's Canterbury to discover an exciting part of the Roman town including the real remains of a house with fine mosaics. Experience everyday life in the reconstructed market place and see exquisite silver and glass. Try your skills on the touch screen computer, and in the hands-on area with actual finds. Use the computer animation of Roman Canterbury to join the search for the lost temple.

Times Open all year, Mon-Sat 10-4 & Sun (Jun-Oct) 1.30-4. (Last admission 4). Closed Good Fri & Xmas period. **Fees** £3.10 (ch 5-18, concessions £2.10). Family ticket £8 (2ad+up to 3 ch).* **Facilities** 🅿 ♿ toilets for disabled shop ⊗

The Canterbury Tales

St. Margaret's St CT1 2TG
☎ 01227 479227 🖹 01227 765584
e-mail: info@canterburytales.org.uk
web: www.canterburytales.org.uk
dir: In heart of city centre, located in St Margaret's St

Step back in time to experience the sights, sounds and smells of the Middle Ages in this reconstruction of 14th-century England. Travel from the Tabard Inn in London, to St. Thomas Becket's Shrine in Canterbury with Chaucer's colourful pilgrims. Their tales of chivalry, romance and intrigue are brought vividly to life along the way.

Times Open all year, Mar-Jun 10-5, Jul-Aug 9.30-5, Sep-Oct 10-5 & Nov-Feb 10-4.30. Closed 25 & 26 Dec, 1 Jan **Fees** £7.75 (ch £5.75, concessions £6.75) Contact for most recent prices. **Facilities** 🅿 ♿ toilets for disabled shop ⊗

Druidstone Park

Honey Hill, Blean CT2 9JR
☎ 01227 765168 🖹 01227 768860
web: www.druidstone.net
dir: 3m NW on A290 from Canterbury

Idyllic garden setting with enchanted woodland walks "where dwells the sleeping dragon". See the mystical Oak Circle with the Old Man of the Oaks. Children's farmyard, play areas, gift shop and cafeteria.

Times Open Etr-Nov, Fri-Mon, 10-5.30; daily during school hols.* **Fees** £4.50 (ch under 3 free). **Facilities** 🅿 ☕ 🛱 (outdoor) ♿ toilets for disabled shop ⊗

Museum of Canterbury

Stour St CT1 2NR
☎ 01227 475202 🖹 01227 455047
e-mail: museums@canterbury.gov.uk
web: www.canterbury-museums.co.uk
dir: in the Medieval Poor Priests' Hospital, just off St Margaret's St or High St

Discover the story of Canterbury in new interactive displays for all the family. See the city's treasures including the famous Canterbury Cross. Try the fun activities in the Medieval Discovery Gallery, find out about the mysteries surrounding Christopher Marlowe's life and death, and spot friend or foe planes in the WW2 Blitz gallery. Meet favourite children's TV character Bagpuss and friends, and enjoy the Rupert Bear Museum.

Times Open all year, Mon-Sat 11-4 & Sun (Jun-Sep) 1.30-4 (last admission 4). Closed Good Fri & Xmas period. **Fees** £3.60 (concessions £2.30). Family ticket £9.20 (2ad+3 ch).* **Facilities** 🅿 ♿ toilets for disabled shop ⊗

Chartwell

TN16 1PS

☎ 01732 866368 (info line) & 868381   🖷 01732 868193
e-mail: chartwell@nationaltrust.org.uk
web: www.nationaltrust.org.uk/chartwell
dir: off A25 onto B2026 at Westerham, Chartwell 2m S of village

The former home of Sir Winston Churchill is filled with reminders of the great statesman, from his hats and uniforms to gifts presented by Stalin, Roosevelt, de Gaulle and many other State leaders. There are portraits of Churchill and other works by notable artists, and also many paintings by Churchill himself. The gardens command breathtaking views over the Weald of Kent.

Times Open House, 13 Mar-Oct, Wed-Sun 11-5. Open BH Mon & Tue in Jul & Aug. (Last admission 4.15). Garden, shop & restaurant open all year, Wed-Sun; Jul-Aug, Tue-Sun. **Fees** Gift Aid admission House, Garden & Studio £11.80 (ch £5.90). Garden & Studio £5.90 (Ch £2.95). Family ticket £29.50. Including a voluntary donation of 10% or more. Visitors can, however, choose to pay the standard admission prices which are displayed at the property & on NT website* **Facilities** 🅿 🍴 licensed ☴ (outdoor) 🚻 (partly accessible) (house stairs to 1st, lower floors & steps, steep slopes in garden) toilets for disabled shop ⊗ 🐾

Dickens World

Leviathan Way ME4 4LL

☎ 01634 890421   🖷 01634 891972
e-mail: enquiries@dickensworld.co.uk
web: www.dickensworld.co.uk
dir: Signposted from junct 1, 3, & 4 of the M2, follow brown anchor signs

Dickens World is an exciting indoor complex themed around the life, books and times of Charles Dickens. It takes visitors on a fascinating journey through the author's lifetime as you step back into Dickensian England and are immersed in the streets, sounds and smells of the 19th century. Dickens World includes The Great Expectations boat ride; The Haunted Man; Victorian School Room; a 4D Hi-def show in Peggotty's Boathouse; Fagin's Den, a soft play area for younger children; and The Britannia Theatre, an animatronic stage show.

Times Open all year, daily from 10, closing time varies seasonally. Closed 25 Dec. **Fees** £12.20 (ch 5-15 £7.30, concessions £10.20)* **Facilities** 🅿 🅿 🖵 🍴 licensed 🚻 (partly accessible) (to board boat ride, wheelchair users must be able to get in/out of chair unaided) toilets for disabled shop ⊗

The Historic Dockyard Chatham

ME4 4TZ

☎ 01634 823807 & 823800   🖷 01634 823801
e-mail: info@chdt.org.uk
web: www.thedockyard.co.uk
dir: M29 junct 6, M2 junct 3 onto A229 towards Chatham. Then A230 and A231, following brown tourist signs. Brown anchor signs lead to visitors entrance

Costumed guides bring this spectacular maritime heritage site alive. Discover over 400 years of maritime history as you explore the most complete dockyard of the Age of Sail, set in a stunning 80-acre estate. Various special events take place throughout the year, please see the website for details.

Times Open daily mid Feb-end Oct, Nov wknds only.* **Facilities** 🅿 🅿 🖵 🍴 licensed ☴ (indoor & outdoor) 🚻 (partly accessible) toilets for disabled shop

Deal Castle

Victoria Rd CT14 7BA

☎ 01304 372762
web: www.english-heritage.org.uk
dir: SW of Deal town centre

Discover the history of this formidable fortress as you explore the long, dark passages that once linked a garrison of 119 guns.

Times Open Apr-Sep, daily 10-6 (Sat 10-5). Closed Oct-Mar. **Fees** £4.30 (concessions £3.70, ch £2.20). Family Ticket £10.80. Please call 0870 333 1181 for the most up to date prices and opening times when planning your visit. **Facilities** 🚻 (partly accessible) (spiral staircase, some steps, narrow doorways) shop ⊗ ♿

Walmer Castle & Gardens

Kingsdown Rd CT14 7LJ

☎ 01304 364288   🖷 01304 364829
web: www.english-heritage.org.uk
dir: 1m S on coast, off A258

Originally built by Henry VIII as a formidable and austere fortress, the castle has since been transformed into an elegant stately home, formerly used by HM The Queen Mother. Many of her rooms are open to view, but the special highlight is the magnificent gardens.

Times Open Apr-Sep, daily 10-6 (Sat 10-4); Oct-1 Nov & Mar, Wed-Sun 10-4. Closed 2 Nov-Feb. (Also closed 10-11 Jul when Lord Warden in residence). **Fees** £6.70 (concessions £5.70, ch £3.40). Family ticket £16.80. Please call 0870 333 1181 for the most up to date prices and opening times when planning your visit. **Facilities** 🅿 🖵 🚻 (partly accessible) (cobbled & flagstone walkway, wooden drawbridge) shop ⊗ ♿

DOVER

Dover Castle & Secret Wartime Tunnels

CT16 1HU
☎ 01304 211067   ▤ 01304 214739
web: www.english-heritage.org.uk

Various exhibitions demonstrate how Dover Castle has served as a vital strategic centre for the Iron Age onwards. In May 1940 the tunnels under the castle became the nerve centre for 'Operation Dynamo' - the evacuation of Dunkirk. These wartime secrets are now revealed for all to see.

Times Open Apr-Jul & Sep, daily 10-6; Aug, daily 9.30-6; Oct-1 Nov, daily 10-5; 2 Nov-Jan, Thu-Mon 10-4; Feb-Mar, daily 10-4. Closed 24-26 Dec & 1 Jan. **Fees** £13.40 (concessions £11.40, ch £6.70). Family £33.50. (Additional charges may apply on event days). Please call 0870 333 1181 for the most up to date prices and opening times when planning your visit. **Facilities** 🅿 ⓟ 🍴 licensed ♿ (partly accessible) (steep slopes) toilets for disabled shop ⊗ ♯

The White Cliffs of Dover

Visitor Centre, Langdon Cliffs, Upper Rd CT16 1HJ
☎ 01304 202756   ▤ 01304 215484
e-mail: whitecliffs@nationaltrust.org.uk
web: www.nationaltrust.org.uk
dir: A2/A258 towards Dover town centre, in 1m turn left into Upper Rd, 0.75m turn right into entrance

The White Cliffs of Dover are one of England's most spectacular natural features, as well as being an important national icon. Visitors enjoy their special appeal through the seasons by taking the cliff top paths offering views of the French coast, and savouring the rare flora and fauna that can be found across this chalk grassland. The visitor centre is full of useful information, as well as a coffee shop and National Trust shop.

Times Open all year. Visitor Centre: Nov-Feb, 11-4, Mar-Oct, 10-5. Car park Nov-Feb, 8-5, Mar-Oct, 8-6. **Fees** Free admission. Parking charges car £3, mobile home £4, coach £7. **Facilities** 🅿 ⛾ 🍴 (outdoor) ♿ (partly accessible) (some uneven and steep paths) toilets for disabled shop

EYNSFORD

Eagle Heights

Lullingstone Ln DA4 0JB
☎ 01322 866466   ▤ 01322 861024
e-mail: office@eagleheights.co.uk
web: www.eagleheights.co.uk
dir: M25 junct 3/A20 towards West Kingsdown. Right after 2 rdbts onto A225. Follow brown signs

Eagle Heights is an impressive display of birds of prey from all over the world. Many are flown out across the Darenth valley twice daily. There are also owls, pygmy goat and rabbits in the paddock. New Africa show including cheetah.

Times Open Mar-Oct daily 10.30-5. Nov, Jan-Feb wknd only 11-4. **Fees** £8.50 (ch £5, concessions £7).* **Facilities** 🅿 ⓟ ⛾ 🍴 (outdoor) ♿ toilets for disabled shop ⊗

GILLINGHAM

Royal Engineers Museum, Library & Archive

Prince Arthur Rd ME4 4UG
☎ 01634 822839   ▤ 01634 822371
e-mail: mail@re-museum.co.uk **web:** www.remuseum.org.uk
dir: follow brown signs from Gillingham & Chatham town centres

The museum covers the work of the Royal Engineers. Learn about the first military divers, photographers, aviators and surveyors; see memorabilia relating to General Gordon and Field Marshal Lord Kitchener, Wellington's battle map from Waterloo and a Harrier jump-jet. Medal displays include 25 Victoria Crosses, among 6,000 medals. Among the exhibits are locomotives, tanks, the first wire guided torpedo, bridges, and models. Some special events take place in conjunction with Chatham Historic Dockyard.

Times Open all year, Tue-Fri 9-5, Sat-Sun & BH Mon 11.30-5. Closed Good Fri, Xmas week & 1 Jan. Library open by appointment (ex wknds).* **Fees** £6.99 (concessions £4.66) Family £18.64. Gift aid ticket for 1yr entry.* **Facilities** 🅿 ⓟ 🍴 (indoor & outdoor) ♿ (partly accessible) (one gallery not easily accessible) toilets for disabled shop ⊗

GROOMBRIDGE PLACE

Groombridge Place Gardens & Enchanted Forest

TN3 9QG
☎ 01892 861444 🖷 01892 863996
e-mail: office@groombridge.co.uk
web: www.groombridge.co.uk
dir: M25 junct 5, follow A21 S, exit at A26 (signed Tunbridge Wells), then take A264 - follow signs to village and Groombridge Place Gardens

This award-winning attraction, set in 200 acres, features a series of magnificent walled gardens set against the backdrop of a romantic 17th-century moated manor. Explore the herbaceous border, the white rose garden, the 'Drunken Topiary', the 'Secret Garden' and the peacock walk. By way of contrast, in the ancient woodland of the 'Enchanted Forest', the imagination is stimulated by mysterious features such as the 'Dark Walk', 'Dinosaur and Dragon Valley' and 'Groms' Village'. Groombridge was used as a major location in the recent movie adaptation of Jane Austen's Pride and Prejudice. There are also bird of prey flying displays, canal boat cruises, and a full programme of special events.

Times Open Apr-Nov, daily 10-5.30* **Facilities** 🅿 🍴 licensed 🎪 (outdoor) ♿ (partly accessible) toilets for disabled shop ⊗

HYTHE

Romney, Hythe & Dymchurch Railway

TN28 8PL
☎ 01797 362353 & 363256 🖷 01797 363591
e-mail: info@rhdr.org.uk
web: www.rhdr.org.uk
dir: M20 junct 11, follow signs to Hythe Station

The world's smallest public railway has its headquarters here. The concept of two enthusiasts coincided with Southern Railway's plans for expansion, and so the 13.5 mile stretch of 15-inch gauge railway came into being, running from Hythe through New Romney and Dymchurch to Dungeness Lighthouse.

Times Open Etr-Oct; daily; Jan-Mar, wknds **Fees** Romney Rover all day ticket £14 (ch over 3 £7). **Facilities** 🅿 🖵 🍴 licensed 🎪 (indoor & outdoor) ♿ toilets for disabled shop

IGHTHAM

Ightham Mote

TN15 0NT
☎ 01732 810378 & 811145 (info line) 🖷 01732 811029
e-mail: ighthammote@nationaltrust.org.uk
web: www.nationaltrust.org.uk
dir: 2.5m S off A227, 6m E of Sevenoaks

This moated manor house, nestling in a sunken valley, dates from 1320. The main features of the house span many centuries and include the Great Hall, an old chapel and crypt, a Tudor chapel with painted ceiling, and a drawing room with Jacobean fireplace, frieze and 18th-century hand-painted Chinese wallpaper. There is an extensive garden as well as interesting walks in the surrounding woodland. Following completion of all conservation work, visitors can enjoy the most extensive visitor route to date, including the bedroom of Charles Henry Robinson who bequeathed Ightham Mote to the National Trust.

Times Open 14 Mar-1 Nov, daily (ex Tue & Wed), 11-5. Open BH & Good Fri. (Last admission 4.30).* **Fees** Voluntary Gift Aid donation £10.40 (ch £5.20). Family ticket £26. Including a voluntary donation of 10% or more. Visitors can, however, choose to pay the standard admission prices which are displayed at the property & on NT website* **Facilities** 🅿 🖵 🍴 licensed 🎪 (outdoor) ♿ (partly accessible) (only gardens & ground floor rooms in house accessible) toilets for disabled shop ⊗ 🐾

LYDD

RSPB Nature Reserve

Boulderwall Farm, Dungeness Rd TN29 9PN
☎ **01797 320588** 🖹 **01797 321962**
e-mail: dungeness@rspb.org.uk
web: www.rspb.org.uk
dir: off Lydd to Dungeness road, 1m SE of Lydd, follow tourist signs

Occupying over 2,000 acres of the Dungeness peninsula, this is the largest shingle beach of its kind in Europe. About 60 species of birds breed on the reserve each year, including large numbers of waterfowl and waders. Marsh harriers and bearded tits nest in the reed beds along with more common reed and sage warblers and reed buntings. In spring and autumn migrating birds such as warblers and waders pass through Dungeness, while in winter the reserve plays host to hundreds of wildfowl, including pintail, smew and goldeneye. Many plants, butterflies and dragonflies can also be seen around the nature trail. The Dungeness Wildlife and Countryside fair takes place in August each year, with free entry to all.

Times Open: Visitor Centre all year, daily 10-5 (10-4 Nov-Feb). Reserve open all year, daily 9am-9pm (or sunset if earlier). Closed 25-26 Dec.* **Fees** £3 (ch £1, concessions £2). RSPB members free.* **Facilities** ❷ 🛲 (outdoor) ♿ (partly accessible) (visitor centre & most trails accessible for wheelchair users & access by car to all but one hide) toilets for disabled shop ⊗

LYMPNE

Port Lympne Wild Animal Park

CT21 4LR
☎ **0844 8424 647** 🖹 **01303 264944**
e-mail: info@howletts.net
web: www.totallywild.net
dir: M20 junct 11, follow brown tourist signs

An historic mansion and landscaped gardens set in 600 acres, Port Lympne Park also houses the largest breeding herd of black rhino outside Africa as well as African elephants, Siberian and Indian tigers, small cats, monkeys, Malayan tapirs, Barbary lions and many more rare and endangered species. Other exciting features include the 'African Experience', Livingstone Safari Lodge, Day and Sunset safaris, Enrichment Centre Workshops and the chance to be a keeper for a day (subject to availability and at an additional charge) Pre-booking essential for some activities, please see website.

Times Open all year, daily 10-6 (summer, last admission 4.30) 10-5 (winter, last admission 3.30). Closed 25 Dec.* **Fees** Please phone for prices or see website.* **Facilities** ❷ 🖵 🍴 licensed 🛲 (outdoor) ♿ (partly accessible) (very limited access for disabled, special route available) toilets for disabled shop ⊗

MAIDSTONE

Kent Life

Lock Ln, Sandling ME14 3AU
☎ **01622 763936**
e-mail: enquiries@kentlife.org.uk
web: www.kentlife.org.uk
dir: from M20 junct 6 onto A229 Maidstone road, follow signs for Aylesford

Kent Life is Kent's premier farm attraction featuring 28 acres of fun including a new indoor play barn and outdoor play area. Lots of hands on activities and an animal cuddle corner. See website for a full list of seasonal events.

Times Open daily 10-5 (term time), 10-6 school hols & wknds (last admission 1 hr before close). Open all year for school & group bookings. See website for further details. **Fees** Prices not confirmed for 2010. Please telephone for details. **Facilities** ❷ ℗ 🖵 🛲 (outdoor) ♿ (partly accessible) (access to upper floors restricted, no lifts) toilets for disabled shop

Leeds Castle

ME17 1PL
☎ **01622 765400** 🖹 **01622 735616**
e-mail: enquiries@leeds-castle.co.uk
web: www.leeds-castle.com
dir: 7m E of Maidstone at junct 8 of M20/A20, clearly signed

Set in 500 acres of beautiful parkland, a visit to Leeds Castle, near Maidstone, Kent is full of discovery. With over 900 years of fascinating history, the castle has been a Norman stronghold, a royal residence for six medieval queens of England, a favourite palace of Henry VIII and a grand country house. Its blend of history and heritage, glorious gardens, aviary and birds of prey, maze and grotto, dog collar museum, craft centre and children's playground, make it the perfect choice for a day out. Special events all year, contact for details or visit the website.

Times Open all year, Grounds: Apr-Sep, daily 10-6 (Castle 10.30-5.30) Last admission 4.30. Grounds: Oct-Mar 10-4 (Castle 10.30-4) Last admission 3. Last entry to the castle is 30min after the last admission time. **Fees** £16.50 (ch £9.50, under 4 free, concessions £13.50). Every ticket purchased for entry to Leeds Castle is valid for unlimited use for an entire year (excluding special ticketed events). Please contact Castle for most recent prices. **Facilities** ❷ 🍴 licensed 🛲 (outdoor) ♿ (partly accessible) (only ground floor of castle accessible) toilets for disabled shop ⊗

Maidstone continued

Maidstone Museum
& Bentlif Art Gallery   FREE

St Faith's St ME14 1LH
☎ 01622 602838
e-mail: museum@maidstone.gov.uk
web: www.museum.maidstone.gov.uk
dir: close to County Hall & Maidstone E train station, opposite Fremlin's Walk

Set in an Elizabethan manor house which has been much extended over the years, this museum contains an outstanding collection of fine and applied arts, including watercolours, furniture, ceramics, and a collection of Japanese art and artefacts. The museum of the Queen's Own Royal West Kent Regiment is also housed here. Please apply for details of temporary exhibitions, workshops etc.

Times Open all year, Mon-Sat 10-5.15, Sun & BH Mon 11-4. Closed 25-26 Dec & 1 Jan. **Facilities** ℗ ⊑ & (partly accessible) shop ⊗

Tyrwhitt Drake
Museum of Carriages   FREE

The Archbishop's Stables, Mill St ME15 6YE
☎ 01622 602838
e-mail: museuminfo@maidstone.gov.uk
web: www.museum.maidstone.gov.uk
dir: close to River Medway & Archbishops Palace, just off A229 in town centre

The museum is home to a unique collection of horse-drawn vehicles and transport curiosities. More than 60 vehicles are on display, from grand carriages and ornate sleighs to antique sedan chairs and Victorian cabs, there is even an original ice-cream cart.

Times Open May-Aug, Wed-Sun & BH, 10.30-4.30.* **Facilities** ℗ & (partly accessible) shop ⊗

Penshurst Place & Gardens

TN11 8DG
☎ 01892 870307   📄 01892 870866
e-mail: enquiries@penshurstplace.com
web: www.penshurstplace.com
dir: M25 junct 5 take A21 Hastings road then exit at Hildenborough & follow brown signs

Built between 1340 and 1345, the original house is perfectly preserved. Enlarged by successive owners during the 15th, 16th and 17th centuries, the great variety of architectural styles creates a dramatic backdrop for the extensive collections of English, French and Italian furniture, tapestries and paintings. The chestnut-beamed Baron's Hall is one of the oldest and finest in the country, and the house is set in magnificent formal gardens. There is a toy museum, venture playground, woodland trail, 10 acres of walled formal gardens and events throughout the season. Penshurst was used as a location for the movie version of The Other Boleyn Girl, and is a popular choice as a movie and television location.

Times Open: wknds from 6-28 Mar, daily from 29 Mar-Oct. Gardens open 10.30-6. House open noon-4. **Fees** House, garden, grounds £9.50 (ch 5-16 £6). Family (2ad+2ch) £25. Grounds including garden £7.50 (ch 5-16 £5.50). Family (2ad+2ch) £22. **Facilities** ℗ ℗ ⊑ ⍾ licensed ⊞ (outdoor) & (partly accessible) (garden accessible from visitor entrance, Baron's Hall and Nether Gallery all on ground floor, DVD show of other state rooms) toilets for disabled shop ⊗

SEVENOAKS

Knole

TN15 0RP
☎ 01732 462100 & 450608 (info line) 📠 01732 465528
e-mail: knole@nationaltrust.org.uk
web: www.nationaltrust.org.uk/knole
dir: From town centre, off A225 Tonbridge road, opposite St. Nicholas' Church

Knole's fascinating links with Kings, Queens and nobility, as well as its literary connections with Vita Sackville-West and Virginia Woolf, make this one of the most intriguing houses in England. Thirteen superb state-rooms are laid out much as they were in the 18th century, to impress visitors with the status of the Sackville family, who continue to live at Knole today. The house includes rare furniture, important paintings, as well as many 17th-century tapestries.

Times House open 13 Mar-Oct, Wed-Sun 12-4; open BH Mon. 27 Jul-5 Sep, Tue-Sun 11-4.30. **Fees** Voluntary Gift Aid donation: £10.45 (ch £5.20). Family ticket £26.10. Garden (standard admission) £2 (ch £1). Including a voluntary donation of 10% or more. Visitors can, however, choose to pay the standard admission prices which are displayed at the property & on NT website **Facilities** 🅿 Ⓟ 🚻 ♿ (partly accessible) (access to the Great Hall, shop & tea room ground floor only) toilets for disabled shop ⊗ 💥

SISSINGHURST

Sissinghurst Castle Garden

TN17 2AB
☎ 01580 710700 📠 01580 710702
e-mail: sissinghurst@nationaltrust.org.uk
web: www.nationaltrust.org.uk
dir: 1m E of Sissinghurst village on A262

Created in the ruins of a large Elizabethan house and set in unspoilt countryside, Sissinghurst Castle Garden is one of the most celebrated gardens made by Vita Sackville-West and her husband Sir Harold Nicolson. Phone for details of special events and info on the bus link.

Times Open: Gardens 13 Mar-Oct, Fri-Tue 11-5.30. (Peace & Tranquillity after 3.30) **Fees** Please telephone or check website for details* **Facilities** 🅿 🚻 🍽 licensed 🪑 ♿ (partly accessible) (some steps in garden, buggy service to vegetable garden when open) toilets for disabled shop ⊗ 💥

STROOD

Diggerland

Medway Valley Leisure Park, Roman Way ME2 2NU
☎ 0871 227 7007 📠 09012 010300
e-mail: mail@diggerland.com
web: www.diggerland.com
dir: M2 junct 2, follow A228 towards Rochester. At rdbt turn right. Diggerland on right

An adventure park with a difference. Experience the thrills of driving real earth-moving equipment. Choose from various types of diggers and dumpers ranging from 1 ton to 8.5 tons. Complete the Dumper Truck Challenge or dig for buried treasure supervised by an instructor. New rides include JCB Robots, Diggerland Dodgems, Go-karts, Landrover Safari, Spin Dizzy and the Diggerland Tractors.

Times Open 12 Feb-end Oct, 10-5, wknds, BHs & school hols only (including half term). **Fees** £15 - all rides & drives included in price. **Facilities** 🅿 Ⓟ 🚻 🪑 (outdoor) ♿ toilets for disabled shop ⊗

TENTERDEN

Kent & East Sussex Railway

Tenterden Town Station, Station Rd TN30 6HE
☎ 01580 765155 📠 01580 765654
e-mail: enquiries@kesr.org.uk
web: www.kesr.org.uk
dir: A28 turn into Station Rd beside The Vine Public House, station 200yds on right

Ten and a half miles of pure nostalgia, this is England's finest rural light railway. Beautifully restored coaches and locomotives dating from Victorian times enable visitors to experience travel and service from a bygone age. The picturesque line weaves between Tenterden and Bodiam, terminating in the shadow of the castle.

Times Open Etr-Sep wkdays & wknds. Other times of the year wknds & school hols. Five trains per day* **Facilities** 🅿 Ⓟ 🚻 🍽 licensed 🪑 (outdoor) ♿ toilets for disabled shop

TUNBRIDGE WELLS (ROYAL)

Tunbridge Wells Museum and Art Gallery FREE

Civic Centre, Mount Pleasant TN1 1JN
☎ **01892 554171 & 526121** 🖹 **01892 554131**
e-mail: museum@tunbridgewells.gov.uk
web: www.tunbridgewellsmuseum.org
dir: adjacent to Town Hall, off A264

This combined museum and art gallery tells the story of the borough of Tunbridge Wells. There are collections of costume, art, dolls and toys along with natural and local history from dinosaur bones to the original Pantiles. There is also a large collection of Tunbridge ware, the intricate wooden souvenirs made for visitors to the Wells. The art gallery features a changing programme of contemporary and historic art, touring exhibitions, and local art and craft.

Times Open all year, daily 9.30-5. Sun 10-4. Closed BHs & Etr Sat. **Facilities** Ⓟ ♿ (partly accessible) (platform lift to first floor) shop ⊗

LANCASHIRE

BLACKPOOL

Blackpool Zoo

East Park Dr FY3 8PP
☎ **01253 830830** 🖹 **01253 830800**
e-mail: info@blackpoolzoo.org.uk
web: www.blackpoolzoo.org.uk
dir: M55 junct 4, follow brown tourist signs

This multi-award-winning zoo, built in 1972, houses over 1500 animals within its 32 acres of landscaped gardens. There is a miniature railway, lots of close encounters and animals in action, a children's play area, animal feeding times and keeper talks throughout the day. New animal attractions include Giraffe Heights and Penguin Pool. Many special events throughout the year.

Times Open all year daily, summer 10-6; winter 10-dusk. Jul-Aug, Wed 10-9. Closed 25 Dec.* **Fees** £12.95 (ch £8.95, concessions £10.95, disabled & carers £6.50). Family (2ad+2ch) £39, (2ad+3 ch) £47.* **Facilities** Ⓟ Ⓟ ⊑⍟ licensed 🗚 (outdoor) ♿ toilets for disabled shop ⊗

CHARNOCK RICHARD

Camelot Theme Park

PR7 5LP
☎ **01257 452100** 🖹 **01257 452395**
e-mail: kingarthur@camelotthemepark.co.uk
web: www.camelotthemepark.co.uk
dir: from M6 junct 27/28, or M61 junct 8 follow brown tourist signs

Join Merlin, King Arthur and the Knights of the Round Table at the magical kingdom of Camelot. Explore five magic lands filled with thrilling rides, spectacular shows, and many more attractions. From white-knuckle thrills on Knightmare, The Whirlwind spinning rollercoaster, to wet-knuckle thrills on Pendragon's Plunge, there's something for everyone.

Times Open 31 Mar-28 Oct.* **Facilities** Ⓟ ⊑ 🗚 (indoor & outdoor) ♿ (partly accessible) toilets for disabled shop ⊗

CHORLEY

Astley Hall Museum & Art Gallery FREE

Astley Park PR7 1NP
☎ **01257 515555** 🖹 **01257 515923**
e-mail: astley.hall@chorley.gov.uk
web: www.astleyhall.co.uk
dir: M61 junct 8, signed Botany Bay. Follow brown signs

A charming Tudor/Stuart building set in beautiful parkland, this lovely Hall retains a comfortable 'lived-in' atmosphere. There are pictures and pottery to see, as well as fine furniture and rare plasterwork ceilings. Special events throughout the year.

Times Open Apr (or Etr)-Oct, Sat-Sun & BH Mon 12-5; By appointment only during the week* **Facilities** Ⓟ Ⓟ 🗚 (outdoor) shop ⊗

CLITHEROE

Clitheroe Castle Museum

Castle Hill BB7 1BA
☎ **01200 424568** 🖹 **01200 421008**
e-mail: clitheroecastlemuseum@lancashire.gov.uk
web: www.lancashire.gov.uk
dir: follow Clitheroe signs from A59 Preston-Skipton by-pass. Museum located in castle grounds near town centre

Clitheroe Castle Museum covers 350 million years of history of the local area. The galleries include displays and hands-on interactives on geology, wildlife, the history of Clitheroe's castle keep and buildings; the history of the town, its people, industry and transport.

Times Open all year, Apr-Oct, daily 11-5, Nov-Mar, daily noon-4. Closed 25-26 Dec & 1 Jan. **Fees** £3.50 (ch under 16 free but must be accompanied by an adult, concessions £2.50). LCMS Xplorer tickets welcome.* **Facilities** Ⓟ ⊑ ♿ toilets for disabled shop ⊗

LANCASTER

Lancaster Maritime Museum

St George's Quay LA1 1RB
☎ 01524 382264   📄 01524 841692
e-mail: lancastermaritimemuseum@lancashire.gov.uk
web: www.lancashire.gov.uk/museums
dir: close to M6, junct 33 & 34. From A6 follow signs to town centre & then brown tourist signs to the Quay

Graceful Ionic columns adorn the front of the Custom House, built in 1764. Inside, the histories of the 18th-century transatlantic maritime trade of Lancaster, the Lancaster Canal and the fishing industry of Morecambe Bay are well illustrated. Changing programme of special exhibitions and holiday events, please ring or see website for details.

Times Open all year, daily, Etr-Oct 11-5; Nov-Etr 12.30-4.
Fees £3 (concessions £2). Free to accompanied children and residents of Lancaster district. **Facilities** 🅿 Ⓟ ⊑ ㅠ (indoor) ♿ (partly accessible) (mezzanine floor inaccessible) toilets for disabled shop ⊗

LEYLAND

British Commercial Vehicle Museum

King St PR25 2LE
☎ 01772 451011   📄 01772 451015
e-mail: enquiries@bcvm.co.uk
web: www.bcvm.co.uk
dir: 0.75m from M6 junct 28 in town centre

A unique line-up of historic commercial vehicles and buses spanning a century of truck and bus building. There are more than 50 exhibits on permanent display, and plenty of special events including transport model shows, transport shows, and the Ford Cortina Mk I gathering.

Times Open Apr-Sep, Sun, Tue-Thu & BH Mon (Oct open Tue & Sun only); 10-5.* **Facilities** 🅿 Ⓟ ⊑ ♿ toilets for disabled shop ⊗

MARTIN MERE

WWT Martin Mere

L40 0TA
☎ 01704 895181   📄 01704 892343
e-mail: info@martinmere.co.uk
web: www.wwt.org.uk/martinmere
dir: signed from M61, M58 & M6, 6m from Ormskirk, off A59

One of Britain's most important wetland sites, where you can get really close to a variety of ducks, geese and swans from all over the world as well as two flocks of flamingos and beavers. Thousands of wildfowl, including pink-footed geese, Bewick's and Whooper swans, winter here. Other features include a children's adventure playground, craft area, shop and an educational centre.

Times Open all year, daily 9.30-5.30 (5 in winter). Closed 25 Dec.* **Fees** £8.75 (ch £4.30, concessions £6.50). Family ticket £23.50.* **Facilities** 🅿 ⊑ ㅠ (indoor & outdoor) ♿ toilets for disabled shop

PRESTON

National Football Museum   FREE

Sir Tom Finney Way, Deepdale PR1 6PA
☎ 01772 908442   📄 01772 908444
e-mail: enquiries@nationalfootballmuseum.com
web: www.nationalfootballmuseum.com
dir: 2m from M6 juncts 31, 31A or 32. Follow brown tourist signs

Take an amazing journey through football history. Discover the world's biggest football museum, packed full of great footballing moments, stories and objects -from the World Cup ball used in the first ever final in 1930, to the ball used in the 1966 World Cup final. There are fun interactive opportunities and the brilliant penalty shoot-out game Goalstriker. Plus events, activities and exhibitions all year round means there's always something new to see and do.

Times Open all year, Tue-Sat 10-5, Sun 11-5. Closed Mon ex BHs and school hols. (Museum closed 15 mins before 'kick off' on match days)* **Facilities** 🅿 Ⓟ ⊑ ♿ toilets for disabled shop ⊗

RUFFORD

Rufford Old Hall

L40 1SG
☎ 01704 821254   📄 01704 823823
e-mail: ruffordoldhall@nationaltrust.org.uk
web: www.nationaltrust.org.uk
dir: M6 junct 27 & follow signs to Rufford. Hall on E side of A59

Rufford is one of Lancashire's finest Tudor buildings, and is where a young William Shakespeare is believed to have performed for its owner, Sir Thomas Hesketh. Visitors can wander around the house and view the fine collections of furniture, arms, armour and tapestries. Outside there are the gardens, topiary and sculptures. Enjoy a walk in the woodlands alongside the canal, and then have some freshly-prepared local food in the tea room.

Times Open 28 Feb-8 Mar, wknds only, 11-5.30; 14-Mar-1 Nov, Sun-Wed 11-5.30 & Sat 1-5.30. Garden, shop & tea room, 6 Nov-21 Dec, Fri-Sun, 12-4.* **Fees** House & Garden: £6 (ch £3). Family ticket £15. Groups £5.10 each. Garden only: £4.20 (ch £2.10). **Facilities** ❷ 🍴 licensed 🎪 (outdoor) ♿ (partly accessible) (ground floor accessible, but steps from Great Hall & some loose cobbles & gravel in grounds) toilets for disabled shop ⊗ 🐾

SILVERDALE

RSPB Leighton Moss Nature Reserve

Myers Farm LA5 0SW

☎ 01524 701601   📄 01524 702092
e-mail: leighton.moss@rspb.org.uk
web: www.rspb.org.uk
dir: M6 junct 35, west on A501(M) for 0.5m. Turn right and head N on A6. Follow brown tourist signs

Leighton Moss is the largest remaining reedbed in north-west England, with special birds, breeding bitterns, bearded tits, marsh harriers, avocets and other spectacular wildlife. You can visit nature trails, look around the RSPB shop and visitor centre and enjoy a meal in the tearoom.

Times Reserve: open daily 9-dusk. Visitor Centre daily Feb-Oct 9.30-5 (Nov-Jan 9.30-4.30). Closed 25 Dec. **Fees** £4.50 (ch £1, concessions £3) Family £9. RSPB members Free* **Facilities** ❷ ⊡ 🍴 licensed 🎪 (outdoor) ♿ (partly accessible) (some nature trails accessible) toilets for disabled shop ⊗

ASHBY-DE-LA-ZOUCH

Ashby-de-la-Zouch Castle

South St LE65 1BR
☎ 01530 413343   📄 01530 411677
web: www.english-heritage.org.uk

Impressive ruins of a late medieval castle. The magnificent 24-metre Hastings Tower offers panoramic views of the surrounding countryside. Ashby was the setting for the famous jousting scene in Sir Walter Scott's classic romance Ivanhoe.

Times Open all year, Apr-Jun & Sep-1 Nov, Thu-Mon 10-5; Jul-Aug, daily 10-6; 2 Nov-Mar, Thu-Mon 12-4. Closed 24-26 Dec & 1 Jan. **Fees** £3.90 (concessions £3.30, ch £2). Family ticket £9.80. Please call 0870 333 1181 for the most up to date prices and opening times when planning your visit. **Facilities** ❷ shop ⊞

BELVOIR

Belvoir Castle

NG32 1PE
☎ 01476 871002   📄 01476 870443
e-mail: info@belvoircastle.com
web: www.belvoircastle.com
dir: between A52 & A607, follow the brown heritage signs from A1, A52, A607 & A46

Although Belvoir Castle has been the home of the Dukes of Rutland for many centuries, the turrets, battlements, towers and pinnacles of the house are a 19th-century fantasy. Amongst the many treasures to be seen inside are paintings by Murillo, Holbein and other famous artists. For children, there's a delightful Regency nursery, schoolroom and an adventure playground. Lovingly restored gardens are also open to visitors. Special events planned every weekend throughout the season, phone for details or visit the website.

Times Open Jun, Sun, Jul, daily ex Sat (closed 22-26); Aug, daily ex Sat (open 28-31); Sep, Sun only; 1-13 Dec.* **Fees** £10 (ch £6) Family £28.* **Facilities** ❷ Ⓟ ⊡ 🍴 licensed 🎪 (outdoor) ♿

(partly accessible) (Castle limited to ground floor, Gardens limited access) toilets for disabled shop ⊗

COALVILLE

Snibston Discovery Museum

Ashby Rd LE67 3LN
☎ 01530 278444   🖷 01530 813301
e-mail: snibston@leics.gov.uk
web: www.snibston.com
dir: 4.5m from M1 junct 22 or from A42/M42 junct 13 on A511 on W side of Coalville

Award winning attraction and up-to-date science centre. In the Extra Ordinary hands-on gallery visitors can see how technology has affected everyday life, by lifting up a Mini Cooper. The Fashion Gallery has a wide selection of historic and modern costumes, while the underground life of a miner can be explored in the colliery tour. There are also rides on a diesel locomotive, or fun in the adventure play area. The Country Park is free, and has two fishing lakes, picnic spots and the Grange Nature Reserve.

Times Open all year, Apr-Oct, daily 10-5; Nov-Mar 10-3. School hols & wknds 10-5. Closed 2 weeks in Jan for maintenance. **Fees** £6.75 (ch £4.50, concessions £4.75). Family ticket £20.* **Facilities** 🅿 🅿 ⬚ 🞧 (indoor & outdoor) ⓖ toilets for disabled shop ⊗

LEICESTER

National Space Centre

Exploration Dr LE4 5NS
☎ 0845 605 2001   🖷 0116 258 2100
e-mail: info@spacecentre.co.uk
web: www.spacecentre.co.uk
dir: off A6, 2m N of city centre midway between Leicester's central & outer ring roads. Follow brown rocket signs from M1 (junct 21, 21a or 22) & all arterial routes around Leicester

The award-winning National Space Centre offers a great family day out, with six interactive galleries, a full-domed Space Theatre, a 42-metre high Rocket Tower, and the new Human Spaceflight Experience with 3D SIM ride. Explore the universe, orbit Earth, join the crew on the lunar base, and take the astronaut fitness tests, all without leaving Leicester! Project Apollo is the latest interactive experience celebrating the 40th anniversary of the Apollo moon landing. Throughout the year there are numerous events relating to space reality and science fiction, so contact the Centre for more details.

Times Open during school term: Tue-Fri, 10-4, Sat-Sun 10-5. During school hols: daily, 10-5.* **Fees** £13 (ch 4-16yrs & concessions £11). Family of 4 £40, of 5 £50. All tickets valid for a full year. **Facilities** 🅿 ⬚ 🍴 licensed 🞧 (outdoor) ⓖ toilets for disabled shop ⊗

LOUGHBOROUGH

Great Central Railway

Great Central Rd LE11 1RW
☎ 01509 230726   🖷 01509 239791
e-mail: sales@gcrailway.co.uk
web: www.gcrailway.co.uk
dir: signed from A6, follow brown tourist signs

This private steam railway runs over eight miles from Loughborough Central to Leicester North, with all trains calling at Quorn & Woodhouse and Rothley. The locomotive depot and museum are at Loughborough Central. A buffet car runs on most trains.

Times Open all year daily, trains run every wknd & BHs throughout the year, May-Sep, Wed; Jun, Jul & Aug daily ex Fri.* **Fees** Runabout (all day unlimited travel) £12 (ch £7 & concessions £10). Family ticket (2ad+3ch) £30 (1ad+3ch) £20* **Facilities** 🅿 🅿 ⬚ 🍴 licensed 🞧 (outdoor) ⓖ toilets for disabled shop

MARKET BOSWORTH

Bosworth Battlefield Visitor Centre & Country Park

Ambion Hill, Sutton Cheney CV13 0AD
☎ 01455 290429   🖷 01455 292841
e-mail: bosworth@leics.gov.uk
web: www.leics.gov.uk
dir: follow brown tourist signs from A447, A444 & A5

The Battle of Bosworth Field was fought in 1485 between the armies of Richard III and the future Henry VII. The visitor centre offers a comprehensive interpretation of the battle, with exhibitions, models and a film theatre. Special medieval attractions are held in the summer months.

Times Open: Country Park daily Apr-Sep, 8.30-5.30, Oct-Mar 8.30-4.40. Heritage Centre open daily Apr-Oct, 10-5, Nov-Mar, 10-4 (last admission 1hr before closing). Closed Jan & 24-27 Dec.* **Fees** £6 (ch 3-16 yrs £3, ch under 3 free, concessions £4). Family ticket (2ad+2ch) £15.* **Facilities** 🅿 🅿 ⬚ 🍴 licensed 🞧 (outdoor) toilets for disabled shop

MOIRA

Conkers

Millennium Av, Rawdon Rd DE12 6GA
☎ **01283 216633**   📠 **01283 210321**
e-mail: info@visitconkers.com **web:** www.visitconkers.com
dir: on B5003 in Moira, signed from A444 and M42

Explore over one hundred indoor interactive exhibits, together with 120 acres that contain lakeside walks and trails, habitats, an assault course, adventure play areas and a miniature train. There are also events in the covered amphitheatre, and many other opportunities for you and your family to be entertained and educated.

Times Open all year, daily, summer 10-6, autumn 10-5, winter 10-4.30. Closed 25 Dec.* **Fees** £7.95 (ch 3-15yrs £5.95, ch under 3 free, concessions £6.95). Family ticket (2ad+2ch) £24.95. Prices include a 10% donation to The Heart of the National Forest. **Facilities** 🅿 ☐ 🍴 licensed 🎪 (indoor & outdoor) ♿ toilets for disabled shop ⊗

SHACKERSTONE

Battlefield Line Railway

Shackerstone Station CV13 6NW
☎ **01827 880754**   📠 **01827 881050**
web: www.battlefield-line-railway.co.uk
dir: located between Ashby-de-la-Zouch & Hinckley. Follow brown signs from A444 & A447

The Battlefield Line is the last remaining part of the former Ashby and Nuneaton Joint Railway which was opened in 1873. It runs from Shackerstone via Market Bosworth to Shenton in Leicestershire and is operated by the Shackerstone Railway Society. There are regular train trips to Bosworth battlefield with a variety of locomotives, steam and diesel-hauled trains and heritage railcars. Special events take place all year - please contact for details.

Times Open all year Sat, 12-5, Sun & BH Mon 10.30-5.30. Closed Xmas. Trains runs Etr-Oct, Santa trains Dec* **Facilities** 🅿 ☐ 🎪 (outdoor) ♿ (partly accessible) (not all carriages & parts of museum suitable for wheelchairs) toilets for disabled shop

TWYCROSS

Twycross Zoo

CV9 3PX
☎ **01827 880250**   📠 **01827 880700**
web: www.twycrosszoo.org
dir: on A444 Burton to Nuneaton road, directly off M42 junct 11

Twycross Zoo appeals to all ages and spans some 50 acres that are home to around 1000 animals, including the most comprehensive collection of primate species in the world. Twycross is the only zoo in Great Britain to house bonobos - humanity's 'closest living relative'. While at the zoo, visitors can visit a genuine Borneo Longhouse, brought to life in the Leicestershire countryside, where many exotic birds, animal species and traditional artefacts can be seen. See also the new Asian elephant walkway and a new children's area with adventure playground, rides for little explorers and pets from around the world.

Times Open all year, daily 10-5.30 (4 in winter). Closed 25 Dec. **Fees** £9.50 (ch £6, pen £7). Family Ticket £29.* **Facilities** 🅿 ☐ 🎪 (outdoor) ♿ toilets for disabled shop ⊗

LINCOLNSHIRE

BELTON

Belton House Park & Gardens

NG32 2LS
☎ **01476 566116**   📄 **01476 579071**
e-mail: belton@nationaltrust.org.uk
web: www.nationaltrust.org.uk
dir: 3m NE Grantham on A607

17th-century country house, set in its own extensive deer park, Belton was designed to impress with opulent décor, stunning silverware and fine furnishings. Delightful gardens, luxuriantly planted Orangery and lakeside walks are a pleasure to explore.

Times Open: House: 1-14 Mar, Sat & Sun 12.30-4.30; 15 Mar-Oct, Wed-Sun. Open BH Mon, 12.30-4.30. Garden: 6-28 Feb, Sat & Sun 12-4; Mar-Oct, Wed-Sun 10.30-5.30 (daily during Lincolnshire school hol Mar-Oct).* **Fees** With Gift Aid donation: House & garden £10.50 (ch £6.50). Family ticket £27.50. Grounds only £8.50 (ch £4.75) Family ticket £21.50.* **Facilities** ❷ 🗗🍴 licensed toilets for disabled shop ⊗ ♨

CLEETHORPES

Pleasure Island Family Theme Park

Kings Rd DN35 0PL
☎ **01472 211511**   📄 **01472 211087**
e-mail: reception@pleasure-island.co.uk
web: www.pleasure-island.co.uk
dir: M180 then A180, follow signs to park

Pleasure Island is packed with over seventy rides and attractions. Hold on tight as the colossal wheel of steel rockets you into the sky at a G-force of 2.5, then hurtles you around 360 degrees, sending riders into orbit and giving the sensation of complete weightlessness. It's not just grown ups and thrill seekers who are catered for at Pleasure Island. For youngsters there's hours of fun in Tinkaboo Town, an indoor themed area full of rides and attractions. There's also five family shows.

Times Open 4 Apr-Oct, daily from 10.30. Plus wknds during Sep-Oct. Park closed Mon-Tue during quiet times. Call for further info. **Fees** £16.50 (ch under 4 free, concessions £9.50). **Facilities** ❷ 🗗🍴 licensed ⊓ (outdoor) ♿ (partly accessible) (shops & restaurants are wheelchair accessible) toilets for disabled shop

GRIMSBY

Fishing Heritage Centre

Alexandra Dock DN31 1UZ
☎ **01472 323345**   📄 **01472 323555**
web: www.nelincs.gov.uk/leisure/museums
dir: follow signs off M180

Sign on as a crew member for a journey of discovery, and experience the harsh reality of life on board a deep sea trawler built inside the Centre. Through interactive games and displays, your challenge is to navigate the icy waters of the Arctic in search of the catch.

Times Open Nov-Apr, Mon-Fri 10-4, Wknds & BHs 11-9*
Facilities ❷ ℗ 🗗 toilets for disabled shop ⊗

GRIMSTHORPE

Grimsthorpe Castle

PE10 0LY
☎ **01778 591205**   📄 **01778 591259**
e-mail: ray@grimsthorpe.co.uk
web: www.grimsthorpe.co.uk
dir: on A151, 8m E of Colsterworth on A1

Seat of the Willoughby de Eresby family since 1516, the castle has a medieval tower and a Tudor quadrangular house with a Baroque north front by Vanbrugh. There are eight state rooms, two picture galleries, and an important collection of furniture, pictures and tapestries. There is also a family cycle trail, woodland adventure playground and ranger-guided tours of the park by minibus. A cycle hire service is in operation allowing visitors to explore trails in the park.

Times Open Apr-May, Sun, Thu & BH Mon; Jun-Sep, Sun-Thu. Park & Gardens 11-6. Castle 1-4.30. **Fees** Park & Gardens £4 (ch £2, concessions £3.50). Combined ticket with castle £9 (ch £3.50, concessions £8).* **Facilities** ❷ 🗗🍴 licensed ⊓ (outdoor) ♿ (partly accessible) (no wheelchair access to 1st floor) toilets for disabled shop

Lincolnshire

Museum of Lincolnshire Life   FREE

Burton Rd LN1 3LY
☎ 01522 528448   📠 01522 521264
e-mail: lincolnshirelife.museum@lincolnshire.gov.uk
web: www.lincolnshire.gov.uk/museumoflincolnshirelife
dir: 5 min walk from Lincoln Castle

A large and varied social history museum, where two centuries of Lincolnshire life are illustrated by enthralling displays of domestic implements, industrial machinery, agricultural tools and a collection of horse-drawn vehicles. The exciting and interactive Royal Lincolnshire Regiment Museum contains videos, an audio tour, and touch screen computers. Various events throughout the year.

Times Open all year, Apr-Sep, daily 10-4; Oct-Mar, Mon-Sat 10-4 (last admission 3.30). Closed 24-26 & 31 Dec, 1 Jan. **Facilities** 🅿️ ⓟ ⟐ ♿ toilets for disabled shop ⊗

Normanby Hall Country Park

Normanby DN15 9HU
☎ 01724 720588   📠 01724 721248
e-mail: normanby.hall@northlincs.gov.uk
web: www.northlincs.gov.uk/normanby
dir: 4m N of Scunthorpe off B1430

A whole host of activities and attractions are offered in the 300 acres of grounds that surround Normanby Hall, including riding, nature trails and a farming museum. Inside the Regency mansion the fine rooms are decorated and furnished in period style. There is a fully restored and working Victorian kitchen garden, and a Victorian walled garden selling a wide range of Victorian and other unusual plants, from barrows located at the gift shop and Farming Museum.

Times Open: Park all year, daily, 9-dusk. Walled garden, daily 10.30-5 (4 in winter). Hall & Farming Museum, Apr-Sep, daily 1-5.* **Fees** Mar-Sep £5 (ch £2.40, under 5s free, concessions £4.40). Family season ticket £19.* **Facilities** 🅿️ ⟐ ¹⁰¹ licensed ⟱ (outdoor) ♿ (partly accessible) (ground floor of Great Hall, walled garden, farming museum, cafe, giftshops & toilets accessible) toilets for disabled shop ⊗

Church Farm Museum

Church Road South PE25 2HF
☎ 01754 766658   📠 01754 898243
e-mail: churchfarmmuseum@lincolnshire.gov.uk
web: www.lincolnshire.gov.uk/churchfarmmuseum
dir: follow brown museum signs on entering Skegness

A farmhouse and outbuildings, restored to show the way of life on a Lincolnshire farm at the end of the 19th century, with farm implements and machinery plus household equipment on display. Temporary exhibitions are held in the barn and there is a restored timber-framed mud and stud cottage on site. Telephone for details of special events held throughout the season.

Times Open Apr-Oct, daily 10-4 (last entry 3.30).* **Fees** Free admission apart from special events. **Facilities** 🅿️ ⟐ ⟱ (outdoor) ♿ (partly accessible) (grounds accessible with care) toilets for disabled shop ⊗

Skegness Natureland Seal Sanctuary

North Pde PE25 1DB
☎ 01754 764345   📠 01754 764345
web: www.skegnessnatureland.co.uk
dir: N end of seafront

Natureland houses seals, penguins, tropical birds, aquarium and reptiles, as well as a pets' corner. Also free-flight tropical butterflies (Apr-Oct). Natureland is well known for its rescue of abandoned seal pups, and has successfully reared and returned to the wild a large number of them. The hospital unit incorporates a public viewing area, and a large seascape seal pool (with underwater viewing).

Times Open all year, daily at 10. Closing times vary according to season. Closed 25-26 Dec & 1 Jan. **Fees** £6.20 (ch £4, pen £5). Family ticket £18.40 (2ad+2ch)* **Facilities** ⓟ ⟐ ¹⁰¹ licensed ⟱ (outdoor) ♿ toilets for disabled shop

SPALDING

Butterfly & Wildlife Park

Long Sutton PE12 9LE
☎ 01406 363833 & 363209   🖹 01406 363182
e-mail: info@butterflyandwildlifepark@.co.uk
web: www.butterflyandwildlifepark.co.uk
dir: off A17 at Long Sutton

The Park contains one of Britain's largest walk-through tropical gardens, in which hundreds of butterflies from all over the world fly freely. The tropical gardens are also home to crocodiles, snakes and lizards. Outside are 15 acres of butterfly and bee gardens, wildflower meadows, nature trail, farm animals, a pets' corner and a large adventure playground. At The Lincolnshire Birds of Prey Centre, there are daily birds of prey displays. In the ant room visitors can observe leaf-cutting ants in their natural working habitat.

Times Open 15 Mar-2 Nov, daily 10-5. Sep & Oct 10-4*
Facilities ❷ ⛾ ㆑ (outdoor) ♿ toilets for disabled shop ⊗

STAMFORD

Burghley House

PE9 3JY
☎ 01780 752451   🖹 01780 480125
e-mail: burghley@burghley.co.uk
web: www.burghley.co.uk
dir: 1.5m off A1 at Stamford

This great Elizabethan palace, built by William Cecil, has all the hallmarks of that ostentatious period. The vast house is three storeys high and the roof is a riot of pinnacles, cupolas and paired chimneys in classic Tudor style. However, the interior was restyled in the 17th century, and the state rooms are now Baroque, with silver fireplaces, elaborate plasterwork and painted ceilings. These were painted by Antonio Verrio, whose Heaven Room is quite awe-inspiring. The Sculpture Garden is dedicated to exhibiting the best in contemporary sculpture, in pleasant surroundings.

Times Open 31 Mar-28 Oct, daily (ex Fri). Please telephone for details.* **Facilities** ❷ ⛾ ⏹ licensed ㆑ (outdoor) toilets for disabled shop ⊗

TATTERSHALL

Tattershall Castle

LN4 4LR
☎ 01526 342543
e-mail: tattershallcastle@nationaltrust.org.uk
web: www.nationaltrust.org.uk
dir: S of A153, 15m NE of Sleaford

Explore the six floors of this 130ft tall, rare red-brick medieval castle built by Ralph Cromwell, Lord Treasurer of England and one of the most powerful men in the country. Let the audio guide create a picture of what life was like at Tattershall Castle in the 15th century. Climb the 150 steps from the basement to the battlements and enjoy the magnificent views of the Lincolnshire countryside, then explore the grounds, moats, bridges and neighbouring church, also built by Ralph Cromwell.

Times Open 1-14 Mar & 3 Nov-16 Dec, Sat & Sun, 12-4; 15 Mar-1 Oct, Mon-Wed & Sat-Sun, 11-5.30; Open Good Fri 11-5.30.* **Fees** With Gift Aid donation: £5 (ch £2.50). Family ticket £12.50* **Facilities** ❷ ♿ (partly accessible) (ramped entrance, ground floor has ramp available. Many stairs to other floors. Some visitors may require assistance) toilets for disabled shop ⊗ ⚘

WOOLSTHORPE

Woolsthorpe Manor

23 Newton Way NG33 5PD
☎ 01476 862826   🖹 01476 860338
e-mail: woolsthorpemanor@nationaltrust.org.uk
web: www.nationaltrust.org.uk
dir: 7m S of Grantham, 1m W of A1

Isaac Newton was born in this modest manor house in the mid 1600s and he made many of his most important discoveries about light and gravity here. A complex figure, Newton notched up careers as diverse as Cambridge Professor and Master of the Royal Mint; spent years studying alchemy and the Bible as well as science, and was President of the Royal Society, which celebrates its 350th anniversary in 2010. You can still see the famous apple tree from Isaac's bedroom window and enjoy the brand new Discovery Centre which is opening at the start of 2010.

Times Open 27 Feb-29 Mar & 4-26 Oct, Sat & Sun 1-5; Apr-28 Jun & 2-27 Sep, Wed-Sun (open BHs) 1-5; 2 Jul-Aug, Sat & Sun 11-5; Wed-Fri, 1-5; 2 Oct -1 Nov, Fri-Sun 1-5* **Fees** With Gift Aid donation: £5.80 (ch £2.90). Family ticket £14.50* **Facilities** ❷ ♿ (partly accessible) (narrow doorways & small rooms, ramps available. Stairs to other floors. Grounds partly accessible, uneven & loose gravel paths, some steps) toilets for disabled shop ⊗ ⚘

LONDON

E2

Geffrye Museum

136 Kingsland Rd, Shoreditch E2 8EA
☎ **020 7739 9893** 📄 **020 7729 5647**
e-mail: info@geffrye-museum.org.uk
web: www.geffrye-museum.org.uk
dir: S end of Kingsland Rd A10 in Shoreditch between Cremer St & Pearson St

The only museum in the UK to specialise in the domestic interiors and furniture of the urban middle classes. Displays span the 400 years from 1600 to the present day, forming a sequence of period rooms which capture the nature of English interior style. The museum is set in elegant, 18th-century buildings, surrounded by delightful gardens including an award-winning walled herb garden and a series of historical gardens which highlight changes in town gardens from the 17th to 20th centuries. One of the museum's historic almshouses has been fully restored to its original condition and is open on selected days (ring for details). Each December, the museum's period rooms are decorated in authentic, festive style to reflect 400 years of Christmas traditions in English homes.

Times Open all year, Tue-Sat 10-5, Sun & BH Mon 12-5. Closed Mon, Good Fri, 24-26 Dec & New Year.* **Facilities** ℗ ⫪ licensed ⊓ (outdoor) ♿ toilets for disabled shop ⊗

V&A Museum of Childhood   FREE

Cambridge Heath Rd E2 9PA
☎ **020 8983 5200** 📄 **020 8983 5225**
e-mail: moc@vam.ac.uk
web: www.museumofchildhood.org.uk
dir: Underground - Bethnal Green

The V&A Museum of Childhood re-opened following an extensive transformation a few years ago. There is a stunning new entrance, fully updated galleries and displays, a brand new gallery and expanded public spaces. Galleries include Creativity, Moving Toys and Childhood Galleries. There is also a full programme of activities. Exhibitions include Sit Down, Seating for kids.

Times Open all year, daily 10-5.45. Closed 25-26 Dec & 1 Jan.
Facilities ℗ ⫪ ⊓ (outdoor) ♿ toilets for disabled shop ⊗

E9

Sutton House

2 & 4 Homerton High St E9 6JQ
☎ **020 8986 2264** 📄 **020 8525 9051**
e-mail: suttonhouse@nationaltrust.org.uk
web: www.nationaltrust.org.uk
dir: 10 min walk from Hackney Central train station

In London's East End, the building is a rare example of a Tudor red-brick house. Built in 1535 by Sir Ralph Sadleir, Principal Secretary of State for Henry VIII, the house has 18th-century alterations and later additions. There are regular exhibitions of contemporary art by local artists.

Times Open Feb-19 Dec, Thu-Sun & BH Mon, 12.30-4.30, closed Good Fri.* **Facilities** ℗ ⫪ ⊞ licensed ♿ (partly accessible) (wheelchair accessible on ground floor) toilets for disabled shop ⊗ ⚘

E14

Museum of London Docklands

No 1 Warehouse, West India Quay E14 4AL
☎ **020 7001 9844**
e-mail: info@museumoflondon.org.uk
web: www.museumoflondon.org.uk/docklands
dir: Signposted from West India Quay DLR

From Roman settlement to Docklands' regeneration, unlock the history of London's river, port and people, in this historic warehouse. Discover a wealth of objects from whale bones to WWII gas masks in state-of-the-art galleries, including Mudlarks, an interactive area for kids; Sailortown, an atmospheric recreation of 19th century riverside Wapping; and London, Sugar & Slavery, which reveals the city's involvement in the transatlantic slave trade.

Times Open all year, daily 10-6. Closed 24-26 Dec. **Fees** £5 (ch16 free, concessions £3)* **Facilities** ℗ ⫪ ⊞ licensed ⊓ (indoor) ♿ toilets for disabled shop ⊗

EC2

Bank of England Museum   FREE

Bartholomew Ln EC2R 8AH
☎ 020 7601 5545   🖷 020 7601 5808
e-mail: museum@bankofengland.co.uk
web: www.bankofengland.co.uk/museum
dir: museum housed in Bank of London, entrance in Bartholomew Lane. Bank underground, exit 2

The museum tells the story of the Bank of England from its foundation in 1694 to its role in today's economy. Interactive programmes with graphics and video help explain its many and varied roles. Popular exhibits include a unique collection of banknotes and a genuine gold bar, which may be handled.

Times Open all year, Mon-Fri 10-5. Closed wknds & BHs. Open on day of Lord Mayor's Show & Open House London **Facilities** Ⓟ ♿ toilets for disabled shop ⊗

Museum of London   FREE

150 London Wall EC2Y 5HN
☎ 0870 444 3851   🖷 0870 444 3853
e-mail: info@museumoflondon.org.uk
web: www.museumoflondon.org.uk
dir: Underground - St Paul's, Barbican. N of St Paul's Cathedral at the end of St Martins le Grand and S of the Barbican. S of Aldersgate St

Dedicated to the story of London and its people, the Museum of London exists to inspire a passion for London in all who visit it. As well as the permanent collection, the Museum has a varied exhibition programme with major temporary exhibitions and topical displays each year. There are also smaller exhibitions in the foyer gallery. A wide programme of lectures and events explore London's history and its evolution into the city of today.

Times Open all year, Mon-Sat 10-5.50, Sun 12-5.50. Last admission 5.30.* **Facilities** ❷ Ⓟ ❑ ⊓ toilets for disabled shop ⊗

EC3

The Monument

Monument St EC3R 8AH
☎ 020 7626 2717   🖷 020 7403 4477
e-mail: enquiries@towerbridge.org.uk
web: www.towerbridge.org.uk
dir: Underground - Monument

Designed by Wren and Hooke and erected in 1671-7, the Monument commemorates the Great Fire of 1666 which is reputed to have started in nearby Pudding Lane. The fire destroyed nearly 90 churches and about 13,000 houses. This fluted Doric column stands 202ft high (Pudding Lane is exactly 202ft from its base) and you can climb the 311 steps to a platform at the summit, and receive a certificate as proof of your athletic abilities.

Times Open all year, daily, 9.30-5.* **Facilities** ⊗

Tower of London

Tower Hill EC3N 4AB
☎ 0870 756 6060
web: www.hrp.org.uk
dir: Underground - Tower Hill

Perhaps the most famous castle in the world, the Tower of London has played a central part in British history. Discover the stories of this awesome fortress; from gruesome tales of torture and escape to fascinating traditions that can still be seen today. Learn the legend of the ravens and be dazzled by the Crown Jewels. Join a Yeoman Warder tour and listen to their captivating tales of pain and passion, treachery and torture, all delivered with a smile and a swagger!

Times Open all year, Mar-Oct, Sun-Mon 10-5.30, Tue-Sat 9-5.30 (last admission 5); Nov-Feb, Tue-Sat 9-4.30, Sun-Mon 10-4.30 (last admission 4). Closed 24-26 Dec & 1 Jan.* **Fees** £17 (ch £9.50 under 5s free, children must be accompanied by an adult) concessions: full-time student, over 60 with ID £14.50). Family ticket (2ad+3ch) £47.* **Facilities** Ⓟ ❑ ⦿ licensed toilets for disabled shop ⊗

N1

The London Canal Museum

12/13 New Wharf Rd N1 9RT
☎ 020 7713 0836   🖷 020 7689 6679
e-mail: info@canalmuseum.org.uk
web: www.canalmuseum.org.uk
dir: Underground - Kings Cross. Follow York Way along East side of King's Cross Stn, turn right at Wharfdale Rd, then left into New Wharf Rd

The museum covers the development of London's canals (particularly Regent's Canal), canal vessels and trade, and the way of life of the canal people. Housed in a former ice warehouse and stables, it also illustrates horse transport and the unusual trade of importing ice from Norway; there are two large ice wells under the floor. Facilities include temporary moorings, so you can arrive by boat if you want. There are regular special exhibitions, and special events include evening illustrated talks, towpath walks, and tunnel boat trips.

Times Open all year, Tue-Sun & BH Mon 10-4.30 (last admission 3.45), 1st Thu each mth 10-7.30. Closed 24-26 & 31 Dec. **Fees** £3 (ch £1.50, concessions £2, under 5s free). Groups 10+ **Facilities** Ⓟ ⊓ (indoor & outdoor) ♿ toilets for disabled shop ⊗

NW1

Madame Tussauds

Marylebone Rd NW1 5LR
☎ **0870 400 3000**
e-mail: csc@madame-tussauds.com
web: www.madame-tussauds.com
dir: Underground - Baker Street

Madame Tussaud's world-famous waxwork collection was founded in Paris in 1770, moved to England in 1802, and found a permanent home in London's Marylebone Road in 1884. The 21st century has brought new innovations and new levels of interactivity. Listen to Kylie Minogue whisper in your ear, become an A-list celeb in the 'Blush' nightclub, and take your chances in a high security prison populated by serial killers.

Times Open all year 9.30-5.30 (9-6 wknds/summer). Closed 25 Dec. **Fees** £25 (ch under 16 £21. (Includes entry into Stardome & The Wonderful World of Stars).* **Facilities** ℗ ⑩ licensed ♿ toilets for disabled shop ⊗

ZSL London Zoo

Regents Park NW1 4RY
☎ **020 7449 6231** 🖷 **020 7586 6177**
e-mail: marketing@zsl.org
web: www.zsl.org
dir: Underground - Camden Town or Regents Park

ZSL London Zoo is home to over 12,000 animals, insects, reptiles and fish. First opened in 1828, the Zoo can claim the world's first aquarium, insect and reptile house. Get closer to your favourite animals, learn about them at the keeper talks and watch them show off their skills at special events. Enjoy Gorilla Kingdom, a walk through the rainforest where you can get close to a group of Western Lowland gorillas. The newest exhibit is Giants of the Galapagos, featuring three Galapagos tortoises.

Times Open all year, daily from 10, (closing time dependant on time of year). Closed 25 Dec.* **Facilities** ℗ ℗ ⌨ ⑩ licensed ⊓ toilets for disabled shop ⊗

NW3

Kenwood House   FREE

Hampstead Ln NW3 7JR
☎ **020 8348 1286** 🖷 **020 7973 3891**
web: www.english-heritage.org.uk
dir: Underground - Hampstead

In splendid grounds beside Hampstead Heath, this outstanding neo-classical house contains one of the most important collections of paintings ever given to the nation. Works by Rembrandt, Vermeer, Turner, Gainsborough and Reynolds are all set against a backdrop of sumptuous rooms. Scenes from Notting Hill and Mansfield Park were filmed here.

Times Open all year, Apr-Mar, daily 11.30-4. Closed 24-26 Dec & 1 Jan. (The park stays open later, please see site notices).
Facilities ℗ ⌨ ⑩ licensed ⊓ toilets for disabled shop ⊞

NW9

Royal Air Force Museum London   FREE

Grahame Park Way, Colindale NW9 5LL
☎ **020 8205 2266** 🖷 **020 8358 4981**
e-mail: groups@rafmuseum.org
web: www.rafmuseum.org
dir: within easy reach of the A5, A41, M1 and North Circular A406 roads. Tube on Northern Line to Colindale. Rail to Mill Hill Broadway station. Bus route 303 passes the door

Take off to the Royal Air Force Museum London and soar through the history of aviation from the earliest balloon flights to the latest Eurofighter. This is a world-class collection of over 100 aircraft, aviation/wartime memorabilia and artefacts together with an impressive sound and light show that takes you back to the Battle of Britain. The Aeronauts Interactive Centre offers hands-on entertainment and education for all ages and includes cockpit controls, co-ordination tests, engine lifting, air speed, drop zone, pilot testing and more. The museum will celebrate the 70th anniversary Battle of Britain 11th to 12th September 2010, various other events throughout the year.

Times Open all year, daily 10-6. (Last admission 5.30). Closed 24-26 Dec, 1 & 11-15 Jan. **Facilities** ℗ ℗ ⌨ ⑩ licensed ⊓ (indoor & outdoor) ♿ toilets for disabled shop ⊗

SE1

Design Museum

Shad Thames SE1 2YD
☎ **0870 909 9009** 🖷 **0870 909 1909**
e-mail: info@designmuseum.org
web: www.designmuseum.org
dir: Turn off Tooley St onto Shad Thames. Underground - London Bridge or Tower Hill

The Design Museum is the first museum in the world to be dedicated to 20th and 21st century design. Since opening in 1989, it has won international acclaim for its ground-breaking exhibition and education programmes. As one of the leading museums of design, fashion and architecture, the Design Museum has a changing programme of exhibitions, combining insights into design history with innovative contemporary design.

Times Open all year, daily 10-5.45 (last entry 5.15). Closed 25-26 Dec.* **Fees** £7 (ch under 12 free, concessions £4)* **Facilities** ℗ ⌨ ⑩ licensed ♿ toilets for disabled shop ⊗

Florence Nightingale Museum

**St Thomas' Hospital, Gassiot House,
2 Lambeth Palace Rd SE1 7EW**
☎ **020 7620 0374** 🖷 **020 7928 1760**
e-mail: info@florence-nightingale.co.uk
web: www.florence-nightingale.co.uk
dir: Underground - Westminster, Waterloo. On the site of St Thomas' Hospital

Florence Nightingale needs no introduction, but this museum shows clearly that she was more than `The Lady with the Lamp'. Beautifully designed, the museum creates a setting in which a large collection of Florence's personal items including childhood souvenirs, her dress, furniture from her houses, and honours awarded to her in old age are displayed. There is a small military history collection of souvenirs from the Crimean War, including military medals and a military nursing uniform. The museum will be closed for refurbishment until Spring 2010.

Times Open all year, Mon-Fri 10-5; wknds & BHs 10-5. (Last admission 1hr before closing). Closed for refurbishment until Spring 2010. **Fees** £5.80 (ch & concessions £4.80). Family ticket £16 (2ad+ up to 5ch). Discounted rates for pre-booked groups of 15+.* **Facilities** 🅿 ♿ toilets for disabled shop ⊗

Golden Hinde Educational Trust

182 Pickfords Wharf, Clink St SE1 9DG
☎ **020 7403 0123** 🖷 **020 7407 5908**
e-mail: info@goldenhinde.org
web: www.goldenhinde.org
dir: On the Thames path between Southwark Cathedral and the new Globe Theatre

An authentic replica of the galleon in which Sir Francis Drake sailed around the world in 1577-1580. This ship has travelled over 140,000 miles, many more than the original. She is now permanently berthed on London's South Bank.

Times Open all year, daily 10-5.30. Visitors are advised to check opening times as they may vary due to closures for functions.* **Facilities** 🅿 ♿ (partly accessible) (stairs on main deck so no access to wheelchairs) shop ⊗

HMS Belfast

Morgans Ln, Tooley St SE1 2JH
☎ **020 7940 6300** 🖷 **020 7403 0719**
e-mail: hmsbelfast@iwm.org.uk
web: www.iwm.org.uk/hmsbelfast
dir: Underground - London Bridge/Tower Hill/Monument. Rail - London Bridge

Europe's last surviving big gun armoured warship from the Second World War, HMS Belfast was launched in 1938 and served in the North Atlantic and Arctic with the Home Fleet. She led the Allied naval bombardment of German positions on D-Day, and was saved for the nation in 1971. A tour of the ship will take you from the Captain's Bridge through nine decks to the massive Boiler and Engine Rooms. You can visit the cramped Mess Decks, Officers' Cabins, Galley, Sick Bay, Dentist and Laundry.

Times Open all year, daily. Mar-Oct 10-6 (last admission 5); Nov-Feb 10-5 (last admission 4). Closed 24-26 Dec.* **Fees** £10.70 (ch under 15 free, concessions £8.60).* **Facilities** 🖵 🍴 (indoor) ♿ (partly accessible) (wheelchair access to main decks, but not all decks) toilets for disabled shop ⊗

Imperial War Museum

Lambeth Rd SE1 6HZ
☎ **020 7416 5320 & 5321** 🖷 **020 7416 5374**
e-mail: mail@iwm.org.uk
web: www.iwm.org.uk
dir: Underground - Lambeth North, Elephant & Castle or Waterloo

Founded in 1917, this museum illustrates and records all aspects of the two World Wars and other military operations involving Britain and the Commonwealth since 1914. There are always special exhibitions and the programme of special and family events includes film shows and lectures. The museum also has an extensive film, photography, sound, document and art archive as well as a library, although some reference departments are open to the public by appointment only. In 2010 it will be 70 years since the Battle of Britain, and the introduction of rationing.

Times Open all year, daily 10-6. Closed 24-26 Dec.* **Fees** Free admission (charges apply for some temporary exhibitions)* **Facilities** 🅿 🖵 🍴 licensed 🍴 (indoor & outdoor) ♿ toilets for disabled shop ⊗

London

SE1 continued

London Aquarium

County Hall, Riverside Building, Westminster Bridge Rd SE1 7PB
☎ 020 7967 8000 ▤ 020 7967 8029
e-mail: info@londonaquarium.co.uk
web: www.londonaquarium.co.uk
dir: Underground-Waterloo & Westminster. On south bank next to Westminster Bridge, nr Big Ben & London Eye

The London Aquarium is one of Europe's largest displays of global aquatic life with over 350 species in over 50 displays, ranging from the mystical seahorse to the deadly stonefish. The huge Pacific display is home to a variety of jacks, stingrays and seven sharks. Come and witness the spectacular Atlantic feed where a team of divers hand-feed rays and native British sharks. The rainforest feed incorporates a frenzied piranha attack with the amazing marksmanship of the archerfish. There is also a range of education tours and literature to enhance any visit.

Times Open all year, daily 10-6. (Last admission 1hr before closing). Closed 25 Dec. Late opening over summer months.*
Facilities Ⓟ ⬚ toilets for disabled shop ⊗

London Eye

Riverside Building, County Hall, Westminster Bridge Rd SE1 7PB
☎ 0870 500 0600 ▤ 0870 990 8882
e-mail: customer.services@londoneye.com
web: www.londoneye.com
dir: Underground - Waterloo/Westminster

The London Eye is one of the most inspiring and visually dramatic additions to the London skyline. At 135m/443ft high, it is the world's tallest observation wheel, allowing you to see one of the world's most exciting cities from a completely new perspective. The London Eye takes you on a gradual, 30 minute, 360 degree rotation, revealing parts of the city, which are simply not visible from the ground. For Londoners and visitors alike, it is the best way to see London and its many celebrated landmarks. The London Eye provides the perfect location for private parties and entertaining, and offers a wide variety of 'in-flight' hospitality packages, like champagne and canapés, which are available to enjoy in the privacy of your own capsule.

Times Open all year, daily, Oct-May 10-8; Jun-Sep, 10-9. Closed 25 Dec & annual maintenance.* **Facilities** Ⓟ ⬚ toilets for disabled shop ⊗

Shakespeare's Globe Theatre Tours & Exhibition

21 New Globe Walk, Bankside SE1 9DT
☎ 020 7902 1500 ▤ 020 7902 1515
e-mail: info@shakespearesglobe.com
web: www.shakespeares-globe.org
dir: Underground - London Bridge, walk along Bankside. Mansion House, walk across Southwark Bridge. St Pauls, walk across Millennium Bridge

Guides help to bring England's theatrical heritage to life at the 'unparalleled and astonishing' recreation of this famous theatre. Discover what an Elizabethan audience would have been like, find out about the rivalry between the Bankside theatres, the bear baiting and the stews, hear about the penny stinkards and find out what a bodger is. Shakespeare's Globe Exhibition is the world's largest exhibition devoted to Shakespeare and the London in which he lived and worked. Housed beneath the reconstructed theatre, the exhibition explores the remarkable story of the Globe, and brings Shakespeare's world to life using a range of interactive display and live demonstrations.

Times Open all year, May-early Oct, daily 9-12 (1-5 Rose Theatre tour); Oct-Apr 10-5.* **Fees** £10.50 (ch 5-15 £6.50, pen & students £8.50). Family ticket (2ad+3ch) £28.* **Facilities** Ⓟ ⬚ ⑩ licensed ♿ toilets for disabled shop ⊗

Tate Modern

Bankside SE1 9TG
☎ 020 7887 8008 (info) & 8888 ▤ 020 7401 5052
e-mail: information@tate.org.uk
web: www.tate.org.uk
dir: Underground - Southwark, Blackfriars

This is the UK's largest museum of modern art and is housed in the impressive Bankside power station. Entrance to the permanent collection, which includes works from artists like Picasso, Warhol and Dalí, is free. Tate Modern also holds world-acclaimed temporary exhibitions as well as education programmes, events and activities.

Times Open all year, Sun-Thu 10-6 (last admission 5.15), Fri & Sat 10am-10pm (last admission 9.15). Closed 24-26 Dec.* **Facilities** Ⓟ ⬚ ⑩ licensed ♿ toilets for disabled shop ⊗

The Tower Bridge Exhibition

Tower Bridge Rd SE1 2UP
☎ **020 7940 3985** 📠 **020 7357 7935**
e-mail: enquiries@towerbridge.org.uk
web: www.towerbridge.co.uk
dir: Underground - Tower Hill or London Bridge

One of the capital's most famous landmarks, its glass-covered walkways stand 142ft above the Thames, affording panoramic views of the river. Much of the original machinery for working the bridge can be seen in the engine rooms. The Tower Bridge Exhibition uses state-of-the-art effects to present the story of the bridge in a dramatic and exciting fashion.

Times Open all year, Apr-Sep 10-6.30 (last ticket 5.30); Oct-Mar 9.30-5.30 (last ticket 5)* **Facilities** Ⓟ 🚻 toilets for disabled shop ⊗

Winston Churchill's Britain at War Experience

64/66 Tooley St SE1 2TF
☎ **020 7403 3171** 📠 **020 7403 5104**
e-mail: info@britainatwar.org.uk
web: www.britainatwar.co.uk
dir: mid way down Tooley St, between London Bridge & Tower Bridge. 2min walk from London Bridge Stn

Step back in time to the 1940s and experience a realistic adventure of life in war-torn London. Take the lift to the underground where many spent sleepless nights. Explore evacuation, food and clothes rationing, the blackout and much more. Uniforms, gas masks and tin helmets are available to try on and photography is allowed. Voted top World War Two tourist attraction.

Times Open all year, Apr-Oct 10-5; Nov-Mar 10-4.30.*
Fees £11.45 (ch under 5 free, ch 5-16 £5.50, concessions £6.50). Family £29 (2ad+2ch).* **Facilities** Ⓟ 🚻 toilets for disabled shop ⊗

SE9

Eltham Palace

Court Yard SE9 5QE
☎ **020 8294 2548 ex209** 📠 **020 8294 2621**
web: www.english-heritage.org.uk

Stephen and Virginia Courtauld's stunning country house shows the glamour and allure of 1930s Art Deco style and is a feast of luxurious design ideas. The house incorporates the medieval Great Hall and stunning moated gardens.

Times Open Apr-1 Nov, Sun-Wed 10-5; 2 Nov-20 Dec & Feb-Mar, Sun-Wed 11-4. Closed 21 Dec-Jan. **Fees** House & Garden: £8.30 (concessions £7.10, ch £4.20). Family ticket £20.80. Garden only: £5.30 (concessions £4.50, ch £2.70). Please call 0870 333 1181 for the most up to date prices and opening times when planning your visit. **Facilities** Ⓟ shop ⊗ 🚫🅿 ⊞

SE10

National Maritime Museum

Romney Rd SE10 9NF
☎ **020 8312 6565** 🖷 **020 8312 6632**
e-mail: RScates@nmm.ac.uk
web: www.nmm.ac.uk
dir: central Greenwich A206

Britain's seafaring history is displayed in this impressive modern museum. Themes include exploration and discovery, Nelson, trade and empire, passenger shipping and luxury liners, maritime London, costume, art and the sea, and the future of the sea. There are interactive displays for children.

Times Open all year, daily 10-5 Closed 24-26 Dec. (Partial closures 31 Dec, 1 Jan & Marathon day). **Fees** Free, except some special exhibtions. **Facilities** ℗ ⏇ ♔ (outdoor) ⅋ toilets for disabled shop ⊗

Royal Observatory Greenwich

Greenwich Park, Greenwich SE10 8XJ
☎ **020 8312 6565** 🖷 **020 8312 6632**
e-mail: bookings@nmm.ac.uk
web: www.nmm.ac.uk
dir: off A2, Greenwich Park, enter from Blackheath Gate only

Charles II founded the Royal Observatory in 1675 'for perfecting navigation and astronomy'. It stands at zero meridian longitude and is the original home of Greenwich Mean Time. Astronomy galleries and the Peter Harrison Planetarium house an extensive collection of historic timekeeping, astronomical and navigational instruments.

Times Open all year, daily 10-5. (Partial closures 31 Dec, 1 Jan and Marathon day) **Fees** Free, except for Planetarium shows from £6 (ch £4). **Facilities** ℗ ⏇ ♔ (outdoor) ⅋ (partly accessible) (narrow staircase to Octagon room) toilets for disabled shop ⊗

SE18

Firepower Royal Artillery Museum

Royal Arsenal, Woolwich SE18 6ST
☎ **020 8855 7755** 🖷 **020 8855 7100**
e-mail: info@firepower.org.uk
web: www.firepower.org.uk
dir: A205, right at Woolwich ferry onto A206, attraction signed

Firepower is the Royal Artillery Museum in the historic Royal Arsenal. It spans 2000 years of artillery and shows the development from Roman catapult to guided missile to self-propelled gun. Put science into action with touchscreen displays and be awed by the big guns.

Times Open all year, Wed-Sun & BHs 11-5.30. Phone for winter opening times.* **Facilities** ℗ ℗ ♔ toilets for disabled shop ⊗

Thames Barrier Information & Learning Centre

1 Unity Way SE18 5NJ
☎ **020 8305 4188** 🖷 **020 8855 2146**
e-mail: learningcentre@environment-agency.gov.uk
web: www.environment-agency.gov.uk
dir: Turn off A102(M) onto A206, turn onto Eastmoor St and follow signs

Spanning a third of a mile, the Thames Barrier is the world's largest movable flood barrier. The visitors' centre and exhibition on the South Bank explains the flood threat and the construction of this £535 million project, now valued at £1 billion. Each month a test closure of all ten gates, lasting over 2 hours, is carried out and the annual full day closure of all ten gates takes place in the autumn.

Times Open Apr-Sep, 10.30-4.30; Oct-Mar, 11-3.30. Closed 25 Dec-3 Jan. **Fees** £3.50 (ch £2, pen £3). **Facilities** ℗ ⏇ ♔ (outdoor) ⅋ toilets for disabled shop ⊗

SE23

The Horniman Museum & Gardens   FREE

London Rd, Forest Hill SE23 3PQ
☎ **020 8699 1872** 🖷 **020 8291 5506**
e-mail: enquiry@horniman.ac.uk **web:** www.horniman.ac.uk
dir: situated on A205

Founder Frederick Horniman, a tea merchant, gave the museum to the people of London in 1901. The collection covers the natural and cultural world including Natural History with displays on Vanishing Birds and African Worlds, The Music Gallery, which displays Britain's largest collection of musical instruments and the Centenary Gallery which showcases world cultures. There are 16 acres of gardens, and the museum hosts a variety of workshops and activities for all ages.

Times Open all year, daily 10.30-5.30. Closed 24-26 Dec. Gardens close at sunset.* **Facilities** ℗ ⏇ ♔ (outdoor) toilets for disabled shop ⊗

SW1

Buckingham Palace

Buckingham Palace Rd SW1A 1AA
☎ **020 7766 7300** 🖹 020 7930 9625
e-mail: bookinginfo@royalcollection.org.uk
web: www.royalcollection.org.uk
dir: Underground - Victoria, Green Park, St James' Park, entrance in Buckingham Palace Road

Buckingham Palace has been the official London residence of Britain's sovereigns since 1837. Today it serves as the home and office of Her Majesty The Queen. Its nineteen State Rooms, which open for eight weeks a year, form the heart of the working palace and more than 50,000 people visit each year as guests at State, ceremonial and official occasions and garden parties. After visiting the State Rooms, visitors can enjoy a walk along the south side of the garden, which offers superb views of the west front of the Palace and the 19th-century lake.

Times Open Aug-Sep 9.45-6 (last admission 3.45). Entry by timed-ticket. **Fees** £17 (ch under 17 £10, ch under 5 free, students & pen £15.50) Family (2ad+3ch) £45. **Facilities** ℗ ₕ toilets for disabled shop ⊗

Churchill Museum & Cabinet War Rooms

Clive Steps, King Charles St SW1A 2AQ
☎ **020 7930 6961** 🖹 020 7839 5897
e-mail: cwr@iwm.org.uk **web:** www.iwm.org.uk/cabinet
dir: Underground - Westminster (exit 6) or St James Park

Learn more about the man who inspired Britain's finest hour at the interactive and innovative Churchill Museum, the world's first major museum dedicated to the life of the 'Greatest Briton'. Step back in time and discover the secret underground headquarters that were the nerve centre of Britain's war effort. Located in the heart of Westminster, visitors can view this complex of historic rooms left as they were in 1945, while at the same time taking in the Churchill Museum.

Times Open all year, daily 9.30-6. (last admission 5). Closed 24-26 Dec.* **Facilities** ℗ 🚻 ₕ (partly accessible) (2 wheelchairs available) toilets for disabled shop ⊗

The Household Cavalry Museum

Horse Guards, Whitehall SW1A 2AX
☎ **020 7930 3070**
e-mail: museum@householdcavalry.co.uk
web: www.householdcavalrymuseum.org.uk
dir: Underground - Charing Cross, Embankment & Westminster

The Household Cavalry Museum is unlike any other military museum because it offers a unique 'behind-the-scenes' look at the work that goes into the ceremonial duties and operational role of the Household Cavalry. Watch troopers working with their horses in the original 18th-century stables (via a glazed screen) and hear accounts of their demanding training. Plus children's trails, activity packs and dressing up areas.

Times Open all year daily, Mar-Sep 10-6, Oct-Feb 10-5.* **Fees** £6 (ch 5-16 & concessions £4). Family ticket (2ad+3ch) £15. Group rate 10% discount.* **Facilities** ℗ ₕ toilets for disabled shop ⊗

The Queen's Gallery

Buckingham Palace, Buckingham Palace Rd SW1A 1AA
☎ **020 7766 7301** 🖹 020 7930 9625
e-mail: bookinginfo@royalcollection.org.uk
web: www.royalcollection.org.uk
dir: Underground - Victoria, Green Park & St. James' Park. Entrance in Buckingham Palace Road).

The Queen's Gallery is a permanent space dedicated to changing exhibitions of items from the Royal Collection, a wide-ranging collection of art, furniture, jewellery and other pieces held in trust by The Queen for the Nation.

Times Open all year, daily 10-5.30 (last admission 4.30). Closed 25-26 Dec. **Fees** £9 (ch under 5 free, ch under 17 £4.50 concessions £8). Family ticket (2ad+3ch) £23. **Facilities** ℗ ₕ toilets for disabled shop ⊗

The Royal Mews

Buckingham Palace, Buckingham Palace Rd SW1W 0QH
☎ **020 7766 7302** 🖹 020 7930 9625
e-mail: bookinginfo@royalcollection.org.uk
web: www.royalcollection.org.uk
dir: Underground - Victoria, Green Park, St. James Park. Entrance in Buckingham Palace Road

Designed by John Nash and completed in 1825, the Royal Mews houses the State Coaches, horse-drawn carriages and motor cars used for Coronations, State Visits, Royal Weddings and the State Opening of Parliament. These include the Gold State Coach made in 1762, with panels painted by the Florentine artist Cipriani. As one of the finest working stables in existence, the Royal Mews provides a unique opportunity for you to see a working department of the Royal Household.

Times Open daily ex Fri. Mar-Oct 11-4; Aug-Sep 10-5. (Last admission 3.15, Aug-Sep 4.15). **Fees** £8 (ch under 17 £5, ch under 5 free, concessions £7) Family (2ad+3ch) £21.50. **Facilities** ℗ ₕ toilets for disabled shop ⊗

SW1 continued

Tate Britain

Millbank SW1P 4RG
☎ **020 7887 8888 & rec info 8008**
e-mail: information@tate.org.uk
web: www.tate.org.uk
dir: Underground - Pimlico

Tate Britain is the national gallery of British art from 1500 to the present day, from Tudors to the Turner Prize. Tate holds the greatest collection of British art in the world, including works by Blake, Constable, Epstein, Gainsborough, Gilbert and George, Hatoum, Hirst, Hockney, Hodgkin, Hogarth, Moore, Rossetti, Sickert, Spencer, Stubbs and Turner. The gallery is the world centre for the understanding and enjoyment of British art.

Times Open all year, daily 10-5.50. Closed 24-26 Dec.* **Facilities** Ⓟ 🖥️🍽️ licensed 🍴 (indoor & outdoor) ♿ toilets for disabled shop ⊗

Westminster Abbey

Broad Sanctuary SW1P 3PA
☎ **020 7222 5152 & 7654 4900** 📄 **020 7233 2072**
e-mail: info@westminster-abbey.org
web: www.westminster-abbey.org
dir: Underground - Westminster, St James's Park. Next to Parliament Square and opposite the Houses of Parliament

Westminster Abbey was originally a Benedictine monastery. In the 11th century, it was re-founded by St Edward the Confessor. The great Romanesque abbey Edward built next to his royal palace became his burial place shortly after it was completed. Over the centuries that followed, many more kings and queens have been buried, and many great figures commemorated, in the abbey. The abbey has been the setting for nearly every coronation since that of William the Conqueror in 1066, and for numerous other royal occasions. The present building, begun by Henry III in 1245, is one of the most visited churches in the world.

Times Open all year, Mon-Fri 9.30-3.45, Sat 9-1.45. Wed late night til 7. (Last admission 1hr before closing). No tourist visiting on Sun, however visitors are welcome at services. The Abbey may at short notice be closed for special services & other events.* **Facilities** Ⓟ 🖥️♿ (partly accessible) toilets for disabled shop ⊗

SW3

National Army Museum   FREE

Royal Hospital Rd, Chelsea SW3 4HT
☎ **020 7730 0717** 📄 **020 7823 6573**
e-mail: info@national-army-museum.ac.uk
web: www.national-army-museum.ac.uk
dir: Underground - Sloane Square

The museum will guide you through Britain's Military History and its effect on Britain and the world today. Permanent gallery displays, exhibitions, celebrity speakers, lectures and special events will both engage and entertain you.

Times Open all year, daily 10-5.30. Closed Good Fri, May Day, 24-26 Dec & 1 Jan.* **Facilities** Ⓟ Ⓟ 🖥️♿ toilets for disabled shop ⊗

SW7

The Natural History Museum

Cromwell Rd SW7 5BD
☎ **020 7942 5000** 📄 **020 7942 5075**
e-mail: feedback@nhm.ac.uk
web: www.nhm.ac.uk
dir: Underground - South Kensington

This vast and elaborate Romanesque-style building, with its terracotta tiles showing relief mouldings of animals, birds and fishes, covers an area of four acres. Holding over 70 million specimens from all over the globe, from dinosaurs to diamonds and earthquakes to ants, the museum provides a journey into Earth's past, present and future. Discover more about the work of the museum through a daily programme of talks from museum scientists or go behind the scenes of the Darwin Centre, the museum's scientific research centre.

Times Open all year, daily 10-5.50 (last admission 5.30). Closed 24-26 Dec. **Fees** Free. Charge made for some special exhibitions. **Facilities** Ⓟ 🖥️🍽️ licensed 🍴 (indoor) ♿ (partly accessible) (top floor/one gallery not accessible) toilets for disabled shop ⊗

Science Museum

Exhibition Rd, South Kensington SW7 2DD
☎ 0870 870 4868 📄 020 7942 4421
e-mail: sciencemuseum@sciencemuseum.org.uk
web: www.sciencemuseum.org.uk
dir: Underground - South Kensington, signed from tube stn

See iconic objects from the history of science, from Stephenson's Rocket to the Apollo 10 command module; be amazed by a 3D IMAX movie; take a ride in a simulator; visit an exhibition; and encounter the past, present and future of technology in seven floors of free galleries, including the famous hands-on section where children can have fun investigating science with the Museum's dedicated Explainers. The Museum is free, but charges apply to the IMAX cinema, special exhibitions and simulators.

Times Open all year, daily 10-6. Closed 24-26 Dec.
Fees Admission free. Charges apply for IMAX 3D cinema, simulators & some special exhibitions. **Facilities** Ⓟ ⛝ 🍽 licensed ⋒ (indoor) ♿ toilets for disabled shop ⊗

Victoria and Albert Museum

Cromwell Rd, South Kensington SW7 2RL
☎ 020 7942 2000
e-mail: vanda@vam.ac.uk
web: www.vam.ac.uk
dir: Underground - South Kensington, Museum situated on A4, Buses C1, 14, 74, 414 stop outside the Cromwell Road entrance

The V&A is the world's greatest museum of art and design. It was established in 1852 to make important works of art available to all, and also to inspire British designers and manufacturers. The Museum's rich and diverse collections span over three thousand years of human creativity from many parts of the world, and include ceramics, furniture, fashion, glass, jewellery, metalwork, sculpture, textiles and paintings. Highlights include the British Galleries 1500-1900, the Jameel Gallery of Islamic Art, and the magnificent John Madejski Garden.

Times Open all year, daily 10-5.45. Fri 10am-10pm* **Facilities** Ⓟ ⛝ 🍽 licensed ⋒ (outdoor) toilets for disabled shop ⊗

SW13

London Wetland Centre

Queen Elizabeth Walk SW13 9WT
☎ 020 8409 4400 📄 020 8409 4401
e-mail: info.london@wwt.org.uk
web: www.wwt.org.uk
dir: A306 (underground - Hammersmith)

An inspiring wetland landscape that stretches over 105 acres, almost in the heart of London. Thirty wild wetland habitats have been created from reservoir lagoon to ponds, lakes and reedbeds and all are home to a wealth of wildlife. The visitor centre includes a café, gift shop, cinema, large glass viewing observatory and optics shop. There is a new Explore adventure centre for 3-11s. The Centre will be celebrating its 10th anniversary in 2010.

Times Openall year: winter 9.30-5 (last admission 4); summer 9.30-6 (last admission 5).* **Fees** £9.50 (ch £5.25, concessions £7.10). Family ticket £26.55. **Facilities** Ⓟ ⛝ 🍽 licensed ⋒ (outdoor) ♿ toilets for disabled shop ⊗

SW19

Wimbledon Lawn Tennis Museum

Museum Building, The All England Club, Church Rd SW19 5AE
☎ 020 8946 6131 📄 020 8947 8752
e-mail: museum@aeltc.com
web: www.wimbledon.org/museum
dir: Underground - Southfields, 15mins walk. By road - from central London take A3 Portsmouth road, just before Tibbet's Corner left onto A219 towards Wimbledon, down Parkside, left onto Church Rd

Visitors to the Wimbledon Lawn Tennis Museum are invited to explore the game's evolution from a garden party pastime to a multi-million dollar professional sport played worldwide. Highlights include the Championship Trophies, a cinema that captures the Science of Tennis using CGI special effects, film and video footage of some of the most memorable matches, an extensive collection of memorabilia dating back to 1555, and a holographic John McEnroe who walks through a recreated 1980s changing room.

Times Open all year, daily 10-5. Closed middle Sun of Championships, Mon immediately following the Championships, 24-26 Dec & 1 Jan. **Fees** £10 (ch £5.50, ch under 5 free, concessions £8.75). Party 15+. **Facilities** Ⓟ Ⓟ ⛝ ♿ toilets for disabled shop ⊗

W1

Apsley House, The Wellington Museum

148 Piccadilly, Hyde Park Corner WIJ 7NT
☎ 020 7499 5676   📄 020 7493 6576
web: www.english-heritage.org.uk
dir: Underground - Hyde Park Corner, exit 1 overlooking rdbt

Number One, London, is the popular name for one of the Capital's finest private residences, 19th-century home of the first Duke of Wellington. Built in the 1770s, its rich interiors have been returned to their former glory, and house the Duke's magnificent collection of paintings, silver, porcelain, sculpture and furniture.

Times Open all year Apr-1 Nov, Wed-Sun & BHs 11-5; 2 Nov-Mar, Wed-Sun 11-4. Closed 24-26 Dec & 1 Jan. **Fees** £5.70 (ch £2.90, concessions £4.80). Please call 0870 333 1181 for the most up to date prices and opening times. **Facilities** ℗ shop ⊗ ♿

Pollock's Toy Museum

1 Scala St W1T 2HL
☎ 020 7636 3452
e-mail: pollocks@btconnect.com
web: www.pollockstoytheatre.com
dir: Underground - Goodge St

Teddy bears, wax and china dolls, dolls' houses, board games, toy theatres, tin toys, mechanical and optical toys, folk toys and nursery furniture, are among the attractions to be seen in this appealing museum. Items from all over the world and from all periods are displayed in two small, interconnecting houses with winding staircases and charming little rooms.

Times Open all year, Mon-Sat 10-5. Closed BH, Sun & Xmas.*
Facilities ℗ ♿ (partly accessible) shop

Royal Academy Of Arts

Burlington House, Piccadilly W1J 0BD
☎ 020 7300 5729   📄 020 7300 8032
e-mail: maria.salvatierra@royalacademy.org.uk
web: www.royalacademy.org.uk
dir: Underground - Piccadilly Circus, head towards Green Park

Known principally for international loan exhibitions, the Royal Academy of Arts was founded in 1768 and is Britain's oldest Fine Arts institution. Two of its founding principles were to provide a free school and to mount an annual exhibition open to all artists of distinguished merit, now known as the Summer Exhibition. The Royal Academy's most prized possession, Michelangelo's Taddei Tondo, 'The Virgin and Child with the Infant St John', one of only four marble sculptures by the artist outside Italy, is on permanent display in the Sackler Wing. The John Madejski Fine Rooms are a suite of six rooms displaying the highlights from the RA collection.

Times Open all year, daily 10-6. Late night opening Fri 10am-10pm. Closed 24-25 Dec. **Fees** £7-£12 (ch, concessions & group visitors reduced price). Prices vary for each exhibition. Free entry to permanent collection. **Facilities** ℗ ⊡ 🍴 licensed ♿ toilets for disabled shop ⊗

The Wallace Collection   FREE

Hertford House, Manchester Square W1U 3BN
☎ 020 7563 9500   📄 020 7224 2155
e-mail: visiting@wallacecollection.org
web: www.wallacecollection.org
dir: Underground - Bond St, Baker St, Oxford Circus, located minutes from Oxford St, in garden square behind Selfridges

Founded by the 1st Marquis of Hertford, the Wallace Collection was bequeathed to the nation in 1897 and came on public display three years later. This is one of the world's finest collections of art ever assembled by one family. The collection is shown in the family home, a tranquil oasis just a few minutes from Oxford Street. There are paintings by Titian, Canaletto, Rembrandt, Rubens, Hals, Fragonard, Velazquez, Gainsborough and many more. There is a very important collection of French porcelain and furniture, much of it of Royal providence, as well as amazing arms and armour, sculpture and Renaissance treasures. Many rooms have been recently restored creating wonderful intimate and opulent settings for the works of art.

Times Open all year, daily 10-5, closed 24-26 Dec & 1 Jan.*
Facilities ℗ ⊡ 🍴 licensed ♿ toilets for disabled shop ⊗

W8

Kensington Palace State Apartments & Royal Ceremonial Dress Collection

Kensington Gardens W8 4PX
☎ 0844 482 7777   📠 020 3166 6110
e-mail: kensingtonpalace@hrp.org.uk
web: www.hrp.org.uk
dir: Underground - High Street Kensington or Notting Hill Gate

Highlights of a visit to Kensington include the King's and Queen's Apartments with a fine collection of paintings from the Royal Collection. The rooms used by Princess Victoria are also shown, including her bedroom, where she was woken to be told she was Queen. The Royal Ceremonial Dress Collection includes representations of tailor's and dressmaker's workshops, and a display of dresses that belonged to Diana, Princess of Wales. Kensington Palace will undergo a major re-presentation with work commencing in 2010.

Times Open all year, Mar-Oct 10-6, Nov-Feb 10-5 (last admission 1hr before closing). Closed 24-26 Dec. **Fees** £12.50 (ch 5-16 £6.25, concessions £11). Family ticket (2ad+3ch) £34.* **Facilities** ℗ 🚻♿ (partly accessible) (ground floor & lower ground floor accessible) toilets for disabled shop ⊗

W11

Museum of Brands, Packaging & Advertising

2 Colville Mews, Lonsdale Rd W11 2AR
☎ 020 7908 0880   📠 020 7908 0950
e-mail: info@museumofbrands.com
web: www.museumofbrands.com
dir: A4026 signed Notting Hill. From Westbourne Grove turn onto Ledbury Rd then left onto Lonsdale Rd

Featuring over 12,000 original items from the Robert Opie Collection, MOBPA details the history of consumer culture, revealed decade by decade in the "time tunnel", from Victorian times to the present day. Exhibits include all aspects of daily cultural consumer life, from washing power packaging to newspapers, from radio and television to the rise of trains and planes. Regular changing exhibitions.

Times Open all year, Tue-Sat, 10-6, Sun & BH Mon, 11-5. Closed 25 Dec & Notting Hill carnival 29-30 Aug 2010 (dates to be confirmed). **Fees** £5.80 (ch 7-16 £2, ch under 7 free, concessions £3.50) Group discount 10%. (adult price includes gift aid donation).* **Facilities** ℗ 🚻♿ toilets for disabled shop ⊗

W12

BBC Television Centre Tours

BBC Television Centre, Wood Ln W12 7RJ
☎ 0370 603 0304   📠 020 8576 7466
e-mail: bbctours@bbc.co.uk
web: www.bbc.co.uk/tours
dir: Underground - Central Line/White City

On a tour of BBC Television Centre you will see behind the scenes of the most famous TV Centre in the world. You may see studios, the News Centre, Weather Centre, the interactive studio, and dressing rooms, but due to the operational nature of the building guarantees cannot be made. The CBBC Experience is aimed at 7-12 year olds - visit the Blue Peter Garden, have fun making a programme in the interactive studio, take part in the Raven challenge, and become 'Diddy Dick & Dom'. Both tours last up to two hours. Tours of Broadcasting House run weekly on Sundays. The UK's first purpose-built broadcast centre has been undergoing a major restoration and modernisation as part of a ten year development project. Tours are fitted round the working building's activities and you will see a range of areas such as the newly restored radio theatre, the council chamber and an interactive radio drama experience. Please telephone for details.

Times Open all year, Mon-Sat 10-6. Tours at 10, 10.20, 10.40, 1.15, 1.30, 1.45, 3.30, 3.45 & 4. Closed Xmas & BHs. All tours must be pre-booked. Also tours at 11, 2, 4.15 Mon-Fri. **Fees** £9.50 (ch & students £7, concessions £8.50). Family £27. **Facilities** ℗ ♿ toilets for disabled shop ⊗

WC1

British Museum

Great Russell St WC1B 3DG
☎ 020 7323 8000   📠 020 7323 8616
e-mail: information@britishmuseum.org
web: www.thebritishmuseum.ac.uk
dir: Underground - Russell Sq, Tottenham Court Rd, Holborn

Of the world and for the world, the British Museum brings together astounding examples of universal heritage, for free. Enter through the largest covered square in Europe. Pick up your audio guide, children's pack or What's On programme. Then discover the world through objects like the Aztec mosaics, the Rosetta Stone, El Anatsui's African textiles or the colossal Ramesses II. And if you want a more intimate look, a fantastic evening meal or some world cinema, come late - every Thursday and Friday.

Times Open all year, Gallery: 10-5.30 selected galleries open late Thu-Fri until 8.30. Great Court: Sun-Wed 9-6, Thu-Sat 9am-11pm. Closed Good Fri, 24-26 Dec & 1 Jan.* **Facilities** ℗ 🚻 🍴 licensed 🍽 (indoor) toilets for disabled shop ⊗

WC1 continued

The Cartoon Museum

35 Little Russell St WC1A 2HH
☎ **020 7580 8155** 📄 **020 7631 0793**
e-mail: info@cartoonmuseum.org
web: www.cartoonmuseum.org
dir: left off New Oxford St into Museum St, then left into Little
Russell St

The main galleries display over 200 original cartoons, comics,
cartoon strips and caricatures by many of the greatest and
funniest of British cartoonists past and present. There is also a
programme of temporary exhibitions which change regularly.

Times Open all year Tue-Sat 10.30-5.30, Sun 12-5.30.*
Facilities ℗ ♿ (partly accessible) (only ground floor acessible to
wheelchairs) toilets for disabled shop ⊗

WC2

London Transport Museum

The Piazza, Covent Garden WC2E 7BB
☎ **020 7379 6344** & **7565 7299** 📄 **020 7565 7250**
e-mail: enquiry@ltmuseum.co.uk
web: www.ltmuseum.co.uk
dir: Underground - Covent Garden, Leicester Sq, Holborn or
Charing Cross

Situated in the old Victorian flower market, London Transport
Museum tells the story of the development of London, its
transport system and how it shaped the lives of people living
and working in the Capital. One of the world's best collections
of graphic art and design is showcased in the 'Design for
Travel' gallery including Harry Beck's famous Underground
map, iconic transport posters, architecture and the story of a
pioneering corporate identity. The museum also features past
and present public transport including the Routemaster bus
and the world's first Underground steam train.

Times Open all year Sat-Thu 10-6, Fri 11-6 (last admission
5.15). See website for Xmas & New Year opening times.*
Fees With voluntary Gift Aid donation: £10 (under 16 free, pen
£8, concessions £6).* **Facilities** ℗ ⊑ 🍴 (indoor) ♿ toilets for
disabled shop ⊗

National Gallery

Trafalgar Square WC2N 5DN
☎ **020 7747 2885** 📄 **020 7747 2423**
e-mail: information@ng-london.org.uk
web: www.nationalgallery.org.uk
dir: Underground - Charing Cross, Leicester Square, Embankment
& Piccadilly Circus. Rail - Charing Cross. Located on N side of
Trafalgar Sq

All the great periods of Western European painting from the
Middle Ages to the early 20th century are represented here.
Artists on display include Leonardo da Vinci, Rembrandt, Titian,
Caravaggio, Turner, Monet and Van Gogh. Major exhibitions
and events throughout the year.

Times Open all year, daily 10-6, (Fri until 9). Special major
changing exhibitions open normal gallery times. Closed 24-26
Dec & 1 Jan. **Fees** Free. Admission charged for some major
exhibitions. **Facilities** ℗ ⊑ 🍴 licensed ♿ toilets for disabled
shop ⊗

National Portrait Gallery

St Martin's Place WC2H 0HE
☎ **020 7306 0055** 📄 **020 7306 0056**
web: www.npg.org.uk
dir: Underground - Charing Cross, Leicester Square. Buses to
Trafalgar Square

The National Portrait Gallery is home to the largest collection
of portraiture in the world featuring famous British men and
woman who have created history from the Middle Ages until
the present day. Over 1000 portraits are on display across three
floors from Henry VIII and Florence Nightingale to The Beatles
and HM The Queen. If you want to rest your weary feet, visit
the fabulous Portrait Restaurant on the top floor with roof-top
views across London. Special events take place throughout the
year, see website for details.

Times Open all year, Mon-Wed & Sat-Sun 10-6, Thu-Fri 10-9.
Closed Good Fri, 24-26 Dec & 1 Jan. (Gallery closure commences
10mins prior to stated time).* **Fees** Free ex special exhibitions
Facilities ℗ ⊑ 🍴 licensed ♿ toilets for disabled shop ⊗

GREATER LONDON

BARNET

Museum of Domestic Design & Architecture

Middlesex University, Cat Hill EN4 8HT
☎ 020 8411 5244　▤ 020 8411 6639
e-mail: moda@mdx.ac.uk
web: www.moda.mdx.ac.uk
dir: from M25, junct 24 signed A111 Cockfosters to Cat Hill rdbt, straight over onto Chase side. Entrance 1st right opposite Chicken Shed Theatre on Cat Hill Campus

MoDA is a museum of the history of the home. It holds one of the world's most comprehensive collections of decorative design for the period 1870 to 1960, and is a rich source of information on how people decorated and lived in their homes. MoDA has two galleries, a lecture theatre for study days, a seminar room with practical workshops for both adults and children, and a study room which gives visitors access to the collections.

Times Open all year, Tue-Sat 10-5, Sun 2-5. Closed Mon, Etr, Xmas & New Year. **Fees** Free entrance. Charges for study days, workshop & group tours **Facilities** ❷ & toilets for disabled shop ⊗

CHESSINGTON

Chessington World of Adventures

Leatherhead Rd KT9 2NE
☎ 0871 663 4477
web: www.chessington.com
dir: M25 junct 9/10, on A243

Explore Chessington - it's a whole world of adventures! Soar on the Vampire roller coaster through the depths of Transylvania, take a fiery spin round Dragon's Fury or discover the mystery of Tomb Blaster in Forbidden Kingdom. Take a walk on the wild side with tigers, lions and gorillas in the Trail of the Kings and come face to face with sharks and curious stingrays in the park's very own Sea Life Centre - all in one place!

Times Open 28 Mar-2 Nov, times vary (main season). Zoo only days wknds from 7 Nov & daily from 12-31 Dec 10-3. Closed 25 Dec.* **Fees** Prices not confirmed for 2010. Please telephone for details. **Facilities** ❷ ▭ ⑪ licensed ⋒ (outdoor) & toilets for isabled shop ⊗

CHISLEHURST

Chislehurst Caves

Old Hill BR7 5NL
☎ 020 8467 3264　▤ 020 8295 0407
e-mail: enquiries@chislehurstcaves.co.uk
web: www.chislehurstcaves.co.uk
dir: off A222 near Chislehurst railway stn. Turn into station approach, then right & right again into Caveside Close

Miles of mystery and history beneath your feet. Grab a lantern and get ready for an amazing adventure. Visit the caves and your whole family can travel back in time as you explore the maze of passageways dug through the chalk deep beneath Chislehurst. Accompanied by an experienced guide on a 45-minute tour you'll see the tunnels made famous as a shelter during the Second World War, visit the cave's church, druid altar, the haunted pool and much more.

Times Open all year, Wed-Sun, 10-4. Daily during local school hols (incl half terms). Closed Xmas. **Fees** £5 (ch & pen £3). **Facilities** ❷ ▭ ⑪ licensed ⋒ (outdoor) & (partly accessible) (Uneven floors in the caves may cause some difficulties) toilets for disabled shop ⊗

HAM

Ham House & Garden

Ham St TW10 7RS
☎ 020 8940 1951 ▤ 020 8940 1950
e-mail: hamhouse@nationaltrust.org.uk
web: www.nationaltrust.org.uk/hamhouse
dir: W of A307, between Kingston & Richmond

Ham House is a fine example of 17th-century fashion and power. Built in 1610, the house was enlarged in the 1670s by the Duchess of Lauderdale, when it was at the heart of Restoration court life and intrigue. It was then occupied by the same family until 1948. The formal garden is significant for its survival in an area known as the cradle of the English Landscape Movement. The outbuildings include an orangery, an ice house, a still house (a 17th-century equivalent of an in-house pharmacy), and a dairy with unusual cast-iron "cow's legs". Open-air theatre and ghost tours, contact for details. The house and gardens celebrates its 400th anniversary in 2010 and a wide range of events are planned.

Times House 13 Feb-28 Feb, Sat-Wed 12-4; 1-12 Mar, Sat-Sun 12-4; 13 Mar-Oct, Sat-Wed 12-4. Garden, shop, cafe Jan-7 Feb, Sat-Sun 11-4; 13 Feb-Oct ,Sat-Wed 11-5; Nov-19 Dec, Sat-Sun 11-5. Close 1 Jan. Open Good Fri (normal opening times). Last admission 30mins before closing time. **Fees** House & Garden* £10.40 (ch £5.80). Family ticket £26.60. Garden only £3.50 (ch £2.35). Family ticket £9.25. Groups £8 (£14 outside normal opening hours). **Facilities** 🅿 Ⓟ ⬚ ⊼ (outdoor) ♿ (partly accessible) (onsite lift suitable for most manual wheelchairs) toilets for disabled shop ⊗ ✿

HAMPTON COURT

Hampton Court Palace

KT8 9AU
☎ 0870 752 7777 ▤ 020 8781 9669
e-mail: hamptoncourt@hrp.org.uk
web: www.hrp.org.uk
dir: A3 to Hook underpass then A309. Train from Waterloo - Hampton Court, 2mins walk from station

Step into a living Tudor world at Henry VIII's favourite palace, celebrating the 500th anniversary of his accession to the throne. As part of our Henry VIII: heads and hearts festivities the palace is hosting a fantastic variety of exciting daily events for all ages. Join Henry as his Tudor Kitchens fire up to prepare a king's feast and be a guest at his royal wedding, to his 6th wife! Creep along the eerie Haunted Gallery, relax in the acres of beautiful gardens running alongside the River Thames, and lose yourself in the world famous Maze.

Times Open all year, palace & maze 29 Mar-24 Oct, daily 10-6. Last ticket sold at 5, last entry into the maze 5.15 ; 25 Oct -27 Mar, daily 10-4.30. Last ticket sold at 3.30, last entry into the maze: 3.45. Closed 24-26 Dec.* **Fees** £14 (ch £7 under 5's free, children must be accompanied by an adult, concessions full-time student, over 60 with ID £11.50). Family ticket (2ad+3ch) £38.*
Facilities 🅿 Ⓟ ⬚ †⊚† licensed ⊼ ♿ toilets for disabled shop ⊗

ISLEWORTH

Syon Park

TW8 8JF
☎ 020 8560 0882 ▤ 020 8568 0936
e-mail: info@syonpark.co.uk
web: www.syonpark.co.uk
dir: A310 Twickenham road into Park Rd

Contained within the 40 acres that make up Syon Park Gardens is one of the inspirations for the Crystal Palace at the Great Exhibition of 1851: a vast crescent of metal and glass, the first construction of its kind in the world and known as the Great Conservatory. Although the horticultural reputation of Syon Park goes back to the 16th century, its beauty today is thanks to the master of landscape design, `Capability' Brown.

Times Open all year, Mar-Oct daily, 10.30-5.30; (4pm Nov-Feb, wkends & 1 Jan)* **Facilities** 🅿 ⬚ toilets for disabled shop ⊗

KEW

Kew Gardens (Royal Botanic Gardens)

TW9 3AB
☎ 020 8332 5655   📄 020 8332 5197
e-mail: info@kew.org
web: www.kew.org
dir: 1m from M4 on South Circular (A205)

Kew Gardens is a paradise throughout the seasons. Lose yourself in the magnificent glasshouses and discover plants from the world's deserts, mountains and oceans. Wide-open spaces, stunning vistas, listed buildings and wildlife contribute to the Gardens' unique atmosphere. As well as being famous for its beautiful gardens, Kew is world renowned for its contribution to botanical and horticultural science.

Times Open all year, Gardens daily 9.30. Closing times vary (seasonal, phone to verify). Closed 24-25 Dec.* **Fees** £13 (ch under 17 free, concessions £11).* **Facilities** 🅿 🅟 ▭ ⑩ licensed ♿ (partly accessible) (access restricted in Palm House basement & galleries, Temperate House & steps to upper level in the Princess of Wales Conservatory) toilets for disabled shop ⊗

Kew Palace

Royal Botanic Gardens TW9 3AB
☎ 0870 751 5179
e-mail: kewpalace@hrp.org.uk
web: www.hrp.org.uk
dir: Underground - Kew Bridge

A fairly modest red-brick building, built in the Dutch style with gables, Kew Palace was built in 1631 and used until 1818 when Queen Charlotte died. Visitors can see artefacts that belonged to George III and his family, and gain access to the second floor, which has never before been open to the public. There are also rooms on the second floor, faithfully recreated with décor and furnishings as George III and his family would have known them in the early 1800s.

Times Open 10 Apr-27 Sep, Mon 11-5, Tue-Sun 10-5 (last admission 4.15).* **Fees** £5 (ch under 16 free, concessions full-time student, over 60 with ID £4.50) Admission ticket to Kew Gardens must be purchased in order to access Kew Palace* **Facilities** 🅿 🅟 ♿ toilets for disabled shop ⊗

OSTERLEY

Osterley Park and House

Jersey Rd TW7 4RB
☎ 020 8232 5050   📄 020 8232 5080
e-mail: osterley@nationaltrust.org.uk
web: www.nationaltrust.org.uk/osterley
dir: signed from A4. Underground - Osterley

This spectacular mansion and its surrounding gardens, park and farmland is one of the last surviving country estates in London. Transformed in the late 18th century for the wealthy Child family by the architect Robert Adam, the house and garden were designed for entertaining and impressing this banking family's friends and clients. With a series of stunning show rooms affording views over extensive parkland, Osterley continues to impress visitors today. The gardens are currently being restored to their former 18th-century splendour and there are pleasant walks around the park as well as wide open green spaces for families to enjoy.

Times House 12 Mar-2 Nov, Wed-Sun + BH's 1-4.30. Garden 12 Mar-2 Nov, Wed-Sun + BH's 11-5. Park, daily until 29 Mar 8-6; 30 Mar-25 Oct 8-7.30; 26 Oct onwards 8-6,* **Fees** House & Garden £8.40 (ch £4.20). Family ticket £21. Group 15+(booked in advance) £7.15. Garden only £3.70 (ch £1.85).* **Facilities** 🅿 🅟 ▭ ⋔ (outdoor) ♿ (partly accessible) (house-steps to principle floor, please call for full details) toilets for disabled shop ⊗ ⅏

TWICKENHAM

World Rugby Museum & Twickenham Stadium Tours

Twickenham Stadium, Rugby Rd TW1 1DZ
☎ 020 8891 8877 📠 020 8892 2817
e-mail: museum@rfu.com
web: www.rfu.com/museum/
dir: A316, follow signs to Twickenham Stadium

Combine a behind-the-scenes guided tour of the world's most famous rugby stadium with a visit to the World Rugby Museum. The tour includes breathtaking views from the top of the Stand, a visit to the England dressing room and ends by walking through the players tunnel to pitch side. The multi-media museum appeals to enthusiasts of all ages and charts the history and world-wide growth of rugby. You can also test your skills on the scrum machine. 100 years of Twickenham Stadium 2009/2010 season.

Times Open all year, Tue-Sat 10-5 (last museum admission 4.30), Sun 11-5 (last admission 4.30). Closed post Twickenham match days, Etr Sun, 24-26 Dec & 1 Jan. On match days museum only available to match ticket holders. Please pre book all tours. **Fees** Museum & Tour £14 (concessions £8). Family (2ad+up to 3ch) £40. **Facilities** 🅿 🛒 †◎† licensed 🔗 toilets for disabled shop ⊗

MERSEYSIDE

LIVERPOOL

The Beatles Story

Britannia Pavilion, Albert Dock L3 4AD
☎ 0151 709 1963 📠 0151 203 3089
e-mail: info@beatlesstory.com
web: www.beatlesstory.com
dir: follow signs to Albert Dock. Located outside Britannia Pavilion, next to Premier Travel Inn

Located within Liverpool's historic Albert Dock, the Beatles Story is a unique visitor attraction that transports you on an enlightening and atmospheric journey into the life, times, culture and music of The Beatles. White Feather: the spirit of Lennon, a new exclusive exhibition telling the emotional personal story of the life of the Lennon family is open until December 2010.

Times Open all year, daily 9-7 (last admission 5). Closed 25-26 Dec.* **Fees** £12.25 (ch 5-16 yrs £6.35 & concessions £8.30). Family ticket (2ad+2ch) £32 (2ad+3ch) £37.* **Facilities** 🅿 🅿 🛒 🔗 toilets for disabled shop ⊗

International Slavery Museum   FREE

Albert Dock L3 4AQ
☎ 0151 478 4499 📠 0151 478 4590
web: www.liverpoolmuseums.org.uk
dir: enter Albert Dock from the Strand

2007 saw the bicentenary of the abolition of the slave trade in Britain, and this museum was opened at Albert Dock. It looks at the impact of the transatlantic slave trade and includes thought-provoking displays on issues such as freedom, identity, human rights, racial discrimination and cultural change.

Times Open all year, daily 10-5 & 24 Dec 10-2. Closed 25-26 Dec & 1 Jan.* **Facilities** 🅿 🅿 🛒 †◎† licensed toilets for disabled shop ⊗

Liverpool Football Club Museum and Stadium Tour

Anfield Rd L4 0TH
☎ 0151 260 6677 📠 0151 264 0149
e-mail: Stephen.done@liverpoolfc.tv
web: www.liverpoolfc.tv

Touch the famous "This is Anfield" sign as you walk down the tunnel to the sound of the crowd at the LFC museum and tour centre. Celebrate all things Liverpool, past and present. Bright displays and videos chart the history of one of England's most successful football clubs.

Times Open all year: Museum daily 10-5 last admission 4. Closed 25-26 Dec. Match days 9 until last admission - 1hr before kick off. Museum & Tour - tours are run subject to daily demand. Advance booking is essential to avoid disappointment.* **Facilities** 🅿 🅿 †◎† licensed toilets for disabled shop ⊗

Merseyside Maritime Museum   FREE

Albert Dock L3 4AQ
☎ 0151 478 4499   📄 0151 478 4590
web: www.liverpoolmuseums.org.uk
dir: enter Albert Dock from the Strand

Discover the story behind one of the world's greatest ports and the people who used it. For many, Liverpool was a gateway to a new life in other countries. For others its importance to the slave trade had less happy consequences. From slavers to luxury liners, submarine hunters to passenger ferries, explore Liverpool's central role.

Times Open all year, daily 10-5 & 24 Dec 10-2. Closed 25-26 Dec & 1 Jan.* **Facilities** 🅿 ⌨ 🍴 licensed ⌂ (outdoor) toilets for disabled shop ⊗

National Conservation Centre   FREE

Whitechapel L1 6HZ
☎ 0151 478 4999   📄 0151 478 4990
web: www.liverpoolmuseums.org.uk
dir: follow brown tourist signs to Whitechapel

Award-winning centre, the only one of its kind, gives the public an insight into the world of museum and gallery conservation. There is a regular changing exhibition programme.

Times Open all year, daily 10-5 & 24 Dec 10-2. Closed 25-26 Dec & 1 Jan. **Facilities** 🅿 Ⓟ ⌨ ♿ toilets for disabled shop ⊗

National Wildflower Centre

Court Hey Park, Roby Rd L16 3NA
☎ 0151 738 1913   📄 0151 737 1820
e-mail: info@nwc.org.uk
web: www.nwc.org.uk
dir: M62 junct 5, take A5080 to rdbt. Exit into Roby Rd, entrance 0.5m on left

Set in a public park on the outskirts of Liverpool, the award-winning National Wildflower Centre promotes the creation of wildflower habitats around the country and provides educational materials, wildflower seeds and interactive facilities. The Centre has demonstration areas, children's activities, a working nursery, compost display and rooftop walk. There is a comprehensive programme of events through the summer. Special Events: Green Fayre in June, Knowsley Flower Show in August, Winter Celebration in December.

Times Open Mar-Aug, daily 10-5. (Last admission 4). **Fees** £3.50 (ch & concessions £1.75). Family ticket (2ad+2ch) £9. Group discount tickets available & supporter packages **Facilities** 🅿 ⌨ ⌂ (outdoor) ♿ toilets for disabled shop ⊗

Sudley House   FREE

Mossley Hill Rd L18 8BX
☎ 0151 724 3245
web: www.liverpoolmuseums.org.uk
dir: near Aigburth Station and Mossley Hill Station

Sudley, Liverpool's hidden gem, is unique, a Victorian merchant's house with an art collection displayed in its original setting. Works on show include paintings by Landseer and Turner, major pre-Raphaelite pictures and a group of 18th-century portraits by Gainsborough, Reynolds, Romney and Lawrence. Sudley houses an introductory display telling the history of the house, a Toy Zone (a display of dolls, toys and doll's house with a children's activities area), a display of items from the historic costume and fashion collection, and a new temporary exhibition gallery.

Times Open all year, daily 10-5 & 24 Dec 10-2. Closed 25-26 Dec & 1 Jan.* **Facilities** 🅿 ⌨ ♿ shop ⊗

Tate Liverpool

Albert Dock L3 4BB
☎ 0151 702 7400 & 7402   📄 0151 702 7401
e-mail: visiting.liverpool@tate.org.uk
web: www.tate.org.uk/liverpool/
dir: within walking distance of Liverpool Lime Street train station, on the Albert Dock. Follow the brown tourist signs from motorway.

Tate Liverpool is one of the largest galleries of modern and contemporary art outside London and is housed in a converted warehouse in the historic Albert Dock. The gallery is home to the National Collection of Modern Art in the North, and has four floors displaying work selected from the Tate Collection, as well as special exhibitions which bring together artwork loaned from around the world.

Times Open all year, Tue-Sun, BH Mon & all Mons in Jun-Aug, 10-5.50. Closed 24-26 Dec & Good Fri **Fees** Admission free. Charge for special exhibitions, phone for details. **Facilities** Ⓟ ⌨ ♿ toilets for disabled shop ⊗

Walker Art Gallery   FREE

William Brown St L3 8EL
☎ 0151 478 4199   📄 0151 478 4190
web: www.liverpoolmuseums.org.uk
dir: city centre adjacent to St George's Hall & Lime St

The National Gallery of the North, this is one of the finest art galleries in Europe, housing an outstanding collection of British and European art from the 14th to the 20th century. Many visitors will already be familiar with some of the much-loved paintings in the gallery's permanent collection, including the tense Civil War scene And when did you last see your father? and The Fever Van by L. S. Lowry. There are also temporary exhibitions and a programme of special events, please see the website for details.

Times Open all year, daily 10-5 & 24 Dec 10-2. Closed 25-26 Dec & 1 Jan.* **Facilities** 🅿 Ⓟ ⌨ 🍴 licensed ♿ toilets for disabled shop ⊗

Liverpool continued

World Museum Liverpool `FREE`

William Brown St L3 8EN
☎ **0151 478 4393** 📄 **0151 478 4350**
web: www.liverpoolmuseums.org.uk
dir: in city centre next to St George's Hall and Lime St, follow brown signs

The World Museum Liverpool offers a journey of discovery from the oceans to the stars. Collections cover natural and physical sciences, ancient history and archaeology, and there are also frequently changing exhibitions, special events and other permanent attractions, such as the Bug House.

Times Open all year, daily 10-5 & 24 Dec 10-2. Closed 25-26 Dec & 1 Jan.* **Facilities** 🅿 🅟 🖵 🍴 licensed 🪑 (indoor) ♿ toilets for disabled shop ⊗

PORT SUNLIGHT

Lady Lever Art Gallery `FREE`

CH62 5EQ
☎ **0151 478 4136** 📄 **0151 478 4140**
web: www.liverpoolmuseums.org.uk
dir: M53 junct 4 or from Liverpool/Birkenhead tunnel follow A41 towards Port Sunlight & follow brown heritage signs

The Lady Lever Art Gallery is one of the most beautiful galleries in the country and the perfect place to introduce younger members of the family to art. Home to the extensive personal collection of founder William Hesketh Lever, first Lord Leverhulme, this wonderful gallery is best known for its outstanding Victorian and pre-Raphaelite paintings by artists such as Leighton and Rossetti as well as other treasures just waiting to be discovered around every corner.

Times Open all year, daily 10-5 & 24 Dec 10-2. Closed 25-26 Dec & 1 Jan. **Facilities** 🅿 🅟 🖵 ♿ toilets for disabled shop ⊗

PRESCOT

Knowsley Safari Park

L34 4AN
☎ **0151 430 9009** 📄 **0151 426 3677**
e-mail: safari.park@knowsley.com
web: www.knowsley.com
dir: M57 junct 2. Follow 'safari park' signs

A five-mile drive through the reserves enables visitors to see lions, tigers, elephants, rhinos, monkeys and many other animals in spacious, natural surroundings. Also a children's amusement park, reptile house, pets' corner plus sealion shows. Other attractions include an amusement park and a miniature railway.

Times Open all year, Mar-Oct, daily 10-4; Nov-Feb, 11-3. Closed 25 Dec. **Fees** £12 (ch & concession £9).* **Facilities** 🅿 🖵 🪑 (outdoor) ♿ toilets for disabled shop ⊗

ST HELENS

World of Glass

Chalon Way East WA10 1BX
☎ **01744 22766** 📄 **01744 616966**
e-mail: info@worldofglass.com
web: www.worldofglass.com
dir: 5mins from M62 junct 7

Ideal for all the family, this fascinating attraction is in the heart of St Helens, a town shaped by glass-making. Features include the world's first continuous glass-making furnace, and two museum galleries that show glass from antiquity and Victorian life in St Helens. Live glass-blowing demonstrations and a special effects film show are the highlight of any visit.

Times Open all year, Etr-Oct, Tue-Sun & BH, 10-5; Nov-Etr, Tue-Sun, 10-4. Closed 25-26 Dec & 1 Jan.* **Fees** £5.30 (ch & pen £3.80) Family & group discounts.* **Facilities** 🅿 🅟 🖵 ♿ toilets for disabled shop ⊗

SPEKE

Speke Hall

The Walk L24 1XD
☎ 0151 427 7231 & 0844 8004799 📄 0151 427 9860
e-mail: spekehall@nationaltrust.org.uk
web: www.nationaltrust.org.uk
dir: on N bank of Mersey, 1m off A561 on W side of Liverpool Airport, follow brown signs

A remarkable timber-framed manor house set in tranquil gardens and grounds. The house has a Tudor Great Hall, Stuart plasterwork, and William Morris wallpapers. Outside are varied grounds, including a rose garden, bluebell woods and woodland walks. Also, live interpretation by costumed guides, children's quiz-trail and adventure playground. Lots of events throughout the year, contact for details.

Times House open: 27 Feb-14 Mar, 6 Nov-12 Dec, Sat & Sun 11-4.30; 17 Mar-Oct, Wed-Sun, 11-5 Garden open 2 Jan-14 Mar, 2 Nov-30 Dec, Tue-Sun 11-4.30 & **Fees** Hall & Garden: £8.40 (ch £4.20). Family ticket £21. Gardens only: £5 (ch £2.60). Family ticket £12.60. **Facilities** 🅿 💻🍽 licensed 🅰 (outdoor) ♿ (partly accessible) (ground floor accessible. Level entrance to shop & restaurant. Accessible route in grounds) toilets for disabled shop ⊗ 🌸

NORFOLK

BANHAM

Banham Zoo

The Grove NR16 2HE
☎ 01953 887771 & 887773 📄 01953 887445
e-mail: info@banhamzoo.co.uk
web: www.banhamzoo.co.uk
dir: on B1113, signed off A11 and A140. Follow brown tourist signs

Set in 35 acres of magnificent parkland, see hundreds of animals ranging from big cats to birds of prey and siamangs to shire horses. Tiger Territory is a purpose-built enclosure for Siberian tigers, including a rock pool and woodland setting. See also Lemur Island and Tamarin and Marmoset Islands. The Heritage Farm Stables and Falconry displays Norfolk's rural heritage with majestic shire horses and birds of prey. Other attractions include Children's Farmyard Barn and Adventure Play Area.

Times Open all year, daily from 10. (Last admission 1 hour before closing). Closed 25 & 26 Dec.* **Facilities** 🅿 🅟 💻🍽 licensed 🅰 toilets for disabled shop ⊗🚭

BLICKLING

Blickling Hall

NR11 6NF
☎ 01263 738030 📄 01263 738035
e-mail: blickling@nationaltrust.org.uk
web: www.nationaltrust.org.uk/blickling
dir: on B1354, 1.5m NW of Aylsham, signposted off A140 Norwich to Cromer road

Flanked by dark yew hedges and topped by pinnacles, the warm red brick front of Blickling is a memorable sight. Fifty five acres of grounds include woodland and a lake, a formal parterre, topiary yew hedges, a Secret Garden, an orangery, and a dry moat filled with roses, camellias and other plants. Inside there are fine collections of furniture, paintings and tapestries, along with a spectacular Jacobean plaster ceiling, and a library of some 12,000 books.

Times Hall: 28 Feb-12 Jul, 15 Jul-6 Sep, 9 Sep-1 Nov, Wed-Sun 11-5, Garden: 2 Jan-27 Feb, 2 Nov-Jan, Thu-Sun 11-4; 28 Feb-1 Nov Wed-Sun10.15-5.15. Park: all year* **Fees** £9.75 (ch £4.85) Family £25.50. Gardens only: £6.50 (ch £3.25) Family £17.10* **Facilities** 🅿 💻🍽 licensed 🅰 (outdoor) ♿ (partly accessible) (stairs to basement rooms) toilets for disabled shop ⊗ 🌸

BRESSINGHAM

Bressingham Steam Museum & Gardens

IP22 2AB
☎ **01379 686900 & 687386** 📄 **01379 686907**
e-mail: info@bressingham.co.uk
web: www.bressingham.co.uk
dir: on A1066 2.5m W of Diss, between Thetford & Diss

Alan Bloom is an internationally recognised nurseryman and a steam enthusiast, and has combined his interests to great effect at Bressingham. There are three miniature steam-hauled trains, including a 15-inch gauge running through two and a half miles of the wooded Waveney Valley. The Dell Garden has 5000 species of perennials and alpines; Foggy Bottom has wide vistas, pathways, trees, shrubs, conifers and winter colour (restricted opening). A steam roundabout is another attraction, and the Norfolk Fire Museum is housed here. Various events are held, including Dad's Army Day, Friends of Thomas the Tank Engine, and the home of the Royal Scot locomotive, please telephone for details.

Times Open: Steam Museum, Dad's Army collection, Foggy Bottom & Dell Garden Mar, Apr, May, Sep & Oct, daily 10.30-4.30. Jun, Jul & Aug, 10.30-5.30. Check before travelling.* **Facilities** 🅿 💻🍽 licensed 🌲 (outdoor) ♿ (partly accessible) (Nursery and Waveney lines accessible to wheelchairs) toilets for disabled shop ⊗

CROMER

Cromer Museum

East Cottages, Tucker St NR27 9HB
☎ **01263 513543** 📄 **01263 511651**
e-mail: cromer.museum@norfolk.gov.uk
web: www.norfolk.gov.uk/tourism/museums
dir: On Church St next to Cromer Church

The museum is housed in five 19th-century fishermen's cottages, one of which has period furnishings. There are pictures and exhibits from Victorian Cromer, with collections illustrating local natural history, archaeology, social history and geology. Items to discover include the scandal of mixed bathing, the daring rescues of Henry Blogg and the Cromer Lifeboatmen, and the incredible story of the West Runton elephant, Britain's oldest and most complete elephant fossil. Contact for details of special events.

Times Open all year, Mar-Oct, Mon-Sat 10-5, Sun 2-5; Nov-Feb, Mon-Sat 10-4. Closed Sun* **Fees** £3 (ch £1.70, concessions £2.50)* **Facilities** 🅿 ♿ (partly accessible) toilets for disabled shop ⊗

RNLI Henry Blogg Museum   FREE

The Rocket House, The Gangway NR27 9ET
☎ **01263 511294** 📄 **01263 513047**
e-mail: cromer_museum@rnli.org.uk
web: www.org.uk/henryblogg
dir: located at the bottom of East Gangway

A lifeboat has been stationed at Cromer since 1804, and the museum at the bottom of The Gangway covers local lifeboat history and the RNLI in general. The main exhibit is the WWII Watson Class lifeboat H F Bailey, the boat Henry Blogg coxed. In ten years he helped to save over 500 lives, and is still the RNLI's most decorated crew member. The exhibition hosts a number of new features including; interactive displays and radio/navigation instruction.

Times Open all year, Apr-Sep, Tue-Sun 10-5; Oct-Nov & Feb-Mar 10-4. Closed Dec-Jan. **Facilities** 🅿 ♿ toilets for disabled shop ⊗

FAKENHAM

See also Thursford Green

Pensthorpe Nature Reserve & Gardens

Pensthorpe NR21 0LN
☎ 01328 851465   📄 01328 855905
e-mail: info@pensthorpe.com
web: www.pensthorpe.co.uk
dir: 1m from Fakenham on the A1067 to Norwich

Explore the beautiful lakes, nature trails and gardens designed by Chelsea Flower Show gold medallists, and look out for the large collection of cranes in the recently opened Conservation Centre. Pensthorpe is currently host to the BBC Springwatch programme.

Times Open Jan-Mar, daily 10-4. Apr-Dec, 10-5. Closed 25-26 Dec* **Fees** £8.50 (ch 4-16 £5, concessions £7). Family ticket (2ad+2ch) £23. Please telephone or see website for more details.* **Facilities** 🅿 🛆 🖵 🏠 (outdoor) ♿ (partly accessible) (suitable paths around some of the reserve) toilets for disabled shop ⊗

FILBY

Thrigby Hall Wildlife Gardens

NR29 3DR
☎ 01493 369477   📄 01493 368256
web: www.thrigbyhall.co.uk
dir: on unclass road off A1064, between Acle & Caister-on-Sea

The 250-year-old park of Thrigby Hall is now the home of animals and birds from Asia, and the lake has ornamental wildfowl. There are tropical bird houses, a unique blue willow pattern garden and tree walk and a summer house as old as the park. The enormous jungled swamp hall has special features such as underwater viewing of large crocodiles.

Times Open all year, daily from 10. **Fees** £9.50 (ch 4-14 £7.50, concessions £8.50). **Facilities** 🅿 🅿 🖵 🏠 (indoor & outdoor) ♿ toilets for disabled shop ⊗

GREAT YARMOUTH

Elizabethan House Museum

4 South Quay NR30 2QH
☎ 01493 855746   📄 01493 745459
e-mail: yarmouth.museums@norfolk.gov.uk
web: www.museums.norfolk.gov.uk
dir: from A12 & A47 follow town centre signs, then Historic South Quay signs, leading onto South Quay

Experience the lives of families who lived in this splendid quayside house from Tudor to Victorian times. Decide for yourself if the death of Charles I was plotted in the Conspiracy Room. Dress the family in Tudor costumes. Discover Victorian life, upstairs and downstairs, and find out what it was like to work in the kitchen and scullery. Children can play in the toy room, while parents relax in the small but delightful walled garden.

Times Open Apr-Nov, Mon-Fri 10-5, Sat & Sun 12-4.* **Fees** £3.30 (ch £1.80, concessions £2.80)* **Facilities** 🅿 ♿ (partly accessible) shop ⊗

Great Yarmouth Row 111 Houses & Greyfriars' Cloister

South Quay NR30 2RQ
☎ 01493 857900
web: www.english-heritage.org.uk
dir: follow signs to dock and south quay

Visit these 17th-century houses unique to Great Yarmouth, and the remains of a Franciscan friary with rare early wall paintings. Guided tours explain how the rich and poor lived in these properties through history.

Times Open Apr-Sep, daily 12-5. **Fees** £3.90 (concessions £3.30, ch £2). Family ticket £9.80. Please call 0870 333 1181 for the most up to date prices and opening times when planning your visit. **Facilities** shop ⊗ ♿

Merrivale Model Village

Marine Pde NR30 3JG
☎ 01493 842097
web: www.merrivalemodelvillage.co.uk
dir: Marine parade seafront, next to Wellington Pier

Set in more than an acre of attractive landscaped gardens, this comprehensive miniature village is built on a scale of 1:12, and features streams, a lake and waterfalls. Among the models are a working fairground, a stone quarry, houses, shops, and a garden railway. At some times of the year there are illuminations at dusk. The Penny Arcade gives you the chance to play old amusements.

Times Open Etr-Oct, daily from 10. **Fees** Please telephone for details **Facilities** 🅿 🖵 🏠 (outdoor) ♿ toilets for disabled shop

Great Yarmouth continued

Time and Tide Museum of Great Yarmouth Life

Tower Curing Works, Blackfriar's Rd NR30 3BX
☎ 01493 743930   📄 01493 743940
e-mail: yarmouth.museums@norfolk.gov.uk
web: www.museums.norfolk.gov.uk
dir: from A12 & A47 follow brown signs

An award-winning museum set in a Grade II listed Victorian herring-curing factory. Time and Tide tells Great Yarmouth's fascinating story, from prehistoric times to the present day; displays include fishing, wreck and rescue, seaside holidays, port and trade, and the World Wars. It also brings to life the herring curing industry and the lives of the people who worked here. The Museum's unique collections are interpreted using both traditional and interactive technology.

Times Open all year, Apr-Oct daily, 10-4; Nov-Mar, Mon-Fri 10-4, Sat & Sun12-4.* **Facilities** ℗ ♿ toilets for disabled shop ⊗

GRESSENHALL

Gressenhall Farm and Workhouse

NR20 4DR
☎ 01362 860563   📄 01362 860385
e-mail: gressenhall.museum@norfolk.gov.uk
web: www.museums.norfolk.gov.uk
dir: on B1146 3m NW of Dereham, follow brown signs

Enjoy a fascinating journey through the story of rural Norfolk with a thrilling woodland adventure playground, an historic workhouse, traditional farm and many indoor displays, Gressenhall is the perfect setting for a day out.

Times Open Mar-Nov, 10-5. **Fees** £8.10 (ch £5.80, under 4s free, concessions £6.90) **Facilities** ℗ ♿ (indoor & outdoor) ♿ toilets for disabled shop ⊗

HOLKHAM

Holkham Hall & Bygones Museum

NR23 1AB
☎ 01328 710227   📄 01328 711707
e-mail: enquiries@holkham.co.uk
web: www.holkham.co.uk
dir: off A149, 2m W of Wells-next-the-Sea, coaches should use B1105 at New Holkham, signed "Holkham Coaches"

This classic Palladian mansion was built between 1734 and 1764 by Thomas Coke, 1st Earl of Leicester, and is home to his descendants. It has a magnificent alabaster entrance hall and the sumptuous state rooms house Roman statuary, fine furniture and paintings by Rubens, Van Dyck, Gainsborough and others. The Bygones Museum, housed in the stable block, has over 5,000 items of domestic and agricultural display - from gramophones to fire engines. The adjacent free History of Farming exhibition illustrates how a great agricultural estate such as Holkham works and has evolved.

Times Open 12-13 Apr, May & Oct, Sun, Mon & Thu; Jun-Sep, Sun-Wed & Thu, 12-4.* **Fees** Hall £8 (ch £4). Bygones £5 (ch £2.50). Combined ticket Hall & Bygones: £10 (ch £5). Family ticket £25.* **Facilities** ℗ ℗ ♿ (outdoor) ♿ toilets for disabled shop ⊗

HORSHAM ST FAITH

City of Norwich Aviation Museum

Old Norwich Rd NR10 3JF
☎ 01603 893080   📄 01603 893080
e-mail: norwichairmuseum@hotmail.com
web: www.cnam.co.uk
dir: follow brown tourist signs from A140 Norwich to Cromer road

A massive Avro Vulcan bomber, veteran of the Falklands War, dominates the collection of military and civilian aircraft at this museum. There are several displays relating to the aeronautical history of Norfolk, including some on the role played by Norfolk-based RAF and USAAF planes during World War II, and a section dedicated to the operations of RAF Bomber Command's 100 group.

Times Open all year, Apr-Oct, Tue-Sat 10-5, Sun & BH Mons 12-5, Nov-Mar, Wed & Sat 10-4, Sun 12-4.* **Fees** £4.25 (ch £2.10, concessions £4). Family £12. **Facilities** ℗ ♿ (outdoor) ♿ (partly accessible) shop ⊗

HOUGHTON

Houghton Hall

PE31 6UE

☎ **01485 528569** 📠 **01485 528167**

e-mail: administrator@houghtonhall.com

web: www.houghtonhall.com

dir: 1.25m off A148. 13m E of King's Lynn & 10m W of Fakenham on A148

Houghton Hall built in the 1720s by Sir Robert Walpole, Britain's first Prime Minister, is one of the grandest surviving Palladian Houses in England. Now owned by the 7th Marquess of Cholmondeley. The spectacular 5-acre walled garden, restored by Lord Cholmondeley, has been divided into areas for fruit and vegetables, spacious herbaceous borders, and formal rose gardens with over 150 varieties. A collection of Model Soldiers contains over 20,000 models laid out in various battle formations. Look out for the herd of fallow deer that live in the grounds, and also a collection of contemporary sculpture. There are musical events in the summer, and the Houghton International Horse Trials in May.

Times Open Park, Walled Garden, Soldier Museum 4 Apr-Sep, Wed, Thu, Sun & BHs 11.30-5.30. House open 1.30-5 (last entry 4.30). **Fees** £8.80 (ch £3.50). Family ticket £22. Grounds only (not house) £6 (ch £2.50) Family ticket £15. **Facilities** ❷ ⭐🍴 licensed ⋔ (outdoor) ♿ toilets for disabled shop ⊗

HUNSTANTON

Hunstanton Sea Life Sanctuary

Southern Promenade PE36 5BH

☎ **01485 533576** 📠 **01485 533531**

web: www.sealsanctuary.co.uk

dir: A149 King's Lynn to Hunstanton, then follow brown sealife signs

With over 30 fascinating displays of marine life, this fascinating aquarium offers close encounters with starfish, sharks, octopus, eels and many other underwater wonders. Feeding demonstrations, talks and special presentations. Also see: Claws. Six displays featuring strange clawed creatures from around the world.

Times Open all year, daily from 10. (Closed 25 Dec)* **Facilities** ❷ ℗ ⬚⋔ toilets for disabled shop ⊗

LENWADE

Dinosaur Adventure Park

Weston Park NR9 5JW

☎ **01603 876310** 📠 **01603 876315**

e-mail: info@dinosaurpark.co.uk

web: www.dinosaurpark.co.uk

dir: From A47 or A1067 follow brown signs to Park

Visitors can help the Ranger 'Track: T-Rex' on the Dinosaur Trail and meet giants from the past including the new spinosaurus. They can also make friends with animals from hedgehogs to wallabies, or bugs and snakes in the secret animal garden. There is also an adventure play area including a Climb-o-saurus, Raptor Racers, Jurassic Putt Crazy Golf, and the Lost World Amazing Adventure.

Times Open daily from 10 Sep & Oct half term; 11 Sep-22 Oct, Fri-Sun.* **Facilities** ❷ ⬚ ⋔ (indoor & outdoor) toilets for disabled shop ⊗

NORWICH

Air Defence Radar Museum

RAF Neatishead NR12 8YB

☎ **01692 631485**

e-mail: curator@radarmuseum.co.uk

web: www.radarmuseum.co.uk

dir: follow brown signs from A1062 at Horning

This multi-award winning Museum, housed in the original 1942 Radar Operations building, features the Battle of Britain Room, 1942 Ground Controlled Interception Room, Radar Engineering, Military Communications Systems, Cold War Operations Room, Royal Observer Corps, Space Defence, Bloodhound Missiles and Original Mobile Radar Vehicles. The newest addition is the RAF Coltishall Memorial Room.

Times Open year round 2nd Sat each month; Apr-Oct, Tue & Thu & BH Mons 10-5* **Fees** £4.50 (ch £3.50, under 13 free, concessions £4)* **Facilities** ❷ ⬚⋔ (outdoor) ♿ (partly accessible) (two rooms not accessible to wheelchairs) toilets for disabled shop ⊗

Norwich continued

Norwich Castle Museum & Art Gallery

Castle Meadow NR1 3JU
☎ **01603 493625** 🖹 **01603 493623**
e-mail: museums@norfolk.gov.uk
web: www.museums.norfolk.gov.uk
dir: in city centre

The Castle keep was built in the 12th century, and the museum houses displays of art, archaeology, natural history, Lowestoft porcelain, Norwich silver, a large collection of paintings (with special emphasis on the Norwich School of Painters) and British ceramic teapots. There are also guided tours of the dungeons and battlements. A programme of exhibitions, children's events, gallery and evening talks takes place throughout the year. Please ring for details.

Times Open all year, Mon-Sat from 10, Sun from 1* **Fees** Castle Ticket £6 (ch £4.40, concessions £5.10), Special exhibitions £3.10 (ch £2.30, concessions £2.70)* **Facilities** ℗ ⬚ 🛏 (indoor) ♿ toilets for disabled shop ⊗

OXBOROUGH

Oxburgh Hall

PE33 9PS
☎ **01366 328258** 🖹 **01366 328066**
e-mail: oxburghhall@nationaltrust.org.uk
web: www.nationaltrust.org.uk/oxburghhall
dir: Signed from A134 at Stoke ferry & Swaffham

The outstanding feature of this 15th-century moated building is the 80ft high Tudor gatehouse which has remained unaltered throughout the centuries. Henry VII lodged in the King's Room in 1487. A parterre garden of French design stands outside the moat. Rare needlework by Mary Queen of Scots and Bess of Hardwick is on display. A particular attraction is a genuine 16th-century priests hole, which is accessible to members of the public.

Times Open House: 28 Feb-8 Mar, Sat & Sun, 11-5; 14 Mar-Jul, 1 Sep-1 Nov, Mon-Sun, 11-5. 1-31 Aug, daily 11-5.* **Fees** £7.45, (ch £3.90). Family Ticket £19.95* Garden only £3.90 (ch £2.25). Includes a voluntary donation but visitors can choose to pay the standard prices displayed at the property and on the website.* **Facilities** ℗ 🍴 licensed 🛏 (outdoor) ♿ (partly accessible) toilets for disabled shop ⊗ ♨

Pettitts Animal Adventure Park

NR13 3UA
☎ **01493 700094 & 701403** 🖹 **01493 700933**
e-mail: pettittsreedham@aol.com
web: www.pettittsadventurepark.co.uk
dir: off A47 at Acle then follow brown signs

Three parks in one, aimed at the younger child. Rides include a railway and roller coaster; the adventure play area has a golf course, ball pond and tearoom; and entertainment is provided by clowns, puppets and live musicians. Among the animals that can be seen are small horses, wallabies, birds of prey, goats, alpacas and reindeer.

Times Open daily 15 Mar-2 Nov, 10-5/5.30; wknds in Nov & Dec. Daily during Xmas hols. Closed 25 Dec.* **Facilities** ℗ ℗ ⬚ 🛏 (outdoor) toilets for disabled shop ⊗

SANDRINGHAM

Sandringham House, Gardens & Museum

PE35 6EN
☎ **01553 612908** 🖹 **01485 541571**
e-mail: visits@sandringhamestate.co.uk
web: www.sandringhamestate.co.uk
dir: off A148

The private country retreat of Her Majesty The Queen, this neo-Jacobean house was built in 1870 for King Edward VII. The main rooms used by the Royal Family when in residence are all open to the public. Sixty acres of glorious grounds surround the House and offer beauty and colour throughout the season. Sandringham Museum contains fascinating displays of Royal memorabilia. The ballroom exhibition changes each year.

Times Open Etr Sat-mid Jul & early Aug-Oct. House open 11-4.45, Museum 11-5 & Grounds 10.30-5.* **Fees** House, Museum & Grounds: £10 (ch £5, pen £8). Family ticket £25. **Facilities** ℗ ⬚ 🍴 licensed 🛏 (outdoor) ♿ toilets for disabled shop ⊗

SHERINGHAM

North Norfolk Railway (The Poppy Line)

Sheringham Station NR26 8RA
☎ 01263 820800 📄 01263 820801
e-mail: enquiries@nnrailway.co.uk
web: www.nnrailway.co.uk
dir: from A148 take A1082. Next to large car park by rdbt in town centre. Just off A149 coast road

A full size heritage railway running between Sheringham and Holt, with an intermediate station at Weybourne. The route runs for 5.5m along the coast, and up through the heathland, and features genuine Victorian stations. The William Marriott Railway Museum at Holt Station is housed in a replica goods shed. There are special events throughout the year, please contact for details. "North Norfolkman" dining train offers timetables lunch and dinner services - contact for dates.

Times Open Apr-Oct, daily. Santa Specials in Dec **Fees** £10.50 (ch 5-15yrs £7, concessions £9.50). Family ticket £35 incl £5 voucher to spend on refreshments. Cycles & dogs £1.* **Facilities** ❷ Ⓟ ⛶ ⋔ (outdoor) ♿ toilets for disabled shop

SOUTH WALSHAM

Fairhaven Woodland & Water Garden

School Rd NR13 6DZ

☎ 01603 270449 & 270683 📄 01603 270449
e-mail: fairhavengarden@btconnect.com
web: www.fairhavengarden.co.uk
dir: follow brown heritage signs from A47 onto B1140 to South Walsham. Through village towards Gt Yarmouth. Left into School Rd, 100yds on left, opposite South Walsham Village Hall

131 acres of ancient woodland and water garden with private broad. Excellent bird-watching from the boat. In spring there are masses of primroses and bluebells, with azaleas and rhododendrons in several areas. Candelabra primulas and some unusual plants grow near the waterways, and in summer the wild flowers provide food for butterflies, bees and dragonflies. Summer flowers include Day Lilies, Ligularia, Hostas, Hydrangeas and flowering shrubs, including Viburnum Mariesii (Wedding Cake Viburnum), Cornus Kousa Chinensis and Cornus Florida Rubra. Special events take place throughout the summer and 2010 marks the 35th anniversary of the opening of the garden.

Times Open all year, daily 10-5, (10-4 winter). Closed 25 Dec. **Fees** £5 (ch £2.50, concessions £4.50). Single membership tickets £18.50. Family membership ticket £45. **Facilities** ❷ Ⓟ ⛶ ⋔ (outdoor) ♿ toilets for disabled shop

THURSFORD GREEN

Thursford Collection

NR21 0AS
☎ 01328 878477 📄 01328 878415
e-mail: admin@thursfordcollection.co.uk
web: www.thursford.com
dir: 1m off A148. Halfway between Fakenham and Holt

Only open during the summer, Thursford Collection is a working museum of mechanical organs, Wurlitzer shows, silent movies, old-fashioned fairground carousels and static displays of both fairground and road engines, along with all kinds of related memorabilia. There are two behind-the-scenes tours: the first goes back stage, taking in dressing rooms, costume stores, wardrobe and Fantasy Land, while the second visits the old forge and engine yard, with videos explaining how the engines would have been used. During November and December, Christmas Spectacular Shows and also Santa's Magical Journey are staged.

Times Open Good Fri-last Sun in Sep, daily, 12-5. Closed Sat.* **Fees** £8 (ch under 4 free, ch 4-14 £4, students & pen £7). Party 20+ £7 each.* **Facilities** ❷ ⛶ 🍴 licensed ⋔ (outdoor) ♿ toilets for disabled shop ⊗

TITCHWELL

RSPB Nature Reserve

PE31 8BB
☎ 01485 210779 📄 01485 210779
e-mail: titchwell@rspb.org.uk
web: www.rspb@org.uk
dir: 6m E of Hunstanton on A149, signed entrance

On the Norfolk coast, Titchwell Marsh is the RSPB's most popular reserve. Hundreds and thousands of migrating birds pass through in spring and autumn and many stay during winter, providing an opportunity to see many species of ducks, waders, seabirds and geese and also the RSPB emblem bird, the Avocet. A great day out for the entire family.

Times Open at all times. Visitor Centre daily 9.30-5 (4 Nov-Mar).* **Fees** Facilities charge for non RSPB members.* **Facilities** ❷ ⛶ ⋔ (outdoor) ♿ toilets for disabled shop

Norfolk

UPPER SHERINGHAM

Sheringham Park

Visitor Centre, Wood Farm NR26 8TL
☎ 01263 820550
e-mail: sheringhampark@nationaltrust.org.uk
web: www.nationaltrust.org.uk/sheringham
dir: 2m SW of Sheringham, main entrance at junct of A148
Cromer-Holt road & B1157

Fabulous displays of rhododendrons and azaleas from mid May
to June, as well as a gazebo and viewing towers with stunning
coastal vistas, make Sheringham one of the finest examples of
landscape design in the country.

Times Open Park: all year, dawn-dusk; Visitor Centre: Feb-14 Mar
& Nov-Jan 11-4 Sat-Sun; 15 Mar-Sep daily 10-5; Oct Wed-Sun
10-5* **Fees** £4* **Facilities** ℗ ⊡ toilets for disabled shop ⊗ ✿

WELNEY

WWT Welney Wetland Centre

Hundred Foot Bank PE14 9TN
☎ 01353 860711   ▤ 01353 863524
e-mail: info.welney@wwt.org.uk
web: www.wwt.org.uk
dir: off A1101, N of Ely

This important wetland site on the beautiful Ouse Washes is
famed for the breathtaking winter spectacle of wild ducks,
geese and swans. Impressive observation facilities, including
hides and a heated main observatory, offer outstanding views
of the huge numbers of wildfowl which include Bewick's and
Whooper swans, wigeon, teal and shoveler. Floodlit evening
swan feeds take place between November and February.
In summer the reserve is alive with over 40% of all British
wetland plant flowers. Butterflies, dragonflies and damselflies
are in abundance, and the summer walk gives a unique access
to the marshes.

Times Open all year, Mar-Oct, daily 9.30-5; Nov-Feb, Mon-
Wed 10-5, Thu-Sun 10-8. Closed 25 Dec.* **Facilities** ℗ ⊡ ㅠ
(outdoor) toilets for disabled shop ⊗

WEST RUNTON

Hillside Shire Horse Sanctuary

Sandy Ln NR27 9QH
☎ 01603 736200
e-mail: contact@hillside.org.uk
web: www.hillside.org.uk
dir: off A149 in village of West Ranton half-way between Cromer
& Sheringham, follow brown signs for Shire Horse Sanctuary

Come and see the heavy horses, ponies and donkeys as well
as sheep, pigs, rabbits, ducks, hens, goats and many more
rescued animals in their home in the beautiful north Norfolk
countryside. Visit the museum and relive the farming days
of yesteryear surrounded by an extensive collection of carts,
wagons and farm machinery. There is lots of space for children
to play in the activity areas. Try 'animal friendly' refreshments
in the cafe and take home a souvenir from the gift shop. You
may even 'adopt' a rescued animal.

Times Open 28 Mar-28 Oct daily; Apr-May after Etr closed Fri &
Sat; Jun-Aug closed Sat; Sep-Oct closed Fri & Sat **Fees** £5.95 (ch
£3.95, pen £4.95). Family ticket (2ad+2ch) £18.* **Facilities** ℗
⊡ ㅠ (outdoor) toilets for disabled shop ⊗

WEYBOURNE

The Muckleburgh Collection

Weybourne Military Camp NR25 7EG
☎ 01263 588210 & 588608   📠 01263 588425
e-mail: info@muckleburgh.co.uk
web: www.muckleburgh.co.uk
dir: on A149, coast road, 3m W of Sheringham

The largest privately-owned military collection of its kind in Norfolk, which incorporates the Museum of the Suffolk and Norfolk Yeomanry. Exhibits include restored and working tanks, armoured cars, trucks and artillery of WWII, and equipment and weapons from the Falklands and the Gulf War. Live tank demonstrations are run daily (except Sat) during school holidays.

Times Open daily 20 Mar-Oct. **Fees** £6 (ch £4, pen £5). Family ticket £17. **Facilities** ❷ ⛟ 🍴 licensed 🛱 (outdoor) ♿ toilets for disabled shop ⊗

CANONS ASHBY

Canons Ashby House

NN11 3SD
☎ 01327 861900   📠 01327 861909
e-mail: canonsashby@nationaltrust.org.uk
web: www.nationaltrust.org.uk
dir: easy access from either M40 junct 11 or M1 junct 16

Canon Ashby was first built by the Dryden family during the Elizabethan period, using stone from the Augustinian priory which previously occupied the site. The private church is all that remains of the priory. The interior is welcoming and atmospheric, with Jacobean wall paintings, plasterwork and tapestries. The house was updated in the 18th century, with the south facing rooms remodelled and again in the 19th century, when Sir Henry Dryden 'The Antiquarian' recorded much of the history of the estate and the surrounding area. The gardens are currently being restored to their colourful 19th-century designs from Sir Henry's records.

Times Open: House & Gardens 28 Feb-8 Mar, Sat-Sun 11-5; 14 Mar-1 Nov, daily (ex Thu & Fri) 11-5; 7 Nov-20 Dec , daily (ex Thu & Fri) 12-4. House 6-21 Dec, Sat-Sun 12-4. Gardens, Park & Church 28 Feb-8 Mar, 11-5.30; 14 Mar-1 Nov, daily (ex Thu & Fri) 11-5; 7 Nov-20 Dec, Sat-Sun 12-4. Open Good Fri 11-5. House tour timed tickets only before 1pm.* **Fees** With Gift Aid donation: £7.95 (ch £3.95) Family (2ad+2ch) £19.85. Garden only £2.95 (ch £1.75). Winter grounds only £1.75 (ch £1).* **Facilities** ❷ ⛟♿ (partly accessible) (access limited, ground floor has steps, uneven floors, little turning space. Stairs to other floors. Grounds have gravel paths & some steps) toilets for disabled shop ⊗ 🦌

ROCKINGHAM

Rockingham Castle

LE16 8TH
☎ 01536 770240   📠 01536 771692
e-mail: a.norman@rockinghamcastle.com
web: www.rockinghamcastle.com
dir: 2m N of Corby, off A6003

Set on a hill overlooking five counties, the castle was built by William the Conqueror. The site of the original keep is now a rose garden, but the outline of the curtain wall remains, as do the foundations of the Norman hall, and the twin towers of the gatehouse. A royal residence for 450 years, the castle was granted to Edward Watson in the 16th century, and the Watson family have lived there ever since.

Times Open Etr-Jun: Sun & BH Mon; Jul-Sep, Sun & BH 12-5. Grounds open from 12. Castle open from 1.* **Facilities** ❷ ⛟ 🛱 (outdoor) ♿ (partly accessible) (Ramps are available. Ground floor accessible, 1st floor & tower not accessible due to spiral staircase) toilets for disabled shop

SULGRAVE

Sulgrave Manor

Manor Rd OX17 2SD
☎ 01295 760205 **📄 01295 768056**
e-mail: enquiries@sulgravemanor.org.uk
web: www.sulgravemanor.org.uk
dir: off B4525 Banbury to Northampton road

A splendid example of a Tudor manor house with a Georgian wing, housing excellent collections of authentic period furniture and fabrics. Set in pleasant gardens in the English formal style.

Times Open Apr-Oct (wknds only in April). From May Tue, Wed and Thu from 2 (Last entry 4). Open for pre-booked groups all year. **Fees** £6.25 (ch £3). Family £17.50. Special event days £7.50 (ch £3.50). Family ticket £20.* **Facilities** 🅿 Ⓟ ⏛ 🍴 (outdoor) ♿ (partly accessible) (fully accessible visitor centre and grounds. House partially accessible on ground floor) toilets for disabled shop

NORTHUMBERLAND

ALNWICK

Alnwick Castle

NE66 1NQ
☎ 01665 510777 **📄 01665 510876**
e-mail: enquiries@alnwickcastle.com
web: www.alnwickcastle.com
dir: off A1 on outskirts of town, signed

Set in a stunning landscape, Alnwick Castle overlooks the historic market town of Alnwick. Although it was originally built for the Percy family, who have lived here since 1309, -the current Duke and Duchess of Northumberland being the current tenants- the castle is best known as one of the locations that served as Hogwarts School in the Harry Potter movies. The castle is full of art and treasures and there are plenty of activities for all the family.

Times Open Etr-Oct, daily 10-6 (last admission 4.30). **Fees** £11.95 (ch 5-16yrs £4.95, concessions £9.95). Family ticket (2ad+4ch) £29.95. Party 14+ £7.95.* **Facilities** Ⓟ ⏛ 🍴 licensed 🍴 (outdoor) ♿ (partly accessible) (Some areas not suitable for wheelchair users) toilets for disabled shop ⊗

The Alnwick Garden

Denwick Ln NE66 1YU
☎ 01665 511350 **📄 01665 511351**
e-mail: info@alnwickgarden.com
web: www.alnwickgarden.com
dir: 1m from A1. Follow signs & access garden from Denwick Lane

The Alnwick Garden is a vision of the Duchess of Northumberland and a leading garden visitor attraction in North East England. The 40-acre landscape is the creation of Belgian designers Wirtz International, and British architect Sir Michael Hopkins designed The Pavilion and Visitor Centre. This unique project in a deprived rural area has transformed a derelict and forgotten plot into a stimulating landscape. Having completed its second phase of development, the garden includes one of the largest wooden tree houses in the world, a Poison Garden, Bamboo Labyrinth and Serpent Garden. An all-weather attraction for all ages and accessible to all. A varied programme of events and activities throughout the year offers inspiring, informal experiences for all visitors.

Times Open all year, Apr-Sep, 10-6; Oct-Mar, 10-4. Closed 25 Dec.* **Fees** Gift Aid donation £10 (concessions £7.50). Without Gift Aid donation £9 (concessions £6.50). Groups 14+ £6.25.* **Facilities** 🅿 Ⓟ ⏛ 🍴 licensed 🍴 (outdoor) ♿ toilets for disabled shop ⊗

ASHINGTON

Woodhorn

Northumberland Museum, Archives & Country Park, QEII Country Park NE63 9YF
☎ 01670 528080 **📄 01670 528083**
e-mail: dtate@woodhorn.org.uk
web: www.experiencewoodhorn.com
dir: Just off A189 E of Ashington

Inspired by monster coal-cutting machines, the Cutter building houses emotive displays about life in the mining community, colourful banners and exhibition galleries. It is also home to the archives for Northumberland with records dating back 800 years. Unique listed colliery buildings have also been brought back to life for the Colliery Experience.

Times Open all year, Apr-Oct, Wed-Sun (Tue in school hols) & BH Mon 10-5; Nov-Mar, Wed-Sun, (Tue in school hols) & BHs 10-4 **Fees** Entrance free (£2.50 parking) **Facilities** 🅿 Ⓟ ⏛ ♿ (partly accessible) (Accessibility limited to 95%, due to Grade II building status) toilets for disabled shop ⊗

Northumberland

BAMBURGH

Bamburgh Castle

NE69 7DF
☎ **01668 214515 & 214208**
web: www.bamburghcastle.com
dir: A1 Belford by-pass, E on B1342 to Bamburgh

Rising dramatically from a rocky outcrop, Bamburgh Castle is a huge, square Norman castle. Last restored in the 19th century, it has an impressive hall and an armoury with a large collection of armour from the Tower of London. These formidable stone walls have witnessed dark tales of royal rebellion, bloody battles, spellbinding legends and millionaire benefactors. Experience the sights, stories and atmosphere of over two thousand years of exhilarating history.

Times Open Mar-Oct, daily 10-5 (last admission 4).* **Fees** £8 (ch under 5 free, ch 5-15yrs £4 & pen £7). **Facilities** 🅿 ⓟ ⚏ ⇝ (outdoor) ♿ (partly accessible) (5 castle rooms accessible to wheelchairs) toilets for disabled shop ⊗

BARDON MILL

Vindolanda (Chesterholm)

Vindolanda Trust NE47 7JN
☎ **01434 344277** 📄 **01434 344060**
e-mail: info@vindolanda.com
web: www.vindolanda.com
dir: signed from A69 or B6318

Vindolanda was a Roman fort and frontier town. It was started well before Hadrian's Wall, and became a base for 500 soldiers. The civilian settlement lay just west of the fort and has been excavated. The excellent museum in the country house of Chesterholm nearby has displays and reconstructions. There are also formal gardens and an open-air museum with Roman Temple, shop, house and Northumbrian croft.

Times Open Feb-Mar, daily 10-5; Apr-Sep, 10-6; Oct & Nov 10-5. Limited winter opening, please contact site for further details.* **Facilities** 🅿 ⚏ ⇝ (outdoor) ♿ (partly accessible) (please contact for further info) toilets for disabled shop ⊗

BELSAY

Belsay Hall, Castle and Gardens

NE20 0DX
☎ **01661 881636** 📄 **01661 881043**
web: www.english-heritage.org.uk
dir: on A696

Beautiful neo-classical hall, built from its own quarries with a spectacular garden deservedly listed Grade I in the Register of Gardens. It is slightly unclear who built the 'Grecian-style hall', however it was designed by Sir Charles in 1807, in Greek Revival style. The magnificent 30 acres of grounds contain the ruins of a 14th-century castle.

Times Open all year, Apr-Sep, daily 10-5; Oct-1 Nov, daily 10-4; 2 Nov-Mar, Thu-Mon 10-4. Closed 24-26 Dec & 1 Jan. **Fees** £6.50 (concessions £5.50, ch £3.30). Family ticket £16.30. Please call 0870 333 1181 for the most up to date prices and opening times when planning your visit. **Facilities** 🅿 ⚏ ⇝ toilets for disabled shop ✣

CAMBO

Wallington House Walled Garden & Grounds

NE61 4AR
☎ **01670 773600** 📄 **01670 774420**
e-mail: wallington@nationaltrust.org.uk
web: www.nationaltrust.org.uk
dir: 6m NW of Belsay

Wallington is the largest country estate protected by the National Trust. With 13,000 acres that include the entire village of Cambo, the main attraction is the country house set among woods and gardens. There is a Pre-Raphaelite central hall, a small museum of curio sites and a display of dolls' houses. There are plenty of walks exploring the historic landscape, and a walled garden created by the Trevelyan family in the 1920s. Contact the estate for details of open-air theatre and rock and classical music concerts.

Times Open: House daily (ex Tue) 13 Mar-Oct 1-5.30. Grounds open all year dawn-dusk (closed 25 Dec) **Fees** House, walled garden & grounds: £9.70 (ch £4.85). Family £24.20; Garden & grounds only £6.75 (ch £3.40). Family £16.80.* **Facilities** 🅿 ⚏ 🍽 licensed ⇝ (outdoor) toilets for disabled shop ♣

Northumberland

GREENHEAD

Roman Army Museum

Carvoran CA8 7JB
☎ **016977 47485**
e-mail: info@vindolanda.com **web:** www.vindolanda.com
dir: follow brown tourist signs from A69 or B6318

Situated alongside the Walltown Grags Section of Hadrian's Wall, the museum is a great introduction to the Roman Army. Find out about Roman weapons, training, pay, off-duty activities and more. See if you can be persuaded to join up by watching the recruitment film, or view the Eagle's Eye film and soar with the eagle over Hadrian's Wall.

Times Open Feb-Mar & Oct-Nov, 10-5; Apr-Sep 10-6 (closed mid Nov-mid Feb)* **Facilities** ❷ Ⓟ ⊑ ﬁ (outdoor) ⟁ toilets for disabled shop ⊗

ROTHBURY

Cragside

NE65 7PX
☎ **01669 620333 & 620150** 📠 **01669 620066**
e-mail: cragside@nationaltrust.org.uk
web: www.nationaltrust.org.uk
dir: 15m NW of Morpeth on A697, left onto B6341, entrance 1m N of Rothbury

The aptly named Cragside was home to Victorian inventor and landscape genius, Lord Armstrong, and sits high above Debden Burn. Crammed with ingenious gadgets it was the first house in the world to be lit by water-powered electricity. In the 1880s it had hot and cold running water, central heating, fire alarms, telephones, and a passenger lift. The estate includes 40 miles of footpaths to explore, including lovely Victorian gardens.

Times Open, Estate & Gardens: 13 Mar-Oct, Tue-Sun & BH Mons 10.30-5.30; Nov-mid Dec, Wed-Sun 11-4 (or dusk if earlier). Last admission 1hr before closing. House 3 Apr-Sep, 1-5.30, 2 Oct-4 Nov, 1-4.30. **Fees** House, Gardens & Estate £13.20 (ch £6.60) Family £33. Garden & Estate £8.50 (ch £3.50) Family ticket £20.50* **Facilities** ❷ ❗️ licensed ﬁ ⟁ (partly accessible) (very steep paths on estate) toilets for disabled shop ⋇

WALWICK

Chesters Roman Fort

Chollerford NE46 4EP
☎ **01434 681379**
web: www.english-heritage.org.uk
dir: 0.5m W of Chollerford on B6318

The best-preserved Roman cavalry fort in Britain. The museum holds displays of carved stones, altars and sculptures from all along Hadrian's Wall.

Times Open all year, Apr-Sep, daily 10-6; Oct-Mar, daily 10-4. Closed 24-26 Dec & 1 Jan. **Fees** £4.50 (concessions £3.80, ch £2.30). Please check web site or call 0870 333 1181 for the most up to date prices and opening times when planning your visit. **Facilities** ❷ ⊑ shop ⋇

WARKWORTH

Warkworth Castle & Hermitage

NE66 0UJ
☎ **01665 711423**
web: www.english-heritage.org.uk

The magnificent eight-towered keep of Warkworth Castle stands on a hill high above the River Coquet, dominating all around it. A complex stronghold, it was home to the Percy family, which at times wielded more power in the North than the King himself.

Times Open all year. Castle: Apr-Sep, daily 10-5; Oct-1 Nov, daily 10-4; 2 Nov-Mar, Sat-Mon 10-4. Hermitage: Apr-Sep, Wed, Sun & BH 11-5. Closed 24-26 Dec & 1 Jan. **Fees** Castle: £4.20 (concessions £3.60, ch £2.10). Family ticket £10.50. Hermitage: £3 (concessions £2.60, ch £1.50). Please check web site or call 0870 333 1181 for the most up to date prices and opening times when planning your visit. **Facilities** ❷ ⟁ (partly accessible) (limited access, steps) toilets for disabled shop ⋇

WYLAM

George Stephenson's Birthplace

NE41 8BP
☎ **01661 853457**
e-mail: georgestephensons@nationaltrust.org.uk
web: www.nationaltrust.org.uk
dir: 1.5m S of A69 at Wylam

Birthplace of the world famous railway engineer, this small stone tenement was built around 1760 to accommodate mining families. The furnishings reflect the year of Stephenson's birth here in 1781, his whole family living in one room.

Times Open 15 Mar-2 Nov, Thu-Sun, 12-5 & BH Mons.* **Facilities** Ⓟ ⊑ ⟁ toilets for disabled ⊗ ⋇

NOTTINGHAMSHIRE

EDWINSTOWE

Sherwood Forest Country Park & Visitor Centre   FREE

NG21 9HN
☎ 01623 823202 & 824490 📄 01623 823202
e-mail: sherwood.forest@nottscc.gov.uk
web: www.nottinghamshire.gov.uk/sherwoodforestcp
dir: on B6034 N of Edwinstowe between A6075 and A616

At the heart of the Robin Hood legend is Sherwood Forest. Today it is a country park and visitor centre with 450 acres of ancient oaks and shimmering silver birches. Waymarked pathways guide you through the forest. A year round programme of events includes the spectacular annual Robin Hood Festival.

Times Open all year. Country Park: open daily dawn to dusk. Visitor Centre: open daily 10-5 (4.30 Nov-Mar). Closed 25 Dec.*
Facilities 🅿 🄿 ⛄🍴 (outdoor) toilets for disabled shop

FARNSFIELD

White Post Farm

NG22 8HL
☎ 01623 882977 & 882026 📄 01623 883499
e-mail: admin@whitepostfarm.co.uk
web: www.whitepostfarm.co.uk
dir: 12m N of Nottingham on A614

With over 25 acres there's lots to see and do at the White Post Farm. There are more than 3000 animals including pigs, goats and sheep, along with more exotic animals like deer, reptiles and wallabies. The new indoor play area is ideal for small children, and there's also a sledge run, trampolines and pedal go-karts.

Times Open daily from 10* **Fees** £8.50 (ch 2-16 £7.75, under 2s free)* **Facilities** 🅿 🄿 ⛄🍴 licensed 🍴 (indoor & outdoor) 🔱 toilets for disabled shop ⊗

NEWARK-ON-TRENT

Newark Air Museum

The Airfield, Winthorpe NG24 2NY
☎ 01636 707170 📄 01636 707170
e-mail: newarkair@onetel.com
web: www.newarkairmuseum.org
dir: easy access from A1, A46, A17 & Newark relief road, follow tourist signs, next to county showground

A diverse collection of transport, training and reconnaissance aircraft, jet fighters, bombers and helicopters, now numbering more than seventy. Two Undercover Aircraft Display Halls and an Engine Hall make the museum an all-weather attraction. Everything is displayed around a WWII airfield. Special events through the year includes the Annual Cockpit Fest and Aeroboot in mid-June.

Times Open all year, Mar-Sep, daily 10-5; Oct-Feb, daily 10-4. Closed 24-26 Dec & 1 Jan. Other times by appointment.
Fees £6.50 (ch £4.25, concessions £6). Family ticket (2ad+3ch) £19.50. Party 15+. **Facilities** 🅿 🄿 ⛄🍴 (outdoor) 🔱 toilets for disabled shop

Newark Millgate Museum   FREE

48 Millgate NG24 4TS
☎ 01636 655730 📄 01636 655735
e-mail: museums@nsdc.info
web: www.newark-sherwooddc.gov.uk/museums
dir: easy access from A1 & A46

The museum is home to diverse social history collections and features fascinating exhibitions - recreated streets, shops and houses in period settings. There are also children's activities. The mezzanine gallery, home to a number of temporary exhibitions shows the work of local artists, designers and photographers.

Times Open all year, Apr-Sep, Tue-Sun, 10.30-4.30; Oct-Mar, Tue-Fri, 10.30-4, Sat-Sun 1-4. Open spring and summer BH Mon.
Facilities 🄿 ⛄🔱 (partly accessible) (access to ground floor only for wheelchair users) toilets for disabled shop ⊗

Newark-on-Trent continued

Vina Cooke Museum of Dolls & Bygone Childhood

The Old Rectory, Cromwell NG23 6JE
☎ 01636 821364
e-mail: info@vinasdolls.co.uk
web: www.vinasdolls.co.uk
dir: 5m N of Newark off A1

All kinds of childhood memorabilia are displayed in this 17th-century house: prams, toys, dolls' houses, costumes and a large collection of Victorian and Edwardian dolls including Vina Cooke hand-made character dolls.

Times Open Apr-Sep, Tue, Thu, Sat-Sun & BH 10.30-4.30. Mon, Wed, Fri and Oct-Mar by appointment, please telephone. **Fees** £3 (ch £1.50, pen £2.50).* **Facilities** ℗ ℗ ♬ (outdoor) ሌ (partly accessible) (5 steps to front door with handrail on both sides) ⊗

NOTTINGHAM

Galleries of Justice

The Shire Hall, High Pavement, Lace Market NG1 1HN
☎ 0115 952 0555   ▤ 0115 993 9828
e-mail: info@nccl.org.uk
web: www.nccl.org.uk
dir: follow signs to city centre, brown heritage signs to Lace Market & Galleries of Justice

The Galleries of Justice are located on the site of an original Court and County Gaol. Recent developments include the arrival of the HM Prison Service Collection, which will now be permanently housed in the 1833 wing. Never before seen artefacts from prisons across the country offer visitors the chance to experience some of Britain's most gruesome, yet often touching, reminders of what prison life would have been for inmates and prison staff over the last three centuries.

Times Open all year, Tue-Sun & BH Mon 10-5 (also open Mon in school hols). (Last admission one hour before closing). Contact for Xmas opening times.* **Facilities** ℗ ☐ ♬ (indoor) toilets for disabled shop ⊗

The Museum of Nottingham Life

Brewhouse Yard, Castle Boulevard NG7 1FB
☎ 0115 915 3640   ▤ 0115 915 3601
e-mail: anni@ncmg.org.uk
web: www.nottinghammuseum.org.uk
dir: follow signs to city centre, the museum is a 5 min walk from city centre with easy access from train, tram and bus

Nestled in the rock below Nottingham Castle and housed in a row of 17th-century cottages, the museum presents a realistic glimpse of life in Nottingham over the last 300 years. Discover the caves behind the museum and peer through 1920s shop windows.

Times Open all year, daily, 10-4.30. Last admission 4. Closed 24-26 Dec, 1-2 Jan.* **Facilities** ℗ ♬ (outdoor) ሌ (partly accessible) (ground floor fully accessible to all, but no lifts in main museum or Rock Cottage) toilets for disabled shop ⊗

Nottingham Castle Museum & Art Gallery

Off Friar Ln NG1 6EL
☎ 0115 915 3700   ▤ 0115 915 3653
e-mail: castle@ncmg.org.uk
web: www.nottinghamcastle.org.uk
dir: Follow signs to city centre, then signs to castle.

This 17th-century building is both museum and art gallery, with major temporary exhibitions, by historical and contemporary artists, as well as the permanent collections. There is a 'Story of Nottingham' exhibition and a gallery designed especially to entertain young children. Guided tours of the underground passages take place on most days.

Times Open all year, daily; Mar-Sep 10-5; Oct-Feb 10-4 (last entry 30 mins before closing)* **Facilities** ℗ ☐ ♬ (outdoor) ሌ toilets for disabled shop ⊗

Wollaton Hall, Gardens & Park

Wollaton NG8 2AE
☎ 0115 915 3900 🖷 0115 915 3942
e-mail: info@wollatonhall.org.uk
web: www.wollatonhall.org.uk
dir: M1 junct 25 signed from A52, A609, A6514, A60 and city centre

Built in the late 16th century, and extended in the 19th, Wollaton Hall and Park holds Nottingham's Natural History Museum, Nottingham's Industrial Museum, the Wollaton Park Visitor Centre, and the Yard Gallery, which has changing exhibitions exploring art and the environment. The Hall itself is set in 500 acres of historic deer park, with herds of red and fallow deer roaming wild. There are also formal gardens, a lake, nature trails and adventure playgrounds.

Times Open all year, daily, Apr-Oct 11-5; Nov-Mar 11-4. (Please phone for Xmas & New Year closing times.)* **Facilities** 🅿 ⬛ 🍴 (outdoor) ♿ toilets for disabled shop ⊗

OLLERTON

Rufford Abbey Country Park

NG22 9DF
☎ 01623 821338 🖷 01623 824840
e-mail: info.rufford@nottscc.gov.uk
web: www.nottinghamshire.gov.uk/ruffordcp
dir: 3m S of Ollerton, directly off A614

At the heart of the wooded country park stand the remains of a 12th-century Cistercian Abbey, housing an exhibition on the life of a Cistercian Monk at Rufford. Many species of wildlife can be seen on the lake, and there are lovely formal gardens with sculptures, plus exhibitions of contemporary crafts in the gallery.

Times Open all year, daily 10-5 (4.30 in winter). Closed 25 Dec.
Fees Free Admission. Small seasonal charge for car parking.
Facilities 🅿 ⬛ 🍴 licensed 🍴 (outdoor) ♿ (partly accessible) (visitor facilities accessible, advanced booking for w/chair loan) toilets for disabled shop

SOUTHWELL

The Workhouse

Upton Rd NG25 0PT
☎ 01636 817250 🖷 01636 817251
e-mail: theworkhouse@nationaltrust.org.uk
web: www.nationaltrust.org.uk
dir: 13m from Nottingham on A612

Discover the most complete workhouse in existence. Meet the Reverend Becher, the founder of the Workhouse, by watching the introductory film and immerse yourself in the unique atmosphere evoked by the audio guide. Based on real archive records, the guide helps bring the 19th-century inhabitants back to life. Discover how society dealt with poverty through the centuries. Explore the segregated work yards, day rooms, dormitories, master's quarters and cellars, then see the recreated working 19th-century garden and find out what food the paupers would have eaten.

Times Open 28 Feb-15 Mar, Sat -Sun 11-5; 18 Mar-1 Nov, Wed-Sun 12-5. Open BH Mons & Good Fri. (Last admission 1hr before closing, normal house admission from noon)* **Fees** With Gift Aid donation: £6.10 (ch £3.15). Family ticket (2ad+3ch) £15.35. Family ticket (1ad) £9.25.* **Facilities** 🅿 🅿 ♿ (partly accessible) (Ground floor accessible, stairs to other floors. Not suitable for motorised wheelchairs. Grounds partly accessible, loose gravel paths) toilets for disabled ⊗ 🌿

SUTTON-CUM-LOUND

Wetlands Waterfowl Reserve & Exotic Bird Park

Off Loundlow Rd DN22 8SB
☎ 01777 818099
dir: signed on A638

The Reserve is a 32-acre site for both wild and exotic waterfowl. Visitors can see a collection of birds of prey, parrots, geese, ducks, and wigeon among others. There are also many small mammals and farm and wild animals, including llamas, wallabies, emus, monkeys, red squirrels, deer and goats.

Times Open all year, daily 10-5.30 (or dusk - whichever is earlier). Closed 25 Dec.* **Facilities** 🅿 ⬛ 🍴 shop ⊗

Nottinghamshire-Oxfordshire

WORKSOP

Clumber Park

The Estate Office, Clumber Park S80 3AZ
☎ **01909 476592**   📄 **01909 500721**
e-mail: clumberpark@nationaltrust.org.uk
web: www.nationaltrust.org.uk
dir: 4.5m SE of Worksop, 6.5m SW of Retford, 1m from A1/A57

Clumber was once the country estate of the Dukes of Newcastle. Although the house no longer exists, the Walled Kitchen Garden, magnificent Gothic Revival Chapel, Pleasure Ground and lake remain as clues to its past. Covering 3,800 acres, Clumber's mosaic of important and varied habitats are home to a world of hidden nature and a haven for visitors. Bikes are available for hire.

Times Open: Park daily.* **Fees** Walled kitchen garden (Gift Aid on entry): £3 (ch free).* **Facilities** 🅿 ⬛ 🍴 licensed ♿ (partly accessible) (ramped access to chapel & walled kitchen garden & from conservatory to garden) toilets for disabled shop 🌿

OXFORDSHIRE

BROUGHTON

Broughton Castle

OX15 5EB
☎ **01295 276070**
e-mail: info@broughtoncastle.com
web: www.broughtoncastle.com
dir: 2m W of Banbury Cross on B4035 Shipston-on-Stour in Broughton village, turn off B4035 by Saye & Sele Arms

Built by Sir John de Broughton, then owned by William of Wykeham, and later by the first Lord Saye and Sele, the castle is an early 14th-and mid 16th-century house with a moat and gatehouse. Period furniture, paintings and Civil War relics are displayed. There are fine borders in the walled garden, and against the castle walls.

Times Open Etr Sun & Mon; May-15 Sep, Wed, Sun & BH Mon 2-5 (also open Thu in Jul & Aug). Last admission 4.30.* **Fees** £7 (ch £3, concessions £6). **Facilities** 🅿 ⬛ ♿ (outdoor) ♿ (partly accessible) (Ground floor & garden only for wheelchair users). toilets for disabled shop

BURFORD

Cotswold Wildlife Park

OX18 4JP
☎ **01993 823006**   📄 **01993 823807**
web: www.cotswoldwildlifepark.co.uk
dir: on A361 2m S of A40 at Burford

This 160-acre landscaped zoological park, surrounds a listed Gothic-style manor house. There is a varied collection of animals from all over the world, many of which are endangered species such as Asiatic lions, leopards, white rhinos and red pandas. There's an adventure playground, a children's farmyard, and train rides during the summer. The park has also become one of the Cotswolds' leading attractions for garden enthusiasts, with its exotic summer displays and varied plantings offering interest all year. 2010 is the 40th anniversary of the park.

Times Open all year, daily from 10, (last admission 4.30 Mar-Sep, 3.30 Oct-Feb). Closed 25 Dec. **Fees** £11.50 (ch 3-16 & over 65's £8). **Facilities** 🅿 ⬛ 🍴 licensed ♿ (indoor & outdoor) ♿ toilets for disabled shop

CHASTLETON

Chastleton House

GL56 0SU
☎ **01608 674981**   📄 **01608 674355**
e-mail: chastleton@nationaltrust.org.uk
web: www.nationaltrust.org.uk
dir: 6m from Stow-on-the-Wold. Approach from A436 towards Chipping Norton

One of England's finest and most complete Jacobean houses, Chastleton House is filled with a mixture of rare and everyday objects, furniture and textiles maintaining the atmosphere of this 400-year-old home. The gardens have a typical Elizabethan and Jacobean layout with a ring of topiary. The National Trust has focussed on conserving rather than restoring the house. Events include Summer Garden Party in July and Christmas concerts in early December.

Times Open 28 Mar-29 Sep 1-5, 3-27 Oct, 1-4. Custodians tour every Wed at 10am throughout season.* **Fees** With Gift Aid donation £8.25 (ch £3.90). Family £20.25.* **Facilities** 🅿 ♿ (partly accessible) (access restricted to lower floor & gardens) toilets for disabled 🚫 🌿

DIDCOT

Didcot Railway Centre

OX11 7NJ
☎ **01235 817200** 📄 **01235 510621**
e-mail: info@didcotrailwaycentre.org.uk
web: www.didcotrailwaycentre.org.uk
dir: M4 junct 13, A34, located on A4130 at Didcot Parkway
Station

Based around the original GWR engine shed, the Centre is
home to the biggest collection anywhere of Great Western
Railway steam locomotives, carriages and wagons. A typical
GWR station has been re-created and a section of Brunel's
original broad gauge track relaid, with a replica of the Fire Fly
locomotive of 1840. There is a full programme of steamdays,
including the now-traditional Thomas the Tank and Santa
specials. Contact for a timetable. 2010 marks the 175th
anniversary of the Great Western Railway.

Times Open all year, Sat-Sun; daily 14-22 Feb; 4-19 Apr ; 23-31
May; 20 Jun-6 Sep; 24 Oct-1 Nov; 27 Dec-3 Jan. Day out with
Thomas 6-8 Mar, 2-4 Oct & 5-23 Dec, Fri-Sun.* **Fees** £5-£10
depending on event (ch £4-£9, concessions £4.50-£9.50).*
Facilities 🅿 ⬚ ⭐ licensed 🍴 (outdoor) ♿ (partly accessible)
(18 awkward steps at entrance) toilets for disabled shop

HENLEY-ON-THAMES

River & Rowing Museum

Mill Meadows RG9 1BF
☎ **01491 415600** 📄 **01491 415601**
e-mail: museum@rrm.co.uk
web: www.rrm.co.uk
dir: off A4130, signed to Mill Meadows

Discover The River Thames, the sport of rowing and the
town of Henley-on-Thames at this award-winning museum,
a contemporary building overlooking the river and bordered
by meadows. You can also meet Mr Toad, Ratty, Badger and
Mole at the Wind in the Willows exhibition. E.H. Shepard's
famous illustrations are brought to life by 3-D models of their
adventures. See Ratty and Mole's picnic on the riverbank, get
lost in the Wild Wood or watch the weasels at Toad Hall.

Times Open: May-Aug 10-5.30; Sep-Apr 10-5. Closed 24-25
& 31 Dec & 1 Jan.* **Facilities** 🅿 🅿 ⬚ ⭐ licensed ♿ (partly
accessible) toilets for disabled shop ⊗

LONG WITTENHAM

Pendon Museum

OX14 4QD
☎ **01865 407365** 📄 **0870 236 8125**
e-mail: sandra@pendon.plus.com
web: www.pendonmuseum.com
dir: follow brown signs from A4130 Didcot-Wallingford or A415
Abingdon-Wallingford road

This charming exhibition shows highly detailed and historically
accurate model railway and village scenes transporting the
visitor back into 1930s country landscapes. Skilled modellers
can often be seen at work on the exhibits.

Times Open Sat & Sun 2-5 (last admission 4.45), BH wknds from
11 also Wed in school hols. Closed Dec. **Fees** £5 (ch £3, under 6
free, pen £4). Family ticket (2ad+3ch) £16. **Facilities** 🅿 🅿 ⬚ ♿
toilets for disabled shop ⊗

OXFORD

Ashmolean Museum of Art & Archaeology FREE

Beaumont St OX1 2PH
☎ 01865 278000   📄 01865 278018
web: www.ashmolean.org
dir: city centre, opposite The Randolph Hotel

The oldest museum in the country, opened in 1683, the Ashmolean contains Oxford University's priceless collections. Many important historical art pieces and artefacts are on display, including work from Ancient Greece through to the twentieth century. The museum has undergone a massive redevelopment, including the building of 39 new galleries, an education centre, conservation studios and a walkway.

Times Open all year, Tue-Sun 10-5, BH Mons 10-5. Closed during St.Giles Fair (7-9 Sept) Xmas & 1 Jan. Facilities ℗ 🖵 †◎¶ licensed ♿ toilets for disabled shop ⊗

Museum of Oxford FREE

St Aldate's OX1 1DZ
☎ 01865 252761   📄 01865 252555
e-mail: museum@oxford.gov.uk
web: www.museumofoxford.org.uk

Permanent displays depict the archaeology and history of the city through the ages. There are temporary exhibitions, facilities for school parties and groups, and an audio tour. A programme of family, community events and activities also operates throughout the year.

Times Open all year, Tue-Fri 10-5, Sat & Sun 12-5. Closed 25-26 Dec.* Facilities 🖵 ♿ (partly accessible) (main entrance steps, alternative access to ground floor via Town Hall next door) toilets for disabled shop ⊗

Museum of the History of Science FREE

Broad St OX1 3AZ
☎ 01865 277280   📄 01865 277288
e-mail: museum@mhs.ox.ac.uk
web: www.mhs.ox.ac.uk
dir: next to Sheldonian Theatre in city centre, on Broad St

The first purpose-built museum in Britain, containing the world's finest collection of early scientific instruments used in astronomy, navigation, surveying, physics and chemistry. Various events through the year.

Times Open all year, Tue-Fri 12-5, Sat 10-5, Sun 2-5. Closed Xmas and Etr Sun. Facilities ℗ ♿ (partly accessible) (lift to basement) toilets for disabled shop ⊗

Oxford Castle - Unlocked

44-46 Oxford Castle OX1 1AY
☎ 01865 260666   📄 01865 260667
e-mail: info@oxfordcastleunlocked.co.uk
web: www.oxfordcastleunlocked.co.uk
dir: in city centre off New Rd

For the first time in 1000 years, the secrets of Oxford Castle will be "Unlocked" revealing episodes of violence, executions, great escapes, betrayal and even romance. Walk through these ancient buildings and experience the stories that connect the real people of the past to these extraordinary events. At weekends enjoy a Sights and Secrets walking tour.

Times Open all year, daily 10-5.30 (last tour 4.20). Closed 25 Dec.* Fees £7.50 (ch £5.35, concessions £6.20).* Facilities ℗ 🖵 ⊞ (outdoor) ♿ (partly accessible) (St Georges Tower & Castle Mound not accessible) toilets for disabled shop ⊗

Oxford University Museum of Natural History FREE

Parks Rd OX1 3PW
☎ 01865 272950   📄 01865 272970
e-mail: info@oum.ox.ac.uk
web: www.oum.ox.ac.uk
dir: opposite Keble College

Built between 1855 and 1860, this museum of "the natural sciences" was intended to satisfy a growing interest in biology, botany, archaeology, zoology, entomology and so on. The museum reflects Oxford University's position as a 19th-century centre of learning, with displays of early dinosaur discoveries, Darwinian evolution and Elias Ashmole's collection of preserved animals. Although visitors to the Pitt-Rivers Museum must pass through the University Museum, the two should not be confused. The museum celebrates its 150th Anniversary in 2010 see website for details.

Times Open daily 10-5. Times vary at Xmas & Etr. Facilities ℗ ⊞ (outdoor) ♿ toilets for disabled shop ⊗

Pitt Rivers Museum   FREE

South Parks Rd OX1 3PP
☎ 01865 270927   📄 01865 270943
e-mail: prm@prm.ox.ac.uk
web: www.prm.ox.ac.uk
dir: 10 min walk from city centre, visitors entrance on Parks Rd
through the Oxford University Museum of Natural History

The museum is one of the city's most popular attractions. It is
part of the University of Oxford and was founded in 1884. The
collections held at the museum are internationally acclaimed,
and contain many objects from different cultures of the world
and from various periods, all grouped by type, or purpose.

Times Open all year, Tue-Sun & BH Mon 10-4.30, Mon 12-4.30.
Contact museum at Christmas & Easter to check times. The upper
gallery, housing the weapons and armour displays, will be closed
until Spring 2010. Facilities ⓟ & toilets for disabled shop ⊗

WATERPERRY

Waterperry Gardens

OX33 1JZ
☎ 01844 339226 & 339254   📄 01844 339883
e-mail: office@waterperrygardens.co.uk
web: www.waterperrygardens.co.uk
dir: 7.5m from city centre. From E M40 junct 8, from N M40
junct 8a. Waterperry 2.5m form A40, exit a Wheatley and follow
brown tourist signs

Waterperry has eight acres of ornamental gardens, including
formal and rose gardens, a river walk, lily canal and classical
herbaceous border. The Gallery and Long Barn feature works of
art, and the shop carries a large range of locally grown apples
and juices. Look out for outdoor theatre in the gardens in the
summer. Ring for details of this and a full programme of events
or visit website.

Times Open daily all year, Jan-Feb & Nov-Dec 10-5; Mar-Oct
10-5.30. Closed Xmas, New Year & during "Art in Action" 16-19
Jul.* Facilities ⓟ ☕ 🍴 licensed ⋒ (outdoor) & toilets for
disabled shop ⊗

WITNEY

Cogges Manor Farm Museum

Church Ln, Cogges OX28 3LA
☎ 01993 772602   📄 01993 703056
web: www.cogges.org
dir: 0.5m SE off A4022

The museum includes the Manor, dairy and walled garden, and
has breeds of animals typical of the Victorian period. The first
floor of the manor contains period rooms. Special events take
place through the season.

Times Open Apr-Oct, Tue-Fri 10.30-5.30, Sat, Sun & BH Mon,
12-5.30. Early closing Oct. Closed Good Fri.* Facilities ⓟ ⓟ ☕
⋒ (outdoor) toilets for disabled shop

WOODSTOCK

Blenheim Palace

OX20 1PP
☎ 08700 602080   📄 01993 810570
e-mail: operations@blenheimpalace.com
web: www.blenheimpalace.com
dir: M40 junct 9, follow signs to Blenheim Palace, on A44 8m N
of Oxford

Home of the Duke and Duchess of Marlborough and birthplace
of Sir Winston Churchill, Blenheim Palace is an English
Baroque masterpiece. Fine furniture, sculpture, paintings
and tapestries are set in magnificent gilded staterooms that
overlook sweeping lawns and formal gardens. 'Capability'
Brown landscaped the 2100-acre park, which is open to visitors
for pleasant walks and beautiful views. A permanent exhibit
'Blenheim Palace: The Untold Story' explores the lives of those
who have lived here, through the eyes of the servants. Please
telephone for details of the full event programme throughout
the year including a Jousting Tournament and the Battle Proms.

Times Open Palace & Gardens 13 Feb-12 Dec (ex Mon-Tue in
Nov & Dec) daily 10.30-6. (last admission 4.45). Park daily all
year 9-6 (last admission 4.45) Closed 25 Dec. Fees Palace, Park
& Gardens £12.30-£17.50 (ch £6.75-£10, concessions £10.80-
£14). Familly £46. Park & Gardens £6.90-£10 (ch £3.30-£5,
concessions £5.70-£7.50). Family £25. Facilities ⓟ ⓟ ☕ 🍴
licensed ⋒ (outdoor) & (partly accessible) (Wheelchair access via
lift in Palace) toilets for disabled shop ⊗

Woodstock continued

Oxfordshire Museum · FREE

Fletcher's House, Park St OX20 1SN
☎ 01993 811456 · 📄 01993 813239
e-mail: oxon.museum@oxfordshire.go.uk
web: www.tomocc.org.uk
dir: A44 Evesham-Oxford, follow signs for Blenheim Palace. Museum opposite church

Situated in the heart of the historic town of Woodstock, the award-winning redevelopment of Fletcher's House provides a home for the new county museum. Set in attractive gardens, the new museum celebrates Oxfordshire in all its diversity and features collections of local history, art, archaeology, landscape and wildlife as well as a gallery exploring the County's innovative industries from nuclear power to nanotechnology. Interactive exhibits offer new learning experiences for visitors of all ages. The museum's purpose-built Garden Gallery houses a variety of touring exhibitions of regional and national interest. A new display of dinosaur footprints from Ardley Quarry and a replica megalosaurus, are located in the walled garden.

Times Open all year, Tue-Sat 10-5, Sun 2-5. Closed Good Fri, 25-26 Dec & 1 Jan. Galleries closed on Mon, but open BH Mons, 2-5. **Facilities** ℗ 🗔 ⭐ licensed 🛋 (outdoor) ♿ toilets for disabled shop ⊗

RUTLAND

OAKHAM

Oakham Castle · FREE

Catmos St LE15 6HW
☎ 01572 758440 · 📄 01572 758445
e-mail: museum@rutland.gov.uk
web: www.rutland.gov.uk/castle
dir: off Market Place

An exceptionally fine Norman Great Hall built in the 12th century. Earthworks, walls and remains of an earlier motte can be seen along with medieval sculptures and unique presentation horseshoes forfeited by peers of the realm and royalty to the Lord of the Manor. The castle is now a popular place for civil marriages, meetings and special events.

Times Open all year, Mon-Sat 10.30-5 (closed 1-1.30), Sun 2-4. Closed Xmas, New Year & Good Fri* **Facilities** ℗ ♿ (partly accessible) shop ⊗

Rutland County Museum & Visitor Centre · FREE

Catmos St LE15 6HW
☎ 01572 758440 · 📄 01572 758445
e-mail: museum@rutland.gov.uk
web: www.rutland.gov.uk/museum
dir: on A6003, S of town centre

Rutland County Museum is the perfect introduction to England's smallest county. The 'Welcome to Rutland' gallery is a guide to its history. The museum includes a shop and study area. On show in the 18th-century Riding School are displays of archaeology, history and an extensive rural life collection.

Times Open all year, Mon-Sat 10.30-5, Sun 2-4. Closed Xmas, New Year & Good Fri.* **Facilities** 🅿 ℗ ♿ (partly accessible) toilets for disabled shop ⊗

SHROPSHIRE

ATCHAM

Attingham Park

SY4 4TP
☎ 01743 708123 · 📄 01743 708175
e-mail: attingham@nationaltrust.org.uk
web: www.nationaltrust.org.uk/attinghampark
dir: 4m SE of Shrewsbury on B4380

Attingham Park is centred on one of Britain's finest regency mansions, set in a landscaped deer park designed by Humphry Repton. The house is undergoing a major project to revive and re-discover the original lavish decorative schemes, with new upstairs rooms open for the first time. The park is an ideal place for a country walk, and there is a programme of events throughout the year.

Times Park & grounds open daily, 9-6. House: daily. 11-5.30, tours 13-28 Nov, 11-3. **Fees** House & grounds: £9.40 (ch £5.70) Family (2ad+3ch) £20.50. Grounds only: £4.20 (ch £2.20) Family £10.40. **Facilities** 🅿 🗔 🛋 (outdoor) ♿ (partly accessible) (level access, lift to first floor, top floor only accessible via stairs) toilets for disabled shop 🌱

BOSCOBEL

Boscobel House and The Royal Oak

Brewood ST19 9AR
☎ 01902 850244   📄 01902 850244
web: www.english-heritage.org.uk
dir: on unclass road between A41 and A5

Built around 1632, Boscobel House has been fully restored and refurbished and is essentially a farmhouse that was converted into a hunting lodge. After his defeat at the Battle of Worcester in 1651, the future King Charles II hid from Cromwell's troops in an oak tree in the grounds, and then in a priest-hole in the attic of the house. The Royal Oak that visitors can see now was grown from an acorn taken from the original tree.

Times Open Apr-Oct, Wed-Sun & BH 10-5. (last entry 1hr before closing). **Fees** £5.20 (concessions £4.40, ch £2.60). Family ticket £13. Please check web site or call 0870 333 1181 for the most up to date prices and opening times when planning your visit. **Facilities** 🅿 ⬚ 🛆 shop ⊗ ♯

BURFORD

Burford House Gardens

WR15 8HQ
☎ 01584 810777   📄 01584 810673
e-mail: info@burford.co.uk
web: www.burford.co.uk
dir: off A456, 1m W of Tenbury Wells, 8m from Ludlow

Burford House and Garden Centre set within 15 acres, incorporates a Georgian mansion, which houses a shop and riverside gardens where you will find the National Clematis Collection.

Times Open all year 9-6 or dusk if earlier. Closed 25-26 Dec.* **Facilities** 🅿 ⬚ 🍴 licensed 🛆 (outdoor) ♿ (partly accessible) toilets for disabled shop ⊗

COSFORD

The Royal Air Force Museum

TF11 8UP
☎ 01902 376200   📄 01902 376211
e-mail: cosford@rafmuseum.org **web:** www.rafmuseum.org
dir: on A41, 1m S of M54 junct 3

The Royal Air Force Museum Cosford has one of the largest aviation collections in the UK, with 70 historic aircraft on display. Visitors will be able to see Britain's V bombers - Vulcan, Victor and Valiant and other aircraft suspended in flying attitudes in the national Cold War exhibition, housed in a landmark building covering 8000sqm.

Times Open all year daily, 10-6 (last admission 4). Closed 24-26 Dec & 1 Jan, 7-11 Jan.* **Facilities** 🅿 ⬚ 🍴 licensed 🛆 (outdoor) ♿ toilets for disabled shop ⊗

CRAVEN ARMS

The Shropshire Hills Discovery Centre

School Rd SY7 9RS
☎ 01588 676000   📄 01588 676030
e-mail: zoe.griffin@shropshire-cc.gov.uk
web: www.shropshirehillsdiscoverycentre.co.uk
dir: on A49, on S edge of Craven Arms

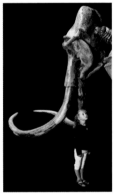

This attraction explores the history, nature and geography of the Shropshire Hills, through interactive displays and simulations. The award-winning Centre has been revamped over the winter and now has a brand new Secret Hills exhibition. Become a landscape detective as you follow the new family Timeline Trail, which takes you from the Ice Age to the present day. On the way meet the Shropshire Mammoth, look inside an Iron Age Round House, dress up in Celtic clothing, make a mediaeval seal and float over Shropshire by watching the panoramic hot air balloon film. Other features include the Ice Age Orienteering trail around Onny Meadows, a Craft Room and a Riverside Ramble.

Times Open all year, daily from 10. (Last admission 3.30 Nov-Mar, 4.30 Apr-Oct).* **Facilities** 🅿 🅿 ⬚ 🍴 licensed 🛆 (outdoor) toilets for disabled shop ⊗

QUATT

Dudmaston Estate

WV15 6QN
☎ 01746 780866   🖷 01746 780744
e-mail: dudmaston@nationaltrust.org.uk
web: www.nationaltrust.org.uk/dudmaston
dir: 4m SE of Bridgnorth on A442

The 17th-century flower paintings which belonged to Francis Darby of Coalbrookdale are exhibited in this house of the same period, with modern works, botanical art and fine furniture. The house stands in an extensive park and garden and there are woodland and lakeside walks.

Times Open House Apr-Sep, Tue, Wed, Sun & BH Mon, 2-5. Garden, tea room & shop Sun-Wed, noon-5.30. Closed Good Fri. **Fees** House & Garden £6.80. Garden only £5.50. Family ticket £17. **Facilities** 🅿 🅿 ☕ 🥤 (outdoor) ♿ (partly accessible) (all ground floors are accessible, first floor galleries are currently unaccessible) toilets for disabled shop ⊗ 🐾

TELFORD

Hoo Farm Animal Kingdom

Preston-on-the-Weald Moors TF6 6DJ
☎ 01952 677917   🖷 01952 677944
e-mail: info@hoofarm.com
web: www.hoofarm.com
dir: M54 junct 6, follow brown tourist signs

Hoo Farm is a real children's paradise where there is always something happening. A clean, friendly farm that appeals to all ages and offers close contact with a wide variety of animals from fluffy chicks and lambs to foxes, llamas, deer and ostriches. A daily programme of events encourages audience participation in the form of bottle feeding lambs, pig feeding, ferret racing and collecting freshly-laid eggs. The Craft Area offers the chance to try your hand at candle dipping, glass or pottery painting or even throwing a pot on the potters wheel. There are junior quad bikes and a rifle range, pony rides, powered mini-tractors as well as indoor and outdoor play areas and a games room. Please telephone for details of special events throughout the year.

Times Open 25 Mar-9 Sep, Tue-Sun 10-6; 10 Sep-24 Nov, Tue-Sun, 10-5. 25; Nov-24 Dec, daily 10-5. Closes at 1 on 24 Dec. Closed 25 Dec to mid March.* **Facilities** 🅿 ☕ 🥤 (indoor & outdoor) ♿ (partly accessible) toilets for disabled shop ⊗

WESTON-UNDER-REDCASTLE

Hawkstone Historic Park & Follies

SY4 5UY
☎ 01948 841700   🖷 01939 200335
e-mail: enquiries@hawkstone.co.uk
web: www.principal-hayley.co.uk
dir: 3m from Hodnet off A53, follow brown heritage signs

Created in the 18th century by the Hill family, Hawkstone is one of the greatest historic parklands in Britain. After almost 100 years of neglect it has now been restored and designated a Grade I historic landscape. Visitors can once again experience the magical world of intricate pathways, arches and bridges, towering cliffs and follies, and an awesome grotto. The Grand Valley and woodlands have centuries-old oaks, wild rhododendrons and lofty monkey puzzles. The park covers nearly 100 acres of hilly terrain and visitors are advised to wear sensible shoes and clothing and to bring a torch. Allow 3-4 hours for the tour, which is well signposted - a route map is included in the admission price. Attractions include 'Hear King Arthur' and meeting the Duke of Wellington in the White Tower to discuss the Battle of Waterloo.

Times Open from 10 Mar, Sat & Sun; Apr-May, & Sep-Oct, Wed-Sun; Jun-Aug, daily. Closed Nov-Mar.* **Fees** Wkdays £6 (ch £4 pen & students £5). Family ticket £17.* **Facilities** 🅿 ☕ 🍽 licensed 🥤 (outdoor) ♿ (partly accessible) (access to tearooms, gift shop and grand valley) toilets for disabled shop

SOMERSET

BARRINGTON

Barrington Court

TA19 0NQ
☎ 01460 241938 & 242614   🖷 01460 243133
e-mail: barringtoncourt@nationaltrust.org.uk
web: www.nationaltrust.org.uk
dir: 5m NE of Ilminster on B3168

The house is a Tudor manor, the interior of which is currently displayed empty, though with changing exhibitions. The gardens were created in the 1920s, with the help (through the post) of Gertrude Jekyll. They are laid out in 'rooms' and there is a large walled kitchen garden supplying fresh fruit and vegetables to the restaurant.

Times Open Mar, Thu-Tue 11-4.30; Apr-Sep daily (ex Wed) 11-5; 2 Oct-2 Nov, Thu-Tue 11-4.30. 6-14 Dec, Sat & Sun 11-4.* **Fees** £9.05 (ch £3.95). Family £21.75. Groups £7.60 **Facilities** 🅿 ☕ 🍽 licensed 🥤 (outdoor) ♿ (partly accessible) (Court House not easily accessible due to many stairs) toilets for disabled shop ⊗ 🐾

BATH

American Museum in Britain

Claverton Manor BA2 7BD
☎ 01225 460503 🖷 01225 469160
e-mail: info@americanmuseum.org
web: www.americanmuseum.org
dir: Signed from city centre & A36 Warminster road

Claverton Manor is just two miles south east of Bath, in a beautiful setting above the River Avon. The house was built in 1820 by Sir Jeffrey Wyatville, and is now a museum of American decorative arts. The gardens are well worth seeing, and include an American arboretum and a replica of George Washington's garden at Mount Vernon. Each year the museum holds special exhibitions and runs a full programme of special events with kids' activities, live music, living history events and Quilting Bees.

Times Open 13 Mar-Oct, Tue-Sun 12-5. Open Mon in Aug & BHs. Also open 26 Nov-19 Dec Tue-Sun 12-4.30. **Fees** £8 (ch £4.50, concessions £7). Family ticket £21.50. **Facilities** 🅿 ⏚ 🎋 (outdoor) ♿ (partly accessible) (grounds not fully accessible) toilets for disabled shop

Bath Postal Museum

27 Northgate St BA1 1AJ
☎ 01225 460333 🖷 01225 460333
e-mail: info@bathpostalmuseum.org
web: www.bathpostalmuseum.org
dir: On entering city fork left at mini rdbt. After all lights into Walcot St. Podium car park facing

The first letter sent with a stamp was sent from Bath, and this museum examines how 18th-century Bath influenced and developed the Postal System, including the story of the Penny Post. Explore the history of written communication from ancient Egyptian clay tablets, to the first Airmail flight from Bath to London in 1912. See the Victorian Post Office and watch video films including the in-house production 'History of Writing'.

Times Open all year, Mon-Sat 11-5. (Last admission Mar-Oct 4.30, Nov-Feb 4).* **Fees** £3.50 (ch under 5 free, ch £1.50,

concessions £3, students £1.50). Family and Party 10+ tickets available.* **Facilities** 🅿 ♿ shop ⊗

Fashion Museum

Bennett St BA1 2QH
☎ 01225 477173 🖷 01225 477743
e-mail: fashion_bookings@bathnes.gov.uk
web: www.fashionmuseum.co.uk
dir: Museum near city centre. Parking in Charlotte Street Car park.

The Fashion Museum showcases a world-class collection of historical and contemporary dress and includes opportunities to try on replica corsets and crinolines. It is housed in Bath's famous 18th-century Assembly Rooms designed by John Wood the Younger in 1771. Entrance to the Assembly Rooms is free. Special exhibitions are held every summer in the Ballroom.

Times Open all year, daily Jan-Feb 10.30-4; Mar-Oct, 10.30-5; Nov-Dec, 10.30-4. Closed 25-26 Dec.* **Fees** £7 (ch £5). Family ticket £20. Combined ticket with Roman Baths, £14.50 (ch £8.70).* **Facilities** 🅿 ⏚ ♿ toilets for disabled shop ⊗

The Herschel Museum of Astronomy

19 New King St BA1 2BL
☎ 01225 446865 🖷 01225 446865
e-mail: herschelbpt@btconnect.com
web: www.bath-preservation-trust.org.uk
dir: in Bath city centre

This 18th-century town house celebrates the achievements of William Herschel and his sister Caroline, who were both distinguished astronomers. William discovered Uranus in 1781. The house is decorated and furnished in the style of the period of Georgian Bath, while the gardens are semi-formal in design and include different plants and herbs popular at the time. There is also a star vault astronomy auditorium. Local Heroes exhibition as part of the Royal Society's 350th anniversary.

Times Open daily Feb-16 Dec, Mon-Tue & Thu-Fri, 1-5, Sat, Sun & BHs 11-5. **Fees** £4, (ch £2.50, students £3, concessions £3.50) Family £10.* **Facilities** 🅿 ♿ (partly accessible) shop ⊗

Bath continued

Museum of Bath at Work

Julian Rd BA1 2RH

☎ 01225 318348 🖷 01225 318348

e-mail: mobaw@hotmail.com **web:** www.bath-at-work.org.uk
dir: from city centre, off Lansdown Rd into Julian Rd. Museum next to church on right

Two thousand years of Bath's commercial and industrial development are explored with exhibits on 'The Story of Bath Stone', a Bath cabinet makers' workshop, a 1914 Horstmann car and a reconstruction of J B Bowlers' engineering and mineral water business. A local history gallery, education room and a display about local inventions add further interest.

Times Open all year, Etr-1 Nov, daily 10.30-5; Nov-Etr, wknds 10.30-5. Closed 25-26 Dec.* **Fees** £5 (concessions £3.50). Family ticket £12.* **Facilities** Ⓟ ☕ ⛩ (indoor) ♿ (partly accessible) shop ⊗

Roman Baths & Pump Room

Abbey Church Yard BA1 1LZ

☎ 01225 477785 🖷 01225 477743

e-mail: romanbaths_bookings@bathnes.gov.uk
web: www.romanbaths.co.uk
dir: M4 junct 18, A46 into city centre

The remains of the Roman baths and temple give a vivid impression of life nearly 2,000 years ago. Built next to Britain's only hot spring, the baths served the sick, and the pilgrims visiting the adjacent Temple of Sulis Minerva. Above the Temple Courtyard, the Pump Room became a popular meeting place in the 18th century. The site still flows with natural hot water and no visit is complete without a taste of the famous hot spa water. Costumed characters every day.

Times Open all year, Mar-Jun & Sep-Oct, daily 9-5; Jul & Aug, daily 9am-9pm; Jan-Feb & Nov-Dec, daily 9.30-4-30. Closed 25-26 Dec. (Last exit 1hr after these times).* **Fees** £11 (£11.50 Jul-Aug) (ch £7.20). Family ticket £32. Combined ticket with Fashion Museum £14.50 (ch £8.70).* **Facilities** Ⓟ 🍴 licensed ♿ (partly accessible) (lift to lower museum) toilets for disabled shop ⊗

CRANMORE

East Somerset Railway

Cranmore Railway Station BA4 4QP

☎ 01749 880417 🖷 01749 880764

e-mail: info@eastsomersetrailway.com
web: www.eastsomersetrailway.com
dir: on A361 between Frome & Shepton Mallet

Steam through the rolling Mendip countryside on a day out at The East Somerset Railway. Take a ride on one of the steam trains and travel back in time to the nostalgic days of steam. There are plenty of events throughout the year, from Thomas the Tank Engine and Santa Specials to Enthusiast Gala Weekends. Telephone for details.

Times Open Apr-Oct, wknds; Jun-Aug, Wed & BHs (& Thu in Aug)* **Fees** £7.50 (ch £5.50 & pen £6.50)* **Facilities** Ⓟ ☕ 🍴 licensed ⛩ ♿ (partly accessible) toilets for disabled shop

CRICKET ST THOMAS

The Wildlife Park at Cricket St Thomas

TA20 4DB

☎ 01460 30111 & 30892 🖷 01460 30817

e-mail: wildlifepark.cst@bourne-leisure.co.uk
web: www.wild.org.uk
dir: 3m E of Chard on A30, follow brown heritage signs

The Wildlife Park offers you the chance to see more than 500 animals at close quarters. Visitors can learn about what is being done to save endangered species, take a walk through the Lemur Wood, or ride on the Safari Train. During peak season, park mascot Larry the Lemur stars in his own show.

Times Open all year, daily 10-6, last admission 4; winter 10-4.30, last admission 3. Closed 25 Dec.* **Fees** £8.75 (ch 3-14 £6.50, under 3's free, concessions £7.50). Family ticket £27.50 (2ad+3ch).* **Facilities** Ⓟ ☕ 🍴 licensed ⛩ (outdoor) ♿ (partly accessible) toilets for disabled shop ⊗

DUNSTER

Dunster Castle

TA24 6SL
☎ **01643 821314 & 823004 (info only)** 📄 **01643 823000**
e-mail: dunstercastle@nationaltrust.org.uk
web: www.nationaltrust.org.uk
dir: 3m SE of Minehead, approach from A39. Approx 2m from Dunster Stn

The castle's picturesque appearance is largely due to 19th-century work, but older features can also be seen, the superb 17th-century oak staircase for example. Sub-tropical plants flourish in the 28-acre park and the terraced gardens are noted for exotica such as a giant lemon tree, yuccas, mimosa and palms as well as the National Collection of Strawberry Trees.

Times Castle: 13 Mar-Oct, daily (ex Thu) 11-5 (last entry 4). Garden & Park: Jan-12 Mar & Nov-Dec, daily 11-4, 13 Mar-Oct daily 10-5. **Fees** Castle, Garden & Park £9 (ch under 16 £4.40). Family ticket £21.50 (1 ad £13.40). Garden & Park only £5 (ch under 16 £2.30). Family ticket £12.20 (1 ad £7.30) **Facilities** ℗ ℗ ⴲ (outdoor) ⴲ (partly accessible) (ground floor wheelchair accessible, wheelchair routes through gardens) toilets for disabled shop ⊗ ⴲ

MINEHEAD

West Somerset Railway

The Railway Station TA24 5BG
☎ **01643 704996** 📄 **01643 706349**
e-mail: info@west-somerset-railway.co.uk
web: www.west-somerset-railway.co.uk
dir: Follow brown WSR sign through Taunton & onto A358. Left after 3m for Bishops Lydeard Station car park

Take a journey of discovery, relive your childhood, or simply sit back and relax as you travel along one of Britain's best and longest Heritage Railways.

Times Open May-Sep, daily; Mar, Apr & Oct, Tue-Thu & Sat-Sun, 10.15-5.15.* **Fees** £14 (ch £7, pen £12.80). Cheaper for shorter journeys.* **Facilities** ℗ ℗ ⴲ ⴲ (outdoor) ⴲ toilets for disabled shop

MONTACUTE

Montacute House

TA15 6XP
☎ **01935 823289** 📄 **01935 826921**
e-mail: montacute@nationaltrust.org.uk
web: www.nationaltrust.org.uk
dir: 4m W of Yeovil, on S side of A3088, 3m E of A303

Set amidst formal gardens, Montacute House was built by Sir Edward Phelips. He was a successful lawyer, and became Speaker of the House of Commons in 1604. Inside there are decorated ceilings, ornate fireplaces, heraldic glass and fine wood panelling. The Long Gallery displays a permanent collection of Tudor and Jacobean portraits from the National Portrait Gallery in London. Montacute has been used as the setting for successful films such as Sense and Sensibility (1995).

Times Open House & Gardens 13 Mar-Oct. **Fees** House & Garden £10.50 (ch £5). Family ticket £24.50. Garden only £6.20 (ch £3). **Facilities** ℗ ⴲ ⴲ licensed ⴲ (outdoor) ⴲ (partly accessible) (wheelchair access restricted to ground floor) toilets for disabled shop ⊗ ⴲ

SPARKFORD

Haynes International Motor Museum

BA22 7LH
☎ **01963 440804** 📄 **01963 441004**
e-mail: info@haynesmotormuseum.co.uk
web: www.haynesmotormuseum.co.uk
dir: from A303 follow A359 towards Castle Cary, museum clearly signed

An excellent day out for everyone - with more than 400 cars and bikes stunningly displayed, dating from 1886 to the present day, this is the largest international motor museum in Britain. If you want a nostalgic trip down memory lane the museum offers a host of familiar names such as Austin, MG and Morris, while for those seeking something more exotic there is a vast array of performance cars, from modern classics such as the Dodge Viper, Jaguar XJ220 and the Ferrari 360, plus the classic Jaguar E Type and AC Cobra. Also on show is a large collection of American cars, including the jewels in the Haynes crown, the V16 Cadillac, and the million-dollar Duesenberg. There's a Kids' Race Track, themed play area, soft play-bus, Super Diggers and plenty of other activities.

Times Open all year, Apr-Sep, daily 9.30-5.30; Oct-Mar, 10-4.30. Closed 24-26 Dec & 1 Jan. **Fees** £7.95 (ch £4.25, concessions £6.95). Family £10.95 (1ad+1ch), £25.75 (2ad+3ch). **Facilities** ℗ ⴲ ⴲ (outdoor) ⴲ toilets for disabled shop ⊗

Cleeve Abbey

TA23 0PS
☎ 01984 640377   📄 01984 641348
web: www.english-heritage.org.uk
dir: 0.25m S of A39

This 13th-century monastic site features some of the finest cloister buildings in England; medieval wall paintings, a mosaic tiled floor and an interesting exhibition.

Times Open Apr-Jun & Sep, daily 10-5; Jul-Aug, daily 10-6; Oct-1 Nov, daily 10-4. Closed 2 Nov- Mar. **Fees** £3.80 (concessions £3.20, ch £1.90). Please check web site or call 0870 333 1181 for the most up to date prices and opening times when planning your visit. **Facilities** ❷ 🍴 shop ♯

Tropiquaria Animal and Adventure Park

TA23 0QB
☎ 01984 640688
e-mail: info@tropiquaria.co.uk
web: www.tropiquaria.co.uk
dir: on A39, between Williton and Minehead

Housed in a 1930s BBC transmitting station, the main hall has been converted into an indoor jungle with a 15-foot waterfall, tropical plants and free-flying birds. (Snakes, lizards, iguanas, spiders, toads and terrapins are caged!) Downstairs is the submarine crypt with local and tropical marine life. Other features include landscaped gardens, the Shadowstring Puppet Theatre, and 'Wireless in the West' museum. Also two new full size pirate adventure ships are moored on the front lawn accessible to pirates of all ages! The park has an indoor playcastle for adventure and fun whatever the weather.

Times Open all year, Apr-Sep, daily 10.30-5 (last entry 4.30); Oct daily 11-5 (last entry 4); Nov-Mar Mon & wknds 11-4 (last entry 3).* **Fees** £7.50 (ch & concessions £6.50).* **Facilities** ❷ 🖵 🍴 (indoor & outdoor) ♿ (partly accessible) (aquarium not accessible) toilets for disabled shop ⊗

The Helicopter Museum

The Heliport, Locking Moor Rd BS24 8PP
☎ 01934 635227   📄 01934 645230
e-mail: helimuseum@btconnect.com
web: www.helicoptermuseum.co.uk
dir: outskirts of town on A371, nr M5 junct 21, follow propellor signs

The world's largest rotary-wing collection and the only helicopter museum in Britain, home of the Queen's Royal flight helicopters. More than 70 helicopters and autogyros are on display - including examples from France, Germany, Poland, Russia and the United States, from 1935 to the present day - with displays of models, engines and other components explaining the history and development of the rotorcraft. Special events include 'Open Cockpit Days', when visitors can learn more about how the helicopter works. Helicopter flights available on set dates throughout the year.

Times Open all year, Nov-Mar, Wed-Sun 10-4.30; Apr-Oct 10-5.30. Open daily during Etr & summer school hols 10-5.30. Closed 24-26 Dec & 1 Jan. **Fees** £5.50 (ch under 5 free, ch 5-16 £3.50, concessions £4.50). Family ticket (2ad+2ch) £15.50, (2ad+3ch) £17.50. Party 12+.* **Facilities** ❷ 🖵 🍴 (outdoor) ♿ toilets for disabled shop

North Somerset Museum

Burlington St BS23 1PR
☎ 01934 621028   📄 01934 612526
e-mail: museum.service@n-somerset.gov.uk
web: www.n-somerset.gov.uk/museum
dir: in centre of Weston-super-Mare

This museum, housed in the former workshops of the Edwardian Gaslight Company, has displays on the seaside holiday, an old chemist's shop, a dairy and Victorian pavement mosaics. Adjoining the museum is Clara's Cottage, a Westonian home of the 1900s with period kitchen, parlour, bedroom and back yard. One of the rooms has an additional display of Peggy Nisbet dolls. Other displays include wildlife gallery, mining and local archaeology, costume and ceramics. There is even a display on secret weapons developed on Birnbeck Island during WWII.

Times Open all year Mon-Sat 10-4.30. Closed 24-26 Dec & 1 Jan.* **Fees** £4.50 (ch free when accompanied by an adult, concessions £3.50)* **Facilities** ℗ 🖵 ♿ (partly accessible) (ground floor of main museum accessible) toilets for disabled shop ⊗

WOOKEY HOLE

Wookey Hole Caves & Papermill

BA5 1BB

☎ 01749 672243 📄 01749 677749

e-mail: witch@wookey.co.uk

web: www.wookey.co.uk

dir: M5 junct 22 follow signs via A38 & A371, from Bristol & Bath A39 to Wells then 2m to Wookey Hole

Britain's most spectacular caves and legendary home of the infamous Witch of Wookey. The 19th-century paper mill houses a variety of fascinating attractions including a Cave Museum, Victorian Penny Arcade, Magical Mirror Maze, Haunted Corridor of Crazy Mirrors, and the Wizard's Castle play area. Visitors can also see paper being made in Britain's only surviving handmade paper mill. Puppet theatre shows, magic lessons, an enchanted fairy garden and Dinosaur Valley round off this family day out in Wookey Gorge.

Times Open all year daily Apr-Oct 10-5; Nov-Mar 10-4; Dec-Jan, open wknds & sch hol. Closed 25-26 Dec.* **Fees** £15 (ch 4-14 & concessions £10, under 3's free)* **Facilities** 🅿 ⏻ 🍽 licensed ᴀ (outdoor) ⅊ (partly accessible) (papermill only accessible) toilets for disabled shop ⊗

YEOVILTON

Fleet Air Arm Museum

Royal Naval Air Station BA22 8HT

☎ 01935 840565 📄 01935 842630

e-mail: info@fleetairarm.com

web: www.fleetairarm.com

dir: on B3151, just off junct of A303 and A37

The Fleet Air Arm Museum is where museum meets theatre! You'll 'fly' by helicopter to the replica flight deck of aircraft carrier HMS Ark Royal. You'll see fighter aircraft and two enormous projection screens showing jet fighters taking off and landing, and even a nuclear bomb. The Museum has Europe's largest collection of naval aircraft and the first British-built Concorde. Go on board and visit the cockpit. There's an adventure playground, and the museum is located alongside Europe's busiest military air station at RNAS Yeovilton.

Times Open all year: Apr-Oct, daily 10-5.30; Nov-Mar, Wed-Sun 10-4.30 (Closed 24-26 Dec)* **Fees** £11 (ch under 17 £8, under 5 free, concessions £9). Family (2ad+3ch) £35.* **Facilities** 🅿 ℗ ⏻ 🍽 licensed ᴀ (outdoor) ⅊ toilets for disabled shop ⊗

STAFFORDSHIRE

ALTON

Alton Towers

ST10 4DB

☎ 08705 204060 📄 01538 704097

e-mail: info@alton-towers.com

web: www.altontowers.com

dir: from S - M1 junct 23a or M6 junct 15. From N - M1 junct 24a or M6 junct 16

Alton Towers is a fantastic day out for all the family. With world first rides and attractions as well as some beautiful gardens, this is more than just a theme park. The Alton Towers Resort is a popular UK short break destination for families. With a unique combination of rides and attractions suitable for all ages, the Resort consists of the Alton Towers Theme Park, waterpark, spa, two fully themed hotels and two nine-hole golf courses.

Times Open daily 14-22 Feb & 28 Mar-1 Nov. Hotels, waterpark, spa and golf open all year.* **Facilities** 🅿 ⏻ 🍽 licensed ᴀ (outdoor) ⅊ toilets for disabled shop ⊗

BIDDULPH

Biddulph Grange Garden

Grange Rd ST8 7SD

☎ 01782 517999 📄 01782 510624

e-mail: biddulphgrange@nationaltrust.org.uk

web: www.nationaltrust.org.uk

dir: access from A527, Tunstall-Congleton road. Entrance on Grange Rd 0.5m N of Biddulph

This exciting and rare survival of a high Victorian garden has undergone extensive restoration. Conceived by James Bateman, the fifteen acres are divided into a number of smaller gardens which were designed to house specimens from his extensive plant collection.

Times Open 3-31 Mar, Wed-Sun 11-5; 9 Apr-Oct, daily 11-5; 6 Nov-19 Dec, Sat-Sun 11-3.30. **Fees** Mar-Oct £6.40 (ch £3.20). Family ticket £14.90; Nov-Dec £2.40 (ch £1.20). Family ticket £5.60.* **Facilities** 🅿 ⏻ ᴀ (outdoor) toilets for disabled shop ⊗ 🌿

Staffordshire

CHEDDLETON

Churnet Valley Railway

The Station ST13 7EE
☎ 01538 360522   📠 01538 361848
e-mail: enquiries@churnetvalleyrailway.co.uk
web: www.churnetvalleyrailway.co.uk
dir: 3m S from Leek, 3m N from Cellarhead along A520. Kingsley & Froghall Station is situated on the Stoke to Ashbourne road, A52

The Churnet Valley Railway runs through the hidden countryside between Cheddleton, with its Grade II Victorian station, and Kingsley and Froghall, with the newly built station and Canal Wharf. The journey incorporates Consall, a sleepy rural station and nature reserve, and Leekbrook with one of the longest tunnels on a preserved railway. Special Events include 1940s weekend Apr, Ghost Train Oct, and Santa & Steam Dec.

Times Open every Mar-Oct, Sun; Jun-Sep, Sat; Jul-Aug, Wed; Aug, Mon & all BH Mon.* **Fees** All day travel £9 (ch £5, concessions £7)* **Facilities** 🅿 ⓟ 🖵 🍴 (outdoor) ♿ toilets for disabled shop

LEEK

Blackbrook Zoological Park

Winkhill ST13 7QR
☎ 01538 308293   📠 01538 308293
e-mail: enquiries@blackbrookzoologicalpark.co.uk
web: www.blackbrookzoologicalpark.co.uk
dir: off A523 Leek to Ashbourne road

Blackbrook Zoological Park is a fun and educational day for all. A continually growing attraction, always with something new to see. The zoo features: mammals, rare birds, reptiles, insects and aquatics; owl flights, pelican, penguin and lemur feeds. Blackbrook Zoological Park is fully accessible for pushchairs and wheelchairs.

Times Open daily 10-5.30; winter 10.30-dusk (last admission 4)* **Facilities** 🅿 🖵 🍴 (outdoor) ♿ toilets for disabled shop ⊗

SHUGBOROUGH

Shugborough Estate

ST17 0XB
☎ 01889 881388   📠 01889 881323
e-mail: shugborough.promotions@staffordshire.gov.uk
web: www.shugborough.org.uk
dir: 6m E of Stafford off A513, signed from M6 junct 13

Journey through the historic estate of Shugborough and discover a bygone era as the costumed living history characters bring the past to life. The story begins in the walled garden - meet the gardeners of 1805 and find out how fruit and vegetables are grown on the estate. At the farm the servants are busy making butter and cheese and the farm hands tend to the animals. Then take a short ride on Lucy the Train or walk across the stunning parkland. The story continues in the Servants' Quarters where cooks and kitchen maids scurry about, preparing food on the range, starching the whites in the laundry and brewing ale in the wood-fired brewery. The Mansion House completes the story, where the 1805 Viscount and Lady Anson are often present. Please contact or see website for details of special events.

Times Open 18 Mar-28 Oct, daily 11-5. Site open all year to pre-booked parties.* **Fees** £12 (ch £7, under 5 free, concessions £9.50). Family ticket (2ad+3ch) £30, (1ad+1ch £15). **Facilities** 🅿 🖵 🍴 licensed 🍴 (outdoor) ♿ (partly accessible) (steps to house, stairclimber available) toilets for disabled shop ⊗

STOKE ON TRENT

Ceramica

Market Place, Burslem ST6 3DS
☎ 01782 832001   📠 01782 823300
e-mail: info@ceramicauk.com
web: www.ceramicauk.com
dir: A4527 (signposted Tunstall). After 0.5m right onto B5051 for Burslem. Ceramica is in Old Town Hall in centre of town.

A unique experience for all the family, Ceramica is housed in the Old Town Hall in the centre of Burslem, Mother Town of the Potteries. Explore the hands-on activities in Bizarreland, and learn how clay is transformed into china. Dig into history with the time team and take a magic carpet ride over the town. Discover the past, present and future of ceramics with the interactive displays in the Pavillions. Explore the Memory Bank and read the local news on Ceramica TV.

Times Open all year, Mon-Sat 9.30-5, Sun 10.30-4.30. For Xmas opening please telephone.* **Facilities** 🅿 ⓟ 🍴 (indoor) toilets for disabled shop ⊗

Gladstone Working Pottery Museum

Uttoxeter Rd, Longton ST3 1PQ
☎ 01782 237777 🖹 01782 237076
e-mail: gladstone@stoke.gov.uk
web: www.stoke.gov.uk/gladstone
dir: A50 then follow brown heritage signs

Located at the heart of the Potteries, Gladstone Pottery Museum is the last remaining Victorian Pottery industry. Whilst touring the original factory building discover what it was like for the men, women and children to live and work in a potbank during the era of the coal firing bottle ovens. In original workshops working potters can be found demonstrating traditional pottery skills. There are also lots of opportunities for you to have a go at pottery making, throw your own pot on the potters wheel, make china flowers and decorate pottery items to take home. Also explore Flushed with Pride, dedicated to the story of the development of the toilet, and The Tile Gallery, a fine collection which traces the development of decorative tiles.

Times Open all year, daily 10-5 (last admission 4). Limited opening Xmas & New Year.* **Facilities** 🅿 ⬛ 🍴 licensed 🎪 toilets for disabled shop ⊗

The Potteries Museum & Art Gallery   FREE

Bethesda St, Hanley ST1 3DW
☎ 01782 232323 🖹 01782 232500
e-mail: museums@stoke.gov.uk
web: www.stoke.gov.uk/museums
dir: M6 junct 15/16 take A500 to Stoke-on-Trent. Follow signs for city centre (Hanley), Cultural Quarter & The Potteries Museum

The history of the Potteries under one roof, including a dazzling display of the world's finest collection of Staffordshire ceramics. Other displays introduce natural, local and archaeological history from in and around The Potteries, and a Mark 16 Spitfire commemorating its locally born designer - Reginald Mitchell.

Times Open all year, Mar-Oct, Mon-Sat 10-5, Sun 2-5; Nov-Feb, Mon-Sat 10-4, Sun 1-4. Closed 25 Dec-1 Jan.* **Facilities** 🅿 🅟 ⬛ toilets for disabled shop ⊗

Wedgwood Visitor Centre

Barlaston ST12 9ER
☎ 01782 282986 🖹 01782 223063
e-mail: bookings@wedgwood.com
web: www.wedgwoodvisitorcentre.com
dir: From M1, via A50 follow tourist signs to Stoke. From M6 junct 15 follow brown tourist signs

Set in 250 acres of lush parkland in the heart of Staffordshire, visitors can take a fascinating trip behind the scenes at one of the world's famous pottery companies. The award winning tour allows visitors to enjoy the entire experience at their own pace. Hands on activities such as throwing your own pot or painting your own plate are available in the demonstration area, where individuals craft artisans demonstrate their skills including Coalport painter, Jewellery Maker, Hand painter and Flower Maker. Add to this, exhibition areas, film theatre and an exclusive Wedgwood shop, the centre offers an all-inclusive day for everyone.

Times Open all year, Mon-Fri 9-5, Sat & Sun 10-5. Shop open Sun 10-4 (ex Etr Sun). Closed Xmas week. **Fees** £4.75 (concessions £3.75). Family £16. **Facilities** 🅿 ⬛ 🍴 licensed 🚾 toilets for disabled shop ⊗

Drayton Manor Theme Park

B78 3TW
☎ 0844 4721950 & 0844 4721960 🖹 01827 288916
e-mail: info@draytonmanor.co.uk
web: www.draytonmanor.co.uk
dir: M42 junct 9, on A4091. Exit at T2 of M6 toll

A popular family theme park with over 100 rides and attractions suitable for all the family, set in 280 acres of parkland and lakes. Drayton Manor has been run by the same family for 60 years, and features world-class rides like rollercoaster sensation G-Force, Apocalypse- the world's first stand-up tower drop, Stormforce 10 and Shockwave - Europe's only stand-up rollercoaster. ThomasLand features Thomas and Percy trains and themed rides for adults and children. There's an award-winning zoo and a penny slot machine museum plus plenty of special events throughout the year.

Times Park & Rides open mid Mar-2 Nov. Rides from 10.30-5, 6 or 7. Zoo open all year. 'ThomasLand' also open 28 Nov-3 Jan (excl 24-26 Dec).* **Fees** £25 (ch under 4 free, 4-11 £21, pen 60+ £12, disabled & helper £19 each).* **Facilities** 🅿 ⬛ 🍴 licensed 🎪 (indoor & outdoor) 🚾 (partly accessible) (some rides limited access due to steps, ramps or lifts to most rides) toilets for disabled shop ⊗

Tamworth continued

Tamworth Castle

Holbway Lodge B79 7NA
☎ 01827 709629 & 709626 📄 01827 709630
e-mail: heritage@tamworth.gov.uk
web: www.tamworthcastle.co.uk
dir: M42 junct 10 & M6 junct 12, access via A5

Tamworth Castle is located in the centre of the town. Owned by six different families over the centuries, the medieval motte and bailey castle has welcomed a number of royal visitors including King Henry II, King James I and his son Prince Charles. The ancient sand stone tower and shell wall still dominate views of the Castle today. While visiting this ancient monument witness the magnificent late medieval Great Hall, grand Tudor chambers and Victorian suite of reception rooms.

Times Open all year, Apr-Sep, Tue-Sun 12-5.15; Oct-Mar, Sat & Sun 12-5.15 (last admission 4.30).* **Fees** £5 (ch under 2 free, 2-4 £1, 5+ £3 & pen £4). Family ticket (2ad+2ch) £14.50. **Facilities** Ⓟ ⊑ ⋤ (outdoor) ⧍ (partly accessible) (ground floor access only) shop ⊗

TRENTHAM

Trentham Gardens

Trentham Estate, Stone Rd ST4 8AX
☎ 01782 646646 📄 01782 644536
e-mail: enquiry@trentham.co.uk **web:** www.trentham.co.uk
dir: M6 junct 15 onto A500 towards Stoke, after 1m take A34 to Trentham & Stone. Estate on right in 1m

This Italianate award-winning landscape garden has a variety of innovative horticultural displays. A mile long lake, fountains and model show gardens displays different techniques, crafts and ideas. For the younger visitor there is an adventure play area and Barfuss Britain's first bare foot walking park.

Times Open all year Northern entrance daily 9-8 (open 9-4 2 Nov-Mar). Southern entrance 9-6. Both entrances 9-4, 2 Nov-Mar. Last entry 1hr before closing at northern entrance. **Fees** £7 (ch 5-15 £5.50, concessions £6) 2 Nov-Mar £5.50 (ch 5-15 £3.50, concessions £4) **Facilities** Ⓟ ⊑ ⋤ (outdoor) toilets for disabled shop

Trentham Monkey Forest

Trentham Estate, Southern Entrance, Stone Rd ST4 8AY
☎ 01782 659845 📄 01782 644699
e-mail: info@monkey-forest.com
web: www.monkey-forest.com
dir: M6 junct 15, 5 mins drive to A34 in direction of Stone

A unique experience for everyone - come to the only place in Britain where you can walk amongst 140 Barbary macaques roaming free in 60 acres of forest. Walking in the park, you are transported into a different world through close contact with the monkeys. Guides are situated all along the path to give information and there are feeding talks every hour.

Times Open Feb-Mar & Nov, wknds & school hols, 10-4; daily Apr-Oct 10-5 (school summer hols 10-6). **Fees** £6 (ch under 3 free, ch 3-14 £4.50). Groups 20+ £5 (ch £3.50).* **Facilities** Ⓟ Ⓟ ⊑ ⋤ (outdoor) ⧍ (partly accessible) (hills in forest) toilets for disabled shop ⊗

WESTON PARK

Weston Park

TF11 8LE
☎ 01952 852100 📄 01952 850430
e-mail: enquiries@weston-park.com
web: www.weston-park.com
dir: on A5 at Weston-under-Lizard, 30min from central Birmingham 3m off M54 junct 3 and 8m off M6 junct 12

Built in 1671, this fine mansion stands in elegant gardens and a vast park designed by 'Capability' Brown. Three lakes, a miniature railway, and a woodland adventure playground are to be found in the grounds, and in the house itself there is a magnificent collection of pictures, furniture and tapestries. There is also an animal centre and Deer Park.

Times Open wknds from 15 Apr-Jul, then daily until 3 Sep.* **Facilities** Ⓟ Ⓟ ⊑ ⫣ licensed ⋤ toilets for disabled shop

SUFFOLK

BURY ST EDMUNDS

Moyse's Hall Museum

Cornhill IP33 1DX
☎ 01284 706183 📄 01284 765373
e-mail: moyses.hall@stedsbc/gov.uk
web: www.stedmundsbury.gov.uk/moyses.htm
dir: take Bury central exit from A14, follow signs for town centre, museum situated in town centre

Moyse's Hall is a 12th-century Norman house built of flint and stone which now serves as a local history museum, and among the fascinating exhibits are memorabilia of the notorious William Corder "Murder in the Red Barn". Other collections include the history of the town, Suffolk Regiment, fine art, toys, clocks and timepieces.

Times Open all year, Mon-Fri 10-5 (last entry at 4), Sat & Sun 11-4. Closed 25-27 Dec & all BH. **Fees** £3 (ch & concessions £2). Free for residents of St Edmondsbury.* **Facilities** ℗ toilets for disabled shop ⊗

EASTON

Easton Farm Park

IP13 0EQ
☎ 01728 746475
e-mail: info@eastonfarmpark.co.uk
web: www.eastonfarmpark.co.uk
dir: signed from A12 at Wickham Market, and from A1120

Award-winning farm park on the banks of the River Deben. There are lots of breeds of farm animals, including Suffolk Punch horses, ponies, pigs, lambs, calves, goats, rabbits, guinea pigs and poultry. Chicks hatching and egg collecting daily. Free hug-a-bunny and pony rides every day.

Times Open Mar-end Sep, daily 10.30-6. Also open Feb & Oct half term hols and wknds in Dec.* **Fees** £6.75 (ch 1-16 £5.50, under 1's free, concessions £6.25). Family £23.* **Facilities** ℗ ⊡ 🍴 (indoor & outdoor) ♿ (partly accessible) (mainly hard standing surfaces) toilets for disabled shop

FRAMLINGHAM

Framlingham Castle

IP8 9BT
☎ 01728 724189
web: www.english-heritage.org.uk
dir: on B1116

Walk the 12th-century battlements that encircle the castle site with their impressive thirteen towers. Exceptional views over the countryside and a very popular audio tour.

Times Open all year, Apr-Jun & Sep-1 Nov, daily 10-5; Jul-Aug, daily 10-6; 2 Nov-Mar, Thu-Mon 10-4. (May close early for events. Please call to check). Closed 24-26 Dec & 1 Jan. **Fees** £5.70 (concessions £4.80, ch £2.90). Family ticket £14.30. Please check web site or call 0870 333 1181 for the most up to date prices and opening times when planning your visit. **Facilities** ℗ ♿ (partly accessible) (steep spiral stairs to upper floors & wall walk) toilets for disabled shop ⊞

HORRINGER

Ickworth House, Park & Gardens

The Rotunda IP29 5QE
☎ 01284 735270 📄 01284 735175
e-mail: ickworth@nationaltrust.org.uk
web: www.nationaltrust.org.uk/ickworth
dir: 2.5m SW of Bury St Edmunds in village of Horringer on A143

The eccentric Earl of Bristol created this equally eccentric house, begun in 1795, to display his collection of European art. The Georgian Silver Collection is considered the finest in private hands. 'Capability' Brown designed the parkland, and also featured are a vineyard, waymarked walks and an adventure playground.

Times Open all year: House 14 Mar-1 Nov, Mon-Tue, Fri-Sun & BHs, 11-5, Oct-2 Nov, Mon-Tue, Fri-Sun & BHs. Garden Feb-13 Mar & 2 Nov-Jan daily, 11-4; 14 Mar-1 Nov daily 10-5. Park: daily 8-8.* **Fees** House, Garden & Park £8.95 (ch £3.30). Family £21. Garden & Park £4.50 (ch £1.10). Family £10.10* **Facilities** ℗ 🍴 licensed 🍴 (outdoor) ♿ (partly accessible) (Grounds partly access, loose gravel paths, steep slopes, terraces, steps) toilets for disabled shop ⊗ 🐾

LEISTON

Long Shop Museum

Main St IP16 4ES
☎ 01728 832189   📄 01728 832189
e-mail: longshop@care4free.net
web: www.longshop.care4free.net
dir: Turn off A12, follow B1119 from Saxmundham to Leiston. Museum is in the middle of town

Discover the Magic of Steam through a visit to the world famous traction engine manufacturers. Trace the history of the factory and Richard Garrett engineering. See the traction engines and road rollers in the very place that they were built. Soak up the atmosphere of the Long Shop, built in 1852 as one of the first production line engineering halls in the world. An award-winning museum with five exhibition halls full of items from the glorious age of steam and covering 200 years of local, social and industrial history.

Times Open Apr-Oct, Mon-Sat 10-5, Sun 11-5.* **Fees** £4.50 (ch £2, ch under 5 free, concessions £4) Family £11.* **Facilities** 🅿 ⓟ 🅰 (outdoor) toilets for disabled shop ⊗

LONG MELFORD

Kentwell Hall

CO10 9BA
☎ 01787 310207   📄 01787 379318
e-mail: info@kentwell.co.uk
web: www.kentwell.co.uk
dir: signed off A134, between Bury St Edmunds & Sudbury

Kentwell Hall is a moated red brick Tudor manor with gardens, woodland walks and a rare breeds farm. Restoration started in 1971 and still continues today. The house and grounds are open to the public at certain times of the year, and recreations of Tudor and 1940s life take place at weekends. Ring for details.

Times Open Mar-Oct. Please contact estate office for opening times.* **Facilities** 🅿 ⊡ 🅰 (outdoor) ♿ (partly accessible) toilets for disabled shop ⊗

Melford Hall

CO10 9AA
☎ 01787 379228 & 376395   📄 01787 379228
e-mail: melford@nationaltrust.org.uk
web: www.nationaltrust.org.uk/melford
dir: off A134, 3m N of Sudbury, next to village green

Set in the unspoilt village of Long Melford, the house has changed little externally since 1578 when Queen Elizabeth I was entertained here, and retains its original panelled banqueting hall. It has been the home of the Hyde Parker Family since 1786. There is a Regency library, Victorian bedrooms, good collections of furniture and porcelain and a small display of items connected with Beatrix Potter, who was related to the family. The garden contains some spectacular specimen trees and a banqueting house and there is an attractive walk through the park.

Times Open all year, Apr, Wed-Mon, 1.30-5; May-Sep, Wed-Sun, 1.30-5; Oct-Nov, Sat & Sun, 1.30-5; BH Mon. Last entry to the house 4.30* **Fees** £6 (ch £3) Family £15.* **Facilities** 🅿 ⓟ ⊡ 🅰 (outdoor) ♿ (partly accessible) (slopes & some steps in grounds) toilets for disabled ⊗ ♨

LOWESTOFT

East Anglia Transport Museum

Chapel Rd, Carlton Colville NR33 8BL
☎ 01502 518459   📄 01502 584658
e-mail: enquiries@eatm.org.uk
web: www.eatm.org.uk
dir: 3m SW of Lowestoft, follow brown signs from A12, A146 & A1117

A particular attraction of this museum is the reconstructed 1930s street scene which is used as a setting for working vehicles: visitors can ride by tram, trolley bus and narrow gauge railway. Other motor, steam and electrical vehicles are exhibited. There is also a woodland picnic area served by trams.

Times Open: Apr-Sep, Sun and BH 11-5. From Jun, Thu and Sat, 2-5.* **Facilities** 🅿 ⊡ 🅰 (outdoor) ♿ (partly accessible) toilets for disabled shop

Pleasurewood Hills

Leisure Way, Corton NR32 5DZ
☎ 01502 586000 (admin)   📄 01502 567393
e-mail: info@pleasurewoodhills.com
web: www.pleasurewoodhills.com
dir: off A12 at Lowestoft

Set in 50 acres of coastal parkland, Pleasurewood Hills has all the ingredients for a great day out for all the family. Adrenalin-fuelled thrills and spills for the bravest adventurers, such as the newest attraction, Wipeout, which claims to be the most extreme rollercoaster in the East of England. Fun rides for all the family including some for younger children. Wonderful shows with sealions, parrots, acrobats and the breathtaking Magic Circus spectacular. When the action gets too much, take a leisurely ride on the alpine chairlift or jump aboard one of two railways that weave their way through the park.

Times Open Apr-Oct. Please telephone for details or visit website.* **Facilities** 🅿 ♿🍴 licensed 🎏 (outdoor) ♿ toilets for disabled shop ⊗

NEWMARKET

National Horseracing Museum and Tours

99 High St CB8 8JH
☎ 01638 667333   📄 01638 665600
web: www.nhrm.co.uk
dir: located in centre of High St

This friendly award-winning museum tells the story of the people and horses involved in racing in Britain. Have a go on the horse simulator in the hands-on gallery and chat to retired jockeys and trainers about their experiences. Special mini bus tours visit the gallops, a stable and horses' swimming pool.

Times Open Etr-Oct, daily 11-5 (also BH Mons). 10am on race days.* **Fees** £6 (ch £3, concessions £5). Family (2ad+2ch) £13.* **Facilities** 🅿 ♿🍴 licensed 🎏 (outdoor) ♿ toilets for disabled shop ⊗

STOWMARKET

Museum of East Anglian Life

IP14 1DL
☎ 01449 612229   📄 01449 672307
e-mail: enquiries@eastanglianlife.org.uk
web: www.eastanglianlife.org.uk
dir: in centre of Stowmarket, signed from A14 & B1115

This 70-acre, all-weather museum is set in an attractive river-valley site with 3km of woodland and riverside nature trails. There are reconstructed buildings, including a working water mill, a smithy and also a wind pump, and the Boby Building houses craft workshops. There are displays on Victorian domestic life, gypsies, farming and industry. These include working steam traction engines, the only surviving pair of Burrell ploughing engines of 1879, and a Suffolk Punch horse. The William Bone Building illustrates the history of Ransomes of Ipswich.

Times Open late March-end Oct.* **Fees** £6.50 (ch 4-16 £3.50, concessions £5.50). Family ticket (2ad+2/3ch) £17.50. 1ad family £11. Party 10+.* **Facilities** 🅿 ♿🎏 (outdoor) toilets for disabled shop

---

SUFFOLK WILDLIFE PARK

Africa Alive!

Kessingland NR33 7TF
☎ 01502 740291   📄 01502 741104
e-mail: info@africa-alive.co.uk
web: www.africa-alive.co.uk
dir: 25min S of Gt. Yarmouth just S of Lowestoft off A12

Set in 80 acres of dramatic coastal parkland, visitors can explore the sights and sounds of Africa at Africa Alive! There are giraffes, rhinos, cheetah, hyenas and many more, including a bird's eye view of the new lion enclosure. There are lots of daily feeding talks and animal encounter sessions, a magnificent bird of prey display, and free journey round the park with live commentary.

Times Open all year, daily from 10. Closed 25-26 Dec.* **Facilities** 🅿 ♿🍴 licensed 🎏 toilets for disabled shop ⊗

WEST STOW

West Stow Anglo Saxon Village

West Stow Country Park, Icklingham Rd IP28 6HG
☎ 01284 728718 📄 01284 728277
e-mail: weststow@stedsbc.gov.uk
web: www.weststow.org
dir: off A1101, 7m NW of Bury St Edmunds. Follow brown heritage signs

The village is a reconstruction of a pagan Anglo-Saxon settlement dated 420-650 AD. Seven buildings have been reconstructed on the site of the excavated settlement. There is a Visitors' Centre which includes a new archaeology exhibition, DVD area and a children's play area. A new Anglo-Saxon Centre houses the original objects found on the site. Located in the 125 acre West Stow Country Park with river, lake, woodland and heath, plus many trails and paths.

Times Open all year, daily 10-5. Last entry 4 (3.30 in Winter) except Xmas period.* **Facilities** 🅿 Ⓟ ⊑ 🎋 (outdoor) ♿ (partly accessible) toilets for disabled shop ⊗

WESTLETON

RSPB Nature Reserve Minsmere

IP17 3BY
☎ 01728 648281 📄 01728 648770
e-mail: minsmere@rspb.org.uk
web: www.rspb.org.uk/reserves/minsmere
dir: signed from A12 at Yoxford & Blythburgh and from Westleton Village

Set on the beautiful Suffolk coast, Minsmere offers an enjoyable day out for all. Nature trails take you through a variety of habitats to the excellent birdwatching hides. Spring is a time for birdsong, including nightingales and booming bitterns. In summer, you can watch breeding avocets and marsh harriers. Autumn is excellent for migrants, and in winter, hundreds of ducks visit the reserve. Look out for otters and red deer. The visitor centre has a well-stocked shop and licensed tearoom, and you can find out more about the reserve. There is a programme of events throughout the year, including several for children and families. Self-guided activity booklets for families.

Times Open all year, daily (ex 25-26 Dec) 9-9 (or dusk if earlier). Visitor centre: 9-5 (9-4 Nov-Jan).* **Facilities** 🅿 Ⓟ ⊑ 🎋 (outdoor) ♿ (partly accessible) (Visitor Centre, parts of nature trail and some hides are accessible) toilets for disabled shop ⊗

WOODBRIDGE

Sutton Hoo

IP12 3DJ
☎ 01394 389700 📄 01394 389702
e-mail: suttonhoo@nationaltrust.org.uk
web: www.nationaltrust.org.uk/suttonhoo
dir: off B1083 Woodbridge to Bawdsey road. Follow signs from A12 avoiding Woodbridge itself

Discovered in 1939 and described as 'page one of English history', this is the site of one of the most important archaeological finds in Britain's history: the complete 7th-century ship burial of an Anglo-Saxon king, which had been missed by grave-robbers, and lay undisturbed for 1300 years. Sutton Hoo displays reveal how Anglo-Saxon nobles lived, went to war and founded a new kingdom in East Anglia. The centre-piece is a full sized replica of an Anglo-Saxon warrior king's burial chamber. The discoveries at Sutton Hoo changed forever our perceptions of the 'Dark Ages', by revealing a culture rich in craftsmanship, trade and legend.

Times Open all year: Jun, Wed-Sun, 10.30-5; Jul-Aug, daily 10.30-5; Sep-Oct, Wed-Sun, 10.30-5; Nov-Feb, Sat-Sun, 11-4. Open: BHs.* **Fees** Gift Aid Admission prices £6.50, (ch £3.40). Family tickets £16.45. Gift aid admission includes a voluntary donation but visitors can choose to pay the standard prices displayed at the property and on the website.* **Facilities** 🅿 🍴 licensed 🎋 ♿ (partly accessible) (Grounds partly access, slopes, burial mound tours not accessible to w/chairs or PMV) toilets for disabled shop ⊗ 🐾

SURREY

CHERTSEY

Thorpe Park

Staines Rd KT16 8PN
☎ **0870 444 4466** 📠 **01932 566367**
web: www.thorpepark.com
dir: M25 junct 11 or 13 and follow signs via A320 to Thorpe Park

For hardcore adrenaline junkies, Thorpe Park is the must-do destination for insanely thrilling rollercoaster fun. Unleash the daredevil within and take on the loops, spins, vertical drops and incredible speeds of the nation's thrill capital.

Times Open 15 Mar-9 Nov. Opening times vary throughout, check in advance.* **Facilities** 🅿 ☖ ⦿ licensed ♨ ♿ toilets for disabled shop ⊗

EAST CLANDON

Hatchlands Park

GU4 7RT
☎ **01483 222482** 📠 **01483 223176**
e-mail: hatchlands@nationaltrust.org.uk
web: www.nationaltrust.org.uk/hatchlands
dir: E of Guildford, off A246

Built in the 1750s for Admiral Boscawen, hero of the battle of Louisburg, and set in a beautiful 430-acre park designed by Humphry Repton, offering a variety of park and woodlands walks, Hatchlands boasts the earliest known decorative works by Robert Adam. Hatchlands is home to the Cobbe collection, the world's largest group of keyboard instruments associated with famous composers. There is also a small garden by Gertrude Jekyll and a beautiful bluebell wood in May. Please telephone for details of family activities and other events.

Times House & Gardens: Apr-Oct, Tue-Thu & Sun, 2-5.30.
Fees Gift Aid donation: £7 (ch £3.50) Family ticket £18. Park walks £3.70 (ch £1.80). Joint ticket with Clandon Park £11.60 (ch £5.80). Family £33.40. Includes a voluntary donation of 10% or more. Visitors can however, choose to pay the standard admission displayed at the property & on NT website* **Facilities** 🅿 ⦿ licensed ♨ (outdoor) ♿ (partly accessible) (park walks unsuitable and not accessible) toilets for disabled shop ⊗ ♣

FARNHAM

Birdworld & Underwaterworld

Holt Pound GU10 4LD
☎ **01420 22140** 📠 **01420 23715**
e-mail: bookings@birdworld.co.uk
web: www.birdworld.co.uk
dir: 3m S of Farnham on A325

Birdworld is the largest bird collection in the country and includes toucans, pelicans, flamingoes, ostriches and many others. Underwater World is a tropical aquarium with brilliant lighting that shows off collections of marine and freshwater fish, as well as the swampy depths of the alligator exhibit. Visitors can also visit some beautiful gardens, the Jenny Wren farm and the Heron Theatre.

Times Open all year, daily, 10-6 (summer), 10-4.30 (winter). Closed 25-26 Dec.* **Fees** £13.95 (ch 3-6 £10.95 & 7-15 £11.95, concessions £11.95). Family ticket (2ad+2ch) £45.* **Facilities** 🅿 ⦿ licensed ♨ (outdoor) ♿ toilets for disabled shop ⊗

Farnham Castle Keep

Castle St GU6 0AG
☎ **01252 713393**
web: www.english-heritage.org.uk
dir: 0.5m N on A287

A motte and bailey castle, once one of the seats of the bishop of Winchester, has been in continuous occupation since the 12th century.

Times Open Apr-Sep, Fri-Sun 1-5. **Fees** £3 (concessions £2.60, ch £1.50). Please check web site or call 0870 333 1181 for the most up to date prices and opening times when planning your visit. **Facilities** 🅿 shop ⌂

GODSTONE

Godstone Farm

RH9 8LX
☎ **01883 742546** 📠 **01883 740380**
e-mail: havefun@godstonefarm.co.uk
web: www.godstonefarm.co.uk
dir: M25 junct 6, S of village, signed

An ideal day out for children, Godstone Farm has lots of friendly animals, big sand pits and play areas, including an indoor play barn for rainy days.

Times Open all year, Mar-Oct, 10-6 (last admission 5); Nov-Feb 10-5 (last admission 4). Closed 25 & 26 Dec.* **Fees** Contact for admission prices.* **Facilities** 🅿 ☖ ♨ (indoor & outdoor) ♿ toilets for disabled shop ⊗

GREAT BOOKHAM

Polesden Lacey

RH5 6BD
☎ 01372 452048   📠 01372 452023
e-mail: polesdenlacey@nationaltrust.org.uk
web: www.nationaltrust.org.uk/polesdenlacey
dir: 2m S off A246 from village of Bookham

King George VI and Queen Elizabeth the Queen Mother spent part of their honeymoon here, and photographs of other notable guests can be seen. The house is handsomely furnished and full of charm, and it is set in spacious grounds. There is also a summer festival, where concerts and plays are performed. Please phone for details of special events.

Times Open all year; Grounds & Garden: daily 10-5. House: 15 Mar-25 Oct,11-5 (last admission 30 mins before closing).* **Fees** Gift Aid donation: Garden £7 (ch £3.50). Family ticket £17.50. House & Garden £11 (ch £5.50). Family £27.50. Group rates 15+. Includes a voluntary donation of 10% or more. Visitors can however, choose to pay the standard admission which is displayed at the property and on NT website.* **Facilities** 🅿 ☕ 🍴 licensed 🍴 (outdoor) ♿ (partly accessible) (no access for w/chairs to house upper floors. Some steps & uneven paths in garden. Courtesy shuttle from car park to front of house) toilets for disabled shop ♨

GUILDFORD

Loseley Park

GU3 1HS
☎ 01483 304440 & 505501   📠 01483 302036
e-mail: enquiries@loseley-park.com
web: www.loseley-park.com
dir: 2m SW of Guildford, off A3 onto B3000

Magnificent Elizabethan mansion, home of the More-Molyneux family for 500 years. Set in magnificent parkland scenery. Based on a Gertrude Jekyll design, the walled garden contains five gardens each with its own theme and character. These include the award-winning Rose Garden, Vine Walk, fruit, vegetable and flower gardens and the Serene White Fountain

Garden. Events throughout the year including RHS talks, medieval festival, Shakespeare performances and music.

Times Open Grounds and Walled Garden: May-Sep, Tue-Sun & BH 11-5. House May-Aug, Tue-Thu, Sun & BH 1-5. **Fees** House & Gardens £7 (ch £4, ch under 5 free, concessions £7.50). Family £20. Gardens only £4.50 (ch £2.25, concessions £4). Discount for pre-booked groups. "Friends of Loseley" ticket £20. **Facilities** 🅿 ☕ 🍴 (outdoor) ♿ (partly accessible) (Only ground floor of house accessible) toilets for disabled shop ⊗

HASCOMBE

Winkworth Arboretum

Hascombe Rd GU8 4AD
☎ 01483 208477   📠 01483 208252
e-mail: winkwortharboretum@nationaltrust.org.uk
web: www.nationaltrust.org.uk/winkwortharboretum
dir: 2m SE of Godalming, E side of B2130, follow brown tourist signs from Godalming

This lovely woodland covers a hillside of nearly 100 acres, with fine views over the North Downs. The best times to visit are April and May, for the azaleas, bluebells and other flowers, and October for the autumn colours. A delightful Victorian boathouse is open Apr-Oct with fine views over Rowes Flashe lake. Many rare trees and shrubs in group plantings for spring and autumn colour effect.

Times Open all year, daily during daylight hours. (Could close when weather is bad). **Fees** Gift Aid donation: £5 (ch £2.50). Family £12.50. Reduction if arriving by public transport/cycle. Includes a voluntary donation of 10% or more. Visitors can however, choose to pay the standard admission which is displayed at the property and on NT website.* **Facilities** 🅿 ☕ toilets for disabled ⊗ ♨

PAINSHILL PARK

Painshill Park

Portsmouth Rd KT11 1JE
☎ 01932 868113   📄 01932 868001
e-mail: info@painshill.co.uk
web: www.painshill.co.uk
dir: W of Cobham on A245

Covering 158 acres, this magnificent 18th-century parkland was created by Charles Hamilton as a series of subtle and surprising vistas. Its landscapes include authentic 18th-century plantings, a working vineyard, unusual follies, and a magical grotto. The Park is also home to the John Bartram Heritage Collection of North American Trees and Shrubs. There are events for the whole family throughout the year and Father Christmas visits the grotto in December.

Times Open all year, Apr-Oct, 10.30-6 (last entry 4.30). Nov-Mar, 10.30-4 (last entry 3). Closed 25-26 Dec. Ltd opening times to grotto.* **Fees** £6.60 (ch 5-16 £3.85, under 5 free, concessions £5.80). Family £22 (2ad & 4ch). Free admission for carer of disabled person. Pre-booked adult groups 10+ £5.80* **Facilities** 🅿 🔄 🚻 (outdoor) ♿ (partly accessible) (accessible route covering 2/3rds of the landscape) toilets for disabled shop ⊗

TILFORD

Rural Life Centre

Reeds Rd GU10 2DL
☎ 01252 795571   📄 01252 795571
e-mail: info@rural-life.org.uk **web:** www.rural-life.org.uk
dir: off A287, 3m S of Farnham, signed

The museum covers village life from 1750 to 1960. It is set in over ten acres of garden and woodland and incorporates purpose-built and reconstructed buildings, including a chapel, pavilion, village hall, schoolroom and 'prefab'. Displays show village crafts and trades, such as wheelwrighting, thatching, ploughing and gardening. The historic village playground provides entertainment for children and a narrow gauge railway operates on Sundays during the summer months. There is an arboretum featuring over 100 trees from around

the world. An extensive programme of events takes place throughout the year, please contact for details.

Times Open mid Mar-end Oct, Wed-Sun & BH 10-5; Winter Wed & Sun only 11-4 **Fees** £8 (ch £6, concessions £7). Family ticket (2ad+2ch) £25. **Facilities** 🅿 🔄 🍴 licensed 🚻 (indoor & outdoor) ♿ (partly accessible) (2 buildings not wheelchair accessible but can be viewed from outside) toilets for disabled shop

WEST CLANDON

Clandon Park

GU4 7RQ
☎ 01483 222482   📄 01483 223479
e-mail: clandonpark@nationaltrust.org.uk
web: www.nationaltrust.org.uk/clandonpark
dir: E of Guildford on A247

A grand Palladian mansion built c.1730 by the Venetian architect Giacomo Leoni, and notable for its magnificent marble hall. The house is filled with the superb Gubbay collection of 18th-century furniture, porcelain, textiles and carpets. The attractive gardens contain a parterre, grotto, sunken Dutch garden and a Maori meeting house. Please telephone or see website for details of special events and family activities.

Times House & Garden: open 14 Mar-Oct, Tue-Thu & Sun 11-5; museum 12-5. **Fees** Gift Aid donation: House & Garden £8.10 (ch £4). Family ticket £22.00. Joint ticket with Hatchlands Park £11.60 (ch £5.80). Family £33.40. Includes a voluntary donation of 10% or more. Visitors can however, choose to pay the standard admission which is displayed at the property and on NT website.* **Facilities** 🅿 🍴 licensed 🚻 (outdoor) ♿ (partly accessible) (7 steps to house entrance with handrail. Grounds partly accessible, grass & loose gravel paths, slopes, some steps & ramped access) toilets for disabled shop ⊗ 🐾

WEYBRIDGE

Brooklands Museum

Brooklands Rd KT13 0QN
☎ 01932 857381   📄 01932 855465
e-mail: info@brooklandsmuseum.com
web: www.brooklandsmuseum.com
dir: M25 junct 10/11, museum off B374, follow brown signs

Brooklands racing circuit was the birthplace of British motorsport and aviation. From 1907 to 1987 it was a world-renowned centre of engineering excellence. The Museum features old banked track and the 1-in-4 Test Hill. Many of the original buildings have been restored including the Clubhouse, the Shell and BP Petrol Pagodas, and the Malcolm Campbell Sheds in the Motoring Village. Many motorcycles, cars and aircraft are on display. Ring for details of special events.

Times Open all year, daily & BHs 10-5 (4 in winter).* **Facilities** 🅿 🔄 🚻 (outdoor) ♿ (partly accessible) (no wheelchair access to aircraft) toilets for disabled shop ⊗

WISLEY

RHS Garden Wisley

GU23 6QB

☎ 01483 224234 📠 01483 211750

web: www.rhs.org.uk

dir: on A3, close to M25 junct 10

With over 100 years of gardening, Wisley is the flagship garden of the Royal Horticultural Society. The garden stretches over 200 acres and there are countless opportunities for visitors to draw inspiration and gather new ideas. A 'must see' is the new glasshouse, one of the highlights, with exotics from around the world in two climate zones. The mixed borders and vegetable garden are glories of summer, while the country garden, Battleston Hill and wild garden are magnificent in spring. Whatever the season the garden is full of interest.

Times Open all year, Mon-Fri 10-6 (4.30 Nov-Feb), Sat-Sun, 9-6 (4.30 Nov-Feb). Closed 25 Dec.* **Facilities** 🅟 ☕ 🍴 licensed ⛩ (outdoor) ♿ (partly accessible) (garden partly accessible, some difficult paths) toilets for disabled shop 🚫

EAST SUSSEX

ALFRISTON

Drusillas Park

Alfriston Rd BN26 5QS

☎ 01323 874100 📠 01323 874101

e-mail: info@drusillas.co.uk

web: www.drusillas.co.uk

dir: off A27 near Alfriston 12m from Brighton & 7m from Eastbourne

Widely regarded as the best small zoo in the country, Drusillas Park offers an opportunity to get nose to nose with nature, with the help of hundreds of exotic animals, from monkeys and crocodiles to penguins and meerkats. Animals are only half the fun there's a fun: Go Bananas! Amazon Adventure and Go Wild! are perfect for energetic kids, and Thomas the Tank Engine offers a train service 362 days a year. Don't miss the Zoolympics Trail and free Spotter Books, Jungle Adventure Golf, Panning for Gold, Explorers' Lagoon or close encounters in Lemurland.

Times Open all year, daily 10-5 (winter 10-4). Closed 24-26 Dec. **Fees** Family of 4: peak £53.20, standard £49.20, off peak £41.20* **Facilities** 🅟 ☕ 🍴 licensed ⛩ (indoor & outdoor) ♿ toilets for disabled shop 🚫

BATTLE

1066 Battle of Hastings Abbey & Battlefield

TN33 0AD
☎ 01424 773792   📄 01424 775059
web: www.english-heritage.org.uk
dir: A21 onto A2100

Explore the site of the Battle of Hastings, where on 14th October 1066, one of the most famous events in English history took place. Free interactive wand tour of the battlefield and atmospheric abbey ruins.

Times Open all year, Apr-Sep, daily 10-6; Oct-Mar, daily 10-4. Closed 24-26 Dec & 1 Jan. **Fees** £6.70 (concessions £5.70, ch £3.40). Family £16.80. For the most recent info on prices please phone 0870 333 118. **Facilities** ❷ ♿ (partly accessible) (steps to enter all abbey buildings) toilets for disabled shop ♯

Yesterday's World

89-90 High St TN33 0AQ
☎ 01424 893938 & 774269   📄 01424 893316
e-mail: shop@yesterdaysworld.co.uk
web: www.yesterdaysworld.co.uk
dir: M25 junct 5, A21 onto A2100 towards Battle, opposite Battle Abbey Gatehouse

Go on a magical time-travel adventure from the reign of Queen Victoria to the psychedelic 1970s. Explore five floors of displays with over 100,000 artefacts, virtual and interactive exhibits, sounds and smells. See an English country garden, a children's play village, the 1930s Nippy's Tea Room, nostalgic gift shop and traditional English sweet shop.

Times Open all year, Winter, daily 9.30-5.30; Summer, daily 9.30-6. Closed 25-26 Dec & 1 Jan.* **Fees** £7 (ch £3.95, concession £5). Family ticket (2ad+2ch - extra child £3) £20. Discount for groups of 15+.* **Facilities** ℗ ⏴ ⛱ (outdoor) ♿ (partly accessible) toilets for disabled shop ⊗

BODIAM

Bodiam Castle

TN32 5UA
☎ 01580 830196   📄 01580 830398
e-mail: bodiamcastle@nationaltrust.org.uk
web: www.nationaltrust.org.uk/bodiamcastle
dir: 2m E of A21 Hurst Green

With its tall round drum towers at each corner, Bodiam is something of a fairytale castle. It was built in 1386 by Sir Edward Dalyngrigge, for comfort and defence. The ramparts rise dramatically above a broad moat and the great gatehouse contains the original portcullis - a very rare example of its kind.

Times Open all year, Jan-12 Feb, Sat-Sun 10.30-4; 13 Feb-Oct, daily 10.30-5.30; Nov-19 Dec, Wed-Sun 10.30-4 (last entry 30 mins before closing). **Fees** Gift Aid donation: £6.20 (ch £3.10). Family ticket £15.50. Group 15+ £5.10 (ch £2.55). Includes a voluntary donation of 10% or more. Visitors can however, choose to pay the standard admission which is displayed at the property and on NT website. **Facilities** ❷ ⏴ ♿ (partly accessible) (ground floor level is fully accessible, spiral staircase to upper levels) toilets for disabled shop ⊗ ♨

BRIGHTON

Brighton Toy and Model Museum

52-55 Trafalgar St BN1 4EB
☎ 01273 749494
e-mail: info@brightontoymuseum.co.uk
web: www.brightontoymuseum.co.uk
dir: underneath Brighton Railway Station

A fascinating collection of over 10,000 exhibits, includes collections of toys from the last one hundred years. Toys from the top toy makers and a priceless model train collection are some examples to be viewed.

Times Open all year, Tue-Fri 10-5, Sat 11-5. Closed Sun & Mon.* **Facilities** ℗ toilets for disabled shop ⊗

Brighton continued

Royal Pavilion

BN1 1EE

☎ 03000 290900 📄 03000 292871

e-mail: visitor.services@brighton-hove.gov.uk
web: www.royalpavilion.org.uk
dir: M23/A23 from London. In city centre near seafront. 15 min walk from rail station

Acclaimed as one of the most exotically beautiful buildings in the British Isles, the Royal Pavilion was the magnificent seaside residence of George IV. This breathtaking Regency palace is decorated in Chinese style, with a romanticised Indian exterior, and surrounded by restored Regency gardens.

Times Open all year, Apr-Sep, daily 9.30-5.45 (last admission 5); Oct-Mar, daily 10-5.15 (last admission 4.30). Closed 25-26 Dec. **Fees** £9 (ch £5.20, concessions £7). Family ticket (1ad+2ch) £14.20, (2ad+2ch) £23.20. Group rates available 15+. **Facilities** Ⓟ 🖵🍴 licensed 🎋 (outdoor) ♿ (partly accessible) (ground floor only accessible) toilets for disabled shop ⊗

Sea Life Centre

Marine Pde BN2 1TB

☎ 01273 604234 📄 01273 681840

e-mail: slcbrighton@merlinentertainments.biz
web: www.sealife.co.uk
dir: next to Brighton Pier between Marine Parade & Madeira Drive

Experience spectacular marine displays, set in the world's oldest functioning aquarium. Take a look at over 100 species in their natural habitat, including seahorses, sharks and rays. Over forty exhibits include Adventures at 20,000 Leagues complete with NASA-designed walkthrough observation tunnel. Features also include a Captain Pugwash quiz trail, a soft play area, a café and a giftshop.

Times Open all year, daily 10-5. (Last admission 4). Open later on wknds in summer & school hols. Closed 25 Dec.* **Fees** £9.95 (ch £7.50, concessions £8.50).* **Facilities** Ⓟ 🖵♿ (partly accessible) toilets for disabled shop ⊗

Bateman's

TN19 7DS

☎ 01435 882302 📄 01435 882811

e-mail: batemans@nationaltrust.org.uk
web: www.nationaltrust.org.uk
dir: 0.5m SW off A265

Rudyard Kipling lived for over 34 years in this 17th-century manor house which remains much the same as it was during his life. His 1928 Rolls Royce Phantom is on display, and the watermill at the bottom of the garden grinds wheat into flour on Saturday afternoons and Wednesdays. 2010 marks the 60th anniversary of the house being given to the National Trust.

Times Open 13 Mar-Oct, Sat-Wed 11-5, also open Good Fri, (last admission 4.30). House closes at 5. **Fees** Gift Aid donation: £8.20 (ch £4.10). Family ticket £20.50. Party £6.45 (ch £3.15). Includes a voluntary donation of 10% or more. Visitors can however, choose to pay the standard admission which is displayed at the property and on NT website. **Facilities** Ⓟ 🖵🍴 licensed 🎋 (outdoor) ♿ (partly accessible) (access to first floor & water mill restricted) toilets for disabled shop ⊗ 🌿

EAST DEAN

Seven Sisters Sheep Centre

Gilberts Dr BN20 0AA

☎ 01323 423302 📄 01323 423302

e-mail: sevensisters.sheepcentre@talk21.com
web: www.sheepcentre.co.uk
dir: 3m W of Eastbourne on A259. Turn left in village of East Dean to Birling Gap and sea, 0.5m on left

Possibly the largest collection of sheep in the world, where over 40 different breeds can be visited at this family run farm. See lambs being born, sheep sheared and milked, cheese making and spinning. Take in the agricultural heritage and history of sheep on the South Downs.

Times Open 3 Mar-7 May & 30 Jun-2 Sep, 2-5 (11-5 wknds/E Sussex school hols)* **Facilities** Ⓟ Ⓟ 🖵🎋 (indoor & outdoor) shop ⊗

EASTBOURNE

"How We Lived Then" Museum of Shops & Social History

20 Cornfield Ter BN21 4NS
☎ 01323 737143
e-mail: howwelivedthen@btconnect.com
web: www.how-we-lived-then.co.uk
dir: just off seafront, between town centre & theatres, signed

Over the last 50 years, Jan and Graham Upton have collected over 100,000 items which are now displayed on four floors of authentic old shops and room-settings, transporting visitors back to their grandparents' era. Other displays, such as seaside souvenirs, wartime rationing and Royal mementoes, help to capture 100 years of social history.

Times Open all year, daily, 10-5 (last entry 4.30). Winter times subject to change, telephone establishment.* **Fees** £4.50 (ch 5-15 £3.50, under 5's free, concession £4). Party 10+.* **Facilities** Ⓟ ♿ (partly accessible) (ground floor access only) shop

FOREST ROW

Ashdown Forest Llama Park

Wych Cross RH18 5JN
☎ 01825 712040 📄 01825 713698
e-mail: info@llamapark.co.uk
web: www.llamapark.co.uk
dir: on A22 between Uckfield & East Grinstead, 250mtrs S of junct with A275

Ashdown Forest Llama Park is home to more than 100 llamas and alpacas and these beautiful and gentle woolly animals, native to the high Andes of South America, are very much at home in Sussex. There are also now three reindeer who, in December, are an important part of the Christmas celebrations and Santa's Grotto. The park has wonderful views over Ashdown Forest and there is a marked trail around the Park, a picnic area and adventure play area. In the information Centre, learn about the fascinating world of llamas and alpacas and other fibre producing animals and plants. The coffee shop is open daily and local produce is used as much as possible. You can visit the coffee shop at any time without paying to visit the park. The park is holder of a Green Tourist Award.

Times Open all year, daily 10-5. Closed 25-26 Dec & 1 Jan*
Facilities Ⓟ ⬚ ⭐ licensed ⊼ (outdoor) ♿ (partly accessible) (Shop and coffee shop accessible, some gravel areas in park but limited access to wheelchair users) toilets for disabled shop ⊗

HALLAND

Bentley Wildfowl & Motor Museum

BN8 5AF
☎ 01825 840573 📄 01825 841322
e-mail: barrysutherland@pavilion.co.uk
web: www.bentley.org.uk
dir: 7m NE of Lewes, signposted off A22, A26 & B2192

Hundreds of swans, geese and ducks from all over the world can be seen on lakes and ponds along with flamingoes and peacocks. There is a fine array of Veteran, Edwardian and Vintage vehicles, and the house has splendid antiques and wildfowl paintings. The gardens specialise in old fashioned roses. Other attractions include woodland walks, a nature trail, education centre, adventure playground and a miniature train.

Times Open 17 Mar-Oct, daily 10.30-4.30. House open from noon, Apr-Nov, Feb & part of Mar, wknds only. Estate closed Dec & Jan. House closed all winter.* **Facilities** Ⓟ ⬚ ⊼ toilets for disabled shop ⊗

HASTINGS

Blue Reef Aquarium

Rock-a-nore Rd TN34 3DW
☎ 01424 718776 📄 01424 721483
e-mail: hastings@bluereefaquarium.co.uk
web: www.bluereefaquarium.co.uk
dir: Follow signs to end of Rock-a-nore Rd on seafront

Undersea safari in Hastings. Come face to face with seahorses, sharks, giant crabs, stingrays and many of other aquatic creatures. At the aquarium's heart is a giant ocean tank where an underwater walkthrough tunnel offers close encounters with giant wrasse, tropical sharks and hundreds of colourful fish. Talks and feeding displays take place throughout the day.

Times Open all year daily 10-5 (10-4 winter). Closed 25 Dec. **Fees** £7.75 (ch £5.75, concessions £6.75, disabled & carers £4.99). Family ticket (2ad+2ch) £24, (2ad+3ch) £27.50.* **Facilities** Ⓟ ⬚ ♿ (partly accessible) (Steps to tunnel) toilets for disabled shop ⊗

1066 Story in Hastings Castle

Castle Hill Rd, West Hill TN34 3RG
☎ 01424 781111 & 781112 (info line) 📄 01424 781186
e-mail: bookings@discoverhastings.co.uk
web: www.hastings.gov.uk
dir: close to A259 seafront, 2m from B2093

The ruins of the Norman castle stand on the cliffs, close to the site of William the Conqueror's first motte-and-bailey castle in England. It was excavated in 1825 and 1968, and old dungeons were discovered in 1894. An unusual approach to the castle can be made via the West Hill Cliff Railway.

Times Open daily, 27 Mar-Sep 10-5; Oct-26 Mar 11-3.30. Closed 24-26 Dec.* **Facilities** Ⓟ ⊼ shop ⊗

Hastings continued

Smugglers Adventure

St Clements Caves, West Hill TN34 3HY
☎ 01424 422964
e-mail: smugglers@discoverhastings.co.uk
web: www.discoverhastings.co.uk
dir: follow brown signs on A259, coast road, through Hastings. Use seafront car park, then take West Cliff railway or follow signed footpath

Journey deep into the heart of Hastings historic West Hill to discover the fascinating world of the Smugglers Adventure in St Cements Caves. Join notorious smuggler 'Hairy Jack' as he leads you through acres of underground caverns, passages and tunnels on a voyage back through time to the heyday of smuggling. Several events throughout the year.

Times Open all year daily, Apr-Sep 10-5; Oct-Mar 11-4.* **Fees** £7 (ch £5, concessions £6). Family ticket (2ad+2ch) £21, (2ad+3ch) £25* **Facilities** Ⓟ ♿ (partly accessible) (40 steps to entrance & exit the attraction) shop ⊗

HERSTMONCEUX

The Observatory Science Centre

BN27 1RN
☎ 01323 832731   📠 01323 832741
e-mail: info@the-observatory.org
web: www.the-observatory.org
dir: 0.75m N of Wartling village

From the 1950s to the 1980s this was part of the Royal Greenwich Observatory, and was used by astronomers to observe and chart movements in the night sky. Visitors can learn about not only astronomy, but also other areas of science in a series of interactive and engaging displays. There are also exhibitions, a discovery park, and a collection of unusual giant exhibits.

Times Open daily from 26 Jan-Nov. Open wknd of Dec 6-7.* **Fees** £7.23 (ch 4-15 £5.41). Family ticket (2ad+3ch or 1ad+4ch) £22.27. Family of 5 £25.40.* **Facilities** Ⓟ ⊑ ⊓ (indoor & outdoor) ♿ (partly accessible) toilets for disabled shop ⊗

LEWES

Lewes Castle & Barbican House Museum

169 High St BN7 1YE
☎ 01273 486290   📠 01273 486990
e-mail: castle@sussexpast.co.uk
web: www.sussexpast.co.uk
dir: N of High St off A27/A26/A275

One of the oldest castles in England, built soon after the Norman Conquest, and one of only two in England to be built on two mounds. The views over Lewes, the River Ouse and surrounding Downs are worth the climb up the Keep. Barbican House Museum, opposite the Castle tells the story of Sussex from the Stone Age to the end of the medieval period, and displays include flint tools, pottery, weapons, jewellery and other archaeological discoveries, as well as a model of Lewes in about 1870. Special family sessions on archaeological and historical themes are run throughout the year. Other events include a Medieval Day in May and open-air theatre.

Times Open all year, daily, Tue-Sat 10-5.30, Sun, Mon & BHs 11-5.30. (Last admission 30 mins before closing). Closed Xmas & Mon in Jan.* **Fees** £5.20 (ch 5-15 £2.60, concessions £4.55). Family ticket (2ad+2ch) £14.30, (1ad+4ch) £14.30. Carer £1.95 each.* **Facilities** Ⓟ ♿ (partly accessible) (Wheelchair access is limited to the lower Gun Garden of the Castle) shop ⊗

NEWHAVEN

Paradise Park, Heritage Trail & Gardens

Avis Rd BN9 0DH
☎ 01273 512123   📠 01273 616005
e-mail: promotions@paradisepark.co.uk
web: www.paradisepark.co.uk
dir: signed off A26 & A259

A perfect day out for plant lovers whatever the season. Discover the unusual garden designs with waterfalls, fountains and lakes, including the Caribbean garden and the tranquil Oriental garden. The Conservatory Gardens complex contains a large variety of the world's flora divided into several zones. There's also a Sussex history trail and Planet Earth with moving dinosaurs and interactive displays, plus rides and amusements for children.

Times Open all year, daily 9-6. Closed 25-26 Dec. **Fees** £8.99 (ch £6.99). Family ticket £24.99 (2ad+2ch).* **Facilities** Ⓟ ⊑ ⍾ licensed ⊓ (outdoor) ♿ toilets for disabled shop ⊗

SHEFFIELD PARK

Sheffield Park Garden

TN22 3QX

☎ **01825 790231** 🖺 **01825 791264**
e-mail: sheffieldpark@nationaltrust.org.uk
web: www.nationaltrust.org.uk/sheffieldpark
dir: midway between East Grinstead & Lewes, 5m NW of Uckfield, on E side of A275, between A272 & A22

Sheffield Park was originally landscaped by 'Capability' Brown, in about 1775 to create a beautiful park with four lakes and cascades. Further extensive planting was done at the beginning of the 20th century, to give emphasis to autumn colour among the trees. In May and June masses of azaleas and rhododendrons bloom and later there are magnificent waterlillies on the lakes. Autumn brings stunning colours from the many rare trees and shrubs. Also visit South Park, a 265 acre historic parkland with stunning views. Special events run throughout the year please, check the website for details.

Times Open all year. Please phone for details or check website.
Fees Gift Aid donation: £7.70 (ch £3.85). Family ticket £19.25. Groups 15+ £6.50. Joint ticket with Bluebell Railway available. RHS members free. Includes a voluntary donation of 10% or more. Visitors can however, choose to pay the standard admission which is displayed at the property and on NT website.* **Facilities** 🅿 ⛱🗚 (outdoor) ♿ (partly accessible) (most of the garden is accessible, please phone for further details) toilets for disabled shop ⊗ 🌺

SHEFFIELD PARK STATION

Bluebell Railway

Sheffield Park Station TN22 3QL

☎ **01825 720800 & & 722370** 🖺 **01825 720804**
e-mail: info@bluebell-railway.co.uk
web: www.bluebell-railway.co.uk
dir: 4.5m E of Haywards Heath, off A275, 10m S of East Grinstead A22-A275

A volunteer-run heritage steam railway with nine miles of track running through pretty Sussex countryside. Please note that there is no parking at Kingscote Station. If you wish to board the train here, catch the bus (service 473) which connects Kingscote and East Grinstead.

Times Open all year, Sat & Sun, daily Apr-Oct & during school hols. Santa Specials run Dec. For timetable and information regarding trains contact above.* **Facilities** 🅿 🅟 ⛱🗚 (indoor) ♿ (partly accessible) toilets for disabled shop

AMBERLEY

Amberley Working Museum

BN18 9LT

☎ **01798 831370** 🖺 **01798 831831**
e-mail: office@amberleymuseum.co.uk
web: www.amberleymuseum.co.uk
dir: on B2139, between Arundel and Storrington, adjacent to Amberley railway station

36 acre open-air museum dedicated to the industrial heritage of the south east of England. Traditional craftspeople on site, working narrow-gauge railway and vintage bus collection, Connected Earth telecommunications display, Seeboard Electricity Hall, stationary engines, print workshop, woodturners, wheelwrights, nature trails, and much more.

Times Open 12 Mar-2 Nov, Wed-Sun & BH Mon 10-5.30 (last admission 4.30). Also open daily during school hols.* **Facilities** 🅿 ⛱🗚 toilets for disabled shop

ARUNDEL

Arundel Castle

BN18 9AB

☎ **01903 882173** 🖺 **01903 884581**
e-mail: info@arundelcastle.org **web:** www.arundelcastle.org
dir: on A27 between Chichester & Worthing

Set high on a hill in West Sussex, this magnificent castle and stately home, seat of the Dukes of Norfolk for nearly 1000 years, commands stunning views across the river Arun and out to sea. Climb to the keep and battlements; marvel at a fine collection of 16th-century furniture; portraits by Van Dyke, Gainsborough, Canaletto and others; tapestries and the personal possessions of Mary, Queen of Scots; wander in the grounds and Victorian flower and vegetable gardens.

Times Open Apr-Oct, Sun-Fri 11-5, Castle open 12-5. (Last admission 4). Closed Sat.* **Facilities** 🅿 🅟 ⛱ toilets for disabled shop ⊗

BIGNOR

Bignor Roman Villa & Museum

RH20 1PH
☎ 01798 869259   ≣ 01798 869259
e-mail: enquiries@bignorromanvilla.co.uk
web: www.bignorromanvilla.co.uk
dir: 6m S of Pulborough & 6m N of Arundel on A29, signed. 8m S of Petworth on A285, signed

Rediscovered in 1811, this Roman house was built on a grand scale. It is one of the largest known, and has spectacular mosaics. The heating system can also be seen, and various finds from excavations are on show. The longest mosaic in Britain (82ft) is on display here in its original position.

Times Open Mar-Apr, Tue-Sun & BH 10-5; May daily 10-5; Jun-Sep daily 10-6, Oct daily 10-5* **Fees** £5.50 (ch under 16 £2.50, pen £4). Family £14. Party 10+ 20% discount. Guided tours by arrangement.* **Facilities** ℗ ⊡ ⊟ (outdoor) ♿ (partly accessible) (most areas accessible) shop ⊗

EAST GRINSTEAD

Standen

West Hoathly Rd RH19 4NE
☎ 01342 323029   ≣ 01342 316424
e-mail: standen@nationaltrust.org.uk
web: www.nationaltrust.org.uk/standen
dir: 2m S of East Grinstead, signed from B2110

Life in a Victorian family home is brought vividly to life in this gem of the Arts & Crafts movement. Standen is hidden at the end of a quiet Sussex lane with fine views over the High Weald and Weir Wood Reservoir. The design of the house, which incorporates the original medieval farmhouse, is a monument to the combined genius of architect Philip Webb and his friend William Morris. All the big names of the Arts & Crafts period are represented including ceramics by William de Morgan, furniture by George Jack and metal work by W. A. S. Benson. The beautiful hillside gardens provide year-round interest and the woodlands now offer a number of easily accessible, and picturesque, walks.

Times House open: 27 Feb-7 Mar, Sat & Sun; 13 Mar-4 Apr, 21 Apr-25 Jul, Sep-24 Oct, Wed-Sun & BH; 5-18 Apr, 26 Jul-30 Aug, 25-31 Oct, Wed-Mon, 11-4.30. **Fees** Gift Aid donation: House & garden £8.50 (ch £4.25). Family ticket £21.25, Groups £7.20. Garden only: £5.10 (ch £2.55). Family ticket £12.65. Includes a voluntary donation of 10% or more. Visitors can however, choose to pay the standard admission which is displayed at the property and on NT website. **Facilities** ℗ ¶⦿¶ licensed ⊟ (outdoor) ♿ (partly accessible) (ground floor of house accessible. Some parts of garden steep with steps) toilets for disabled shop ⊗ ⛊

FISHBOURNE

Fishbourne Roman Palace

Salthill Rd PO19 3QR
☎ 01243 785859   ≣ 01243 539266
e-mail: adminfish@sussexpast.co.uk
web: www.sussexpast.co.uk
dir: off A27 onto A259 into Fishbourne. Turn right into Salthill Rd & right into Roman Way

The remains of the Roman Palace at Fishbourne were discovered in 1960. Here you can see Britain's largest collection of in-situ Roman floor mosaics. More everyday Roman objects found during the excavations are displayed in the museum gallery. An audio-visual presentation uses computer-generated images to interpret the site. Outside the garden has been replanted to its original plan, using plants that may have grown there when the palace was inhabited. The Collections Discovery Centre displays more artefacts from both Fishbourne and Chichester district. Join a 'behind the scenes' tour for an opportunity to handle some of these.

Times Open all year, daily Feb-15 Dec. Feb, Nov-mid Dec 10-4; Mar-Jul & Sep-Oct 10-5; Aug 10-6. Winter wknds 10-4.* **Facilities** ℗ ⊡ ⊟ (outdoor) ♿ toilets for disabled shop ⊗

HANDCROSS

Nymans

RH17 6EB
☎ 01444 405250   ≣ 01444 400253
e-mail: nymans@nationaltrust.org.uk
web: www.nationaltrust.org.uk/nymans
dir: on B2114 at Handcross, 4m S of Crawley

One of the great 20th-century gardens, with an important collection of rare plants, set around a romantic house and ruins in a beautiful woodland estate. Theatrically designed with plants from around the world, Nymans is internationally renowned for its garden design, rare plant collection and intimacy. Visit the Messel family rooms in the house, and see the dramatic ruins, which form a backdrop to the main lawn. Enjoy fine views across the Sussex countryside and explore the wide estate with walks through ancient woodland, lakes and wild flowers. Nymans is one of the leading 'green' gardens in the National Trust, actively engaging visitors with its methods of sustainable gardening. Buggy tours are available, along with learning opportunities for the kids, and an all-round programme of events and workshops.

Times Garden: Open all year, Wed-Sun & BH 10-5; Nov-Jan 10-4. Last admission 30mins before closing. House: open 11 Mar-1 Nov, 11-4. Closed 25-26 Dec & 1 Jan. (Last admission to house 3.45pm).* **Fees** Gift Aid donation: £9 (ch £4.50), Family ticket (2ad + 3ch) £22. Includes a voluntary donation of 10% or more. Visitors can however, choose to pay the standard admission which is displayed at the property and on NT website. **Facilities** ℗ ⊡ ¶⦿¶ licensed ⊟ (outdoor) ♿ toilets for disabled shop ⊗ ⛊

HIGHDOWN

Highdown   FREE

Highdown Gardens BN12 6PE
☎ 01903 501054   📄 01903 218757
e-mail: chris.beardsley@worthing.gov.uk
web: www.worthing.gov.uk/wbc
dir: N off A259 between Worthing & Littlehampton. Access off dual carriageway, when coming from E proceed to rdbt

Set on downland countryside this unique garden overlooks the sea, and has been deemed a National Collection due to the unique assortment of rare plants and trees. The garden was the achievement of Sir Frederick and Lady Stern, who worked for fifty years to prove that plants could grow on chalk. Many of the original plants were collected in China and the Himalayas.

Times Open all year: Apr-Sep, Mon-Fri 10-6. Winter: Oct-Nov & Feb-Mar, Mon-Fri, 10-4.30; Dec-Jan, 10-4. **Facilities** 🅿 🎋 (outdoor) ♿ (partly accessible) (gardens on a sloping site, may prove difficult for wheelchair users) toilets for disabled ⊗

LITTLEHAMPTON

Harbour Park

Seafront BN17 5LL
☎ 01903 721200   📄 01903 716663
e-mail: fun@harbourpark.com
web: www.harbourpark.com
dir: A259 & A284 connect Littlehampton. Take B2140 follow signs to seafront, attraction is next to Windmill Theatre and River Arun.

Located on the east bank of the River Arun and close beaches and seafront, Harbour Park includes amusements, traditional rides, like the Waltzer and Dodgems, wide grass picnic areas and stunning views of the River Arun and Marina. With its New England 'fishing village' setting, this attraction offers something for all the family.

Times Open all year. Closed 25 Dec. Outdoor attractions closed Nov-Feb, open wknds until Etr and every day during holidays. **Fees** Admission free. Rides £15, book 10 tickets, or tokens can be purchased individually. Play area £3. **Facilities** 🅿 🅟 ⊑ 🍴 licensed 🎋 (outdoor) ♿ toilets for disabled shop

PETWORTH

Petworth House & Park

GU28 0AE
☎ 01798 342207 & 343929   📄 01798 342963
e-mail: petworth@nationaltrust.org.uk
web: www.nationaltrust.org.uk/petworth
dir: in town centre, A272/283

Petworth House is an impressive 17th-century mansion set in a 700 acre Deer Park, landscaped by 'Capability' Brown, and immortalised in Turner's paintings. At Petworth you will find the National Trust's finest art collection including work by Van Dyck, Titian, Blake and Turner, as well as sculpture, ceramics and fine furniture. Fascinating Servants' Quarters show the domestic side of life of this great estate.

Times Open Mar-Oct, Sat-Wed 11-5 (last entry 4.30)*
Fees With voluntary Gift Aid donation: £10.40 (ch £5.20). Family ticket £26. NT members free. Pleasure Ground £4 (ch £2.10).*
Facilities 🅿 🅟 ⊑ 🍴 licensed ♿ (partly accessible) (staircase to first floor bedrooms and steps down into chapel) toilets for disabled shop ⊗ 🦮

PULBOROUGH

RSPB Pulborough Brooks Nature Reserve

Uppertons Barn Visitor Centre, Wiggonholt RH20 2EL
☎ 01798 875851
e-mail: pulborough.brooks@rspb.org.uk
web: www.rspb.org.uk
dir: signed on A283, 2m SE of Pulborough & 2m NW of Storrington

Set in the scenic Arun Valley and easily reached via the visitor centre at Wiggonholt, this is an excellent reserve for year-round family visits. A nature trail winds through hedgerow-lined lanes to viewing hides overlooking water-meadows. Breeding summer birds include nightingales and warblers, ducks and wading birds, and nightjars and hobbies on nearby heathland. Unusual wading birds and hedgerow birds regularly pass through on spring and autumn migration. Contact for details of special events or see website.

Times Open daily, Reserve: 9-9, (or sunset if earlier). Visitor centre: 9.30-5. Reserve closed 25 Dec, Visitor Centre closed 25-26 Dec. **Fees** £3.50 (ch £1, concessions £2.50). Family ticket £7.* **Facilities** 🅿 🅟 ⊑ 🎋 (outdoor) toilets for disabled shop ⊗

SINGLETON

Weald & Downland Open Air Museum

PO18 0EU
☎ 01243 811348   📄 01243 811475
e-mail: office@wealddown.co.uk
web: www.wealddown.co.uk
dir: 6m N of Chichester on A286

A showcase of English architectural heritage, where historic buildings have been rescued from destruction and rebuilt in a parkland setting. Vividly demonstrating the evolution of building techniques and use of local materials, these fascinating buildings bring to life the homes, farms and rural industries of the south east of the past 500 years. See also working Shire horses, cattle and traditional breeds of farm animals.

Times Open daily all year, during BST, 10.30-6 & 10.30-4 the rest of year. Winter opening days vary, see website for details. **Fees** £8.95 (ch £4.70, pen £7.95). Family ticket (2ad+3ch) £24.25.* **Facilities** ● ⏛ 🎪 (indoor & outdoor) & (partly accessible) (some areas of museum not suitable for disabled visitiors, but most key areas and exhibits are accessible) toilets for disabled shop

SOUTH HARTING

Uppark

GU31 5QR
☎ 01730 825415 & 825857   📄 01730 825873
e-mail: uppark@nationaltrust.org.uk
web: www.nationaltrust.org.uk/uppark
dir: A3 take A272, B2146 to South Harting, follow signs to Uppark

A late 17th-century house set high on the South Downs with magnificent sweeping views to the sea. The elegant Georgian interior houses a famous Grand Tour collection that includes paintings, furniture and ceramics. An 18th-century dolls' house with original features is one of the more impressive items. The servants' quarters appear as they did in Victorian days, when H G Wells' mother was housekeeper, while the garden is restored in the early 19th-century 'Picturesque' style.

Times Open 21 Mar-Oct, Sun-Thu. Garden 11.30-5. House: 12.30-4.30 **Fees** Gift Aid donation: £7.50 (ch £3.75). Family £18. Garden only £3.50 (ch £1.75). Includes a voluntary donation of 10% or more. Visitors can however, choose to pay the standard admission which is displayed at the property and on NT website.* **Facilities** ● ⏛ 🎪 licensed 🎪 (outdoor) & toilets for disabled shop ⊗ 🦋

WISBOROUGH GREEN

Fishers Farm Park

Newpound Ln RH14 0EG
☎ 01403 700063   📄 01403 700823
e-mail: info@fishersfarmpark.co.uk
web: www.fishersfarmpark.co.uk
dir: follow brown & white tourist boards on all roads approaching Wisborough Green

All weather, all year farm and adventure park, providing a mixture of farmyard and dynamic adventure play. Please contact for details of special events.

Times Open all year, daily, 10-5. Closed 26-26 Dec. **Fees** Please phone for details. **Facilities** ● ℗ ⏛ 🎪 licensed 🎪 (outdoor) & (partly accessible) (woodland walkway inaccessible to wheelchairs) toilets for disabled shop ⊗

TYNE & WEAR

GATESHEAD

Baltic Centre for Contemporary Art   FREE

South Shore Rd, Gateshead Quays NE8 3BA
☎ 0191 478 1810 & 440 4944   📄 0191 478 1922
e-mail: info@balticmill.com
web: www.balticmill.com
dir: follow signs for Quayside, Millennium Bridge. 15 mins' walk from Gateshead Metro & Newcastle Central Station

Once a 1950s grain warehouse, part of the old Baltic Flour Mills, Baltic Centre for Contemporary Art is an international centre presenting a dynamic and ambitious programme of complementary exhibitions and events. It consists of five art spaces, cinema, auditorium, library and archive, eating and drinking areas and a shop. Check website for current events information.

Times Open all year daily 10-6 (Tue 10.30-6). Closed 25-26 Dec & 1 Jan. **Facilities** 🅿 Ⓟ ⏼🍽 licensed ♿ toilets for disabled shop ⊗

JARROW

Bede's World

Church Bank NE32 3DY
☎ 0191 489 2106   📄 0191 428 2361
e-mail: visitor.info@bedesworld.co.uk
web: www.bedesworld.co.uk
dir: off A185 near S end of Tyne tunnel

Bede's World is an ambitious museum based around the extraordinary life and work of the Venerable Bede (AD673-735) early Medieval Europe's greatest scholar and England's first historian. Attractions include an 'Age of Bede' exhibition in the museum, which displays finds excavated from the site of St Paul's monastery. Alongside the museum, Bede's World has developed Gyrwe, an Anglo-Saxon demonstration farm, which brings together the animals, timber buildings, crops and vegetables that would have featured in the Northumbrian Landscape of Bede's Day.

Times Open all year, Apr-Oct, Mon-Sat 10-5.30, Sun noon-5.30; Nov-Mar, Mon-Sat 10-4.30 & Sun 12-4.30. Please contact for Xmas/New Year opening times.* **Facilities** 🅿 Ⓟ ⏼🍽 licensed 🏖 (outdoor) toilets for disabled shop ⊗

NEWCASTLE UPON TYNE

Discovery Museum   FREE

Blandford Square NE1 4JA
☎ 0191 232 6789   📄 0191 230 2614
e-mail: discovery@twmuseums.org.uk
web: www.twmuseums.org.uk/discovery
dir: off A6115/A6125. 5 mins walk from Newcastle Central Station

Newcastle Discovery Museum offers something for everyone. There are displays covering fashion, military history, maritime splendours and scientific curiosities. Local history is covered in the fascinating Great City story. There is a gallery housing Turbinia, once the world's fastest ship.

Times Open all year, Mon-Sat 10-5; Sun 2-5. (Closed 25-26 Dec & 1 Jan). **Facilities** 🅿 Ⓟ ⏼♿ toilets for disabled shop ⊗

Hancock Museum

Barras Bridge NE2 4PT
☎ 0191 222 7418   📄 0191 261 7537
e-mail: hancock@twmuseums.org.uk
web: www.twmuseums.org.uk/hancock
dir: follow exit signs for city centre A167, off A1

Newcastle's premier Natural History museum unravels the natural world, through sensational galleries and close encounters with resident reptiles and insects. For more than 100 years the Hancock Museum has provided visitors with a glimpse of the animal kingdom and the powerful and often destructive forces of nature. From the dinosaurs to live animals, the Hancock is home to creatures past and present and the odd Egyptian mummy or two.

Times Open all year, Mon-Sat, 10-5, Sun 2-5. Closed 25-26 Dec & 1 Jan.* **Facilities** 🅿 Ⓟ ⏼🏖 toilets for disabled shop ⊗

Life Science Centre

Times Square NE1 4EP
☎ 0191 243 8210   📄 0191 243 8201
e-mail: info@life.org.uk
web: www.life.org.uk
dir: A1M, A69, A184, A1058 & A167, follow signs to Centre for Life or Central Station

Life is an exciting place where science comes alive in a fun and funky environment. Aiming to inspire curiosity and encourage visitors to uncover new things about life, whatever age. If you are curious about the world around you, there is something for all the family at Life. Step inside for a hands-on, minds-on, hearts-on experience and see what Life has to offer.

Times Open all year Mon-Sat 10-6, Sun 11-6 . Closed 25-26 Dec & 1 Jan. (Last entry subject to seasonal demand).* **Fees** £8 (ch 5-16 £5.85, concessions £6.95). Family ticket (1ad&3ch) £24.20 (2ad&2ch) £24.20.* **Facilities** 🅿 Ⓟ ⏼🍽 licensed 🏖 (indoor) ♿ toilets for disabled shop ⊗

Tyne & Wear

ROWLANDS GILL

Gibside

NE16 6BG
☎ 01207 541820 📄 01207 541830
e-mail: gibside@nationaltrust.org.uk
web: www.nationaltrust.org.uk
dir: 3m W of Metro Centre & 6m SW of Gateshead, on B6314, clearly signposted from the A1

This 18th-century landscaped garden is the former home of the Bowes-Lyon family, with miles of walks through the wooded slopes and riverside of the Derwent valley. Discover hidden vistas, wildlife or wild flowers, or just enjoy a Georgian style lunch in the tea room. Lots of events and activities for children and families. Anglican weddings can be held in the unique Palladian Chapel.

Times Grounds open: all year daily 5 Mar-8 Oct 10-6 (last entry 4.30); 23 Oct-4 Mar 10-4 (last entry 3.30). Closed 23-26 Dec, 30 Dec-2 Jan; Chapel open 13 Mar-Oct 11-4.30 **Fees** £6.50 (ch £4). Family (2ad+4ch), £18.50, family (1ad+3ch), £13.* **Facilities** ℗ 🍴 🎠 toilets for disabled shop 🌿

SOUTH SHIELDS

Arbeia Roman Fort & Museum

Baring St NE33 2BB
☎ 0191 456 1369 📄 0191 427 6862
web: www.twmuseums.org.uk
dir: 5 mins' walk from town centre

In South Shields town are the extensive remains of Arbeia, a Roman fort in use from the 2nd to 4th century. It was the supply base for the Roman army's campaign against Scotland. On site there are full size reconstructions of a fort gateway, a barrack block and part of the commanding officer's house. Archaeological evacuations are in progress throughout the summer.

Times Open all year, Apr-Oct, Mon-Sat 10-5.30, Sun 1-5; Nov-Mar, Mon-Sat 10-3.30. Closed 25-26 Dec & 1 Jan* **Fees** Fort & Museum free of charge ex for 'Timequest' Archaeological Interpretation Gallery £1.50 (ch & concessions 80p).* **Facilities** ℗ 🎠 (outdoor) 🦽 (partly accessible) toilets for disabled shop

SUNDERLAND

Monkwearmouth Station Museum FREE

North Bridge St SR5 1AP
☎ 0191 567 7075
dir: off A1018

Time stands still in this beautifully restored Victorian station. Travel and transport in the early 1900s are recorded with a look behind the scenes of the booking offices and guard's van. The brand new 'Play Station' activities area has been specifically designed for young visitors with regular organised events for children.

Times Open all year, Mon-Sat 10-5, Sun 2-5. Closed 25-26 Dec & 1 Jan* **Facilities** ℗ 🦽 (partly accessible) toilets for disabled shop ⊗

National Glass Centre FREE

Liberty Way SR6 0GL
☎ 0191 515 5555 📄 0191 515 5556
e-mail: info@nationalglasscentre.com
web: www.nationalglasscentre.com
dir: A19 onto A1231, signposted from all major roads

The National Glass Centre offers galleries showing an international programme of exhibitions. Home to the largest art glass making facility for kiln forming, a unique venue and a hub for activity inspired by glass. Artists' studios, glass production facilities and much more and located in an innovative glass and steel building on the banks of the River Wear. Explore with a behind-the-scenes tours.

Times Open all year, daily 10-5 (last admission to glass tour 4.30). Closed 25 Dec & 1 Jan. **Facilities** ℗ 🍴 licensed 🦽 toilets for disabled shop ⊗

162

Sunderland Museum & Winter Gardens   FREE

Burdon Rd SR1 1PP
☎ 0191 553 2323   📄 0191 553 7828
e-mail: sunderland@twmuseums.org.uk
web: www.twmuseums.org.uk/sunderland
dir: in city centre on Burdon Rd, short walk from Sunderland metro and mainline stations

An award-winning attraction with wide-ranging displays and many hands-on exhibits that cover the archaeology and geology of Sunderland, the coal mines and shipyards of the area and the spectacular glass and pottery made on Wearside. Other galleries show the changes in the lifestyles of Sunderland women over the past century, works by LS Lowry and wildlife from all corners of the globe. The Winter Gardens are a horticultural wonderland where the exotic plants from around the world can be seen growing to their full natural height in a spectacular glass and steel rotunda.

Times Open all year, Mon-Sat 10-5, Sun 2-5.* **Facilities** Ⓟ ⌷ 🍽 licensed ♿ toilets for disabled shop ⊗

TYNEMOUTH

Blue Reef Aquarium

Grand Pde NE30 4JF
☎ 0191 258 1031   📄 0191 257 2116
e-mail: tynemouth@bluereefaquarium.co.uk
web: www.bluereefaquarium.co.uk
dir: follow A19, taking A1058 (coast road), signed Tynemouth. Situated on seafront

From its position overlooking one of the North East's prettiest beaches, Blue Reef is home to a dazzling variety of creatures. Enjoy close encounters with seals, seahorses, sharks, stingrays, giant octopus, frogs, otters and hundreds of other aquatic lifeforms. Explore a dazzling coral reef and journey through the spectacular tropical ocean display in a transparent underwater tunnel. Informative, entertaining talks and feeding displays throughout the day.

Times Open all year, daily from 10. Closed 25 Dec.* **Fees** £7.75 (ch £5.75, concessions £6.75). Family (2ad+2ch) £24 (2ad+3ch) £27.50.* **Facilities** Ⓟ Ⓟ ⌷ 🍴 (outdoor) ♿ toilets for disabled shop ⊗

Segedunum Roman Fort, Baths & Museum

Buddle St NE28 6HR
☎ 0191 236 9347   📄 0191 295 5858
e-mail: segedunum@twmuseums.org.uk
web: www.twmuseums.org.uk/sege
dir: A187 from Tyne Tunnel, signposted

Hadrian's Wall was built by the Roman Emperor Hadrian in 122AD, Segedunum was built as part of the Wall, serving as a garrison for 600 soldiers until the collapse of Roman rule around 410AD. This major historical venture shows what life would have been like then, using artefacts, audio-visuals, reconstructed buildings and a 34m high viewing tower. Plenty of special events including craft activities and re-enactments from Roman cavalry and soldiers. Contact for details.

Times Open all year, Apr-Oct 10-5; Nov-Mar, 10-3. **Fees** £4.25 (ch, pen & concessions £2.50). (ch 16 and under free) **Facilities** Ⓟ Ⓟ ⌷ 🍴 (outdoor) ♿ toilets for disabled shop ⊗

WASHINGTON

WWT Washington Wetland Centre

Pattinson NE38 8LE
☎ 0191 416 5454   📄 0191 416 5801
e-mail: info.washington@wwt.org.uk
web: www.wwt.org.uk/visit/washington
dir: signposted off A195, A1231 & A182

Explore 45 hectares of wetland, woodland and wildlife reserve at Washington Wetland Centre - one of the North East's biggest conservation success stories. Home to exotic birds, amazing insects and beautiful wild scenery. Get nose to beak with rare waterbirds at Close Encounters and meet the pink Chilean Flamingos. See Grey Herons at Wade Lake, Great-spotted Woodpeckers in Hawthorn Wood and tiny ducklings at Waterfowl Nursery (May-July). Plus wildflower meadows, dragonflies, frogs, bats, goats and ancient woodland. Excellent year-round events calendar, award-winning educational programmes, excellent disabled access and free wheelchair hire.

Times Open all year. Summer: 9.30-5.30. (Last admission 5pm). Winter: 9.30-4.30. (Last admission 4pm). Closed 25 Dec. **Fees** £6.31 (ch £3.18, concessions £4.85). Family £17.08 Please contact for current prices.* **Facilities** Ⓟ ⌷ 🍴 licensed 🍴 (outdoor) ♿ (partly accessible) (majority of pathways are tarmacced and most hides are accessible) shop ⊗

WHITBURN

Souter Lighthouse & The Leas

Coast Rd SR6 7NH
☎ **0191 529 3161 & 01670 773966** 📄 **0191 529 0902**
e-mail: souter@nationaltrust.org.uk
web: www.nationaltrust.org.uk
dir: on A183 coast road, 2m S of South Shields, 3m N of
Sunderland

When it opened in 1871, Souter was the most advanced
lighthouse in the world, and warned shipping off the notorious
rocks in the river approaches of the Tyne and the Wear. Painted
red and white and standing at 150ft high, it is a dramatic
building and hands-on displays and volunteers help bring it
to life. Visitors can explore the whole building with its engine
room and lighthouse keeper's cottage. You can take part
in activities concerning shipwrecks and the workings of the
lighthouse. Climb to the top of the lighthouse, or walk along
the Leas, a 2.5 mile stretch of spectacular coastline.

Times Open 13 Mar-Oct daily (ex Fri but open Good Fri) 11-5.
Fees £4.85 (ch £3.15) Family ticket £12.65. Group 10+ £4.*
Facilities 🅿 ⓟ 🍽 licensed ⊼ toilets for disabled shop ⊗ ♨

WARWICKSHIRE

ALCESTER

Ragley Hall

B49 5NJ
☎ **01789 762090** 📄 **01789 764791**
e-mail: info@ragleyhall.com
web: www.ragleyhall.com
dir: 8m SW of Stratford-upon-Avon, off A46/A435, follow brown
tourist signs

Built in 1680, Ragley is the family home of the Marquess and
Marchioness of Hertford, and has been for nine generations.
Set in 400 acres of parkland, woodland and landscaped
gardens, Ragley has something for all the family. Younger
visitors will enjoy Adventure Wood with its swings, trampoline,
3-D maze, rope bridges and wooden fortress, while the
Lakeside Café is ideal for parents to rest and enjoy a cuppa
while the kids play safely. There are also 27 acres of formal
gardens, the Woodland Walk featuring the Jerwood Sculpture
Park, and the 18th-century stable block that houses a collection
of historic carriages and equestrian memorabilia.

Times House & Park Sun & school hols, Feb-Jun & Sep Oct;
Sun-Fri, Jul & Aug. Park only open Sat. Park 10-6 (last admission
4.30). House & State Rooms 12-4. Please phone or see website
to confirm opening times. **Fees** £8.50 (ch £5, concessions £7).
Family £27.* **Facilities** 🅿 ⊡ ⊼ (outdoor) ♿ (partly accessible)
(some areas of garden accessible) toilets for disabled shop ⊗

BADDESLEY CLINTON

Baddesley Clinton Hall

B93 0DQ
☎ **01564 783294** 📄 **01564 782706**
e-mail: baddesleyclinton@nationaltrust.org.uk
web: www.nationaltrust.org.uk
dir: 0.75m W off A4141, 7.5m NW of Warwick

A romantically-sited medieval moated house, dating from the
15th century, that has changed very little since 1634. With
family portraits, priest's holes, chapel, garden, ponds, nature
trail and lake walk.

Times Open Garden: 11 Feb-1 Nov, Wed-Sun 11-5; 4 Nov-20
Dec, Wed-Sun 11-4. House 11 Feb-1 Nov, Wed-Sun 11-5.*
Fees Garden only £4.40 (ch £2.20). House & Garden £8.80 (ch
£4.40). Family ticket £22. Joint ticket with Packwood House
£12.70 (ch £6.35). Family ticket £31.75. Joint ticket for gardens
only £6.60 (ch £3.30).* **Facilities** 🅿 🍽 licensed ⊼ (outdoor)
♿ (partly accessible) (grounds partly accessible,some steps and
gravel paths) toilets for disabled shop ⊗ ♨

COMPTON VERNEY

Compton Verney

CV35 9HZ
☎ 01926 645500 📠 01926 645501
e-mail: info@comptonverney.org.uk
web: www.comptonverney.org.uk
dir: 9m from Stratford-upon-Avon/Warwick/Leamington Spa on B4086 between Wellesbourne & Kineton

Visitors of all ages are warmly welcomed to this award-winning art gallery, housed in a restored 18th century mansion. Explore works of art from around the world in the permanent collections, be enthralled by the diverse programme of changing exhibitions and events before relaxing in the 120 acres of landscaped parkland.

Times Open 27 Mar-12 Dec, Tue-Sun, 11-5. Closed Mon except BH. Fees £8 (ch under 5's free, 5-16 £2, concessions £6) Family £18 (2+up to 4 ch). Facilities 🅿 🏧 🍴 licensed 🍴 (outdoor) ♿ toilets for disabled shop ⊗

COUGHTON

Coughton Court

B49 5JA
☎ 01789 400777 & 400702 📠 01789 765544
e-mail: coughtoncourt@nationaltrust.ork.uk
web: www.nationaltrust.org.uk
dir: 2m N of Alcester on E side of A435

This imposing Tudor house is set in beautiful gardens, and has been home to the Throckmortons for 600 hundred years. The house contains many family portraits, and much in the way of fascinating furniture, fabrics and ornaments. The estate has two churches, a 19th-century Catholic church, and the parish church of St Peter's. The Throckmorton family created and maintain the grounds, including the walled garden and the award-winning displays of roses.

Times House & Gardens open 15 Mar-29 Jun, Wed-Sun 11-5; Jul-Aug, Tue-Sun 11-5, 3-28 Sep, Wed-Sun 11-5; 4 Oct-2 Nov, wknds only 11-5.* Fees House and Garden: £9.20 (ch £4.60). Family £23. Garden only: £6.40 (ch £3.20). Family £16. Walled

garden: £2.50 for NT members. (inc. in admission price for non-members)* Facilities 🅿 🍴 licensed 🍴 (outdoor) ♿ (partly accessible) (access only to to ground floor of mansion house, loose gravel and hoggin paths in garden) toilets for disabled shop ⊗ 🌿

GAYDON

Heritage Motor Centre

Banbury Rd CV35 0BJ
☎ 01926 641188 📠 01926 641555
e-mail: enquiries@heritage-motor-centre.co.uk
web: www.heritage-motor-centre.co.uk
dir: M40 junct 12 and take B4100. Attraction signed

The Heritage Motor Centre is home to the world's largest collection of historic British cars. The museum boasts exciting and interactive exhibitions which uncover the story of the British motor industry from the 1890s to the present day. Fun for all the family with children's activity packs, special school holiday and lecture programs, plus free guided tours twice a day, onsite café and gift shop and a selection of outdoor activities including children's play area, picnic site, 4x4 Experience and Go-Karts.

Times Open all year, daily 10-5. (Closed over Xmas, check website or call 01926 641188 for details) Fees £9 (ch 5-16 £7, under 5 free, & concessions £8). Family ticket £28. (Additional charges apply to outdoor activities). Group & education rates available.* Facilities 🅿 🏧 🍴 (outdoor) ♿ toilets for disabled shop ⊗

KENILWORTH

Kenilworth Castle

CV8 1NE
☎ 01926 852078 📠 01926 851514
web: www.english-heritage.org.uk

Explore the largest and most extensive castle ruin in England, with a past rich in famous names and events. Its massive red sandstone towers, keep and wall glow brightly in the sunlight. Discover the history of Kenilworth through the interactive model in Leicester's Barn.

Times Open all year, Mar-1 Nov, daily 10-5; 2 Nov-Feb, daily 10-4. Closed 24-26 Dec & 1 Jan. Fees £7 (concessions £6, ch £3.50). Family ticket £17.50. Please check web site or call 0870 333 1181 for the most up to date prices and opening times when planning your visit. Facilities 🅿 🏧 🍴 ♿ (partly accessible) (uneven surfaces, steep slopes, steps) toilets for disabled shop ⊞

Kenilworth continued

Stoneleigh Abbey

CV8 2LF
☎ 01926 858535 & 858585 📄 01926 850724
e-mail: enquire@stoneleighabbey.org
web: www.stoneleighabbey.org
dir: entrance off B4115 close to junct of A46 and A452

Stoneleigh Abbey is one of the finest country house estates in the Midlands and has been the subject of considerable restoration work. The abbey, founded in the reign of Henry II, is now managed by a charitable trust. Visitors will experience a wealth of architectural styles spanning more than 800 years. The magnificent state rooms and chapel, the medieval Gatehouse and the Regency stables are some of the major areas to be admired. Set in 690 acres of parkland, 'Through the Keyhole' tours enable visitors to see parts of the Abbey that are not generally open to the public and on Sundays and Wednesdays to explore the Abbey's close links with Jane Austen.

Times Open Good Fri-Oct, Tue-Thu, Sun & BHs for guided tours at 11, 1 & 3. Grounds open 10-5. **Fees** Grounds only, £3. Guided tour of house, £6.50 (1ch 5-12 free, additional ch £3) pen £5.50. **Facilities** 🅿 ☐ ♿ (partly accessible) (access over exterior gravel paths will require assistance & lift access to state rooms) toilets for disabled shop ⊗

MIDDLETON

Ash End House Children's Farm

Middleton Ln B78 2BL
☎ 0121 329 3240 📄 0121 329 3240
e-mail: contact@thechildrensfarm.co.uk
web: www.childrensfarm.co.uk
dir: signed from A4091

Ideal for young children, this is a small family-owned farm with many friendly animals to feed and stroke, including some rare breeds. Café, new farm shop stocking local produce, play areas, picnic barns and lots of undercover activities. A recent addition is the New Farm Education Classroom to complement Food and Farming Year and an improved Toddlers Barn.

Times Open all year, daily 10-5 or dusk in winter. Closed 25 Dec until 2nd weekend in Jan* **Facilities** 🅿 ☐ 🍴 (indoor & outdoor) ♿ toilets for disabled shop ⊗

Packwood House

B94 6AT
☎ 01564 782024 📄 01564 787920
e-mail: packwood@nationaltrust.org.uk
web: www.nationaltrust.org.uk
dir: on unclass road off A3400

Dating from the 16th century, Packwood House has been extended and much changed over the years. An important collection of tapestries and textiles is displayed. Equally important are the stunning gardens with renowned herbaceous borders, attracting many visitors, and the almost surreal topiary garden based on the Sermon on the Mount. During summer months there is open air theatre in the garden.

Times House & Gardens open: 11 Feb-1 Nov 11-5, Wed-Sun, BH Mon & Good Fri. Park open all year.* **Fees** House & Garden £7.70 (ch £3.85, ch under 5 free.). Family ticket £19.25. Garden only £4.40 (ch £2.20). Joint ticket with Baddesley Clinton £12.70 (ch £6.35). Family ticket £31.75, joint ticket for gardens only £6.60 (ch £3.30).* **Facilities** 🅿 🍴 (outdoor) ♿ (partly accessible) (ground floor of house, apart from great hall, accessible and loose gravel and some steps in garden) toilets for disabled shop ⊗ 🦮

STRATFORD-UPON-AVON

Stratford Butterfly Farm

Tramway Walk, Swan's Nest Ln CV37 7LS
☎ 01789 299288 📄 01789 415878
e-mail: sales@butterflyfarm.co.uk
web: www.butterflyfarm.co.uk
dir: south bank of River Avon opposite RSC

The UK's largest live butterfly and insect exhibit. Hundreds of the world's most spectacular and colourful butterflies, in the unique setting of a lush tropical landscape, with splashing waterfalls and fish-filled pools. See also the strange and fascinating Insect City, a bustling metropolis of ants, stick insects, beetles and other remarkable insects. See the dangerous and deadly in Arachnoland!

Times Open all year, daily 10-6 (winter 10-dusk). Closed 25 Dec.* **Fees** £5.75 (ch £4.75, concessions £5.25). Family £16.75.*
Facilities ℗ 🍴 (outdoor) ♿ shop ⊗

WARWICK

Warwick Castle

CV34 4QU
☎ 0870 442 2000 📄 0870 442 2394
e-mail: customer.information@warwick-castle.com
web: www.warwick-castle.com
dir: 2m from M40 junct 15

From the days of William the Conqueror to the reign of Queen Victoria, Warwick Castle has provided a backdrop for many turbulent times. Today it offers family entertainment with a medieval theme. Attractions include the world's largest siege engine, thrilling jousting tournaments, birds of prey, daredevil knights, and entire castleful of colourful characters. The newest addition is the immersive and interactive "Dream of Battle".

Times Open all year, daily 10-6 (5pm Nov-Mar). Closed 25 Dec.*
Facilities ℗ ℗ ☕ 🍴 licensed 🍴 toilets for disabled shop ⊗

BIRMINGHAM

Birmingham Botanical Gardens & Glasshouses

Westbourne Rd, Edgbaston B15 3TR
☎ 0121 454 1860 📄 0121 454 7835
e-mail: admin@birminghambotanicalgardens.org.uk
web: www.birminghambotanicalgardens.org.uk
dir: 2m W of city centre, follow signs for Edgbaston, then brown heritage signs

Originally opened in 1832, the gardens include the Tropical House, which has a 24ft-wide lily pool and lush vegetation. The Mediterranean house features a wide variety of citrus fruits and the Arid House has a desert scene with its giant agaves and opuntias. Outside, a tour of the gardens includes rhododendrons and azalea borders and a collection of over 200 trees. Young children's discovery garden and a sculpture trail. There are a large amount of events to choose from, contact the gardens for a brochure.

Times Open all year, wkdays 9-7, Sun 10-7. **Fees** £7.50 (concessions £4.75). Family £22. Groups 10+ £6.50 (concessions £4.50). **Facilities** ℗ ℗ ☕ 🍴 licensed 🍴 (outdoors) ♿ toilets for disabled shop ⊗

West Midlands

Birmingham continued

Birmingham Museum & Art Gallery

Chamberlain Sq B3 3DH
☎ 0121 303 2834   📄 0121 303 1394
e-mail: bmag-enquiries@birmingham.gov.uk
web: www.bmag.org.uk
dir: 5 mins walk from Birmingham New St Station, by Town Hall, Council House & Central Library

One of the world's best collections of Pre-Raphaelite paintings can be seen here, including important works by Burne-Jones, a native of Birmingham. Also on display are fine silver, ceramics and glass. The archaeology section has prehistoric Egyptian, Greek and Roman antiquities, and also objects from the Near East, Mexico and Peru. New galleries explore the creation of art, while the In Touch gallery includes talking sculptures, and Samurai armour. The Bull Ring explores the 800 year history of this well-known area. There is a regular programme of temporary art and history exhibitions every year.

Times Open all year, Mon-Thu & Sat 10-5, Fri 10.30-5 and Sun 12.30-5. Fees Admission free but small charge may be made for some temporary exhibitions Facilities ℗ ⬚ ꭯◉ licensed ⚿ toilets for disabled shop ⊗

Museum of the Jewellery Quarter   FREE

75-80 Vyse St, Hockley B18 6HA
☎ 0121 554 3598   📄 0121 554 9700
e-mail: bmag-enquiries@birmingham.gov.uk
web: www.bmag.org.uk
dir: off A41 into Vyse St, museum on left after 1st side street

The Museum tells the story of jewellery making in Birmingham from its origins in the Middle Ages right through to the present day. Discover the skill of the jeweller's craft and enjoy a unique tour of an original jewellery factory frozen in time. For over eighty years the family firm of Smith and Pepper produced jewellery from the factory. This perfectly preserved 'time capsule' workshop has changed little since the beginning of the 20th century. The Jewellery Quarter is still very much at the forefront of jewellery manufacture in Britain and the Museum showcases the work of the city's most exciting new designers.

Times Open all year* Facilities ℗ ⚿ toilets for disabled shop ⊗

Thinktank at Millennium Point

Millennium Point, Curzon St B4 7XG
☎ 0121 202 2222   📄 0121 202 2280
e-mail: findout@thinktank.ac
web: www.thinktank.ac

Thinktank offers a fun-packed day out for all the family. From steam engines to intestines this exciting museum has over 200 amazing artefacts and interactive exhibits on science and discovery. A state-of-the-art planetarium means you can tour the night sky and fly through the galaxy without stepping outside. There is an ever-changing programme of demonstrations, workshops and events. Contact for details.

Times Open daily 10-5 (last entry 4). Closed 24-26 Dec. Fees £9 (ch £7.15, concessions £7.15). Family ticket £27.40 (2ad+2ch).* Facilities ℗ ℗ ⬚ ꭯ (indoor) toilets for disabled shop ⊗

BOURNVILLE

Cadbury World

Linden Rd B30 2LU
☎ 0845 450 3599   📄 0121 451 1366
e-mail: cadbury.world@csplc.com
web: www.cadburyworld.co.uk
dir: 1m S of A38 Bristol Rd, on A4040 Ring Rd. Follow brown signs from M5 junct 2 and junct 4

Get involved in the chocolate making process, and to find out how the chocolate is used to make famous confectionery. Visitors can learn about the early struggles and triumphs of the Cadbury business, and follow the history of Cadbury television advertising. Two recently added attractions are: Essence, where visitors can create their own unique product by combining liquid chocolate with different tastes, and Purple Planet, where you can chase a creme egg, grow cocoa beans, and see yourself moulded in chocolate. A new visitor centre explores the innovative values of the Cadbury Brothers that make Bournville the place it is. 2010 is the 20th anniversary of Cadbury World.

Times Opening times vary throughout the year please contact the information line 0845 450 3599.* Fees £13.45 (ch 4-15yrs £10.10, concessions £10.30).* Facilities ℗ ⬚ ꭯◉ licensed ꭯ (outdoor) ⚿ (partly accessible) (limited access to landing area) toilets for disabled shop ⊗

COVENTRY

Coventry Transport Museum   FREE

Millennium Place, Hales St CV1 1JD
☎ 024 7623 4270   📄 024 7623 4284
e-mail: enquiries@transport-museum.com
web: www.transport-museum.com
dir: just off junct 1, Coventry ring road, Tower St in city centre

Coventry is the traditional home of the British motor industry, and the museum's world-renowned collection displays over 150 years of its history. You can design your own car, feel what its like to break the sound barrier at 763mph and even travel into the future. The Festival of Motoring takes place over the fist weekend in September and features vintage, veteran and classic vehicles with family activities and stunt show riders culminating in a car and motorcycle rally around the region.

Times Open all year, daily 10-5. Closed 24-26 Dec & 1 Jan
Facilities 🅿 🚻 ♿ toilets for disabled shop ⊗

Herbert Art Gallery & Museum   FREE

Jordan Well CV1 5QP
☎ 024 7683 2386
e-mail: info@theherbert.org
web: www.theherbert.org
dir: in city centre near Cathedral

The Herbert Art and Gallery Museum, located next to Coventry Cathedral, has undergone a £20 million redevelopment. The site has eight permanent galleries, history centre and media suites. There is also an active programme of temporary exhibitions, and plenty of events and activities for children. Please contact for details of forthcoming events. The Museum will celebrate its 50th Anniversary in 2010.

Times Open all year, Mon-Sat 10-5.30, Sun 12-5. Closed 24-26, 31 Dec & 1 Jan.* Facilities 🅿 🚻 ♿ toilets for disabled shop ⊗

Jaguar Daimler Heritage Centre   FREE

Browns Ln, Allesley CV5 9DR
☎ 024 7620 3322   📄 024 7620 2835
e-mail: jagtrust@jaguar.com
web: www.jdht.com
dir: on A45, follow signs for Browns Lane Plant

Established in 1983, the Jaguar-Daimler Heritage Trust maintains a unique collection of motor vehicles and artefacts manufactured by Jaguar Cars Ltd, and the many other renowned marques associated with the company.

Times Open wkdays by appointment, no appointment required on last Sun of mth.* Facilities 🅿 🚻 toilets for disabled shop ⊗

Lunt Roman Fort

Coventry Rd, Baginton CV8 3AJ
☎ 024 7678 5173 & 7683 2565   📄 024 7622 0171
e-mail: info@theherbert.org
web: www.theherbert.org
dir: S side of city, off Stonebridge highway, A45

The turf and timber Roman fort from around the end of the 1st century has been faithfully reconstructed. An Interpretation Centre is housed in the granary.

Times Open 27 Mar-Oct, Sat-Sun & BH Mon 10-5; mid Jul-end Aug, Thu-Tue 10-5; Spring BH wk, Thu-Tue 10-5.* Facilities 🅿 🚻 (outdoor) toilets for disabled shop ⊗

DUDLEY

Black Country Living Museum

Tipton Rd DY1 4SQ
☎ 0121 557 9643 & 520 8054   📄 0121 557 4242
e-mail: info@bclm.co.uk
web: www.bclm.co.uk
dir: on A4037, near Showcase cinema

On the 26-acre site is a recreated canal-side village, with shops, houses and workshops. Meet the costumed characters and find out what life was like around 1900. Ride on a tramcar, explore the underground mine, venture into the limestone caverns or visit the olde tyme fairground (additional charge). There are also demonstrations of chainmaking, glass engraving and sweet-making. Watch a silent movie in the Limelight cinema, taste fish and chips cooked on a 1930s range, and finish your visit with a glass of real ale or dandelion and burdock in the Bottle and Glass Inn. Lots of varied events throughout the year, contact for details.

Times Open all year, Mar-Oct, Mon-Sun 10-5; Nov-Feb, Wed-Sun 10-4. (Telephone for Xmas closing)* Fees £12.95 (ch & student with NUS card £6.95, pen £10.50). Family (1ad+1ch) £18 & (2ad+3ch) £34.95* Facilities 🅿 🚻 🍴 licensed 🚻 (indoor & outdoor) ♿ (partly accessible) (access to most buildings requires use of temporary ramp. Staff will assist visitors with restricted mobility) toilets for disabled shop ⊗

Dudley continued

Dudley Zoological Gardens

2 The Broadway DY1 4QB
☎ 01384 215313   🖹 01384 456048
e-mail: marketing@dudleyzoo.org.uk
web: www.dudleyzoo.org.uk
dir: M5 junct 2 towards Wolverhampton/Dudley, signed

From lions and tigers to snakes and spiders, enjoy animal encounters and feeds. Get closer to some furry, and some not so furry creatures, and have fun on the fair rides, land train, and the adventure playground. Step back in time and see history come to life in the castle.

Times Open all year, Etr-mid Sep, daily 10-4; mid Sep-Etr, daily 10-3. Closed 25 Dec.* **Fees** £11.90 (ch 3 £7.70 under 3's free, concessions £8.70).* **Facilities** 🅿 🅟 ⊑ 🍴 licensed 🎪 (outdoor) ♿ (partly accessible) (not all accessible for wheelchairs due to hilly site) toilets for disabled shop ⊗

SOLIHULL

National Motorcycle Museum

Coventry Rd, Bickenhill B92 0EJ
☎ 01675 443311   🖹 0121 711 3153
web: www.nationalmotorcyclemuseum.co.uk
dir: M42 junct 6, off A45 near NEC

The National Motorcycle Museum is recognised as the finest and largest motorcycle museum in the world, with machines always being added to the collection. It is a place where legends live on and it is a tribute to and a living record of this once great British industry that dominated world markets for some sixty years. The museum records for posterity the engineering achievements of the last century.

Times Open all year, daily 10-6. Closed 24-26 Dec. **Fees** £6.95 (ch 12 & pen £4.95). Party 20+ £5.95. **Facilities** 🅿 🍴 licensed ♿ toilets for disabled shop ⊗

STOURBRIDGE

The Falconry Centre

Hurrans Garden Centre, Kidderminster Road South, Hagley DY9 0JB
☎ 01562 700014   🖹 01562 700014
e-mail: info@thefalconrycentre.co.uk
web: www.thefalconrycentre.co.uk
dir: off A456

The centre houses some 70 birds of prey including owls, hawks and falcons and is also a rehabilitation centre for sick and injured birds of prey. Spectacular flying displays are put on daily from midday. There are picnic areas, special fun days and training courses available.

Times Open all year, daily 10-5 & Sun 11-5. Closed 25, 26 Dec & Etr Sun.* **Facilities** 🅿 ⊑ 🎪 toilets for disabled shop ⊗

WALSALL

The New Art Gallery Walsall   FREE

Gallery Square WS2 8LG
☎ 01922 654400   🖹 01922 654401
e-mail: info@artatwalsall.org.uk
web: www.artatwalsall.org.uk
dir: signed from all major routes into town centre

Opened in 2000, this exciting new art gallery has at its core the Garman Ryan Collection, and a Children's Discovery Gallery that offers access to the very best in contemporary art in the only interactive art gallery designed especially for young people.

Times Open all year, Tue-Sat 10-5, Sun noon-5. Closed Mon ex BH Mon, 25-28 Dec & 1 Jan. Please telephone to confirm.* **Facilities** 🅿 ⊑ ♿ toilets for disabled shop ⊗

WORDSLEY

The Red House Glass Cone   FREE

High St DY8 4AZ
☎ 01384 812750   🖹 01384 812751
e-mail: redhouse.cone@dudley.gov.uk
web: www.redhousecone.co.uk
dir: A491 just N of Stourbridge

One of only four cones left in the UK and one of the most complete glass cone sites in Europe, over one hundred feet tall, Red House was built in the 18th century. The cone was in use until 1936, and housed a furnace around which men blew glass. This is a busy heritage site hosting exhibitions, events, children's activities, tours, a schools' programme, live glass-making and craft studios. International Festival of Glass is being held 27-30 August 2010.

Times Open all year, daily, 10-4. Please check for Xmas opening times.* **Facilities** 🅿 ⊑ 🎪 (outdoor) ♿ (partly accessible) toilets for disabled shop ⊗

ALUM BAY

The Needles Old Battery & New Battery

West High Down PO30 0JH
☎ 01983 754772 📄 01983 756978
e-mail: isleofwight@nationaltrust.org.uk
web: www.nationaltrust.org.uk/isleofwight
dir: at Needles Headland, W of Freshwater Bay and Alum Bay, B3322

The threat of a French invasion prompted the construction in 1862 of this spectacularly sited fort, which now contains exhibitions on the Battery's involvement in both World Wars. Two of the original gun barrels are displayed in the parade ground and a 60-yard tunnel leads to a searchlight emplacement perched above the Needles Rocks giving magnificent views of the Dorset coastline beyond. An exhibition about the secret rocket testing programme is housed further up the headland at the Needles New Battery. Opening times vary, phone for details.

Times Old battery open: 13 Mar-Oct, daily 10.30-5 (last admission 4.30). New battery 13 Mar-Oct, Sat-Sun & Tue 11-4. (both properties close in high winds). **Fees** Old battery with Gift Aid: £4.85 (ch £2.45). Family ticket £12.10. New battery free.*
Facilities ℗ ⬚ & (partly accessible) (Access to the tunnel at Old Battery via spiral staircase. Uneven surfaces & steep paths. Access to New battery via steps to exhibition room). toilets for disabled shop ♻

The Needles Park

PO39 0JD
☎ 0871 720 0022 📄 01983 755260
e-mail: info@theneedles.co.uk
web: www.theneedles.co.uk
dir: signed on B3322

Overlooking the Needles on the western edge of the island, the park has attractions for all the family: included in the wide range of facilities is the spectacular chair lift to the beach to view the famous coloured sand cliffs, Needles Rocks and lighthouse. Other popular attractions are Alum Bay Glass and the Isle of Wight Sweet Manufactory. Kids will enjoy the Junior Driver roadway, the Jurassic golf course and the Spins and Needles tea cup ride. Please contact for special events.

Times Open Etr-Oct, daily from 10am. (Some attractions available in winter). **Fees** No admission charged for entrance to Park, pay to park your car. Pay as you go attractions or Supersaver Attraction discount tickets. **Facilities** ℗ ⬚ ⛷ licensed ⛲ (outdoor) & (partly accessible) (Some slopes) toilets for disabled shop

ARRETON

Robin Hill Country Park

Downend PO30 2NU
☎ 01983 527352 📄 01983 527347
e-mail: dj@robin-hill.com
web: www.robin-hill.com
dir: 0.5m from Arreton next to Hare & Hounds pub

Set in 88 acres of beautiful woodland gardens and countryside, Robin Hill provides fun for all the family, with a wide variety of activities and attractions. There are twice-daily falconry displays at 11.30 and 2.45, and plenty of rides, like the Toboggan Run, Colossus Galleon and Time Machine. New attractions include a Roman villa interpretation barn and The Cows Express children's train ride. Robin Hill is also well-known as a great place to spot red squirrels.

Times Open Mar-Oct, daily 10-5 (last admission 4). **Fees** £8.50 (pen & disabled £5.50). Saver ticket (4) £31.* **Facilities** ℗ ⬚ ⛷ licensed ⛲ (outdoor) & (partly accessible) (most areas accessible, but some steep paths & rides may be unsuitable) toilets for disabled shop ⊗

BLACKGANG

Blackgang Chine Fantasy Park

PO38 2HN
☎ 01983 730330 📄 01983 731267
e-mail: info@blackgangchine.com
web: www.blackgangchine.com
dir: follow signs from Ventnor for Whitnell & Niton. From Niton follow signs for Blackgang

Opened as scenic gardens in 1843 covering some 40 acres, the park has imaginative play areas, water gardens, maze and coastal gardens. Set on the steep wooded slopes of the chine are the themed areas Smugglerland, Nurseryland, Dinosaurland, Fantasyland and Frontierland. St Catherine's Quay has a maritime exhibition showing the history of local and maritime affairs. Newer attractions include Cliffhanger: the roller coaster, and Pirate's Lair, an adventure play area. Recent themes include 'Chocolate Heaven', and a helicopter film cinema 'Wight Experience'.

Times Open late Mar-end Oct daily, 10-5; school summer hols open until 6. **Fees** Combined ticket (as from 15 May) to chine, sawmill & quay £9.50. Saver ticket (4 people) £35.* **Facilities** ℗ ⬚ ⛲ (outdoor) & (partly accessible) (park on cliff edge, sloping paths) toilets for disabled shop

Isle of Wight

BRADING

Brading The Experience

46 High St PO36 0DQ
☎ 01983 407286 📄 01983 402112
e-mail: info@bradingtheexperience.co.uk
web: www.bradingtheexperience.co.uk
dir: on A3055, in Brading High St

Brading The Experience is more than just a waxworks. Comprising Great British Legends Gallery, this 16th-century rectory mansion is filled with famous and infamous characters from the past. There's also a Chamber of Horrors, award-winning courtyards, Animal World, World of Wheels and The Pier.

Times Open all year, Etr-Oct 10-5, (Nov-Etr please contact establishment for details). (Last admission 1.5 hrs before closing). **Fees** £7.25 (ch 5-15 £5.25, under 5 free, concessions £6.25). Family £23 (2ad+2ch), Family £28 (2ad+3ch). Party 20+.* **Facilities** ℗ ℗ ☞ toilets for disabled shop

Lilliput Antique Doll & Toy Museum

High St PO36 0DJ
☎ 01983 407231
e-mail: lilliput.museum@btconnect.com
web: www.lilliputmuseum.org.uk
dir: A3055 Ryde/Sandown road, in Brading High Street

This private museum contains one of the finest collections of antique dolls and toys in Britain. There are over 2000 exhibits, ranging in age from 2000BC to 1945 with examples of almost every seriously collectable doll, many with royal connections. Also dolls' houses, teddy bears and rare and unusual toys.

Times Open all year, daily, 10-5.* **Fees** £2.50 (ch £1.25, ch under 5 free, concessions £1.50). Party on request.* **Facilities** ℗ ♿ shop

CARISBROOKE

Carisbrooke Castle

Castle Hill PO30 1XY
☎ 01983 522107 📄 01983 528632
web: www.english-heritage.org.uk
dir: 1.25m SW of Newport, off B3401

A royal fortress and prison to King Charles I, Carisbrooke is set on a sweeping ridge at the heart of the Isle of Wight. Don't miss the donkeys that can be seen working a 16th-century wheel to draw water from the well.

Times Open all year, Apr-Sep, daily 10-5; Oct-Mar, daily 10-4. Closed 24-26 Dec & 1 Jan. **Fees** £6.70 (concessions £5.70, ch £3.40). Family £16.80. Please check web site or call 0870 333 1181 for the most up to date prices and opening times when planning your visit. **Facilities** ℗ ☞ toilets for disabled shop ♯

FRESHWATER

Dimbola Lodge Museum

Terrace Ln, Freshwater Bay PO40 9QE
☎ 01983 756814 📄 01983 755578
e-mail: administrator@dimbola.co.uk
web: www.dimbola.co.uk
dir: off A3054, visible from Freshwater Bay

Home of Julia Margaret Cameron, the pioneer Victorian portrait photographer. The house has the largest permanent collection of Cameron prints on display in the UK, as well as galleries exhibiting work by young, up and coming, and acclaimed modern photographers; and a large display of cameras and accessories.

Times Open all year Tue-Sun. Closed 5 days at Xmas. Open BH Mons & daily during school summer hols.* **Fees** £4 (ch 16 free) £3.50 student rate upon showing NUS card.* **Facilities** ℗ ℗ 🍴 licensed ♿ toilets for disabled shop ⊗

MOTTISTONE

Mottistone Manor Garden

PO30 4ED
☎ 01983 741302 🖹 01983 741302
e-mail: isleofwight@nationaltrust.org.uk
web: www.nationaltrust.org.uk/isleofwight
dir: Situated between Brighstone & Brook on B3399

This magical garden is set in a sheltered valley with views to the sea, and surrounds an Elizabethan manor house, which is tenanted. With its colourful borders, shrub-filled banks and grassy terraces, it provides a tranquil and interesting place to visit. There is also a small organic kitchen garden, children's activity packs, a flowerpot trail, and some delightful walks onto the downs across the adjoining Mottistone Estate.

Times Open 14 Mar-28 Oct, Sun-Thu 11-5. (Last admission 4.30 or dusk if earlier). **Fees** With voluntary Gift Aid donation: £3.85 (ch £1.95). Family £9.65.* **Facilities** ℗ ⊑ ⅋ (partly accessible) (Access to entrance has steps, with loose gravel paths & some slopes & steps in garden) toilets for disabled shop ❧

OSBORNE HOUSE

Osborne House

PO32 6JY
☎ 01983 200022 🖹 01983 281380
web: www.english-heritage.org.uk
dir: 1m SE of East Cowes

The beloved seaside retreat of Queen Victoria offers a glimpse into the private life of Britain's longest reigning monarch. The royal apartments are full of treasured mementos; and Queen Victoria's role as Empress of India is celebrated in the decoration of the Durbar Room. Visit the gardens and the charming Swiss Cottage.

Times Open all year, Apr-Sep, daily 10-6 (house 10-5); Oct-1 Nov, daily 10-4; 4 Nov-Mar, Wed-Sun 10-4 (pre-booked guided tours, last tour 2.30. Xmas tour season 18 Nov-3 Jan). May close early for special events on occasional days in Jul & Aug. **Fees** House & Grounds: £10.20 (concessions £8.70, ch £5.10). Family £25.50. Grounds only: £8.40 (concessions £7.20, ch £4.20). Family £21. Please check web or call 0870 333 1181 for the most up to date prices and opening times. **Facilities** ℗ ⊑ ⅋ shop ⊗ ♯

PORCHFIELD

Colemans Animal Farm

Colemans Ln PO30 4LX
☎ 01983 522831
e-mail: chris@colemansfarmpark.co.uk
web: www.colemansfarmpark.co.uk
dir: A3054 Newport to Yarmouth road, follow brown tourist signs

Ideal for young children, this extensive petting farm has donkeys, goats, rabbits, guinea pigs, pigs, Highland Ankole cattle, llamas, Shetland ponies, chickens, ducks and geese. There is also a straw fun barn with slides and swings, an adventure playground, a Tractor Fun Park, and an Old Barn Café for adults who need to relax. Visitors can cuddle, stroke and feed the animals at special times throughout the day. Other special events run all day.

Times Open mid Mar-end Oct, Tue-Sun, 10-4.30 (last admission recommended 3.30). (Closed Mon, ex during school and BHs). Open for pre-booked events out of season.* **Fees** £7 (ch £6, concessions £5).* **Facilities** ℗ ⊑ ⅋ (indoor & outdoor) ⅋ (partly accessible) (90% accessible) toilets for disabled shop

SANDOWN

Dinosaur Isle

Culver Pde PO36 8QA
☎ 01983 404344 🖹 01983 407502
e-mail: dinosaur@iow.gov.uk
web: www.dinosaurisle.com
dir: In Sandown follow brown tourist signs to Dinosaur Isle, situated on B3395 on seafront

Britain's first purpose-built dinosaur attraction where, in a building reminiscent of a Pterosaur flying across the Cretaceous skies, you can walk back through fossilised time. In recreated landscape meet life-sized models of the island's five famous dinosaurs - Neovenator, Eotyrannus, Iguandon, Hypsilophodon and Polacanthus. Look out for the flying Pterodactyls and skeletons as they are found, watch volunteers preparing the latest finds or try the many hands-on activities. A guided fossil hunt (which must be pre-booked) has proven a popular addition.

Times Open all year daily, Apr-Sep 10-6; Oct 10-5; Nov-Mar 10-4. (Closed 24-26 Dec & 1 Jan). Please phone to confirm opening 5 Jan-6 Feb. (Last admission 1hr before closing.) **Fees** £5 (ch 3-15 £3, concessions £4). Family (2ad+2ch) £14.50* **Facilities** ℗ ℗ ⅋ (outdoor) ⅋ toilets for disabled shop ⊗

SHANKLIN

Shanklin Chine

12 Pomona Rd PO37 6PF
☎ **01983 866432** 📠 **01983 866145**
e-mail: jillshanklinchine1@msn.com
web: www.shanklinchine.co.uk
dir: turn off A3055 at lights, left into Hope Rd & continue onto Esplanade for entrance

Part of Britain's national heritage, this scenic gorge at Shanklin is a magical world of unique beauty and a haven for rare plants and wildlife. A path winds through the ravine with overhanging trees, ferns and other flora covering the steep sides. 'The Island - Then and Now' is an exhibition detailing the history of the Isle of Wight, including its military importance in WWII.

Times Open 31 Mar-25 May, 10-5. 26 May-10 Sep, 10-10. 11 Sep-29 Oct, 10-5.* **Facilities** ℗ 🚻 toilets for disabled shop

WROXALL

Appuldurcombe House

PO38 3EW
☎ **01983 852484**
web: www.english-heritage.org.uk
dir: off B3327, 0.5m W

The shell of Appuldurcombe, once the grandest house on the Isle of Wight, stands in its own grounds, designed by 'Capability' Brown. An exhibition of prints and photographs depicts the house and its history.

Times Open 22 Mar-Sep, daily 10-4 (Sat closes noon). (Last entry 1hr before closing).* **Fees** £3.50 (concessions £3.25, ch £2.50). Family ticket £12. Please check web site or call 0870 333 1181 for the most up to date prices and opening times when planning your visit.* **Facilities** ℗ shop ⊗ ♯

WILTSHIRE

CALNE

Bowood House & Gardens

SN11 0LZ
☎ **01249 812102** 📠 **01249 821757**
e-mail: houseandgardens@bowood.org
web: www.bowood.org
dir: off A4 Chippenham to Calne road, in Derry Hill village

Built in 1624, the house was finished by the first Earl of Shelburne, who employed celebrated architects, notably Robert Adam, to complete the work. Adam's library is particularly admired, and also in the house is the laboratory where Dr Joseph Priestley discovered the existence of oxygen in 1774. The house overlooks terraced gardens towards the 40-acre lake and some beautiful parkland. The gardens were laid out by 'Capability' Brown in the 1760s, and are carpeted with daffodils, narcissi and bluebells in spring. For children between 2 and 12 years there is the superb adventure playground, which boasts a life size pirate galleon and the famous space dive. There is also an indoor soft play palace for younger children.

Times Open daily Apr-Oct 11-6, incl BH. Rhododendron Gardens (separate entrance off A342) open 6 weeks during mid Apr-early Jun, 11-6.* **Fees** House & Gardens £8.40 (ch 2-4 £4.75; 5-15 £6.85; pen £7.40). Family ticket (2ad+2ch) £26. Rhododendrons only £5.60 (pen £5.10). £1 discount if house visited on same day.* **Facilities** ℗ 🚻 🍴 licensed 🎪 (outdoor) ♿ (partly accessible) (restricted access to upper exhibition rooms) toilets for disabled shop ⊗

LACOCK

Lacock Abbey, Fox Talbot Museum & Village

SN15 2LG
☎ **01249 730227 (abbey)** & **730459** 📠 **01249 730501**
e-mail: lacockabbey@nationaltrust.org.uk
web: www.nationaltrust.org.uk
dir: 3m S of Chippenham, E of A350, car park signed

Lacock Abbey is the former home of William Henry Fox Talbot, who invented the photographic negative process. The oldest negative in existence is of a photograph of Lacock Abbey. As well as the museum there are newly-restored botanic gardens and greenhouse and a well-preserved country village. The Abbey has also been used as a film location, and can be seen in Harry Potter, Pride and Prejudice, Cranford, The Other Boleyn Girl and Wolfman.

Times Cloisters & Grounds, Mar-2 Nov, daily 11-5.30. Closed Good Fri. Abbey, 15 Mar-2 Nov, daily, ex Tue, 1-5.30. Closed Good Fri. Museum 23 Feb-2 Nov, daily 11-5.30; 8 Nov-21 Dec, Sat & Sun 11-4; 3-31 Jan, Sat & Sun 11-4* **Facilities** ℗ 🎪 (outdoor) toilets for disabled shop ⊗ ♿

LONGLEAT

Longleat

The Estate Office BA12 7NW
☎ 01985 844400 01985 844885
e-mail: enquiries@longleat.co.uk
web: www.longleat.co.uk
dir: turn off A36 Bath-Salisbury road onto A362 Warminster-Frome road

Nestling within magnificent 'Capability' Brown landscaped grounds in the heart of Wiltshire, Longleat House is widely regarded as one of the most beautiful stately homes open to the public. Built by Sir John Thynne and completed in 1580, it has remained the home of the same family ever since. Many treasures are contained within the house: paintings by Tintoretto and Wootton, exquisite Flemish tapestries, fine French furniture and elaborate ceilings by John Dibblee Crace. The murals in the family apartments in the West Wing were painted by Alexander Thynne, the present Marquess, and are fascinating and remarkable additions to the collection. Apart from the ancestral home, Longleat is also renowned for its safari park, which was the first of its kind in the UK. Here, visitors have the rare opportunity to see hundreds of animals in natural woodland and parkland settings. Among the most magnificent sights are the famous pride of lions, wolves, rhesus monkeys and zebra. Other attractions which ensure a fun family day out include the Longleat Hedge Maze, the Adventure Castle, Longleat Railway, Pets' Corner and the Safari Boats.

Times Open daily 14-22 Feb, wknds only 28 Feb-29 Mar; daily 4 Apr-1 Nov. Longleat House open daily (ex 25 Dec).* **Facilities** licensed (outdoor) (partly accessible) toilets for disabled shop

LYDIARD PARK

Lydiard Park

Lydiard Tregoze SN5 3PA
☎ 01793 770401 01793 770968
e-mail: lydiardpark@swindon.gov.uk
web: www.lydiardpark.org.uk
dir: M4 junct 16, follow brown tourist signs

Set in country parkland, Lydiard Park belonged to the St John family (the Bolingbrokes) for 500 years up until 1943 when the Swindon Corporation purchased it. Since then the house has been restored and many of the original furnishings returned, together with a family portrait collection dating from Elizabethan to Victorian times. Exceptional plaster work, early wallpaper, a rare painted glass window, and a room devoted to the talented 18th-century artist, Lady Diana Spencer (Beauclerk), can also be seen. The restored 18th-century ornamental fruit and flower walled garden opened in 2007.

Times Open all year, House & walled garden, Tue-Sun & BH Mons 11-5. Nov-Feb closing 4. Park: all year, daily closing at dusk. Times may be subject to change, please call 01793 770401 or check website* **Fees** House £3.50 (ch £1.75, concessions £3). House & Walled Garden £4.50 (ch £2.25, pen £4). Walled Garden only £1.85 (ch £1, pen £1.50) Entry to grounds is free.* **Facilities** (outdoor) toilets for disabled shop

STONEHENGE

Stonehenge

SP4 7DE
☎ 0870 333 1181 & 01722 343834 01722 343831
web: www.english-heritage.org.uk
dir: 2m W of Amesbury on junct A303 and A344/A360

Britain's greatest prehistoric monument and a World Heritage Site. What visitors see today are the substantial remains of the last in a series of monuments erected between around 3000 and 1600BC.

Times Open all year, 16 Mar-May & Sep-15 Oct, daily 9.30-6; Jun-Aug, daily 9-7; 16 Oct-15 Mar, daily 9.30-4; 26 Dec & 1 Jan, 10-4. Closed 24-25 Dec. (opening times may vary around Summer Solstice 20-22 Jun). **Fees** £6.60 (concessions £5.60, ch £3.30). Family ticket £16.50. NT members free. Please check web site or call 0870 333 1181 for the most up to date prices and opening times when planning your visit. **Facilities** shop #

STOURHEAD

Stourhead

Stourhead Estate Office BA12 6QD
☎ 01747 841152   📄 01747 842005
e-mail: stourhead@nationaltrust.org.uk
web: www.nationaltrust.org.uk
dir: At Stourton off B3092, 3m NW Mere A303, follow brown tourist signs

An outstanding example of the English landscape style, this splendid garden was designed by Henry Hoare II and laid out between 1741 and 1780. Classical temples, including the Pantheon and Temple of Apollo, are set around the central lake at the end of a series of vistas, which change as the visitor moves around the paths and through the mature woodland with its extensive collection of exotic trees.

Times Garden open all year 9-7 (or dusk if earlier). House open 15 Mar-2 Nov, 11.30-4.30 (closed Wed & Thu); King Alfred tower open 15 Mar-2 Nov, daily 11.30-4.30.* **Facilities** ℗ ☕ 🍴 licensed 🌲 (outdoor) toilets for disabled shop ⊗ 🐾

STOURTON

Stourton House Flower Garden

Stourton House BA12 6QF
☎ 01747 840417
dir: 3m NW of Mere, on A303

Set in the attractive village of Stourton, the house has more than four acres of beautifully maintained flower gardens. Many grass paths lead through varied and colourful shrubs and trees. Stourton House also specialises in unusual plants and dried flowers, many of which are for sale. It also has collections of daffodils, delphiniums and hydrangeas, along with a nature garden where visitors can sit and watch the birds, butterflies and other wildlife.

Times Open last 2 Sun Feb & Apr-end Nov, Wed, Thu, Sun & BH Mon 11-6 (or dusk if earlier). Also open Dec-Mar, wkdays for plant/dried flower sales.* **Facilities** ℗ ℗ ☕ toilets for disabled shop ⊗

SWINDON

STEAM - Museum of the Great Western Railway

Kemble Dr SN2 2TA
☎ 01793 466646   📄 01793 466615
e-mail: steampostbox@swindon.gov.uk
web: www.steam-museum.org.uk
dir: from M4 junct 16 & A420 follow brown signs to 'Outlet Centre' & Museum

This fascinating day out tells the story of the men and women who built, operated and travelled on the Great Western Railway. Hands-on displays, world-famous locomotives, archive film footage and the testimonies of ex-railway workers bring the story to life. A reconstructed station platform, posters and holiday memorabilia recreate the glamour and excitement of the golden age of steam. Good value group packages, special events, exhibitions and shop.

Times Open daily 10-5. Closed 25-26 Dec & 1 Jan* **Facilities** ℗ toilets for disabled shop ⊗

Swindon & Cricklade Railway

Blunsdon Station, Tadpole Ln, Blunsdon SN25 2DA
☎ 01793 771615
e-mail: randallchri@yahoo.co.uk
web: www.swindon-cricklade-railway.org
dir: M4 junct 15, take A419, follow signs to Blunsdon Stadium, past station, continue for 2.5m follow brown signs

Heritage railway in the process of being restored. Steam and diesel locomotives, historic carriages, wagons and a large variety of railway structures from a past era. Last extension to the line opened in May 2008.

Times Open 10 Jan-19 Dec, Sat-Sun. Also open BHs (often special events) & Wed in local school hols. **Fees** £5 (ch £3.50). Family £15. Different prices apply for some special events.* **Facilities** ℗ ☕ 🌲 (outdoor) ♿ toilets for disabled shop

TEFFONT MAGNA

Farmer Giles Farmstead

SP3 5QY
☎ 01722 716338   📠 01722 716147
e-mail: farmergiles@farmergiles.co.uk
web: www.farmergiles.co.uk
dir: 11m W of Stonehenge, off A303 to Teffont. Follow brown signs

Forty acres of Wiltshire downland with farm animals to feed, ponds, inside and outside play areas, exhibitions, tractor rides, and gift shop. Working farm with hands-on rare breed animal feeding, cuddling and grooming. Pony rides, tractor rides, vast indoor and outdoor play areas and exhibitions. Special events during 2010 to celebrate Farmer Giles' 21st year.

Times Open mid Mar-mid Nov, daily 10-6 (last entry 4pm), wknds in winters & school hols, 10-dusk. Party bookings all year. Closed 25 & 26 Dec. **Fees** £5.50 (ch £4.50, under 2's free & pen £5) Family ticket £18.* **Facilities** 🅿 ℗ 🍴 licensed 🎍 (indoor & outdoor) ♿ toilets for disabled shop ⊗

WESTBURY

Brokerswood Country Park

Brokerswood BA13 4EH
☎ 01373 822238 & & 823880   📠 01373 858474
e-mail: info@brokerswood.co.uk
web: www.brokerswood.co.uk
dir: off A36 at Bell Inn, Standerwick. Follow brown signs from A350

Brokerswood Country Park's nature walk leads through 80 acres of woodlands, with a lake and wildfowl. Facilities include a woodland visitor centre (covering wildlife and forestry), two children's adventure playgrounds (Etr-Oct school holidays & wknds only) and the woodland railway, over a third of a mile long.

Times Open all year; Park open daily 10-5. Closed 24-26 Dec & 1 Jan. Ring for museum opening hours.* **Fees** £3.50 (ch 3-16 £2.50, concessions £2.50)* **Facilities** 🅿 🖳 🎍 (outdoor) ♿ (partly accessible) (ramp access to cafe) toilets for disabled shop

WILTON (NEAR SALISBURY)

Wilton House

SP2 0BJ
☎ 01722 746720 & 746729(24 hr line)   📠 01722 744447
e-mail: tourism@wiltonhouse.com
web: www.wiltonhouse.com
dir: 3m W of Salisbury, on A30, 10m from Stonehenge & A303

This fabulous Palladian mansion amazes visitors with its treasures, including magnificent art, fine furniture and interiors by Inigo Jones. The traditional and modern gardens, some designed by the 17th Earl, are fabulous throughout the season and continue to delight visitors, whilst the adventure playground is a firm favourite with children.

Times Open House: 10-13 Apr, 2 May-Aug generally closed each Fri & Sat, open BHs Sat 2 May-23 May. The House will not be open on Sat 29 Aug, noon - 5 (last admission 4.15pm). Grounds: 4-19 Apr, 2 May-Aug, daily & wknds in Sep, 11-5.30 (last admission 4.30pm). For further details see www.wiltonhouse.com* **Fees** House and Grounds: £12 (ch5-15 £6.50, concessions £9.75) Family ticket (2ad+2ch 5-15) £29.50. Grounds, including Adventure Playground £5 (ch 5-15 £3.50, concessions £4.50). Family ticket (2ad+2ch 5-15) £15. For further details see www.wiltonhouse.com* **Facilities** 🅿 🖳 🍴 licensed 🎍 (outdoor) ♿ toilets for disabled shop ⊗

BEWDLEY

West Midland Safari & Leisure Park

Spring Grove DY12 1LF
☎ 01299 402114   📠 01299 404519
e-mail: info@wmsp.co.uk
web: www.wmsp.co.uk
dir: on A456 between Kidderminster & Bewdley

Located in the heart of rural Worcestershire, this 200-acre site is the home to a drive-through safari and an amazing range of exotic animals. Animal attractions include Leopard Valley, Twilight Cave, Creepy Crawlies, the Reptile House, Sealion Theatre, and Seaquarium exhibit. There are also a variety of rides, amusements and live shows suitable for all members of the family.

Times Open daily mid Feb-early Nov. Times may change. Seasonal wknd opening early Nov-mid Feb. Check website for up to date opening times and information.* **Fees** £11.50 (ch 3-15yrs £10.50, ch under 3 free, concessions £10.50). Amusement rides extra.* **Facilities** 🅿 🖳 🍴 licensed 🎍 (outdoor) ♿ shop ⊗

Avoncroft Museum of Historic Buildings

Stoke Heath B60 4JR
☎ 01527 831886 & 831 363 📠 01527 876934
e-mail: admin@avoncroft.org.uk
web: www.avoncroft.org.uk
dir: 2m S, off A38

A visit to Avoncroft takes you through nearly 700 years of history. Here you can see 25 buildings rescued from destruction and authentically restored on a 15 acre rural site. There are 15th and 16th-century timber framed buildings, 18th-century agricultural buildings and a cockpit. There are industrial buildings and a working windmill from the 19th century, and from the 20th a fully furnished pre-fab.

Times Open all year, Apr-Oct, Tue-Sun 10.30-5, daily Jul-Aug; Nov-Dec & Mar, Fri-Sun 10.30-4.30; Closed Mon (except BHs), 24-26 Dec.* **Fees** £6.60 (ch £3, concessions £5.50). Family (2ad+3ch) £16.50. Members free.* **Facilities** ❷ ▭ ▭ ᴩ (outdoor) ♿ (partly accessible) (some building interiors may not be fully accessible) toilets for disabled shop

Hanbury Hall

School Rd WR9 7EA
☎ 01527 821214 📠 01527 821251
e-mail: hanburyhall@nationaltrust.org.uk
web: www.nationaltrust.org.uk
dir: 4.5m E of Droitwich, 1m N of B4090 and 1.5m W of B4091

This William and Mary style red-brick house, completed in 1701, was built by a prosperous local family. The house contains outstanding painted ceilings and staircase by Thornhill, and the Watney collection of porcelain. The 18th-century garden has recently been restored with many features including parterre, bowling green and working orangery. 395 Acres of beautiful park allow you to enjoy lovely views across the Worcestershire countryside.

Times House & gardens open 6-21 Feb, Sat-Sun 11.30-3.30 (downstairs only tours); 27 Feb-Oct, Sat-Wed 11-5; 26 Jun-26 Aug, Sat-Thu 11-5; 6 Nov-19 Dec, Sat-Sun 11.30-3.30 (downstairs only tours). Garden & Grounds, open 2 Jan-21 Feb, Sat-Sun 11-4; 27 Feb-Oct, daily 11-5; 6 Nov-26 Dec, Sat-Sun 11-4; 26-31 Dec open daily 11-4. **Fees** House & Garden £7.25 (ch £3.60). Family ticket £18.15. Garden & grounds £4.90 (ch £2.45). Family ticket £12.25. **Facilities** ❷ ▭ ᴩ (outdoor) ♿ (partly accessible) (gardens and ground floor of house are accessible) toilets for disabled shop ⊗ ❖

Severn Valley Railway

Comberton Hill DY10 1QN
☎ 01299 403816 📠 01299 400839
web: www.svr.co.uk
dir: on A448, clearly signed

The leading standard gauge steam railway, with one of the largest collections of locomotives and rolling stock in the country. Services operate from Kidderminster and Bewdley to Bridgnorth through 16 miles of picturesque scenery along the River Severn. Special steam galas take place during the year along with Santa Specials and many other events.

Times Trains operate wknds throughout the year, daily, early May-end of Sep, school hols & half terms, Santa Specials, phone for details. **Fees** Subject to Review. (Train fares vary according to journey. Main through ticket £13 return, Family ticket £33)* **Facilities** ❷ ℗ ▭ ⍅◎ licensed ᴩ (outdoor) ♿ (partly accessible) toilets for disabled shop

Worcestershire County Museum

Hartlebury Castle, Hartlebury DY11 7XZ
☎ 01299 250416 📄 01299 251890
e-mail: museum@worcestershire.gov.uk
web: www.worcestershire.gov.uk/museum
dir: 4m S of Kidderminster clearly signed from A449

Housed in the north wing of Hartlebury Castle, the County Museum contains a delightful display of crafts and industries. There are unique collections of toys and costume, displays on domestic life, period room settings and horse-drawn vehicles. Visitors can also see a reconstructed forge, a schoolroom, scullery and nursery. Family events at least one weekend each month. Children's craft activities Tue-Fri in school holidays. Phone for details of special events.

Times Open 5 Jan-23 Dec, Tue-Fri 10-5; Sat, Sun & BHs 11-5. Closed Good Fri. **Fees** £4 (ch & concession £2). Family ticket (2ad+2ch) £10.* **Facilities** 🅿 🅟 ⬚ 🍴 (outdoor) ♿ toilets for disabled shop ⊗

Forge Mill Needle Museum & Bordesley Abbey Visitor Centre

Forge Mill, Needle Mill Ln, Riverside B98 8HY
☎ 01527 62509
e-mail: museum@redditchbc.gov.uk
web: www.forgemill.org.uk
dir: N side of Redditch, off A441

The Needle Museum tells the fascinating and sometimes gruesome story of how needles are made. Working, water-powered machinery can be seen in an original needle-scouring mill. The Visitor Centre is an archaeological museum showing finds from excavations at the nearby Bordesley Abbey. Children can become an archaeologist for the day and explore the ruins of this fascinating ancient monument. Regularly changing temporary exhibits.

Times Open all year, Etr-Sep, Mon-Fri 11-4.30, Sat-Sun 11-4; Oct-Nov, Tue-Fri 11-4 & Sat-Sun 1-4.* **Fees** £4.15 (ch £1.10, pen £3, Reddicard concessions). Family ticket £8.50. Free admission Wed for Redditch residents.* **Facilities** 🅿 🅟 ⬚ 🍴 (outdoor) ♿ (partly accessible) toilets for disabled shop ⊗

EAST RIDING OF YORKSHIRE

BEMPTON

RSPB Nature Reserve

YO15 1JD
☎ 01262 851179 📄 01262 851533
web: www.rspb.org.uk
dir: take cliff road from B1229, Bempton Village and follow brown tourist signs

Part of the spectacular chalk cliffs that stretch from Flamborough Head to Speeton. This is one of the best sites in England to see thousands of nesting seabirds, including gannets and puffins at close quarters. Viewpoints overlook the cliffs, which are best visited from April to July. There are over two miles of chalk cliffs rising to 400ft with numerous cracks and ledges. Enormous numbers of seabirds nest on these cliffs including guillemots, razorbills, kittiwakes, fulmars, herring gulls and several pairs of shag. This is the only gannetry in England and is growing annually. Many migrants pass offshore including terns, skuas and shearwaters. Wheatears, ring ouzels and merlins frequent the clifftop on migration. Grey seal and porpoise are sometimes seen offshore.

Times Visitor centre open all year, Mar-Oct, daily 10-5. Nov -Dec 9.30-4.* **Facilities** 🅿 ⌑ 🎪 (outdoor) toilets for disabled shop

BURTON AGNES

Burton Agnes Hall

Estate Office YO25 0ND
☎ 01262 490324 📄 01262 490513
e-mail: office@burtonagnes.com
web: www.burton-agnes.co.uk
dir: on A614 between Driffield & Bridlington

Built in 1598, this exquisite Elizabethan house is filled with furniture, pictures and china amassed by one family over four centuries. Lawns with topiary bushes surround the Hall and an award-winning walled garden contains a maze, potager, giant games, jungle garden and more than four thousand plant species, including campanula and geranium collections. There is a woodland walk, children's playground and picnic area. The Red Bus Gallery presents works by local artists in a London RouteMaster bus.

Times Open Hall & Gardens Apr-Oct, daily 11-5. (Xmas opening 14 Nov-21 Dec).* **Fees** Hall & gardens: £7 (ch £3.50 5-15, pens £6.50). Gardens only: £4 (ch 5-15 £2.50, pens £3.50). **Facilities** 🅿 ⌑ 🎪 (outdoor) ♿ (partly accessible) (ground floor of hall, garden, woodland areas, courtyard cafe & shop all toilets for disabled shop

GOOLE

The Yorkshire Waterways Museum

Dutch River Side DN14 5TB
☎ **01405 768730**   📄 **01405 769868**
e-mail: info@waterwaysmuseum.org.uk
web: www.waterwaysmuseum.org.uk
dir: M62 junct 36, enter Goole, turn right at next 3 sets of lights onto Dutch River Side. 0.75m and follow brown signs

Discover the story of the Aire & Calder Navigation and the growth of the 'company town' of Goole and its busy port. Find out how to sail and, in the interactive gallery, see how wooden boats were built. Enjoy the unique 'Tom Pudding' story, brought to life through the vessels on the canal and the boat hoist in South Dock. Rediscover the Humber keels and sloops, and Goole's shipbuilding history through the objects, photos and memories of Goole people. 2010 is the 100th anniversary of the museums Humber keel called Sobriety.

Times Open all year Mon-Fri 9-4, Sat-Sun 10-4. (Closed Xmas & New Year).* **Fees** Free entry to museum. Boat trip £4 (ch under 12 £3).* **Facilities** ❷ ⌷ 🎋 (outdoor) ♿ toilets for disabled shop ⊗

HORNSEA

Hornsea Museum

11 Newbegin HU18 1AB
☎ **01964 533443**
web: www.hornseamuseum.com
dir: turn off A165 onto B1244

A former farmhouse whose outbuildings now illustrate local life and history. There are 19th-century period rooms and a dairy, plus craft tools and farming implements. Photographs, local personalities and industries are also featured along with a large display of Hornsea pottery.

Times Open Etr-Sep & Oct half-term hols, Tue-Sat 11-5, Sun 2-5 (last admission 4). Also open BH Mon.* **Fees** £2.50 (concessions £2). Family £7.50* **Facilities** ℗ 🎋 (outdoor) ♿ (partly accessible) (two thirds of museum accessible) toilets for disabled shop

KINGSTON UPON HULL

`Streetlife' - Hull Museum of Transport
FREE

High St HU1 1PS
☎ **01482 613902**   📄 **01482 613710**
e-mail: museums@hullcc.gov.uk
web: www.hullcc.gov.uk
dir: A63 from M62, follow signs for Old Town

This purpose-built museum uses a 'hands-on' approach to trace 200 years of transport history. With a vehicle collection of national importance, state-of-the-art animatronic displays and authentic scenarios, you can see Hull's Old Town brought vividly to life. The mail coach ride uses the very latest in computer technology to recreate a Victorian journey by four-in-hand.

Times Open all year, Mon-Sat 10-5, Sun 1.30-4.30. Closed 24-25 Dec & Good Fri* **Facilities** ℗ 🎋♿ toilets for disabled shop ⊗

The Deep

HU1 4DP
☎ **01482 381000**   📄 **01482 381018**
e-mail: info@thedeep.co.uk
web: www.thedeep.co.uk
dir: follow signs from city centre

The Deep is a conservation and educational charity which runs one of the deepest and most spectacular aquariums in the world. It is a unique blend of stunning marine life, the latest interactives and audio-visual presentations which together tell the dramatic story of the world's oceans. Highlights include 40 sharks and 3500 fish, Europe's deepest viewing tunnel and a glass lift ride through a 10m deep tank. Includes 3D movie. The Deep has an annual programme of events all available online.

Times Open all year, daily 10-6. Closed 24-25 Dec (last entry 5). **Fees** £8.75 (ch under 16 £6.75). Family ticket (2ad+2ch) £28, (2ad+3ch) £33.25.* **Facilities** ❷ ℗ ⌷ 🍴 licensed 🎋 (indoor & outdoor) ♿ toilets for disabled shop ⊗

SPROATLEY

Burton Constable Hall

HU11 4LN
☎ 01964 562400   📄 01964 563229
e-mail: helendewson@btconnect.com
web: www.burtonconstable.com
dir: Follow signs for A165 Bridlington Road towards Sirlaugh, then right towards Hornsea and follow brown historic house signs to Burton Constable

This superb Elizabethan house was built in 1570, but much of the interior was remodelled in the 18th century. There are magnificent reception rooms and a Tudor long gallery with a pendant roof: the contents include pictures and furniture along with a unique collection of 18th-century scientific instruments. Outside are 200 acres of parkland landscaped by 'Capability' Brown, with oaks and chestnuts, and a lake with an island. Various events through the season include a classic car rally in June and a country fair in July.

Times Open, Hall & Grounds Etr Sat-end Oct. Grounds 12.30-5, Hall 1-5. (Last admission 4). Closed Fri. **Fees** House £6 (ch £3, pen £5.50). Family ticket £14.50. Grounds only £2.50 (ch £1.25). Family ticket £6.25. **Facilities** 🅿 ⬛ 🎋 (outdoor) ♿ (partly accessible) (3 bedrooms not accessible) toilets for disabled shop ⊗

NORTH YORKSHIRE

BENINGBROUGH

Beningbrough Hall & Gardens

YO30 1DD
☎ 01904 472027
e-mail: beningbrough@nationaltrust.org.uk
web: www.nationaltrust.org.uk/beningbrough
dir: off A19, 8m NW of York

Beningbrough Hall is a Georgian mansion built in 1716 housing over a hundred 18th century portraits on loan from the National Portrait Gallery in London, including seven interpretation galleries 'Making Faces: Eighteenth Century Style'. A working walled garden supplies the Walled Garden Restaurant. There is a wilderness play area and equipped Victorian laundry and giftshop.

Times Open Sun-Thu (ex Thu & Fri) open Good Fri, 12-5. Grounds 11-5.30 (3.30 in winter). Galleries winter wknds Nov-Feb, 11-3.30, Feb half term also open Mon-Wed. **Fees** Summer £8.40 (ch £4.20) Winter £5.50 (ch £2.60) **Facilities** 🅿 🍴 licensed 🎋 (outdoor) ♿ (partly accessible) (all floors of Georgian mansion & 7 interpretation galleries accessible) toilets for disabled shop ⊗ 🐾

ELVINGTON

Yorkshire Air Museum & Allied Air Forces Memorial

Halifax Way YO41 4AU
☎ 01904 608595   📄 01904 608246
e-mail: museum@yorkshireairmuseum.co.uk
web: www.yorkshireairmuseum.co.uk
dir: from York take A1079 then immediate right onto B1228, museum is signposted on right

This award-winning museum and memorial is based around the largest authentic former WWII Bomber Command Station open to the public. There is a restored tower, an air gunners museum, archives, an Airborne Forces display, Squadron memorial rooms, and much more. Among the exhibits are replicas of the pioneering Cayley Glider and Wright Flyer, along with the Halifax Bomber and modern jets like the Harrier GR3, Tornado GR1 and GR4. A new exhibition 'Against The Odds' tells the story of the RAF Bomber Command.

Times Open all year, daily, 10-5 (summer); 10-3.30 (winter). Closed 25-26 Dec.* **Fees** £7 (ch £4 & pen £6). Prices under review **Facilities** 🅿 ⬛ 🍴 licensed 🎋 (outdoor) ♿ toilets for disabled shop

FAIRBURN

RSPB Nature Reserve Fairburn Ings

The Visitor Centre, Newton Ln WF10 2BH
☎ **01977 628191**
e-mail: fairburn.ings@rspb.org.uk
web: www.rspb.org.uk/fairburnings
dir: W of A1, N of Ferrybridge. Signed from Allerton Bywater off A656. Signed Fairburn Village off A1

One-third of the 700-acre RSPB reserve is open water, and over 270 species of birds have been recorded. A visitor centre provides information, and there is an elevated boardwalk, suitable for disabled visitors.

Times Access to the reserve via car park, open 9-dusk. Centre open 9-5 everyday. Car park open: 9-5. Closed 25-26 Dec.
Fees Car park fee £2 all day, first 1/2 hr free, RSPB members free. **Facilities** ❷ ⊞ (outdoor) ᕕ (partly accessible) (immediate boardwalk & visitor centre accessible, trails not accessible to wheelchairs) toilets for disabled shop ⊗

HARROGATE

RHS Garden Harlow Carr

Crag Ln, Otley Rd HG3 1QB
☎ **01423 565418** 📠 **01423 530663**
e-mail: harlowcarr@rhs.org.uk
web: www.rhs.org.uk/harlowcarr
dir: off B6162 Otley Rd, 1.5m from Harrogate centre

One of Yorkshire's most relaxing and surprising gardens at the gateway to the Yorkshire Dales! Wander through tranquil surroundings and find inspiration in the innovative and dramatic Rose Revolution and Main Borders. Stroll along the Streamside Garden and explore 'Gardens through Time'; savour the Scented Garden, and take practical ideas from the extensive Kitchen Garden. Year round events for all the family - sculpture, outdoor theatre, guided walks, quiz trails, workshops and free demonstrations.

Times Open all year, daily 9.30-6, Nov-Mar 9.30-4 (last admission 1hr before closing). Closed 25 Dec.* **Fees** £7 (ch under 6 free, ch 6-16 £2.50).* **Facilities** ❷ ⓟ 🖵 ◉ licensed ⊞ (outdoor) ᕕ toilets for disabled shop ⊗

HAWES

Dales Countryside Museum & National Park Centre

Station Yard DL8 3NT
☎ **01969 666210** 📠 **01969 666239**
e-mail: hawes@yorkshiredales.org.uk
web: www.yorkshiredales.org.uk
dir: off A684 in Old Station Yard

Fascinating museum telling the story of the people and landscape of the Yorkshire Dales. Static steam loco and carriages with displays. Added features include hands-on interactive displays for children, temporary exhibitions and special events. Free family exhibition every summer with activities for visitors of all ages!

Times Open all year daily 10-5. Closed 24-26 Dec 1 Jan & Jan following Xmas hol period. **Fees** Museum: £3 (ch free, concessions £2). National park centre, temporary exhibitions free.* **Facilities** ❷ ⓟ ⊞ (outdoor) ᕕ toilets for disabled shop ⊗

HELMSLEY

Duncombe Park

YO62 5EB
☎ **01439 778625** 📠 **01439 771114**
e-mail: liz@duncombepark.com
web: www.duncombepark.com
dir: located within North York Moors National Park, off A170 Thirsk-Scarborough road, 1m from Helmsley market place

Duncombe Park stands at the heart of a spectacular 30-acre early 18th-century landscape garden which is set in 300 acres of dramatic parkland around the River Rye. The house, originally built in 1713, was gutted by fire in 1879 and rebuilt in 1895. Its principal rooms are a fine example of the type of grand interior popular at the turn of the 19th century. Home of the Duncombes for 300 years, for much of this century the house was a girls' school. In 1985 the present Lord and Lady Feversham decided to make it a family home again and after major restoration, opened the house to the public in 1990. Part of the garden and parkland were designated a 250-acre National Nature Reserve in 1994. Special events include a Country Fair (May), an Antiques Fair (June), Steam Fair (July), Antiques Fair (November). Please telephone for details.

Times Open 12 Apr-25 Oct, Sun-Thu; Gardens, Parkland Centre tea room & shop & Parkland walks 11-5.30. House by guided tour only every hour from 12.30-3.30. (Closed 10, 11 & 15 Jun).* **Fees** House & Gardens £8.25 (ch 5-16, £3.75, concessions £6.25) Gardens & Parkland £5 Parkland only £3.* **Facilities** ❷ ⓟ ◉ licensed ⊞ (outdoor) ᕕ (partly accessible) (garden limited due to steps) toilets for disabled shop ⊗

Helmsley continued

Helmsley Castle

Castlegate YO6 5AB
☎ 01439 770442 🖨 01439 771814
web: www.english-heritage.org.uk

An atmospheric ruin with formidable double earthworks. There is an exhibition of the history of the castle.

Times Open all year, Apr-Sep, daily 10-6; Oct-1 Nov & Mar, daily 10-5; 2 Nov-Feb, Thu-Mon 10-4. Closed 24-26 Dec & 1 Jan.
Fees £4.50 (concessions £3.80, ch £2.30). Family ticket £11.30. Please check web site or call 0870 333 1181 for the most up to date prices and opening times when planning your visit. **Facilities** ℗ ♿ (partly accessible) shop ♯

KIRBY MISPERTON

Flamingo Land Theme Park & Zoo

The Rectory YO17 6UX
☎ 01653 668287 🖨 01653 668280
e-mail: info@flamingoland.co.uk
web: www.flamingoland.co.uk
dir: turn off A64 onto A169, Pickering to Whitby road

Set in 375 acres of North Yorkshire countryside with over 100 rides and attractions there's something for everyone at Flamingo Land. Enjoy the thrills and spills of 12 white knuckle rides or enjoy a stroll through the extensive zoo where you'll find tigers, giraffes, hippos and rhinos. The theme park also boasts 6 great family shows.

Times Open daily, 30 Mar-28 Oct.* **Fees** £22 (ch under 3 free, concessions £11). Family ticket (4 people) £82.* **Facilities** ℗ ℗ 🖥 🍽 licensed 🅰 (outdoor) toilets for disabled shop

KIRKHAM

Kirkham Priory

Whitwell-on-the-Hill YO6 7JS
☎ 01653 618768
web: www.english-heritage.org.uk
dir: 5m SW of Malton on minor road off A64

Discover the ruins of this Augustinian priory, which includes a magnificent carved gatehouse, set in a peaceful and secluded valley by the River Derwent.

Times Open Apr-Jul & Sep, Thu-Mon 10-5; Aug, daily 10-5.
Fees £3 (cconcessions £2.60, ch £1.50). Please check web site or call 0870 333 1181 for the most up to date prices and opening times when planning your visit. **Facilities** ℗ ♿ (partly accessible) (steep steps cloister to refectory) ♯

KNARESBOROUGH

Knaresborough Castle & Museum

Castle Yard HG5 8AS
☎ 01423 556188 🖨 01423 556130
e-mail: museums@harrogate.gov.uk
web: www.harrogate.gov.uk/museums
dir: off High St towards Market Square, right at police station into Castle Yard

Towering high above the town of Knaresborough, the remains of this 14th-century castle look down over the gorge of the River Nidd. This imposing fortress was once the hiding place of Thomas Becket's murderers and a summer home for the Black Prince. Visit the King's Tower, the secret underground tunnel and the dungeon. Discover Knaresborough's history in the museum and find out about 'Life in a Castle' in the hands-on gallery. Play the new computer game "Time Gate: The Prisoner of Knaresborough Castle". Special events include a Medieval Day annually on the third Sunday in June.

Times Open Good Fri-4 Oct, daily 10.30-5. Guided tours regularly available* **Fees** £2.80 (ch £1.50, concessions £1.80). Family ticket (2ad+3ch) £7.50 Party 10+. Annual season tickets available for Knaresborough Castle & Museum & The Royal Pump Room Museum.* **Facilities** ℗ ℗ ♿ (partly accessible) (ground floor of King's Tower accessible) toilets for disabled shop ⊗

LAWKLAND

Yorkshire Dales Falconry & Wildlife Conservation Centre

Crows Nest LA2 8AS
☎ 01729 822832 & 825164 (info line) 📄 01729 825160
e-mail: mail@falconryandwildlife.com
web: www.falconryandwildlife.com
dir: on A65 follow brown signs

The first privately owned falconry centre in the north of England. The main aim of the centre is to educate and promote awareness that many of the world's birds of prey are threatened with extinction. Successful captive breeding and educational programmes will help to safeguard these creatures. Regular free flying demonstrations throughout the day and falconry courses throughout the week.

Times Open all year summer 10-6; winter 10-4. Closed 25-26 Dec & 1 Jan.* **Fees** £5.90 (ch £3.90, pen £4.80). Family ticket £18.50 (2ad+2ch). Group 20+ £4.90 (ch £3.50). 1 Ad free with 10 ch.* **Facilities** 🅿 ⬚ 🗲 (indoor & outdoor) ♿ toilets for disabled shop ⊗

MALTON

Castle Howard

YO60 7DA
☎ 01653 648333 📄 01653 648529
e-mail: house@castlehoward.co.uk
web: www.castlehoward.co.uk
dir: off A64, follow brown heritage signs

A magnificent 18th-century house situated in breathtaking parkland. House guides share the history of the house, family and collections, while outdoor guided tours reveal the secrets of the gardens and architecture. Visitors can also enjoy a changing programme of exhibitions and events; boat trips, adventure playground and various cafes and shops including a farm shop and a chocolate shop. New exhibition "Brideshead Restored" - telling the story of restoration of Castle Howard and the filming of both the TV and movie versions of Brideshead Revisited.

Times House: Mar-Oct open Mar-1 Nov & 28 Nov-20 Dec, daily from 11. Gardens, shops & cafes open all year from 10.* **Fees** £10.50 (ch £6.50, concessions £9.50). Grounds only £8.00 (ch £5.50, concessions £7.50).* **Facilities** 🅿 ⬚ 🍽 licensed ♿ (partly accessible) toilets for disabled shop ⊗

Malton continued

Eden Camp Modern History Theme Museum

Eden Camp YO17 6RT
☎ 01653 697777 ▤ 01653 698243
e-mail: admin@edencamp.co.uk
web: www.edencamp.co.uk
dir: junct of A64 & A169, between York & Scarborough

House within the unique setting of an original prisoner of war camp built in 1942 to house Italian and German POWs, this regional and national award winning museum presents the most comprehensive display of British civilian life during WWII. The period is brought to life through life size tableaux and dioramas which incorporate sound, light and even smell effects to create the atmosphere of the 1940s. Other sections of the museum cover military and political events of WWII and British military history of the 20th century from WWI to the war in Iraq and Afghanistan. The museum also houses an extensive collection of military vehicles, artillery and associated equipment. Special Events: WWII re-enactment weekend; Reunion of Escapers and Evaders April; All Services Commemorative Day and Parade September; Palestine Veterans Reunion Day in Oct.

Times Open 2nd Mon in Jan-23 Dec, daily 10-5. (Last admission 4) **Fees** £5.50 (ch & concessions £4.50). Party 10+, £1 discount on individual admission prices. **Facilities** ❷ ⊡ ⛺ (indoor & outdoor) toilets for disabled shop

MIDDLEHAM

Middleham Castle

Castle Hill DL8 4RJ
☎ 01969 623899
web: www.english-heritage.org.uk
dir: 2m S of Leyburn on A6108

Explore the maze of rooms and passageways at this impressive castle, the boyhood home of the ill-fated Richard III. Oak viewing gallery of the magnificent views of the 12th-century keep and exhibition.

Times Open all year, Apr-Sep, daily 10-6; Oct-Mar, Sat-Wed 10-4. Closed 24-26 Dec & 1 Jan. **Fees** £4 (concessions £3.40, ch £2). Please check web site or call 0870 333 1181 for the most up to date prices and opening times when planning your visit. **Facilities** ℗ ⛺ ♿ (partly accessible) (steep spiral staircase to top of keep) shop ⌗

MIDDLESBROUGH

Captain Cook Birthplace Museum   FREE

Stewart Park, Marton TS7 8AT
☎ 01642 311211 ▤ 01642 515659
e-mail: captcookmuseum@middlesbrough.gov.uk
web: www.captcook-ne.co.uk
dir: 3m S on A172

Opened to mark the 250th anniversary of the birth of the voyager in 1728, this museum illustrates the early life of James Cook and his discoveries with permanent and temporary exhibitions. Located in spacious and rolling parkland, the site also offers outside attractions for the visitor. The museum has a special resource centre which has fresh approaches to presentation with computers, films, special effects, interactives and educational aids.

Times Open all year: Mar-Oct, Tue-Sun, 10-5.30. Nov-Feb 9-4.00. (Last entry 45 mins before closure). Closed Mon & some BH, 24-26 Dec, 1 Jan & 1st full week Jan.* **Facilities** ❷ ℗ ⊡ ⛄ licensed ⛺ (outdoor) ♿ toilets for disabled shop ⊗

NEWBY HALL & GARDENS

Newby Hall & Gardens

HG4 5AE
☎ 01423 322583 ▤ 01423 324452
e-mail: info@newbyhall.com
web: www.newbyhall.com
dir: 4m SE of Ripon & 2m W of A1M, off B6265, between Boroughbridge and Ripon

One of Britain's finest Adam houses with Chippendale furniture, Gobelins tapestries and classical statuary, Newby Hall boasts 25 acres of award winning gardens including one of Europe's largest double herbaceous borders. With an enchanting woodland walk and a delightful contemporary sculpture park, younger visitors will also enjoy the miniature railway and exciting adventure gardens.

Times Open Apr-Sep, Tue-Sun & BHs, also Mon in Jul & Aug; Gardens 11-5.30; House 12-5. (Last admission 5 Gardens, 4.30 House)* **Facilities** ❷ ⊡ ⛄ licensed ⛺ outdoor ♿ toilets for disabled shop ⊗

NORTH STAINLEY

Lightwater Valley Theme Park

HG4 3HT
☎ 0871 720 0011 📄 0871 721 0011
e-mail: leisure@lightwatervalley.co.uk
web: www.lightwatervalley.co.uk
dir: 3m N of Ripon on A6108

Set in 175 acres of beautiful North Yorkshire parkland, Lightwater Valley Theme park, Shopping Village and Birds of Prey Centre offers an exciting choice of activities. The thrilling theme park line-up comprises some amazing rides, including Europe's longest rollercoaster - The Ultimate, as well as the stomach-churning mighty Eagle's Claw and The Hornet's Nest - the ride with a sting in its tail! If you prefer to take things at a more leisurely pace, enjoy a gentle stroll around the picturesque lake, play crazy golf or just climb aboard the Lightwater Express for a round-the-park train ride. Also on site, the Birds of Prey Centre was established to raise awareness of a wide selection of breathtaking birds. The purpose-built raptor complex offers the opportunity to see possibly the largest Golden Eagle in England, as well as learning how these amazing birds are trained and handled, as well as being treated to dramatic flying shows every day.

Times Open 31 Mar-15 Apr, wknds only; 21 Apr-27 May inc BH Mon; daily from 26 May-2 Sep, wknds only, 8 Sep-21 Oct, daily 22-28 Oct. Gates open at 10, closes 4.30, depending on time of year.* **Fees** £17.95 over 1.3mtrs, £15.45 under 1.3mtrs, free under 1m (concessions £8.95). Family (2ad+2ch or 1ad+3ch under 16) £62.* **Facilities** 🅿 ⬛🍽 licensed ☂ (outdoor) ♿ (partly accessible) toilets for disabled shop ⊗

ORMESBY

Ormesby Hall

TS7 9AS
☎ 01642 324188 📄 01642 300937
e-mail: ormesbyhall@nationaltrust.org.uk
web: www.nationaltrust.org.uk
dir: 3m SE of Middlesborough, W of A19 take the A174 to the A172 . Follow signs for Ormesby Hall. Car entrance on Ladgate Lane B1380

An 18th-century mansion, Ormesby Hall has stables attributed to John Carr of York. Plasterwork, furniture and 18th-century pictures are on view. Exhibiting a large model railway.

Times Open 17 Mar-4 Nov Sat, Sun & BHs 1.30-5* **Facilities** 🅿 ⬛ ☂ (outdoor) ♿ (partly accessible) toilets for disabled ⬥

PICKERING

North Yorkshire Moors Railway

Pickering Station YO18 7AJ
☎ 01751 472508 📄 01751 476970
e-mail: admin@nymr.pickering.fsnet.co.uk
web: www.northyorkshiremoorsrailway.com
dir: from A169 take road towards Kirkbymoorside, right at traffic lights, station 400yds on left

Operating through the heart of the North York Moors National Park between Pickering and Grosmont, steam trains cover a distance of 18 miles. The locomotive sheds at Grosmont are open to the public. Events throughout the year include Day Out with Thomas, Steam Gala, Santa Specials.

Times Open 29 Mar-Oct, daily; Dec, Santa specials and Xmas to New Year running. Further information available from Pickering Station.* **Facilities** 🅿 🅿 ⬛🍽 licensed ☂ (outdoor) toilets for disabled shop

Pickering Castle

Castlegate YO6 5AB
☎ 01751 474989
web: www.english-heritage.org.uk

Splendid 12th-century castle, on the edge of the Yorkshire Moors, originally built by William the Conqueror. Visit the exhibition on the castle's history and take in the views from the keep.

Times Open Apr-Sep, daily 10-6. **Fees** £3.50 (concessions £3, ch £1.80). Family ticket £8.80. Please check web site or call 0870 333 1181 for the most up to date prices and opening times when planning your visit. **Facilities** 🅿 ☂ ♿ (partly accessible) (no w/chair access to motte) toilets for disabled shop ⊞

RICHMOND

Richmond Castle

Tower Castle DL10 4QW
☎ 01748 822493
web: www.english-heritage.org.uk

Overlooking the River Swale and market town of Richmond, the views from the keep are stunning. Built by William the Conqueror to subdue the rebellious North, the castle now houses an exciting interactive exhibition.

Times Open all year, Apr-Sep, daily 10-6; Oct-Mar, Thu-Mon 10-4. Closed 24-26 Dec & 1 Jan. **Fees** £4 (concessions £3.40, ch £2). Please check web site or call 0870 333 1181 for the most up to date prices and opening times when planning your visit. **Facilities** 🅿 ☂♿ (partly accessible) toilets for disabled shop ⊞

RIEVAULX

Rievaulx Abbey

☎ 01439 798228
web: www.english-heritage.org.uk
dir: 2.25m W of Helmsley on minor road off B1257

Explore the magnificent romantic ruin set in a tranquil wooded valley of the River Rye. Find out about monastic life with the help of the audio tour and exhibition.

Times Open all year, Apr-Sep, daily, 10-6; Oct-1 Nov, Thu-Mon, 10-5; 2 Nov-Mar, Thu-Mon, 10-4. Closed 24-26 Dec & 1 Jan **Fees** £5 (concessions £4.30, ch £2.50). Please check web site or call 0870 333 1181 for the most up to date prices and opening times when planning your visit. **Facilities** ♿ 🍴 ⚐ (partly accessible) (some steps, site on slight slope) shop 🅿 ⚑

RIPLEY

Ripley Castle

HG3 3AY
☎ 01423 770152   📠 01423 771745
e-mail: enquiries@ripleycastle.co.uk
web: www.ripleycastle.co.uk
dir: off A61, Harrogate to Ripon road

Ripley Castle has been home to the Ingilby family for 26 generations and stands at the heart of an estate with deer park, lakes and Victorian walled gardens. The Castle has a rich history and a fine collection of Royalist armour housed in the 1555 tower. There are also tropical hot houses, a children's play trail, tearooms, woodland walks, pleasure grounds and the National Hyacinth Collection in spring.

Times Open Nov-8 Mar, Tue, Thu, Sat & Sun 10.30-3; Apr-Oct, daily 10.30-3; Dec-Feb wkends only, also BH and school hols. Groups all year by prior arrangement. Gardens open daily 9-5.* **Fees** Castle & Gardens £8 (ch £5, pen £7). Gardens only £5.50 (ch £3.50, concession £5). Party £5.* **Facilities** ♿ ⚐ 🍴 licensed ⚑ (partly accessible) (two of the rooms in the castle on view are upstairs) toilets for disabled shop ⊗

RIPON

Fountains Abbey & Studley Royal

HG4 3DY
☎ 01765 608888   📠 01765 601002
e-mail: fountainsenquiries@nationaltrust.org.uk
web: www.fountainsabbey.org.uk
dir: 4m W of Ripon off B6265

A World Heritage Site comprising the ruin of a 12th-century Cistercian abbey and monastic watermill, an Elizabethan mansion and one of the best surviving examples of a Georgian water garden. Elegant ornamental lakes, canals, temples and cascades provide eye-catching vistas. The site also contains the Victorian St Mary's Church and medieval deer park.

Times Open all year, daily, Nov-Feb 10-4, Mar-Oct 10-5. Closed Fri Nov-Jan & 24-25 Dec.* **Facilities** ♿ ⚐ 🍴 licensed ⚑ (outdoor) ⚐ (partly accessible) toilets for disabled shop ⊗ ⚑

SCARBOROUGH

Scarborough Castle

Castle Rd YO11 1HY
☎ 01723 372451   📠 01723 372451
web: www.english-heritage.org.uk
dir: E of town centre

This 12th-century fortress housed many important figures in history. Enjoy the spectacular coastal view and see the remains of the great keep still standing over three storeys high. Discover the castle's exciting history through the free audio tour.

Times Open all year, Apr-Sep, daily 10-6; Oct-Mar, Thu-Mon 10-4. Closed 24-26 Dec & 1 Jan. **Fees** £4.50 (concessions £3.80, ch £2.30). Family ticket £11.30. Please check web site or call 0870 333 1181 for the most up to date prices and opening times when planning your visit. **Facilities** ℗ ⚐ ⚑

Sea Life & Marine Sanctuary

Scalby Mills Rd, North Bay YO12 6RP
☎ **01723 376125**   📄 **01723 376285**
web: www.sealife.co.uk
dir: follow brown tourist signs after entering Scarborough. Centre in North Bay Leisure Parks area of town

Made up of three large white pyramids, this impressive marine sanctuary overlooks the white sandy beaches of the North Bay, Scarborough's Castle, and Peasholm Park. The sanctuary features Jurassic seas, jellyfish, Otter River, penguins, and sea turtles.

Times Open all year daily. Closed 25 Dec.* **Fees** Prices to be confirmed.* **Facilities** 🅿 🅟 ⊑ 🎪 toilets for disabled shop ⊗

SKINNINGROVE

Cleveland Ironstone Mining Museum

Deepdale TS13 4AP
☎ **01287 642877**   📄 **01287 642970**
e-mail: visits@ironstonemuseum.co.uk
web: www.ironstonemuseum.co.uk
dir: in Skinningrove Valley, just off A174 near coast between Saltburn and Whitby

On the site of the old Loftus Mine, this museum offers visitors a glimpse into the underground world of Cleveland's ironstone mining past. Discover the special skills and customs of the miners who helped make Cleveland the most important ironstone mining district in Victorian and Edwardian England. The museum is not a glass case museum but an experience.

Times Open Apr-Oct, Mon-Fri 10.30-3.30, Sat 1-3.30. **Fees** £5 (ch 5-16 £2.50, concessions £4.50). Family ticket (2ad+2ch) £12. **Facilities** 🅿 🅟 🎪 (outdoor) ♿ (partly accessible) (electric wheelchairs unable to navigate the tour through a narrow doorway) toilets for disabled shop ⊗

Skipton Castle

BD23 1AW
☎ **01756 792442**   📄 **01756 796100**
e-mail: info@skiptoncastle.co.uk
web: www.skiptoncastle.co.uk
dir: in town centre at head of High Street

Skipton Castle is one of the most complete and well-preserved medieval castles in England. Some of the castle dates from the 1650s when it was rebuilt after being partially damaged following the Civil War. However, the original castle was erected in Norman times and became the home of the Clifford family in 1310 and remained so until 1676. Illustrated tour sheets are available in a number of languages. Please see website for special events.

Times Open all year, daily from 10, (Sun from noon). Last admission 6 (4pm Oct-Feb). Closed 25 Dec. **Fees** £6 (incl illustrated tour sheet) (ch under 18 £3.50, under 5 free, concessions £5.40). Family ticket £18.90. Party 15+.* **Facilities** 🅟 ⊑ 🎪 (indoor & outdoor) ♿ (partly accessible) (access to grounds, shops, tea room) shop ⊗

Falconry UK - Birds of Prey Centre

Sion Hill Hall, Kirby Wiske YO7 4EU
☎ **01845 587522**
e-mail: mail@falconrycentre.co.uk
web: www.falconrycentre.co.uk
dir: follow brown tourist signs, situated on A167 between Northallerton and Topcliffe

Set up to ensure that birds of prey would survive to provide the public with a rare opportunity to see and enjoy these beautiful birds. Enjoy the excitement of falconry with over 70 birds and 30 species. Three different flying displays with public participation where possible. After each display, handling birds brought out for public to hold.

Times Open Mar-Oct daily, 10.30-5. 3 Daily flying displays (different birds in each display) at 11.30, 1.30, 3.30. **Fees** £6.50 (ch £4.50, under 3 free, pen £5.50). Family ticket £19 (2ad+2ch) **Facilities** ❷ ℗ ⏛ ᴚ (outdoor) ♿ toilets for disabled shop ⊗

Monk Park Farm Visitor Centre

Bagby YO7 2AG
☎ **01845 597730** 🖹 **01845 597730**
web: www.monkpark.co.uk
dir: just off A170 Scarborough road or A19 from York

Monk Park, once a haven for the monks generations ago who made their living from the land, is now a favourite for children. There is something for all ages to see and do, with indoor and outdoor viewing and feeding areas. The park has also been the venue for filming Blue Peter and Vets in Practice.

Times Open Feb half term-Oct, daily, 11-5.30.* **Facilities** ℗ ⏛ ᴚ (indoor & outdoor) toilets for disabled shop ⊗

Whitby Abbey

YO22 4JT
☎ **01947 603568** 🖹 **01947 825561**
web: www.english-heritage.org.uk
dir: on clifftop E of Whitby town centre

Uncover the full story of these atmospheric ruins in their impressive clifftop location above the picturesque fishing town with associations ranging from Victorian jewellery and whaling, to Count Dracula.

Times Open all year, Apr-Sep, daily 10-6; Oct-Mar, Thu-Mon 10-4. Closed 24-26 Dec & 1 Jan. **Fees** £5.50 (concessions £4.70, ch £2.80). Family ticket £13.80. Please check web site or call 0870 333 1181 for the most up to date prices and opening times when planning your visit. **Facilities** ❷ ⏛ ᴚ shop ♯

DIG

St Saviourgate YO1 8NN
☎ **01904 615505** 🖹 **01904 627097**
e-mail: jorvik@yorkat.co.uk
web: www.digyork.co.uk
dir: follow A19 or A64 to city centre then pedestrian signs for attraction

Grab a trowel and dig to see what you can find in DIG's specially designed excavation pits. Rediscover some of the amazing finds that the archaeologists have uncovered under the streets of York. Understand how these finds explain how people lived in Roman, Viking, Medieval and Victorian times. Touch real artefacts and work out what they would be used for. Special events scheduled throughout the year.

Times Open all year, daily 10-5. Closed 24-26 Dec. **Fees** £5.50. (ch, concessions £5). Family of 4 £18.50. Family of 5 £19.60. Group rates available on request.* **Facilities** ℗ ᴚ (indoor & outdoor) ♿ toilets for disabled shop ⊗

Jorvik Viking Centre

Coppergate YO1 9WT
☎ 01904 615505 📄 01904 627097
e-mail: jorvik@yorkat.co.uk
web: www.jorvik-viking-centre.com
dir: follow A19 or A64 to York. Jorvik in Coppergate shopping area (city centre) signed

Explore York's Viking history on the very site where archaeologists discovered remains of the city of Jorvik. See over 800 of the items discovered on site and meet the famous Jorvik Vikings in our three exciting exhibitions, learn what life was like here more than 1000 years ago, and journey through a reconstruction of actual Viking streets. A new feature is 'Are You A Viking?', which uses scientific evidence to discover if you have Viking ancestors. 'Unearthed' tells how the people of ancient York lived and died, as revealed by real bone material. Special events throughout the year.

Times Open all year, summer, daily 10-5; winter, daily 10-4. Closed 24-26 Dec. Opening times subject to change. **Fees** £8.50 (ch 5-15 £6.00, under 5 free, concessions £7) Family of 4 £26 & family of 5 £29. Telephone bookings on 01904 615505 (£1 booking fee per person at peak times).* **Facilities** Ⓟ ☐ & (partly accessible) (wheelchair users are advised to pre-book) toilets for disabled shop ⊗

National Railway Museum

Leeman Rd YO26 4XJ
☎ 01904 621261 📄 01904 611112
e-mail: nrm@nrm.org.uk
web: www.nrm.org.uk
dir: behind rail station. Signed from all major roads and city centre

The National Railway Museum is the world's largest railway museum. From record breakers to history makers the museum is home to a vast collection of locomotives, carriages and wagons, including The Royal Trains, a replica of Stephenson's Rocket, the Japanese Bullet Train and the elegant Duchess. With three enormous galleries, interactive exhibits and daily events, the National Railway Museum mixes education with fun. This attraction is also free. NB: There is a charge for certain special events.

Times Open all year 10-6. Closed 24-26 Dec. **Fees** Admission is free but there may be charges for special events and rides. **Facilities** Ⓟ Ⓟ ☐ ⍾◯⍾ licensed ⊓ (outdoor) & toilets for disabled shop ⊗

Treasurer's House

Minster Yard YO1 7JL
☎ 01904 624247 📄 01904 647372
e-mail: treasurershouse@nationaltrust.org.uk
web: www.nationaltrust.org.uk
dir: in Minster Yard, on N side of Minster, in the centre of York

Named after the Treasurer of York Minster and built over a Roman Road, the house is not all it seems. Nestled behind the Minster, the size, splendour and contents of the house are a constant surprise to visitors - as are the famous ghost stories. Children's trails and access to the tea room free.

Times Open Apr-Oct, daily (ex Fri) 11-5. **Fees** £5.90 (ch £3). Family ticket £14.80 (2ad+3ch). House and Ghost Cellar £8.30 (ch £4.60)* **Facilities** Ⓟ ☐ ⍾◯⍾ licensed & (partly accessible) ⊗ ⚘

North Yorkshire-South Yorkshire

York continued

York Castle Museum
The Eye of York YO1 1RY
☎ 01904 687687
e-mail: castle.museum@ymt.org.uk
web: www.yorkcastlemuseum.org.uk
dir: city centre, next to Clifford's Tower

Fascinating exhibits that bring memories to life, imaginatively displayed through reconstructions of period rooms and Victorian indoor streets, complete with cobbles and a Hansom cab. The museum is housed in the city's former prison and is based on an extensive collection of 'bygones' acquired at the beginning of the twentieth century. It was one of the first folk museums to display a huge range of everyday objects in an authentic scene. The Victorian street includes a pawnbroker, a tallow candle factory and a haberdasher's. There is even a reconstruction of the original sweet shop of the York chocolate manufacturer, Joseph Terry. An extensive collection of many other items ranging from musical instruments to costumes. The museum also has one of Britain's finest collections of Militaria. A special exhibition called 'Seeing it Through' explores the life of York citizens during the Second World War. The museum includes the cell where highwayman Dick Turpin was held. Please contact the museum for details of exhibitions and events.

Times Open all year, daily 9.30-5 **Fees** £7.50 (ch £4 under 5's free, concessions £6.50). Family tickets available* **Facilities** Ⓟ ▯ & (partly accessible) (main galleries accessible, no access up stairs) toilets for disabled shop ⊗

Yorkshire Museum
Museum Gardens YO1 7FR
☎ 01904 551800 ▤ 01904 551802
e-mail: yorkshire.museum@york.gov.uk
web: http://www.york.gov.uk
dir: park & ride service from 4 sites near A64/A19/A1079 & A166, also 3 car parks within short walk

The Yorkshire Museum is set in 10 acres of botanical gardens in the heart of the historic City of York, and displays some of the finest Roman, Anglo-Saxon, Viking and Medieval treasures ever discovered in Britain. The Middleham jewel, a fine example of English Gothic jewellery, is on display, and in the Roman Gallery, visitors can see a marble head of Constantine the Great. The Anglo-Saxon Gallery houses the delicate silver-gilt Ormside bowl and the Gilling sword.

Times Open all year, daily 10-5.* **Facilities** Ⓟ ☈ toilets for disabled shop ⊗

SOUTH YORKSHIRE

DONCASTER

Brodsworth Hall & Gardens
Brodsworth DN5 7XJ
☎ 01302 722598 ▤ 01302 337165
web: www.english-heritage.org.uk
dir: between A635 & A638

This Victorian country house has survived largely intact. Imagine how the serving classes fared below stairs, then experience, in contrast, the opulent 'upstairs' apartments. Outside, visitors can enjoy a leisurely stroll around the extensive newly restored gardens.

Times House: open Apr-Sep, Tue-Sun & BHs, 1-5; Oct, Sat-Sun 12-4. Gardens: open Apr-1 Nov, daily 10-5.30; 2 Nov-Mar, Sat-Sun 10-4. (including Servant's Wing). (Last admission half an hour before closing). Closed 24-26 & 1 Jan. **Fees** House & Gardens £8.30 (concessions £7.10, ch £4.20). Gardens only £5 (concessions £4.30, ch £2.50). Please check web site or call 0870 333 1181 for the most up to date prices and opening times when planning your visit. **Facilities** Ⓟ ▯ & (partly accessible) (limited access, some steps, steep slopes) toilets for disabled shop ⊗ ⊞

Doncaster Museum & Art Gallery   FREE
Chequer Rd DN1 2AE
☎ 01302 734293 ▤ 01302 735409
e-mail: museum@doncaster.gov.uk
web: www.doncaster.gov.uk/museums
dir: off inner ring road

The wide-ranging collections include fine and decorative art and sculpture. Also ceramics, glass, silver, and displays on history, archaeology and natural history. The historical collection of the Kings Own Yorkshire Light Infantry is housed here. A recent addition is the 'By River and Road' gallery, which details the history of the Doncaster area. Temporary exhibitions are held.

Times Open all year, Mon-Sat 10-5, Sun 2-5. (Closed Good Fri, 25-26 Dec & 1 Jan).* **Facilities** Ⓟ Ⓟ & toilets for disabled shop ⊗

192

ROTHERHAM

Magna Science Adventure Centre

Sheffield Rd, Templeborough S60 1DX
☎ 01709 720002 🖷 01709 820092
e-mail: aholdsworth@magnatrust.co.uk
web: www.visitmagna.co.uk
dir: M1 junct 33/34, follow Templeborough sign off rdbt, then brown heritage signs

Magna is the UK's first Science Adventure Centre, an exciting exploration of Earth, Air, Fire and Water. A chance for visitors to create their own adventure through hands-on interactive challenges. Visit the four Adventure Pavilions, live show and outdoor playgrounds Sci-Tek and Aqua-Tek.

Times Open all year, daily (Check website for Mondays), 10-5. Closed 24-26 Dec. **Fees** £9.95 (ch under 4's free, ch & concessions £8.95). Family ticket (2ad+1ch) £25 **Facilities** 🅟 Ⓟ ☕ 🍴 licensed ⛩ (indoor & outdoor) ♿ toilets for disabled shop 🚫

SHEFFIELD

Abbeydale Industrial Hamlet FREE

Abbeydale Industrial Hamlet, Abbeydale Road South S7 2QW
☎ 0114 236 7731
e-mail: postmaster@simt.co.uk
web: www.simt.co.uk
dir: Turn off A61 south, follow A621 Abbeydale road to Abbeydale Road South towards Bakewell

Worker's houses, water wheels, crucible steel, furnaces, tilt hammers and workshops create a unique atmosphere of life at home and at work in a scythe and steel works, dating back to the 18th century. The works gallery tells the story of one of the largest water powered industrial complex, on Sheffield's River Sheaf. Look out for Abbeydale family Sunday events.

Times Open Apr-Oct. Open all year for pre-booked school and group visits. **Facilities** 🅟 Ⓟ ☕ ♿ (partly accessible) shop 🚫

Kelham Island Museum

Alma St S3 8RY
☎ 0114 272 2106 🖷 0114 275 7847
e-mail: postmaster@simt.co.uk
web: www.simt.co.uk
dir: 0.5m NW of city centre, from Sheffield Parkway (A57), take A6 North ringroad and follow signs

The story of Sheffield, its industry and life, with the most powerful working steam engine in Europe, reconstructed workshops, and craftspeople demonstrating traditional 'made in Sheffield' skills - this is a 'living' museum. During the year Kelham Island stages events, displays and temporary exhibitions culminating in the annual Christmas Victorian Market. Coming soon - The Hawley Gallery - the story of tool making in Sheffield.

Times Open Mon-Thu 10-4, Sun 11-4.45. Closed Fri & Sat. Check opening days & times at Xmas & New Year before travelling. **Fees** £4 (accompanied ch under 16 free, concessions £3). Sheffield's school hol, admission free for all. **Facilities** 🅟 Ⓟ ☕ ♿ (partly accessible) (all main areas fully accessible) toilets for disabled shop 🚫

Millennium Gallery

Arundel Gate S1 2PP
☎ 0114 278 2600 🖷 0114 278 2604
e-mail: info@museums-sheffield.org.uk
web: www.museums-sheffield.org.uk
dir: Follow signs to city centre, then follow the brown signs marked M).

With four different galleries under one roof, the Millennium Gallery has something for everyone. Enjoy new blockbuster exhibitions drawn from the collections of Britain's national galleries and museums, including the Victoria & Albert Museum and Tate Gallery. See the best of contemporary craft and design in a range of exhibitions by established and up-and-coming makers. Be dazzled by Sheffield's magnificent and internationally important collection of decorative and domestic metalwork and silverware. Discover the Ruskin Gallery with its wonderful array of treasures by Victorian artist and writer John Ruskin.

Times Open all year, daily Mon-Sat 10-5, Sun 11-5.*
Fees Admission prices apply for some special exhibitions (concessions available). **Facilities** Ⓟ ☕ 🍴 licensed toilets for disabled shop 🚫

WEST YORKSHIRE

BRADFORD

Bolling Hall   FREE

Bowling Hall Rd BD4 7LP
☎ 01274 431826   📄 01274 726220
web: www.bradfordmuseums.org
dir: 1m from city centre off A650

A classic West Yorkshire manor house, complete with galleried 'housebody' (hall), Bolling Hall dates mainly from the 17th century but has medieval and 18th-century sections. It has panelled rooms, plasterwork in original colours, heraldic glass and a rare Chippendale bed.

Times Open all year, Wed-Fri 11-4, Sat 10-5, Sun 12-5. Closed Mon ex BH, Good Fri, 25-26 Dec.* **Facilities** 🅿 Ⓟ shop ⊗

Bradford Industrial Museum and Horses at Work   FREE

Moorside Mills, Moorside Rd, Eccleshill BD2 3HP
☎ 01274 435900   📄 01274 636362
web: www.bradfordmuseums.org
dir: off A658

Moorside Mills is an original spinning mill, now part of a museum that brings vividly to life the story of Bradford's woollen industry. There is the machinery that once converted raw wool into cloth, and the mill yard rings with the sound of iron on stone as shire horses pull trams, haul buses and give rides. Daily demonstrations and changing exhibitions.

Times Open all year, Tue-Sat 10-5, Sun 12-5. Closed Mon ex BH, Good Fri & 25-26 Dec* **Facilities** 🅿 ⊑ toilets for disabled shop ⊗

National Media Museum

Pictureville BD1 1NQ
☎ 01274 202030   📄 01274 723155
e-mail: talk@nationalmediamuseum.org.uk
web: www.nationalmediamuseum.org.uk
dir: 2m from end of M606, follow signs for city centre

Journey through popular photography and visit IMAX - the world's powerful giant screen experience, discover the past, present and future of television in Experience TV, watch your favourite TV moments in TV Heaven, play with light, lenses and colour in the Magic Factory and explore the world of animation - watch a real animator at work in the Animation Gallery. There are also temporary exhibitions and various special events are planned, please see the website for details.

Times Open all year, Tue-Sun 10-6, BH Mon & school hols. Closed 24-26 Dec.* **Fees** Admission to permanent galleries free, IMAX Cinema £6.95 (concessions £4.95). DMR (Feature length films) £8 (£6 concesssions). Groups 20% discount.* **Facilities** 🅿 Ⓟ ⊑ 🍽 licensed 🍴 (Indoor) & toilets for disabled shop ⊗

CASTLEFORD

Diggerland

Willowbridge Ln, Whitwood WF10 5NW
☎ 0871 227 7007   📄 09012 01300
e-mail: mail@diggerland.com
web: www.diggerland.com
dir: M62 junct 31 then north on A655 towards Castleford. Diggerland 0.5m on left immediately before petrol station

An adventure park with a difference. Experience the thrills of driving real earth moving equipment. Choose from various types of diggers and dumpers ranging from 1 ton to 8.5 tons. Complete the Dumper Truck Challenge or dig for buried treasure supervised by an instructor. New rides include JCB Robots, Diggerland Dodgems, Go-karts, Landrover Safari, Spin Dizzy and the Diggerland Tractors.

Times Open 12 Feb-end Oct, 10-5, wknds, BH & school hols only (including half terms). **Fees** £15 - all rides & drives included in price. **Facilities** 🅿 Ⓟ ⊑ 🍴 (outdoor) & toilets for disabled shop ⊗

HALIFAX

Eureka! The National Children's Museum

Discovery Rd HX1 2NE
☎ 01422 330069   📠 01422 330275
e-mail: info@eureka.org.uk
web: www.eureka.org.uk
dir: M62 junct 24 follow brown heritage signs to Halifax centre
- A629

With over 400 'must touch' exhibits, interactive activities and challenges, visitors are invited to embark upon a journey of discovery through six main gallery spaces. They can find out how their bodies and senses work, discover the realities of daily life, travel from the familiar 'backyard' to amazing and faraway places and experiment with creating their own sounds and music.

Times Open all year, daily 10-5. Closed 24-26 Dec* **Fees** £7.25 (ch 1-2 £2.25, ch under 1 free) Family Saver ticket £31. Special group rates available.* **Facilities** 🅿 Ⓟ ⊔ 🍴 (indoor & outdoor) ♿ toilets for disabled shop ⊗

HAREWOOD

Harewood House & Bird Garden

LS17 9LG
☎ 0113 218 1010   📠 0113 218 1002
e-mail: info@harewood.org
web: www.harewood.org
dir: junct A61/A659 Leeds to Harrogate road

Designed in 1759 by John Carr, Harewood House is home to the Queen's cousin, the Earl of Harewood. His mother, HRH Princess Mary, Princess Royal lived at Harewood for 35 years and much of her memorabilia is still displayed. The house, renowned for its stunning architecture and exquisite Adam interiors, contains a rich collection of Chippendale furniture, fine porcelain and outstanding art collections from Italian Renaissance masterpieces and Turner watercolours to contemporary works. The old kitchen contains the best collection of noble household copperware in the country

giving visitors a glimpse into below stairs life. The grounds include a restored parterre terrace, oriental rock garden, Himalayan Garden with Buddist Stupa, walled garden, lakeside and woodland walks, a bird garden and for youngsters, an adventure playground.

Times Open wknds 12 Feb-1 Apr & Nov-12 Dec 10-4 (grounds only). Full opening 2 Apr-Oct 10-6, House 12-4. **Fees** With Gift Aid donation: 28 Jun-7 Sep plus all BH wknds, £13.50 (ch/student £8.50, pen £12.20) Family (2ad+3ch) £46.50. Without Gift Aid donation: £12 (ch/student £7.70, pen £11) Family (2ad+3ch) £42. Prices will change in the lower season. Grounds & Below Stairs £7.50-£10, Freedom ticket £11-£14.30. **Facilities** 🅿 Ⓟ ⊔ 🍴 (outdoor) ♿ (partly accessible) (the house is fully accessible. The grounds are on a natural slope with some gravel paths) toilets for disabled shop ⊗

HAWORTH

Brontë Parsonage Museum

Church St BD22 8DR
☎ 01535 642323   📠 01535 647131
e-mail: bronte@bronte.org.uk
web: www.bronte.info
dir: A629 & A6033 follow signs for Haworth, take Rawdon Rd, pass 2 car parks, next left, then right

Haworth Parsonage was the lifelong family home of the Brontës. An intensely close-knit family, the Brontës saw the parsonage as the heart of their world and the moorland setting provided them with inspiration for their writing. The house contains much personal memorabilia, including the furniture Charlotte bought with the proceeds of her literary success, Branwell's portraits of local worthies, Emily's writing desk and Anne's books and drawings. The museum is currently holding a two year exhibition focusing on Branwell Brontë, who as a child was considered the greatest genius of the family. Branwell declined into alcoholism while his sisters went on to write great novels.

Times Open all year, Apr-Sep, daily 10-5.30; Oct-Mar, daily 11-5 (final admission 30 min before closing). Closed 24-27 Dec & 2-31 Jan. **Fees** £6 (ch 5-16 £3, concessions £4.50). Family ticket £15.* **Facilities** 🅿 Ⓟ ♿ (partly accessible) (please contact the musuem for info) shop ⊗

Haworth continued

Keighley & Worth Valley Railway & Museum

Keighley BD22 8NJ
☎ 01535 645214 & 677777 📄 **01535 647317**
e-mail: admin@kwvr.co.uk
web: www.kwvr.co.uk
dir: 1m from Keighley on A629 Halifax road, follow brown signs

The line was built mainly to serve the valley's mills, and passes through the heart of Brontë country. Beginning at Keighley (shared with Network Rail), it climbs up to Haworth, and terminates at Oxenhope, which has a storage and restoration building. At Haworth there are locomotive workshops and at Ingrow West, an award-winning museum. Events take place throughout the year, please telephone for details.

Times Open every wknd, please phone for other times.* **Facilities** 🅿 Ⓟ 🚻 🚬 (outdoor) ♿ (partly accessible) toilets for disabled shop

KEIGHLEY

East Riddlesden Hall

Bradford Rd BD20 5EL
☎ 01535 607075 📄 **01535 691462**
e-mail: eastriddlesden@nationaltrust.org.uk
web: www.nationaltrust.org.uk
dir: 1m NE of Keighley on S side of Bradford Rd

The interior of this 17th-century manor house is furnished with textiles, Yorkshire oak and pewter, together with fine examples of 17th-century embroidery. The honeysuckle and rose covered façade ruin of the Starke Wing, provides the backdrop to the garden. Wild flowers, perennials, and a fragrant herb border provide a transition of colour throughout the year.

Times Open 27 Feb-Oct daily (ex Thu & Fri) 12-5. Open Good Fri. **Fees** £5.30 (ch £2.70). Family ticket £12. **Facilities** 🅿 🚬 🚬 (outdoor) ♿ (partly accessible) shop ⊗ 🌿

LEEDS

Abbey House Museum

Abbey Walk, Abbey Rd, Kirkstall LS5 3EH
☎ 0113 230 5492 📄 **0113 230 5499**
e-mail: abbey.house@leeds.gov.uk
web: www.leeds.gov.uk
dir: 3m W of city centre on A65

Displays at this museum include an interactive childhood gallery, a look at Kirkstall Abbey, and an exploration of life in Victorian Leeds. Three reconstructed streets allow the visitor to immerse themselves in the sights and sounds of the late 19th century, from the glamourous art furnishers shop to the impoverished widow washerwoman.

Times Open all year Tue-Fri 10-5, Sat noon-5, Sun 10-5. Closed Mon ex BH Mon (open 10-5)* **Facilities** Ⓟ Ⓟ 🚬 🍴 licensed 🚬 (outdoor) toilets for disabled shop ⊗

Leeds Industrial Museum at Armley Mills

Canal Rd, Armley LS12 2QF
☎ 0113 263 7861
web: www.leeds.gov.uk/armleymills
dir: 2m W of city centre, off A65

Once the world's largest woollen mill, Armley Mills evokes memories of the 18th-century, showing the progress of wool from the sheep to knitted clothing. The museum has its own 1930s cinema illustrating the history of cinema projection, including the first moving pictures taken in Leeds. The Museum is set in some lovely scenery, between the Leeds & Liverpool Canal and the River Aire. There are demonstrations of static engines and steam locomotives, a printing gallery and a journey through the world of textiles and fashion.

Times Open all year, Tue-Sat 10-5, Sun 1-5. Last entry 4pm. Closed Mon ex BHs.* **Facilities** 🅿 🚬 (indoor & outdoor) ♿ (partly accessible) toilets for disabled shop ⊗

Royal Armouries Museum   FREE

Armouries Dr LS10 1LT
☎ 0113 220 1999 & 0990 106 666 📄 **0113 220 1955**
e-mail: enquiries@armouries.org.uk
web: www.royalarmouries.org
dir: off A61 close to Leeds centre, follow brown heritage signs.

The museum is an impressive contemporary home for the renowned national collection of arms and armour. The collection is divided between five galleries: War, Tournament, Self-Defence, Hunting and Oriental. The Hall of Steel features a 100ft-high mass of 3000 pieces of arms and armour. Visitors are encouraged to take part in and handle some of the collections. Live demonstrations and interpretations take place throughout the year.

Times Open all year, daily, from 10-5. Closed 24-25 Dec*
Facilities 🅿 🚬 🍴 licensed 🚬 (indoor) toilets for disabled shop ⊗

Temple Newsam Estate

Temple Newsam Rd, Off Selby Rd, Halton LS15 0AE
☎ 0113 264 7321 (House) & 264 5535 (Estate)
🖹 0113 232 6485
e-mail: temple.newsam.house@leeds.gov.uk
web: www.leeds.gov.uk/templenewsam
dir: 4m from city centre on A63 or 2m from M1 junct

Temple Newsam is celebrated as one of the country's great historic houses and estates. Set in 1500 acres of stunning parkland, Temple Newsam House is home to outstanding collections of fine and decorative art, many of national importance. The Estate includes a working Rare Breeds farm and national plant collections.

Times Open all year. House: Tue-Sun 10.30-5, Nov-28 Dec & Mar, Tue-Sat 10.30-4. Open BHs. Home Farm: Tue-Sun, 10-5 (4 in winter), also open Mon in school hols; Gardens: 10-dusk. Estate: daily, dawn-dusk.* **Facilities** 🅿 ☕ 🌲 (outdoor) ♿ toilets for disabled shop ⊗

Tropical World

Roundhay Park LS8 2ER
☎ 0113 214 5715
e-mail: parks@leeds.gov.uk
web: www.leeds.gov.uk
dir: 3m N of city centre off A58 at Oakwood, also accessible from A610

The atmosphere of the tropics is recreated here as visitors arrive on the beach and walk through the depths of the swamp into the rainforest. A waterfall cascades into a rock-pool and other pools contain terrapins and carp. There are reptiles, insects, meerkats and more than 30 species of butterfly. Feel the dry heat of the desert and the darkness of the nocturnal zone, and watch out for the piranhas and other exotic fish in the depths of the aquarium.

Times Open all year, winter daily 10-4 (last admission 3.30); summer 10-6 (last admission 5.30). Closed 25-26 Dec.* **Facilities** 🅿 🅿 ☕ ♿ toilets for disabled shop ⊗

MIDDLESTOWN

National Coal Mining Museum for England ~~FREE~~

Caphouse Colliery, New Rd WF4 4RH
☎ 01924 848806   🖹 01924 844567
e-mail: info@ncm.org.uk
web: www.ncm.org.uk
dir: on A642 between Huddersfield & Wakefield

A unique opportunity to go 140 metres underground down one of Britain's oldest working mines. Take a step back in time with one of the museum's experienced local miners who will guide parties around the underground workings, where models and machinery depict methods and conditions of mining from the early 1800s to present day. Other attractions include the Hope Pit, pithead baths, Victorian steam winder, nature trail and adventure playground and meet the last ever working pit ponies. You are strongly advised to wear sensible footwear and warm clothing.

Times Open all year, daily 10-5. Closed 24-26 Dec & 1 Jan.*
Facilities 🅿 ☕ 🍴 licensed 🌲 (outdoor) ♿ toilets for disabled shop ⊗

WEST BRETTON

Yorkshire Sculpture Park

WF4 4LG
☎ 01924 832631   🖹 01924 832600
e-mail: info@ysp.co.uk
web: www.ysp.co.uk
dir: M1 junct 38, follow brown heritage signs to A637. After 1m, left at rdbt, attraction signed

Set in the beautiful grounds and gardens of a 500 acre, 18th-century country estate, Yorkshire Sculpture Park is one of the world's leading open-air galleries and presents a changing programme of international sculpture exhibitions. The landscape provides a variety of magnificent scenic vistas of the valley, lakes, estate buildings and bridges. By organising a number of temporary exhibitions each year in four magnificent galleries, the park ensures that there is always something new to see. The Visitor Centre provides all-weather facilities including a large restaurant, shop, coffee bar, audio-visual auditorium and meeting rooms. Major exhibition by David Nash in summer 2010.

Times Open all year, daily 10-6 (summer) 10-5 (winter). Closed 23-25 Dec. **Fees** Free. (Donations welcome). Car parking £4, coaches £10 by prior arrangement. **Facilities** 🅿 ☕ 🍴 licensed 🌲 (outdoor) ♿ (partly accessible) (some paths difficult for wheelchair users, all galleries accessible) toilets for disabled shop ⊗

GUERNSEY

ROCQUAINE BAY

Fort Grey Shipwreck Museum

GY7 9BY
☎ **01481 265036** 📄 **01481 263279**
e-mail: admin@museums.gov.gg
web: www.museum.gov.gg
dir: on coast road at Rocquaine Bay

The fort is a Martello tower, built in 1804, as part of the Channel Islands' extensive defences. It is nicknamed the `cup and saucer' because of its appearance, and houses a museum devoted to ships wrecked on the treacherous Hanois reefs nearby.

Times Open 26 Mar-Oct, daily 10-5 **Fees** £3.50 (ch over 7 & students £1, concessions £2.75). Season ticket available.
Facilities Ⓟ ⨅ (outdoor) shop ⊗

ST MARTIN

Sausmarez Manor

Sausmarez Rd GY4 6SG
☎ **01481 235571** 📄 **01481 235572**
e-mail: sausmarezmanor@cwgsy.net
web: www.sausmarezmanor.co.uk
dir: halfway between airport & St Peter Port

The Manor has been owned and lived in by the same family for centuries. The style of each room is different, with collections of Oriental, French and English furniture and paintings. Outside take a train ride, enjoy a game of pitch and putt or visit the Formal Garden with its herbaceous borders and the subtropical Woodland Garden, set around two small lakes and a stream, is planted with colourful shrubs, bulbs and wild flowers. Also on view, a sculpture park which is now the most comprehensive in Britain.

Times Open Etr-Oct 10-5. **Fees** House £6.90 (ch £5.50, concessions £6.50). Woodland Garden £5 (accompanied ch & concessions £4.50, disabled free). Sculpture Park £5 (accompanied ch & concessions £4.50, disabled free).* **Facilities** 🅿 Ⓟ ⊑🛆 (partly accessible) (partial access to garden) shop ⊗

ST PETER PORT

Guernsey Museum & Art Gallery

Candie Gardens GY1 1UG
☎ **01481 726518** 📄 **01481 715177**
e-mail: admin@museums.gov.gg
web: www.museums.gov.gg
dir: On the outskirts of St Peter Port set in the Victorian 'Candie gardens'

The museum, designed around a Victorian bandstand, tells the story of Guernsey and its people. There is an audio-visual theatre and an art gallery, and special exhibitions are arranged throughout the year. It is surrounded by beautiful gardens with superb views over St Peter Port harbour. In 2010 a summer exhibition on arts and crafts made by Guernsey people deported during WW2.

Times Open Feb-Dec, daily 10-5 (winter 10-4) **Fees** £4.50 (ch over 7 & students £1, pen £3.75). Season ticket available.
Facilities Ⓟ ⊑🛆 toilets for disabled shop ⊗

JERSEY

GOREY

Mont Orgueil Castle

JE3 6ET
☎ **01534 853292** 📄 **01534 854303**
e-mail: marketing@jerseyheritagetrust.org
web: www.jerseyheritagetrust.org
dir: A3 or coast road to Gorey

Standing on a rocky headland, on a site which has been fortified since the Iron Age, this is one of the best-preserved examples in Europe of a medieval concentric castle, and dates from the 12th and 13th centuries.

Times Open daily, Mar-Nov 10-6 (last admission 5). Winter open Fri-Mon 10-4 (last admission 3).* **Facilities** Ⓟ ⊑⨅ (outdoor) 🛆 (partly accessible) (castle keep accessible) toilets for disabled shop ⊗

GROUVILLE

La Hougue Bie

JE2 7UA
☎ 01534 853823 📄 01534 856472
e-mail: marketing@jerseyheritagetrust.org
web: www.jerseyheritagetrust.org
dir: A6 or A7 to Five Oaks, at mini-rdbt take B28 to site

This Neolithic burial mound stands 40ft high, and covers a stone-built passage grave that is still intact and may be entered. The passage is 50ft long, and built of huge stones, the mound is made from earth, rubble and limpet shells. On top of the mound are two medieval chapels, one of which has a replica of the Holy Sepulchre in Jerusalem below. Also on the site is an underground bunker built by the Germans as a communications centre, now a memorial to the slave workers of the Occupation.

Times Open Mar-Nov, daily 10-5.* **Facilities** 🅿 🎴 (outdoor) shop ⊗

ST CLEMENT

Samarès Manor

JE2 6QW
☎ 01534 870551 📄 01534 768949
e-mail: enquiries@samaresmanor.com
web: www.samaresmanor.com
dir: 2m E of St Helier on St Clements Inner Rd

Samares Manor is a beautiful house, surrounded by exceptional gardens. These include the internationally renowned herb garden, Japanese garden, water gardens and exotic borders. There are tours of the manor house and of the Rural Life and Carriage Museum. Talks on herbs and their uses take place each week day and there is a plant trail and activities for children.

Times Open 3 Apr-16 Oct. **Fees** £6.75 (ch under 5 free, 5-16 & students £2.35, concessions £6.20). **Facilities** 🅿 🎴🍴 licensed ♿ (partly accessible) (ground floor only of the house and part of the water garden as small paths) toilets for disabled shop ⊗

ST HELIER

Elizabeth Castle

JE2 3WU
☎ 01534 723971 📄 01534 610338
e-mail: marketing@jerseyheritagetrust.org
web: www.jerseyheritagetrust.org
dir: access by causeway or amphibious vehicle

The original Elizabethan fortress was extended in the 17th and 18th centuries, and then refortified by the Germans during the Occupation. Please telephone for details of events.

Times Open Mar-Nov, daily 10-6 (last admission 5)* **Facilities** 🅿 🎴 (outdoor) ♿ (partly accessible) (castle keep & parade ground accessible) toilets for disabled shop ⊗

Maritime Museum & Occupation Tapestry Gallery

New North Quay JE2 3ND
☎ 01534 811043 📄 01534 874099
e-mail: marketing@jerseyheritagetrust.org
web: www.jerseyheritagetrust.org
dir: alongside Marina, opposite Liberation Square

This converted 19th-century warehouse houses the tapestry consisting of 12 two-metre panels that tells the story of the occupation of Jersey during World War II. Each of the 12 parishes took responsibility for stitching a panel, making it the largest community arts project ever undertaken on the island. The Maritime Museum celebrates the relationship of islanders and the sea, including an award winning hands-on experience, especially enjoyed by children.

Times Open all year, daily summer 9.30-5; winter 10-4.* **Facilities** 🅿 ♿ toilets for disabled shop ⊗

ST LAWRENCE

Hamptonne Country Life Museum

La Rue de la Patente JE3 1HS
☎ 01534 863955 📄 01534 863935
e-mail: marketing@jerseyheritagetrust.org
web: www.jerseyheritagetrust.org
dir: 5m from St Helier on A1, A10 & follow signs

Here visitors will find a medieval 17th-century home, furnished in authentic style and surrounded by 19th-century farm buildings. Guided tours every weekday. Living history interpretation and daily demonstrations.

Times Open Mar-Nov, daily 10-5.* **Facilities** 🅿 🎴 (outdoor) ♿ (partly accessible) (courtyard & garden accessible) toilets for disabled shop ⊗

Jersey-Isle of Man

Channel Islands-Isle of Man

St Lawrence continued

Jersey War Tunnels

Les Charrieres Malorey JE3 1FU
☎ 01534 860808   📄 01534 860886
e-mail: info@jerseywartunnels.com
web: www.jerseywartunnels.com
dir: bus route 8A from St Helier

On 1 July 1940 the Channel Islands were occupied by German forces, and this vast complex dug deep into a hillside is the most evocative reminder of that Occupation. A video presentation, along with a large collection of memorabilia, illustrates the lives of the islanders at war and a further exhibition records their impressions during 1945, the year of liberation.

Times Open 14 Feb-19 Dec, daily 9.30-5.30 (last admission 4).*
Facilities 🅿 🅟 ⬜ 🍴 licensed toilets for disabled shop ⊗

ST PETER

The Living Legend

Rue de Petit Aleval JE3 7ET
☎ 01534 485496   📄 01534 485855
e-mail: info@jerseyslivinglegend.co.je
web: www.jerseyslivinglegend.co.je
dir: from St Helier, along main esplanade & right to Bel Royal. Left and follow road to attraction, signed from German Underground Hospital

Pass through the granite archways into the landscaped gardens and the world of the Jersey Experience where Jersey's exciting past is recreated in a three dimensional spectacle featuring Stephen Tompkinson, Tony Robinson and other well-known names. Learn of the heroes and villains, the folklore and the story of the island's links with the UK and its struggles with Europe. Other attractions include an adventure playground, street entertainment, the Jersey Craft and Shopping Village, a range of shops and the Jersey Kitchen Restaurant. Two 18-hole adventure golf courses are suitable for all ages. Jersey Karting is a formula one style experience. A unique track featuring adult and cadet karts.

Times Open Apr-Oct, daily; Mar & Nov, Sat-Wed; 9-5.* **Facilities** 🅿 ⬜ 🍴 licensed ♿ (partly accessible) (Adventure Golf has lots of steps and uneven surfaces) toilets for disabled shop ⊗

TRINITY

Durrell Wildlife Conservation Trust

Les Augres Manor, La Profunde Rue JE3 5BP
☎ 01534 860000   📄 01534 860001
e-mail: info@durrell.org
web: www.durrell.org
dir: From St Hellier follow A8 to Trinity until B31. Turn right & follow B31, signed

Gerald Durrell's unique sanctuary and breeding centre for many of the world's rarest animals. Visitors can see these remarkable creatures, some so rare that they can only be found here, in modern, spacious enclosures in the gardens of the 16th-century manor house. Major attractions are the magical Aye-Ayes from Madagascar and the world-famous family of Lowland gorillas. There is a comprehensive programme of keeper talks, animal displays and activities.

Times Open all year, daily 9.30-6 (summer); 9.30-5 (winter). Closed 25 Dec.* **Fees** £12.90 (ch £9.40, pen £10.50). Family ticket £39.95.* **Facilities** 🅿 ⬜ 🍴 licensed 🍽 (outdoor) ♿ (partly accessible) (some indoor areas cannot accommodate wheelchairs/scooters) toilets for disabled shop ⊗

ISLE OF MAN

BALLAUGH

Curraghs Wild Life Park

IM7 5EA
☎ 01624 897323   📄 01624 897327
e-mail: curraghswlp@gov.im
web: www.gov.im/wildlife
dir: on main road halfway between Kirk Michael & Ramsey

This park has been developed adjacent to the reserve area of the Ballaugh Curraghs and a large variety of animals and birds can be seen. A walk-through enclosure lets visitors explore the world of wildlife, including local habitats along the Curraghs Nature Trail. The miniature railway runs on Sundays.

Times Open all year Etr-Oct, daily 10-6. (Last admission 5). Oct-Etr, Sat-Sun 10-4.* **Fees** £7 (ch £3.50, under 3's free, pen £5). Family ticket (2ad+2ch) £17.50.* **Facilities** 🅿 ⬜ 🍽 (outdoor) ♿ (partly accessible) (some paths in winter not accessible to wheelchairs) toilets for disabled shop ⊗

200

CASTLETOWN

Castle Rushen

The Quay IM9 1LD
☎ 01624 648000 📄 01624 648001
e-mail: enquiries@mnh.gov.im
web: www.storyofmann.com
dir: centre of Castletown

One of the world's best preserved medieval castles, Castle Rushen is a limestone fortress rising out of the heart of the old capital of the Island, Castletown. Once the fortress of the Kings and Lords of Mann, Castle Rushen is brought alive with rich decorations, and the sounds and smells of a bygone era.

Times Open daily, Etr-Oct, 10-5.* **Fees** £5 (ch £2.50) Family £12. Group from £4.50 each.* **Facilities** Ⓟ shop ⊗

Old Grammar School   FREE

IM9 1LE
☎ 01624 648000 📄 01624 648001
e-mail: enquiries@mnh.gov.im
web: www.storyofmann.com
dir: centre of Castletown, opposite the castle

Built around 1200AD, the former capital's first church, St Mary's, has had a significant role in Manx education. It was a school from 1570 to 1930 and evokes memories of Victorian school life.

Times Open daily, Etr-late Oct, 10-5.* **Facilities** Ⓟ Ⓟ ⊼ (outdoor) ♿ (partly accessible) (restricted access narrow door, 3 steps) shop ⊗

CREGNEASH

The National Folk Museum at Cregneash

☎ 01624 648000 📄 01624 648001
e-mail: enquiries@mnh.gov.im
web: www.storyofmann.com
dir: 2m from Port Erin/Port St Mary, signed

The Cregneash story begins in Cummal Beg - the village information centre which shows what life was really like in a Manx crofting village during the early 19th century. As you stroll around this attractive village, set in beautiful countryside, call into Harry Kelly's cottage, a Turner's shed, a Weaver's house, and the Smithy. The Manx Four-horned Loghtan Sheep can be seen grazing along with other animals from the village farm.

Times Open Etr-Oct, daily 10-5.* **Fees** £3.50 (ch £1.70) Family £8.50. Group rates from £2.80* **Facilities** Ⓟ ⊔ ⊼ (outdoor) shop ⊗

DOUGLAS

Manx Museum   FREE

IM1 3LY
☎ 01624 648000 📄 01624 648001
e-mail: enquiries@mnh.gov.im
web: www.storyofmann.com
dir: signed in Douglas

The Island's treasure house provides an exciting introduction to the "Story of Mann" where a specially produced film portrayal of Manx history complements the award-winning displays. Galleries depict natural history, archaeology and the social development of the Island. There are also examples of famous Manx artists in the National Art Gallery, together with the Island's National archive and reference library. Events and exhibitions throughout the year, please visit website for details.

Times Open all year, Mon-Sat, 10-5. Closed 25-26 Dec & 1 Jan.* **Facilities** Ⓟ Ⓟ ⊔ ⫟⦿ licensed ⊼ (outdoor) ♿ toilets for disabled shop ⊗

LAXEY

Great Laxey Wheel & Mines Trail

☎ 01624 648000 📄 01624 648001
e-mail: enquiries@mnh.gov.im
web: www.storyofmann.com
dir: signed in Laxey village

Built in 1854, the Great Laxey Wheel, 22 metres in diameter, is the largest working water wheel in the world. It was designed to pump water from the lead and zinc mines, and is an acknowledged masterpiece of Victorian engineering. The wheel is also known as 'Lady Isabella', after the wife of the then Lieutenant Governor of the Isle of Man.

Times Open Etr-Oct 10-5* **Fees** £3.50 (ch £1.80) Family £8.50. Group rates from £2.80* **Facilities** Ⓟ Ⓟ ⊼ (outdoor) shop ⊗

Isle of Man

House of Manannan

Mill Rd IM5 1TA
☎ **01624 648000** 📄 **01624 648001**
e-mail: enquiries@mnh.gov.im
web: www.storyofmann.com
dir: signed in Peel

The mythological sea-god Manannan guides visitors through the Island's rich Celtic, Viking and maritime past. Step inside reconstructions of a Manx Celtic roundhouse and a Viking longhouse, discover the stories on magnificent Manx stone crosses, and see Odin's Raven, a splendid Viking longship. Displays and exhibitions throughout the year please see website.

Times Open all year, daily 10-5. Closed 25-26 Dec & 1 Jan*
Fees £5.70 (ch £2.80) Family £14. Group rates from £4.60.*
Facilities 🅿 Ⓟ ♿ toilets for disabled shop ⊗

Peel Castle

IM5 1TB
☎ **01624 648000** 📄 **01624 648001**
e-mail: enquiries@mnh.gov.im
web: www.storyofmann.com
dir: on St Patrick's Isle, facing Peel Bay, signed

One of the Island's principle historic centres, this great natural fortress with its imposing curtain wall set majestically at the mouth of Peel Harbour is part of Man's Viking heritage. The sandstone walls of Peel Castle enclose an 11th-century church and Round Tower, the 13th-century St German's Cathedral and the later apartments of the Lords of Mann.

Times Open Etr-Oct, daily 10-5* **Fees** £3.50 (ch £1.80). Family £8.50. Group rates from £2.80.* **Facilities** Ⓟ ⊗

Loch Ard, Stirling

Scotland

CITY OF ABERDEEN

ABERDEEN

Aberdeen Art Gallery   FREE

Schoolhill AB10 1FQ
☎ **01224 523700** 📄 **01224 632133**
e-mail: info@aagm.co.uk
web: www.aberdeencity.gov.uk
dir: located in city centre

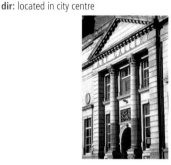

Aberdeen's splendid art gallery houses an important fine art collection, a rich and diverse applied art collection and an exciting programme of special exhibitions.

Times Open all year Tue-Sat 10-5, Sun 2-5. Closed Xmas & New Year* **Facilities** ℗ 🖵 toilets for disabled shop ⊗

Aberdeen Maritime Museum   FREE

Shiprow AB11 5BY
☎ **01224 337700** 📄 **01224 213066**
e-mail: info@aagm.co.uk
web: www.aberdeencity.gov.uk
dir: located in city centre

The award-winning Maritime Museum brings the history of the North Sea to life. Featuring displays and exhibitions on the offshore oil industry, shipbuilding, fishing and clipper ships.

Times Open all year, Tue-Sat, 10-5, Sun 2-5.* **Facilities** ℗ 🖵 🍴 licensed ♿ (partly accessible) (2 rooms in Provost Ross's house not accessible due to stairs) toilets for disabled shop ⊗

The Gordon Highlanders Museum

St Luke's, Viewfield Rd AB15 7XH
☎ **01224 311200** 📄 **01224 319323**
e-mail: museum@gordonhighlanders.com
web: www.gordonhighlanders.com

Presenting a large collection of artefacts, paintings, films and reconstructions, the Gordon Highlanders Museum is the perfect day out for anyone interested in Scottish military history, and is also the former home of 19th century artist, Sir George Reid. The exhibition includes interactive maps, original film footage, scaled reproductions, life-size models, touch screens, uniforms, medals and an armoury. The grounds also contain a tea-room, shop and gardens. See the website for details of changing exhibitions and events.

Times Open Apr-Oct, Tue-Sat 10-4.30, Sun 12.30-4.30. (Closed Mon). Nov, Feb & Mar Thu-Sat 10-4. Open by appointment only at other times.* **Facilities** 🅿 ℗ 🖵 ♿ toilets for disabled shop ⊗

Satrosphere Science Centre

179 Constitution St AB24 5TU
☎ **01224 640340** 📄 **01224 622211**
e-mail: info@satrosphere.net
web: www.satrosphere.net
dir: located very close to Beach Esplanade. Follow signs to fun beach, then attraction

Satrosphere is Scotland's first science and discovery centre and with over 50 hands-on exhibits and live science shows, a visit to Satrosphere will not only inspire the scientist within but will entertain the whole family. Satrosphere's exhibits offer interactive ways for visitors to discover more about the world around them and the science of how things work.

Times Open all year, Mar-Oct, daily 10-5; Nov-Feb, Tue-Sun 10-5. Closed 25-26 Dec & 1 Jan.* **Facilities** 🅿 ℗ 🖵 ♿ toilets for disabled shop ⊗

PETERCULTER

Drum Castle

AB31 5EY

☎ 0844 493 2161　📄 0844 493 2162
e-mail: information@nts.org.uk
web: www.nts.org.uk
dir: Off A93, 3m W of Peterculter

The great 13th-century Square Tower is one of the three oldest tower houses in Scotland and has associations with Robert the Bruce. The handsome mansion, added in 1619, houses a collection of family memorabilia. The grounds contain the 100-acre Old Wood of Drum, a natural oak wood and an old rose garden.

Times Castle:May-Jun & Sep, daily (closed Tues & Fri) 11.30-5; Jul-Aug, daily 11.30-5. Garden of Historic Roses: Apr-Oct, daily 10-6. Grounds: all year, daily; Jul-Aug open guided, daily 11.30-5. Last admission 45 mins before closing. Property open BH wknds from Fri-Mon inclusive.* **Fees** £8.50 (concessions £5.50) Family £21 (1 Parent £16).* **Facilities** 🅿 ⊡ ⊓ ♿ (partly accessible) (access to ground floor, but limited access to main floor) shop ⊗ ☗

ABERDEENSHIRE

ALFORD

Alford Valley Railway

AB33 8AD

☎ 019755 64236　& 07879 293934
e-mail: info@alfordvalleyrailway.org.uk
web: www.alfordvalleyrailway.org.uk
dir: A944 Alford Village

Alford Valley Railway is a narrow-gauge passenger railway between Alford and Haughton Park, about one mile long. Santa specials at Christmas (first two week-ends in December).

Times Open Apr, May & Sep, wknds 1-5; Jun-Aug, daily from 1 (30 min service). Party bookings also available at other times. **Fees** £2.50 (ch £1.50) return fare.* **Facilities** 🅿 ℗ ⊓ (outdoor) ♿ toilets for disabled shop

Craigievar Castle

AB33 8JF

☎ 0844 493 2174　📄 0844 493 2163
e-mail: information@nts.org.uk
web: www.nts.org.uk
dir: on A980, 6m S of Alford

A fairytale like castle, the Great Tower completed in 1626. The collection includes family portraits and 17th and 18th century furniture. There are extensive wooded grounds with a waymarked trail.

Times Castle: Mar-Jun, Fri-Tues 12-5.30; Jul-Aug, daily 12-5.30. Castle is undergoing restoration please telephone for more information.* **Facilities** 🅿 ⊓ ♿ (partly accessible) (access to castle difficult, many steps & spiral stairs to all rooms) shop ⊗ ☗

BALMORAL

Balmoral Castle Grounds & Exhibition

AB35 5TB

☎ 013397 42534　📄 013397 42034
e-mail: info@balmoralcastle.com
web: www.balmoralcastle.com
dir: on A93 between Ballater & Braemar

Queen Victoria and Prince Albert first rented Balmoral Castle in 1848, and Prince Albert bought the property four years later. He commissioned William Smith to build a new castle, which was completed by 1856 and is still the Royal Family's Highland residence. Explore the exhibitions, grounds, gardens and trails as well as the magnificent Castle Ballroom.

Times Open Apr-Jul, daily 10-5 (last admission 4.30)* **Fees** £7 (ch £3, concessions £6). Family (2ad+4ch) £15.* **Facilities** 🅿 ⊡ ⊓ (outdoor) ♿ toilets for disabled shop

Scotland

205

CRATHES

Crathes Castle Garden & Estate

AB31 5QJ
☎ 0844 4932166 📠 0844 4932169
e-mail: information@nts.org.uk
web: www.nts.org.uk
dir: On A93, 3m E of Banchory, 15m W of Aberdeen

This impressive 16th-century castle with magnificent interiors has royal associations dating from 1323. There is a large walled garden and a notable collection of unusual plants, including yew hedges dating from 1702. The grounds contain six nature trails, one suitable for disabled visitors, and an adventure playground.

Times Open daily 1-19 Apr & then wknds until 4 May, 10.30-4.30 (last entry 3.45); 4 May-Jun & Sep-Oct, Sat-Thu 10.30-4.30 (last entry 3.45); Jul-Aug, daily 10.30-5.30 (last entry 4.45). Gardens & Estate open all year, daily 9-sunset.* **Fees** £10.50 (concessions £7.50). Family ticket £26 (1 Parent £20).* **Facilities** 🅿 🍽 licensed ⅊ ᨷ (partly accessible) (only lower garden accessible for wheelchairs) toilets for disabled shop ⊗ ♨

KEMNAY

Castle Fraser

AB51 7LD
☎ 0844 493 2164 📠 0844 493 2165
e-mail: information@nts.org.uk
web: www.nts.org.uk
dir: off A944, 4m N of Dunecht

The massive Z-plan castle was built between 1575 and 1636 and is one of the grandest of the Castles of Mar. The interior was remodelled in 1838 and decoration and furnishings of that period survive in some of the rooms. A formal garden inside the old walled garden, estate trails, a children's play area and a programme of concerts are among the attractions.

Times Castle open Apr-Jun, Thu-Sun 12-5; Jul-Aug, daily 11-5; Sep-Oct, Thu-Sun 12-5 & B.H Mon's.* **Fees** £8.50 (concessions £5.50). Family £21 (1 Parent £16).* **Facilities** 🅿 ⊑ ⅊ ᨷ (partly accessible) (access restricted to ground floor of Castle & walled garden) toilets for disabled shop ⊗ ♨

MACDUFF

Macduff Marine Aquarium

11 High Shore AB44 1SL
☎ 01261 833369 📠 01261 831052
e-mail: macduff.aquarium@aberdeenshire.gov.uk
web: www.macduff-aquarium.org.uk
dir: off A947 and A98 to Macduff, aquarium signed

Exciting displays feature local sealife. The central exhibit, unique in Britain, holds a living kelp reef. Divers feed the fish in this tank. Other displays include an estuary exhibit, splash tank, rock pools, deep reef tank and ray pool. Young visitors especially enjoy the touch pools. There are talks, video presentations and feeding shows throughout the week.

Times Open all year, daily 10-5 (last admission 4.15). Closed 25-26 Dec & 31 Dec-2 Jan* **Facilities** 🅿 🅿 ⅊ (outdoor) ᨷ toilets for disabled shop ⊗

MARYCULTER

Storybook Glen

AB12 5FT
☎ 01224 732941 📠 01224 732941
web: www.storybookglenaberdeen.co.uk
dir: 5m W of Aberdeen on B9077

This is a child's fantasy land, where favourite nursery rhyme and fairytale characters are brought to life. Grown-ups can enjoy the nostalgia and also the 20 acres of Deeside country, full of flowers, plants, trees and waterfalls.

Times Open all year, Mar-Oct, daily 10-6; Nov-Feb, 10-4.* **Fees** £5.40 (ch £3.85, concessions £4.05).* **Facilities** 🅿 ⊑ 🍽 licensed ⅊ (outdoor) ᨷ toilets for disabled shop ⊗

MINTLAW

Aberdeenshire Farming Museum FREE

Aden Country Park AB42 5FQ
☎ 01771 624590 ▤ 01771 623558
e-mail: museums@aberdeenshire.gov.uk
web: www.aberdeenshire.gov.uk/museums
dir: 1m W of Mintlaw on A950

Housed in 19th-century farm buildings, once part of the estate which now makes up the Aden Country Park. Two centuries of farming history and innovation are illustrated, and the story of the estate is also told. The reconstructed farm of Hareshowe shows how a family in the north-east farmed during the 1950s - access by guided tour only.

Times Open May-Sep, daily 11-4.30; Apr & Oct, wknds only noon-4.30. (Last admission 30 mins before closing). Park open all year, Apr-Sep 7-10; winter 7-7.* **Facilities** ❷ ℗ ⊑ ⊼ (outdoor) ⅃ (partly accessible) (1st floor not accessible) toilets for disabled shop ⊗

OYNE

Archaeolink Prehistory Park

Berryhill AB52 6QP
☎ 01464 851500 ▤ 01464 851544
e-mail: info@archaeolink.co.uk
web: www.archaeolink.co.uk
dir: 1m off A96 on B9002

A stunning audio-visual show, a Myths and Legends Gallery and a whole range of interpretation techniques help visitors to explore what it was like to live 6000 years ago. In addition there are landscaped walkways, and outdoor activity areas including an Iron Age farm, Roman marching camp and Stone Age settlement in the 40-acre park. Enjoy daily hands-on activities for all ages, guided tours with costumed guides or relax in the coffee shop. Special weekend events held regularly.

Times Open Apr-Oct, daily 10-5 **Fees** £5.75 (ch £3.70, concessions £4.90) Family from £12.15* **Facilities** ❷ ℗ ⊑ ⦸️ licensed ⊼ (outdoor) toilets for disabled shop ⊗

RHYNIE

Leith Hall, Garden & Estate

Kennethmont AB54 4NQ
☎ 0844 493 2175 ▤ 0844 493 2176
e-mail: information@nts.org.uk
web: www.nts.org.uk
dir: on B9002, 1m W of Kennethmont

Home of the Leith family for over 300 years, the house, which is no longer open to the public, dates back to 1650. It is surrounded by charming gardens and extensive grounds, with marked trails.

Times Garden: all year, daily 9-sunset. Grounds: all year, daily.* **Fees** £8.50 (concessions £5.50). Family £21 (1 Parent £16).* **Facilities** ❷ ⊑ ⊼ ⅃ (partly accessible) (sloping walled garden, path to viewpoint & pond walk accessible with assistance) toilets for disabled ⊗ ⽝

ANGUS

BRECHIN

Pictavia Visitor Centre

Brechin Castle Centre, Haughmuir DD9 6RL
☎ 01356 626241 ▤ 01307 467357
e-mail: ecdev@angus.gov.uk **web:** www.pictavia.org.uk
dir: off A90 at Brechin

Find about more about the ancient pagan nation of the Picts, who lived in Scotland nearly 2000 years ago. Visitors can learn about Pictish culture, art and religion through film, interactive displays and music. There are also nature and farm trails, a pets' corner, and an adventure playground in the adjacent country park (operated by Brechin Castle Centre). 2010 will see the introduction of new interactive computer games, a temporary exhibition and re-enactment weekends.

Times Open all year, Mar-Oct, Mon-Sat 9-5, Sun 10-5; Nov-Feb, Sat 9-5, Sun 10-5. **Fees** £3.25 (ch & concessions £2.25, ch under 5 free). Family ticket £10. Group rates available for large parties & educational groups. **Facilities** ❷ ⊑ ⦸️ licensed ⊼ (outdoor) ⅃ toilets for disabled shop ⊗

Angus

GLAMIS

Angus Folk Museum

Kirkwynd Cottages DD8 1RT
☎ 0844 493 2141 🖷 0844 493 2141
e-mail: information@nts.org.uk
web: www.nts.org.uk
dir: off A94, in Glamis, 5m SW of Forfar

A row of stone-roofed, late 18th-century cottages now houses the splendid Angus Folk Collection of domestic equipment and cottage furniture. Across the wynd, an Angus stone steading houses 'The Life on the Land' exhibition.

Times Open 4 Apr-28 Jun, wknds only 12-5, 29 Jun-Aug daily 12-5, 5 Sep-1 Nov wknds only 12-5, BH Mon's.* **Fees** £5.50 (concessions £4.50), Family £15 (1 parent £10).* **Facilities** 🅿 & toilets for disabled ⊗ ⚏

Glamis Castle

DD8 1RJ
☎ 01307 840393 🖷 01307 840733
e-mail: enquiries@glamis-castle.co.uk
web: www.glamis-castle.co.uk
dir: 5m W of Forfar on A94

Glamis Castle is the family home of the Earls of Strathmore and Kinghorne and has been a royal residence since 1372. It is the childhood home of the late Queen Mother, the birthplace of her daughter the late Princess Margaret, and the setting for Shakespeare's play Macbeth. Though the Castle is open to visitors it remains the home of the Strathmore family. Each year there are Highland games, a transport extravaganza, the Scottish Prom Weekend, and a countryside festival. Contact venue for exact dates.

Times Open all year, Mar-Oct, 10-6 (last admission 4.30), Nov-Dec 10.30-5 (last admission 3.30).* **Facilities** 🅿 🅟 ♨ licensed 🛱 (outdoor) & (partly accessible) toilets for disabled shop ⊗

KIRRIEMUIR

J M Barrie's Birthplace

9 Brechin Rd DD8 4BX
☎ 0844 493 2142 🖷 0844 493 2142
e-mail: information@nts.org.uk
web: www.nts.org.uk
dir: on A90/A926 in Kirriemuir, 6m NW of Forfar

The creator of Peter Pan, Sir James Barrie, was born in Kirriemuir in 1860. The upper floors of No 9 Brechin Road are furnished as they may have been when Barrie lived there, and the adjacent house, No 11, houses an exhibition about him. The wash-house outside was his first 'theatre' and gave him the idea for Wendy's house in Peter Pan.

Times Open 4 Apr-28 Jun, Sat-Wed 12-5; 29 Jun-30 Aug, daily 11-5; 31 Aug-1 Nov, Sat-Wed 12-5.* **Fees** £5.50 (concessions £4.50). Family £15,(1 Parent £10).* **Facilities** 🅟 ⊑ 🛱 & (partly accessible) (steps to reception room, wheelchair access restricted to museum & wash house) shop ⊗ ⚏

MONTROSE

House of Dun

DD10 9LQ
☎ 0844 493 2144 🖷 0844 493 2145
e-mail: information@nts.org.uk
web: www.nts.org.uk
dir: on A935, 3m W of Montrose

This Georgian house, overlooking the Montrose Basin, was built for Lord Dun in 1730 and is noted for the exuberant plasterwork of the interior. Family portraits, fine furniture and porcelain are on display, and royal mementos connected with a daughter of King William IV and the actress Mrs Jordan, who lived here in the 19th century. There is a walled garden and woodland walks.

Times Open House: Apr-28 Jun & 2 Sep-Oct, Wed-Sun 12-5; 29 Jun-Aug, daily 11-5. (Last admission 45 mins before closing). Garden: All year, daily 9-sunset. Grounds: All year daily. Open BH wknds from Fri-Mon incl. (Occasional closures for weddings).* **Fees** £8.50 (concessions £5.50). Family £21, (1 Parent £16).* **Facilities** 🅿 ♨ licensed 🛱 & (partly accessible) (access to first floor & basement via a stair lift) toilets for disabled shop ⊗ ⚏

Scotland

ARGYLL & BUTE

ARROCHAR

Argyll Forest Park   FREE

Forestry Commission, Ardgartan Visitor Centre G83 7AR
☎ 01301 702597   📄 01301 702597
e-mail: katy.freeman@forestry.gsl.gov.uk
dir: on A83 at foot of "The Rest and Be Thankful"

This park extends over a large area of hill ground and forest, noted for its rugged beauty. Numerous forest walks and picnic sites allow exploration; the Arboretum walks and the route between Younger Botanic Gardens and Puck's Glen are particularly lovely. Wildlife viewing facilities include live footage of nesting birds in season.

Times Open Etr-Oct, daily.* **Facilities** 🅿 ⛺ (outdoor) shop

BARCALDINE

Scottish Sea Life Sanctuary

PA37 1SE
☎ 01631 720386   📄 01631 720529
e-mail: obansealife@merlinentertainments.biz
web: www.sealsanctuary.co.uk
dir: 10m N of Oban on A828 towards Fort William

Set in one of Scotland's most picturesque locations, the Scottish Sea Life Sanctuary provides dramatic views of native undersea life including stingrays, seals, octopus and catfish. There are daily talks and feeding demonstrations and during the summer young seals can be viewed prior to their release back into the wild. Recent additions include Otter Creek - a large naturally landscaped enclosure with deep diving pool with underwater viewing and cascading streams through other pools, and 'Into the Deep', a themed interactive area displaying living creatures from the deep. There is a restaurant, gift shop, children's play park and a nature trail.

Times Open daily at 10am. Please call for last admissions.*
Fees Please telephone 01631 720386 for prices or book online.*
Facilities 🅿 ⛺ 🍴 (outdoor) ♿ toilets for disabled shop ⊗

BENMORE

Benmore Botanic Garden

PA23 8QU
☎ 01369 706261   📄 01369 706369
e-mail: benmore@rbge.org.uk
web: www.rbge.org.uk
dir: 7m N of Dunoon on A815

From the formal gardens, through the hillside woodlands, follow the paths to a stunning viewpoint with a spectacular outlook across the garden and the Holy Loch to the Firth of Clyde and beyond. Amongst many highlights are the stately conifers, the magnificent avenue of giant redwoods, and an extensive magnolia and rhododendron collection. Visit the restored Victorian Fernery.

Times Open Mar & Oct, daily 10-5, Apr-Sep, daily 10-6* **Fees** £5 (ch 5-16yrs £1, concessions £4). Family £10. **Facilities** 🅿 ⛺ 🍴 licensed toilets for disabled shop ⊗

LOCHAWE

Cruachan Power Station

Visitor Centre, Dalmally PA33 1AN
☎ 01866 822618   📄 01866 822509
e-mail: visit.cruachan@scottishpower.com
web: www.visitcruachan.co.uk
dir: A85 18m E of Oban

A vast cavern hidden deep inside Ben Cruachan, which contains a 400,000-kilowatt hydro-electric power station, driven by water drawn from a high-level reservoir up the mountain. A guided tour takes you inside the mountain and reveals the generators in their underground cavern.

Times Open Etr-Nov, daily 9.30-5 (last tour 4.15). (Winter hours available on request).* **Fees** £5 (ch 6-16 £2, concessions £4.50).* **Facilities** 🅿 ⛺ ⛺ toilets for disabled shop ⊗

DUMFRIES & GALLOWAY

CAERLAVEROCK

Caerlaverock Castle

Glencaple DG1 4RU
☎ 01387 770244
web: www.historic-scotland.gov.uk
dir: 8m SE of Dumfries, on B725

This ancient seat of the Maxwell family is a splendid medieval stronghold dating back to the 13th century. It has high walls and round towers, with machicolations added in the 15th century.

Times Open all year, Apr-Sep, daily 9.30-5.30; Oct-Mar, daily 9.30-4.30. Closed 25-26 Dec & 1-2 Jan.* **Fees** £5.20 (ch £2.60, concessions £4.20). Please phone or check website for further details.* **Facilities** ❷ ⓟ ⓣ licensed ⌐ toilets for disabled shop ▨

WWT Caerlaverock

Eastpark Farm DG1 4RS
☎ 01387 770200 📄 01387 770539
e-mail: info@caerlaverock@wwt.org.uk
web: www.wwt.org.uk
dir: 9m SE of Dumfries, signed from A75

This internationally important wetland is the winter home of the Barnacle goose, whose entire Svalbard population spend the winter on the Solway Firth. Observation facilities include 20 hides, 3 towers and a heated observatory. A wide variety of other wildlife can be seen, notably the rare Natterjack Toad and a family of Barn Owls and ospreys which can be observed via a CCTV system. Swan feeds daily at 11-2. For our wide range of special events please see website for details.

Times Open daily 10-5. Closed 25 Dec.* **Fees** £6.30 (ch £3.10 , concessions £4.75). Family ticket £16.95.* **Facilities** ❷ ⏛ ⌐ (outdoor) ♿ (partly accessible) (all hides and observatories accessible except farmhouse tower and small avenue hides) toilets for disabled shop ⊗

CASTLE DOUGLAS

Threave Castle

DG7 1TJ
☎ 07711 223101
web: www.historic-scotland.gov.uk
dir: 3m W on A75

Archibald the Grim built this lonely castle in the late 14th century. It stands on an islet in the River Dee, and is four storeys high with round towers guarding the outer wall. The island is reached by boat.

Times Open Apr-Sep, daily 9.30-5.30.* **Fees** £4.20 (ch £2.10, concessions £3.20). Charge includes ferry trip. Please phone or check website for further details.* **Facilities** ❷ ⌐ toilets for disabled ⊗ ▨

CREETOWN

Creetown Gem Rock Museum

Chain Rd DG8 7HJ
☎ 01671 820357 & 820554   📄 01671 820554
e-mail: enquiries@gemrock.net
web: www.gemrock.net
dir: follow signs from A75 at Creetown bypass

The Gem Rock is the leading independent museum of its kind in the UK, and is renowned worldwide. Crystals, gemstones, minerals, jewellery and fossils, the Gem Rock displays some of the most breathtaking examples of nature's wonders. See the audio-visual 'Fire in the Stones', the latest attraction 'Olga', a 50,000 year old cave bear skeleton, explore the Crystal Cave, relax in the Prospector's Study, and sample the home-baked Scottish cakes in the café.

Times Open daily, Feb-Mar 10-4; Apr-Sep 9.30-5.30, Oct-22 Dec 10-4. Closed 23 Dec-Jan. **Fees** £3.75 (ch £2.25, under 5 free, concessions £3.25). Family ticket (2ad+3ch) £9.75. **Facilities** ❷ ⓟ ⏛ ⌐ (outdoor) ♿ toilets for disabled shop ⊗

KIRKCUDBRIGHT

Galloway Wildlife Conservation Park

Lochfergus Plantation DG6 4XX
☎ 01557 331645   🖹 01557 331645
e-mail: info@gallowaywildlife.co.uk
web: www.gallowaywildlife.co.uk
dir: follow brown signs from A75, 1m from Kirkcudbright on B727

Galloway is the wild animal conservation centre for southern Scotland, set in 27 acres of mixed woodland. A varied zoological collection of over 150 animals from all over the world. Close animal encounters and bird of prey displays are some of the features giving an insight into wildlife conservation.

Times Open Feb-Nov, daily 10-6 (last admission 5).* **Facilities** 🅿 🚻 🎍 (outdoor) ♿ (partly accessible) (due to the rising terrain, the nature trail is not accessible) toilets for disabled shop ⊗

NEW ABBEY

National Museum of Costume Scotland

Shambellie House DG2 8HQ
☎ 0131 247 4030
e-mail: info@nms.ac.uk
web: www.nms.ac.uk/costume
dir: 7m S of Dumfries, on A710

Become a dedicated follower of fashion. Shambellie House, a 19th-century country home in wooded grounds, is the perfect setting for discovering 100 years of costume, from the 1850s through to the 1950s. Put yourself in the shoes of those who wore the trends of the time. The museum holds special events and activities throughout the year.

Times Open Apr-Oct, daily, 10-5. **Fees** £3.50 (ch under 12 & members free, concessions £2.50). **Facilities** 🅿 🚻 🎍 (outdoor) ♿ (partly accessible) (ramp & wheelchair lift provide access to ground floor of museum, tearoom & toilets) shop ⊗

THORNHILL

Drumlanrig Castle, Gardens & Country Park

DG3 4AQ
☎ 01848 331555   🖹 01848 331682
e-mail: enquiries@drumlanrig.com
web: www.drumlanrig.com
dir: 4m N of Thornhill off A76

This unusual pink sandstone castle was built in the late 17th century in Renaissance style. It contains a outstanding collection of fine art. There is also French furniture, as well as silver and relics of Bonnie Prince Charlie. The old stable block has a craft centre with resident craft workers, and the grounds offer an extensive garden plant centre, mountain bike hire and woodland walks. The Scottish cycle museum and shop have been recently renovated. For details of special events phone 01848 331555.

Times Castle open 2 Apr-Aug, daily 11-4 (last tour). **Fees** £8 (ch £4.50 & pen £6.50). Grounds only £4. Party 20+ £6 each. **Facilities** 🅿 🅿 🍴 licensed 🎍 (outdoor) ♿ (partly accessible) (some areas of garden not easily accessible to wheelchair users) toilets for disabled shop ⊗

WANLOCKHEAD

Hidden Treasures Museum of Lead Mining

ML12 6UT

☎ 01659 74387 📄 01659 74481

e-mail: miningmuseum@hotmail.com
web: www.leadminingmuseum.co.uk
dir: signed from M74 and A76

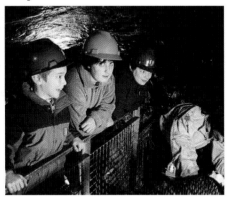

Wanlockhead is Scotland's highest village, set in the beautiful Lowther Hills. Visitors can see miners' cottages, and the miners' library as well as the 18th-century lead mine. Visitors can also pan for gold.

Times Open Apr-Nov, daily 11-4.30; Jul-Aug & BHs 10-5.*
Fees £6.25 (ch & concessions £4.50). Family tickets available.*
Facilities 🅿 🅿 ⬛ ⑂ licensed ⼍ (outdoor) ⅙ toilets for disabled shop ⊗

CITY OF DUNDEE

DUNDEE

Camperdown Country Park

Coupar Angus Rd DD2 4TF

☎ 01382 431818 📄 01382 431810

e-mail: leisure.communities@dundeecity.gov.uk
web: www.camperdownpark.com
dir: A90 to Dundee then onto A923 (Coupar-Angus road), left at 1st rdbt to attraction

Camperdown is Dundee's largest park, covers an area of over 400 acres and is home to some 190 species of tree. There is a good range of facilities, including an 18-hole golf course, a putting green, boating pond, children's play area, footpaths and woodland trails, and Camperdown Wildlife Centre. There is also a year-round calendar of special events, contact for details.

Times Open Park: all year. Wildlife Centre: daily Mar-Sep, 10-4.30 (last admission 3.45), Oct-Feb, daily 10-3.30 (last admission 2.45).* **Fees** Park - free admission. Wildlife Centre charged, £3.40 (ch £2.75 under 3 £1, concessions £2.75), family (2ad+3ch) £9.80, accompanied group £3.90pp, unaccompanied group £2.75pp.* **Facilities** 🅿 ⬛ ⼍ (outdoor) ⅙ toilets for disabled shop ⊗

Discovery Point & RRS Discovery

Discovery Quay DD1 4XA

☎ 01382 309060 📄 01382 225891

e-mail: info@dundeeheritage.co.uk
web: www.rrsdiscovery.com
dir: follow brown heritage signs for Historic Ships

Discovery Point is the home of RRS Discovery, Captain Scott's famous Antarctic ship. Spectacular lighting, graphics and special effects re-create key moments in the Discovery story. The restored bridge gives a captain's view over the ship and the River Tay. Learn what happened to the ship after the expedition, during the First World War and the Russian Revolution, and find out about her involvement in the first survey of whales' migratory patterns.

Times Open all year, Apr-Oct, Mon-Sat 10-6. Sun 11-6; Nov-Mar, Mon-Sat 10-5, Sun 11-5.* **Fees** £7.50 (ch £4.50, concessions £5.75). Family ticket £20.* **Facilities** 🅿 🅿 ⬛ ⑂ licensed ⼍ (outdoor) ⅙ (partly accessible) (access to exhibition on top deck, no access to lower deck, but virtual tour available) toilets for disabled shop ⊗

Mills Observatory

Balgay Park, Glamis Rd DD2 2UB
☎ **01382 435967** 🖹 **01382 435962**
e-mail: mills.observatory@dundeecity.gov.uk
web: www.dundeecity.gov.uk/mills
dir: 1m W of city centre, in Balgay Park, on Balgay Hill. Vehicle entrance at Glamis Rd gate to Balgay Park

Mills Observatory is Britain's only full-time public observatory. See breathtaking views of the stars and planets through the impressive Victorian refracting telescope. The telescope with state-of-the-art 'go to' technology, allows you to 'hop' from one object to another more quickly than ever before! During October to March, the Planetarium Shows provide the chance to learn about constellations, planets and other jewels of the night sky. There are also displays on the solar system and space exploration.

Times Open all year, Apr-Sep, Tue-Fri 11-5, Sat & Sun 12.30-4; Oct-Mar, Mon-Fri 4pm-10pm, Sat & Sun 12.30-4. Closed 25-26 Dec & 1-3 Jan.* **Fees** Free entry, small charge for public Planetarium shows and groups* **Facilities** 🅿 Ⓟ 🅰 (outdoor) ♿ (partly accessible) (ground floor accessible) toilets for disabled shop ⊗

Verdant Works

West Henderson's Wynd DD2 5BT
☎ **01382 309060** 🖹 **01382 225891**
e-mail: info@dundeeheritage.co.uk
web: www.verdantworks.com
dir: follow brown tourist signs

Dating from 1830, this old Jute Mill covers 50,000 square feet and has been restored as a living museum of Dundee and Tayside's textile history and award-winning European Industrial Museum. Phase I explains what jute is, where it comes from and why Dundee became the centre of its production. Working machinery illustrates the production process from raw jute to woven cloth. Phase II deals with the uses of jute and its effects on Dundee's social history.

Times Open all year, Apr-Oct; Mon-Sat 10-6, Sun 11-6; Nov-Mar, Mon-Sat 10-4.30, Sun 11-4.30. Venue closes 1hr after last entry. (Please check for winter opening times). Closed 25-26 Dec & 1-2 Jan.* **Fees** £7 (ch £4, concessions £5.25). Family ticket (2ad+2ch) £17.* **Facilities** 🅿 Ⓟ 🖵 🍽 licensed ♿ toilets for disabled shop ⊗

EAST AYRSHIRE

GALSTON

Loudoun Castle Theme Park

KA4 8PE
☎ **01563 822296** 🖹 **01563 822408**
e-mail: loudouncastle@btinternet.com
web: www.loudouncastle.co.uk
dir: signed from A74(M), from A77 and from A71

Loudoun Castle Theme Park is a great day out for the whole family. Theme park rides, live entertainment and McDougals Farm are just a taster of what's on offer.

Times Open Etr-end of Sep. Please phone for further details.* **Facilities** 🅿 🖵 🍽 licensed 🅰 (indoor & outdoor) toilets for disabled shop ⊗

EAST DUNBARTONSHIRE

MILNGAVIE

Mugdock Country Park　　　FREE

Craigallian Rd G62 8EL
☎ **0141 956 6100 & 6586**
e-mail: rangers@mcp.ndo.co.uk
web: www.mugdock-country-park.org.uk
dir: N of Glasgow on A81, signed

This country park incorporates the remains of Mugdock and Craigend castles, set in beautiful landscapes as well as an exhibition centre, craft shops, orienteering course and many walks.

Times Open all year, daily.* **Facilities** 🅿 Ⓟ 🖵 🍽 licensed 🅰 (outdoor) toilets for disabled shop

Scotland

EAST LOTHIAN

ABERLADY

Myreton Motor Museum

EH32 0PZ
☎ **01875 870288 & 07947 066666** 🖎 **01368 860199**
e-mail: myreton.motor.museum@aberlady.org
dir: 1.5m from A198, 2m from A1

The museum has on show a large collection, from 1899, of cars, bicycles, motor cycles and commercials. There is also a large collection of period advertising, posters and enamel signs.

Times Open all year, Mar-Oct daily 10.30-4.30, Nov-Feb, wknds only 11-3.* **Fees** £7 (ch £3, concessions £6). **Facilities** 🅿 ㅈ (outdoor) ♿ ⊗

EAST FORTUNE

National Museum of Flight Scotland

East Fortune Airfield EH39 5LF
☎ **0131 247 4238**
e-mail: info@nms.ac.uk
web: www.nms.ac.uk
dir: signed from A1 near Haddington. Onto B1347, past Athelstaneford, 20m E of Edinburgh

The National Museum of Flight is situated on 63 acres of one of Britain's best preserved wartime airfields. The museum has four hangars, with more than 50 aeroplanes, plus engines, rockets and memorabilia. Items on display include two Spitfires, a Vulcan bomber and Britain's oldest surviving aeroplane, built in 1896; recent exhibits also include a Phantom jet fighter, and a Harrier jump-jet. The Concorde Experience is free with admission to the Museum, but boarding passes are limited. The Concorde Experience explores the story of this historic plane through the lives of those who worked or travelled on it.

Times Open all year, Apr-Oct, daily, 10-5. Nov-Mar, wknds only, 10-4. (Contact for details of seasonal variations in opening times.) **Fees** £8.50 (ch under 12 & NMS members free, concessions £6.50). **Facilities** 🅿 ⊑ ㅈ (outdoor) ♿ (partly accessible) (no wheelchair access to Concorde's passenger cabin, most display areas are on ground floor) toilets for disabled shop ⊗

NORTH BERWICK

Scottish Seabird Centre

The Harbour EH39 4SS
☎ **01620 890202** 🖎 **01620 890222**
e-mail: info@seabird.org
web: www.seabird.org
dir: A1 from Edinburgh, then A198 to North Berwick. Brown heritage signs clearly marked from A1

Escape to another world at this award-winning wildlife visitor attraction. Breathtaking panoramic views over the sea and sandy beaches. See wildlife close up with amazing live cameras - puffins spring-cleaning their burrows, gannets with fluffy white chicks, seals sunning themselves and occasional sightings of dolphins and whales. The Discovery Centre has a Wildlife cinema, Environment Zone, Kid' Playzone and Migration Flyway. There's a packed programme of festivals and events, see the website for details.

Times Open all year, Feb, Mar & Oct Mon-Fri 10-5, Sat-Sun 10-5.30. Apr-Sep 10-6 every day. Nov-Jan Mon-Fri 10-4, Sat-Sun 10-5.30.* **Facilities** 🅿 ⓟ ⊑ ⑪ licensed ㅈ (outdoor) ♿ toilets for disabled shop ⊗

Tantallon Castle

EH39 5PN
☎ **01620 892727**
web: www.historic-scotland.gov.uk
dir: 3m E, off A198

A famous 14th-century stronghold of the Douglases facing towards the lonely Bass Rock from the rocky Firth of Forth shore. Nearby 16th and 17th century earthworks.

Times Open all year, Apr-Sep, daily, 9.30-5.30; Oct, 9.30-4.30; Nov-Mar, Mon-Wed & Sat-Sun, 9.30-4.30. Closed 25-26 Dec & 1-2 Jan.* **Fees** £4.70 (ch £2.35, concessions £3.70). Please phone or check website for further details.* **Facilities** 🅿 ㅈ shop ⊗ 🚩

PRESTONPANS

Prestongrange Museum   FREE

Prestongrange
☎ 0131 653 2904 📠 01620 828201
e-mail: elms@eastlothian.gov.uk
web: www.prestongrange.org
dir: on B1348 coast road between Prestonpans & Musselburgh

The oldest documented coal mining site in Scotland, with 800 years of history, this museum shows a Cornish Beam Engine and on-site evidence of associated industries such as brickmaking and pottery. It is located next to a 16th-century customs port. Contact for details of special events or see website.

Times Open Apr-Oct, daily, 11-4.30. **Facilities** 🅿 ⬚ 🍴 (outdoor) ♿ (partly accessible) (grounds partly accessible) toilets for disabled shop ⊗

CITY OF EDINBURGH

EDINBURGH

Camera Obscura

Castlehill, Royal Mile EH1 2ND
☎ 0131 226 3709 📠 0131 225 4239
e-mail: info@camera-obscura.co.uk
web: www.camera-obscura.co.uk
dir: next to Edinburgh Castle

A unique view of Edinburgh - as the lights go down, a brilliant moving image of the surrounding city appears. See three other floors of optical illusions and hands on inter-active fun. The exhibition space will be expanded in the summer of 2010 introducing more hands-on exhibits.

Times Open all year, daily, Apr-Oct 9.30-6: Nov-Mar 10-5. Closed 25 Dec. Open Jul-Aug, 9.30-7.30. **Fees** £9.15 (ch £6.25). **Facilities** shop

Dynamic Earth

Holyrood Rd EH8 8AS
☎ 0131 550 7800 📠 0131 550 7801
e-mail: enquiries@dynamicearth.co.uk
web: www.dynamicearth.co.uk
dir: on edge of Holyrood Park, opposite Palace of Holyrood House

How the Earth works. Take a walk through Scotland's geological history. Travel back in time to follow the creation of Planet Earth. Be shaken by a volcano, feel the chill of polar ice and get caught in a tropical rainstorm. Please visit website for details of events running throughout the year.

Times Open all year, Apr-Oct daily & Nov-Mar Wed-Sun 10-5, (last entry 3.50); Jul-Aug daily, 10-6, (last entry 4.50).* **Facilities** 🅿 🅿 ⬚ 🍴 (indoor & outdoor) toilets for disabled shop ⊗

Edinburgh Castle

EH1 2NG
☎ 0131 225 9846
web: www.historic-scotland.gov.uk

This historic stronghold stands on the precipitous crag of Castle Rock. One of the oldest parts is the 11th-century chapel of the saintly Queen Margaret, but most of the present castle evolved later, during its stormy history of sieges and wars, and was altered again in Victorian times. The Scottish crown and other royal regalia are displayed in the Crown Room. Also notable is the Scottish National War Memorial.

Times Open all year, Apr-Sep, daily, 9.30-6; Oct-Mar 9.30-5; 1 Jan, 11-4.30. Closed 25-26 Dec.* **Fees** £10.30 (ch £4.50, concessions £8.50). Please phone or check website for further details.* **Facilities** 🅿 ⬚ 🍴 licensed toilets for disabled shop ⊗ ▮

Edinburgh Zoo

134 Corstorphine Rd, Murrayfield EH12 6TS
☎ 0131 334 9171 📠 0131 314 0382
e-mail: info@rzss.org.uk
web: www.edinburghzoo.org.uk
dir: 3m W of city centre on A8 towards Glasgow

Scotland's largest wildlife attraction set in 82 acres of leafy hillside parkland, just ten minutes from the city centre. With over 1,000 animals ranging from the UK's only koalas to massive Indian rhinos, including many other threatened species. See the world's largest penguin pool or visit our chimpanzees in the world-class, Budongo Trail.

Times Open all year, daily Apr-Sep, 9-6; Oct & Mar, 9-5; Nov-Feb, 9-4.30.* **Fees** £12.60 (ch £8.50, concessions £10.80). Family ticket (2ad+2ch) £42.* **Facilities** 🅿 🅿 ⬚ 🍴 licensed 🍴 (indoor & outdoor) ♿ (partly accessible) (Zoo is on a hillside, but there is a free hilltop safari to the top of the hill) toilets for disabled shop ⊗

Edinburgh continued

Museum of Childhood   FREE

42 High St, Royal Mile EH1 1TG
☎ 0131 529 4142   📄 0131 558 3103
e-mail: moc@edinburgh.gov.uk
web: www.cac.org.uk
dir: On the Royal Mile

One of the first museums of its kind, this was the brainchild of a local councillor, and first opened in 1955. It has a wonderful collection of toys, games and other belongings of children through the ages, to delight visitors both old and young. Ring for details of special events.

Times Open all year, Mon-Sat 10-5, Sun 12-5.* **Facilities** Ⓟ ♿ (partly accessible) toilets for disabled shop ⊗

National Gallery Complex

The Mound, Princess St EH2 2EL
☎ 0131 624 6200   📄 0131 343 3250
e-mail: enquiries@nationalgalleries.org
web: www.nationalgalleries.org
dir: off Princes St

The National Gallery complex consists of three magnificent buildings, right in the heart of Edinburgh: The National Gallery of Scotland, home to Scotland's prestigious national collection; The Royal Scottish Academy, one of Europe's premier exhibition centres; and The Weston Link which houses the café, restaurant and lecture rooms.

Times Open all year, daily 10-5, Thu until 7. 1 Jan noon-5. Closed 25-26 Dec. **Fees** Free. Admission charged to some major exhibitions. **Facilities** Ⓟ ⬚ ⓧ licensed ♿ toilets for disabled shop ⊗

National Museum of Scotland   FREE

Chambers St EH1 1JF
☎ 0131 225 7534
e-mail: info@nms.ac.uk
web: www.nms.ac.uk
dir: situated in Chambers St in Old Town. A few mins walk from Princes St and The Royal Mile

Scotland - past, present and future. The Museum's collections tell you the story of Scotland - land, people and culture. What influence has the world had on Scotland, and Scotland on the world? Your journey of discovery starts here. For generations the museum has collected key exhibits from all over Scotland and beyond. Viking brooches, Pictish stones, ancient chessmen and Queen Mary's clarsach. There's more! Connect with Dolly the sheep, design a robot, test drive a Formula One car or blast off into outer space. See website for special exhibitions and events. Part of the Victorian Royal museum building is closed for refurbishment and will re-open in 2011.

Times Open all year, daily 10-5. **Facilities** Ⓟ ⬚ ⓧ licensed ♿ toilets for disabled shop ⊗

National War Museum Scotland

Edinburgh Castle EH1 2NG
☎ 0131 225 7534   📄 0131 225 3848
e-mail: info@nms.ac.uk
web: www.nms.ac.uk
dir: at Edinburgh Castle, a few minutes walk up the Royal Mile to Castlehill

Explore the Scottish experience of war and military service over the last 400 years. A chance to experience the poignant stories of the Scots who went to war, through their letters and personal treasures. See website for special exhibitions and events.

Times Open all year, daily, Apr-Sep, 9.45-5.45; Oct-Mar, 9.45-4.45. Closed 25-26 Dec. **Fees** Standard Fares £12 (ch £6, ch under 5 free, concessions £10). NMS members £10.80. Free entry to museum with admission to Edinburgh Castle. Peak Fares £13 (ch £6.50, concessions £10.50). NMS Members £11.70. **Facilities** Ⓟ ♿ toilets for disabled shop ⊗

Palace of Holyroodhouse

EH8 8DX
☎ 0131 556 5100   📄 020 7930 9625
e-mail: bookinginfo@royalcollection.org.uk
web: www.royalcollection.org.uk
dir: at east end of Royal Mile

The Palace grew from the guest house of the Abbey of Holyrood, said to have been founded by David I after a miraculous apparition. Mary, Queen of Scots had her court here from 1561 to 1567, and 'Bonnie' Prince Charlie held levees at the Palace during his occupation of Edinburgh. Today the Royal Apartments are used by HM The Queen for state ceremonies and official entertaining, and are finely decorated with works of art from the Royal Collection.

Times Open all year, daily, Apr-Oct 9.30-6 (last admission 5); Nov-Mar 9.30-4.30 (last admission 3.30). Closed Good Fri, 25-26 Dec and when The Queen is in residence.* **Fees** £10.50 (ch £6.50, concessions £9.50). Family ticket (2ad+3ch) £28. Provides unlimited admission for 12 months. **Facilities** ⓟ Ⓟ ⬚ ♿ (partly accessible) (historic apartments accessible by spiral staircase) toilets for disabled shop ⊗

The Royal Yacht Britannia

Ocean Terminal, Leith EH6 6JJ
☎ 0131 555 5566 📄 0131 555 8835
e-mail: enquiries@tryb.co.uk
web: www.royalyachtbritannia.co.uk
dir: follow signs to North Edinburgh & Leith. Situated within Ocean Terminal

Visit the Royal Yacht Britannia, now in Edinburgh's historic port of Leith. The experience starts in the Visitor Centre where you can discover Britannia's fascinating story. Then step aboard for a self-led audio tour which takes you around five decks giving you a unique insight into what life was like for the Royal Family, officers and yachtsmen. Highlights include the State Apartments, Admiral's Cabin, Engine Room, Laundry and Sick Bay. Visit the new Royal Deck tearoom.

Times Open all year daily from 10 (Jul & Aug from 9.30). Last admission 4 (Apr-Jul, Sep-Oct), 4.30 (Aug) or 3.30 (Nov-Mar). Closed 25 Dec & 1 Jan. **Fees** £10.50 (ch 5-17 £6.25, concessions £9) Family ticket (2ad+3ch) £29.75. **Facilities** 🅿 Ⓟ ⬚ ♿ toilets for disabled shop ⊗

Scottish National Gallery of Modern Art

75 Belford Rd EH4 3DR
☎ 0131 624 6200 📄 0131 343 3250
e-mail: enquiries@nationalgalleries.org
web: www.nationalgalleries.org
dir: in West End, 20min walk from Haymarket station

An outstanding collection of 20th-century painting, sculpture and graphic art. Includes major works by Matisse, Picasso, Bacon, Moore and Lichtenstein and an exceptional group of Scottish paintings. Set in leafy grounds with a sculpture garden.

Times Open all year, daily 10-5. New Year's Day noon-5. Closed 25-26 Dec. **Fees** Free. Admission charged to some major exhibitions. **Facilities** 🅿 ⬚ ♿ toilets for disabled shop ⊗

SOUTH QUEENSFERRY

Hopetoun House

EH30 9SL
☎ 0131 331 2451 📄 0131 319 1885
e-mail: marketing@hopetounhouse.com
web: www.hopetounhouse.com
dir: 2m W of Forth Road Bridge, off A904

Hopetoun House at South Queensferry is just a short drive from Edinburgh and has all the ingredients for a great family day out. Whether it is a leisurely stroll, afternoon tea or a touch of nostalgia, Hopetoun fits the bill. Built around 300 years ago, it is a delight to wander the corridors and historical rooms of one of the most splendid examples of the work of Scottish architects, Sir William Bruce and William Adam. It shows some of the finest examples in Scotland of carving, wainscoting and ceiling painting. With 100 acres of parkland including a deer park, the gardens are a colourful carpet of seasonal flowers. Summer fair in July, Christmas shopping fair in November.

Times Open daily Etr-26 Sep. **Fees** £8 (ch £4.25). Grounds £3.70 (ch £2.20).* **Facilities** 🅿 Ⓟ ⬚ ⊓ (outdoor) ♿ (partly accessible) (ramps to tearoom, lift to first floor of house) toilets for disabled shop ⊗

FALKIRK

BIRKHILL

Birkhill Fireclay Mine

EH51 9AQ
☎ 01506 825855 & 822298 📄 01506 828766
e-mail: mine@srps.org.uk
web: www.srps.org.uk
dir: A706 from Linlithgow, A904 from Grangemouth, follow brown signs to Steam Railway & Fireclay Mine. Main access is by train from Bo'ness

Tour guides will meet you at Birkhill Station and lead you down into the ancient woodland of the beautiful Avon Gorge, and then into the caverns of the Birkhill Fireclay mine. See how the clay was worked, what it was used for and find the 300-million-year-old fossils in the roof of the mine.

Times Open wknds Apr-Oct, daily in Jul-Aug. **Fees** Mine & Train £9 (ch £5, concessions £7.50) Family ticket (2ad+2ch) £23. Mine only £3.10 (ch £2.10, concessions £2.60) Family ticket £8.25.* **Facilities** 🅿 Ⓟ ⊓ (outdoor) toilets for disabled

Scotland

BO'NESS

Bo'ness & Kinneil Railway

Bo'ness Station, Union St EH51 9AQ
☎ 01506 825855 & 822298 📄 01506 828766
e-mail: enquiries.railway@srps.org.uk
web: www.srps.org.uk
dir: A904 from all directions, signed

Historic railway buildings, including the station and train shed, have been relocated from sites all over Scotland. The Scottish Railway Exhibition tells the story of the development of railways and their impact on the people of Scotland. Take a seven mile return trip by steam train to the tranquil country station at Birkhill. Thomas the Tank Engine weekends in May, August and September, and Santa Specials in December.

Times Open wknds Apr-Oct, daily Jul-Aug. **Fees** Return fare £9 (ch 5-15 £5, concessions £7.50). Family ticket £23. (Ticket for return train fare & tour of Birkhill Fireclay Mine).* **Facilities** 🅿 Ⓟ ⊑ 🎠 (outdoor) 🐾 toilets for disabled shop

FALKIRK

Callendar House   FREE

Callendar Park FK1 1YR
☎ 01324 503770 📄 01324 503771
e-mail: calendar.house@falkirk.gov.uk
web: www.falkirk.gov.uk/cultural
dir: On southside of town centre, Callendar House is signposted. Easily accessible from M9

Mary, Queen of Scots, Oliver Cromwell, Bonnie Prince Charlie, noble earls and wealthy merchants all feature in the history of Callendar House. Costumed interpreters describe early 19th-century life in the kitchens and the 900-year history of the house is illustrated in the 'Story of Callendar House' exhibition. The house is set in parkland, offering boating and woodland walks. Regular exhibitions in Callendar House's Large Gallery.

Times Open all year, Mon-Sat, 10-5 (Sun Apr-Sep only 2-5).*
Facilities 🅿 Ⓟ ⊑ 🎠 (outdoor) 🐾 (partly accessible) (ramped access, lift to all floors, no wheelchair access to shop/reception) toilets for disabled shop

FIFE

ANSTRUTHER

Scottish Fisheries Museum

St Ayles, Harbour Head KY10 3AB
☎ 01333 310628 📄 01333 310628
e-mail: info@scotfishmuseum.org
web: www.scotfishmuseum.org
dir: A917 through St Monans & Pittenweem to Anstruther

This award-winning national museum tells the story of Scottish fishing and its people from the earliest times to the present. With 10 galleries, 2 large boatyards, and a restored fisherman's cottage, which contain many fine paintings and photographs, boat models and 17 actual boats, clothing and items of daily life to see, a visit to the museum makes for an exceptional day out. Contact the museum for details of events. 2009 was the 40th anniversary of the opening of the museum.

Times Open all year, Apr-Sep, Mon-Sat 10-5.30, Sun 11-5; Oct-Mar, Mon-Sat 10-4.30, Sun 12-4.30. Closed 25-26 Dec & 1-2 Jan. (Last admission 1 hr before closing).* **Fees** £5 (ch in school groups £1.50, accompanied ch free, concessions £4).* **Facilities** 🅿 ⊑ 🐾 toilets for disabled shop ⊗

CUPAR

The Scottish Deer Centre

Bow-of-Fife KY15 4NQ
☎ 01337 810391 📄 01337 810477
e-mail: info@tsdc.co.uk
web: www.tsdc.co.uk
dir: From South M90 junct 8 to A91 Cupar, from North M90 junct 9 to A912, join A91. Follow brown tourist sign

Guided tours take about 30 minutes and allow you to meet and feed deer. There are indoor and outdoor adventure play areas. Other features include daily falconry displays and a tree top walkway. European Wolves are fed every-day (except Friday) at 3pm.

Times Open all year, daily, Winter 10-4, Summer 10-5, 5.30 Jul-Aug. **Fees** £6.95 (ch 3-15 £4.95).* **Facilities** 🅿 ⊑ 🎠 (indoor & outdoor) 🐾 toilets for disabled shop ⊗

DUNFERMLINE

Abbot House Heritage Centre

Abbot House, Maygate KY12 7NE
☎ **01383 733266** 📠 **01383 624908**
e-mail: dht@abbothouse.co.uk
web: www.abbothouse.co.uk
dir: in city centre

For the better part of a millennium, pilgrims have beaten a path to Dumfermline's door. Today visitors can still share the rich royal heritage of the capital of Fife's Magic Kingdom. The volunteer-run Abbot House Heritage Centre - dubbed 'The People's Tardis' - propels the traveller through time from the days of the Picts - a time warp peopled by a veritable Who's Who of characters from Dumfermline's past: Scotland's royal saint, Braveheart's Wallace and Bruce, Scotland's Chaucer, steel magnate Andrew Carnegie and a whole panoply of kings, ending with the birth of ill-starred Charles I.

Times Open Mar-Oct daily, 10-5; Nov-Feb, Sun-Fri 10-4, Sat 10-5. Closed 25-26 Dec & 1 Jan.* **Fees** £4 (accompanied ch under 16 free, concessions £3). Party 20+.* **Facilities** ℗ 🚻 ♿ (partly accessible) (ground floor fully accessible) toilets for disabled shop ⊗

Andrew Carnegie Birthplace Museum   FREE

Moodie St KY12 7PL
☎ **01383 724302** 📠 **01383 749799**
e-mail: info@carnegiebirthplace.com
web: www.carnegiebirthplace.com
dir: 400yds S from Abbey

The museum tells the story of the handloom weaver's son, born here in 1835, who created the biggest steel works in the USA and then became a philanthropist on a huge scale. The present-day work of the philanthropic Carnegie Trust is also explained. 175th anniversary of the birth of Andrew Carnegie on 25th November 2010.

Times Open Apr-Oct, Mon-Sat 11-5, Sun 2-5. **Facilities** ℗ ℗ 🚻 ♿ (partly accessible) (cottage inaccessible, main hall and shop accessible) toilets for disabled shop ⊗

FALKLAND

Falkland Palace & Garden

KY15 7BU
☎ **0844 493 2186** 📠 **0844 493 2188**
e-mail: information@nts.org.uk
web: www.nts.org.uk
dir: off A912, 10m from M90, junct 8

The hunting palace of the Stuart monarchs, this fine building, with a French-Renaissance style south wing, stands in the shelter of the Lomond Hills. The beautiful Chapel Royal and King's Bedchamber are its most notable features, and it is also home to the oldest royal tennis court in Britain (1539). The garden has a spectacular delphinium border. Recorded sacred music is played hourly in the Chapel. Please telephone for details of concerts, recitals etc.

Times Palace & Garden: 2 Mar-Oct, Mon-Sat 10-5, Sun 1-5.* **Fees** £10.50 (concessions £7.50). Family £26 (1 Parent £20).* **Facilities** ℗ ℗ ♿ (partly accessible) (building not suitable for wheelchairs, some gravel paths in garden) shop ⊗ 🐾

KELLIE CASTLE & GARDENS

Kellie Castle & Gardens

KY10 2RF
☎ **0844 493 2184** 📠 **0844 493 2183**
e-mail: information@nts.org.uk
web: www.nts.org.uk
dir: On B9171, 3m NNW of Pittenweem

The oldest part dates from about 1360, but it is for its 16th and 17th-century domestic architecture (designed by Sir Robert Lorimer) that Kellie is renowned. It has notable plasterwork and painted panelling, and there are also interesting Victorian gardens.

Times Castle: 3 Apr-May & Sep-Oct, Fri-Tue 1-5; Jun-Aug, daily 1-5. Garden: same dates as Castle, 10-5.* **Fees** £8.50 (concessions £5.50). Family £21, (1 Parent £16).* **Facilities** ℗ 🚻 ⊞ (outdoor) toilets for disabled shop ⊗ 🐾

NORTH QUEENSFERRY

Deep Sea World

Forthside Ter KY11 1JR
☎ 01383 411880   📄 01383 410514
e-mail: info@deepseaworld.co.uk
web: www.deepseaworld.com/
dir: from N, M90 take exit for Inverkeithing. From S follow signs to Forth Rd Bridge, 1st exit left

The UK's longest underwater tunnel gives you a diver's eye view of an underwater world. Come face to face with Sand Tiger sharks, and watch divers hand-feed a wide array of sea life. Visit the Amazon Experience with ferocious piranhas and the amazing amphibian display featuring the world's most poisonous frog. Also featuring the Seal Sanctuary, dedicated to the rehabilitation and release of injured and orphaned seal pups. Please telephone or visit website for details of events running throughout the year.

Times Open all year, daily from 10. See website for seasonal closing times. **Fees** £11.75 (ch 3-15 £8, under 3 free, concessions £10). Family ticket discount available.* **Facilities** ❷ ℗ ☐ ☶ (outdoor) ♿ toilets for disabled shop ⊗

ST ANDREWS

Castle & Visitor Centre

KY16 9AR
☎ 01334 477196

This 13th-century stronghold castle was the scene of the murder of Cardinal Beaton in 1546. The new visitor centre incorporates an exciting multi-media exhibition describing the history of the castle and nearby cathedral.

Times Open all year, Apr-Sep, daily 9.30-6.30; Oct-Mar, daily 9.30-4.30. Closed 25-26 Dec & 1-2 Jan.* **Facilities** ℗ toilets for disabled shop ⊗

St Andrews Aquarium

The Scores KY16 9AS
☎ 01334 474786   📄 01334 475985
web: www.standrewsaquarium.co.uk
dir: signed in town centre

This continually expanding aquarium is home to shrimps, sharks, eels, octopi, seals and much much more. Special features include the Seahorse Parade, and the Sea Mammal Research Unit, which is committed to the care of sea mammals and their environment.

Times Open all year, daily from 10. Please phone for winter opening* **Facilities** ❷ ℗ ☐ ❢⊙❢ licensed ☶ toilets for disabled shop ⊗

CITY OF GLASGOW

GLASGOW

Burrell Collection   FREE

Pollok Country Park, 2060 Pollokshaws Rd G43 1AT
☎ 0141 287 2550   📄 0141 287 2597
e-mail: museums@csglasgow.org
web: www.glasgowmuseums.com
dir: 3.5m S of city centre, signposted from M77 junct 2

Set in Pollok Country Park, this award-winning building makes the priceless works of art on display seem almost part of the woodland setting. Shipping magnate Sir William Burrell's main interests were medieval Europe, Oriental art and European paintings. Colourful paintings and stained glass show the details of medieval life. Furniture, paintings, sculpture, armour and weapons help to complete the picture. Rugs, ceramics and metalwork represent the art of Islam. There is also a strong collection of Chinese and other Oriental ceramics. Paintings on display include works by Bellini, Rembrandt and the French Impressionists.

Times Open all year, Mon-Thu & Sat 10-5, Fri & Sun 11-5. Closed 25-26 & 31 (pm) Dec & 1-2 Jan **Facilities** ❷ ☐ ❢⊙❢ licensed ♿ toilets for disabled shop ⊗

Clydebuilt - Scottish Maritime Museum at Braehead

Braehead Shopping Centre, King Inch Rd G51 4BN
☎ 0141 886 1013 📄 0141 886 1015
e-mail: clydebuilt@scotmaritime.org.uk
web: www.scottishmaritimemuseum.org
dir: M8 junct 25A, 26, follow signs for Braehead Shopping Centre, then Green car park

On the banks of the River Clyde, home of the Scottish shipbuilding industry, visitors can discover how Glasgow's famous ships were built, from the design stages through to the launch. There are also displays on the textile and cotton industries, iron and steel, and tobacco. Hands-on activities allow you to operate a real ship's engine, become a ship's riveter, and steer a virtual ship up the Clyde. See the QE2 exhibition celebrating her last visit to the place of her birth.

Times Open all year, daily 10-5.30.* **Fees** £4.25 (ch £2.50, concessions £3). Family ticket £10.* **Facilities** ❷ Ⓟ ⴲ (outdoor) & toilets for disabled shop ⊗

Glasgow Botanic Gardens   FREE

730 Great Western Rd G12 0UE
☎ 0141 276 1614 📄 0141 276 1615
e-mail: gbg@land.glasgow.gov.uk
dir: From M8 junct 17 onto A82 Dumbarton. Approx 2-3m the Botanic Gardens are on the right

Home of the national collections of Dendrobium Orchids, Begonias and tree ferns, the Gardens consist of an arboretum, herbaceous borders, a herb garden, rose garden, and unusual vegetables. The Kibble Palace contains carnivorous plants, island flora and temperate plant collections.

Times Open all year. Gardens open daily 7-dusk. Glasshouses 10-6 (4.15 in winter).* **Facilities** Ⓟ toilets for disabled ⊗

Glasgow Science Centre

50 Pacific Quay G51 1EA
☎ 0141 420 5000 📄 0871 540 1006
e-mail: admin@glasgowsciencecentre.org
web: www.glasgowsciencecentre.org
dir: M8 junct 24 or M77 junct 21, follow brown signs, across Clyde from SECC

The centre is home to many entertaining and exciting attractions and contains hundreds of interactive exhibits apart from over 2 acres of science floors. Highlights include the Planetarium, Scotland's only IMAX cinema and the 127 metre Glasgow Tower, a remarkable free-standing structure that gives breathtaking views of the city (check availability before visiting). GSC presents the world of science and technology in new and exciting ways.

Times Open all year, 29 Oct-30 Mar, 10-5 Tue-Sun; 30 Mar-29 Oct daily 10-5.* **Fees** £8.25 (ch & concessions £6.25). Tower, Planetarium, & Imax Science Film £2.50 each.* **Facilities** ❷ Ⓟ ⴲ (indoor & outdoor) & toilets for disabled shop ⊗

Holmwood House

61-63 Netherlee House, Cathcart G44 3YG
☎ 0844 493 2204 📄 0844 493 2204
e-mail: information@nts.org.uk
web: www.nts.org.uk
dir: off Clarkston Rd

Completed in 1858, Holmwood is considered to be the finest domestic design by the architect Alexander 'Greek' Thomson. Many rooms are richly ornamented in wood, plaster and marble.

Times Open Apr-Oct, Thu-Mon 12-5.* **Fees** £5.50 (concessions £4.50). Family £15, (1 Parent £10).* **Facilities** ❷ Ⓟ ⴲ & (partly accessible) (access to first floor via lift) shop ⊗ ✻

House for an Art Lover

10 Dumbreck Rd, Bellahouston Park G41 5BW
☎ 0141 353 4770 📄 0141 353 4771
e-mail: info@houseforanartlover.co.uk
web: www.houseforanartlover.co.uk
dir: M8 W junct 23 signed B768, left at top of slip road onto Dumbreck Rd. Bellahouston Park on right

Inspired by a portfolio of drawings by Charles Rennie Mackintosh in 1901, this fascinating artistic attraction and private dining venue opened in 1996. Visitors can view the Mackintosh suite of rooms and learn from a DVD presentation about the development of the building and its contents. There is a full programme of changing art exhibitions, dinner concerts and afternoon musical recitals. Contact for more details.

Times Open all year, Apr-Sep, Mon-Wed 10-4 & Thu-Sun 10-1; Oct-Mar, Sat-Sun 10-1, telephone for wkday opening times.* **Fees** £4.50 (ch under 10 free, concessions £3).* **Facilities** ❷ ⏀ licensed & toilets for disabled shop ⊗

Scotland

City of Glasgow

Scotland

Glasgow continued

Hunterian Art Gallery   FREE

82 Hillhead St, The University of Glasgow G12 8QQ
☎ 0141 330 5431   📄 0141 330 3618
e-mail: hunter@museum.gla.ac.uk
web: www.hunterian.gla.ac.uk
dir: on University of Glasgow Campus in Hillhead District, 2m W of city centre

The founding collection is made up of paintings bequeathed in the 18th century by Dr William Hunter, including works by Rembrandt and Stubbs. The Gallery now has works by Whistler, major displays of paintings by the Scottish Colourists, and a graphics collection holding some 300,000 prints. A popular feature of the Charles Rennie Mackintosh collection is the re-construction of the interiors of The Mackintosh House.

Times Open all year, Mon-Sat 9.30-5. Telephone for BH closures.* **Facilities** Ⓟ ♿ toilets for disabled shop ⊗

Hunterian Museum   FREE

Gilbert Scott Building, The University of Glasgow G12 8QQ
☎ 0141 330 4221   📄 0141 330 3617
e-mail: hunter@museum.gla.ac.uk
web: www.hunterian.gla.ac.uk
dir: on University of Glasgow campus in Hillhead District, 2m W of city centre

Named after the 18th-century physician, Dr William Hunter, who bequeathed his large and important collections of coins, medals, fossils, geological specimens and archaeological and ethnographic items to the university. The exhibits are shown in the main building of the university, and temporary exhibitions are held.

Times Open all year, Mon-Sat 9.30-5. Closed certain BHs phone for details.* **Facilities** Ⓟ toilets for disabled shop ⊗

Kelvingrove Art Gallery & Museum

Argyle St G3 8AG
☎ 0141 276 9599   📄 0141 276 9540
e-mail: museums@csglasgow.org
web: www.glasgowmuseums.com
dir: 1m W of city centre

Glasgow's favourite building re-opened in July 2006 after a three-year, £35 million restoration project. On display are 8000 objects, including a Spitfire, a 4-metre ceratosaur and Salvador Dali's Christ of St John of the Cross. A new 'Mackintosh and the Glasgow Style Gallery' explores the genius of Charles Rennie Mackintosh. Exciting temporary exhibitions take place throughout the year. Organ recitals take place each day and there are a range of tours and activities available for all ages.

Times Open all year, Mon-Thu & Sat 10-5; Fri & Sun 11-5. Closed 25-26 Dec & 31 Dec (pm) & 1-2 Jan. **Fees** Free admission to venue & permanent displays, some exhibitions have an entrance fee. Please check website for details. **Facilities** Ⓟ Ⓟ ♿ ⑪ licensed 🪑 (outdoor) ♿ toilets for disabled shop ⊗

Museum of Transport   FREE

1 Bunhouse Rd G3 8DP
☎ 0141 287 2720   📄 0141 287 2692
e-mail: museums@csglasgow.org
web: www.glasgowmuseums.com
dir: 1.5m W of city centre

Visit the Museum of Transport and the first impression is of gleaming metalwork and bright paint. All around you there are cars, caravans, carriages and carts, fire engines, buses, steam locomotives, prams and trams. The museum uses its collections of vehicles and models to tell the story of transport by land and sea, with a unique Glasgow flavour. Visitors can even go window shopping along the recreated Kelvin Street of 1938. Upstairs 250 ship models tell the story of the great days of Clyde shipbuilding. The Museum of Transport has something for everyone.

Times Open all year, Mon-Thu & Sat 10-5, Fri & Sun 11-5 until Apr 2010 when museum closes due to collections moving to a new museum. **Facilities** Ⓟ Ⓟ ♿ ♿ toilets for disabled shop ⊗

People's Palace   FREE

Glasgow Green G40 1AT
☎ 0141 276 0788   📄 0141 276 0787
e-mail: museums@csglasgow.org
web: www.glasgowmuseums.com
dir: 1m SE of city centre

Glasgow grew from a medieval town located by the Cathedral to the Second City of the British Empire. Trade with the Americas, and later industry, made the city rich. But not everyone shared in Glasgow's wealth. The People's Palace on historic Glasgow Green shows how ordinary Glaswegians worked, lived and played. Visitors can discover how a family lived in a typical one-room Glasgow 'single end' tenement flat, see Billy Connolly's amazing banana boots, learn to speak Glesga, take a trip 'doon the watter' and visit the Winter Gardens.

Times Open all year, Mon-Thu & Sat 10-5, Fri & Sun 11-5. Closed 25-26 & 31 Dec (pm) & 1-2 Jan **Facilities** Ⓟ ♿ toilets for disabled shop ⊗

222

Scotland Street School Museum FREE

225 Scotland St G5 8QB
☎ 0141 287 0500   🖹 0141 287 0515
e-mail: museums@csglasgow.org
web: www.glasgowmuseums.com

Designed by Charles Rennie Mackintosh between 1903 and 1906 for the School Board of Glasgow, and now a museum telling the story of education in Scotland from 1872 to the late 20th century. Also hosts temporary exhibitions.

Times Open all year daily 10-5, Fri & Sun 11-5. (closed 25,26,31 Dec & pm 1 & 2 Jan) Facilities ℗ 🚻♿ toilets for disabled shop ⊗

The Tenement House

145 Buccleuch St, Garnethill G3 6QN
☎ 0844 493 2197   🖹 0844 493 2197
e-mail: information@nts.org.uk
web: www.nts.org.uk
dir: N of Charing Cross

This shows an unsung but once-typical side of Glasgow life: it is a first-floor flat, built in 1892, with a parlour, bedroom, kitchen and bathroom, furnished with the original recess beds, kitchen range, sink, and coal bunker, among other articles. The home of Agnes Toward from 1911 to 1965, the flat was bought by an actress who preserved it as a `time capsule'. The contents vividly portray the life of one section of Glasgow society.

Times Open Mar-Oct, daily 1-5.* Fees £5.50 (concessions £4.50). Family £15 (1 Parent £10).* Facilities ℗ ♿ (partly accessible) (steps to first floor) shop ⊗ ♨

BOAT OF GARTEN

RSPB Loch Garten Osprey Centre

RSPB Reserve Abernethy Forest, Forest Lodge, Nethybridge PH25 3EF
☎ 01479 821894   🖹 01479 821069
dir: signed from B970 & A9 at Aviemore, follow 'RSPB Ospreys' signs

Home of the Loch Garten Osprey site, this reserve holds one of the most important remnants of Scots Pine forest in the Highlands. Within its 30,760 acres are forest bogs, moorland, mountain top, lochs and crofting land. In addition to the regular pair of nesting ospreys, there are breeding Scottish crossbills, capercaillies, black grouse and many others. The ospreys can be viewed through telescopes and there is a live TV link to the nest. Please telephone for details of special events running throughout the year.

Times Osprey Centre open daily, Apr-Aug 10-6.* Facilities ℗ toilets for disabled shop ⊗

CARRBRIDGE

Landmark Forest Adventure Park

PH23 3AJ
☎ 01479 841613 & 0800 731 3446   🖹 01479 841384
e-mail: landmarkcentre@btconnect.com
web: www.landmark-centre.co.uk
dir: off A9 between Aviemore & Inverness

This innovative centre is designed to provide a fun and educational visit for all ages. Microworld takes a close-up look at the incredible microscopic world around us. There is a 70ft forest viewing tower and a treetop trail. There are also demonstrations of timber sawing, on a steam-powered sawmill and log hauling by a Clydesdale horse throughout the day. Attractions include a 3-track Watercoaster, a maze and a large covered adventure play area, mini electric cars and remote-controlled truck arena. New features include; 'RopeworX', the Tarzan Trail aerial highwire obstacle courses, and 'Skydive', a parachute jump simulator.

Times Open all year, daily, Apr-mid Jul 10-6; mid Jul-mid Aug 10-7; Sep-Oct 10-5.30; Nov-Mar 10-5. Closed 25 Dec, 1 Jan. Fees Apr-Oct £10.55 (ch & pen £8.25), Nov-Mar £3.50 (ch & pen £2.65). Facilities ❶ ℗ 🚻🍴 licensed ♿ (partly accessible) (all areas accessible, some attractions not suitable) toilets for disabled shop

DRUMNADROCHIT

Official Loch Ness Exhibition Centre, Loch Ness 2000

IV3 6TU
☎ 01456 450573 & 450218   📄 01456 450770
web: www.lochness.com
dir: on A82, 12m S Inverness

This award-winning centre has a fascinating and popular multi-media presentation lasting 30 minutes. Seven themed areas cover the story of the Loch Ness Monster, from the pre-history of Scotland, through the cultural roots of the legend in Highland folklore, and into the 50-year controversy which surrounds it. The centre uses the latest technology in computer animation, lasers and multi-media projection systems.

Times Open all year; Nov-end Jan, 10-3.30, Xmas hols 10-5, Feb-end May & Oct 9.30-5, Jun & Sep, 9-6, Jul & Aug 9-6.30*
Facilities 🅿 Ⓟ ⌑ 🍴 licensed 🪑 (outdoor) ♿ toilets for disabled shop ⊗

HELMSDALE

Timespan

Dunrobin St KW8 6JX
☎ 01431 821327   📄 01431 821058
e-mail: enquiries@timespan.org.uk
web: www.timespan.org.uk
dir: off A9 in centre of village, by Telford Bridge

Located in a historic fishing village, this museum relates to the social and natural history of the area, and the art gallery has changing exhibitions of contemporary art and works by local artists. The garden has over 100 varieties of herbs and plants. There is a gift shop, and a café with beautiful views of the Telford Bridge.

Times Open Etr-end Oct, Mon-Sat 10-5, Sun 12-5.* **Fees** £4 (ch £2, concessions £3). Family ticket £10.* **Facilities** 🅿 Ⓟ ⌑ ♿ toilets for disabled shop ⊗

KINCRAIG

Highland Wildlife Park

PH21 1NL
☎ 01540 651270   📄 01540 651236
e-mail: info@highlandwildlifepark.org
web: www.highlandwildlifepark.org
dir: on B9152, 7m S of Aviemore

As you drive through the main reserve, you can see awe-inspiring European bison grazing alongside wild horses, red deer and highland cattle plus a wide variety of other species. Then in the walk-round forest, woodland and moorland habitats prepare for close encounters with animals such as wolves, capercaillie, arctic foxes, wildcats, pine martens, otters and owls. Visit the snow monkeys in their beautiful lochside enclosure and the red pandas usually found climbing high up the trees.

Times Open all year, weather permitting. Apr-Oct, 10-5 (last entry 4); Nov-Mar 10-4. (Last entry 3).* **Fees** £11.50 (ch £8.75, concessions £9.50). Family ticket (2ad+2ch) £37; (2ad+3ch) £42.* **Facilities** 🅿 Ⓟ ⌑ 🪑 (outdoor) ♿ (partly accessible) (some steep inclines & rocky roads can restrict wheelchair access) toilets for disabled shop ⊗

NEWTONMORE

Highland Folk Museum   FREE

Aultlarie Croft PH20 1AY
☎ 01540 673551   📄 01540 673693
e-mail: highland.folk@highland.gov.uk
web: www.highlandfolk.com
dir: on A86, follow signs off A9

An early 18th-century farming township with turf houses has been reconstructed at this award-winning museum. A 1930s school houses old world maps, little wooden desks and a teacher rules! Other attractions include a working croft and tailor's workshop. Squirrels thrive in the pinewoods and there is an extensive play area at reception. A vintage bus runs throughout the site.

Times Open daily Etr-Aug, 10.30-5.30; Sep-Oct, 11-4.30.
Facilities 🅿 ⌑ 🪑 (outdoor) toilets for disabled shop ⊗

STRATHPEFFER

Highland Museum of Childhood

The Old Station IV14 9DH
☎ 01997 421031
e-mail: info@highlandmuseumofchildhood.org.uk
web: www.highlandmuseumofchildhood.org.uk
dir: 5m W of Dingwall on A834

Located in a renovated Victorian railway station of 1885, the museum tells the story of childhood in the Highlands amongst the crofters and townsfolk; a way of life recorded in oral testimony, displays and evocative photographs. An award-winning video, A Century of Highland Childhood is shown. There are also doll and toy collections.

Times Open Apr-Oct, daily 10-5, (Sun 2-5). Other times by arrangement. **Fees** £2.50 (ch £1.50, concessions £2). Family ticket (2ad+4ch) £6. **Facilities** 🅿 Ⓟ ⌑ 🪑 (outdoor) ♿ shop ⊗

WICK

Wick Heritage Museum

18-27 Bank Row KW1 5EY
☎ **01955 605393**   ▤ **01955 605393**
e-mail: museum@wickheritage.org
web: www.wickheritage.org
dir: close to the harbour

The heritage centre is near the harbour in a complex of eight houses, yards and outbuildings. The centre illustrates local history from Neolithic times to the herring fishing industry. In addition, there is a complete working 19th-century lighthouse, and the famous Johnston collection of photographs.

Times Open Apr-Oct, Mon-Sat 10-5, last admission 3.45. (Closed Sun).* **Facilities** ❷ ⊼ (outdoor) ♿ (partly accessible) toilets for disabled

MIDLOTHIAN

DALKEITH

Edinburgh Butterfly & Insect World

Dobbies Garden World, Mellville Nursery, Lasswade EH18 1AZ
☎ **0131 663 4932**   ▤ **0131 654 2774**
e-mail: info@edinburgh-butterfly-world.co.uk
web: www.edinburgh-butterfly-world.co.uk
dir: 0.5m S of Edinburgh city bypass at Gilmerton exit or at Sherrifhall rdbt

Rich coloured butterflies from all over the world can be seen flying among exotic rainforest plants, trees and flowers. The tropical pools are filled with giant waterlilies, colourful fish and are surrounded by lush vegetation. There are daily animal handling sessions and opportunities to see the leaf-cutting ants, scorpions, poison frogs, snakes, tarantulas and other remarkable creatures. There is also a unique honeybee hive that can be visited in season. 2010 is the 25th anniversary.

Times Open all year, summer daily 9.30-5.30; winter daily 10-5. Closed 25-26 Dec & 1 Jan. **Fees** £6.50 (ch 3-15 £4.50, concessions £5.50). Family ticket from £21 (2ad+2ch). Party

rates. **Facilities** ❷ ⎚ ⍾ licensed ⊼ (outdoor) ♿ toilets for disabled shop ⊗

NEWTONGRANGE

Scottish Mining Museum

Lady Victoria Colliery EH22 4QN
☎ **0131 663 7519**   ▤ **0131 654 0952**
e-mail: visitorservices@scottishminingmuseum.com
web: www.scottishminingmuseum.com
dir: 10m S of Edinburgh on A7, signed from bypass

Based at Scotland's National Coalmining Museum offering an outstanding visit to Britains' finest Victorian colliery. Guided tours with miners, magic helmets, exhibitions, theatres, interactive displays and a visit to the coal face. Home to Scotland's largest steam engine.

Times Open all year, daily Mar-Oct, 10-5. Nov-Feb, daily, 10-4.*
Fees £6.50 (ch & concessions £4.50). Family ticket £19.95. Party 12+ (£5.50, ch £3.50)* **Facilities** ❷ ℗ ⎚ ⍾ licensed ⊼ (outdoor) ♿ toilets for disabled shop ⊗

MORAY

SPEY BAY

The WDCS Wildlife Centre   FREE

IV32 7PJ
☎ **01343 829109**   ▤ **01343 829065**
e-mail: enquiries@mfwc.co.uk
web: www.mfwc.co.uk
dir: off A96 onto B9014 at Fochabers, follow road approx 5m to village of Spey Bay. Turn left at Spey Bay Hotel and follow road for 500mtrs

The centre, owned and operated by the Whale and Dolphin Conservation Society, lies at the mouth of the River Spey and is housed in a former salmon fishing station, built in 1768. There is a free exhibition about the Moray Firth dolphins and the wildlife of Spey Bay. Visitors can browse through a well-stocked gift shop and enjoy refreshments in the cosy tea room.

Times Open Apr-Oct 10.30-5. Check for winter opening times*
Facilities ❷ ℗ ⎚ ⊼ (outdoor) toilets for disabled shop ⊗

Scotland

NORTH AYRSHIRE

LARGS

Kelburn Castle and Country Centre

Fairlie KA29 0BE
☎ 01475 568685   📄 01475 568121
e-mail: admin@kelburncountrycentre.com
web: www.kelburncountrycentre.com
dir: 2m S of Largs, on A78

Historic home of the Earls of Glasgow, Kelburn is famous for its romantic Glen, family gardens, unique trees and spectacular views over the Firth of Clyde. Glen walks, riding and trekking centre, adventure course, Kelburn Story Cartoon Exhibition and a family museum. The "Secret Forest" at the centre, Scotland's most unusual attraction, is a chance to explore the Giant's Castle, maze of the Green Man and secret grotto. Also included is an indoor Sawmill Adventure Playground.

Times Open all year, Etr-end Oct, daily 10-6; Nov-Mar, 11-dusk. Grounds and Adventure Playbarn, wknds only* **Fees** £7.50 (ch & concessions £5) Family ticket £25.* **Facilities** 🅿 Ⓟ 🛒🍽 licensed 🍴 (outdoor) ♿ (partly accessible) (wheelchair access limited to main square area) toilets for disabled shop

NORTH LANARKSHIRE

COATBRIDGE

Summerlee Industrial Museum   FREE

Heritage Way, West Canal St ML5 1QD
☎ 01236 638460   📄 01236 638454
e-mail: museums@northlan.gov.uk
web: www.visitlanarkshire.com/summerlee
dir: follow main routes towards town centre, adjacent to Coatbridge central station

A 20-acre museum of social and industrial history centering on the remains of the Summerlee Ironworks which were put into blast in the 1830s. The exhibition hall features displays of social and industrial history including working machinery, hands-on activities and recreated workshop interiors. Outside, Summerlee operates the only working tram in Scotland, a coal mine and reconstructed miners' rows with interiors dating from 1840.

Times Open summer 10-5, winter 10-4. **Facilities** 🅿 Ⓟ 🛒🍴 (outdoor) ♿ (partly accessible) (coal mine tour not accessible, miner's cottages narrow doors and single step) toilets for disabled shop 🚫

MOTHERWELL

Motherwell Heritage Centre   FREE

High Rd ML1 3HU
☎ 01698 251000   📄 01698 268867
e-mail: museums@northlan.gov.uk
web: www.nlcmuseums.bravehost.com
dir: A723 for town centre. Left at top of hill, after pedestrian crossing and just before railway bridge

This award-winning audio-visual experience, 'Technopolis', traces the history of the area from Roman times to the rise of 19th-century industry and the post-industrial era. There is also a fine viewing tower, an exhibition gallery and family history research facilities. A mixed programme of community events and touring exhibitions occur throughout the year.

Times Open all year Wed-Sat 10-5 (Thu 10-7), Sun 12-5. Also open BHs. Local studies library closed Sun* **Facilities** 🅿 Ⓟ ♿ toilets for disabled shop 🚫

PERTH & KINROSS

BLAIR ATHOLL

Blair Castle

PH18 5TL
☎ 01796 481207   📄 01796 481487
e-mail: office@blair-castle.co.uk
web: www.blair-castle.co.uk
dir: 7m NW of Pitlochry, off A9 at Blair Atholl & follow signs to attraction

Blair Castle is at the heart of the Atholl Estates set among glorious Highland scenery. The castle has been the ancient seat of the Dukes and Earls of Atholl for almost 740 years and is home to the Atholl Highlanders, Europe's only remaining private army. There are 30 rooms open to visitors, as well as historic gardens and grounds which include a magnificent walled garden, a peaceful wooded grove, a ruined Celtic Kirk, a red deer park and a whimsical gothic folly. Children will also enjoy the castle's woodland adventure playground. Highland Games in May, Horse Trials and Country Fair in August.

Times Open daily Etr-end Oct, 9.30-5.30 (last admission 4.30).
Fees £8.25 (ch £5.10, pen £7.20). Family ticket £22.50.*
Facilities ℗ ⚏ 🍽 licensed ⛱ (outdoor) ♿ (partly accessible)
(access to ground floor only) shop ⊗

KINROSS

RSPB Nature Reserve Vane Farm

By Loch Leven KY13 9LX
☎ 01577 862355   📠 01577 862013
e-mail: vane.farm@rspb.org.uk
web: www.rspb.org.uk
dir: 2m E of M90 junct 5, on S shore of Loch Leven, entered off
B9097 to Glenrothes

Well placed beside Loch Leven, with a heritage trail to Kinross,
hides overlooking the Loch and a woodland trail with stunning
panoramic views. Noted for its pink-footed geese. The area
also attracts whooper swans, greylag geese and great spotted
woodpeckers amongst others. Details of special events are
available from the Visitors' Centre and the RSPB website.

Times Open all year daily, 10-5. Closed 25-26 Dec & 1-2
Jan.* **Fees** £3 (ch 50p, concessions £2). Family ticket £6. RSPB
members free.* **Facilities** ℗ ⚏ ⛱ (outdoor) ♿ (partly accessible)
(Visitor Centre accessible but not reserve without assistance)
toilets for disabled shop ⊗

PERTH

Caithness Glass Factory & Visitor Centre   FREE

Inveralmond PH1 3TZ
☎ 01738 492320   📠 01738 492300
e-mail: visitorcentre@caithnessglass.co.uk
web: www.caithnessglass.co.uk
dir: on Perth Western Bypass, A9, at Inveralmond Roundabout

All aspects of paperweight-making can be seen from the
purpose-built viewing galleries. Visitors can now enter the
glasshouse on a route which enables them to watch the
glassmakers closely. There are talks in the glasshouse regularly
throughout the day from Monday to Friday. There is also a
factory shop, a best shop, children's play area and tourist
information centre with internet access.

Times Open all year, Factory shop & restaurant Mon-Sat 9-5, Sun
10-5 (Jan-Feb 12-5). Glassmaking Mon-Sun 9-4.30.* **Facilities**
℗ 🍽 licensed ⛱ (outdoor) ♿ toilets for disabled shop ⊗

PITLOCHRY

Scottish Hydro Electric Visitor Centre, Dam & Fish Pass   FREE

PH16 5ND
☎ 01796 473152   📠 01796 473152
dir: off A9, 24m N of Perth

The visitor centre features an exhibition showing how
electricity is brought from the power station to the customer,
and there is access to the turbine viewing gallery. The salmon
ladder viewing chamber allows you to see the fish as they
travel upstream to their spawning ground.

Times Open Apr-Oct, Mon-Fri 10-5. Wknd opening Jul, Aug &
BHs **Facilities** ℗ ♿ ♿ (partly accessible) (access to shop only)
toilets for disabled shop ⊗

SCONE

Scone Palace

PH2 6BD
☎ 01738 552300   📠 01738 552588
e-mail: visits@scone-palace.co.uk
web: www.scone-palace.co.uk
dir: 2m NE of Perth on A93

Visit Scone Palace, the crowning place of Scottish Kings and
the home of the Earls of Mansfield. The Palace dates from 1803
but incorporates 16th century and earlier buildings, and is a
unique treasury of furniture, fine art and other objets d'art. As
well as beautiful gardens the grounds are home to the Murray
Star Maze, the Pinetum, an adventure playground, livestock,
Highland cattle and champion trees.

Times Open Apr-Oct, daily 9.30-5.30, Sat last admission 4.
Fees Palace & Grounds £8.50 (ch £5.30, concessions £7.30).
Family ticket £24. Grounds only £4.80 (ch £3.20, concessions
£4.20). Group £7.30 (ch £4.80 concessions £6.30)* **Facilities** ℗
⚏ 🍽 licensed ⛱ (outdoor) ♿ toilets for disabled shop ⊗

Scotland

RENFREWSHIRE

LANGBANK

Finlaystone Country Estate

PA14 6TJ
☎ 01475 540505 📄 01475 540505
e-mail: info@finlaystone.co.uk
web: www.finlaystone.co.uk
dir: off A8 W of Langbank, 10m W of Glasgow Airport, follow Thistle signs

A beautiful country estate with historic formal gardens which are renowned for their natural beauty, with extensive woodland walks, picnic, BBQ and play areas. A tea room in the old walled garden, a gift shop and The 'Dolly Mixture', an international collection of dolls, can be seen in the Visitor Centre.

Times Open all year. Woodland & Gardens daily, 10-5 (winter 12-4).* **Fees** Garden & Woods £4 (ch & pen £2.50). 'The Dolly Mixture' Doll Museum free.* **Facilities** ❷ 🖵 🍴 (outdoor) ♿ (partly accessible) (gardens and most walks accessible for wheelchairs) toilets for disabled shop

LOCHWINNOCH

RSPB Lochwinnoch Nature Reserve

Largs Rd PA12 4JF
☎ 01505 842663 📄 01505 843026
e-mail: lochwinnoch@rspb.org.uk
web: www.rspb.org.uk/reserves/lochwinnoch
dir: on A760, Largs road, opposite Lochwinnoch station, 16m SW of Glasgow

The reserve, part of Clyde Muirshiel Regional Park and a Site of Special Scientific Interest, comprises two shallow lochs fringed by marsh which in turn is fringed by scrub and woodland. There are two trails with hides and a visitor centre with a viewing area. Please visit website for details of events running throughout the year.

Times Open all year, daily 10-5. Closed 1-2 Jan & 25-26 Dec.
Fees Trails £2 (concessions £1, ch 50p). Family ticket £4.
Facilities ❷ ℗ 🍴 (outdoor) ♿ (partly accessible) (trails and hides all accessible, tower inaccessible) toilets for disabled shop

SCOTTISH BORDERS

COLDSTREAM

The Hirsel

Douglas & Angus Estates, Estate Office, The Hirsel TD12 4LP
☎ 01890 830279 & 7 830293 📄 01890 830279
e-mail: john.letham2@btinternet.com
web: www.hirselcountrypark.co.uk
dir: 0.5m W on A697, on N outskirts of Coldstream

The seat of the Home family, the grounds of which are open all year. The focal point is the Homestead Museum, craft centre and workshops. From there, nature trails lead around the lake, along the Leet Valley and into woodland noted for its rhododendrons and azaleas.

Times Garden & Grounds open all year, daylight hours. Museum 10-5. Craft Centre Mon-Fri, 10-5, wknds noon-5.* **Fees** £2.50 per car* **Facilities** ❷ 🖵 🍴 licensed 🍴 (outdoor) ♿ toilets for disabled shop ⊗

INNERLEITHEN

Robert Smail's Printing Works

7/9 High St EH44 6HA
☎ 0844 493 2259
e-mail: information@nts.org.uk
web: www.nts.org.uk
dir: 30m S of Edinburgh, A272, 6m from Peebles. (Innerleithen Road)

These buildings contain a Victorian office, a paper store with reconstructed waterwheel, a composing room and a press room. The machinery is in full working order and visitors may view the printer at work and experience typesetting in the composing room.

Times Open 2 Apr-Oct , Thu-Mon 12-5, Sun 1-5.* **Fees** £5.50 (concessions £4.50). Family £15 (1 Parent £10).* **Facilities** ℗ ♿ (partly accessible) (stairs to caseroom) shop ⊗ 🍴

Bowhill House and Country Estate

TD7 5ET
☎ 01750 22204   📄 01750 23893
e-mail: bht@buccleuch.com
web: www.bowhill.org
dir: 3m W of Selkirk off A708

An outstanding collection of pictures, including works by Van Dyck, Canaletto, Reynolds, Gainsborough and Claude Lorraine are displayed here. Memorabilia and relics of people such as Queen Victoria and Sir Walter Scott, and a restored Victorian kitchen add further interest inside the house. Outside, the wooded grounds are perfect for walking. A small theatre provides a full programme of music and drama.

Times House open: daily Jul 11-5 (last entry 4); Aug Guided Tours only 2 & 3.30. Park open: Apr-Jun, 10-5 wknd and BHs only; Jul-Aug daily 10-5.* **Fees** House & grounds £7 (ch under 3 free, pen & groups £5). Grounds only £3.* **Facilities** 🅿 ⛶ 🍴 licensed ᴘ (outdoor) ♿ toilets for disabled shop ⊗

Halliwells House Museum   FREE

Halliwells Close, Market Place TD7 4BC
☎ 01750 20096   📄 01750 23282
e-mail: museums@scotborders.gov.uk
dir: off A7 in town centre

A row of late 18th-century town cottages converted into a museum. Displays recreate the building's former use as an ironmonger's shop and home, and tell the story of the Royal Burgh of Selkirk. The Robson Gallery hosts a programme of contemporary art and craft exhibitions.

Times Open Apr-Sep, Mon-Sat 10-5, Sun 10-12; Jul-Aug, Mon-Sat 10-5.30, Sun 10-12; Oct, Mon-Sat 10-4.* **Facilities** 🅿 🅿 ♿ toilets for disabled shop ⊗

Traquair House

EH44 6PW
☎ 01896 830323   📄 01896 830639
e-mail: enquiries@traquair.co.uk
web: www.traquair.co.uk
dir: at Innerleithen take B709, house in 1m

Said to be Scotland's oldest inhabited house, dating back to the 12th century, 27 Scottish monarchs have stayed at Traquair House. William the Lion Heart held court here, and the house has associations with Mary, Queen of Scots and the Jacobite risings. The Bear Gates were closed in 1745, not to be reopened until the Stuarts should once again ascend the throne. There is a maze and woodland walks by the River Tweed, craft workshops and a children's adventure playground. Also an 18th-century working brewery with museum shop and tastings. Award-winning 1745 Cottage Restaurant open for lunches and teas.

Times Open daily Apr-May & Sep 12-5, Jun-Aug 10.30-5, Oct 11-4, Nov 11-3 (wknds only). **Fees** House & Grounds £7.50 (ch £4, pen £6.80). Family £21. Grounds only £4 (concessions £2.50). **Facilities** 🅿 ⛶ 🍴 licensed ᴘ (outdoor) ♿ (partly accessible) (ground floor of house only accessible) toilets for disabled shop

SOUTH AYRSHIRE

ALLOWAY

Burns National Heritage Park

Murdoch's Lone KA7 4PQ
☎ 01292 443700 📄 01292 441750
e-mail: info@burnsheritagepark.com
web: www.burnsheritagepark.com
dir: 2m S of Ayr

The birthplace of Robert Burns, Scotland's National Poet set in the gardens and countryside of Alloway. An introduction to the life of Robert Burns, with an audio-visual presentation - a multi-screen 3D experience describing the Tale of Tam O'Shanter. This attraction consists of the museum, Burn's Cottage, visitor centre, tranquil landscaped gardens and historical monuments. Please telephone for further details.

Times Open all year, Apr-Sep 10-5.30, Oct-Mar 10-5. Closed 25-26 Dec & 1-2 Jan* **Facilities** ❷ ℗ ⬚ ⍟ licensed ⅙ (partly accessible) (access limited in some parts of property) toilets for disabled shop ⊗

CULZEAN CASTLE

Culzean Castle & Country Park

KA19 8LE
☎ 0844 493 2149 📄 0844 493 2150
e-mail: information@nts.org.uk
web: www.nts.org.uk
dir: 4m W of Maybole, off A77, 12m S of Ayr

This 18th-century castle stands on a cliff in spacious grounds and was designed by Robert Adam for the Earl of Cassillis. It is noted for its oval staircase, circular drawing room and plasterwork. The Eisenhower Room explores the American General's links with Culzean. The 563-acre country park has a wide range of attractions - shoreline, woodland walks, parkland, an adventure playground and gardens.

Times Castle, Visitor centre & other facilities: Apr-1 Nov, daily 10.30-5 (last entry 4). (Visitor centre off season: 2 Nov-29 Mar, Sat-Sun 11-4). Walled garden: all year, daily 9.30-5 (sunset if earlier). Country Park: open all year 9.30-sunset.* **Fees** £13 (concessions £9). Family £32 (1 Parent £25). Country Park only: £8.50 (concessions £5.50). Family £21 (1 Parent £16).* **Facilities** ❷ ⬚ ⍟ licensed ⊟ (outdoor) ⅙ (partly accessible) toilets for disabled shop ⊗ ⍟

SOUTH LANARKSHIRE

BLANTYRE

David Livingstone Centre

165 Station Rd G72 9BT
☎ 0844 493 2207 📄 0844 493 2206
e-mail: information@nts.org.uk
web: www.nts.org.uk
dir: M74 junct 5 onto A725, then A724, follow signs for Blantyre, right at lights. Centre is at foot of hill

Share the adventurous life of Scotland's greatest explorer, from his childhood in the Blantyre Mills to his explorations in the heart of Africa, dramatically illustrated in the historic tenement where he was born. Various events are planned throughout the season.

Times Open Apr-24 Dec, Mon-Sat 10-5, Sun 12.30-5.*
Fees £5.50 (concessions £4.50) Family £15 (1 Parent £10).*
Facilities ❷ ℗ ⬚ ⊟ ⅙ toilets for disabled shop ⊗ ⍟

EAST KILBRIDE

National Museum of Rural Life Scotland

Wester Kittochside, Philipshill Rd, (off Stewartfield Way) G76 9HR
☎ 0131 225 7534
e-mail: info@nms.ac.uk
web: www.nms.ac.uk/rural
dir: From Glasgow take A749 to East Kilbride. From Edinburgh follow M8 to Glasgow, turn off junct 6 onto A725 to East Kilbride. Kittochside is signed before East Kilbride

Get a healthy dose of fresh air. Take in the sights, sounds and smells as you explore this 170-acre farm. Discover what life was like for country people in the past and how this has shaped Scotland's countryside today. Would you cope with life on a 1950s farm? Try milking 'Clover' by hand, hitch a ride on the farm explorer, meet Mairi the horse and the sheep, cows and hens. See the website for details of a wide range of special events and exhibitions.

Times Open daily 10-5. (Closed 25-26 Dec & 1Jan). **Fees** £5.50 (ch under 12 free, concessions £4.50) NMS and NTS members free. Charge for some events.* **Facilities** ❷ ℗ ⬚ ⊟ (outdoor) ⅙ (partly accessible) (wheelchair users have access to ground floor of farmhouse only, some steep paths) toilets for disabled shop ⊗

Scotland

NEW LANARK

New Lanark Visitor Centre

Mill 3, New Lanark Mills ML11 9DB
☎ **01555 661345** ▤ **01555 665738**
e-mail: trust@newlanark.org
web: www.newlanark.org
dir: 1m S of Lanark. Signed from all major routes. Less than 1hr from Glasgow (M74/A72) and Edinburgh (A70).

Founded in 1785, New Lanark became well known in the early 19th century as a model community managed by enlightened industrialist and educational reformer Robert Owen. Surrounded by woodland and situated close to the Falls of Clyde, this unique world heritage site explores the philosophies of Robert Owen, using theatre, interactive displays, and the 'Millennium Experience', a magical ride through history. (Accommodation is available at the New Lanark Mill Hotel, and there's also a Youth Hostel.) Delicious meals and home-baking are available at the Mill Pantry, and the village is also home to the Scottish Wildlife Trust's Falls of Clyde Reserve. A wide variety of exciting, fun and educational events take place every year. There is a new roof garden and viewing platform which provides a bird's eye view of this historic village and surrounding woodland.

Times Open all year daily. Jun-Aug 10.30-5; Sep-May 11-5. Closed 25 Dec & 1 Jan. **Fees** £6.95 (ch, concessions £5.95). Family ticket (2ad+2ch) £21.95. Family ticket (2ad+4ch) £27.95.* **Facilities** ❶ ⏥ ⦿ licensed ☒ (outdoor) ♿ toilets for disabled shop ⊗

STIRLING

BANNOCKBURN

Bannockburn

Glasgow Rd FK7 0LJ
☎ **0844 493 2139** ▤ **0844 493 2138**
e-mail: information@nts.org.uk
web: www.nts.org.uk
dir: 2m S of Stirling off M80/M9 junct 9, on A872

The Heritage Centre stands close to what is traditionally believed to have been Robert the Bruce's command post before the 1314 Battle of Bannockburn, a famous victory for the Scots and a turning point in Scottish history.

Times Heritage Centre 2 Mar-Oct daily, 10-5. Grounds all year daily, until dusk.* **Fees** £5.50 (concession £4.50) Family £15 (1 Parent £10).* **Facilities** ❶ ⏥ ♿ (partly accessible) toilets for disabled shop ⊗ ⥮

BLAIR DRUMMOND

Blair Drummond Safari & Leisure Park

FK9 4UR
☎ **01786 841456 & 841396** ▤ **01786 841491**
e-mail: enquiries@blairdrummond.com
web: www.blairdrummond.com
dir: M9 junct 10, 4m on A84 towards Callander

Drive through the wild animal reserves where zebras, North American bison, antelope, lions, tigers, white rhino and camels can be seen at close range. Other attractions include the sea lion show, a ride on the boat safari through the waterfowl sanctuary and around Chimpanzee Island, an adventure playground, giant astraglide, and pedal boats. There are also African elephants, giraffes and ostriches.

Times Open 19 Mar-3 Oct, daily 10-5.30. (Last admission 4.30)* **Facilities** ❶ ⏥ ⦿ licensed ☒ (outdoor) toilets for disabled shop ⊗

STIRLING

Stirling Castle

Upper Castle Hill FK8 1EJ
☎ **01786 450000**
web: www.historic-scotland.gov.uk

Sitting on top of a 250ft rock, Stirling Castle has a strategic position on the Firth of Forth. As a result it has been the scene of many events in Scotland's history. James II was born at the castle in 1430. Mary, Queen of Scots spent some years there, and it was James IV's childhood home. Among its finest features are the splendid Renaissance palace built by James V, and the Chapel Royal, rebuilt by James VI.

Times Open all year, Apr-Sep, daily 9.30-6; Oct-Mar, daily 9.30-5. Closed 25-26.* **Fees** £9 (ch £4.50, concessions £7). Please phone or check website for further details.* **Facilities** ❶ ⦿ licensed ☒ toilets for disabled shop ⊗ ▮

Stirling Old Town Jail

Saint John St FK8 1EA
☎ **01786 450050** ▤ **01786 471301**
e-mail: info@oldtownjail.com
web: www.oldtownjail.com
dir: Located on St John's St (main route to Stirling Castle)

Step inside an authentic Victorian jail at the heart of historic Stirling for a fascinating live prison tour. You'll meet the warden, the convict desperate to escape, and even the hangman. Look out from the rooftop viewpoint for a wonderful view, visit the exhibition area, and just for children, join the Beastie Hunt.

Times Open 8 Jun-1 Nov daily 10-5.* **Fees** £5-£5.95 (ch £3.20-£3.80, concessions £3.80-£4.50). Family ticket £13.25-£15.70.* **Facilities** ❶ Ⓟ ⏥ toilets for disabled shop ⊗

WEST LOTHIAN

LIVINGSTON

Almond Valley Heritage Trust

Millfield EH54 7AR
☎ 01506 414957 🖹 01506 497771
e-mail: info@almondvalley.co.uk
web: www.almondvalley.co.uk
dir: 2m from M8 junct 3

A combination of fun and educational potential ideal for children, Almond Valley has a petting zoo of farm animals, an interactive museum on the shale oil industry, a narrow gauge railway, and tractor rides. Please telephone for details of events running throughout the year.

Times Open all year, daily 10-5. Closed Dec 25-26, Jan 1-2. **Fees** £5 (ch £3.50). Family (2ad+4ch) £17. **Facilities** 🅿 ☕ 🍴 (indoor & outdoor) ♿ toilets for disabled shop

SCOTTISH ISLANDS

ISLE OF ARRAN

BRODICK

Brodick Castle, Garden & Country Park

KA27 8HY
☎ 0844 493 2152 🖹 0844 493 2153
e-mail: information@nts.org.uk
web: www.nts.org.uk
dir: Ferry from Ardrossan-Brodick or Lochranza-Kintyre - frequent in summer, limited in winter

The site has been fortified since Viking times, but the present castle dating from the 13th century was a stronghold of the Dukes of Hamilton. Splendid silver, fine porcelain and paintings acquired by generations of owners can be seen, including many sporting pictures and trophies. There is a magnificent woodland garden, started by the Duchess of Montrose in 1923, world famous for its rhododendrons and azaleas.

Times Castle Apr-Oct, Sun-Thu 11-4, (closed at 3 in Oct). Country Park all year, daily 9.30-sunset. Reception Centre, Walled Garden & shop Apr-Oct, daily 10-4.30, Nov-21 Dec, Fri-Sun 10-3.30. Goatfell all year, daily.* **Fees** £10.50 (concessions £7.50). Family £26 (1 Parent £20).* **Facilities** 🅿 🍽 licensed 🍴 ♿ (partly accessible) (access limited to ground floor castle & some areas of the garden unsuitable for wheelchairs) toilets for disabled shop 🚫 ❦

Isle of Arran Heritage Museum

Rosaburn KA27 8DP
☎ 01770 302636
e-mail: tom.macleod@arranmuseum.co.uk
web: www.arranmuseum.co.uk
dir: right at Brodick Pier, approx 1m

The setting is an 18th-century croft farm, including a cottage restored to its pre-1920 state and a 'smiddy' where a blacksmith worked until the late 1960s. There are also several demonstrations of horse-shoeing, sheep-shearing and weaving and spinning throughout the season - please ring for details. There is a large archaeology and geology section with archive, where help with research is available. Also, a school room set in the 1940's and a new geology display which reflects the importance of Arran in geological terms.

Times Open Apr-Oct, daily 10.30-4.30. **Fees** £3 (ch £1.50, pen £2). Family £7. **Facilities** 🅿 ☕ 🍴 (outdoor) toilets for disabled shop 🚫

St Govan's Chapel, Pembrokeshire

Wales

Wales

ISLE OF ANGLESEY

BRYNSIENCYN

Anglesey Sea Zoo

LL61 6TQ
☎ **01248 430411** 📄 **01248 430213**
e-mail: info@angleseyseazoo.co.uk
web: www.angleseyseazoo.co.uk
dir: 1st turning off Britannia Bridge onto Anglesey then follow Lobster signs along A4080 to zoo

Nestling by the Menai Straits, this all-weather undercover attraction contains a shipwreck bristling with conger eels, a lobster hatchery, a seahorse nursery, crashing waves and the enchanting fish forest.

Times Open Feb half term-late Oct half term. Telephone for times.* **Facilities** 🅿 🅟 ⊑🍴 licensed 🪑 (outdoor) toilets for disabled shop ⊗

HOLYHEAD

RSPB Nature Reserve
South Stack Cliffs   FREE

Plas Nico, South Stack LL65 1YH
☎ **01407 764973**
e-mail: south.stack@rspb.org.uk
web: www.rspb.org.uk/reserves/southstack
dir: A5 or A55 to Holyhead follow town centre then follow brown heritage signs

South Stack Cliffs is an expanse of heathland with dramatic sea cliffs and tremendous views. In summer breeding seabirds, including puffins, can be seen from the Information Centre at Ellins Tower where telescopes are provided and staff are on hand to help. There are also large screen televisions displaying live images of the seabirds which staff can control from the information centre to give visitors an amazing 'Big Brother' type view of the breeding seabirds.

Times Open: Information Centre daily, Etr-Sep, 10-5.30. Reserve open daily at all times. **Facilities** 🅿 🅟 ♿ (partly accessible) (natural surface paths and tracks) toilets for disabled

PLAS NEWYDD

Plas Newydd

LL61 6DQ
☎ **01248 714795** 📄 **01248 713673**
e-mail: plasnewydd@nationaltrust.org.uk
web: www.nationaltrust.org.uk
dir: 2m S of Llanfairpwll, on A4080

Set amidst breathtakingly beautiful scenery and with spectacular views of Snowdonia, this elegant 18th-century house was built by James Wyatt and is an interesting mixture of Classical and Gothic. The comfortable interior, restyled in the 1930s, is famous for its association with Rex Whistler, whose largest painting is here. There is also an exhibition about his work. A military museum contains campaign relics of the 1st Marquess of Anglesey, who commanded the cavalry at the Battle of Waterloo. There is a fine spring garden and Australasian arboretum with an understorey of shrubs and wild flowers, as well as a summer terrace and, later, massed hydrangeas and autumn colour. A woodland walk gives access to a marine walk on the Menai Strait.

Times Open Apr-Oct, Sat-Wed. House 12-5, Garden 11-5.30. (Last admission 4.30)* **Facilities** 🅿 ⊑ 🪑 (outdoor) ♿ (partly accessible) (ground floor accessible for manual wheelchairs) toilets for disabled shop ⊗ 🐾

CAERPHILLY

CAERPHILLY

Caerphilly Castle

CF8 1JL
☎ **029 2088 3143**
web: www.cadw.wales.gov.uk
dir: on A469

The concentrically planned castle was begun in 1268 by Gilbert de Clare and completed in 1326. It is the largest in Wales, and has extensive land and water defences. A unique feature is the ruined tower - the victim of subsidence - which manages to out-lean even Pisa! The south dam platform, once a tournament-field, now displays replica medieval siege-engines.

Times Openall year, Apr-Oct, daily 9-5; Nov-Mar, Mon-Sat 9.30-4, Sun 11-4.* **Fees** £3.60 (ch 5-15, concessions £3.20, disabled visitors and assisting companion free). Family ticket (2ad+all ch/grandch under 16) £10.40. Group rates available. Please contact or visit website for most recent prices. **Facilities** 🅿 shop ⊗ ❁

Llancaiach Fawr Manor

Gelligaer Rd, Nelson CF46 6ER
☎ **01443 412248**   📠 **01443 412688**
e-mail: llancaiachfawr@caerphilly.gov.uk
web: www.llancaiachfawr.co.uk
dir: M4 junct 32, A470 to Merthyr Tydfil. Towards Ystrad Mynach
A472, follow brown heritage signs

Step back in time to the Civil War period at this fascinating
living history museum. The year is 1645 and visitors are invited
into the Manor to meet the servants of 'Colonel' Edward
Prichard - from the puritanical to the gossipy. Please telephone
for details of events running throughout the year.

Times Open daily 10-5 (last admission 1hr before closing). Closed
Mon, Nov-Feb and 24 Dec-1 Jan **Fees** £6 (ch £4.50, concessions
£5). Family (2ad+2ch) £18.* **Facilities** ℗ 🍽 licensed 🛏
(outdoor) ♿ (partly accessible) (2nd & 3rd floors not accessible as
no lift) toilets for disabled shop ⊗

CWMCARN

Cwmcarn Forest & Campsite

Nantcarn Rd NP11 7FA
☎ **01495 272001**   📠 **01495 279306**
e-mail: cwmcarn-vc@caerphilly.gov.uk
web: www.cwmcarnforest.co.uk
dir: 8m N of Newport on A467, follow brown tourist signs

A seven-mile scenic drive with spectacular views over the
Bristol Channel and surrounding countryside. Facilities include
barbecues, picnic and play areas, and forest and mountain
walks. There is also a mountain bike trail and downhill trail on
site. Special events are held throughout the year, please ring
for details or visit the website.

Times Open Forest Drive: Mar & Oct 11-5; Apr-Aug 11-7 (11-9
wknds during Jul & Aug); Sep, 11-6; Nov-Feb 11-4 (wknds only).
Visitor Centre open daily; Etr-Sep Mon-Thu 9-5, Fri-Sun 9-5; Oct-
Etr, Mon-Thu & Sat-Sun 9-5, Fri 9-4.30. Please phone for Xmas &
New Year opening times.* **Fees** Cars & Motorcycles £5, Minibus
£10, Coaches £20. Car season ticket £20.* **Facilities** ℗ 🛏
(outdoor) ♿ toilets for disabled shop

CARDIFF

Cardiff Castle

Castle St CF10 3RB
☎ **029 2087 8100**   📠 **029 2023 1417**
e-mail: cardiffcastle@cardiff.gov.uk
web: www.cardiffcastle.com
dir: from M4, A48 & A470 follow signs to city centre

Cardiff Castle is situated in the heart of the city. Contained
within its mighty walls is a history spanning nearly 2000
years, dating from the coming of the Romans to the Norman
Conquest and beyond. Discover spectacular interiors on your
guided tour, and enjoy magnificent views of the city from the
top of the 12th-century Norman keep. The new Interpretation
Centre includes a film presentation and a multimedia guide
around the Castle grounds. Regular events throughout the year
include a teddy bear's picnic, open air theatre, medieval and
Roman re-enactments and much more.

Times Open all year, daily (ex 25-26 Dec & 1 Jan) including
guided tours, Mar-Oct, 9.30-6 (last tour 5); Nov-Feb, 9.30-5.00
(last tour 4). Royal Regiment of Wales Museum closed Tue.*
Facilities ℗ ♿ (partly accessible) (Castle apartments and
Norman Keep not accessible to wheelchair users, cobblestone
path at entrance) toilets for disabled shop ⊗

Millennium Stadium Tours

Millennium Stadium, Westgate St, Gate 3 CF10 1JA
☎ **029 2082 2228**   📠 **029 2082 2151**
e-mail: mgibbons@wru.co.uk
web: millenniumstadium.com/tours
dir: A470 to city centre. Westgate St opposite Castle far end. Turn
by Angel Hotel on corner of Westgate Street.

In the late 1990s this massive stadium was completed as part
of an effort to revitalise Welsh fortunes. It replaced Cardiff
Arms Park, and now hosts major music events, exhibitions, and
international rugby and soccer matches. Its capacity of around
75,000 and its retractable roof make it unique in Europe. The
home of Welsh Rugby and Welsh Football.

Times Open all year, Mon-Sat, 10-5; Sun 10-4* **Facilities** ℗ ♿
toilets for disabled shop ⊗

Cardiff continued

National Museum Cardiff

Cathays Park CF10 3NP

☎ 029 2039 7951 📄 029 2057 3321

e-mail: post@museumwales.ac.uk

web: www.museumwales.ac.uk

dir: in Civic Centre. M4 junct 32, A470, 5 mins walk from city centre & 20 mins walk from bus & train station

National Museum Cardiff is home to spectacular collections from Wales and all over the world. The Museum showcases displays of art, archaeology, geology and natural history all under one roof. The new archaeology gallery, 'Origins in search of early Wales', traces life in Wales from the earliest humans 230,000 years ago. Explore the past through themes such as conflict, power, wealth, family and the future - are we really so different today? Discover stories behind some of Wales' most famous works of art in the new art galleries, which now include activity stations and touch screens to help bring the paintings to life. You can also enjoy changing displays drawn from the collection of Impressionist and Post-Impressionist paintings, including work by Monet, Renoir and Cézanne. Or how about a close encounter with The Big Bang, erupting volcanoes, dinosaurs and woolly mammoths on the journey through time and space?

Times Open all year, Tue-Sun 10-5. Closed Mon (ex BHs). Telephone for Xmas opening times. **Fees** Free admission but charge may be made for some events. **Facilities** 🅟 Ⓟ ☕ 🍽 licensed ♿ toilets for disabled shop 🚫

Techniquest

Stuart St CF10 5BW

☎ 029 2047 5475 📄 029 2048 2517

e-mail: info@techniquest.org

web: www.techniquest.org

dir: A4232 to Cardiff Bay

Located in the heart of the Cardiff Bay, there's always something new to explore at this exciting science discovery centre. Journey into space in the planetarium, enjoy an interactive Science Theatre Show or experience one of the 120 hands-on exhibits. Please visit website for details of events running throughout the year.

Times Open all year, school days 9.30-4.30; all other times 10-5. Closed Xmas. **Fees** £7 (ch & concessions £5). Family ticket (2ad+3ch) £23. Friends season ticket available. Discounts for groups **Facilities** Ⓟ ☕ ♿ toilets for disabled shop 🚫

ST FAGANS

St Fagans: National History Museum

CF5 6XB

☎ 029 2057 3500 📄 029 2057 3490

web: www.museumwales.ac.uk

dir: 4m W of Cardiff on A4232. From M4 exit at junct 33 and follow brown signs

A stroll around the indoor galleries and 100 acres of beautiful grounds will give you a fascinating insight into how people in Wales have lived, worked and spent their leisure hours since Celtic times. You can see people practising the traditional means of earning a living, the animals they kept and at certain times of year, the ways in which they celebrated the seasons.

Times Open all year daily, 10-5. (Closed 24-26 Dec). **Fees** Free. Charge may apply to some events. **Facilities** 🅟 ☕ 🍽 licensed 🛖 (outdoor) ♿ (partly accessible) (wheelchair access possible to most parts) toilets for disabled shop 🚫

CARMARTHENSHIRE

ABERGWILI

Carmarthenshire County Museum

FREE

SA31 2JG

☎ 01267 228696 📄 01267 223830

e-mail: museums@carmarthenshire.gov.uk

web: www.carmarthenshire.gov.uk/

dir: 2m E of Carmarthen, just off A40, at Abergwili rdbt

Housed in the old palace of the Bishop of St David's and set in seven acres of grounds, the museum offers a wide range of local subjects to explore, from geology and prehistory to butter making, Welsh furniture and folk art. Temporary exhibitions are held.

Times Open all year, Mon-Sat 10-4.30. Closed Xmas-New Year.* **Facilities** 🅟 Ⓟ ☕ 🛖 (outdoor) ♿ toilets for disabled shop 🚫

DRE-FACH FELINDRE

National Woollen Museum

SA44 5UP
☎ **01559 370929** 📠 **01559 371592**
e-mail: post@museumwales.ac.uk
web: www.museumwales.ac.uk
dir: 16m W of Carmarthen off A484, 4m E of Newcastle Emlyn

The museum is housed in the former Cambrian Mills and has a comprehensive display tracing the evolution of the industry from its beginnings to the present day. Demonstrations of the fleece to fabric process are given on 19th-century textile machinery.

Times Open all year, Apr-Sep, daily 10-5; Oct-Mar, Tue-Sat 10-5. Phone for details of Xmas opening times. **Fees** Free admission but charge may be made for some events. **Facilities** ❷ ⓟ ⌂ ㄓ (outdoor) ♿ toilets for disabled shop ⊗

LLANARTHNE

The National Botanic Garden of Wales

SA32 8HG
☎ **01558 668768** 📠 **01558 668933**
e-mail: info@gardenofwales.org.uk
web: www.gardenofwales.org.uk
dir: 8m E of Carmarthen on A48, dedicated intersection - signed

Set amongst 568 acres of parkland in the beautiful Towy Valley in West Wales. The Garden's centrepiece is the Great Glasshouse, an amazing tilted glass dome with a six-metre ravine. The Mediterranean landscape enables the visitor to experience the aftermath of an Australian bush fire, pause in an olive grove or wander through Fuchsia collections from Chile. The Tropical House features orchids, palms and other tropical plants. A 220 metre herbaceous board walk forms the spine of the garden and leads to the children's play area and our 360°-surround screen cinema to the Old Stables Courtyard. Here the visitor can view art exhibitions, wander in the gift shop or enjoy a meal in the restaurant. Land train tours will take the visitor around the necklace of lakes, which surround the central garden.

Times Open all year, 24 Mar-26 Oct 10-6; 27 Oct-22 Mar 10-4.30* **Facilities** ❷ ⌂ 🍽 licensed ㄓ (outdoor) toilets for disabled shop ⊗

LLANELLI

WWT National Wetland Centre Wales

Llwynhendy SA14 9SH
☎ **01554 741087** 📠 **01554 744101**
e-mail: info.llanelli@wwt.org.uk
web: www.wwt.org.uk
dir: 3m E of Llanelli, off A484

Stretching over 97 hectares on the Burry Inlet, the centre is Wales' premier site for water birds and waders and is home to countless wild species as diverse as dragonflies and Little Egrets. The beautifully landscaped grounds are home to over 650 of some of the world's most spectacular ducks, swans, geese and flamingos - many so tame they feed from the hand. There is also a discovery centre and outdoor activities for visitors including a Canoe Safari, Water Vole City, Pond Dipping Zone and Bike Trail.

Times Open all year, daily 9.30-5 (ex 24-25 Dec). Grounds open until 6 in the summer.* **Fees** Gift Aid donation: £7.30 (ch £4 age 4-16, ch under 4 and disability helpers free, concessions £5.50). Family (2ad+2ch) £20.35. WWT members free.* **Facilities** ❷ ⌂ 🍽 licensed ㄓ (indoor & outdoor) ♿ (partly accessible) (tower inaccessible) toilets for disabled shop ⊗

PUMSAINT

Dolaucothi Gold Mines

SA19 8US
☎ **01558 650177** 📠 **01588 651919**
e-mail: dolaucothi@nationaltrust.org.uk
web: www.nationaltrust.org.uk
dir: on A482, signed both directions

Here is an opportunity to spend a day exploring the gold mines and to wear a miner's helmet and lamp while touring the underground workings. It is the only Roman gold mine in the UK.

Times Open 13 Mar-Jun & Sep-Oct, daily 11-5, Jul-Aug 10-6. **Fees** £3.27 (ch £1.64) Family £8.18. With Gift Aid £3.60 (ch £1.80) Family £9. Guided underground tours £3.80 (ch £1.19) Family £9.50. **Facilities** ❷ ⌂ ㄓ (outdoor) ♿ (partly accessible) (only one underground tour accessible, most other areas accessible) toilets for disabled shop ⅍

CEREDIGION

ABERYSTWYTH

The National Library of Wales

Penglais SY23 3BU
☎ **01970 632800** 📠 **01970 632882**
e-mail: holi@llgc.org.uk
web: www.llgc.org.uk
dir: Off Penglais Hill, A487 in N area of Aberystwyth

The largest library in Wales. Its collections include books, manuscripts, archival documents, maps and photographs as well as paintings, film, video and sound recordings. The library is recognised as the leading research centre for Welsh and Celtic studies, and is popular with those studying family history. Lectures, screenings and conferences throughout the year. There are constantly changing exhibitions in the galleries and exhibition halls. Free guided tour every Monday morning at 11am. Group guided tours available by prior arrangement.

Times Open on selected BHs. Please check details before travelling* **Fees** Free. Admission to reading rooms available by readers ticket, two proofs of identity required, one including address. Free admission to all exhibitions **Facilities** 🅿 🍴 licensed 🥢 (outdoor) ♿ toilets for disabled shop ⊗

EGLWYS FACH

RSPB Nature Reserve Ynys-hir

Visitor Centre, Cae'r Berllan SY20 8TA
☎ **01654 700222** 📠 **01654 700333**
e-mail: ynyshir@rspb.org.uk
web: www.rspb.org.uk
dir: 6m S of Machynlleth on A487 in Eglwysfach. Signed from main road

The mixture of different habitats is home to an abundance of birds and wildlife. The saltmarshes in winter support the only regular wintering flock of Greenland white-fronted geese in England and Wales, in addition to peregrines, hen harriers and merlins. The sessile oak woodland is home to pied flycatchers, wood warblers, and redstarts in the summer, but woodpeckers, nuthatches, red kites, sparrowhawks and buzzards are here all year round. Otters, polecats, 30 butterfly and 15 dragonfly species are also present. Guided walks and children's activities. Please telephone for details of events running throughout the year.

Times Open all year, daily, 9am-9pm (or sunset if earlier). Visitor Centre: Apr-Oct 9-5 daily; Nov-Mar 10-4 (Wed-Sun)* **Facilities** 🅿 Ⓟ 🥢 (outdoor) shop ⊗

CONWY

BETWS-Y-COED

Conwy Valley Railway Museum

Old Goods Yard LL24 0AL
☎ **01690 710568** 📠 **01690 710132**
e-mail: info@conwyrailwaymuseum.co.uk
web: www.conwyrailwaymuseum.co.uk
dir: signed from A5 into Old Church Rd, adjacent to train station

The two large museum buildings have displays on both the narrow and standard-gauge railways of North Wales, including railway stock and other memorabilia. There are working model railway layouts, a steam-hauled miniature railway in the grounds, which cover over four acres, and a 15inch-gauge tramway to the woods. The latest addition is the quarter-size steam 'Britannia' loco that is now on display. For children there are mini-dodgems, Postman Pat, a school bus and Toby Tram. There is a large model railway in the B R Coach.

Times Open all year daily, 10-5.30. Closed Xmas.* **Fees** £1.50 (ch & concessions 80p). Family ticket £4. Steam train ride £1.50. Tram ride £1.* **Facilities** 🅿 Ⓟ 🍴 licensed 🥢 (outdoor) ♿ toilets for disabled shop

COLWYN BAY

Welsh Mountain Zoo

Old Highway LL28 5UY
☎ **01492 532938** 📠 **01492 530498**
e-mail: info@welshmountainzoo.org
web: www.welshmountainzoo.org
dir: A55 junct 20 signed Rhos-on-Sea. Zoo signed

Set high above Colwyn Bay with panoramic views and breath-taking scenery, this caring conservation zoo is set among beautiful gardens. Among the animals are many rare and endangered species, and there are daily shows which include Penguins' Playtime, Chimp Encounter, Sealion Feeding and Birds of Prey.

Times Open all year, Mar-Oct, daily 9.30-6; Nov-Feb, daily 9.30-5. Closed 25 Dec. **Fees** £8.95 (ch & students £6.60, pen £7.80). Family ticket (2ad+2ch or 1ad+3ch) £28.25* **Facilities** 🅿 🍴 licensed 🥢 (outdoor) ♿ (partly accessible) toilets for disabled shop ⊗

CONWY

Conwy Castle

LL32 8AY
☎ **01492 592358**
web: www.cadw.wales.gov.uk
dir: via A55 or B5106

The castle is a magnificent fortress, built 1283-7 by Edward I. There is an exhibition on castle chapels on the ground floor of the Chapel Tower. The castle forms part of the same defensive system as the extensive town walls, which are among the most complete in Europe.

Times Open all year, Apr-Oct, daily 9-5; Nov-Mar, Mon-Sat 9.30-4, Sun 11-4.* **Fees** £4.60 (ch 5-15, concessions £4.10, disabled visitors & assisting companion free). Family ticket £13.30. Joint ticket for both monuments £6.85 (ch 5-15 & concessions £5.85, family £19.55, disabled visitors & assisting companion free). Group rates available. Please contact or visit website for most recent prices. **Facilities** ℗ toilets for disabled shop ⊗ ⊕

LLANDUDNO

Great Orme Bronze Age Copper Mines

Pyliau Rd, Great Orme LL30 2XG
☎ **01492 870447**
e-mail: gomines@greatorme.freeserve.co.uk
web: www.greatormemines.info
dir: Follow 'copper mine' signs from Llandudno Promenade

Browse in the visitor centre with a model of a Bronze Age village depicting life in Bronze Age times. Take a look at some original 4,000 year old Bronze Age artefacts and a selection of Bronze Age mining tools. After watching two short films take a helmet and make your way down to the mines. Walking through tunnels mined nearly 4,000 years ago look into some of the smaller tunnels and get a feel for the conditions our prehistoric ancestors faced in their search for valuable copper ores. Excavation on the surface will continue for decades and one of the team is usually available to answer visitors' questions as they walk around the site and view the prehistoric landscape being uncovered.

Times Open mid Mar-end Oct, daily 10-5.* **Fees** £6 (ch £4, under 5's free). Family ticket (2ad+2ch) £16, extra child £3.* **Facilities** ℗ Ⓟ ⊑ ♒ (outdoor) ♿ (partly accessible) (no wheelchair access to underground mine) toilets for disabled shop

LLANDUDNO JUNCTION

RSPB Nature Reserve Conwy

LL31 9XZ
☎ **01492 584091**
e-mail: conwy@rspb.org.uk
web: www.rspb.org.uk
dir: signed from junct 18 of A55

Explore the quiet nature trails, get close up experience with birds and other wildlife, or enjoy a leisurely cup of coffee or lunch while drinking in the magnificent views of Conwy Castle and Snowdonia. Lots of activities to keep small people happy and lots to interest big kids too.

Times Open all year, daily, 9.30-5. Closed 25 Dec. **Fees** £2.50 (ch £1, concessions £1.50). Family £5. **Facilities** ℗ ⊑ ♒ (outdoor) ♿ toilets for disabled shop ⊗

PENMACHNO

Ty Mawr Wybrnant

LL25 0HJ
☎ **01690 760213**
e-mail: tymawrwybrnant@nationaltrust.org.uk
web: www.nationaltrust.org.uk
dir: From A5 3m S of Betws-y-Coed take B4406 to Penmachno. House is 2.5m NW of Penmachno by forest road

Situated in the beautiful, secluded Wybrnant Valley, Ty Mawr was the birthplace of Bishop William Morgan (1545-1604), the first translator of the Bible into Welsh. The house has been restored to give an idea of its 16th-17th century appearance. The Wybrnant Nature Trail, a short walk, covers approximately one mile.

Times Open 5 Apr-28 Oct, Thu-Sun & BH Mon 12-5; Oct, Thu, Fri & Sun 12-4. (Last admission 30 mins before closing).* **Fees** £3 (ch £1.50). Family ticket £7.50. Party 15+(£2.50 each).* **Facilities** ℗ ♒ (outdoor) ⊗ ♨

DENBIGHSHIRE

BODELWYDDAN

Bodelwyddan Castle

LL18 5YA
☎ 01745 584060   📄 01745 584563
e-mail: enquiries@bodelwyddan-castle.co.uk
web: www.bodelwyddan-castle.co.uk
dir: just off A55, near St Asaph, follow brown signs

Bodelwyddan Castle houses over 100 portraits from the National Portrait Gallery's 19th-century collection. The portraits hang in beautifully refurbished rooms and are complemented by sculpture and period furnishings. Interactive displays show how portraits were produced and used in the Victorian era. The Castle Gallery hosts a programme of temporary exhibitions and events. The castle is set within 200 acres of parkland, including formal gardens, an aviary, woodlands, a butterfly glade and an adventure playground. Lots of events, contact the castle for details.

Times Please telephone for details. **Fees** £6 (ch 5-16 £2.50, ch under 4 free, concessions £5). Family ticket (2ad+2ch) £15 (1ad+2ch) £12.* **Facilities** 🅿 🅟 ☒ 🍴 licensed 🍽 (outdoor) ♿ (partly accessible) toilets for disabled shop ⊗

CORWEN

Ewe-Phoria Sheepdog Centre

Glanrafon, Llangwm LL21 0PE
☎ 01490 460369
e-mail: info@adventure-mountain.co.uk
web: www.ewe-phoria.co.uk
dir: off A5 to Llangwm, follow signs

Ewe-Phoria is an Agri-Theatre and Sheepdog Centre that details the life and work of the shepherd on a traditional Welsh farm. The Agri-Theatre has unusual living displays of sheep with accompanying lectures on their history and breed, while outside sheepdog handlers put their dogs through their paces. Try your hand at quad biking and off-road rally karting on Adventure Mountain.

Times Open Etr-end Oct, Wed-Fri & Sun. Closed Sat & Mon ex BHs* **Facilities** 🅿 ☒ 🍴 licensed 🍽 ♿ toilets for disabled shop ⊗

LLANGOLLEN

Horse Drawn Boats Centre

The Wharf, Wharf Hill LL20 8TA
☎ 01978 860702 & 01691 690322   📄 01978 860702
e-mail: bill@horsedrawnboats.co.uk
web: www.horsedrawnboats.co.uk
dir: A5 onto Llangollen High St, across river bridge to T-junct. Wharf opposite, up the hill

Take a horse drawn boat trip along the beautiful Vale of Llangollen. There is also a narrow boat trip that crosses Pontcysyllte Aqueduct, the largest navigable aqueduct in the world. Full bar on board, commentary throughout. Tea room serving light meals & breakfast.

Times Open Etr-end Oct, daily, 9.30-5; Tea room Nov-Mar, wknds 10-4.30. **Fees** Horse Drawn Boat Trip from £5 (ch £2.50). Family £12.50 Aquaduct Trip £11 (ch £9).* **Facilities** 🅟 ☒ ♿ (partly accessible) (no access to motor boat, access to tea room & Horse Drawn Boats) toilets for disabled shop ⊗

GWYNEDD

BEDDGELERT

Sygun Copper Mine

LL55 4NE
☎ 01766 890595 & 510101 📄 01766 890595
e-mail: sygunmine@hotmail.com
web: www.syguncoppermine.co.uk
dir: 1m E of Beddgelert on A498

Spectacular audio-visual underground experience where visitors can explore the workings of this 19th-century coppermine and see the magnificent stalactite and stalagmite formations. Other activities include archery, panning for gold, metal detecting and coin making. Marvel at the fantastic coin collection from Julius Caesar to Queen Elizabeth II, and visit the Time-Line Museum with Bronze Age and Roman artefacts.

Times Open Mar-end Oct 9.30-5. Feb half term, 10-4* **Facilities**
🅿 🅟 🖵 🛱 (outdoor) ♿ (partly accessible) (gift shop, cafe & museum accessible for wheelchairs) shop

BLAENAU FFESTINIOG

Llechwedd Slate Caverns

LL41 3NB
☎ 01766 830306 📄 01766 831260
e-mail: quarrytours@aol.com
web: www.llechwedd-slate-caverns.co.uk
dir: beside A470, 1m from Blaenau Ffestiniog

The Miners' Tramway travels deep into the mountainside with tour guides who introduce you to the tools of the trade and working conditions underground. There is also an audio-visual tour through ten spectacular caverns. Free surface attractions include various exhibitions, museums, and the Victorian village with shops, bank, Miners Arms pub, chemist and viewpoint.

Times Open all year, daily from 10. (Last tour Etr-Sep, 5.15, Sep-Etr, 4.15). Closed 25-26 Dec & 1 Jan. **Fees** Single Tour £9.45 (ch £7.15, sen £7.95). Both tours £15.20 (ch £11.60, pen £12.95). Group discounts, 10% family discount when taking both tours. **Facilities** 🅿 🖵 🍽 licensed 🛱 (outdoor) ♿ (partly accessible) (access to underground mine tours via steps, some areas of loose slate chipping) toilets for disabled shop ⊗

CAERNARFON

Caernarfon Castle

LL55 2AY
☎ 01286 677617
web: www.cadw.wales.gov.uk

Edward I began building the castle and extensive town walls in 1283 after defeating the last independent ruler of Wales. Completed in 1328, it has unusual polygonal towers, notably the 10-sided Eagle Tower. There is a theory that these features were copied from the walls of Constantinople, to reflect a tradition that Constantine was born nearby. Edward I's son and heir was born and presented to the Welsh people here, setting a precedent that was followed in 1969, when Prince Charles was invested as Prince of Wales.

Times Open all year, Apr-Oct, daily 9-5; Nov-Mar, Mon-Sat 9.30-4, Sun 11-4.* **Fees** £4.95 (ch 5-15, pen & students £4.60, disabled visitors & assisting compainion free). Family ticket (2 ad & all ch/grandch under 16) £14.50. Group rates available. Please contact or visit website for most recent prices. **Facilities** 🅿 shop ⊗ ⊕

Caernarfon continued

Segontium Roman Museum   FREE
Beddgelert Rd LL55 2LN
☎ 01286 675625 🖹 01286 678416
e-mail: info@segontium.org.uk
web: www.segontium.org.uk
dir: on A4085 to Beddgelert approx 1m from Caernarfon

Segontium Roman Museum tells the story of the conquest and occupation of Wales by the Romans and displays the finds from the auxiliary fort of Segontium, one of the most famous in Britain. You can combine a visit to the museum with exploration of the site of the Roman Fort, which is in the care of Cadw: Welsh Historic Monuments. The exciting discoveries displayed at the museum portray the daily life of the soldiers stationed in this most westerly outpost of the Roman Empire.

Times Open all year, Tue-Sun 12.30-4. Closed Mon except BH*
Facilities Ⓟ shop ⊗

Welsh Highland Railway
St. Helen's Rd LL55 2YD
☎ 01286 677018 & 01766 516000 🖹 01286 677018
e-mail: enquiries@festrail.co.uk
web: www.festrail.co.uk
dir: SW of Caernarfon Castle beside harbour. Follow brown signs

The Welsh Highland Railway is the latest of the Great Little Trains of Wales. It runs from Caernarfon, beside the famous castle to the beautiful village of Beddgelert and on through the Aberglaslyn Pass. The final stretch of line to Porthmadog is expected to open in 2010. Passengers can sit back, enjoy the nostalgia of a steam train and the stunning scenery of north Snowdonia whilst travelling in modern comfortable carriages with heating and refreshment service. A first class panorama vehicle is at the rear of some trains. It is a great way of accessing the national park.

Times Open Etr-end Oct, limited service in Winter
Fees Caernarfon-Rhyd Ddu £17.50, Beddgelert £22, Hafody Hyn £25 (1 ch free for each adult, concessions 10% discount)*
Facilities Ⓟ Ⓟ ♿ (partly accessible) (most main service trains, main stations & buildings accessible) toilets for disabled shop ⊗

Fairbourne Railway
Beach Rd LL38 2EX
☎ 01341 250362 🖹 01341 250240
web: www.fairbournerailway.com
dir: on A493 follow signs for Fairbourne, main terminus is just past level crossing on left

One of the most unusual of Wales's 'little trains'; built in 1890 as a horse-drawn railway to carry building materials it was later converted to steam, and now covers two-and-a-half miles. Its route passes one of the loveliest beaches in Wales, with views of the beautiful Mawddach Estuary.

Times Open Feb half term (ex Fri). Apr-23 Sep (closed most Fri ex late Jul & all of Aug). Oct wknds & 20-28 Oct (ex Fri).*
Fees Return £7.60 (ch £4, pen £6). Family £18.75 (2ad+3ch).*
Facilities Ⓟ 🚻♿ (partly accessible) toilets for disabled shop

Harlech Castle
LL46 2YH
☎ 01766 780552
web: www.cadw.wales.gov.uk
dir: from A496

Harlech Castle was built in 1283-89 by Edward I, with a sheer drop to the sea on one side. Owain Glyndwr starved the castle into submission in 1404 and made it his court and campaigning base. Later, the defence of the castle in the Wars of the Roses inspired the song Men of Harlech. Today the sea has slipped away, and the castle's great walls and round towers stand above the dunes.

Times Open all year, Apr-Oct, daily 9-5; Nov-Mar, Mon-Sat 9.30-4, Sun 11-4.* **Fees** £3.60 (ch 5-15, concessions £3.20, disabled visitors & assisting companion free). Family ticket (2ad+all ch/grandch under 16) £10.40. Group rates available. Please contact or visit website for most recent prices.
Facilities Ⓟ shop ⊗ ✲

LLANBERIS

Snowdon Mountain Railway

LL55 4TY
☎ **01286 870223** 📄 **01286 872518**
e-mail: info@snowdonrailway.co.uk
web: www.snowdonrailway.co.uk
dir: on A4086, Caernarfon to Capel Curig road. 7.5m from Caernarfon

The journey of just over four-and-a-half miles takes passengers more than 3,000ft up to the summit of Snowdon; breathtaking views include, on a clear day, the Isle of Man and the Wicklow Mountains in Ireland. The round trip to the summit and back takes two and a half hours including a half hour at the summit.

Times Open daily mid Mar-Oct, (weather permitting).*
Fees Return £23 (ch £16). Early bird discount on 9am train, pre-booking only. 3/4 distance return £16 (ch £12). **Facilities** 🅿 Ⓟ 🖵 🍴 (outdoor) ♿ (partly accessible) (some carriages suitable for wheelchairs - must notify) toilets for disabled shop ⊗

Welsh Slate Museum

Gilfach Ddu, Padarn Country Park LL55 4TY
☎ **01286 870630** 📄 **01286 871906**
e-mail: slate@museumwales.ac.uk
web: www.museumwales.ac.uk
dir: 0.25m off A4086. Museum within Padarn Country Park

Set among the towering quarries at Llanberis, the Welsh Slate Museum is a living, working site located in the original workshops of Dinorwig Quarry, which once employed 15,000 men and boys. You can see the foundry, smithy, workshops and mess room which make up the old quarry, and view original machinery, much of which is still in working order.

Times Open all year, Etr-Oct, daily 10-5; Nov-Etr, Sun-Fri 10-4.
Fees Some events may incur a charge. **Facilities** 🅿 Ⓟ 🖵 🍴 ♿ (partly accessible) toilets for disabled shop ⊗

LLANUWCHLLYN

Bala Lake Railway

The Station LL23 7DD
☎ **01678 540666**
web: www.bala-lake-railway.co.uk
dir: off A494 Bala to Dolgellau road

Steam locomotives which once worked in the slate quarries of North Wales now haul passenger coaches for four-and-a-half miles from Llanuwchllyn Station along the lake to Bala. The railway has one of the few remaining double-twist lever-locking framed GWR signal boxes, installed in 1896. Some of the coaches are open and some closed, so passengers can enjoy the beautiful views of the lake and mountains in all weathers.

Times Open Etr-last wknd in Sep, daily. (Closed certain Mon & Fri, telephone for details).* **Fees** £8.50 (pen £8). Family ticket (2ad+2ch) £18.* **Facilities** 🅿 Ⓟ 🖵 🍴 (outdoor) ♿ (partly accessible) shop

LLANYSTUMDWY

Lloyd George Museum

LL52 0SH
☎ **01766 522071** 📄 **01766 522071**
e-mail: amgueddfeydd-museums@gwynedd.gov.uk
web: www.gwynedd.gov.uk/museums
dir: on A497 between Pwllheli & Criccieth

Explore the life and times of David Lloyd George in this museum. His boyhood home is recreated as it would have been when he lived there between 1864 and 1880, along with his Uncle Lloyd's shoemaking workshop.

Times Open Etr, daily 10.30-5; Apr-May, Mon-Fri 10.30-5 (open Sat in Jun); Jul-Sep daily 10.30-5; Oct, Mon-Fri, 11-4. Open BHs; Other times by appointment, telephone 01286 679098 for details.* **Facilities** 🅿 Ⓟ 🍴 (outdoor) toilets for disabled shop ⊗

Wales

Wales

PORTHMADOG

Ffestiniog Railway

Harbour Station LL49 9NF
☎ **01766 516000** 📠 **01766 516006**
e-mail: enquiries@festrail.co.uk
web: www.festrail.co.uk
dir: SE end of town beside the harbour, on A487

One of the Great Little Train of Wales, this railway runs
for 13.5 through Snowdonia. Originally built to carry slate
from the quarries at Blaenau Ffestiniog to the harbour at
Porthmadog, the little trains now carry passengers through the
beautiful scenery of the national park. A licensed at-your-seat
refreshment service is available on all main trains. Day rover
tickets allow you to break your journey to make the most of
your day. First class observation carriage on all trains.

Times Open daily late Mar-late Oct. Limited Winter service mid
wk trains Nov & early Dec. Santa specials in Dec. Open Feb
half term. **Fees** Full distance return £17.95 (1 ch under 16 free,
concessions £16.15). Other fares available.* **Facilities** 🅿 🅿 ⊑
🍴 licensed 🛱 (outdoor) ♿ (partly accessible) (most train services
accessible, phone in advance, main station/platforms & restaurant
accessible) toilets for disabled shop ⊗

PORTMEIRION

Portmeirion

LL48 6ER
☎ **01766 770000** 📠 **01766 771331**
e-mail: info@portmeirion-village.com
web: www.portmeirion-village.com
dir: off A487 at Minffordd

Welsh architect Sir Clough Williams Ellis built his fairy-tale,
Italianate village on a rocky, tree-clad peninsula on the
shores of Cardigan Bay. A bell-tower, castle and lighthouse
mingle with a watch-tower, grottoes and cobbled squares
among pastel-shaded picturesque cottages let as holiday
accommodation. The 60-acre Gwyllt Gardens include miles of
dense woodland paths and are famous for their fine displays
of rhododendrons, azaleas, hydrangeas and sub-tropical flora.
There is a mile of sandy beach and a playground for children.
The village is probably best known as the major location for
1960s cult TV show, The Prisoner.

Times Open daily Oct-Mar, 9.30-5.30; Apr-Sep, 9.30-7.30.
Fees £7.50 (ch £4, concessions £6). Family ticket (2ad+2ch)
£19.* **Facilities** 🅿 ⊑ 🍴 licensed 🛱 (outdoor) ♿ (partly
accessible) (steep slopes and many steps make access difficult to
some areas) toilets for disabled shop ⊗

Y FELINHELI

GreenWood Forest Park

LL56 4QN
☎ **01248 670076** 📠 **01248 670069**
e-mail: info@greenwoodforestpark.co.uk
web: www.greenwoodforestpark.co.uk
dir: A55 junct 11, follow Llanberis signs onto A4244, signed from
next rdbt. Located between Bangor and Caernarfon

Family adventure and forest fun, whatever the weather. Ride
the eco-friendly Green Dragon Rollercoaster, zoom down
the 70 metre sledge slide, scramble through Tunnel Warren
- tunnels, slides, ropes and towers for the under 7s, plus the
giant Jumper - the biggest Bouncing Pillow ever and the first
one in Wales. Enjoy the Jungle Boat Adventure, drive mini-
tractors, shoot traditional Longbows and build dens in the
woods. Tackle the challenge of the Treetop Towers and find a
crocodile in the Maze, Adventure Playgrounds, Puzzle Barn and
Toddlers' Village plus the indoor interactive exhibition in the
Great Hall. There'll be entertainment in the Forest Theatre, and
you can try the newest ride: Moon Karts - Formula One Fun!

Times Open mid Mar-late Oct, daily 10-5.30 (Sep & Oct 10-5);
Feb half-term* **Facilities** 🅿 ⊑ 🍴 licensed 🛱 (indoor & outdoor)
♿ (partly accessible) (grounds mostly accessible, some activities
may not be accessible for visitors with disabilities) toilets for
disabled shop

MERTHYR TYDFIL

MERTHYR TYDFIL

Brecon Mountain Railway

Pant Station Dowlais CF48 2UP
☎ 01685 722988   📄 01685 384854
web: www.breconmountainrailway.co.uk
dir: follow Mountain Railway signs from A470 or A465 N of Merthyr Tydfil

Opened in 1980, this narrow-gauge railway follows part of an old British Rail route which closed in 1964 when the iron industry in South Wales fell into decline. The present route starts at Pant Station and continues for 3.5 miles through the beautiful scenery of the Brecon Beacons National Park, as far as Taf Fechan reservoir. The train is pulled by a vintage steam locomotive and is one of the most popular railways in Wales.

Times Opening times on application to The Brecon Mountain Railway, Pant Station, Merthyr Tydfil.* **Fees** Fares are under review, please ring for details.* **Facilities** ℗ 🖵 🍽 licensed ⊓ (indoor & outdoor) ♿ (partly accessible) (no disabled access to toilets at Pontsticill Station) toilets for disabled shop

MONMOUTHSHIRE

CALDICOT

Caldicot Castle & Country Park

Church Rd NP26 4HU
☎ 01291 420241   📄 01291 435094
e-mail: caldicotcastle@monmouthshire.gov.uk
web: www.caldicotcastle.co.uk
dir: M4 junct 23A onto B4245. From M48 junct 2 follow A48 & B4245. Signed from B4245

Caldicot Castle's well-preserved fortifications were founded by the Normans and fully developed by the late 14th century. Restored as a family home by a wealthy Victorian, the castle offers the chance to explore medieval walls and towers in a setting of tranquil gardens and wooded country parkland, plus the opportunity to play giant chess or draughts. Plenty of events are planned throughout the year, see website for details.

Times Open Apr-Oct, daily, 11-5. **Fees** £3.75 (ch, pen, student & disabled £2.50). Family (2ad+3ch) £12. Party 10+.* **Facilities** ℗ Ⓟ 🖵 ⊓ (outdoor) ♿ (partly accessible) (access to courtyard) toilets for disabled shop

GROSMONT

Grosmont Castle   FREE

☎ 01981 240301
web: www.cadw.wales.gov.uk
dir: on B4347

Grosmont is one of the 'trilateral' castles of Hubert de Burgh (see also Skenfrith and White Castle). It stands on a mound with a dry moat, and the considerable remains of its 13th-century great hall can be seen. Three towers once guarded the curtain wall, and the western one is well preserved.

Times Open all year, access available at all reasonable times, which will normally be 10-4 daily.* **Facilities** 🚫 ⌖

MONMOUTH

The Nelson Museum & Local History Centre   FREE

New Market Hall, Priory St NP25 3XA
☎ 01600 710630
e-mail: nelsonmuseum@monmouthshire.gov.uk
dir: in town centre

One of the world's major collections of Admiral Nelson-related items, including original letters, glass, china, silver, medals, books, models, prints and Nelson's fighting sword feature here. The local history displays deal with Monmouth's past as a fortress market town, and include a section on the co-founder of the Rolls Royce company, Charles Stewart Rolls, who was also a pioneer balloonist, aviator and, of course, motorist. A major exhibition on C S Rolls and his family will take place between January and August 2010. 12 July 2010 commemorates the centenary of the death of C S Rolls.

Times Open all year, Mar-Oct, Mon-Sat & BH 11-1 & 2-5, Sun 2-5; Nov-Feb, Mon-Sat 11-1 & 2-4, Sun 2-4. **Facilities** ℗ ♿ (partly accessible) (mezzanine display area accessible only by stairs - 25% of whole museum display area) toilets for disabled shop 🚫

Wales

SKENFRITH

Skenfrith Castle   FREE

☎ 01443 336000
web: www.cadw.wales.gov.uk
dir: on B4521

This 13th-century castle has a round keep set inside an imposing towered curtain wall. Hubert de Burgh built it as one of three 'trilateral' castles to defend the Welsh Marches.

Times Open all year, access available at all reasonable times, which will normally be 10-4 daily. Key keeper arrangement.*
Facilities ❷ ⊗ ✛ ♨

WHITE CASTLE

White Castle

NP7 8UD
☎ 01600 780380
web: www.cadw.wales.gov.uk
dir: 7m NE of Abergavenny, unclass road N of B4233

The impressive 12th to 13th-century moated stronghold was built by Hubert de Burgh to defend the Welsh Marches. Substantial remains of walls, towers and a gatehouse can be seen. This is the finest of a trio of castles, the others being at Skenfrith and Grosmont.

Times Open Apr-Oct, 10-5 daily. Open 10-4 daily and unstaffed with no admission charge at all other times.* **Fees** £2.60 (ch 5-15, concessions £2.25, disabled visitors & assisting companion free). Family ticket (2ad+all ch/grandch under 16) £7.45. Group rates available. Please contact or visit website for most recent prices. **Facilities** ❷ ⊗ ✛

NEATH PORT TALBOT

CRYNANT

Cefn Coed Colliery Museum   FREE

SA10 8SN
☎ 01639 750556   🖺 01639 750556
e-mail: colliery@btconnect.com
web: www.neath-porttalbot.gov.uk
dir: 1m S of Crynant, on A4109

The museum is on the site of a former working colliery, and tells the story of mining in the Dulais Valley. A steam-winding engine has been kept and is now operated by electricity, and there is also a simulated underground mining gallery, boilerhouse, compressor house, and exhibition area. Outdoor exhibits include a stationary colliery locomotive. Exhibitions relating to the coal mining industry are held on a regular basis. The museum is now home to the Dulais Valley Historical Model Railway Society who, with the help from the Heritage Lottery Fund have created an ever increasing layout depicting the Neath-Brecon railway through the valley. 2010 is the 30th anniversary of the museum.

Times Open Apr-Oct, daily 10.30-5; Nov-Mar, groups welcome by prior arrangement.* **Facilities** ❷ ⊞ (outdoor) ♿ (partly accessible) (access to exhibition areas, but not to underground gallery) toilets for disabled shop

NEATH

Neath Abbey   FREE

SA10 7DW
☎ 01443 336000
web: www.cadw.wales.gov.uk
dir: 1m W off A465

These ruins were originally a Cistercian abbey founded in 1130 by Richard de Grainville.

Times Open all year, access available at all reasonable times, which will normally be 10-4 daily. Key keeper arrangement.*
Facilities ❷ ⊗ ✛

NEWPORT

CAERLEON

National Roman Legion Museum FREE
High St NP18 1AE
☎ 01633 423134   📄 01633 422869
e-mail: roman@museumwales.ac.uk
web: www.museumwales.ac.uk
dir: close to Newport, 20 min from M4, follow signs from Cardiff & Bristol

The museum illustrates the history of Roman Caerleon and the daily life of its garrison. On display are arms, armour and equipment, with a collection of engraved gemstones, a labyrinth mosaic and finds from the legionary base at Usk. Please telephone for details of children's holiday activities.

Times Open all year: Mon-Sat 10-5, Sun 2-5.* **Facilities** Ⓟ toilets for disabled shop ⊗

PEMBROKESHIRE

CRYMYCH

Castell Henllys Iron Age Fort
Pant-Glas, Meline SA41 3UT
☎ 01239 891319   📄 01239 891319
e-mail: celts@castellhenllys.com
web: www.castellhenllys.com
dir: off A487 between Cardigan and Newport

This Iron Age hill fort is set in the beautiful Pembrokeshire Coast National Park. Excavations began in 1981 and three roundhouses have been reconstructed, another roundhouse has been completed and is the largest on the site. Celtic roundhouses have been constructed in the original way using hazel wattle walls, oak rafters and thatched conical roofs. A forge, smithy and looms can be seen, with other attractions such as trails and a herb garden. Please telephone for details of special events.

Times Open all year, Etr-Oct, daily 10-5 (last entry 4.30); Nov-Mar 11-3 (last entry 2.30). Closed 24-31 Dec. **Fees** £3.90 (concessions £2.75). Family £10.50.* **Facilities** Ⓟ ⊓ (outdoor) ♿ toilets for disabled shop

FISHGUARD

OceanLab
The Parrog, Goodwick SA64 0DE
☎ 01348 874737   📄 01348 872528
e-mail: fishguardharbour.tic@pembrokeshire.gov.uk
web: www.ocean-lab.co.uk
dir: A40 to Fishguard, turn at by-pass, follow signs for Stenaline ferry terminal, pass 2 garages, turn right at rdbt & follow signs to attraction

Overlooking the Pembrokeshire coastline, OceanLab is a multifunctional centre, which aims to provide a fun-filled experience for the family. There is also a hands-on ocean quest exhibition, a soft play area and a cybercafé. An exhibition is centred around 'Ollie the Octopus's Garden', with hands-on displays and activities.

Times Open Apr-Oct, 9.30-5 (6 wk summer hols 9.30-6); Nov-Mar 10-4. **Fees** Free admission. £1 soft play under 5's, £2 cyber cafe for 30 mins. **Facilities** Ⓟ Ⓟ ⊡ ⊓ (outdoor) ♿ toilets for disabled shop ⊗

NARBERTH

Oakwood Park
Canaston Bridge SA67 8DE
☎ 01834 861889   📄 01834 891380
e-mail: info@oakwoodthemepark.co.uk
web: www.oakwoodthemepark.co.uk
dir: M4 W junct 49, take A48 to Carmarthen, signed

Oakwood Theme Park has over 30 rides and attractions. Thrill seekers can brave Speed, the UK's first roller-coaster with a beyond vertical drop, the award-winning wooden roller coaster Megafobia, the 50 metre high sky coaster Vertigo and shot 'n' drop tower coaster The Bounce, or cool off on Hydro, the steepest and wettest ride in Europe! There are also plenty of family rides and lots of fun to be had for smaller kids with a designated children's area available with smaller rides.

Times Open Etr-Oct, days & times vary please call for details* **Fees** £14.95 (under 2's free, ch 3-9 £13.50, pen £10 & disabled £11.50). Family ticket (4) £53, (6) £77. Party 20+ tickets available £12.95* **Facilities** Ⓟ ⊡ 🍴 licensed ⊓ (outdoor) ♿ (partly accessible) (most areas of park are accessible apart from a few rides) toilets for disabled shop ⊗

Wales

PEMBROKE

Pembroke Castle

SA71 4LA
☎ 01646 681510 & & 684585 📄 01646 622260
e-mail: info@pembrokecastle.co.uk
web: www.pembrokecastle.co.uk
dir: W end of main street

This magnificent castle commands stunning views over the Milford estuary. Discover its rich medieval history, and that of Henry VII, the first Tudor king, through a variety of exhibitions. There are lively guided tours and events each Sunday in July and August. Before leaving, pop into the Brass Rubbing Centre and make your own special souvenir. To complete the day, wander round the tranquil millpond and medieval town walls, which surround other architectural gems from Tudor and Georgian times. Special Events: 1st week in Sep 'Pembroke Festival'. Please telephone for details.

Times Open all year, daily, Apr-Sep 9.30-6; Mar & Oct 10-5; Nov-Feb, 10-4. Closed 24-26 Dec & 1 Jan.* **Facilities** ℗ ⛁ 🏠 (outdoor) toilets for disabled shop

SCOLTON

Scolton Manor Museum & Country Park

Scolton Manor SA62 5QL
☎ 01437 731328 (Museum) & & 731457 (Park)
📄 01437 731743
dir: 5m N of Haverfordwest, on B4329

Scolton Manor Museum is situated in Scolton Country Park. The early Victorian mansion, refurbished stables and the exhibition hall illustrate the history and natural history of Pembrokeshire. There are new displays in the house and stables, plus a 'Pembrokeshire Railways' exhibition. The 60-acre grounds, partly a nature reserve, have fine specimen trees and shrubs. Environmentally friendly Visitor Centre, alternative energy and woodland displays, guided walks and children's play areas. Classic Car show in June and Model Air show in July.

Times Open Museum Etr-Oct, daily & BHs 10.30-5.30 (last entry 4.30); Country Park all year, Apr-Oct 9.30-5.30, Nov-Mar 9.30-4.30. Closed 25-26 Dec **Fees** Museum: £2 (ch £1, concessions £1.50). Country Park car park £1 all day* **Facilities** ℗ ℗ ⛁ 🏠 (outdoor) ♿ (partly accessible) (ground floor only accessible only for wheelchairs) toilets for disabled shop ⊗

POWYS

ABERCRAF

Dan-Yr-Ogof The National Showcaves Centre for Wales

SA9 1GJ
☎ 01639 730284 📄 01639 730293
e-mail: info@showcaves.co.uk
web: www.showcaves.co.uk
dir: M4 junct 45, midway between Swansea & Brecon on A4067, follow brown tourist signs for Dan-Yr-Ogof

This award-winning attraction includes three separate caves, dinosaur park, Iron Age Farm, museum, shire horse centre and covered children's play area.

Times Open daily Apr-Oct, from 10.30 (last admission 3)* **Facilities** ℗ ⛁ 🏠 (outdoor) toilets for disabled shop ⊗

LLANFAIR CAEREINION

Welshpool & Llanfair Light Railway

SY21 0SF

☎ **01938 810441**   📄 **01938 810861**

e-mail: info@wllr.org.uk
web: www.wllr.org.uk
dir: beside A458, Shrewsbury-Dolgellau road

The Llanfair Railway is one of the Great Little Trains of Wales. It offers a 16-mile round trip through glorious scenery by narrrow-gauge steam train. The line is home to a collection of engines and coaches from all round the world. Please ring for details for special events.

Times Open Etr-late Oct wknds, (some extra days during Jun, Jul & Sep) daily during holiday periods, phone for timetable enquiries.* **Fees** £11.60 return (one ch free per adult, extra ch £5.80, concessions £10.60).* **Facilities** ❷ Ⓟ ☕ 🍴 (outdoor) ♿ (partly accessible) (both termini have ramped access. No access from intermediate stations) toilets for disabled shop

MACHYNLLETH

Bards' Quest

Corris Craft Centre, Corris SY20 9RF

☎ **01654 761584**   📄 **01654 761575**

e-mail: info@kingarthurslabyrinth.co.uk
web: www.kingarthurslabyrinth.com
dir: Situated at Corris Craft Centre on main A487 rd between Machynlleth & Dolgellau

Take on the Bard's Quest and search the maze of time for myths and legends. Once found, enjoy the stories told by animated figures. The maze is a self-guided outdoor maze and easy to get around, with level paths and seating.

Times Open daily 22 Mar-Oct, 10-5. **Fees** £4.10 (ch £2.35, concessions £3.60).* **Facilities** ❷ ☕ 🍴 (outdoor) ♿ (partly accessible) (restricted access King Arthur's labyrinth - underwater boat ride and walk through caverns) toilets for disabled shop ⊗

Centre for Alternative Technology

SY20 9AZ

☎ **01654 705950**

e-mail: info@cat.org.uk
web: www.cat.org.uk
dir: 3m N of Machynlleth, on A487

The Centre for Alternative Technology promotes practical ideas and information on sustainable technologies. The exhibition includes displays of wind, water and solar power, organic gardens, low-energy buildings, and a unique water-powered railway which ascends a 200ft cliff from the car park. Free children's activities and guided tours during the summer holidays.

Times Open all year (closed 23-27 Dec & 3-14 Jan), 10-5.30 or dusk in winter.* **Fees** Summer £8.40 (ch over 5 £4.20, concessions £7.40); Winter, £6.40 (ch over 5 £4.20, concessions £5.40). Discounts available for cyclists, walkers and users of public transport.* **Facilities** ❷ 🍴 licensed 🍴 (indoor & outdoor) ♿ toilets for disabled shop ⊗

King Arthur's Labyrinth

King Arthur's Labyrinth, Corris SY20 9RF

☎ **01654 761584**   📄 **01654 761575**

e-mail: info@kingarthurslabyrinth.co.uk
web: www.kingarthurslabyrinth.com
dir: on A487 between Machynlleth and Dolgellau

An underground storytelling adventure where visitors travel by boat deep inside the vast caverns of the labyrinth, and far back into the past. Tales of King Arthur and other legends are re-told as you explore the spectacular underground setting. Complete with colourful scenes, and sound and light effects, this is a fascinating attraction for all ages.

Times Open daily, 22 Mar-end Oct, 10-5. **Fees** £6.50 (ch £4.65, concessions £5.85).* **Facilities** ❷ ☕ 🍴 (outdoor) ♿ (partly accessible) (full access to reception, shop & units of craft centre. Labyrinth tour includes 0.5m walk through caverns) toilets for disabled shop ⊗

PRESTEIGNE

The Judge's Lodging

Broad St LD8 2AD
☎ 01544 260650
e-mail: info@judgeslodging.org.uk
web: www.judgeslodging.org.uk
dir: in town centre, off B4362, signed from A44 & A49

A restored Victorian town house with integral courtroom, cells and service areas - step back into the 1860s, accompanied by an 'eavesdropping' audio tour of voices from the past. Explore the fascinating world of the Victorian judges, their servants and felonious guests at this award-winning, historic house. Various special events take place throughout the year, please telephone for details.

Times Open Mar-Oct, Tue-Sun 10-5; Nov, Wed-Sun & Dec, Sat-Sun 10-4. (closed Mon ex BH). **Fees** £5.50 (ch £3.95, concessions £4.75). Family ticket £15. Party rates available. **Facilities** ℗ & (partly accessible) (access to ground floor only) shop ⊗

RHAYADER

Gilfach Nature Discovery Centre and Reserve

St Harmon LD6 5LF
☎ 01597 823298
e-mail: info@rwtwales.org
web: www.rwtwales.org
dir: From A470 turn right into reserve, before cattle grid turn right and follow road

Situated in the Cambrian Mountains, Gilfach is locally unique due to its wide variety of habitats; high moorland to enclosed meadow, oak woodland to rocky upland river. The reserve therefore supports a tremendous abundance of plants and animals within a relatively small area. This richness of wildlife has adapted to living in the various habitats created over the centuries through the practice of traditional farming. Visitors can take a number of planned walks including the Nature Trail, the Monks Trod Trail, and the Oakwood Path. The Nature Discovery Centre offers the opportunity to learn about the various habitats and wildlife featuring footage from cameras in nestboxes, games and quizzes. Please see the website or ring 01597 823298.

Times Open Reserve all year. Visitor Centre & Nature Discovery Centre open Etr-Sep during wknds, BHs & school hols.*
Fees Donations for parking. **Facilities** ❷ ℗ ⊑ ⧮ (outdoor) & (partly accessible) (the centre & otter hide is accessible) toilets for disabled shop ⊗

TREHAFOD

Rhondda Heritage Park

Lewis Merthyr Colliery, Coed Cae Rd CF37 7NP
☎ 01443 682036 📄 01443 687420
e-mail: info@rhonddaheritagepark.com
web: www.rhonddaheritagepark.com
dir: between Pontypridd & Porth, off A470, follow brown heritage signs from M4 junct 32

Based at the Lewis Merthyr Colliery, the Heritage Park is a fascinating 'living history' attraction. You can take the Cage Ride to 'Pit Bottom' and explore the underground workings of a 1950s pit, guided by men who were miners themselves. There are children's activities, an art gallery and a museum illustrating living conditions in the Rhondda Valley. Special events throughout the year, phone for details.

Times Open all year, daily 10-6. Closed Mon from Oct-Etr. (Last admission 4). Closed 25 Dec-early Jan.* **Fees** £5.60 (ch £4.30, pen £4.95). Family(4)ticket from £16.50, (6) £21.* **Facilities** ❷ ℗ ⊑ 🍴 licensed ⧮ (indoor & outdoor) & (partly accessible) toilets for disabled shop ⊗

PARKMILL

Gower Heritage Centre

Y Felin Ddwr SA3 2EH
☎ 01792 371206 📄 01792 371471
e-mail: info@gowerheritagecentre.co.uk
web: www.gowerheritagecentre.co.uk
dir: follow signs for South Gower on A4118 W from Swansea. W side of Parkmill village

Based around a 12th-century water-powered cornmill, the site also contains a number of craft workshops, two play areas, animals, a museum and a miller's cottage, all set in attractive countryside in an Area of Outstanding Natural Beauty.

Times Open all year, daily, Mar-Oct 10-5.30; Nov-Feb 10-4.30. Closed 25 Dec.* **Facilities** ❷ ℗ ⊑ 🍴 licensed ⧮ toilets for disabled shop

TORFAEN

BLAENAVON

Big Pit National Coal Museum   FREE

NP4 9XP
☎ **01495 790311**   📄 **01495 792618**
e-mail: post@museumwales.ac.uk
web: www.museumwales.ac.uk
dir: M4 junct 25/26, follow signs on A4042 & A4043 to
Pontypool & Blaenavon. Signed off A465

The Real Underground Experience, Big Pit is the UK's leading
mining museum. It is a real colliery and was the place of work
for hundreds of men, woman and children for over 200 years.
A daily struggle to extract the precious mineral that stoked
furnaces and lit household fires across the world.

Times Open all year 9.30-5. Please call for underground guided
tour availability* **Facilities** ❷ 🚽 ♿ (partly accessible) toilets for
disabled shop ⊗

Blaenavon Ironworks   FREE

North St NP4 9RN
☎ **01495 792615**
web: www.cadw.wales.gov.uk

The Blaenavon Ironworks were a milestone in the history of
the Industrial Revolution. Constructed in 1788-99, they were
the first purpose-built, multi-furnace ironworks in Wales. By
1796, Blaenavon was the second largest ironworks in Wales,
eventually closing down in 1904.

Times Open all year, Apr-Oct, daily 10-5; Nov-Mar, Fri-Sat
9.30-4, Sun 11-4.* **Facilities** ❷ ⊗ ⊕

CWMBRAN

Greenmeadow Community Farm

Greenforge Way NP44 5AJ
☎ **01633 647662**   📄 **01633 647671**
e-mail: greenmeadowcommunityfarm@torfaen.gov.uk
web: www.greenmeadowcommunityfarm.org.uk
dir: M4 junct 26. Follow signs for Cwmbran then brown signs
with white sheep

Greenmeadow Community Farm has been a working farm
for over 250 years. Set in over 150 acres, it has a wide range
of pedigree and rare animals which you can meet up close.
Nestled in the heart of Cwmbran, this is a community farm in
every sense of the word, working closely with and serving the
local community and welcoming visitors from far and wide. The
cosy farmhouse café offers a selection of homemade specials.
Milking demonstrations held daily, tractor and trailer rides, a
farm trail and lots more.

Times Open all year, daily, Apr-Oct, 10-6 (last admission 5); Nov-
Mar, 10-4.30 (last admission 3.30). **Fees** £4.50 (ch £3.50). Family
(2ad+3ch) £16. Season tickets available. **Facilities** ❷ ❿ 🚽 ⊼
(outdoor) ♿ (partly accessible) (some slopes and uneven paths,
some rooms accessible by stairs only) toilets for disabled shop ⊗

VALE OF GLAMORGAN

BARRY

Welsh Hawking Centre

Weycock Rd CF62 3AA
☎ **01446 734687**   📄 **01446 739620**
e-mail: norma@welsh-hawking.co.uk
dir: on A4226

There are over 200 birds of prey here, including eagles,
hawks, owls, buzzards and falcons. They can be seen and
photographed in the mews and some of the breeding aviaries.
There are flying demonstrations at regular intervals during the
day. A variety of tame, friendly animals, such as guinea pigs,
horses and rabbits will delight younger visitors.

Times Open late Mar-late Sep, daily 10.30-5 (1hr before dusk
in winter)* **Facilities** ❷ 🚽 ⊼ (outdoor) ♿ toilets for disabled
shop ⊗

Wales

Wales

PENARTH

Cosmeston Lakes Country Park & Medieval Village

Lavernock Rd CF64 5UY
☎ 029 2070 1678 ▤ 029 2070 8686
e-mail: NColes@valeofglamorgan.gov.uk
web: www.valeofglamorgan.gov.uk
dir: on B4267 between Barry and Penarth

Deserted during the plagues and famines of the 14th century, the original village was rediscovered through archaeological excavations. The buildings have been faithfully reconstructed on the excavated remains, creating a living museum of medieval village life. Special events throughout the year include re-enactments and Living History.

Times Open all year, daily 11-5 in Summer, 11-4 in Winter. Closed 25 Dec. Country park open at all times.* **Facilities** ❷ ❏ ❿ licensed ⪫ toilets for disabled shop

WREXHAM

CHIRK

Chirk Castle

LL14 5AF
☎ 01691 777701 ▤ 01691 774706
e-mail: chirkcastle@nationaltrust.org.uk
dir: 8m S of Wrexham, signed off A483, 5m from Llangollen signed off A5

Chirk Castle is one of a chain of late 13th-century Marcher castles. Its high walls and drum towers have hardly changed, but the inside shows the varied tastes of 700 years of occupation. One of the least altered parts is Adam's Tower. Many of the medieval-looking decorations were created by Pugin in the 19th century. Varied furnishings include fine tapestries. In the garden there are beautiful views that take in seven counties.

Times Open 3 Mar-Oct, Wed-Sun 11-5, Garden & Tower 10-6, Full Castle 11-5. Closed BH Mon, Tue in Jul & Aug, 1 wk early Oct. **Fees** Full Castle £9.60 (ch £4.80) Family £24. Garden & Tower £6.80 (ch £3.40), Family £17. **Facilities** ❷ ❏ ⪫ (outdoor) ⪪ (partly accessible) (access to east wing, garden, laundries, servants hall) toilets for disabled shop ✿

WREXHAM

Erddig

LL13 0YT
☎ 01978 355314 ▤ 01978 313333
e-mail: erddig@nationaltrust.org.uk
web: www.nationaltrust.org.uk
dir: off A525, 2m S of Wrexham & A483/A5152

Built in 1680, the house was enlarged and improved by a wealthy London lawyer with a passion for gilt and silver furniture. Original furnishings remain, including a magnificent state bed in Chinese silk. The house is notable for the view it gives of both 'upstairs' and 'downstairs' life. The gardens, unusually, have been changed very little since the 18th century. The country park includes part of Wat's Dyke, a cup and saucer waterfall, examples of ridge and furrow field systems and a motte and bailey castle. Woodland walks and carriage rides available. Special events take place in spring, summer and autumn, please contact for details.

Times Open 13 Mar-Oct, Sat-Wed (open Good Fri & Thu in Jul-Aug), house 12-5, garden 11-6. **Fees** House & garden £10.30 (ch £5.15). Family £25.75. **Facilities** ❷ ❏ ❿ licensed ⪫ (outdoor) ⪪ (partly accessible) (no access to first floor of house) toilets for disabled shop ⊗ ✿

Giant's Causeway, Co Antrim

Ireland

Northern Ireland

CO ANTRIM

BALLYMENA

Ecos Visitor & Conference Centre   FREE

Ecos Centre, Kernohams Ln, Broughshane Rd BT43 7QA
☎ 028 2566 4400 ⦿ 028 2563 8984
e-mail: www.ballymena.gov.uk/ecos
web: www.ballymena.gov.uk/ecos
dir: follow signs from M2 bypass at Ballymena

Plenty of fun and adventure for all the family with duck feeding, toy tractors and sand pit. The centre hosts two interactive galleries, one on sustainability and one on biodiversity, and you can stroll through the willow tunnel and enjoy the play park.

Times Open Etr-Oct, Mon-Fri 9-5; Jun-Aug, Sat-Sun 12-5 (last admission 4). **Facilities** ❷ ⬚ ⚲ (outdoor) & toilets for disabled shop ⊗

BALLYMONEY

Leslie Hill Open Farm

Leslie Hill BT53 6QL
☎ 028 2766 6803 ⦿ 028 2766 6803
web: www.lesliehillopenfarm.co.uk
dir: 1m NW of Ballymoney on MacFin Rd

An 18th-century estate with a Georgian house, magnificent period farm buildings, and fine grounds with paths, lakes and trees. Attractions include an extensive collection of rare breeds, poultry, horsedrawn machinery and carriages, exhibition rooms, a museum, working forge, deer park, walled garden and an adventure playground.

Times Open Jul-Aug, Mon-Sat 11-6, Sun 2-6; Jun, Sat-Sun & BHs 2-6; Etr-May, Sun & BHs 2-6, open all Etr wk 11-6.* **Fees** £4 (ch £3). Family ticket £12.* **Facilities** ❷ ⬚ ⚲ (indoor & outdoor) & toilets for disabled shop ⊗

CARRICK-A-REDE

Carrick-a-Rede Rope Bridge and Larrybane Visitor Centre

BT54 6LS
☎ 028 2076 9839 & 2073 1582 (office)
⦿ 028 2073 2963
e-mail: carrickarede@nationaltrust.org.uk
web: www.nationaltrust.org.uk
dir: E of Ballintoy on B15

On the North Antrim Coastal Path is one of Northern Ireland's best-loved attractions: Carrick-a-Rede Rope Bridge and the disused limestone quarry of Larrybane. The island of Carrick is known as 'the rock in the road', as it is an obstacle on the path of migrating salmon, and fishermen have taken advantage of this to net the fish here for over 300 years.

Times Open Bridge daily (weather permitting), 28 Feb-24 May & Sep-1 Nov 10-6, 25 May-Aug 10-7. (Last admission 45 mins before closing. Coastal path open all year.* **Facilities** ❷ ⬚ ⚲ (outdoor) toilets for disabled ⚲

GIANT'S CAUSEWAY

Giant's Causeway Centre

44 Causeway Rd BT57 8SU
☎ 028 2073 1855 ⦿ 028 2073 2537
e-mail: causewaytic@hotmail.com
web: www.northantrim.com
dir: 2m N of Bushmills on B146

This dramatic rock formation is undoubtedly one of the wonders of the natural world. The Centre provides an exhibition and audio-visual show, and Ulsterbus provides a minibus service to the stones and there are guided walks, and special facilities for the disabled.

Times Open all year, daily from 10 (closes 7 Jul & Aug). Closed 1 wk Xmas.* **Facilities** ❷ ⬚ ⦿ licensed ⚲ toilets for disabled shop ⊗

CO ARMAGH

ARMAGH

Armagh County Museum   FREE

The Mall East BT61 9BE
☎ 028 3752 3070   📄 028 3752 2631
e-mail: acm.info@nmni.com
web: www.magni.org.uk
dir: in city centre

Housed in a 19th-century schoolhouse, this museum contains an art gallery and library, as well as a collection of local folkcrafts and natural history. Special events are planned thoughout the year.

Times Open all year, Mon-Fri 10-5, Sat 10-1 & 2-5. **Facilities** ℗ & toilets for disabled shop ⊗

Armagh Planetarium

College Hill BT61 9DB
☎ 028 3752 3689 & 4725   📄 028 3752 6187
e-mail: info@armaghplanet.com
web: www.armaghplanet.com
dir: on Armagh-Belfast road close to mall, city centre

The Planetarium is home to The Digital Theatre, a multi-media environment equipped with the latest Planetarim projector technology and state-of-the-art sound system. Also featured are the space displays in the Galileo Hall, Copernicus Hall, Tycho, Cassini and Kepler rooms and surrounding the Planetarium is the Astropark, a 25-acre area where you can walk through the Solar System and the Universe.

Times Open all year, Sat 11.30-5. Sun 11.30-5, Mon during term time; May-Jun & Sep-Dec wkdys 1-5, July-Aug wkdys 11.30-5.*
Facilities ❷ ℗ ⛟ ☴ (outdoor) & toilets for disabled shop ⊗

Navan Centre & Fort

81 Killylea Rd BT60 4LD
☎ 028 3752 9655   📄 028 3752 6431
e-mail: navan@armagh.gov.uk
web: www.navan.com
dir: 2.5m W on A28

Navan was once known as Emain Macha, the ancient seat of kings and earliest capital of Ulster. Today it is an impressive archaeological site with its own museum and visitor centre located in a building that blends into the landscape. The Navan Centre uses audio-visuals and interactive devices to unravel history from myth. Travel into the 'Real World' of archaeology and the 'Other World' to hear the legends of the Ulster Cycle.

Times Open daily Jul-Sep 10-7, Oct-Dec 10-4.* **Fees** £5.15 (ch £3.45, concessions £4.20). Family ticket £14.95.* **Facilities** ❷ ⛟ ☴ (outdoor) & toilets for disabled shop ⊗

Saint Patrick's Trian Visitor Complex

40 English St BT61 7BA
☎ 028 3752 1801   📄 028 3751 0180
e-mail: info@saintpatrickstrian.com
web: www.visitarmagh.com
dir: in city centre

An exciting visitor complex in the heart of the city. Incorporating three major exhibitions - The Armagh story: traces Armagh's historic Pagan monuments through to the coming of St Patrick and Celtic Christianity to the modern day city. Patrick's Testament: takes a closer look at Ireland's patron saint through the writings found in ancient manuscript The Book of Armagh. The Land of Lilliput: Jonathan Swift's most famous book, Gulliver's Travels is narrated by a 20-foot giant.

Times Open all year, Mon-Sat 10-5, Sun 2-5. Closed 12 Jul.*
Fees £5.15 (ch £3.45, concessions £4.20). Family ticket £14.95.*
Facilities ❷ ℗ 🍴 licensed & toilets for disabled shop ⊗

Northern Ireland

255

Northern Ireland

Lough Neagh Discovery Centre

Oxford Island National Nature, Reserve BT66 6NJ
☎ 028 3832 2205   ▤ 028 3831 1699
e-mail: oxford.island@craigavon.gov.uk
web: www.oxfordisland.com
dir: signed from M1 junct 10

In a spectacular setting on the water's edge, discover natural history, wildlife, family walks and much more.

Times Open all year, Apr-Sep, Mon-Fri 9-5, Sat 10-5, Sun 10-6; Oct-Mar, Mon-Fri 9-5, Sat-Sun 10-5.* **Fees** Free except for events. **Facilities** ❷ ℗ 立 ㄒ (outdoor) 丈 toilets for disabled shop ⊗

BELFAST

BELFAST

Belfast Zoological Gardens

Antrim Rd BT36 7PN
☎ 028 9077 6277   ▤ 028 9037 0578
e-mail: info@belfastzoo.co.uk
web: www.belfastzoo.co.uk
dir: M2 junct 4 signed to Glengormley. Follow signs off rdbt to Zoo

The 50-acre zoo has a dramatic setting on the face of Cave Hill, enjoying spectacular views. Attractions include the primate house (gorillas and chimpanzees), penguin enclosure, free-flight aviary, African enclosure, and underwater viewing of sealions and penguins. There are also red pandas, lemurs and a group of very rare spectacled bears. Recent additions to the collection include capybara, crowned lemurs, tawny frogmouth and laughing kookaburra, tree kangaroo and giant anteater.

Times Open all year, Apr-Sep, daily 10-7 (last admission 5); Oct-Mar 10-4 (last admission 2.30). Closed 25-26 Dec.* **Fees** Summer: £8.30 (ch £4.40), Winter: £6.90 (ch £4.40, ch under 4, pen and disabled free).* **Facilities** ❷ ℗ 立 ㄒ◉ licensed ㄒ (outdoor) 丈 toilets for disabled shop ⊗

Ulster Museum   FREE

Botanic Gardens BT9 5AB
☎ 028 9038 3000   ▤ 028 9038 3003
e-mail: uminfo@nmni.com
web: www.nmni.com
dir: 1m S of city centre on Stranmillis road

The Ulster Museum is the perfect place to explore the arts, ancient and modern history, and the nature of Ireland. Art displays change regularly but always include a rich variety of Irish and international paintings, drawings and sculpture, along with ceramics, glass and costume. The history galleries tell the story of the north of Ireland from the Ice Age to the present day. The natural environment is explored in the Habitas galleries.

Times Please phone or check website for further details.* **Facilities** ℗ 立 toilets for disabled shop ⊗

W5 at Odyssey

2 Queens Quay BT3 9QQ
☎ 028 9046 7700   ▤ 028 9046 7707
web: www.w5online.co.uk

W5 investigates Who? What? Where? When? Why?... and that pretty much sums up the intent behind Ireland's first purpose built discovery centre. Visitors of any age will want to get their hands on interactive science and technology displays that include the laser harp, the fog knife, microscopes, robots and computers. W5 is part of a massive Millennium Landmark Project in the heart of Belfast.

Times Open all year Mon-Sat 10-6, Sun 12-6. Closed 25-26 Dec & 12 Jul.* **Facilities** ❷ ℗ ㄒ◉ licensed ㄒ toilets for disabled shop ⊗

CO DOWN

DOWNPATRICK

Down County Museum   FREE

The Mall BT30 6AH
☎ 028 4461 5218   ▤ 028 4461 5590
e-mail: museum@downdc.gov.uk
web: www.downcountymuseum.com
dir: on entry to town follow brown signs to museum

The museum is located in the restored buildings of the 18th-century county gaol. In addition to restored cells that tell the stories of some of the prisoners, there are exhibitions on the history of County Down. Plus temporary exhibits, events, tea-room and shop.

Times Open all year, Mon-Fri 10-5, wknds 1-5* **Facilities** ℗ 立 ㄒ (outdoor) toilets for disabled shop ⊗

HOLYWOOD

Ulster Folk and Transport Museum

Cultra BT18 0EU
☎ **028 9042 8428** 📄 **01232 428728**
e-mail: uftm.info@magni.org.uk
web: www.uftm.org.uk
dir: 12m outside Belfast on A2, past Holywood on main road to Bangor

Voted Northern Ireland's Best Visitor Attraction and Irish Museum of the Year, this attraction illustrates the way of life and traditions of Northern Ireland. The galleries of the Transport Museum display collections of horse drawn carts, cars, steam locomotives and the history of ship and aircraft building. Please telephone for details of special events running throughout the year.

Times Open all year Mar-Jun, Mon-Fri 10-5, Sat 10-6, Sun 11-6; Jul-Sep, Mon-Sat 10-6, Sun 11-6; Oct-Feb, Mon-Fri 10-4, Sat 10-5, Sun 11-5.* **Facilities** 🅿 🅟 ⊑ 🎋 (outdoor) toilets for disabled shop

PORTAFERRY

Exploris Aquarium

The Rope Walk, Castle St BT22 1NZ
☎ **028 4272 8062** 📄 **028 4272 8396**
e-mail: info@exploris.org.uk
web: www.exploris.org.uk
dir: A20 or A2 or A25 to Strangford Ferry Service

Exploris Aquarium is Northern Ireland's only public aquarium and now includes a seal sanctuary. Situated in Portaferry on the shores of Strangford Lough it houses some of Europe's finest displays. The Open Sea Tank holds 250 tonnes of sea water. The complex includes a park with duck pond, picnic area, children's playground, caravan site, woodland and bowling green.

Times Open all year, Mon-Fri 10-6, Sat 11-6, Sun 1-6. (Sep-Mar closing 1 hr earlier).* **Facilities** 🅿 🅟 ⊑ 🎋 (outdoor) 🦽 toilets for disabled shop ⊗

STRANGFORD

Castle Ward

BT30 7LS
☎ **028 4488 1204** 📄 **028 4488 1729**
e-mail: castleward@nationaltrust.org.uk
web: www.nationaltrust.org.uk
dir: 0.5m W of Strangford on A25

Explore this exceptional 820-acre walled demesne dramatically set overlooking Strangford Lough and marvel at the quirky mid-Georgian mansion. An architectural curiosity, it is built inside and out in distinctly different styles of classical and gothic. Winding woodland, lakeside and parkland walks afford amazing unexpected vistas.

Times Open Ground Oct-Mar, daily 10-4; Apr-Sep, daily 10-8. House; 21 Feb-29 Jun, wknds, BH/PH 1-5; 10-19 Apr & 4 Jul-Aug, daily 1-5; 5 Sep-1 Nov, wknds 1-5. Wildlife Centre 21-22 Feb, noon-5 & 28 Feb-May, noon-5 wknds & BH/PH* **Fees** Grounds, £4.54 (ch £2.27) Family £11. Group £3.70. Grounds & Wildlife Centre, £5 (ch £2.50). Family £12.50. House £2.80 (ch £1.90) Family £7.50. Group £2.10* **Facilities** 🅿 ⊑ 🎋 (outdoor) 🦽 (partly accessible) (no access to upper floor of house) toilets for disabled shop 🌿

CO FERMANAGH

BELLEEK

Belleek Pottery

3 Main St BT93 3FY
☎ **028 6865 9300 & 6865 8501** 📄 **028 6865 8625**
e-mail: visitorcentre@belleek.ie
web: www.belleek.ie
dir: A46 from Enniskillen to Belleek. Pottery at entrance to village

Discover the secrets that make Belleek Pottery one of the most enduring success stories in Irish craftsmanship. The award winning visitor centre offers guided tours along with a restaurant, audiovisual centre, showroom and museum.

Times Open all year, Jan-Feb, Mon-Fri 9-5.30; Mar-Jun, Mon-Fri 9-5.30, Sat 10-5.30, Sun 2-5.30; Jul-Oct, Mon-Fri 9-6, Sat 10-6, Sun 12-5.30; Nov-Dec, Mon-Fri 9-5.30, Sat 10-5. Closed Xmas, New Year & 17 Mar* **Fees** Guided tours £4 (ch under 12 free, concessions £2).* **Facilities** 🅿 🅟 🍴 licensed 🎋 (outdoor) 🦽 toilets for disabled shop ⊗

Northern Ireland

ENNISKILLEN

Marble Arch Caves Global Geopark

Marlbank Scenic Loop BT92 1EW
☎ 028 6634 8855 📄 028 6634 8928
e-mail: mac@fermanagh.gov.uk
web: www.marblearchcaves.net
dir: off A4 Enniskillen to Sligo road. Left onto A32 and follow signs

One of Europe's finest cave systems, under Cuilcagh Mountain. Visitors are given a tour of a wonderland of stalagmites, stalactites and underground rivers and lakes, starting with a boat trip on the lower lake. The streams, which feed the caves, flow down into the mountain then emerge at Marble Arch, a 30ft detached limestone bridge. The geological, historical and economic benefits of Marble Arch Caves and Cuilcagh Mountain Park were recognised on an international scale when they were jointly awarded the title of European Geopark by UNESCO in 2001.

Times Open late Mar-Sep daily 10-4.30, Jul & Aug 10-5. **Fees** £8 (ch £5, pen & concessions £5.25). Family £18. Group rates available. **Facilities** ❷ ☐ ㅈ (outdoor) ♿ (partly accessible) (cave not accessible) toilets for disabled shop ⊗

CO LONDONDERRY

LONDONDERRY

Tower Museum

Union Hall Place BT48 6LU
☎ 028 7137 2411 📄 028 7137 7633
e-mail: museums@derrycity.gov.uk
web: www.derrycity.gov.uk/museums
dir: behind city wall, facing Guildhall

Opened in 1992, the museum has won the Irish and British Museum of the Year Awards. It has two permanent exhibitions as well as hosting temporary and travelling exhibitions throughout the year. The multimedia 'Story of Derry' exhibition has reopened following extensive refurbishment. There is also an exhibition about the Spanish Armada which includes artefacts from a galleon shipwrecked in Kinnagoe Bay in 1588.

Times Open all year, Sep-Jun, Tue-Sat 10-5. Jul-Aug, Mon-Sat 10-5, Sun 12-4. Please check local press for opening details on BH.* **Fees** £4 (concessions £2.50)* **Facilities** ❷ ♿ toilets for disabled ⊗

CO TYRONE

BALLYGAWLEY

U S Grant Ancestral Homestead

Dergenagh Rd BT70 1TW
☎ 028 8555 7133 📄 028 8555 7133
e-mail: killymaddy.reception@dungannon.gov.uk
web: www.dungannon.gov.uk
dir: off A4, 2m on Dergenagh road, signed

Ancestral homestead of Ulysses S Grant, 18th President of the United States of America. The homestead and farmyard have been restored to the style and appearance of a mid-19th-century Irish smallholding. There are many amenities including a children's play area, purpose built barbecue and picnic tables and butterfly garden. Bike hire available (£1/hr).

Times Open all year daily 9-5. **Fees** Free admission. Advisable to book in advance for audio visual show.* **Facilities** ❷ ㅈ (outdoor) ♿ ⊗

OMAGH

Ulster American Folk Park

2 Mellon Rd, Castletown BT78 5QY
☎ 028 8224 3292 📄 028 8224 2241
e-mail: uafpinfo@nmni.com
web: www.nmni.com
dir: 5m NW Omagh on A5

An award winning outdoor museum of emigration which tells the story of millions of people who emigrated from these shores throughout the 18th and 19th centuries. The Old World and New World layout of the park illustrates the various aspects of emigrant life on both sides of the Atlantic. Traditional thatched buildings, American log houses and a full-scale replica emigrant ship plus the dockside gallery help to bring a bygone era back to life. Costumed demonstrators go about their everyday tasks including spinning, open hearth cookery, printing and textiles. The museum also includes an indoor Emigrants Exhibition and a centre for Migration Studies/library which is accessible to all visitors if they wish to find further information on the history of emigration and the place of their families in it.

Times Open all year Apr-Oct daily 10.30-6, Sun & BH 11-6.30; Nov-Mar Mon-Fri 10.30-5. (Last admission 1hr 30mins before closing).* **Facilities** ❷ ℗ ☐ ⏹ licensed ㅈ (outdoor) ♿ toilets for disabled shop ⊗

CO CLARE

BUNRATTY

Bunratty Castle & Folk Park
☎ 061 360788 📄 061 361020
e-mail: reservations@shannonheritage.com
web: www.shannonheritage.com
dir: approx 11km from Shannon Airport just off the main dual carriageway (N18) between Limerick and Ennis. Follow the tourist sign from the N18

Magnificent Bunratty Castle was built around 1425. The restored castle contains mainly 15th and 16th century furnishings and tapestries. Within its grounds is Bunratty Folk Park where 19th-century Irish life is tellingly recreated. Rural farmhouses, a village street and Bunratty House with its formal Regency gardens are recreated and furnished, as they would have appeared at the time. Medieval Banquets in the castle throughout the year (5.30pm & 8.45pm sitting , booking necessary) and an Irish Night operates in the Folk Park from April to October (reservations necessary).

Times Open all year, Jan-May & Sep-Dec 95.30; Jun-Aug, Mon - Fri 95.30 (last admission 4.15) & Sat & Sun 9- 6 (last admission 5.15). Last admission to the castle is 4pm year round. Closed Dec 24-26. Opening times may be subject to change* **Fees** Castle & Folk Park €15.75 (ch €9.45) Family tickets, senior, student tickets also available.* **Facilities** ℗ 🖵 🍴 licensed 🎍 (outdoor) ♿ (partly accessible) (castle is not accessible to wheelchair users) toilets for disabled shop

KILLALOE

Brian Boru Heritage Centre
☎ 061 360788 📄 061 361020
e-mail: reservations@shannonheritage.com
web: www.shannonheritage.com
dir: off the N7 between Limerick & Nenagh, take the R494 to Killaloe & Ballina

The 11th century High King of Ireland, Brian Boru one of the most influential and colourful figures in Irish history. The heritage centre reveals the story of Brian Boru is through a series of colourful exhibits, graphic illustrations and inter-active audio-visual presentation.

Times Open May-Sep, daily 10-5 (last admission 4.30) Opening times may be subject to change* **Fees** €3.35 (ch €1.75) family tickets, senior, student tickets also available.* **Facilities** ℗ shop 🚫

LISCANNOR

Cliffs of Moher Visitors Experience
☎ 065 7086141 📄 065 7086142
e-mail: info@cliffsofmoher.ie
web: www.cliffsofmoher.ie
dir: 6m NW of Lahinch

The Cliffs of Moher stand as a giant natural rampart against the aggressive might of the Atlantic Ocean. They rise in places to 700ft, and stretch for almost 5 miles. O'Brien's Tower was built in the early 19th century as a viewing point for tourists on the highest point. The famous site is the location for a Visitor Experience, including a state-of-the-art interpretation element, Atlantic Edge, as well as extensive visitor facilities. Cliffs of Moher Rangers are now on site for visitor safety as well as cliff edge guiding and information.

Times Open all year, Jan-Feb, 9-5.30; Mar-Apr & Oct, 9-6.30; May, 9-7; Jun-Aug, 9-9.30; Sep, 9-7.30; Nov-Dec, 9-5. **Fees** Atlantic Edge: €4.95 (ch under 4 free ch 4-16 €2.95, concessions €3.95). Family ticket (2ad+4ch) €13.95. O'Brien's Tower: €2 (ch €1). Facillities charge per vehicle: car €8, mtrcycle €2, summer special after 7.30pm €5.* **Facilities** ℗ 🖵 🍴 licensed 🎍 (outdoor) ♿ toilets for disabled shop

QUIN

Craggaunowen The Living Past Experience
☎ 061 360788 📄 061 361020
e-mail: reservations@shannonheritage.com
web: www.shannonheritage.com
dir: off the R469 near Quin

Craggaunowen is situated on 50 acres of wooded grounds and interprets Ireland's pre-historic and early Christian eras. It features a stunning recreation of some of the homesteads, animals and artefacts which existed in Ireland during those times. Visitors can see a replica of a Crannog (Lake dwelling), Ring Fort, an Iron Age roadway and an outdoor cooking site. Other features include the Brendan Boat and 16th-century Craggaunowen Castle. See rare animal breeds such as Soay sheep and wild boar - specimens of the pre-historic era.

Times Open mid Apr-Sep, daily 10-5 (last admission 4). Opening times may be subject to change* **Fees** €9.40 (ch €5.50). Family tickets, senior, student tickets also available* **Facilities** ℗ 🖵 🎍 (outdoor) ♿ (partly accessible) (castle not accessible) toilets for disabled shop

Quin continued

Knappogue Castle & Walled Garden
☎ 061 360788 ⧉ 061 361020
e-mail: reservations@shannonheritage.com
web: www.shannonheritage.com
dir: on R469 near Quin

Built in 1467, Knappogue has a long and varied history. Occupied by Cromwell's troops in 1641 and completely restored in the mid-19th century, the castle fell into disrepair in the 1900s. In 1966 the careful restoration was completed and today the castle is famous for its medieval events. The attractive restored Victorian walled garden includes among many of its features a collection of plants from the Victorian era. Medieval banquets operate in the castle on evenings from April to October (reservations necessary)'

Times Open May-mid Sep daily 10-4.30. Last admission 4pm. Opening times may be subject to change* **Fees** €7.70 (ch €3.50) Family tickets, senior, student tickets also available* **Facilities** ℗ ⌷ (partly accessible) (ground floor & garden) toilets for disabled shop

CO CORK

BLARNEY

Blarney Castle & Rock Close
☎ 021 4385252 ⧉ 021 4381518
e-mail: info@blarneycastle.ie
web: www.blarneycastle.ie
dir: 5m from Cork on main road towards Limerick

The site of the famous Blarney Stone, known the world over for the eloquence it is said to impart to those who kiss it. The stone is in the upper tower of the castle, and, held by your feet, you must lean backwards down the inside of the battlements in order to receive the 'gift of the gab'. There is also a large area of garden open to the public all year round, woodland walks, lake, fern garden, rock close (laid out in the 18th century) and stable yard.

Times Open Blarney Castle & Rock Close. Mon-Fri, May & Sep 10-4, Jun-Aug 9-7. Oct-Apr 9-sundown or 6. Sun, Summer 9.30-5.30, Winter 9.30-sundown. Closed 24-25 Dec. **Fees** Blarney Castle & Rock Close €10 (ch 8-14 €3.50, concessions €8). Family ticket (2ad+2ch) €23.50* **Facilities** ℗ ℗ ⌷ (partly accessible) shop ⊗

Fota Arboretum & Gardens
Fota Estate
☎ 021 4812728 ⧉ 021 4812728
e-mail: info@heritageireland.ie
web: www.heritageireland.ie
dir: 14km from Cork on Cobh road

Fota Arboretum contains an extensive collection of trees and shrubs extending over an area of approx 27 acres and includes features such as an ornamental pond and Italian walled gardens. The collection includes many tender plants that could not be grown at inland locations, with many examples of exotic plants from the Southern Hemisphere.

Times Arboretum: Open all year, Apr-Oct, daily 9-6; Nov-Mar, daily 9-5. Walled Gardens: Apr-Oct, Mon-Thu 9-4.30, Fri 9-3.30, Apr-Sep, Sat & BH 11-5, Sun 2-5.* **Fees** Free admission. Parking fee €3.* **Facilities** ℗ ⌷ toilets for disabled

Fota Wildlife Park
Fota Estate
☎ 021 4812678 ⧉ 021 4812744
e-mail: info@fotawildlife.ie
web: www.fotawildlife.ie
dir: 16km E of Cork. From N25 (Cork to Waterford road) take Cobh road

Established with the primary aim of conservation, Fota has more than 90 species of exotic wildlife in open, natural surroundings. Many of the animals wander freely around the park. Giraffes, zebras, ostriches, antelope, cheetahs and a wide array of waterfowl are among the species here.

Times Open all year, 17 Mar-Oct, daily, 10-6 (Sun 11-6) (last admission 5); Nov-17 Mar 10-4.30 (Sun 11-4.30). (Last admission 3.30).* **Facilities** ℗ ⌷ ⌷ (outdoor) ⌷ toilets for disabled shop ⊗

CLONAKILTY

West Cork Model Village Railway

Inchydoney Rd
☎ 023 33224
e-mail: modelvillage@eircom.net
web: www.modelvillage.ie
dir: From Cork N71 West Cork left at junct for Inchydoney Island, signed at road junct. Village on bay side of Clonakilty

This miniature world depicts Irish towns as they were in the 1940s, with models of the West Cork Railway and various animated scenes. The tea room is set in authentic railway carriages that overlook picturesque Clonakilty Bay. Also take a guided tour of Clonakilty and the surrounding area on the road train.

Times Open daily Feb-Oct 11-5; Jul-Aug, 10-6.* **Facilities** Ⓟ Ⓟ ⊡ ⼊ toilets for disabled shop ⊗

COBH

The Queentown Story

Cobh Railway Station
☎ 021 4813591 🖹 021 4813595
e-mail: info@cobhheritage.com
web: www.cobhheritage.com
dir: off N25, follow signs for Cobh. Attraction at Deepwater Quay, adjacent to train station

A dramatic exhibition of the origins, history and legends of Cobh. Between 1848 and 1950 over 6 million people emigrated from Ireland; over 2.5 million left from Cobh. Visitors can explore the conditions onboard these vessels and learn about the harbour's connections with the RMS Lusitania and the RMS Titanic.

Times Open daily 5 Jan-22 Dec, 9.30-5, Jun-1 Sep, 9.30-6 (last admission 1hr before closing). **Fees** €7.10 (ch €4, concessions €6). Family ticket €20* **Facilities** Ⓟ Ⓟ ⊡ ⍥ licensed ♿ toilets for disabled shop ⊗

CORK

Cork City Gaol

Convent Av, Sundays Well
☎ 021 4305022 🖹 021 4307230
e-mail: corkgaol@indigo.ie
web: www.corkcitygaol.com
dir: 2km NW from Patrick St off Sundays Well Rd

A restored 19th-century prison building. Furnished cells, lifelike characters and sound effects combine to allow visitors to experience day-to-day life for prisoners and gaoler. There is an audio-visual presentation of the social history of Cork City. Individual sound tours are available in a number of languages. A permanent exhibition, the Radio Museum Experience, is located in the restored 1920s broadcasting studio, home to Cork's first radio station, 6CK. Unfortunately the 1st and 2nd floors are not accessible to wheelchair users.

Times Open all year Mar-Oct, daily 9.30-5; Nov-Feb, daily 10-4. Closed 23-28 Dec.* **Facilities** Ⓟ Ⓟ ⊡ ⼊ (outdoor) ♿ (partly accessible) (3 cells on the first floor inaccessible) toilets for disabled shop ⊗

KINSALE

Desmond Castle

Cork St
☎ 021 4774855
e-mail: desmondcastle@opw.ie **web:** www.desmondcastle.ie
dir: R600 from Cork city to Kinsale. From post office, 1st left then right, opposite Regional Museum then left and right again, castle on left

Built by the Earl of Desmond around the beginning of the 16th century, this tower was originally a custom house, but has also served as an ordnance office, prison, workhouse, stable and meeting place for the Local Defence Force during World War II. In 1938 it was declared a National Monument and restored. The Castle now houses the International Museum of Wine.

Times Open early Apr-late Sep, daily 10-6. (Last admission 45mins before closing).* **Fees** €3, (ch & students €1, pen €2) Family €8.* **Facilities** Ⓟ ⊗

CO DONEGAL

LETTERKENNY

Glenveagh National Park & Castle
Churchill
☎ 074 9137090 & 9137262 📄 074 9137072
e-mail: claire.bromley@environ.ie
web: www.glenreaghnationalpark.ie
dir: left off N56 from Letterkenny

Over 40,000 acres of mountains, glens, lakes and woods. A Scottish-style castle is surrounded by one of the finest gardens in Ireland, contrasting with the rugged surroundings.

Times Open all year, daily 9.30-6 (winter times may change). **Fees** Park: free, Castle €3 (ch & students €1.50, pen €2). Family ticket €7, group 20+ €2. Buses €1 & €2* **Facilities** ℗ ⌨ ⅋ licensed ☂ (outdoor) ☕ (partly accessible) (no lift access to first floor) toilets for disabled ⊗

CO DUBLIN

MALAHIDE

Malahide Castle
☎ 01 8462184 📄 01 8462537
e-mail: malahidecastle@dublintourism.ie
web: www.malahidecastle.com
dir: from Dublin city centre follow signs for Malahide, then approaching village, main entrance to castle is signed to right off main road

One of Ireland's oldest castles, this romantic and beautiful structure, set in 250 acres of grounds, has changed very little in 800 years. Tours offer views of Irish period furniture and historical portrait collections. Additional paintings from the National Gallery depict figures from Irish life over the last few centuries.

Times Open Jan-Dec, Mon-Sat 10-5; Apr-Sep, Sun & PHs, 10-6; Oct-Mar, Sun & PHs 11-5* **Facilities** ℗ ℗ ⌨ ⅋ licensed ☂ (outdoor) shop ⊗

SKERRIES

Skerries Mills
☎ 01 8495208 📄 01 8495213
e-mail: skerriesmills@indigo.ie
web: www.skerriesmills.org
dir: signed off M1 via Lusk or Balbriggan

A collection of restored mills, including a watermill, a five-sail, and a four-sail windmill, all in working order. The site dates from the 16th century and was originally part of a monastic establishment. It came into private ownership in 1538, and there has been a bakery there since 1840. Nature lovers will enjoy the millpond, nearby wetlands and town park, of which the mills are the focal landmark.

Times Open all year, daily Apr-Sep 10-5.30; Oct-Mar 10-4.30. (Closed 24-27 Dec & 31 Dec-2 Jan). **Fees** Guided tours €6.50 (ch €3.50, pen & students €5). Family ticket €13. Groups on request. **Facilities** ℗ ⌨ ⅋ licensed ☕ (partly accessible) toilets for disabled shop ⊗

DUBLIN

DUBLIN

Chester Beatty Library   FREE
Dublin Castle
☎ 01 4070750 📄 01 4070760
e-mail: info@cbl.ie
web: www.cbl.ie
dir: 2 min walk from Dame St via the Palace St gate of Dublin Castle, 5 mins from Trinity College

Situated in the heart of the city centre, the Chester Beatty Library is an art museum and library which houses the great collection of manuscripts, miniature paintings, prints, drawings, rare books and decorative arts assembled by Sir Alfred Chester Beatty (1875-1968). The exhibitions open a window on the artistic treasures of the great cultures and religions of the world. Egyptian papyrus texts, beautifully illustrated copies of the Qur'an and the Bible, and European medieval and renaissance manuscripts are among the highlights of the collection. Turkish and Persian miniatures and striking Buddhist paintings are also on display, as are Chinese dragon robes and Japanese woodblock prints. 2010 is the 10th anniversary of the library moving to Dublin Castle.

Times Open all year, May-Sep, Mon-Fri 10-5; Oct-Apr, Tue-Fri 10-5, Sat 11-5, Sun 1-5. Closed 24-26 Dec, 1 Jan, Good Fri & BH Mons. **Facilities** ℗ ⅋ licensed ☕ toilets for disabled shop ⊗

Dublinia & The Viking World

St Michael's Hill, Christ Church
☎ 01 6794611   🖺 01 6797116
e-mail: info@dublinia.ie
web: www.dublinia.ie
dir: in city centre

The story of medieval Dublin. Housed in the former Synod Hall beside Christ Church Cathedral and developed by the Medieval Trust, Dublinia recreates the period from the arrival of Strongbow and the Anglo-Normans in 1170 to the closure of the monasteries by Henry VIII in 1540. Also included is the exhibition on the Viking World which tells the story of their way of life and turbulent voyages.

Times Open all year daily 10-5 (last admission 4.15) **Fees** €6.25 (ch €3.95, concessions €5). Family ticket (2ad+3ch) €17*
Facilities Ⓟ 🗗 ᕱ (partly accessible) (2 floors accessible, but bridge and tower are not) toilets for disabled shop ⊗

Dublin Zoo

Phoenix Park
☎ 01 4748900   🖺 01 6771660
e-mail: info@dublinzoo.ie
web: www.dublinzoo.ie
dir: 10mins bus ride from city centre

Dublin Zoo first opened to the public in 1830, making it one of the oldest zoos in the world and has consistently been Ireland's favourite attraction. The Kaziranga Forest Trail is the latest development within Dublin Zoo. Visitors wander along winding paths to glimpse a breeding herd of Asian elephants. Dublin Zoo is a modern zoo with conservation, education and study as its mission. The majority of the animals here have been born and bred in zoos and are part of global breeding programmes to ensure their continued survival.

Times Open all year, Mar-Oct, Mon-Sat 9.30-6, Sun 10.30-6; Nov-Feb, daily 10.30-dusk.* **Facilities** Ⓟ Ⓟ 🗗 †○Ⅰ licensed ⋤ (outdoor) ᕱ (partly accessible) toilets for disabled shop ⊗

National Gallery of Ireland

Merrion Square
☎ 01 6615133   🖺 01 6615372
e-mail: info@ngi.ie
web: www.nationalgallery.ie
dir: N11, M50, follow signs to City Centre

The gallery, founded in 1854 by an Act of Parliament, houses the national collections of Irish art and European Old Masters including Rembrandt, Caravaggio, Poussin, and El Greco. There is also a special room dedicated to Jack B Yeats, and a National Portrait Collection.

Times Open all year, Mon-Sat 9.30-5.30 (Thu 9.30-8.30), Sun 12-5. Closed 24-26 Dec & Good Fri.* **Facilities** Ⓟ 🗗†○Ⅰ licensed ᕱ toilets for disabled shop ⊗

National Library of Ireland   FREE

Kildare St
☎ 01 6030200   🖺 01 6766690
e-mail: info@nli.ie
web: www.nli.ie

Founded in 1877 and based on collections from The Royal Dublin Society. The National Library holds an estimated 8 million items. There are collections of printed books, manuscripts, prints and drawings, photos, maps, newspapers, microfilms and ephemera. Included in the library's collection is the most significant exhibition on the life and works of the 20th century poet WB Yeats. The library's research facilities are open to all those with genuine research needs. In addition to research facilities, services include a regular programme of exhibitions open to the public and Genealogy Service.

Times Open all year, Mon-Wed 9.30-9 (Kildare Street); Thu-Fri 9.30-5. Sat 9.30-1 (reading rooms); 9.30-4.30 (Yeats exhibition). Opening times may vary during public hols. **Facilities** Ⓟ 🗗 ᕱ toilets for disabled shop ⊗

Natural History Museum   FREE

Merrion St
☎ 01 6777444   🖺 01 6777828
e-mail: education.nmi@indigo.ie
dir: in city centre

The Natural History Museum, which is part of The National Museum of Ireland, is a zoological museum containing diverse collections of world wildlife. The Irish Room, on the ground floor, is devoted largely to Irish mammals, sea creatures and insects. It includes the extinct giant Irish deer and the skeleton of a basking shark. The World Collection, has as its centre piece, the skeleton of a 60ft whale suspended from the roof. Other displays include the Giant Panda and a Pygmy Hippopotamus.

Times Open all year, Tue-Sat 10-5, Sun 2-5. Closed Mon, 25 Dec & Good Fri* **Facilities** Ⓟ ⊗

CO GALWAY

GALWAY

Galway Atlantaquaria

Salthill
☎ 091 585100   🖺 091 584360
e-mail: atlantaquaria@eircom.net
web: www.nationalaquarium.ie
dir: follow signs for Salthill. Next to Tourist Office at seafront rdbt

Concentrating on the native Irish marine ecosystem, the Galway Atlantiquaria contains some 170 species of fish and sealife, and features both fresh and saltwater exhibits.

Times Open all year, Apr-Jun & Sep, daily 10-5; Jul & Aug, daily,10-6; Oct-Mar, Wed-Sun, 10-5. Closed Mon & Tue.*
Facilities Ⓟ Ⓟ 🗗†○Ⅰ licensed toilets for disabled shop ⊗

ROSSCAHILL

Brigit's Garden

Pollagh
☎ 091 550905 📄 091 550491
e-mail: info@brigitsgarden.ie
web: www.brigitsgarden.ie
dir: signed from N59 between Moycullen & Oughterard

At the heart of Brigit's Garden are four unique gardens based on the old Celtic festivals and representing the cycle of life. Features include Irish sculpture and crafts designed to reflect the West of Ireland landscape. There are 11 acres of woodland and wildflower meadows to explore with a nature trail, a wind chamber, an original ring fort and the impressively large Brigit's Sundial. Special events all year round, including on Bealtaine (May Day) and the Summer Solstice.

Times Open Feb-Oct, daily, 10-5.30 (6pm in Jul & Aug)
Fees €7.50 (ch €5, under 5 free, concessions €6). Family (2ad+3ch) €22. **Facilities** 🅿 ⊡ 🜆 (outdoor) ♿ (partly accessible) (buildings and gardens fully accessible, only section of nature trail not accessible) toilets for disabled shop

KINVARA

Dunguaire Castle

☎ 061 360768 📄 061 361020
e-mail: reservations@shannonheritage.com
web: www.shannonheritage.com
dir: near Kinvara off N18 Limerick/Galway road

Picturesque Dunguaire Castle, situated on the shores of Galway Bay, was built in 1520. Explore the castle and learn about the people who have lived there since the 16th century. Banquets are also held in the castle on evenings from April to October. (reservations necessary)

Times Open mid Apr-Sep, daily 10-5 (last admission 4.30). Opening times may be subject to change* **Fees** €6 (concessions €3.40). Family tickets, senior, student tickets also available* **Facilities** ℗ shop ⊗

ROUNDSTONE

Roundstone Music, Crafts & Fashion   FREE

Craft Centre
☎ 095 35875 📄 095 35980
e-mail: bodhran@iol.ie
web: www.bodhran.com
dir: N59 from Galway to Clifden. After approx 50m turn left at Roundstone sign, 7m to village. Attraction at top of village

The Roundstone Music Craft and Fashion shop is located within the walls of an old Franciscan Monastery. Here you can see Ireland's oldest craft: the Bodhran being made, and regular talks and demonstrations are given. The first RiverDance stage drums were made here and are still on display in the Craftsman's Craftshop. There is an outdoor picnic area in a beautiful location alongside the bell tower by the water where the dolphins swim up to the wall in summer. 2010 is the 30th anniversary of making Bodhrans in Roundstone.

Times Open Apr-Oct 9.30-6, Jul-Sep 9-7, Winter 6 days 9.30-6.*
Facilities 🅿 ℗ ⊡ 🜆 (indoor & outdoor) ♿ toilets for disabled shop ⊗

CO KERRY

CASTLEISLAND

Crag Cave

☎ 066 7141244 📄 066 7142352
e-mail: info@cragcave.com
web: www.cragcave.com
dir: 1m N, signed off N21

Crag Cave is one of the longest surveyed cave systems in Ireland, with a total length of 3.81km. It is a spectacular world, where pale forests of stalagmites and stalactites, thousands of years old, throw eerie shadows around vast echoing caverns complemented by dramatic sound and lighting effects. Now features new indoor and outdoor soft play areas, which are priced seperately. Tours of the caves last about 30 minutes.

Times Open daily all year, 10-6. (Dec-Mar telephone for times).*
Facilities 🅿 ℗ ⊡ 🍴 licensed 🜆 (outdoor) ♿ (partly accessible) toilets for disabled shop ⊗

KILLARNEY

Muckross House, Gardens & Traditional Farms

Muckross
☎ 064 6670144   🖹 066 33926
e-mail: mucros@iol.ie
web: www.muckross-house.ie
dir: 4m on Kenmare road

The 19th-century mansion house of the formerly private Muckross Estate. It now houses a museum of Kerry folklife. In the basement craft centre, a weaver, blacksmith and potter demonstrate their trades. The grounds include Alpine and bog gardens, rhododendrons, azaleas and a rock garden.

Times Open all year Nov-mid Mar, daily 9.30-5; mid Mar-Jun & Sep-Oct, daily 9-6; Jul-Aug, daily 9-7.* **Fees** €7 (ch & students €3, pen €5.50) Family ticket €17.50. Group ticket €5.50.*
Facilities ❷ ℗ 🍴 licensed 🪑 toilets for disabled shop ⊗

TRALEE

Kerry County Museum

Ashe Memorial Hall, Denny St
☎ 066 7127777   🖹 066 7127444
e-mail: info@kerrymuseum.com
web: www.kerrymuseum.com
dir: in town centre, follow signs for museum & tourist information office

The museum tells the story of Kerry (and Ireland) from the Stone Age to the present day. Archaeological treasures are displayed in the Museum Gallery, while a stroll through the Medieval Experience reveals the streets of Tralee as they were in 1450, with all the sights, sounds and smells of a bustling community. Discover what people wore, what they ate and where they lived, and find out why the Earls of Desmond, who founded the town, also destroyed it.

Times Open all year, Jan-Mar, Tue-Fri 10-4.30; Apr-May, Tue-Sat 9.30-5.30; Jun-Aug, daily 9.30-5.30; Sep-Dec, Tue-Sat 9.30-5; BH wknds Sun & Mon 10-5.* **Facilities** ❷ ℗ 🚻 toilets for disabled shop ⊗

VALENCIA ISLAND

The Skellig Experience

☎ 066 9476306   🖹 066 9476351
e-mail: info@skelligexperience.com
web: www.skelligexperience.com
dir: Ring of Kerry road, signed after Cahersiveen then Valentia bridge, or ferry from Rena Rd Point

The Skellig Rocks are renowned for their scenery, sea bird colonies, lighthouses, Early Christian monastic architecture and rich underwater life. The two islands - Skellig Michael and Small Skellig - stand like fairytale castles in the Atlantic Ocean, rising to 218 metres and their steep cliffs plunging 50 metres below the sea. The Heritage Centre, (on Valentia Island, reached from the mainland via a bridge), tells the story of the Skellig Islands in an exciting multimedia exhibition. Cruises around Valentia Habour are also available.

Times Open May-Jun 10-6; Jul-Aug 10-7; Sep 10-6. Mar, Apr & Oct-Nov 10-5* **Facilities** ❷ 🚻 toilets for disabled shop ⊗

CO KILDARE

KILDARE

Irish National Stud, Gardens & Horse Museum

Irish National Stud, Tully
☎ 045 521617   🖹 045 522964
e-mail: japanesegardens@eircom.net
web: www.irish-national-stud.ie
dir: off M7, exit 13 then R415 towards Nurney & Kildare. Attraction well signed from rdbt

Situated in the grounds of the Irish National Stud, the gardens were established by Lord Wavertree between 1906 and 1910, and symbolise 'The Life of Man' in a Japanese-style landscape. You can also visit the Horse Museum which includes the skeleton of Arkle, an Irish racehorse that won a number of major races in the 1960s. The Commemorative Millennium Garden of St Fiachra has 4 acres of woodland and lakeside walks and features a Waterford Crystal garden and monastic cells of limestone.

Times Open 12 Feb-23 Dec, daily, 9.30-5.* **Facilities** ❷ 🚻 🍴 licensed 🪑 (outdoor) ♿ (partly accessible) (all parts of stud, garden & house accessible. Japanese gardens partly accessible) toilets for disabled shop ⊗

Republic of Ireland

CO LIMERICK

BRUFF

Lough Gur Stone Age Centre

Bruff Rd
☎ 061 360788 📄 061 361020
e-mail: reservations@shannonheritage.com
web: www.shannonheritage.com
dir: 17km S of Limerick, off R512 towards Kilmallock

Lough Gur introduces visitors to the habitat of Neolithic Man on one of Ireland's most important archaeological sites. The visitor centre interprets the history of the area which dates back to 3000BC.

Times Open May-mid Sep, daily 10.30-5 (last admission 4.30). Opening times may be subject to change* **Fees** €5 (concessions €3). Family tickets, senior, student tickets also available* **Facilities** 🍴 (outdoor) ⚓ toilets for disabled shop ⊗

CO MAYO

BALLYCASTLE

Céide Fields

☎ 096 43325 📄 096 43261
e-mail: ceidefields@opw.ie
web: www.heritageireland.ie
dir: 5m W of Ballycastle on R314

Beneath the wild boglands of North Mayo lies Céide Fields, the most extensive Stone Age monument in the world; field systems, dwelling areas and megalithic tombs of 5,000 years ago. In addition, the wild flora of the bog is of international importance and is bounded by some of the most spectacular rock formations and cliffs in Ireland.

Times Open early Apr-May & until mid Oct, 10-5; Jun-Sep, daily 10-6. Available for group bookings in winter months. (Last tour 1hr before closing).* **Fees** €4 (ch & students €2, pen €3). Family ticket €10. Group rate €3 each.* **Facilities** 🅿 🚻 toilets for disabled ⊗

CO ROSCOMMON

BOYLE

King House - Georgian Mansion

☎ 071 9663242 📄 071 9663243
e-mail: kinghouse@roscommoncoco.ie
web: www.kinghouse.ie
dir: in town centre

King House is a magnificently restored Georgian mansion built around 1730 by Sir Henry King, whose family were one of the most powerful and wealthy in Ireland. After its first life as a home, King House became a military barracks to the famous Connaught Rangers from 1788-1922. In more recent years it has also been a barracks for the National Irish Army. Today visitors can explore and delve into its history with interactive presentations on: Gaelic Ireland, the lives of the King family, the architecture and restoration of the building and its military history. Visitors can also discover the connection between the famous Hollywood actress Maureen O'Sullivan and King House. The Boyle Arts Festival takes place in the last week of July.

Times Open Apr-Sep, daily 10-6 (last admission 5). Pre-booked groups welcome all year round, telephone for details.* **Fees** €7 (ch €4, concessions €5). Family ticket €18. Group rates available. **Facilities** 🅿 🍴 licensed 🍴 (outdoor) ⚓ toilets for disabled shop ⊗

CO TIPPERARY

CASHEL

Brú Ború Heritage Centre

☎ 062 61122 📄 062 62700
e-mail: bruboru@comhaltas.com
web: www.comhaltas.com
dir: below Rock of Cashel in town

At the foot of the Rock of Cashel, a 4th-century stone fort, this Heritage Centre is dedicated to the study and celebration of native Irish music, song, dance, story telling, theatre and Celtic studies. There's a Folk Theatre where performances are held daily in the summer, and in the evening, banquets evoke the Court of Brian Ború, 11th-century High King of Ireland with music, song and dance. There is also a subterranean, 'Sounds of History', experience.

Times Open all year, Jan-May & Oct-Dec, Mon-Fri 9-5; Jun-Sep, Mon-Sat 9-11.30. **Fees** Admission to centre free. Night show €20. Exhibition, 'Sounds of History' €5 (students €3. Dinner Show/Option €50 (ch €25)). **Facilities** 🅿 🍴 licensed ⚓ toilets for disabled shop ⊗

CO WEXFORD

FERRYCARRIG

The Irish National Heritage Park
☎ 053 9120733 📠 053 9120911
e-mail: info@inhp.com
web: www.inhp.com
dir: 3m from Wexford, on N11

Sixteen historical sites set in a magnificent 35-acre mature forest explaining Ireland's history from the Stone and Bronze Ages, through the Celtic period and concluding with the Vikings and Normans. Among the exhibits are a reconstructed Mesolithic camp, a Viking boatyard with two full-size ships and a Norman motte and bailey. Please visit website for details of events running throughout the year.

Times Open all year, daily, Oct-Mar 9.30-5.30; Apr-Sep 9.30-6.30.* Facilities 🅿 💻 🍴 licensed 🍴 (outdoor) ♿ toilets for disabled shop ⊗

NEW ROSS

John F Kennedy Arboretum
☎ 051 388171 📠 051 388172
e-mail: jfkarboretum@opn.ie
dir: 12km S of New Ross, off R733

The Arboretum covers 623 acres across the hill of Slievecoiltia which overlooks the Kennedy ancestral home at Dunganstown. There are 4,500 types of trees and shrubs representing the temperate regions of the world, and laid out in botanical sequence. There's a lake and a visitor centre.

Times Open all year, Oct-Mar daily 10-5; Apr & Sep daily 10-6.30; May-Aug daily 10-8. (Last admission 45mins before closing).* Fees €3 (ch & student €1, pen €2). Family ticket €8.* Facilities 🅿 💻 🍴 toilets for disabled shop

The Irish Agricultural Museum
Johnstown Castle Estate
☎ 053 9184671 & 9171247
e-mail: info@irishagrimuseum.ie
web: www.irishagrimuseum.ie
dir: 4m SW of town, signed off N25

This museum is located in the old farm and stable buildings of the Johnstown Castle Estate. There are a vast range of artefacts relating to a bygone era. Farming and rural life are the main themes explored, with exhibits covering rural transport, farming and the activities of the farmyard and farmhouse; and includes a large exhibition on the history of the potato and the Great Famine (1845-49). Large scale replicas of different workshops, including a blacksmith, cooper and basket worker, and include displays on the Ferguson tractor system and the history of the estate. Johnstown Castle Garden is a delightful 50 acres of ornamental grounds surrounding a Victorian castle. Famous architect Daniel Robertson designed both Johnstown Castle Gardens and Powerscourt Gardens. The grounds contain a wide variety of trees and shrubs, as well as two lakes and various follies.

Times Open all year: Museum Apr-Nov, Mon-Fri 9-5, Sat-Sun & BHs 11-5; Dec-Mar, Mon-Fri 9-5 (closed for lunch 12.30-1.30, wknds & BHs). Grounds open daily 9-5. Fees Museum €6 (ch & students €4, concessions & group €5). Facilities 🅿 💻 🍴 (outdoor) ♿ (partly accessible) (ground floor accessible) toilets for disabled shop ⊗

Johnstown Castle Gardens
Johnstown Castle Estate
☎ 053 9184671 & 9171247
e-mail: info@irishagrimuseum.ie
web: www.irishagrimuseum.ie
dir: 4m SW of town, signed off N25

Johnstown Castle Garden is a fairy setting consisting of an exquisite Victorian castle set within 50 acres of onarmental grounds. The famous architect Daniel Robertson designed both Johnstown Castle grounds and Powerscourt gardens. The grounds contain a wide variety of trees and shrubs representing the best aspects of a formal and wild garden. The grounds are greatly enhanced by two lakes with folly towers and are populated with a wide range of waterfowl. The Irish Agricultural Museum is located in the old farm and stable buildings of Johnstown Castle estate. Please note that Johnstown Castle itself is not open to the public.

Times Open all year, daily 9-5.30. Closed 25 Dec.* Fees Car (inc passengers) €6. Pedestrians €2 (ch & students €0.50). Small coach €20, large coach €30. Charges apply May-Sep, Oct-Apr free. Facilities 🅿 💻 🍴 (outdoor) ♿ toilets for disabled ⊗

Republic of Ireland

Wexford continued

Wexford Wildfowl Reserve   FREE

North Slob
☎ 053 9123129   📄 053 24785
e-mail: info@heritageireland.ie
dir: 8km NE from Wexford

The reserve is of international importance for Greenland white-fronted geese, Brent geese, Bewick's swans and wigeon. The reserve is a superb place for birdwatching and there are hides and a tower hide available as well as a visitor centre.

Times Open all year, daily 9-5. Other hours by arrangement with the warden. Closed 25 Dec. Notice on gate if reserve closed.*
Facilities 🅿 🎋 toilets for disabled ⊗

CO WICKLOW

ENNISKERRY

Powerscourt House & Gardens

Powerscourt Estate
☎ 01 2046000   📄 01 2046900
web: www.powerscourt.ie
dir: From Dublin city centre take N11 S, after 12m take exit left to Bray S, Enniskerry. Left at rdbt, over flyover, rejoin N11 N. Take 1st left for Enniskerry Village, entrance 600mtrs out of village

In the foothills of the Wicklow Mountains, these gardens were begun by Richard Wingfield in the 1740s, and are a blend of formal plantings, sweeping terraces, statuary and ornamental lakes together with secret hollows, rambling walks and walled gardens. The gardens cover 19 hectares and contain more than two hundred varieties of trees and shrubs. The house itself incorporates an audio visual exhibition which traces the history of the estate, and tells the story of the disastrous fire of 1974 which gutted the house. The grounds also contain Powerscourt Waterfall, Ireland's highest at 398ft, 6km from the main estate.

Times Open all year: Gardens & House daily 9.30-5.30 (Gardens close at dusk in winter), closed 25-26 Dec. Waterfall open daily, Mar-Apr & Sep-Oct 9.30-5.30; May-Aug 9.30-7; Nov-Feb 10.30-4 (closed 2 weeks before Xmas). Ballroom & Garden rooms open every Sun & Mon 9.30-1.30 (May-Sep) **Fees** House & Gardens €8 (ch under 13 €5 ch under 5 free, concessions €7). Waterfall €5 (ch under 13 €3.50 ch under 2 free, concessions €4.50). **Facilities** 🅿 🅟 ⊑ 🍴 licensed ♿ (partly accessible) (some areas in gardens are flat and suitable for wheelchair users) toilets for disabled shop ⊗

RATHDRUM

Avondale House & Forest Park

☎ 0404 46111   📄 0404 46333
e-mail: costelloe_j@coillte.ie
web: www.coillteoutdoors.ie
dir: S of Dublin on N11. At Rathnew on R752 to Glenealy and Rathdrum, L2149 to Avondale

It was here in 1846 that one of the greatest political leaders of modern Irish history, Charles Stewart Parnell, was born. Parnell spent much of his time at Avondale until his death in October 1891. The house is set in a magnificent forest park with miles of forest trails, plus a children's play area, deer pen, orienteering courses and picnic areas.

Times Open: Apr-May & Sep-Oct, Sat-Sun, 12-4, Jun, Tue-Sun 12-4, July-Aug daily 11.30-4.30 (last admission 1hr before closing).* **Fees** €6.50 (pen €6). Family ticket (2ad+2ch) €18.50. **Facilities** 🅿 ⊑ 🍴 licensed 🎋 (outdoor) ♿ (partly accessible) (ground floor in house & one forest trail accessible) ⊗